The 351st Bomb Group in WWII
The Duty to Remember
1942 - 1945

Compiled by Ken Harbour & Peter Harris

The 351st Bomb Group in WWII
The Duty to Remember

Published by:
  Cross Roads
  P.O. Box 83
  Kimberly, WI 54136-0083
  USA

All rights reserved. No part of this book may be reproduced or transmitted in any form or by any means, electronic or mechanical, including photocopying, recording or by any information storage and retrieval system without the written permission from Cross Roads, except for the inclusion of brief quotations in a review.

Copyright © 2008 Cross Roads

Printed in the United States of America

Compiled by Ken Harbour and Peter Harris

First Edition 1980
Revised 2001
Revised 2008

  Harbour, Ken.
      The 351st Bomb Group in WWII : the duty to remember /
  [compiled by Ken Harbour and Peter Harris]. -- Rev.
  [ed.].
     p. cm.
     LCCN: 2008928278
     ISBN-13: 978-0-9675003-7-9
     ISBN-10: 0-9675003-7-0

     1. United States. Army Air Forces. Bombardment Group
  (Heavy), 351st--History. 2. World War, 1939-1945--
  Regimental histories--United States. 3. World War,
  1939-1945--Aerial operations, American.   I. Harris,
  Peter. II. Title.

  D790.H293 2008   940.54'4973
                           QBI08-600156

TABLE OF CONTENTS

Acknowledgements		iv
Introduction		v
Chapter 1	The Beginnings	1
Chapter 2	Baptism of Fire	7
Chapter 3	In Earnest	35
Chapter 4	The End in Sight	69
Chapter 5	Home Run	81
Chapter 6	Ground Personnel	83
Chapter 7	Commanding Officers	89
Chapter 8	The Duty to Remember	91
Chapter 9	351st B.G. Mission Log	101
Chapter 10	Their Aircraft	109
Chapter 11	All Gave Some, Some Gave All	119
Chapter 12	Group Personnel	133
Aircraft Recognition and Markings		168
Group Photos		173
Glossary		295

ACKNOWLEDGEMENT

We are truly indebted to Clint Ball, Elzia Ledoux and Mike Balkovich for their unstinting efforts, and thanks are also extended to the following, for contributions which have assisted us in the compilation of this History.

Joe Anderson, Earl Anderson, E. B. Apperson, Ted Argiropulos (Randall), Chas. Armstrong, Jim Atkins, Robert Bailey, Jim Barker, Elmer Beatty, Billy Berger, Walter Bergstrom, Lloyd Best, Fred Beucler, Roy Birkley, Stan Bishop, C. A. Blanchard, Stephen Bodnar, Jim Blaney, Lloyd Bogle, Jim Bradley, Earl Branaman, John Brolan, Charles Bromley, Gus Bunescu, Frank Burchinal, Bob Burns, Bo Byers, Roland Cadoret, Harold Cannon, George Catlett, Rocky Civizzio, Wm. Clark Jr., Oliver Clegg, Orville Click, Chicago Daily News, Bruce J. Z. Comfort, Bill Cramer, Ralph Crane, Jim Craven, Bill Crockett, Don Cutler, Jack Danby, Malcolm Dawson, Emerson Davis, Ralph Dickman, Joe Donahay, Leon Donnelly, Bill Dortch, Texas Red Drake, Frank Drew, Stan Drury, Jack Duchesneau, Fred Dundas, Clyde Dunlap, John Dunnigan, Junior Edwards, Carl Ekblad, Al Elsaesser, Bob Englert, Stuart Evans, First National Bank of McConnelsville, Seldon Flemming, Del Foigate, Charles Fouzie, John Fowler, Lebren Fox, Dick Franklin, Harold Freeman, Roger Freeman, Russ Fultz, Jose Garcia, Henry Gates, Jim Garrett, Don Gaylord, Jerry Geiger, Mike Gibson, John Goodwin, John Greenwood, John Griffith, George Gross, Harold Haft, Charles Hammack, Roy Handforth, Matthew Harbour, John Harper, Jim Harris, Clement Hayes, Chuck Henry, Carl Hinkle, Dick Hobt, Ken Horsey, Dick Hough, Sam Irwin, Joe Isoardi, Ed Jacobson, Millard G. Jantz, Sheldon Johnson, Louis Kaczor, Jack Keeler, Edward Kicmol, Joe Koffend, Al Kogelman, Veikko Koski, Wayne Kittleson, Charlie Langenbahn, Ladies Home Journal, Dave Litsinger, Leonard London, Ben Love, Ed Lukaszuk, Clarice Lyon, Lewis Maginn, Jim Mahaffey, Charles Majors, Tauno Maki, Richard Manning, Howard Maser, Nelson Matthews, Edgar Matlock via Leon Roper, C. J. McCoy, Clyde McClelland, J. R. McCurdy, Neville McNerney, Carlton Mendell, C. R. Mordecai, Nick Morello, Mal Morgan, Morgan County Herald, McConnelsville, Bill Moriarity, Whitney Miller, Harry Morse, Hank Morris, Dick Moulton, Joe Normile, Louis Nowack, Reg Norwood, Jack Omohundro, John Paige, Joe Peck, Jim Penrod, Frank Pershing, Roger Peterson, Roscoe Pierson, Evan Poston, Peter Provenzale, Jim Quillin, Fred Ralph, Reed Raser, Jim Redmond, Paul Reilley, Tom Richardson, Frank Richardson, Matt Rimmer, Wm. Rohrbacher, Eugene Romig, Don Rude, Elmer Ruschman, Norman St. Pierre, Roy Sage, Art Schoen, Ben Schohan, John Scott, Bob Seaman, Charles Shaw, Smitty Smetana, Norman Snyder, Jack Spence, Carl Stackhouse, Roy Stealey, Jim Stewart, Howard Stickford, Everett Strautman, Jim Strouse, Pete Swangin, Jim Theys, Bill Thompson, Henry Triwush, Joe Valento, Don Wassner, John Watson, Walt Wefel, Bill White, Peck Wilcox, Kenneth Williams, Barry Wilsher, Les Winchester, Joe Wroblewski, Jack Wyatt, Pete Zibas, Tony Zotollo.

A special thank you for to following people who gave of their time to make the 2008 update and reprint possible: Robert Booth, Roberta Bosetti, Randy Burton, Brian Freeman, Ken Harbour, Amber Jakubowski, Marvin Nauman, Jeff Rogers, Rick & Fern School, Luke School, Rachel School, Carolyn White, Kim Zimmerman.

INTRODUCTION

In all the literature that has been published about the United States 8th Air Force there has been a significant omission. The 351st Bomb Group (Heavy) has seldom been mentioned.

This history has been written in an attempt to rectify that omission. It is a factual account of the events written some thirty-five years later by "outsiders" who had no experience of the emotions associated with the Group during its stay at Station 110.

These latter-day writers could not know the fear, the excitement, the despair and the boredom associated with fighting an air war thousands of miles from one's home country. However with the help of many former members of the 351st this, their story, has been written. It is a story of heroism and sacrifice dedicated to those who gave their lives and to those who gave a part of their young lives so many years ago. May their endeavors never be forgotten.

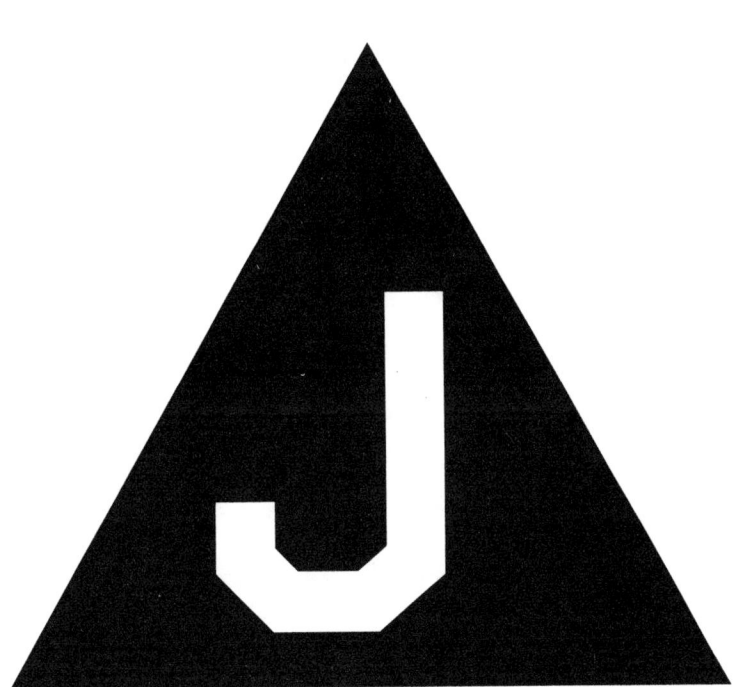

351st Bomb Group Aircraft Recognition Marking

Chapter One
THE BEGINNINGS

Four miles to the west of Spokane, Washington lay the Army Air Force Base of Geiger Field, home of the 34th Bomb Group.

It was here on the morning of November 24, 1942 that paragraph three of Special Orders 327 announced the birth of the 351st Bomb Group. The first paragraph of the first Special Orders of the 351st on the following day confirmed the assignment of the Commanding Officer, Lt. Colonel William A. Hatcher Jr. from Headquarters 2nd Air Force, Fort George Wright, Washington to the Group as of that date.

The orders also confirmed the initial Staff Officer appointments, the men who would assist Colonel Hatcher in molding the 351st into an effective fighting force. The constituent squadrons were also designated the 508th, 509th, 510th and 511th Bomb Squadrons. Over the next few weeks the staff gradually increased and the following formed the nucleus of the new outfit:

Commander	Colonel William A. Hatcher
Dept. Commander	Major Robert W. Burns
Executive Officer	Major Robert W. Bowles
Operations Officer	Major Theodore R. Milton
Adjutant	Captain Fletcher M. Craig
Intelligence Officer	Captain John L. Scott
Surgeon	Major Louis W. Nowack
Engineering Officer	Captain Arren A. Akins
Asst. Eng. Officer	Captain Otto R. Vasak
Chaplain	Lt. Thomas B. Richards
Comm. Officer	Lt. Stuart B. McLaughlin

Squadron Commanders

508th	Lt. Keith G. Birlem
509th	Captain Elzia Ledoux
510th	Captain William R. Forsythe
511th	Lt. Clinton F. Ball

At this time Group Headquarters for the 351st was a small section of Geiger Field Building 414 which was the Headquarters of the 34th Bomb Group.

On November 28, 250 officers and men gathered to hear Colonel Hatcher emphasize that their motive and purpose must be to always put the bombs on the target, this before the Group even had its first aircraft. Another more ominous pronouncement was that after January 1, 1943 no one would be permitted to live off base and all personnel were to consider themselves "restricted to post" except for one 24-hour pass each week.

The Group and Squadron departments began establishing their organizations and assigning responsibilities within the overall structure. Combat crews and other personnel were arriving daily. Within this intake were the four "Model Crews," assigned for their experience and ability to lead the squadrons into the forthcoming combat. Each was assigned to a Squadron as follows:

508th

508 Insignia

Lt. Edward C. Boykin
Lt. Theodore Argiropulos
Lt. Lawrence P. Stover
Lt. Carl D. Potter
Sgt. Raymond E. Miller
Sgt. Joseph S. Cebulak
Sgt. Phillip G. Hulse
Sgt. Kenneth L. Huls
Sgt. Torrido Marcial

509th

509 Insignia

Lt. Roy Snipes
Lt. George F. Cotherman
Lt. Rupert L. Torrey
Lt. Jack E. Danby
Sgt. Charles E. Chadbourne
Sgt. James H. Hart
Sgt. Maurice R. Marquis
Sgt. Edward C. Chiler
Sgt. John Wellnitz

510th

510 Insignia

Lt. R. C. Stewart
Lt. Edwin S. Boyd
Lt. Sydney Rosberger
Lt. Harry J. McTighe
Sgt. Eddie E. Hamlin
Sgt. Julian N. Gurbindo
Sgt. Joseph W. Keen
Sgt. Hugo R. Johnson

511th

511 Insignia

Sgt. Robert J. McAkinden
Lt. Harry B. Morse
Lt. Joseph A. Meli
Lt. Richard C. Theis
Lt. Harvey H. Wallace
Sgt. Joseph E. Hill
Sgt. George R. Lee
Sgt. James H. Vanderlaan
Sgt. Dewey A. Paxon
Sgt. Carl Pettus

The individual Squadrons and the buildup of their own functional structures were established as follows:

508th

The Commander, Lt. Keith Birlem, had in civilian life been a professional footballer, consequently he decided to call the Squadron "The Redskins" after his college team.

Lt. Birlem's staff:

Operations Officer	Lt. Boykin
Asst. Operations	Lt. Oldham
Adjutant	Lt. Morgan, replaced by Captain Seltzer
Intelligence Officer	Captain Davis, replaced by Lt. Rempe
Asst. Intelligence Officer	Lt. M. J. Balkovich

509th

Captain Ledoux entered the pilot training program in December 1940 at Hicks Field, Fort Worth, Texas, graduated, and was commissioned on August 15, 1941. He completed basic training at Randolph Field, Texas, and the advanced course at Kelly Field. He was assigned to Orlando Army Air Base, Florida flying B-18s and later B-25s. In January 1941 he transferred to a B-17 unit, the 34th Bomb Group at Portland, Oregon. The group moved via Tucson, Arizona to Geiger Field, Washington where it became a parent training group, from which the main cadre of the 351st was drawn.

Captain Ledoux's staff:

Operations Officer	Lt. John Blaylock
Adjutant	Lt. William Nichols
Supply	Lt. John Houck
Engineering	Lt. Robert Rollman
Surgeon	Lt. Lewellen
Sqd. Navigator	Lt. Jack Danby
Sqd. Bombardier	Lt. Rupert Torrey
First Sergeant	Sgt. Bill Breeding

510th

Commander Captain William R. Forsythe.

Captain Forsythe's staff:

Adjutant	Lt. Joseph Sweeney
Operations Officer	Lt. Leonard B. Roper
Asst. Operations	Lt. Joseph Turley
Engineering	Lt. Snyder, replaced by Lt. Geiss
Ordnance	Lt. Harry Olsen
Armament	Lt. William Leslie, replaced by Lt. Norman Snyder
First Sergeant	Sgt. Robert Mills
Intelligence Officer	Capt. Frank Reeves, transferred, replaced by Lt. R. Van Beynum
Surgeon	Lt. Thelbert Wilson
Supply	Lt. Alvin Israel
Mess	Lt. Thomas Conlon
Communications	Lt. Joseph Barber
Bombsight/Equip.	Lt. Reginald McDermott

511th

Commander Lt. Clinton F. Ball, 25, from Waco, Texas. Lt. Ball graduated from the Newark, Delaware High School in 1936, then entered the United States Military Academy. He left West Point in 1941 with a BS degree in engineering and a lieutenant's commission in the infantry. He transferred into the Air Corps as a cadet in the class of 42C, went through primary at the Spartan School in Tulsa, basic at Ellington Field and advanced at Randolph Field.

Lt. Ball's staff:

Adjutant	Lt. Verl Shaffer
Operations Officer	Lt. Bob Adams
Intelligence Officer	Lt. Stephen R. Calahan, replaced by Capt. Walter Holloran
Engineering	Lt. Carl Ekblad
Supply	Lt. Paul Weikel

Communications	Lt. George Balgenorth
Ordnance	Lt. George Mihuc
Surgeon	Lt. John Beckman
First Sergeant	Sgt. Donald R. Wells
Armament	Lt. Jesse Effron
Mess	Lt. "Big" Fred Thomas

On December 4 at 1745 hours most of the Group personnel were out on the flight line in a raging snowstorm proudly watching a B-17 circling the field. The aircraft eventually landed with Colonel Hatcher at the controls. The Group's first aircraft, 42-5186, had arrived. Ten minutes later Lt. Morse arrived in aircraft 42-5190. The other two assigned ships, 42-5192 and 42-5187, experienced difficulties. The former landed at Boise with engine trouble; the latter at Ephrata when caught in adverse weather.

It was still snowing very hard on December 8 when the ships took off for the Combat School at Biggs Field, El Paso, Texas. On board were most of the officers. During the next five days of intensive training the foundations of tight formation techniques were firmly impressed upon them.

Prior to the return to Geiger, the Group suffered its first accident. Captain Forsythe's ship was forced off the runway and into a ditch by a landing aircraft, while he was taxiing to a hangar to have the landing lights repaired. The return flight took much longer than expected with the ships forced down by bad weather at Ephrata. Most of the officers pushed on to Geiger by road and rail, while skeleton crews waited for the weather to clear.

The ground echelon marched to the train on December 28 and embarked on a four day journey to Biggs Field where they were met by Major Burns. The air echelon followed on January 2, 1943 with Geiger once again in the grips of a ferocious snowstorm. The southerly flight was interrupted by the crews and passengers being stricken with stomach pains sufficiently severe to necessitate emergency landings at Gowen Field, Boise. The Group's first casualties were detained in the hospital overnight from ptomaine poisoning. Everyone was sufficiently recovered the following day to continue the flight.

At Biggs, the training program commenced in earnest, telescoping first and second phase training into less than two months. Missions went on day and night for weeks, except on the occasions when the Texas winds whipped up sufficient sand to close the field.

The snow of Geiger and the good times at the Davenport Hotel in Spokane were quickly forgotten. In their places came the sand, the bombing range at Alamagordo, more sand, the Wilcox Dry Lake Range, even more sand, the Biggs Air to Ground Range and Juarez.

One day each week a contingent of the 351st fought the battle of Juarez. While bombardiers and gunners steadily improved their aim in the glaring sunlight of Texas and New Mexico, those who were so inclined found little difficulty in "hitting their targets" in the blackness of the Mexican night where a man's wages could quickly disappear with a senorita and a scotch. There were even daytime diversions in Juarez when the men would strain international relations by attending the bullfights and making it known vehemently that their affinity lay solely with the bull.

Others may recall the visits to the El Paso Hilton and its sound architectural structure that repeatedly withstood the violent storms "who" passed through it.

On January 28, 1943, 1st Lt. Clark Gable and 2nd Lt. Andrew J. McIntyre joined the Group and were assigned to the 508th Bomb Squadron. The Hollywood superstar and his team were to make a propaganda film showing the day-to-day activities of a typical Heavy Bombardment Group in training and in action. General "Hap" Arnold had commissioned the film to help encourage aerial gunner recruitment. Lt. Gable was to appear in the film while Lt. McIntyre and two cameramen were to take care of the shooting. A short time later a third officer, 1st Lt. John L. Mahin, joined the team to write the script.

The first and only serious accident during training occurred at 2119 hours on February 26 when aircraft '528 crashed and burned during takeoff on a night time practice mission. Only the pilot, Lt. Edward Kelly, survived. Those killed were: co-pilot Flight Officer Charles G. Novak, bombardier Lt. Ernest Pasqua, navigator Lt. James Bishop, waist gunner S/Sgt. Joseph Baucon, waist gunner S/Sgt. Alvin Simms, top turret gunner Sgt. Victor Berreth, ball turret gunner Sgt. Woodrow Erwin, radio operator Sgt. Adelberg Burke, tail gunner Pvt. Robert Parchman and cameraman Sgt. Howard Speak.

An advanced party under Major Bowles left on February 23 for Pueblo, Colorado, where they were to set up shop for the Group to commence the third phase of training. The ground and air echelons arrived the same day, March 1.

The northward move reintroduced the personnel to the wintry conditions and once again they experienced a snow covered field. Bad weather enforced postponement of a flight to the West Coast on March 4, but practice navigation and bombing flights continued. However, the next day the weather cleared and the crews were briefed for their longest mission to date. The destination: Muroc Dry Lake near Bakersfield, California. Here the crews laid over till the next morning, March 6, when they took off on a sea mission to look for a United States Navy cruiser. They were unsuccessful and the following day set out on a repeat mission. Flying over the Santa Monica Mountains, Lt. Rosewall and Lt. Winter (in the nose of Lt. Pinkerton's 511th ship), thought they had been given the bail out signal. Unquestioning they jumped. The order had not been given. The pair descended somewhere in the mountains where they were met by friendly but somewhat bemused natives, to whom Lt. Rosewall expounded the art of parachute jumping in intricate detail, only to learn that one of the women who listened with what he thought was the most rapture was herself a professional parachutist.

The crews returned to Pueblo on March 9 and commenced formation practice. From then on flights were to be in formation, and to add reality to the situation briefings were held showing routes and targets plotted on European maps as well as on United States air maps.

Missions were flown on March 11 and 13, plus several fuel consumption tests, and on March 16 a ferry mission to Blythe just about wound up phase three.

On March 20 Major Burns announced that there would be no more practice, and that Group activities would be solely directed at preparations for the journey that would take the 351st into combat. The entire air echelon was granted leave from March 22-31. The wives and loved ones of many of the men had, at their own expense and not inconsiderable inconvenience, followed the Group by road and rail from base to base for some four months. These final days of leave would indeed be precious.

At 1100 hours on April 2, the air echelon took off on the first leg of the overseas flight to Kearney, Nebraska. Here they stayed until April 5 being processed and having the ships put through engineering checks. The next hop was to Selfridge Field, Michigan, and from there to Presque Isle, Maine, where the very final processing and ship checks took place.

It was not unknown during the movement eastwards for a ship to "stray" over a hometown for a rehearsal buzz-job, which no doubt, all the offending crews hoped to repeat upon the successful completion of missions. These navigational "errors" were doubtless put down to inexperience.

April 15 was the day the air echelon finally bade farewell to the United States. As thoughts were inevitably of home, families and loved ones, so it was an inwardly subdued air echelon that made the penultimate stage of the overseas flight to Gander Lake, Newfoundland.

Gander Lake, a sprawling muddy place, was positively the last contact with the American continent and the following morning on April 16 the 351st made an uneventful Atlantic crossing. After refueling at Prestwick, Scotland, they flew south to the base at Polebrook, Northamptonshire. This was to be "home" to the 351st until the end of the war in Europe.

Following the departure of the air echelon, the ground personnel spent the next 10 days dividing their time between training and packing enormous amounts of equipment. Finally, on April 12, they moved on to Camp Williams near the sparsely populated town of Camp Douglas, Wisconsin. Here they tasted tent life and generally went on drilling, with cross country hikes often the order of the day. Camp Williams also provided a new, unpleasant but valuable experience to the men, when they were subjected to a surprise gas attack by aircraft crewed by Group personnel. A general pass was issued, which was used in nearby Chicago or Milwaukee. Then, on April 24, they went by train to

Camp Shanks, New York on the Hudson River arriving at 0130 hours on April 26. The next day the men received a final pass to enable them to see the sights of New York and then it was back to final preparations. Equipment shortages were made up, defective items replaced and the last medical examinations completed. Then, on May 4, they took a short train ride to the 42nd Street Ferry and crossed the river to a ship which would take them overseas, the *Queen Elizabeth*. So now, they too bade farewell to the homeland, struggling under the weight of their packs, pockets bulging with chocolate and cigarettes so generously given by the Red Cross. The ship was very crowded and the men had to sleep in shifts. They also experienced the English "queue" or "line" as it was known at home. The introduction to the queue would not be quickly forgotten as they were the longest that the men had ever stood in to obtain their meals.

Apart from the daily fire drills and the rumors of U-boats, the crossing was uneventful. The *Queen Elizabeth* docked at Glasgow at 1100 hours on May 11. From here the men boarded a train which took them southward through the night arriving at the small town of Oundle early on the morning of May 12, from there they traveled the two miles to Station 110, Polebrook, arriving at 0530 hours. This is how one of the "Squadron Historians" described the initial impressions of Polebrook. "The Group had found its operational base. A fairly compact one it was, in comparison to other fields that had been seen, compact except that it was in two separate sections, one a quarter of a mile on the other side of the woods from the main site. But it looked quite good; paved streets and sidewalks, Nissan huts (a couple of boards, a piece of tin, and a stove at one end), no dust, not too much mud, bicycles, and hot water occasionally. The natives seemed to be quite civilized, except that they drank tea, talked with a difficult accent, and handled cigarette coupons as though they were real money. But the strangeness of the new place wasn't for long. The vicinity of Oundle and Peterborough broke that down, and it wasn't long before the men and officers claimed the neighborhood as its own."

The Ground crews and the service units, namely men of the 201st Finance Section, 1206th Q. M. Company, 11th Station Complement Squadron, 1629th Ordnance Company, 2098th Fire-Fighting Platoon, 1061st Military Police Company, 854th Chemical Company, 447th Sub Depot and 252nd Medical Dispensary, settled in for what would prove to be a three-year stay.

Having followed the courses of the two main parties, we must make mention of the very first 351st unit to arrive at Polebrook.

On January 15, 1943 the 304th Service Group arrived and began preparations to receive and organize the air and ground echelons.

The 304th Service Group was comprised of the Headquarters and Headquarters Squadron, the 320th Service Squadron, 1052nd Ordnance Squadron, 1629th Squadron and the 166th Quartermaster Company.

An advance party of the air echelon arrived on April 15 when aircraft 42-29491 landed carrying Major Bowles, Major Milton, Captain Scott, and other key personnel.

The following day the main force arrived. These early days were spent on training and acclimatization flights. During the off duty periods the men would familiarize themselves with the local surroundings. Staging practice missions was a particularly arduous task, bearing in mind that the men who would normally prepare and service the ships were breathing the fresh Atlantic breezes. It was all hands to the task. Key engineering personnel had accompanied the crews on the outward flight and under their guidance and instruction, anyone and everyone tackled the many and varying duties required to put a bomb group in the air.

On May 7 during the completion of a practice bombing mission to Scares Rock, Walney Island, tragedy struck the Group. Two of the best crews were lost when their planes collided in mid-air over the base. Those killed were: Major Keith Birlem, 508th Squadron Commander, Lt. Harry Bartholomew, Lt. Courtland Young, Lt. Harry Summers, Lt. Clarence Yunt, T/Sgt. Thomas Broderick, S/Sgt. Oscar Tipton, S/Sgt. Walter Lappage, S/Sgt. Robert Brooke and S/Sgt. Paul Fennel, all from the 508th Squadron and Lt. Roy Snipes, Lt. Rupert Torrey, Lt. George Cotherman, T/Sgt. Harold Wellnitz, S/Sgt. Irving Berger, S/Sgt. Edward Cihar, S/Sgt. Harry Kelly, S/Sgt. Maurice Marquis and S/Sgt. Charles Chadbourne, all from the 509th Squadron.

Major Birlem had been particularly disappointed with his Squadron's formation flying, and in an effort to demonstrate how it should be done he had pilots on board and the remainder of his staff out on the flight line to watch. However, while leading the second element, Major Birlem's ship overran the first colliding with that of Lt. Snipes who was flying right wingman to the Group Leader. The tail section of Lt. Snipes' ship and the wing of Major Birlem's aircraft were severed, sending both planes plummeting to the ground where they burst into flames.

Prior to the commencement of the 351st operational activities, Colonel Hatcher, the Squadron Commanders and other senior staff flew their first combat missions as observers with the 303rd Bomb Group from Molesworth.

They were now ready.

L to R: Maj. Louis Nowack, GP Surgeon, Lt. Col. Robert Bowles and Lt. Col. William Hatcher. (C. Ball)

Chapter Two

BAPTISM OF FIRE

The Group had trained hard. Confident in the invincibility of their B-17s, they were prepared to attack the fortress of Nazi occupied Europe. Imbued with the enthusiasm of the untried, they were sure that it would all be over by Christmas.

MAY 13, 1943   **MISSION NO. 1**

The target was the Fort Rouge Airfield at St. Omer, France. Starting at 1341 hours, 14 ships took off. The raid was led by Colonel Hatcher with Lt. J. T. Stewart as copilot, Lt. R. W. Menees as navigator and Lt. Stevens as bombardier. The Group turned back at mid-Channel because the high squadron fell behind and was unable to get back into formation.

MAY 14, 1943   **MISSION NO. 2**

A maximum effort was ordered for the Group with Courtrai Airfield in Belgium as the target. Eighteen planes took off starting at 1030 hours, this time led by Colonel Hatcher with Major L. E. Lyle as copilot, Lt. Menees as navigator and Lt. Stevens as bombardier. The Group led the combat wing and bombing results were fairly good. Two ships were lost on this mission. Aircraft 42-29859, piloted by Captain William P. Forsythe, 510th Squadron Commander, fell out of formation with one engine smoking four miles before reaching the target. It was seen being attacked by six enemy aircraft. The second casualty, 42-29862 from the 508th Squadron, piloted by Lt. C. J. McCoy, was flying in the number three position in the lead element. This ship was knocked out by enemy aircraft near Ypres after the bomb run.

After this misson, Lt. James T. Stewart was appointed 508th Squadron Commander.

MAY 15, 1943   **MISSION NO. 3**

The Group's second completed mission was a maximum effort to Emden. Nineteen planes took off at 0730 hours led by Major Wurzbach and Major Burns with Lt. Stover as navigator and Lt. Stevens as bombardier. Due to clouds, ground haze and smoke, bombing results could not be observed.

Returning across the Frisian Islands, the Group came under attack from FW 190s with a few Me 109s and Me 110s. Lt. Meli of the 511th Squadron, flying 42-3173, was seen lagging out of formation, a possible result of flak damage. His B-17 then fell into a slow spiral whereupon five Me 109s attacked him. Five or six parachutes were seen before the plane broke up about 500 feet above the water, approximately 40 miles northeast of Borkum.

MAY 17, 1943

Captain John R. Blaylock was appointed 510th Squadron Commander.

MAY 19, 1943   **MISSION NO. 4**

For the raid on Kiel, 21 planes took off led by Colonel Hatcher with Captain Calhoun as copilot, Captain Menees as navigator and Lt. Stevens as bombardier. On this mission the Group ran into the biggest concentration of enemy fighters they had encountered up to that time. Lt. Mansfield's ship, 42-29701, was damaged by flak over the target but went on with its number three engine smoking and dropped its bombs. It was last seen going down seemingly under control. Just as Lt. W. R. Smith in 42-29852 started the bomb run, a 20mm shell exploded just above the ball turret, severing the oxygen lines. This left the four gunners without oxygen at 25,000 feet. The left waist gunner, T/Sgt. Baker, attempted to bail out but his parachute became snagged on the escape hatch. The plight of the gunners, all suffering from anoxia, went unnoticed until after the bomb run when the rest of the crew heard T/Sgt. Baker's body banging against the fuselage. All but the pilot came back to assist. The ball gunner was unconscious from lack of oxygen when he was removed from his turret. The right waist gunner and tail gunner were almost unconscious. Together they managed to pull T/Sgt. Baker back into the plane, but he was dead from banging against the plane and frozen from the intense cold. Lt. Smith landed at the earliest opportunity, an emergency strip on the coast of England.

MAY 21, 1943   **MISSION NO. 5**

Nineteen planes, led by Major Wurzbach and Major Milton with Lt. Shaw as navigator and Lt. Wallace as bombardier, took off to bomb submarine slips and dock installations at Wilhelmshaven. The bombing results were reported as good, although bombing had to be done through broken clouds. About 50 German fighters attacked the formation and pressed home their attacks until they were well out over the sea on the way back. Battle damage and fuel shortage caused all but one ship to divert to other airfields

During the climb-out over the North Sea, Lt. Carl B. Wilson in 42-3136, *Eight Ball*, experienced a minor problem with the propeller governor on the number two engine, which caused difficulty in keeping the aircraft in close formation, but was insufficient to break formation. At a point near the Frisian Islands and at an altitude in excess of 20,000 feet, the number two engine ran away. The pilot's efforts to feather the propeller were unsuccessful. A decision was made to abort the mission and attempt a return to base. The aircraft disengaged from the formation and headed back to England with the number two propeller windmilling out of control. The runaway engine created a unique situation during the descent to a lower altitude. The vibration from the windmilling propeller would increase during the descent, causing the pilots to pull the aircraft up into a semi-stall position. This reduced the flying speed to about 125 mph and slowed the windmilling propeller and lessened the vibration.

As the pilots gained experience flying the aircraft in its crippled condition and as the aircraft seemed to survive the continuous engine vibration, hope of reaching England without ditching emerged from the crew. However, observation of the engine from the nose section of the aircraft indicated that the reduction gear housing between the engine and the propeller showed metal discoloration caused by extreme heat. This indicated the possibility that the housing might disintegrate. Rivets around the engine cowling and wing sections adjacent to the engine were observed to be popped. (This condition was found to be much more extensive upon closer inspection on the ground.) Although the aircraft had left the formation and was alone and heading in the most direct and descending route for England at minimum airspeed, no German fighters attacked *Eight Ball* to the amazement of the crew. German fighters were observed in the distance, but for unknown reasons did not attack and quickly disappeared.

Upon reaching the English coast, with the aircraft under reasonable control, but with the propeller windmilling and engine vibration continuing, a new crisis was created when the planetary gears in the reduction gear assembly apparently froze and disintegrated. This caused the shaft between the engine and the propeller to shear. Only the force of air against the windmilling propeller held the propeller from falling out of the engine. The possibility of such a separation occurring became obvious when the aircraft was flown in a slight nose-down attitude in that Lt. Wilson could see the windmilling propeller and propeller shaft protrude forward away from the engine. By bringing the nose of the aircraft to a slightly nose-up attitude, the propeller and shaft would settle back into what appeared to be a more normal state, certainly one which seemed more conducive to survival.

Notwithstanding this condition, the pilots and engineer kept the aircraft flying and headed for Polebrook. An emergency landing was considered after crossing the English coastline but was rejected on the basis that the aircraft was controllable, although badly wounded, and that if the windmilling propeller would remain on the engine, a landing at Polebrook was more desirable than at an unfamiliar field. The crew welcomed this decision, having survived the return flight over the North Sea and the possibility of a ditching. The aircraft landed safely at Polebrook, except that during the landing roll the propeller and shaft from the number two engine fell off about 200 yards after touchdown. One or more propeller blades struck the .50 caliber machine gun mounted in the left nose section of the aircraft, causing the gun to strike the navigator who was in the nose section during the landing. The propeller striking the gun, rather than slicing through the nose section of the aircraft probably prevented serious injury to the navigator who was unhurt, although the gun was destroyed. The propeller did, however, cause extensive skin and structural damage to *Eight Ball* as she literally ran over the propeller that had dropped from the number two engine during the landing roll.

Inspection of the aircraft after landing revealed extensive skin and structural damage to the left wing, fuselage and number two engine nacelle. The engine was heavily damaged probably as the result of a fragment of the propeller governor entering the reduction gear assembly, disintegration of the gear assembly, and subsequent failure and disintegration of the gear housing and shearing the propeller shaft.

The damage to *Eight Ball* was extensive and she remained in the major repair hangar for some time. Although repairs were extensive, she lived to fly again with the 8th Air Force, but only after being renamed *No Balls at All*, for obvious reasons. All members of her original crew survived the experience and the required number of combat missions to complete a combat tour, some of which were flown in the repaired and renamed *Eight Ball*.

MAY 29, 1943   **MISSION NO. 6**

This was a raid on the St. Nazaire submarine slips. Twenty-one planes took off, starting at 1350 hours led by Colonel Hatcher and Major Milton, with Captain Menees as navigator and Lt. Stevens as bombardier. The trip was an introduction to the most accurate flak yet encountered. Despite this, the bombing was excellent with many hits on docks, warehouses, gasworks and workshops.

Just after bombs away 42-29838, piloted by Lt. Russell, was hit in the open bomb bay by an 88mm shell. The blast almost completely tore away the ball turret, along with the gunner, Sgt. Bader. The same blast killed Sgt. Welk in the radio room and Sgt. Baldwin, the waist gunner, and started a fire in the bomb bay. With numbers three and four engines also knocked out, the plane dropped out of formation. Immediately it was attacked by several FW 190s which scored hits almost at will. Lt. Russell put the plane into a dive which extinguished the flames, but number three propeller was "running away" and shaking the entire ship violently. Leveling out at roughly 22,000 feet, Lt. Russell gave the order to bail out. Sgt. Williams, tail gunner, and Sgt. Eaton, top turret, went out through the hole torn by the blast. Lts. Russell and Gritkas went through the bomb bay and Lt. Woerhle, bombardier, through the front hatch. As Lt. Stealey, navigator, sat on the edge of the hatch, the plane blew up. Regaining consciousness, he looked up to see his parachute streaming in tatters. He just had time to brace himself before he hit the water. After 90 minutes he was rescued by some French people and taken to a hospital where it was established that he had a broken left arm, two broken ribs, and a hairline fracture of the skull. The rest of the crew landed on the shore and were captured immediately, except Lt. Russell who evaded capture and lived with a Free French Group for several months before being betrayed.

Lt. Boyd's ship, 42-29874, was slightly damaged. A 2,000 pound bomb which dropped from another ship above took off his wing tip.

JUNE 11, 1943   **MISSION NO. 7**

A maximum effort was ordered against an electric plant in Bremen. Twenty-four planes took off led by Major Burns and Major Wurzbach with Lt. Shaw as navigator and Lt. Wallace as bombardier. About 150 FW 190s and Me 109s jumped the formation over Germany, coming in for close attacks at nose, waist and tail. These attacks caused much damage, especially to 42-29843, piloted by Lt. R. E. Smith, in which S/Sgt. Putaansuu, the tail gunner, was killed. Lt. Norris' ship, 42-3150, was badly hit in the nose, killing the navigator, Lt. Angel.

On this raid it was first reported that a B-17 was being used by the Germans to fly along with the formation to gather information. This report proved to be correct.

JUNE 13, 1943   **MISSION NO. 8**

The mission orders called for another attack on Bremen. Fourteen aircraft arrived over the target, led by Captain Ball with Captain Menees as navigator and Lt. Wallace as bombardier. Two planes were lost. Lt. Jackson in 42-5815 was seen going down over Bremen with three engines damaged. The other ship, 42-5814 piloted by Lt. W. T. Forrest, got into trouble soon after crossing the German coast and was forced to turn back. The plane ditched in the North Sea and eight crew members were picked up by the Air Sea Rescue Service after eight and a half hours.

JUNE 15, 1943 **MISSION NO. 9**

Twenty-one planes led by Colonel Hatcher and Captain Ledoux, with Captain Menees as navigator and Lt. Wallace as bombardier took off on a mission to the Rhone Motor Works at Le Mans, France. They approached the target but 10/10 cloud cover prevented completion of the mission and no bombs were dropped.

JUNE 22, 1943 **MISSION NO. 10**

This was one of the most successful missions to date. Twenty-one planes led by Major Burns and Lt. Col. Wurzbach with Lt. Stover as navigator and Lt. Watts as bombardier, took off to bomb the synthetic rubber plant at Huls, Germany. In spite of intense flak, strong fighter opposition and 4/10 cloud in the target area, direct hits were scored on the aiming point. About 125 red and yellow-nosed Me 109s, FW 190s and Ju 88s attacked the formation at nose and tail, dropping parachute bombs. The Group shot down 17 of them, probably destroyed one and damaged two. Several ships were damaged, including Lt. Omohundro's aircraft in which Sgt. Myszka was killed by German machine gun fire. Lt. Turgeon, piloting 42-29826, was seen going down with a badly damaged wing and two engines on fire.

JUNE 23, 1943 **MISSION NO. 11**

The target was the aircraft workshops at Villacoublay, France. The Group, led by Major Milton and Captain Ball with Lt. Danby as navigator and Lt. Stevens as bombardier, was recalled without dropping bombs because of solid cloud cover.

JUNE 25, 1943 **MISSION NO. 12**

This next mission was to Hamburg. Twenty planes led by the same team as the previous mission took off, but were unable to bomb the primary target because of poor visibility. However, the town of Nordenham, Germany, was picked as a last resort target and bombed with good results.

JUNE 26, 1943 **MISSION NO. 13**

Twenty-one planes, led by Colonel Hatcher and Major Ledoux with Lt. Shaw as navigator and Lt. Wallace as bombardier, made another try for Villacoublay. Again the target was covered by cloud and the planes were forced to turn back without dropping bombs.

JUNE 28, 1943 **MISSION NO. 14**

The Group flew another raid on the St. Nazaire submarine slips. Twenty planes took off, led by Major Milton and Captain Ball with Lt. Danby as navigator and Lt. Wallace as bombardier. The bombing was excellent. Several direct hits were scored on the Eastern lock gate which was the aiming point. The Group arrived in the target area at 1800 hours with the bomb run scheduled from north to south. At the start of the bomb run, the P-47 escorts turned back and were immediately replaced by about 100 Me 109s and FW 190s.

At this time the leader of the second element of the high squadron decided to move his flight from the normal position of above and behind the lead element to below and behind. In doing so 42-29847, piloted by Lt. Adams, hit the prop wash of the lead squadron. The plane, completely out of control, was flipped out of the formation. By the time Lt. Adams had recovered control, the plane was about 1,000 feet below and behind the rest of the Group. Taking advantage of this, 10 fighters immediately attacked. Coming in from six o'clock low, they attacked in single file. The first burst hit the number three engine setting it on fire, with the flames extending beyond the tail. Just as Sgt. Yareff, the ball turret gunner, was describing the damage to the plane, the second fighter attacked. Its bursts hit squarely in the waist, killing Sgt. Yareff, Sgt. Young, the radio operator, and both waist gunners, Sgts. Brannen and Wolfe. The pilot, Lt. Adams, attempted to extinguish the fire, but was unable to do so and eventually rang the bail-out bell. The crew, with the exception of the dead gunners, jumped and watched '847 go into a flat spin and crash not too far from where they then landed. Lt. Adams and Lt. Sage, the bombardier, together with the top turret and tail gunners, Sgt. Claggett and Sgt. Capper, were quickly captured. However, the copilot, Lt. Gloudeman, and the navigator, Lt. Normile, were picked up by the French underground. They eventually arrived back in England via Spain about one month later.

Extremely accurate flak at the target accounted for three more ships. 42-29817, piloted by Lt. King, went down over the target with all four engines on fire. Lt. Copeland in 42-29887 and Lt. Moss in 42-29843 fell out of the formation after the target.

In addition 42-29858, piloted by Lt. Kern, took a direct hit on the ball turret, blowing it and the gunner, S/Sgt. McKeen, away.

JUNE 29, 1943   MISSION NO. 15
As a result of the hectic battles of the last few days, the Group had only eight planes and 14 crews in a condition to fly. However, seven planes, led by Major Burns and Lt. Stewart with Lt. Stover as navigator and Lt. Watts as bombardier, took off for Triqueville, France. They flew the entire route as briefed but were unable to bomb because of solid cloud cover over the target.

JULY 4, 1943   MISSION NO. 16
The holiday was fittingly celebrated by a highly successful raid on the Gnome-Rhone Aircraft Engine factory at Le Mans, France. Eighteen planes took off, led by Major Ball and Lt. Stewart with Lt. Shaw as navigator and Lt. Wallace as bombardier. Only 10 to 15 enemy fighters were encountered, three of which were destroyed. The bombing was excellent.

JULY 10, 1943   MISSION NO. 17
Twenty planes, led by Major Ledoux and Major Burns with Lt. Danby as navigator and Lt. Stevens as bombardier, took off to bomb Villacoublay, France. Because of solid cloud cover over the target, no bombs were dropped. Between 35 and 100 enemy fighters came up to intercept the formation. Seven of them were destroyed, one probable and one damaged.

JULY 14, 1943   MISSION NO. 18
This mission was a raid on the Amiens/Glisy Aerodrome in France. Eighteen aircraft, led by Major Ball and Captain Stewart with Captain Menees as navigator and Lt. Watts as bombardier, took off. All bombed the target and returned. Bombing results were excellent with many direct hits in the northeast dispersal area. Only about 10 enemy fighters were encountered and these did not attack with much determination. Two of them were destroyed.

JULY 17, 1943   MISSION NO. 19
The ordered target was the Continental Tire Company at Hanover, Germany. Twenty-six planes took off, 21 in the 351st and five as part of the composite group. Major Ledoux and Major Milton led, with Lt. Kitko as navigator and Lt. Danby as bombardier. Because the target area was obscured by 9/10 cloud, bombs were dropped on an unidentified town in Germany. About 50 to 60 enemy fighters jumped the formation just before the enemy coast on the way home. They continued the attack for half an hour concentrating on the low squadron. Seventeen were destroyed, three probable and three damaged. Flak was meager and inaccurate.

Aircraft 42-29872, piloted by Lt. W. E. Peters, was attacked by fighters over the Dutch coast and hit in the number four engine which caught fire and had to be feathered. The nose was shattered by a 20mm shell and the bombardier, Lt. Shanes, knocked unconscious. The navigator, Lt. Wattles, was struck by a shell and killed. Then number one engine was hit badly. It could not be feathered in time and ran away. By this time the plane was down to 16,000 feet over the North Sea. The nose, tail and ball turret guns were inoperative or out of ammunition and German fighters were still swooping into attack.

Aircraft '872 was riddled with shell holes; controls and stabilizers shot away. Lt. Peters gave the order "prepare for ditching." The plane, losing altitude at 3,000 feet per minute, hit the water at 125 miles per hour. It bounced back and then down again and sank within 45 seconds. Lt. Peters and his copilot, Lt. Eastlund, went out through the copilot's window, the rest of the crew through the radio room hatch. Lt. Wattles went down with the ship. The left raft had been struck by a shell and only partially inflated. Six men climbed into the right raft and helped to hold up the other three men in the half-inflated left raft. They had been in the rafts an hour when an Ensign circled and dropped smoke bombs. About 45 minutes later, two Walrus seaplanes landed and rescued the crew.

JULY 24, 1943   MISSION NO. 20
Twenty-one planes took off to bomb the magnesium works at Heroya, Norway. The Group was led by Major Burns and Captain Blaylock with Lt. Danby as navigator and Lt. Winter as bombardier. The planes flew most of the way over 10/10 cloud which broke just in time for Lt. Winter to get a lead

on the target and do an excellent job of bombing. Flak was meager and not very accurate and no enemy fighters were seen.

JULY 25, 1943 — MISSION NO. 21

This next target was the aero-engine works of the Klockner Flugmotorenban in Hamburg, Germany. Twenty-four planes took off, led by Major Ball and Captain Morse with Lt. Shaw as navigator and Lt. Stevens as bombardier. An effective smoke screen made it impossible to see exactly where the bombs landed, but 68,000 pounds of incendiaries were dropped somewhere on the city. From 15 to 30 German fighters attacked the formation over the target and on the way home, most of them staying out of range below the formation to attack stragglers. Of those that did venture within range, four were shot down, two probably destroyed and one damaged. Flak over the target was intense and accurate.

Lt. E. S. Boyd, flying 42-3272, was seen falling out of formation in the target area with the number three engine smoking. The pilot seemed to be making a desperate effort to rejoin the formation, but was never able to do so. After losing about 5,000 feet he was attacked by enemy fighters and last seen going into a steep dive.

JULY 26, 1943 — MISSION NO. 22

The destruction of Hamburg continued, with the Blohm-Voss submarine works as the specific target. Twenty-four planes took off, led by Captain Stewart and Major Ledoux with Lt. Stover as navigator and Lt. Stevens as bombardier. Haze, smoke screens and smoke from the already blazing city made it impossible to tell exactly where the bombs landed. About 20 to 30 enemy fighters were seen, but did not attack. Flak was heavy and consisted of pink, white, black and brown bursts. In aircraft 42-5807, the last bomb stuck in its rack. The engineer, T/Sgt. Norman Michel, left his turret to kick the bomb out over the target area. He got the bomb out, but passed out from lack of oxygen, suffering head and back injuries as he was thrown around inside the plane.

JULY 28, 1943 — MISSION NO. 23

Twenty-one planes took off for the Henschel Motor works at Kassel, Germany, led by Major Milton and Captain W. R. Smith with Lt. Danby as navigator and Lt. Winter as bombardier. The planes encountered cirrus fog and thick cloud cover which caused the formation to be recalled over Holland.

JULY 29, 1943 — MISSION NO. 24

This mission was a raid on the Kriegsmarinewerft at Kiel, Germany. Twenty planes took off, led by Major Ledoux and Captain Johnson with Lt. Kitko as navigator and Lt. Bradley as bombardier. In spite of considerable fighter opposition and accurate flak, the bombing was excellent and all ships returned. About 50 to 60 fighters attacked after the formation turned away from the target. The inevitable Me 109s and FW 190s, plus Ju 88s, Me 110s and a few Me 210s came in from all around the clock. Eight were destroyed, one probable and 13 were damaged. Lt. Robert Roessler, a navigator of the 509th Squadron, was killed by a fragment of a 20mm shell and three other crewmen were slightly injured by shell fragments.

JULY 30, 1943 — MISSION NO. 25

Twenty-one planes took off for another crack at Kassel, this time a successful one. Led by Captain Stewart and Lt. Geiger, with Lt. Stover navigating and Lt. Stevens as bombardier, the Group encountered moderate but accurate flak.

About 75 enemy fighters came up as the formation was nearing the enemy coast on the way home. They attacked mostly from seven to one o'clock, some attacking through the entire formation and some attacking in formation of as many as eight fighters in trail. Eight of them were destroyed and four damaged.

Just before the target, Lt. Maginnis in 42-29726 encountered problems. With the supercharger on number four engine frozen, he had to feather the propeller. However, by cutting corners and using extra power he was able to keep up with the formation until the bombs were dropped. After turning for home, however, he was no longer able to keep up with the Group.

Immediately the plane came under attack from enemy fighters. The story is now told by T/Sgt. William Glenn, top turret gunner. "In the cabin we knew that if the barrage of 20mm's continued, we were going to be hit in a vital part of the plane. When a shell hit the oxygen tanks, the concussion made us almost deaf and started a fire in the cabin. Lt. Peterson, the copilot, handed me a fire extinguisher and I managed to put out the fire. Lt. Maginnis put the plane into a dive into some cloud cover, successfully eluding the fighters. As we pulled out of the dive I saw Lt. Peterson reach behind his seat and grab a parachute and strap it on. I thought that we were going to bail out, so I looked for my chute.

"I could not find it, so assumed that it had fallen through the hole in the floor made by the 20mm shells. I certainly felt bad, but I thought no one is going to bail out unless I rode one of them down piggyback style. Later, when we were on the ground I thought that I recognized the chute that Lt. Peterson was wearing. I lifted it up and saw that my name was printed on it. I said nothing, but looked him in the eyes. He was really embarrassed, albeit he had taken it by mistake. It had been his chute that had gone out through the hole in the floor. Later on I went to the armament shop and had a hook made. From then on I kept my chute in the corner of the cabin where no one could get it.

"After the dive into the clouds we found that T/Sgt. McCurdy, the radio man, had been severely wounded by a piece of armored plating that had been shattered by the 20mm shells. The tail gunner, S/Sgt. Reeder, had been shot in the leg and both pilots had been wounded in the legs by shell fragments. We were sure that we would have to ditch, so we gathered in the radio room as ordered by Lt. Maginnis. I then heard shouting from the flight deck, the pilots had spotted land. They gave instructions for everyone to start lightening the plane. This we did, throwing out guns, radios, etc. One of the gunners even threw out his chute.

"As we neared the coast I spotted a runway under construction. Lt. Maginnis made for it, putting the plane down between rolls of large bales of steel mesh. The right hand tire had been shot out, causing it to catch fire before the plane rolled to a stop. We quickly pulled the wounded men from the plane and ran with them behind a pile of dirt in case the plane blew up. We made T/Sgt. McCurdy as comfortable as possible, before an RAF rescue crew arrived. Unfortunately he died the next day."

Another crew also faced the prospect of an uncertain landing. While crossing the French coast on the way back, the four fuel warning lights came on in 42-3046. This was quite unexpected and caused consternation in the cockpit. Lt. Maser elected to stay with the formation, but halfway across the Channel one engine stopped. Feathering the engine, Lt. Maser put the ship into a shallow dive towards the English coast, aiming for the emergency airstrip at Sutton Bridge. Lining up for the runway, Lt. Maser discovered that the undercarriage would not lower as gunfire from fighter attacks had damaged it. Going around again, praying that the remaining engines would not cut out, Lt. Maser set the plane down on the grass. None of the crew were hurt, but the ship was damaged beyond repair.

AUGUST 12, 1943   MISSION NO. 26

This mission was a long haul to Gelsenkirchen, Germany, where the target was the synthetic oil refinery. Twenty-one planes took off, led by Major Milton and Captain Carraway with Lt. Miller as navigator and Lt. Bradley as bombardier. Stiff enemy opposition was encountered and the formation did not reach the briefed target. Instead they did an excellent job of bombing the blast furnace area of the Vereinigte Stahlwerke at Bochum, Germany. About 15 minutes before the target, 25 to 35 German fighters appeared. They attacked up to the bombing run and again afterwards until the P-47 escort came up and drove them off. The Group's gunners shot down four of them and damaged two.

El Conquistador, 42-29874, flown by Lt. Garcia, was badly shot up on this mission. Just after bombs away, flak knocked out the number two engine causing the plane to drop behind the formation. Immediately they were spotted by fighters, who attacked continuously for the next two hours, across Germany, Belgium and three-quarters of the way across the English Channel. The fighters knocked out the number three and four engines, leaving just the number one engine to battle against the headwind. The oxygen system was shot out when 20mm shells came through the bomb bay doors and exploded inside the plane. Another burst hit the pilot's instrument panel, knocking out the hydraulic and electrical systems. The wings, flaps, fuselage and tail were full of holes, but still *El Conquistador* kept flying.

With no interphone it was impossible to know what was happening at the back of the plane, so

Lt. Schohan, the navigator, went to find out. There he found Sgt. E. W. Henninger, the tail gunner, dead. The radio operator, T/Sgt. Ralph Crane, was seriously injured in the face and leg, and both waist gunners, Sgts. Zeitler and Bent, were wounded.

Upon crossing the English coast, Lt. Garcia yelled for everybody to prepare for a crash landing. He had spotted an airfield under construction, Leiston, and headed down towards it. With no flaps and the wheels still up, the plane glided about one-third along the runway before touching down on her belly. At the end of the runway there were about 30 workmen laying the concrete and the ship, with no means of stopping, was hurtling towards them. Lt. Garcia had to kick the rudder, veering the plane over to the right into a pile of earth, to avoid hitting them. Fortunately, no one was hurt in the landing and the injured were rushed to the hospital.

AUGUST 15, 1943   MISSION NO. 27

Nineteen planes, led by Major Blaylock and Colonel Burns with Lt. Stockman navigating and Lt. Watts as bombardier, took off with the aerodrome at Brussels as their primary target. However, they bombed the secondary, the airfield at Flushing, Holland. No enemy fighters were encountered. Flak was moderate and not very accurate and all planes returned unharmed.

AUGUST 16, 1943   MISSION NO. 28

Twenty-one planes, led by Major Blaylock and Major Ball with Lt. Stockman as navigator and Lt. Winter as bombardier, took off for the airfield at Le Bourget. All the planes bombed the target scoring hits on the workshops, barracks and dispersal areas. All ships returned without casualties as only 10 enemy fighters were seen and flak was meager and inaccurate.

AUGUST 17, 1943   MISSION NO. 29

Twenty-eight planes, including the 511th Squadron led by Major Ball which flew in a composite group, took off for Schweinfurt, Germany, to bomb the ball bearing factory. The 351st was led by Colonel Hatcher, Major Blaylock and Captain Carraway with Captain Menees as navigator and Lt. Wallace as bombardier. Spitfires gave excellent support on the way in, but as soon as they turned back over Holland, German fighters closed in, attacking until the target area was reached. On the route home fighters attacked again near the Rhur valley. They continued attacking until the Dutch coast where they were driven off by P-47s. Most of the attacks were made in formations of from three to twenty or more. Coming in from all sides and from both above and below, they pressed home the attacks until they were within 50 feet before breaking off. Many seasoned crew members said it was the toughest fighter opposition they had ever seen. Most of the fighters were Me 109s and FW 190s, plus a few Ju 88s and Me 110s. Flak was only moderate and not very accurate.

Two planes failed to return from this mission. Aircraft 42-5812, piloted by Lt. Pinkerton and flying Tail-end Charlie of the high squadron, composite group, was attacked by a swarm of fighters. After about 10 passes they succeeded in knocking out the number three engine. The plane started going down south of the Rhur. The entire crew bailed out. Lt. Hansen, flying 42-29839 in the number three position of the second element, lead squadron, lead group, was hit in the number three engine. The engine lost all oil pressure and could not be feathered. With the windmilling propeller, the plane could not maintain speed and was forced to leave the formation. As the bombs were salvoed to reduce weight, a fighter hit the plane with four bursts of 20mm. The first came through the nose, taking the plexiglass and nose gun completely away, and exploded under the cockpit among the oxygen bottles, starting a fire. The second burst hit the radio room, starting another fire. The third hit in the waist and the fourth in the tail, taking away the tail guns and leaving the gunner staring into space.

With the aircraft burning fiercely, Lt. Hansen gave the order to bail out before bailing out of the side window himself. He was on the wing of the plane, but found that he could not get his right foot out. Looking back, he saw that it was caught in his parachute which he had forgotten to take with him! Turning back he grabbed the parachute, wrapped the harness around his hand and slipped off the wing. When the parachute opened he was left hanging by one foot and one hand. All the crew, except the top turret gunner, managed to get clear before the ship exploded, but all had severe burns.

Despite the intense opposition, bombing was excellent with hits on the factory and marshaling yards. Of the 150 to 200 German fighters encountered, 25 were shot down by the Group's gunners, two were probably destroyed and 21 damaged.

AUGUST 19, 1943   **MISSION NO. 30**

The target was the airfield at Gilze-Rijen in Holland. Only nine planes took part in the mission, flying in a composite group led by Captain Johnson and Lt. Fontaine with Lt. Kitko as navigator and Lt. Taylor as bombardier. Two runs were made at the target. The fighter escort was forced to leave during the second run. This gave the opportunity for about 25 FW 190s and Me 109s to attack, following the formation as far as Overflakkee Island on the way back. Most of the attacks were at nose and tail positions, singly and in formations of two or three. A couple of Ju 88s were also present, stooging around out of range and firing rockets broadside. The group was credited with having destroyed five of the enemy fighters.

AUGUST 24, 1943   **MISSION NO. 31**

Twenty-two planes took off, including four aircraft which flew as a low element of a composite group, for the airfield at Villacoublay, France. The Group was led by Colonel Hatcher, Captain Stewart and Lt. Kern with Lt. Stover as navigator and Lt. Watts as bombardier. About 20 German fighters were seen, but the P-47 escort very effectively kept them away. The formation went in to do an excellent job of bombing, scoring direct hits in the hangar and workshop areas. Flak was moderate and accurate. Nevertheless all the ships bombed the target and returned safely without casualties.

AUGUST 27, 1943   **MISSION NO. 32**

Twenty-two planes took off to bomb an uncompleted secret weapon construction at Watten, France. The Group was led by Major Ledoux and Lt. Omohundro with Lt. Danby as navigator and Lt. Wallace as bombardier. About 20 to 25 FW 190s and Me 109s attacked just before the I.P., coming in close from above and below on the right side of nose and tail positions. Five destroyed and one damaged was the credited total. Flak at the target and at a few other points was moderate and generally inaccurate. 42-29716, piloted by Lt. Suit, was shot down by German fighters about 10 minutes before the target.

AUGUST 31, 1943   **MISSION NO. 33**

The ordered target was the Romilly-sur-Seine Airfield. Twenty-one planes took off, led by Major Blaylock and Captain Carraway with Lt. Stockman as navigator and Lt. Bradley as bombardier. The target was found to be covered by 10/10 cloud, so the airfield at Amiens-Glisy was bombed instead with excellent results. Hits were scored on barracks, workshops and dispersal areas. Only six enemy fighters were seen. Three of them made a pass at a B-17 and shot it down. Flak was meager to moderate over the target, but very accurate, damaging several planes, however without causing casualties.

SEPTEMBER 2, 1943   **MISSION NO. 34**

Twenty planes took off for the Conche and Evreaux-Fauville Aerodrome in France. The mission was recalled without bombs being dropped.

SEPTEMBER 3, 1943   **MISSION NO. 35**

Another mission to Romilly-sur-Seine. Nineteen planes took off, led by Captain Stewart and Lt. Geiger with Lt. Maze as navigator and Lt. Watts as bombardier. About 25 enemy fighters were encountered. They came up about 50 miles northwest of Paris and attacked on and off over the target and back to a point south of Paris. They attacked in twos and threes, but most of the attacks were weak. The crews destroyed three and damaged three. Flak was light to moderate and all planes returned without casualties.

SEPTEMBER 6, 1943   **MISSION NO. 36**

Cloud obscured the Bosch Component factory at Stuttgart, Germany, so the briefed secondary target, Offenburg, was bombed. Hits were scored on the marshaling yard. Twenty-three planes took off, led by Colonel Hatcher, Major Ledoux and Lt. Johnson with Lt. Kitko as navigator and Lt. Baird as bombardier. From 20 to 30 enemy fighters were seen, but they did not press home many attacks and only one was destroyed.

Fuel shortage on the way home caused 14 planes to land at other airfields to refuel, two planes to ditch and one to crash land. Captain Hathaway, in 42-29684, ditched 20 miles off the English coast. All of the crew were picked up by Air Sea Rescue.

The Air Sea Rescue services were not required when Lt. Norris ditched 42-3150 just below the cliffs at Beachy Head. The crew swam ashore! The cliff tops at New Romney were chosen by Lt. Spika on which to crash land 42-29841.

SEPTEMBER 7, 1943   MISSION NO. 37

Nineteen planes, led by Major Ball and Lt. Spika with Lt. Danby as navigator and Lt. Winter as bombardier, took off to bomb the aerodrome at Brussels-Evere, Belgium. There was little opposition and the formation was able to attack the target very successfully, hitting barracks, a workshop and a hangar. Only six enemy fighters were encountered and they were kept at a distance by excellent P-47 escort.

SEPTEMBER 9, 1943   MISSION NO. 38

Lille-Norde aerodrome was the target. Nineteen aircraft took off, led by Colonel Burns, Major Ledoux and Captain Johnson with Lt. Kitko as navigator and Lt. Baird as bombardier. P-47s gave excellent close cover throughout the mission. No enemy fighters were seen! Flak was encountered at only two places and all planes returned without casualties.

On this mission T/Sgt. Martin M. Keniston of the 508th Squadron became the first member of the Group to complete 25 combat missions.

SEPTEMBER 15, 1943   MISSION NO. 39

This mission took the group back to Romilly-sur-Seine airfield. Nineteen planes took off, led by Major Stewart and Lt. Geiger with Lt. Maze as navigator and Lt. Watts as bombardier. Only eight to ten enemy fighters were seen during the mission and most of these did not attack the formation.

The planes carried a heavy bomb load on this mission. In addition to the twelve 500 pound General Purpose bombs in the bomb bay they carried two 1,000 pounders attached to pylons under the wings. These additional bombs caused high drag thus causing the planes to use much more fuel than planned. This fuel shortage and the fact that the Group returned in the dark caused some confusion. As soon as the English coastline was crossed, planes started to drop out of formation. Lts. Kern, Maser and Argiropulos landed at West Malling, Lt. Maginnis at Duxford, Lt. D. Harris at Ridgewell, Lt. Roberts at Wittering and Lt. Holsapple at Bassingbourne. Lt. Omohundro in 42-3140 thought that he could make it back to Polebrook, however, he could not. Number two engine stopped and Lt. Omohundro was afraid to start transferring fuel for fear of starving the other engines. While they were trying to call up "Darky" on the VHF, number three engine stopped. Now desperately he looked for an airfield while he still had some power to maneuver. He then saw three searchlights ahead, a method of indicating a base. He headed for the lights with the two engines wide open. Lt. Omohundro started in a final approach, but red flares were fired. Somehow he went around again, lined up, and again red flares. Not daring to go around again, he started in, but then saw the reason for the red flares. A Short Stirling bomber was lined up ready for takeoff. "Slipping" his plane, Lt. Omohundro landed on the grass alongside the runway. When the plane stopped he could see what he had achieved. He had managed to land between rows of parked Horsa gliders. The RAF personnel at the base, Wratting Common, were not pleased that he had ignored their flares, but were somewhat mollified when he explained his predicament.

Major Stewart in 42-29825 made it back to Polebrook, but as he made his approach another plane cut in causing him to go around. As he gained height the number three engine cut out, starved of fuel. Lining up again, the same thing happened, another plane cut in again. This time the number two engine quit. Another approach and then the remaining two engines cut out. The plane dropped onto a hedge a half mile short of the runway. The crew escaped with minor injuries, but the plane was written off, as was Colonel Hatcher's personal transport. Lt. Colonel Ball in the Control Tower, seeing Major Stewart's ship hit the deck, rushed out, commandeered the Colonel's jeep and roared off towards where he last saw the lights. As he approached the crash site he met a truck speeding from the opposite direction. Thinking he had room to pass he swung the wheel to the left, straight into a six foot dyke. Again fortunately, no injuries but another write-off.

SEPTEMBER 16, 1943   MISSION NO. 40

Nineteen planes, led by Major Ball and Lt. Morse with Lt. Shaw as navigator and Lt. Winter as bombardier, were sent out to the harbor at Nantes. Their briefed M.P.I., a refueling vessel, was obscured by smoke so the marshaling yards and dock area were bombed instead with very good results. Twenty-five FW 190s and Me 109s, with one Ju 88, attacked the formation. They made a few passes from the tail, above and below, and from the nose above. Yellow-nosed FW 190s and green Me 109s attacked in elements of three to six ships abreast. Fighter escort was excellent and the gunners could not claim any victories. Flak was meager and inaccurate.

In the morning as soon as they returned to Polebrook from the previous day's flight, Lt. Omohundro and crew were ordered to go on this mission. Lt. Omohundro was assigned "his" aircraft, 42-29749, *Belle of the Bayous*. He had been assigned this new B-17 at Morrison Field, West Palm Beach, Florida. On March 31, 1943 with orders to report to the Commanding General, 12th Air Force at Oran, North Africa, they set off for Borinquen Field, Puerto Rico. From there they flew to Marrakesh via Georgetown, British Guiana, Belem, Brazil, Natal, Ascension Island and Dakar, French West Africa. At Marrakesh they were informed that they were not going to the 12th Air Force at Oran, but to the 8th in England. Arriving in England they were ordered to leave the *Belle* at Wharton and proceed to Polebrook.

In June a replacement aircraft was assigned to the 509th Squadron. It was 42-29749 with her name still painted on the nose. When he saw her on the base Lt. Omohundro pleaded with his C. O., Major Elzia Ledoux, another Louisianan, to let him have his "old" plane back. At last he had his wish fulfilled and now flew most of his missions in her.

After leaving the target, Lt. Omohundro saw that he was getting low on fuel. After the previous day's escapade on two engines, he did not want to take too many chances. Leaving the formation he headed back alone. Keeping close to cloud cover he reached the English coast, finding it fog covered. Eventually he found somewhere to land, a small grass field with a windsock and no other planes. He started in on final and again was greeted by red flares. Seeing nothing to hinder him he started in again but more red flares were fired. Remembering the two engine episode, he decided to land. It was then that Lt. Omohundro found out why the red flares had been fired. The field was grass, the grass was wet and the field was small. He managed to get the plane slowed and by ground-looping her, got her stopped with no damage at all.

The crew discovered that the field was used as an auxiliary field by the Royal Navy for very light aircraft and staffed by WRENS. These were a very astonished and excited group of young ladies to think that a B-17 had landed at their field. These young ladies informed the crew that there was an RAF field only 10 minutes flying time away. This was fog bound, but they sent a truck and the crew spent the night there.

The next morning they went back to the field, North Cornwall, with a bowser (fuel truck). After refueling they tried to figure out how to get the plane off that tiny field. They took out all the guns, ammunition and other weighty objects. They decided that only the two pilots, Lts. Omohundro and Carson, the navigator, Lt. Banton, and the engineer, Sgt. Brown, would be in the plane for takeoff. They had walked the length of the field and had found that they could get a downhill run of about 800 yards towards the sea. Lt. Omohundro held the brakes, opened the throttles and started to roll. When they were rolling at a speed that he thought fast enough, Lt. Carson put down some flaps. The B-17 jumped off the ground in less than the 800 yards. The nose was lowered slightly and the plane dropped off the cliff, gained speed and started to climb. Overhead, several RAF planes circled. It was learned later that there had been several bets that the "fool Yank" would not make it.

SEPTEMBER 23, 1943   MISSION NO. 41
Nineteen planes went out again after the supply vessel at Nantes. This time they scored several direct hits on it. They were led by Colonel Burns, Major Blaylock and Captain Carraway with Captain Menees as navigator and Lt. Bradley as bombardier. About 50 to 70 enemy fighters were encountered of which four were shot down and one damaged. Flak at the target was moderate but very accurate for both height and deflection. The task of the flak gunners was made somewhat easier because the formation was forced down to 18,000 feet over the target by cloud. Two men, Lt. Henry and S/Sgt. Nadeau, were wounded. However, all ships returned to base.

SEPTEMBER 26, 1943   MISSION NO. 42
The aircraft assembly plant at Meulan, France was the target for the 18 planes led by Major Ledoux and Lt. Homstad with Lt. Danby as navigator and Captain Wallace as bombardier. No bombs were dropped because of 10/10 cloud cover over the target. No enemy fighters were seen and the only flak encountered was a few inaccurate bursts over Dieppe.

SEPTEMBER 27, 1943   MISSION NO. 43

Nineteen planes, led by Captain Morse and Major Ball with Lt. Shaw as navigator and Lt. Winter as bombardier, took off to bomb the dock installations at Emden. The Germans sent up 20 to 25 FW 190s and Me 109s against the formation. They attacked principally head-on from level and above, concentrating on the lead and low groups. One enemy aircraft was damaged. All planes returned to base.

One this day, Captain Harry Morse assumed command of the 511th Squadron.

OCTOBER 1, 1943

Captain John B. Carraway relieved Captain Morse as 511th Squadron Commander. This left Captain Morse to go on with his missions instead of waiting for his turn as Group Leader.

OCTOBER 2, 1943   MISSION NO. 44

This was another mission to Emden by 19 planes, led by Captain Stewart and Lt. Reed with Lt. Maze as navigator and Lt. Watts as bombardier. About 20 German fighters were seen, but excellent P-47 escort made most of them keep their distance. Only about 20 passes, mostly from the nose and tail, were made. One enemy aircraft was destroyed.

On this and the preceding mission, the Group had its first experience in blind bombing. This technique, developed by the RAF, involved dropping bombs through cloud on flares and marker smoke bombs, dropped by Pathfinder ships in the lead of each combat wing formation.

OCTOBER 4, 1943   MISSION NO. 45

Nineteen planes left England to bomb the city of Frankfurt, Germany. The formation was led by Major Blaylock and Captain Roper with Lt. Stockman as navigator and Lt. Bradley as bombardier. The German Air Force went all out to stop this one. About 100 enemy aircraft of all types attacked. Ten were destroyed, six probable and eleven damaged. There was light flak continuously along the route in, but it was not very accurate. However, at the target it was moderate and accurate both for height and deflection. Two planes were lost in the target area, Lt. Reed in 42-30785 and Lt. Nauman in 42-5807.

OCTOBER 8, 1943   MISSION NO. 46

Major Ledoux and Captain Johnson, with Lt. Danby as navigator and Lt. Baird as bombardier, led 21 planes to the submarine slips and dock area at Bremen. The target was effectively covered by a smoke screen so it was difficult to tell where the bombs hit. Some bombs landed southeast of the target area and four planes dropped their bombs on the aerodrome at Quackenbruck. Over 100 enemy planes were seen, but most of them concentrated on the low group of the Combat Wing. The 351st, flying high group, had only a few attacks from the tail which resulted in the Germans losing two destroyed and six damaged. Flak at the target was intense and accurate, but the Group returned without casualties.

OCTOBER 9, 1943   MISSION NO. 47

The Group was briefed to attack the Arado Aircraft Factory at Anklam, Germany. The crews were very concerned when confronted by the mission details. It was the longest flight to date, with expected moderate to heavy flak concentrations. After the briefing, Sgt. Pete Zibas, the engineer on Lt. Garcia's aircraft, recalls the gunners clamoring for an additional four cans of ammunition per gun.

Twenty-one planes were led by Colonel Burns, Captain Carraway and Lt. Norris with Lt. Stackhouse navigating and Lt. Winter as bombardier. The formation crossed the North Sea at 4,000 feet and prior to climbing to bombing altitude, the fuel was cross-fed into the main tanks and the bomb bay tanks jettisoned. As this operation was being carried out in Flight Officer Warring's ship, 42-3152, fire broke out, but the crew managed to extinguish the flames and the ship continued in formation.

Shortly after crossing the Danish coast, the first fighter attacks commenced. Thirty to fifty Me 109s pressed home many close attacks. The first plane to be hit was the second element lead, 42-30790, flown by Captain Morse. A burst of 20mm exploded in the left wing setting it on fire. Captain Morse dropped his wheels and left the formation under control. All the crew bailed out safely.

At the start of the bomb run the enemy fighters broke off their attacks, leaving the formation to suffer the attentions of the Anklam flak gunners. Smoke from the bombs of the preceding combat wing obscured the target and as a consequence most of the bombs fell in the center of the city.

Flight Officer Warring was still experiencing mechanical difficulties. He was forced to jettison his bombs after the target when the bomb bay doors had to be hand-cranked open.

The formation turned for home and flew straight into the Luftwaffe's assembled forces. Me 110s and a few Ju 88s stood off and fired rockets into the formation. Lt. Maser's aircraft, 42-29603, left the formation with its ailerons shot out and number three engine on fire. All ten crewmen bailed out from the stricken aircraft, but only nine survived. What happened to Sgt. Gorsuch, the ball turret gunner, is not known. Sgt. Gorsuch was on his 25th mission, having substituted for the regular crew member, Sgt. Nadeau, who had been wounded on a previous mission.

At the same time Lt. Christman, in 42-30867, and the luckless Flight Officer Warring went down. Despite injuries to several of Flight Officer Warring's crew, they all managed to bail out. Eight members of Lt. Christman's crew survived. Sgts. Blais and Butterback were killed in the fighter attack.

The fighter attacks persisted for some three and a half hours after leaving the target. In the final stages, Me 109s and FW 190s from coastal fields joined in the attacks. It is believed that it was these fighters that shot down 42-29868, flown by Lt. Turley. Only Lt. Williams, the copilot, and Sgt. Curtis, the top turret gunner, survived the crash into the North Sea. They were picked up by the Germans near the Danish coast.

When the Group landed at Polebrook it was found that Lt. Nardi's ship, 42-29877, had returned with an unexploded rocket wedged in the main spar.

OCTOBER 10, 1943　　　　　MISSION NO. 48
The next target was the city of Munster, Germany. Strike photographs showed that the bombing was good, including some hits in the marshaling yard area. Eighteen planes took off, led by Major Stewart and Lt. Hull with Lt. Maze as navigator and Lt. Watts as bombardier, but only nine aircraft reached the target. The others turned back because of engine trouble or fuel shortage. About 25 enemy planes attacked, of which three were destroyed, one probably destroyed and two damaged. Flak over the target was intense and accurate, but all planes returned. However, Lt. Argiropulos and crew abandoned 42-29851 over England when the plane ran out of fuel. The crew landed safely near Norwich and the plane crashed into the sea at Clovehithe.

OCTOBER 14, 1943　　　　　MISSION NO. 49
Eighteen planes took off for Schweinfurt, but only 10 bombed the target. They were led by Major Blaylock and Captain Roper with Lt. Stockman as navigator and Lt. Bradley as bombardier. Study of photographs indicated that the bombing was good, with hits on the marshaling yards and factory buildings. Fighter opposition was very strong. About 200 enemy planes attacked. FW 190s and Me 109s came in as soon as the fighter escort left. Sometime before the target and at the I.P. the attacking fighters were joined by Me 110s, Me 210s, Ju 88s, FW 189s and Do 217s equipped with rocket guns. The Group destroyed four of them, probably destroyed one and damaged seven. One plane, 42-6096, piloted by Lt. Crismon, was hit by a rocket shell near the target and caught fire before exploding in mid-air.

OCTOBER 20, 1943　　　　　MISSION NO. 50
The target ordered for the 50th mission was the marshaling yards at Duren, Germany. Only seven planes flew the mission in a composite box. No bombing was carried out. The Pathfinder plane turned back before reaching the target and led the Wing back with it. Fighter escort was excellent all the way and no enemy planes were seen.

NOVEMBER 3, 1943　　　　　MISSION NO. 51
Twenty-six planes, including a Pathfinder ship flown by Major Ball with Major Danby as navigator, led the Combat Wing and took off for the port area of Wilhelmshaven. The Group's 25 aircraft, led by Major Stewart and Lt. Bohney with Lt. Maze as navigator and Lt. Watts as bombardier, formed the high box of a composite combat wing. All planes bombed the target using Pathfinder markers. Results were unobserved because of solid cloud cover. About 30 enemy fighters were seen, but they made few passes at the formation.

While in the turn to the bomb run, a B-17 from another group collided with 42-29852 piloted by Lt. Nardi. This collision severely damaged the right wing of Lt. Nardi's plane. The aileron was torn off and several feet of the wing were bent upwards. This damage forced Lt. Nardi to abandon the bomb run and jettison the bomb load while he headed for home. Immediately the plane was attacked by three FW 190s until the tail gunner, Sgt. Gates, shot one down, and Sgt. Burton, the ball turret gunner, shot down the other two. Just as Sgt. Burton shouted that he had downed the second fighter, the B-17 exploded or possibly the right wing broke off completely. The ship went into a tight spin, throwing out the crew members with the exception of the two pilots and the ball turret gunner who went to their deaths with the doomed plane.

NOVEMBER 5, 1943

Captain Clark Gable and his staff returned to the United States upon completion of his filming assignment. Following the death of his wife, Carole Lombard, on January 16, 1943, Clark Gable was described as "inconsolable" and "unapproachable". She died in a plane crash on Potosi Mountain a few minutes out of Las Vegas, Nevada while on a War Bonds campaign. Rumors spread around Hollywood that he was contemplating quitting the movies and enlisting. This prompted an approach from Henry Harley "Hap" Arnold, Lieutenant General Chief of the Army Air Forces.

On August 12, 1942, Clark Gable superstar enlisted at the Los Angeles recruiting office and was sworn into the Air Corps as a private. Private Gable, 19125741, applied for admission to Officers Candidate School and became Corporal Gable, assigned to Miami Beach.

On August 15, Clark Gable and an MGM cameraman, Andrew McIntyre, were inducted. Then followed a 13-week course of grueling 18-hour days, seven days a week. He tackled the job with great dedication and enthusiasm and on October 27, Corporal Gable was discharged to accept his Commission. Now 2nd Lt. Gable 0565390, learned that Hap Arnold required his services to make a propaganda film to provide aerial gunner recruitment which was lagging due to heavy casualties. He and Andy McIntyre proceeded via Gunnery School at Tyndall Field, Florida to Fort Wright, Spokane, Washington where they underwent aerial gunnery and photographic training.

In December they went on Christmas leave. On January 28, 1943, after further training, they were assigned to the 508th Bomb Squadron of the 351st Bomb Group which was based at Pueblo, Colorado. The film was to be made around the Group's activities, and to aid the project Lt. Gable enlisted the assistance of Johnny Mahin as his writer. Mahin was in Intelligence, teaching aircraft identification. Colonel Hatcher personally flew Lt. Gable to fetch Mahin who was based in New Mexico.

Lt. Gable, Mahin and McIntyre together with two cameramen, went to England with the vanguard of the 351st. The "Little Hollywood Group" as they were known set up shop.

The "little group" was initially thought of as the glamour or glory boys, but it turned out somewhat differently. Lt. Gable, although offered special facilities, stayed in the Officers Quarters and ate in the Officers Mess. He went on to complete five combat missions. He participated on the raids to Antwerp, Courtrai, Gelsenkirchen, Heroya and Nantes. His first mission was flown on May 4, 1943 with the 303rd Bomb Group based at Molesworth. He flew with Captain Calhoun in the B-17, *Eight Ball*.

Lt. Gable managed to secure certain concessions from the Group Commanders. Colonel Hatcher at Polebrook gave every assistance with regard to camera installation in the 351st aircraft and allowed crew members to operate cameras to supplement the work of the two official cameramen. Permission was also given for prepared sequences to be shot in the hangars. The now Captain Gable was a familiar visitor to the local villages. These he toured on his small motorcycle, which was perhaps the only privilege he allowed himself. He drank in the local pubs and played an active part in the Group's activities, participating in the softball games which he enjoyed immensely.

Although officially a Group Operations Officer, he was allowed to pursue filmmaking for the greater part of his time. He was also called upon to give morale boosting appearances at many bases. His combat participation was indeed a great inspiration for the men.

Captain Gable's furloughs were usually spent in London, where he was in great demand. He was invited to attend functions, dinners, and all kinds of activities by the press, the military, dignitaries, other celebrities, the English aristocracy and even Royalty. It was difficult for him to really relax. His most restful days were spent with David Niven at his Windsor country home or in the countryside around Polebrook. He often went shooting with the Rothschilds at Ashton Wold, the land on which the base was established.

Prior to returning to the States, Captain Gable was awarded the Air Medal. The "little group" had shot some 50,000 feet of film, so they gathered together the material which had been accumulated over nine months with the 351st and returned to California.

A few months later and with the additional assistance of MGM's top editor, Blanche Sewell, Mahin and Gable completed their task. Air gunner recruitment had picked up, so the theme of the film was changed. It highlighted the general appeal and successes of the Army Air Force and the daytime strategic bombing policy.

On the February 15, 1945 in the Staff Officers Mess and in Consolidated Mess number one, the film entitled Combat America was shown.

NOVEMBER 5, 1943   MISSION NO. 52
The target was the city of Gelsenkirchen, Germany. Twenty-one planes took off, but seven of them returned for various reasons before reaching the target. The Group was led by Captain Carraway and Major Blaylock, with Lt. Stackhouse as navigator and Lt. Winter as bombardier. About 25 enemy fighters were encountered, of which four were destroyed, one probable, and three damaged. Bombing results were unobserved, but photos indicate that the bombs hit somewhere in the city. Flak was meager and inaccurate until the formation neared the Rhur valley, where an intense barrage of accurate, continuous, following fire was put up. Lt. Gaylord's ship, 42-3532, had three engines damaged by flak. Over the English coast all three cut out. Lt. Gaylord ordered his crew to bail out, then headed his crippled ship towards the sea. As he prepared to bail out himself he saw that the ship was veering and heading down towards a large factory on the outskirts of Ipswich. Lt. Gaylord stayed with his plane and made a successful crash landing. Total casualties on this mission were two men killed and four wounded.

NOVEMBER 7, 1943   MISSION NO. 53
A mission to the marshaling yard at Wesel, Germany was ordered. Twenty-one planes, led by Major Blaylock and Lt. Kelley with Lt. Stockman as navigator and Lt. Bradley as bombardier, took off. Two ships returned before reaching the target because of supercharger trouble. The rest of the planes bombed on Pathfinder markers, with unobserved results. Enemy fighter opposition was nil and flak was meager and inaccurate. All planes returned to base without casualties.

NOVEMBER 10, 1943
Several captured German aircraft visited the base. A Ju 88, Me 109 and He 111 were on a tour of bases in order to familiarize the combat crews with their appearance and performance. Late in the afternoon two of the aircraft attempted to land on the same runway, one from each end. The He 111 coming in from the west applied power and attempted to turn and gain altitude. However, it stalled, slid off one wing, hit the ground and cartwheeled, bursting into flames. M/Sgt. Bob Bailey and S/Sgt. Francis Drew, working on the 509th Squadron dispersals, were the nearest to the crash. They grabbed a large CO_2 extinguisher and somehow scrambled through the barbed wire perimeter fence and raced to the wreckage. They were amazed to see the number of dying and injured scattered in and around the wreckage. Apparently, several "joyriders" were in the plane. Sgts. Bailey and Drew set about dragging the men clear. Fortunately, they were wearing parachute harnesses which made it much easier to pick them up.

After several minutes the fire truck turned up but did nothing. It was an English foam truck and the only operator that had received any training had been left behind in the control tower! This was not the only grisly bit of humor. The first ambulance to arrive picked up a dead man and started to leave, but was stopped by the 509th engineering officer who made them unload the man beyond help and pick up some of the still living. As Sgts. Bailey and Drew stumbled exhausted from the wreckage, they were immediately admonished by a military policeman who ordered them from the scene under the threat of immediate arrest.

The wreckage burned all night. Seven men were killed and four seriously injured.

NOVEMBER 13, 1943

Another tragedy occurred over the base. An RAF Mosquito was doing high speed aerobatics and as it tried to pull out of a dive its wing broke off. The plane crashed into the woods between the base and the ground crew domestic area. When the duty officer, Lt. Balkovich, and the medics arrived there was very little left. However, it was established that there had been two crew members. They found two hands and three feet!

NOVEMBER 16, 1943   MISSION NO. 54

Twenty-one planes took off to bomb the molybdenum combine at Knaben, Norway. They were led by Major Ledoux and Lt. Spika with Captain Menees as navigator and Lt. Wallace as bombardier. Three planes returned early. An excellent bombing job was done on the difficult target. Strike photographs showed many direct hits. Only six to eight enemy fighters were seen which did not attack. The only flak encountered was a few inaccurate bursts over the target.

NOVEMBER 26, 1943   MISSION NO. 55

The ordered target was the industrial area of Bremen. Nineteen planes, led by Major Blaylock with Lt. Stockman as navigator in a Pathfinder ship, flew the lead box of the Combat Wing. Twenty planes, led by Lt. Cruthirds and Captain Oldham with Lt. Sullivan navigating and Lt. Watts as bombardier, flew in the low box. Two planes turned back before reaching the target. A third, 42-3560 piloted by Lt. Blaisdell, also turned back early. Near the German border, two superchargers went out. Unable to keep up, Lt. Blaisdell left the formation and turned toward England. Off the Dutch coast a fire broke out. The crew was unable to extinguish it. Lt. Blaisdell gave the order "prepare for ditching". This he did successfully. The whole crew was picked up by Air Sea Rescue 20 miles from the English coast. Lt. Blaisdell's crew was credited with a sortie.

Ten Me 109s and FW 190s were seen but they made few effective attacks. Moderate, continuous, following flak was encountered at several points along the route and at the target.

The plane, 42-39839, piloted by Lt. Lemley, was also in trouble as described by Lt. Dunnigan, the bombardier. "We had some engine trouble when we first hit altitude, but were able to keep up with the Group. We then hit two areas of heavy flak which peppered the plane, but nobody was hit. However this flak caused further damage to two of our engines and we could no longer keep up with the Group. Lt. Lemley asked for a heading to allow us to get as much protection as possible from other groups coming and going to the target. We pulled out of formation and headed back towards the North Sea, the way that we had come in. I salvoed the bombs on the Frisian Islands. We struggled along on the two engines and then the German fighters spotted us. They came up from below, protected by the poor visibility, and raked the ship with machine gun and cannon fire. The B-17 reared and bucked, but she kept right on flying on those two engines. As was the procedure, the crew checked in to me on the intercom. I then discovered that we had been badly hit in the radio room and that we had wounded. There was a large hole in the nose and the wind blast was unbearable. The navigator went up to the flight deck and I took an oxygen bottle and went to check the wounded and assess the damage. The crawl from the nose to the radio room seemed endless. When I reached the radio room I was almost sick. It was shot full of holes and covered in T/Sgt. Barbiero's blood. Sgt. Barbiero was standing up, still full of fight, but his lower leg had been shot off. He was in semi-shock, but had had the presence of mind to apply a wire tourniquet around his thigh. S/Sgt. Anderson, the tail gunner, had been hit in the leg, and S/Sgt. Foubert had been blown out of the ball turret. Sgt. Barbiero would not let me give morphine, he wanted to know what was going on. It was just as well as at that time we did not know what we were going to do. He was a big guy and would have been a dead weight under the influence of drugs.

"I went back to the flight deck where Lt. Lemley was doing a masterful job in keeping the ship flying. We discussed our chances and choices, eventually deciding to make for England. At that point we threw out everything that we did not need. After a couple of tough hours I assembled all the crew, with the exception of the pilots, in the radio room and we prepared for either a crash landing or ditching. The crew was all in position when I noticed the radio equipment on the wall opposite us. If this was torn loose on impact it could crush us. I stood up and was throwing the equipment out of the top hatch when we hit. I went flying and took an awful whack, but Sgt. Barbiero, in all his agony, reached up and pulled me back into the plane.

"Lt. Lemley had to take the plane straight in as we had so little power. The plane plowed right through the roof of a farmhouse and tore up a lot of trees and ground before stopping. The farmer and his family came to our rescue and within five minutes an RAF rescue crew arrived from RAF Marham."

Lt. Lemley's men were not the only crew who had to battle for survival. The original plane assigned to Lt. Castle and his crew had an engine failure before takeoff. They transferred to 42-37817, taking off some 10 minutes after the rest of the group. Their story is now taken up by Lt. Williams, navigator.

"After we had taken off we could not find the 351st since there were planes all over the sky. Finally, we attached ourselves as Tail-end Charlie to a group that was just starting out over the English Channel.

"When we arrived over Holland we could not see the fighter escort that was supposed to meet us. However as we crossed into Germany I could see many German fighters taking off from an airfield below us. Within minutes they were at our altitude and firing at the formation. Then the flak came up thick and fast. It continued as we passed over the target at about noon. Just after bombs away a burst of flak hit the chin turret directly below me, and a fragment barely missed me as it flew right up into the plane. I moved back to the flexible gun on the right side of the nose compartment. In doing so I accidentally disconnected my intercom, losing communication with the rest of the crew. The flak had knocked several large holes in the wings, but all the engines were functioning normally as we emerged from the flak area. The group to which we had attached ourselves began a turn to the right to return to England. We did not turn with them but kept flying straight into Germany. I assume that the flak had damaged the controls and the pilot could not turn the plane.

"When we were all alone in the sky many German fighters attacked our ship. Six Me 109s lined up in formation about 1,000 yards out from my gun position; just beyond the range of my gun. I do not know how many fighters were at other positions around our plane. The first two fighters turned towards us and began firing. Bullet holes began to pop in the nose window and the side of the aircraft. The first two fighters passed below us, and the next two came in for a pass. By the time those two passed below us the first two were back in position, ready to attack again. I always had two fighters coming in on my position and I continually fired my gun at them. Not one bullet hit me, nor did I shoot down a single fighter.

"I had lost communication with the rest of the crew, but I sensed that something was wrong. I moved from my gun position and looked back through the tunnel that led to the flight deck. Lt. Castle, the pilot, was down in the tunnel banging on the escape hatch with a heavy ammunition box. Directly behind the pilot was a solid wall of flame. It looked as if the entire plane, except for the nose compartment was engulfed in flames.

"I crawled back to see if I could help the pilot with the escape hatch. As I crawled towards him he managed to force it open with his foot. He then grabbed me by the waist and forced me out head first. As I fell clear I felt a sense of relief that I had escaped that fire. My next thought was, did I put on my parachute? I looked down at my chest, no chute. Then I felt something tugging at my shoulders and looked up to see my unopened parachute a few feet above my head. Evidently I had clipped the chute on to my harness but the force of the pilot pushing me through the hatch had ripped the risers loose.

"As I was falling, the pilot fell past me with a look of horror on his face. I thought that when we got on the ground I would kid him about how scared he looked. I found out later that both the pilot and copilot had jumped without their parachutes. Evidently their chutes had burned in the fire.

"We had been told that if we had to bail out, to delay opening the parachute so that we would fall away from the fighting. I looked at my chute and decided to open it right away. I pulled it down to me hand over hand and pulled the ripcord. It opened immediately, but I was wearing a harness that was too big for me. The force of the opening jerked the harness up and tight around my throat. There I hung at about 20,000 feet above Germany unable to breathe. I grabbed the risers and gradually pulled myself up until I could breathe again.

"Immediately after landing, and having managed to free myself from the chute, a German sergeant and several soldiers came over a small hill and made me their prisoner."

NOVEMBER 29, 1943   MISSION NO. 56

Again, Bremen was the assigned target. Twenty-four planes took off, led by Captain Carraway and Lt. Gaylord with Lt. Stackhouse as navigator and Lt. Huff as bombardier. The formation turned back before reaching the target. No bombs were dropped, with the exception of one ship which bombed a target of opportunity in the Frisian Islands.

DECEMBER 1, 1943   MISSION NO. 57

The briefed target was Solingen, Germany. Nineteen 351st planes and two Pathfinders flew the lead box of the Combat Wing, led by Major Stewart and Lt. Maze flying one of the Pathfinders. Another 21 planes were put up flying in the high box, led by Captain Carraway and Lt. Gaylord with Lt. Stackhouse as navigator and Lt. Winter as bombardier. Five planes returned early. From 30 to 50 Me 109s and FW 190s were encountered in the vicinity of the I.P. where the fighter escort turned back. Most of the attacks were from head-on.

42-37847, piloted by Lt. Plant, was lost to enemy fighters, spiraling down out of control just after the target. Captain Eugene Harris in 42-3140, nicknamed *Patty Ann II*, ran into trouble over the target when the number three engine went out of action. The bombardier salvoed the bombs, but those in the left hand rack did not fall. Then number four engine cut out and the propeller would not feather. Immediately the ship dropped out of formation and began to lose height rapidly.

S/Sgt. Harold R. Mellot, waist gunner, and S/Sgt. Raymond L. Smith, ball turret gunner, went into the bomb bay to try to release the bombs. While they were struggling to free the bombs, an Me 110 and a Ju 88 made a single pass at the plane, riddling her wings with cannon fire. By the time the two sergeants had released the bombs a half an hour had passed and the Fortress was down to 4,200 feet. Relieved of the weight of the bombs, Captain Harris was able to pull the plane up to 5,000 feet.

The next moment an Me 110 roared in on the right, high and from the front. His guns cut a line along the fuselage. Shell fragments struck S/Sgt. Lucyk, waist gunner, in the thigh and knee. Despite his wounds he stayed at his gun. T/Sgt. Tigue in the top turret had the last word. He hit the Me 110 and it was last seen going down with an engine on fire.

Patty Ann II limped on towards the coast, sneaking into the clouds to hide every time she came to a city. Not far from the French coast, she rode through thick flak and 20mm that had her range. However, she still survived. The gunners, preparing to ditch, threw everything they could overboard, ammunition, flak suits, guns and radio equipment. Near Dunkirk, after the last of the ammunition had gone over the side, S/Sgt. Miles, the tail gunner, caught sight of an Me 109 taking off from an airfield below. The fighter came up, circled the Fort a couple of times and then disappeared. Apparently the pilot realized that the plane could never struggle back to England. By this time *Patty Ann II* was practically at water level, and most of the crew had assembled in the radio room for ditching. One of the two good engines started to splutter. When the pilot tilted the wings, the engine would roar normally for a brief interval, then choke and die again. However, Captain Harris managed to coax the ship five miles beyond the French coast before calling, "This is it." The plane skimmed the water in a perfect landing, scarcely jarring her crew.

Swiftly the 10 airmen started to launch the life rafts. Sgt. Miles sprang into one of the rafts and made for Captain Harris, who was in the water. Sgt. Smith, slipping from the fuselage, plunged into the sea on the right of the ship. Grabbing an insulator, he worked his way onto the wing, pulled a life raft from the Fort and hopped into it. Sgt. Lucyk joined him, as did Lt. Tommy Briscoe, navigator, and S/Sgt. John J. McLain, nose gunner. The life raft drifted towards the tail of the plane, which was slapping hard against the water. Within a few seconds the raft half collapsed, but the men clung to it and it kept them afloat. Sgt. Click had climbed into a five-man life raft on the left side of the plane. Before anyone could join him, the raft had broken loose and drifted almost 100 yards towards the French coast. Sgts. Tigue, Mellott and Lt. James J. O'Donoghue, the copilot, crowded into the one-man life raft. They had the emergency radio set with them. Wind and tide seemed to have been at cross currents, for these three were carried towards England. From time to time, they yelled to keep in touch with the others. The last anyone saw of them, they were bobbing towards the English coast.

By paddling hard, Sgt. Click worked his large raft to the damaged one. The men lashed it to the side that had collapsed and both rafts stayed afloat. Then Sgt. Miles pulled up in his small raft with Captain Harris clinging to the side. They pulled Harris into one of the large life rafts and tied Miles' little raft on behind.

Patty Ann II had landed in the Channel at 1400 hours. Two minutes later she sank. From their rafts, some of the crew watched her nose dip under the water until only part of the tail stayed at an angle above the waves. The radio operator had not managed to get off an SOS; his equipment had been too badly shot up.

The Channel wasn't especially rough and the weather wasn't bad so the men didn't worry much. Knowing the efficiency of Air Sea Rescue, they assumed they'd be picked up in three hours at the most. To make themselves as comfortable as possible, they shifted about in the rafts. Harris, Briscoe and Click in the large undamaged one; Smith, Lucyk and McLain in the other and Miles in the small one behind. They tried to paddle but the waves were too high for that, so they just drifted and waited to be rescued.

Shortly before dark the sea became choppy and the skies overcast. Far towards the English coast, the men faintly saw the barrage balloons of a convoy and they hopefully shot half a dozen flares that went unseen. A wind came up after sunset and Miles joined the men in one of the larger rafts where it was warmer. The fliers were cold and they couldn't carry on much conversation above the noise of the wind, but they weren't discouraged. At 2200 hours, when the weather had cleared slightly, they saw searchlight beams crisscrossing in the sky over Dunkirk. They discussed the idea of paddling into the French coast, which wasn't very far away, and trying to make a break from there. Most of them were certain they'd be rescued in the morning, so waiting until help came seemed the wisest course.

At midnight it started to rain. The rafts filled with water and the men took turns bailing them out. The damaged raft kept losing pressure. Someone had to pump for five or ten minutes an hour to keep it sufficiently inflated. Although there were rations and drinking water aboard, no one wanted any. They huddled under their tarpaulins, when they could, and tried to sleep. Harris and Briscoe seemed to doze a little, but for the others sleep wouldn't come.

When *Patty Ann II* had taken off that morning, Harris had a bad cold that he had concealed from the flight surgeon. With only two missions remaining, he had insisted on going in hopes of finishing his combat tour so he could be home by Christmas to see his wife, Eloise, who was expecting a baby. Late that first night he became delirious and began to lose his voice.

Someone passed around the rations. Most of them ate a few malted milk tablets and drank a swallow of water. Harris and Miles got sick from the food and said they didn't want any more. The wounds in his knee and thigh were hurting Lucyk, but he tried not to show it. Not once did he complain about them.

When daylight came around 0900 hours, a fog had settled over the Channel. The men knew that searching parties wouldn't be able to find them that day either. Throughout that Thursday, between spells of light rain, they marveled among themselves that they had been able to bring *Patty Ann II* back alone over such a long stretch of heavily defended enemy territory. There was no point in trying to paddle, the waves were still too high. The bad raft continued to leak air. The others in it being too fatigued, Smith alone worked the pumps that kept it afloat. They hoped the English fliers would spot them and radio Air Sea Rescue. Later more rain fell. Harris, in a stupor, was worse. As best he could, Briscoe cared for him and tried to keep him warm.

In the darkness of early Friday morning, the airmen heard the lingering booms of huge guns off both the French and English coasts.

Getting a bearing from the navigator, some of the men headed the raft northwest and paddled for almost two hours. Then they ran into heavy dark clouds, wind and rain. They pulled the tarpaulins over them and tried to sleep. Smith lay with one hand where he could feel when air pressure in the leaking raft had reached the danger point. Harris, who had gradually been growing worse, moaned intermittently. McLain, too, had been losing strength little by little. That long Friday afternoon was hell for all of them. At nightfall, Click first noticed that Miles had lost practically all of his resistance. Eventually Miles slid from his seat into the water-filled bottom of the life raft. Click pulled him out, slapped him and pinched him, but Miles was dead.

An hour or so later while the rafts were hung on the crest of a large wave, a second wave suddenly plunged Briscoe, Harris, Click and Miles' body into the Channel. Click grabbed the pump on the raft when he popped out of the water and forced a leg over the side. Smith clasped him and held him there. Lucyk meanwhile managed to drag Briscoe back into the raft. Then the three pulled Click all the way to safety. They couldn't find Harris' or Miles' bodies.

The survivors thought they had drifted into the North Sea; for huge, rough waves slapped up into their faces and a strong wind splashed them with a cold drizzle. The rafts were so full of water that bailing was useless. The men made themselves as comfortable as they could. As the waves had washed some of the tarpaulins overboard, Briscoe and Click pulled in the one-man raft and cut it up for covering. Still there wasn't enough material to shelter both. Click gave the covering to Briscoe. Then he crawled through the water to one end of the raft. He huddled there for a long time.

One long miserable hour dragged on to the next. Hunched at his end of the raft, a dazed Click couldn't prevent weird thoughts from coming into his head, so he got up and started to bail out the life raft again. Water kept coming in as fast as he threw it overboard, but the work didn't let his mind wander.

Then he realized that his hands were freezing. When they were out of the water where the wind could strike them they were numb. He stuck them into the water and kept them there. The water was icy cold, but it was warmer than the air.

Saturday morning brought no change in the weather. McLain was completely exhausted. Sitting upright, looking straight ahead, he pounded his arms rhythmically on the sides of the life raft in an effort to warm himself. He babbled and moaned. After a time, the beating became slower and slower, feebler and feebler. Finally, he stiffened, and his arms remained motionless on the sides of the raft. The others knew that he was dead.

Soon after, Smith and Lucyk joined Briscoe and Click in the good life raft. They carried along their tarpaulin, but that didn't keep the waves from splashing over their bodies and drenching them, or a bitter wind from knifing their bodies. Freezing, exhausted and almost beaten, they knew they couldn't last another day. They gave up what little hope remained.

Then they saw two Spitfires circling overhead, but Briscoe who had been on his final mission, slumped to the floor of the life raft and died.

The three surviving sergeants were picked up by an Air Sea Rescue launch 10 miles off the French coast. They had been adrift for 70 long cold hours.

Although the survivors would fly no more combat missions, the Grim Reaper would again call. Sgt. Paul Lucyk lived through the hell of the Solingen mission only to die in the flaming wreck of a B-17 on a Welsh hillside in June 1945.

DECEMBER 5, 1943   MISSION NO. 58
This mission was to bomb a ball bearing factory in western Paris. Thirty-five planes took off. Seventeen were in the lead box, led by Major Ledoux and Lt. Carson with Lt. Danby as navigator and Captain Wallace as bombardier. The 18 planes in the low box were led by Lt. Harris and Lt. Kelley, with Lt. Marquardt as navigator and Lt. Baird as bombardier. Solid cloud cover prevented the Group from bombing the target. Bombs were jettisoned in the Channel or brought back to base.

DECEMBER 11, 1943   MISSION NO. 59
Two combat boxes from the 351st took off for the port area and city of Emden. One box of 21 planes was the lead group of the Combat Wing, led by Captain Oldham and Lt. Floden with Lt. Maze as navigator and Lt. Watts as bombardier. The other box of 21 planes was led by Lt. Cruthirds and

Captain Boykin, with Lt. Sullivan as navigator and Lt. Tynan as bombardier.

Eighteen ships in the lead box and 16 in the high box attacked the target. Results were not accurately observed because of ground haze and a smoke screen in the target area. Only six enemy fighters were seen, concentrating their attacks on the lower echelons. Flak was moderate and inaccurate. All ships returned without casualties.

DECEMBER 13, 1943   MISSION NO. 60

Twenty-three planes, including a Pathfinder piloted by Colonel Lacey and Lt. Stockman, took off to bomb the submarine building yards at Keil. Only five enemy fighters were seen throughout the mission, none of them coming close enough to bother the formation. Flak was moderate and fairly accurate. Bombing results were not observed because of clouds over the target.

DECEMBER 16, 1943   MISSION NO. 61

This mission took the group back to the city of Bremen. Two 18-plane boxes were put up. A high box was led by Captain Norris and Lt. D. Harris, with Lt. Provenzale as navigator and Lt. Shames as bombardier. A low box was led by Lt. Gaylord and Captain Boykin, with Lt. Stackhouse as navigator and Captain Wallace as bombardier. The planes turned back in mid-Channel on the orders of the Wing Commander and no bombs were dropped.

DECEMBER 20, 1943   MISSION NO. 62

Another attack on Bremen was ordered. The 351st put up a high box of 19 planes, led by Lt. Lynch and Lt. Kelley with Lt. Stockman as navigator and Lt. Smith as bombardier, and a low box of 19 planes, led by Lt. Gaylord and Captain Boykin with Lt. Stackhouse as navigator and Captain Wallace as bombardier.

Twenty-six of these planes attacked the target. A smoke screen made observation of results difficult, but photographs indicate that bombs fell in the southeastern part of the city. About 25 German fighters were seen, but not many pressed home with attacks. Of those that did, three were destroyed and one probably destroyed. Flak at the target was intense and accurate. A tail gunner in the 509th Squadron suffered a serious head injury from a 20mm shell.

Aircraft 42-30866, piloted by Lt. Peters, suffered a runaway propeller on number three engine, losing both propeller and engine cowling. In the ensuing confusion two crew members bailed out. The bombardier, Lt. Gardiner, bailed out about 25 miles southeast of Emden and the radio operator, S/Sgt. Albro, already wounded in the leg, left the plane in the vicinity of Zuidlaarber Lake.

DECEMBER 22, 1943   MISSION NO. 63

Thirty-four planes took off to bomb the marshaling yards and steel mill at Osnabruck, Germany. The mission was abandoned by the Combat Wing Commander before the target was attacked because of bad weather. Fighter opposition was very weak, consisting of only a few attacks by FW 190s and Me 109s. Light inaccurate flak was encountered at a few points along the route.

Group leaders in the high box on this mission were Captain D. Harris and Lt. Colonel Cobb, with Lt. Pullen as navigator and Lt. Baird as bombardier. Lt. Carson and Captain Boykin led the low box, with Lt. Heldman as navigator and Lt. Spinning as bombardier.

Lt. Maginn, in 42-39778, was forced to ditch in the North Sea when returning with engine trouble. This incident is described by Lt. Maginn:

"Our aircraft, *Lucky Ball*, had just completed an overhaul and had two engines replaced with rebuilt ones. It was our fifth mission and the target was Osnabruck, Germany. The weather was damp and cold with very strong winds blowing from the west. Even though our plane was pronounced in A1 condition, I was nevertheless concerned about the engines and felt that I would be much happier with them after they had accumulated some more hours of running time. From the start things went wrong. Two of our regular crew could not go on the mission, so two spares were assigned to fill their positions in the ball turret and tail gun. The mission plan was to assemble over a radio beacon on the East coast, then the Group in formation was to join the other Bomb Groups and start the climb to the proper altitude en route to the target. For some reason our Group Commander did not join the stream of Bomb Groups crossing the English Channel at the proper time, and it was only when we saw B-24 Groups approaching, and they were supposed to be behind us, was it realized that we were far behind our assigned location in the stream of Bomb Groups. To regain our position, the lead aircraft of our Group gradually increased power both to gain speed and altitude. We soon found ourselves running at near full power and we were still falling far behind in our formation, as were many others of our Group. We had not yet reached bombing altitude when the oil pressure on our number four engine started dropping. We took all corrective measures possible, but the oil pressure continued to drop and before it reached the critical point, I pressed the feathering button to stop the engine and turn the propeller blades so that they would provide no drag. By this time we were quite some distance behind our squadron, but the target was not far and I felt that we might still stand a chance to catch up even with three engines running at near full power. However, our position changed drastically a few minutes later when the oil pressure on our number three engine started dropping rapidly and I had only a very short time to try corrective measures before it was necessary to push the feathering button on the number three engine.

"Now, with two engines out on the same side, it was no longer possible to catch up, or remain airborne indefinitely for that matter, so reluctantly we turned back. With no targets of opportunity in sight we jettisoned our bomb load into the Zuider Zee, and then also jettisoned most of our ammunition and other unneeded equipment. I trimmed our plane as best as possible to maintain a true course but we continued to lose altitude gradually, even with our number one and two engines running at near full power. At this point I felt we had sufficient altitude and short enough distance to go to the English coast, and that we would not have to ditch in the sea, but our situation changed a few minutes later.

"The tail gunner called out, 'Fighter six o'clock high,' but could not identify it immediately. In our crippled condition we would have been an easy victim for an enemy fighter so we promptly dove to a cloud cover at about 10,000 feet. Just as we reached this altitude, the gunner identified the fighter as a P-47. We leveled off and the fighter came up alongside us and after waving his wings at us flew on ahead. We had lost precious altitude in our dive and then to make matters even worse, the oil pressure on our second engine started to fluctuate and then drop. At about the same time we started to get some flak from the German guns, although l don't recall that any hit us. Anyway we had to take some evasive action which cost us more altitude and with the oil pressure still dropping on the number two engine, I had to feather it. We immediately jettisoned all remaining expendable equipment including our guns and ammunition, but with only one engine now running we were losing altitude rapidly.

"We still felt, however, that we might get to the English coast and crash land wherever possible. Nevertheless, we prepared to ditch, running through the ditching procedure and assembling the crew in the radio room. The radio operator, Sgt. Palmer, started sending the SOS signal. We were heading for Norwich across the North Sea and with a very strong headwind it soon became apparent we would not reach land, even though the English coast was now in view. I could see that the water was choppy. No chance to land in the trough of a wave as the "book" says you're to do. We dragged along on one engine until we were just above the wave tops, then I had to cut the remaining engine because it was causing the plane to swerve and I wanted to land as straight as possible. At about 85 mph we hit the water, and for a few seconds both Lt. Brooks, my copilot, and I blacked out as we were thrown violently forward by the rapid deceleration. I actually thought we were underwater, and in fact we were until the nose of the plane started to rise and then I could see that we were floating.

"Brooks at once pulled the emergency release cord on his copilot's window which allowed the window to fall away, and started to climb out. I opened my window but became stuck in the small opening, so I rapidly backed away and climbed out of the copilot's window. Just as I stepped onto the wing it started to sink, so both Brooks and I inflated our Mae Wests and went into the water. The shock of the cold water was instantly numbing, but even worse was the shock I experienced when I looked at the rear of our plane. The tail from the radio compartment back was sticking up in the air indicating that the plane had broken in half on landing. This fracture had jammed shut the escape hatch from the radio room and therefore the rest of the crew could not get out. Brooks and I immediately started swimming to the side of the plane to see what we could do. Then gradually the nose and wings started to sink, causing the radio hatch to break open, and one by one the crew scrambled out. I called to Dave Shrom, our engineer, to pull the cables to release the life rafts, but he replied that they were jammed and bent and that he was unable to release them. Unfortunately, the plane had no exterior release cables so we could not get at the rafts, therefore the men had to take to the water.

"We assembled together in the water and watched *Lucky Ball* sink. Our efforts to remain together proved fruitless. The first big wave came crashing over us and we could no longer hold on to each other. Palmer assured me that the air rescue squadrons had a "first class fix" on us and that a rescue boat was probably already on the way. However 30 minutes and finally 45 went by before the boat appeared. By this time we were scattered over a 100 yards of sea making it difficult for the boat to find us all, much less to pick us up. I'm sure that by this time some of my crew were overcome by exposure; the wind and bitter cold water took its toll rapidly. I had just about given myself up, when the boat threw me a line. I caught it and hung on for dear life while they hauled me aboard. Three others were already on the ship and shortly after a fifth was brought into the small cabin in which we were huddled. I then discovered Lts. Brooks and Rufeisen and Sgts. Shrom, Palmer and myself had survived. Lt. McMorrow, Sgts. Bucceri, Meyer, Nadeau and Rowlinson were not found."

DECEMBER 24, 1943   MISSION NO. 64

The briefed target was two of the many new rocket launching installations in the Pas de Calais area. Two boxes of two squadrons each took off, for a total of 34 planes. The lead box was led by Lt. Colonel Burns and Lt. Wendt, with Captain Menees and Captain Matthews as navigators and Captain Wallace as bombardier. In the high box was Captain Carraway and Lt. Boyle, with Captain Danby and Lt. Schwartz as navigators and Captain Winter as bombardier.

Bombing was by squadrons with good results. There was little opposition from fighters or flak. All planes returned without casualties.

DECEMBER 30, 1943   MISSION NO. 65

Two boxes were put up to bomb the IG Farbenindustrie Chemical and Explosive Factory at Ludwigshafen, Germany. The high box was led by Lt. Gaylord and Lt. Smith, with Lt. Schwartz as navigator and Lt. Huff as bombardier. The low box was led by Lt. Cruthirds and Lt. Floden, with Lt. Sullivan as navigator and Lt. Tynan as bombardier.

A total of 36 planes attacked the target, but bombing results were not observed because of solid cloud cover over the target. About 15 enemy fighters were encountered, but only a few ineffective attacks were made on the formation. Flak at the target was moderate to intense and only fairly accurate.

One plane, 42-31162, piloted by Lt. Parsons, turned away from the target with one engine burning. As the ship dropped out of formation the crew bailed out.

On the bomb run, 42-39780 was hit by flak in the number three engine. Lt. Adamiak, the pilot, directed the copilot, Lt. Crockett, to feather the propeller. However, because of the loss of the oil pressure he was unable to do so. The bombs were salvoed to lighten the load, but the ship was unable to maintain its position in the formation because of the drag created by the windmilling propeller. Deciding to go home, Lt. Adamiak made a left turn that carried them over Heidelburg, crossing the Rhine between Wiesbaden and Frankfurt, heading for Calais and Dover. Still at the mission altitude near Frankfurt the plane met heavy flak, receiving hits in the number four engine. By this time the number three propeller had broken loose from the shaft and the extreme heat caused by the windmilling propeller had caused the engine to catch fire. With the plane vibrating badly and with the loss of power on the right side, the two pilots had to use all their strength to keep control.

Sometime later over the German border, several fighters were spotted so Lt. Adamiak decided to go into the overcast. The dive into the overcast put the fire out, leaving the engine smoking badly and red hot. With the propeller throwing hot metal from the disintegrating engine through the right side of the cockpit, flak suits were used to line the wall between the pilots and the engine.

Due to the erratic course that the plane had been flying, the navigator was unable to plot the position accurately. Therefore, Lt. Adamiak decided to fly under the cloud to find their position. This he did successfully and after sending an emergency signal the plane was picked up by a flight of RAF Spitfires just off the coast of France. The Spitfires escorted the damaged ship to RAF Hawkinge near Dover. Lt. Adamiak decided to crash land the plane in an open field, rather than the airfield. This was accomplished without injury to the three occupants of the plane, the two pilots and Sgt. David, the radio operator. Unbeknown to the pilots, the rest of the crew had bailed out as soon as the plane reached the coast of England. Unfortunately, at such a low altitude, the parachutes of only two men opened in time. The other five were killed when they hit the ground.

DECEMBER 31, 1943   MISSION NO. 66

The briefed target for the last mission of the year was the aircraft assembly plant at Bordeaux, France. However, it was found to be covered by solid cloud, so the secondary was bombed, the aerodrome at Cognac. Seventeen planes flew in the lead box, led by Colonel Hatcher and Major Blaylock with Captain Danby as navigator and Captain Smith as bombardier. Another 17 flew in the low box, led by Lt. Lynch and Lt. White with Captain Matthews as navigator and Lt. Lyttle as bombardier. The bombing, as shown on strike photographs, was excellent, with direct hits on nine hangars and a concrete apron, and possible hits on the fuel dump, main runway, taxi strip, perimeter track and aircraft on the ground. From 40 to 50 enemy planes were seen. Starting in the area of Bordeaux, they continued attacking until within 30 minutes from the English coast. Flak at Cognac was intense and extremely accurate.

Despite being hit, Colonel Hatcher's plane, 42-37731, completed the bomb run and dropped on the target. Captain Jack Danby was on the lead ship to check out a new lead navigator, Lt. Taylor. As they neared the target, Danby went forward to assist Captain Smith with identification. As he did so the flak began and the ship was instantly hit. They managed to complete the bomb run by which time they had sustained another direct hit. As efforts to contact Captain Boykin in the tail failed, one of the waist gunners crawled back to see what had happened. Part of the tail section was gone and Captain Boykin was dead. The ship was hit again and Lt. Taylor slumped to the floor, mortally wounded. He died in Captain Danby's arms as he tried to administer medical aid. By this time the starboard inboard engine had been partially shot off and was burning badly. The abandon aircraft order was given and up front Colonel Hatcher and Major Blaylock bailed out, followed by Captains Smith and Danby.

Colonel Hatcher and the two captains were immediately captured as they landed on the very edge of what must have been the only German military camp in western France. Major Blaylock's parachute did not open.

Lt. Marvin Bender's crew was forced to bail out when 42-39823 was crippled by flak. Lts. Wilcox and Freeman and Sgt. E. Anderson were befriended by French partisans and evaded capture. However, the rest of the crew was captured.

Lt. Saville's ship, 42-3495, was badly hit and he sounded the alarm bell. The crew jumped, but Lt. Saville and Lt. Bill Playford, copilot, stayed with the doomed ship in a desperate attempt to aid the ball turret gunner, T/Sgt. John Myrick, who was seriously injured and unable to jump. They skillfully effected the crash landing in Vichy, France and eventually escaped over the Pyrennes, but T/Sgt. Myrick died of his wounds and was buried in France.

Two other ships went down in the target area. Lt. Putman and crew were forced to abandon 42-31179 when it caught fire. Lt. Wells, in 42-29948, losing fuel from holed tanks and with only one engine operating, was forced to ditch just off the French coast. Fortunately they were all quickly rescued by a French fishing boat.

The low Combat Box leader, Lt. Nick Lynch, was in no position to perform his lead duties. He was flying Tail-end Charlie with his number four engine on fire and number three throwing oil badly. A fire had started in the cockpit and with Lt. Lynch unable to see, they soon became detached from the formation and became an inviting prey for the Me 109s which had followed the formation for most of the flight. The waist gunners, Sgts. Norquist and Suddock, were wounded along with Lt. John White, the copilot. To make the situation worse, Lt. Bill Lyttle was temporarily blinded when accidentally sprayed in the face with a fire extinguisher. Sgt. John Paige, the radio man, recalls S/Sgt. Peppard standing up to his knees in the flames desperately fighting the fire which threatened to engulf the pilots. Although all three sustained burns, the fire was extinguished and they eventually reached an RAF field on the south coast.

Soon after bombs away, 42-29630, *Piccadilly Commando*, flown by Lt. Willis Smith, shuddered as a heavy caliber shell burst close by, knocking out one of the engines and damaging the oxygen and electrical systems. Immediately the plane lost speed and altitude but no crew members were injured.

Lt. Smith headed '630 out into the Bay of Biscay along with the rest of the formation, but because of the battle damage she steadily fell behind along with the rest of the stragglers. Inevitably, the German fighters began attacking the damaged aircraft as they struggled northwards on the long flight back to their bases. Without the concentrated fire power of the formation to help protect them, several of the bombers fell victim to their onslaughts. The crew of *Piccadilly Commando* knew it was only matter of time before the fighters turned their attention to them.

They were not to be kept waiting long, but if the Luftwaffe pilots had thought it was going to be an easy kill, then they were in for a surprise. *Piccadilly Commando* and her crew still had a great deal of fight in them and although repeated attacks were made on the ship, it was at least two of the Luftwaffe which went down in flames and not the battle scarred bomber. For the second time that day the crew emerged unscathed. She had, however, received many more hits which resulted in the loss of a second engine, further reducing her airspeed. Consequently, the aircraft continued to lose altitude at a steady rate. Strong headwinds too, were having a serious affect on her performance and as they passed over the North Brittany coast it became all too obvious that she would not have sufficient fuel left to complete the Channel crossing.

As they headed out over the cold grey waters, Lt. Smith gave the order to lighten the ship. Soon the crew was busy throwing out everything which was detachable such as machine guns, radio tuning units, frequency meters, flak suits, etc. From his radio room, Sgt. Stephen Bodnar observed Sgt. Carl Linblad throwing his .50 caliber machine gun out of the left waist window and watching to see how big a splash it made when it hit the sea. When he mentioned this to Carl later he had no recollection of his action. The nine men then assembled in the radio room while Sgt. Bodnar pounded out an SOS together with the aircraft's position on his Morse Key. He managed to get a feeble reading on the output meter but cannot be certain if the Allied aircraft they saw later had responded to his call or that of some other bomber experiencing difficulties.

In the cockpit, Lt. Smith with the aid of Lt. Harlan Bixby, copilot, concentrated on the task of setting the big bomber safely down on the water. Coming up to starboard he could see the island of Guernsey and decided to put down as close as possible to the shore to afford his crew the best chance of being rescued, albeit by the enemy. *Piccadilly Commando* was now down to a few hundred feet above the waves as she flew slowly up the west coast of the island, when suddenly a new hazard faced the crew. The coastal defenses plus the Luftwaffe light and medium flak opened fire on the dying aircraft and subjected her to an intense barrage as she descended slowly towards the sea. Yet again their luck held and although it seems certain that the aircraft must have been hit, incredibly her crew once again escaped serious injury.

When the alarm bell was sounded, the nine men took up their ditching positions and waited. The first impact was very gentle, little more than a slight drag, but the second was heavier followed by rapid deceleration. Seconds later the cold salt water was flooding in and the airmen began to evacuate through the hatch in the roof of the radio compartment. Lts. Smith and Bixby seem to have experienced considerable difficulty in exiting through the cockpit windows, but eventually joined the rest of the crew in the sea.

Only one of the life rafts inflated, the other perhaps having been damaged by the various attacks on the bomber. The non-swimmers were placed on the raft while the others hung on to the side ropes. One of the last to leave the sinking craft was Sgt. Norman St. Pierre who ran the length of the wing before diving into the sea and joining his companions. Sadly, they watched *Piccadilly Commando* settle lower in the choppy water, then amid the noise of snapping control cables, she broke in half and slid under the waves to her last resting place many fathoms below. Lt. Smith had done a magnificent job in the face of appalling difficulties in successfully ditching his severely damaged bomber, which at the last moment had lost all power, in a choppy sea and under an intense barrage of gunfire.

A combination of wind and tide drove the raft toward the dangerous rocky coast and it was not long before it grounded upon a reef of rocks some 300 yards off shore. Here the men landed and climbed up the rocks out of reach of the waves. Once there, they tried to attract the attention of some troops nearby with their shouts and by firing flares. Shortly afterwards they became aware of automatic and small arms fire being directed towards the reef and quickly took cover, believing that it was being aimed at them. They later realized the target was an Allied fighter aircraft which was circling the reef, presumably assessing their situation.

After a long wait on their cold and windy ledge they sighted a small patrol boat heading in their direction which eventually stopped a short distance away. A life raft was then launched from it and paddled to the reef from where it conveyed two men per trip to the waiting boat. Once the rescue was completed the vessel set a course which took it around the northern tip of Guernsey, down the east coast and into the safety of St. Peter Port Harbor. Darkness had fallen by the time the airmen came ashore. They were met, Sgt. Bodnar recalls, by a German Officer dressed in a long black leather coat who, after some discussion, informed the men that they would be taken to the "Happy Landings Hotel." One can only imagine the crew's thoughts at this information!

Lt. Willis Smith and his crew were not the only ones to have an unplanned visit to the Island of Guernsey. Lt. Albert Jones, flying 42-29877, *Speed Ball*, had escaped damage by flak and left the target area with the main force. German fighters attacked the formation as it flew back over the Brest Peninsula and some persisted in these actions to within 30 miles of the English coast. During these attacks, 42-29877 was hit. One engine was put out of action, another suffered a serious loss of power and Sgt. Bittner, the tail gunner, was severely wounded.

Lt. Jones was forced to ditch his crippled ship at approximately 1430 hours some 12 miles north of Guernsey; the nine surviving crew members taking to the life rafts. Lt. Charles Bronako, the bombardier, recalled a British fighter circling their ditched aircraft shortly before she sank beneath the waves and spirits rose in the belief that rescue would soon arrive. Sadly this was not to be and as the short winter daylight drew to a close, the crew, in their now saturated clothing, huddled together for warmth against the bitter cold of the winter's night.

Throughout the night of December 31, 1943 and into the morning hours of January 1, 1944 the nine survivors of *Speedball's* crew struggled against the elements in an open life raft on the bitterly cold sea. Sometime between 2200 hours and midnight Lt. Dearborn, the navigator, succumbed to exposure; his body being committed to the deep, with all the dignity possible under the circumstances, by his fellow airmen. During this time, the tide turned and by the early hours of the morning the life rafts were being carried towards the northwest coast of Guernsey, close in fact to where Lt. Willis Smith and his crew had landed some hours previously. The life rafts grounded on an exposed reef, said to have been the Saut Rocher, and the drenched airmen thankfully climbed upon the rocks and tried to alert the attention of the Germans by firing flares at half-hourly intervals. Little seems to have been done to effect the rescue of the stranded men by the occupying force who could not have failed to see the flares.

By 0630 hours the rapidly rising tide began washing over the reef. Sgt. Carl Bekken, the ball turret gunner, who had taken off his life vest to use as a pillow on the rocks, was swept away at 0650 hours, followed shortly afterwards by the rest of the men. Now, weakened by exposure, they became the playthings of the waves. Only Lt. Kenneth Vaughn and Lt. Charles Bronako survived to be washed ashore by the surf where they were found by German soldiers. Following treatment they were taken to the "Happy Landings Hotel."

The 27 ships which had survived had many more dangers to endure. They were all desperately short of fuel and heading for home in the darkness of a winter's afternoon, worsened by a thick fog. All were experiencing acute radio communication difficulties and to add to this, there were still enemy fighters scanning the homeward flight paths. Understandably, many of the ships sought the nearest field for refuge while the tattered remnants of the two boxes proceeded inland, the lead group landing at Rattlesden, Suffolk, and the low group at Thruxton, Hampshire.

The last ship to be lost on this day was 42-37774, flown by Lt. Edward Apperson. Lt. Apperson recalls, "When it was finally time to descend, all fuel gauges indicated very close to empty. The sun was sinking below the cloud layer now, ground visibility was obscured by fog, our "G" navigation equipment was inoperative and it was my judgment that we would probably have no fuel for maneuvering flight after breaking through the overcast. I decided we would make a nylon let down. I trimmed the aircraft for level flight, headed it at 90 degrees, engaged the Automatic Pilot and we bailed out." The crew landed safely between Bassingbourne and Cambridge. The plane eventually ran out of fuel and crashed near Witwell, Cambridgeshire. Lt. Dave Litsinger emphasizes the critical fuel shortage when he recalls following his element leader, Lt. Milton Sherman, into RAF Wyton, Huntingdonshire and having to avoid him parked on the runway out of gas!

Lt. Al Kogelman was also in trouble, one engine out, a critical fuel situation and urgently seeking somewhere to land as the weather worsened.

The sudden appearance of a Spitfire eased the tension and gesturing to explain his predicament, Lt. Kogelman followed the fighter down through the clouds to be presented with the welcoming sight of a coastal field. Although it was a very small fighter strip Lt. Kogelman went straight in, managing to avert the obvious problem of going off the end of the runway. As he turned his ship on the perimeter, a B-24 obviously with similar problems came in over his head and affected a perfect belly landing finishing up at the other end of the runway!

The inhabitants of what turned out to be a Fleet Air Arm training establishment near Bournemouth reveled in the excitement of what was for most of them their first taste of combat activities and their first encounter with American bomber crews. Needless to say, they treated their guests royally at the New Year's Eve Party!

Maj. John Blaylock, 510th CO. KIA December 31, 1943. (F. Richardson)

Rear: Lt. Robert Wilcox, Lt. Harold Freeman, Lt. Marvin Bender, Lt. William Grupp.
Front: Sgt. Lawrence Anderson, Sgt. Francis Rollins, Sgt. Robert Plunkett, Sgt. Francis Anderson, Sgt. Harold Long, Sgt. Veikko Koski. Shot down December 31, 1943. (R. Wilcox)

Rear: Lt. Edward Apperson, Lt. John Ledyard, S/Sgt. Lawrence Koslev, Lt. William Connors, Lt. David Proctor. Front: T/Sgt. William Pappas, S/Sgt. Charles Matthews, S/Sgt. Raymond Bailey, Sgt. David Gaitskill. Shot down December 31, 1943. (J. Tynan)

Chapter Three
IN EARNEST

The war was not over by Christmas. The last raid of 1943 brought about the end of an era. Colonel Hatcher, who had been with the Group since its foundation, had been shot down. In November the Group became a 70 ship establishment. The aircrew complement was increased by diverting crews who were destined for the 401st Bomb Group to the 351st.

JANUARY 3, 1944

The weather was too bad and the Group could not assemble enough ships to go on missions.

Colonel Romig was assigned as Group Commanding Officer to replace Colonel Hatcher who was shot down on the December 31, 1943 mission. Eugene Romig graduated from the United States Military Academy at West Point in the class of 1939. Upon completion of flying training, he was assigned to the 2nd Bomb Group at Langley Field, Virginia. As the European war heated up and the Army Air Corps expanded, he was assigned to the 34th Bomb Group (H), newly activated and stationed at Westover Field, Massachusetts. There he flew anti-submarine patrols until, in a further expansion he was assigned to the newly formed 303rd Bomb Group (H), as Squadron Commander, Headquarter Squadron.

In October 1942 the 303rd went overseas with Major Romig as C. O. of the 359th Squadron. In February 1943 he became Operations Officer for the 303rd and was promoted to Lt. Colonel. In the late spring he moved to the newly activated 41st Combat Wing to serve as Executive Officer for Brigadier General Robert Travis.

JANUARY 4, 1944   MISSION NO. 67

Seventeen planes took off for a raid on Kiel, led by Major Stewart and Lt. Cruthirds, with Captain Maze and Lt. Sullivan as navigators and Captain Watts as bombardier. Fifteen of these planes bombed the target. However, results could not be observed because of solid cloud cover. The only enemy fighters seen were three or four Me 109s attacking stragglers. Flak was fairly accurate, both at the target and at various points on the route in and out. All planes returned without casualties.

JANUARY 5, 1944   MISSION NO. 68

Eighteen planes, led by Lt. Gaylord and Lt. Smith with Lt. Schwartz as navigator and Captain Wallace as bombardier, took off on a mission to the Aerodrome at Tours, France. Sixteen aircraft bombed the target, scoring hits on hangars, ammunition and fuel storage, dumps and aircraft on the ground. About 10 Me 109s and a few FW 190s were seen during the 15 minutes after the target. These aircraft were taken care of by the escort. Flak was weak and inaccurate. All planes returned unharmed.

JANUARY 7, 1944   MISSION NO. 69

The briefed target was a chemical factory at Ludwigshafen. Twenty planes took off, led by Major Ledoux and Lt. Carson with Lt. Heldman as navigator and Captain Wallace as bombardier. Bad weather over England caused great difficulty in forming, forcing 13 planes to return without attacking. Bombing was on Pathfinder markers, but dense cloud in the target area made it impossible to observe the results. About 25 enemy planes were seen, which included the inevitable Me 109s and FW 190s and a couple of Me 110s. None of these attacked the Group. Flak was meager and inaccurate. All planes returned to England. However, as Lt. H. J. Anderson, piloting 42-29821, was descending over the coast, the ship was caught in prop-wash and disintegrated in mid-air. The plane crashed at Sutton Bridge with Lt. Anderson, Lt. O.E. Webb, Lt. W.H. Udick, S/Sgt. R.J. Allen, S/Sgt. F.H. McNamara and S/Sgt. Leonard Edwards being killed. Lt. B.L. Finnell was injured, but the other crew members escaped.

JANUARY 11, 1944   MISSION NO. 70

The assigned target was an aircraft factory and assembly plant at Oschersleben, Germany. Only six planes from the 511th Squadron, flying in a composite box, bombed the primary target. The other planes attacked a target of opportunity at Konigslutter. Twenty-two planes flew the mission, led by Captain Oldham and Lt. Floden with Lt. Badger as navigator and Lt. Trollinger as bombardier. The bombing of the squadron in the composite box was unobserved, but the others dropped their bombs in the northeast section of Konigslutter.

The German Air Force evidently made an all out effort to stop this raid, sending up from 100 to 150 fighters. This included FW 189s, FW 100s, Me 109s, Me 110s, Me 210s, Do 217s, Ju 88s and even a few Stukas. They began their attacks immediately after the fighter escort left a few minutes before the I.P. and continued for 45 minutes. The single-engine fighters employed their familiar tactics, peeling off in echelons of from two to five and barrel rolling through the formation from all directions. The Ju 88s tried air-to-air bombing, while the twin-engine planes used rocket firing guns. Me 210s flying behind the wing in similar formation were not recognized for what they were until they suddenly peeled off in trail for vicious tail attacks.

Six planes were shot down by the fighters. Lt. Cannon in 42-29861, Lt. Garner in 42-39905, Lt. Case in 42-31481 and Lt. Procak in 42-3523 went down between the I.P. and the target. Lt. Myers in 42-30780 and Lt. White in 42-39761 went down after bombing the target. The loss of Lts. Cannon and Myers ended a remarkable run. The 509th Squadron had flown 52 missions during some of the fiercest air battles the Group was to encounter. These were the first losses due to enemy action since June 13, 1943. All surviving aircraft had to land at coastal airfields on their return to England as 9/10 stratus covered Polebrook.

JANUARY 14, 1944   MISSION NO. 71

Ten planes made another trip to the Pas de Calais. The target was one of the rocket-launching installations near Abbeville. The formation was led by Captain Roper and Lt. Kelley, with Captain Matthews as navigator and Lt. Lyttle as bombardier. The bombing was good, with direct hits on the assigned M.P.I. and other buildings in the immediate area. Escorting fighters were very effective. No enemy aircraft were seen. Flak was light but accurate. All planes returned without casualties.

JANUARY 21, 1944   MISSION NO. 72

The target was another rocket-launching site near St. Omer. The formation of 20 planes was led by Lt. Kelley and Captain Richardson, with Captain Matthews as navigator and Lt. Lyttle as bombardier. Because of 8/10 cloud there was some difficulty in making a bombing run and results of the bombing were not clearly observed. Escort support was excellent. There was very little flak and all planes returned without casualties.

JANUARY 24, 1944   MISSION NO. 73

Frankfurt was the assigned target, but the planes were recalled before reaching it because of bad weather. Twenty-eight planes took off, led by Major Ball and Lt. Nesmith with Lt. Korf as navigator and Lt. Huff as bombardier.

JANUARY 29, 1944   MISSION NO. 74

Frankfurt again was the assigned target. This time the formation reached the target and bombed it on Pathfinder markers through solid cloud cover. Nineteen planes attacked the target in the lead box and five in the high squadron of a composite box. The 351st was led by Major Ball and Lt. Gaylord, with Lt. Schwartz as navigator and Captain Wallace as bombardier. Twenty-five to thirty German fighters attacked from the I.P. to the target and for about 20 minutes afterwards. Close attacks were made on the lead group by Me 109s, FW 190s, Ju 88s, Me 110s, Me 210s, Me 410s, FW 189s and Do 217s. Attacks came from all around the clock. Most of the twin-engine fighters had rocket guns which they fired at close range from formations of four abreast. The single-engine fighters imitated the escort tactics and queued up before making head-on attacks. Flak at the target was intense but inaccurate. All planes returned without casualties.

JANUARY 30, 1944   MISSION NO. 75

Twenty-nine planes took off for Brunswick, 11 of them forming the lead and low squadrons of a composite group and 18 in the low group. One plane in the low group had to turn back early because of mechanical trouble. The low group was led by Major Ledoux and Lt. Carson, with Lt.

Heldman as navigator and Lt. Spinning as bombardier. Captain Roper and Lt. Kelley led the composite group, with Captain Matthews as navigator and Lt. Lyttle as bombardier. Moderate enemy opposition was encountered. About 25 to 50 German fighters were seen from near the I.P. until shortly after leaving the target. Most of the opposition was furnished by Me 109s and FW 190s which pressed home attacks from above and head-on. Some dropped aerial bombs and Me 110s and Me 210s fired rockets.

Aircraft 42-3509, piloted by Lt. Robertson, fell out of formation soon after bombing with number four engine on fire. After some maneuvering, the fire went out and the plane straggled on behind the formation. At this point Lt. Robertson had to dive into cloud cover to escape from four German fighters. Coming out of the clouds, he met up with four P-47s who provided cover. However, Lt. Robertson could not make it and he was forced to land in occupied territory.

FEBRUARY 3, 1944   MISSION NO. 76

The first mission for the month of February was flown to Wilhelmshaven. Sixteen planes flew in the lead group, led by Major Stewart and Lt. Cruthirds with Captain Maze as navigator and Captain Watts as bombardier. The high group consisted of 11 planes, led by Major Carraway and Lt. Nesmith with Lt. Livesay as navigator and Lt. Davis as bombardier. Bombs were dropped on Pathfinders through 10/10 cloud and results were unobserved. Only about 15 enemy fighters were seen and flak was meager. While opposition was light, Lt. Walby's crew in 42-31509 had a bad day. T/Sgt. Vernon R. Schnuelle, waist gunner, was in the bomb bay cranking the doors closed when he lost his footing and fell from the aircraft without his parachute. Lt. William N. Finn, bombardier, had his foot crushed when it was caught in the mechanism of the ball turret.

FEBRUARY 4, 1944   MISSION NO. 77

Twenty-five planes flew a Pathfinder mission to Frankfurt, led by Major Roper and Lt. Lynch with Captain Matthews as navigator and Lt. Lyttle as bombardier. Observation of the bombing results was impossible due to the 10/10 cloud cover over the target. There was considerable flak, but no enemy fighters and all aircraft returned without casualties.

FEBRUARY 5, 1944   MISSION NO. 78

Two formations were put up to bomb the aerodrome at Chateauroux, France. A lead group of 17 planes was led by Colonel Romig and Lt. Gaylord, with Captain Menees and Lt. Korf as navigators and Captain Winter as bombardier. Eight other planes in a composite box were led by Lt. Kelley and Lt. Grunow, with Captain Matthews as navigator and Lt. Lyttle as bombardier. The bombing was excellent with direct hits on hangars and runways. Enemy fighter opposition was weak. About 10 to 15 Me 109s and a few FW 190s were seen, but no attacks were made. The only flak was light and inaccurate. No losses or casualties were suffered.

FEBRUARY 6, 1944   MISSION NO. 79

The assigned target was the aerodrome at Dijon. As this area was covered by solid cloud, bombs were dropped instead on the aerodrome at Caen with excellent results. Heavy concentrations of hits were seen in the area of repair shops an administrative buildings, with several direct hits on four hangars.

Twenty planes flew in the low box led by Major Ledoux and Lt. Clay, with Lt. Pullen as navigator and Captain Matthews as bombardier. Fourteen planes in a composite high box were led by Captain Fishburne and Lt. Floden, with Lt. Sullivan as navigator and Lt. Trollinger as bombardier. About 10 FW 190s and Me 109s were encountered, but extremely good fighter cover prevented any persistent attacks. Flak was generally meager and not very accurate. There were no losses and no casualties.

FEBRUARY 11, 1944   MISSION NO. 80

Another mission to Frankfurt was flown by 24 planes, led by Lt. Colonel Burns and Lt. Schwartz as navigator flying in the Pathfinder ship. Bombs were dropped on Pathfinder markers, but partial visibility enabled some crews to observe smoke and fires in the target area. About 25 Me 109s and FW 190s were seen, but excellent escort made most of them keep at a reasonable distance. Some, however, were able to make sneak attacks by simulating escort tactics and then coming in fast from the tail. Flak at the target was moderate and accurate.

The plane piloted by Captain Carson, 42-29863, was seen lagging behind the formation with one feathered propeller about 10 minutes after the target. Later he was heard calling for fighter support, but to no avail. Captain Carson was forced to land in occupied territory. The plane piloted by Lt. Turbyne, 42-31694, was forced to crash land at Southend where the ship caught fire and burned out. Unfortunately the bombardier, Lt. John A. McCall, was killed. The rest of the crew escaped with cuts and bruises.

FEBRUARY 20, 1944   **MISSION NO. 81**

The target was Leipzig. Sixteen planes flew the mission as high box of a First Combat Wing composite led by Major Roper and Lt. Lynch, with Lt. Lyttle as bombardier and Captain Matthews as navigator. Seventeen planes flew the low box of the 94th Combat Wing, led by Major Stewart and Lt. Floden with Lt. Dixey and Lt. Badger as navigators and Lt. Lee as bombardier. The low box bombed Leipzig with good results. The high box was forced to choose a target of opportunity, an industrial plant at Stazfurt. As many as 40 enemy fighters were encountered. Attacking before and after the target, they came in from all around the clock, sometimes lining up in groups of six to twelve planes before pressing home concentrated attacks. Flak at the target was moderate and accurate.

The plane piloted by Lt. Nelson, 42-31763, *Ten Horsepower*, was heavily attacked. Lt. Nelson was originally scheduled to fly right wing off the Group Leader, but the plane had run off the perimeter track and had been stuck in the mud. When they eventually became airborne they were almost an hour behind the Group. Lt. Nelson was able to make up time, however, catch the Group, and settle into the Tail-end Charlie position. Just as they were approaching the I.P., a fighter attacked from head-on. A 20mm cannon shell came through the copilot's window. It just about decapitated Flight Officer Bartley, ricocheted off the armor plate behind him, and hit Lt. Nelson in the right side of his face. Lt. Nelson managed to hit the alarm bell before becoming unconscious. Upon hearing this, Lt. Martin, the bombardier, salvoed the bombs, called for the rest of the crew to abandon the aircraft, then immediately bailed out.

At that point the plane went into a steep, spiraling descent. T/Sgt. Carl Moore, top turret gunner, somehow managed to reach the controls and get the plane leveled off, but not before it had dropped some 15,000 feet. As soon as the plane was under control, Sgt. Archie Mathies, ball turret gunner, moved quickly to the front of the plane. He immediately asked for help in moving Flight Officer Bartley's body. Sgt. Joe Rex, the radio operator, helped move Flight Officer Bartley into the nose of the aircraft. Sgt. Mathies then sat in the copilot's seat and started to fly the plane back to England. From time to time he had to call back to ask for help in flying the plane. One person could not stand the cold from the wind coming in the completely broken windshield. Fortunately Lt. Nelson had insisted, during training, that each crew member should have at least two hours experience flying the plane, just in case they were ever forced to do so.

During the attack the command radio had been destroyed. Sgt. Rex had to rig the high power radio to send out SOS signals. As he did so the German fighters came in to attack again, hitting the plane with 20mm shells in the radio room and injuring Sgt. Rex with shell fragments. However, the fighters were driven off by the fire of the gunners.

Against all the odds late in the afternoon 42-31763, *Ten Horsepower*, appeared over Polebrook. Lt. Truemper radioed the tower explaining their predicament, but emphasizing their intention to get the aircraft down as Lt. Nelson's injuries were such as to prevent him from bailing out.

Major Ledoux, Tower Officer of the Day, immediately summoned the C. O., Colonel Romig, who when presented with the facts and the knowledge that neither Lt. Truemper or Sgt. Mathies had ever effected a landing, ordered Mathies to head the ship for the coast and bail out. However, Sgt. Mathies' resolve forced a compromise. The remaining five gunners, Sgts. Carl Moore, Joseph Rex, Russell Robinson, Thomas Sowell and Magnus Hagbo, bailed out over the field while he and Lt. Truemper listened to landing instructions and advice being transmitted from the tower.

Colonel Romig and Major Ledoux decided to take up another B-17, *My Princess*, 42-30499, to try to "talk them down" while flying alongside providing confidence and instructions. This however, proved to be more of a problem than a help as the damaged aircraft was flying a very erratic course. Collision was more of a probability than a possibility.

Therefore from a comfortable distance in the aircraft flown by Major Ledoux, Colonel Romig talked them through two approaches to the field. Both were too high and too fast. Another attempt was made at Molesworth, set in differing terrain, but again without success. The decision was then made to try to set the aircraft down in the countryside near Polebrook. A large rolling field to the east of the airfield was selected. This time the approach was more purposeful, but they chose, probably without thought as they fought the controls, the up gradient rather than the down. The result was that the nose dug in and the ship disintegrated. Lt. Truemper and Sgt. Mathies died instantly.

The first rescue services on the scene retrieved Lt. Nelson alive from the wreckage but, mortally wounded, he died later that day. On July 4, 1944 on the lawn of their home at 807 North Avenue, Aurora, Illinois, Mrs. Henry E. Truemper, with her son's Navigator Wings pinned on her blouse, received the Medal of Honor awarded for her son from Brigadier General R. E. O'Neill. A similar ceremony took place on July 23, 1944 at the First Presbyterian Church in Finleyville, Pennsylvania where Mrs. Mary Mathies received her son's Medal of Honor from Major General A. Craig.

The B-17 Lt. Nelson and crew took to Leipzig belonged to another crew that was on a 48-hour pass. One of the crew members on leave was Corporal William Stroh, a radio operator and gunner. His pilot was Lt. Horace "Hoppy" Hopkins. Lt. Hopkins' crew felt they would be flying 42-31763 quite often. Because there were 10 men on the crew, and their pilot's name was Horace, they had named 42-31763 *Ten Horace Power* although it was never painted on the aircraft. Lt. Hopkins and his crew returned to Polebrook just in time to see two B-17s flying low over the base. Only later did they learn that one of the planes they had seen was theirs. Corporal Stroh recorded the day's events in his diary. "Today our plane *Ten Horace Power*, No. 763, crashed. We returned from a 48-hour pass in London this afternoon to find that Lt. Nelson and his crew was out on a mission in our ship. It was a long mission to Leipzig. Enemy fighters attacked Lt. Nelson's plane firing 20mm shells. Two came through the windshield, killing the copilot, Lt. Bartley, and seriously wounding the pilot. They went into a tight spin. The bombardier, thinking they would surely crash, was the only one who finally managed to get out of the plane, parachuting down into enemy territory. The navigator and the engineer finally got the ship under control and followed the formation back to England. Over our base we saw 5 of the crew bail out at a low altitude and got down with a few injuries, sprains, etc. The navigator and engineer then tried to land at another field but crashed, killing them both. God rest their souls. They stuck with their ship trying to land it with their wounded pilot aboard."

FEBRUARY 21, 1944   MISSION NO. 82
The target assigned was Gutersloh, Germany, but bad weather forced the planes to bomb elsewhere. The airfield at Achmer was picked as a target of opportunity. Sixteen planes were assigned to the lead box led by Colonel Cobb.

Scheduled number three to take off in this lead box, Lt. Evans in 42-29858 lost an engine just after takeoff. Struggling to gain height he turned to the left to try to land from the west. Flying below tree-top height around the field, he eventually crash landed one mile from Oundle.

The second formation, a low box led by Lt. Cruthirds and Lt. Craven with Lt. Sullivan as navigator and Lt. Lee as bombardier, also lost one ship on takeoff. 42-29848, piloted by Lt. Ritzema, failed to get off the ground, skidding off the end of the runway, fortunately without exploding or injuring the crew.

Over the target 15 to 25 enemy fighters were encountered, including several twin-engine planes. Most of these did not make vigorous attacks, but considerable accurate flak was encountered.

The gunners targeted 42-30866, *Pistol Packin Mama*, knocking out number two and three engines. Lt. Al Kogelman feathered number two, but found his efforts to feather number three unsuccessful so the bomb run was undertaken with a windmilling propeller. Away from the target area, *Pistol Packin Mama* understandably began to struggle under her impediment, her two operative engines straining well beyond safety limits. As the mission continued, she dropped further and further back creating a situation which the Luftwaffe were ever eager to exploit.

S/Sgt. Sheldon Johnson was scanning the sky from his left waist position when suddenly he saw the left horizontal stabilizer disappear. It had been sheared off about a foot from the fuselage by 20mm cannon fire. There were also six large holes in the left wing. A FW 190 veered off to the left trailing black smoke and the intercom suddenly came alive with an excited jumble of voices all shouting at the same time.

Lt. Kogelman quickly restored order and reported control of the ship. S/Sgt. Gil Dennison, the tail gunner, claimed the FW 190 while other reports established the presence of more enemy fighters.

Sgt. Johnson saw an Me 109 flying a parallel course at eight o'clock high. The fighter turned and came in for the attack. A long burst from the .50 caliber machine gun hit its mark. The Me 109 broke out in black smoke, banked off to the right and spiraled into the waters of the Wester Schelde. Excited claims for two more fighters were being called over the intercom, but to whose guns they fell to will remain a mystery as a lone P-47 had joined the melee. The presence of the fighter gave Lt. Kogelman the opportunity to dive for cloud cover at a lower altitude. The ship still seemed willing so they took up a course flying on instruments in the clouds. Out over the North Sea the crew began jettisoning equipment in an effort to aid the ailing engines. About 15 miles from the English coast, at 2,000 feet and 115 mph, *Pistol Packin Mama* finally succumbed to her aggressors. Two passes by an Me 109 and his wingman riddled both wings and damaged both the remaining engines. *Pistol Packing Mama* was not to die alone. The gunners claimed both fighters, which crashed in the sea nearby. Barely 30 feet above the waves '866 stuck to her task. By this time number four engine had gone and ditching was inevitable. Everyone except Lt. Kogelman and Lt. Haynes assumed the ditching position. S/Sgt. Rawdon transmitted SOS signals until the last possible moment.

The ship clipped the top of an 18 to 20 foot swell and bounced back into the air. The second impact was tremendous. The ship came to an abrupt stop and the tail section snapped off. '866 immediately filled with water and sank within a minute. The crew scrambled out of the top hatch while the pilots escaped from their side windows as she went down.

Within a few seconds six of the crew were in or clinging to a raft. Lt. Armour, S/Sgt. Locke and S/Sgt. Spicer were clustered together calling for help a few feet away, but before the raft could reach them they disappeared under a huge wave and were never seen again. Lt. Haynes, a very strong swimmer, retrieved the other raft, but it was full of holes and deflated. Sgt. Johnson was lying on the edge of the raft with his arm around Sgt. Dennison. Sgt. Dunlap was in the raft holding Sgt. Rawdon out of the water and Lts. Kogelman and Shafer were also in the raft holding on to Lt. Haynes.

The three men in the water soon showed signs of drowsiness due to the extreme cold, but spirits rose when a squadron of A30s flew over. One ship peeled off, circled the raft and rejoined his flight, but an hour or so later gloom had set in. The raft was now filling with water and both Sgt. Dennison and Lt. Haynes showed no signs of life. Then suddenly, they heard the drone of an aircraft. Moments later a P-47 appeared overhead, commenced a circling pattern and dipped its wings. Using their last remaining dregs of strength and spirit, the remnants of *Pistol Packin Mama's* crew gave a cheer when a British Air Sea Rescue launch appeared on the horizon. Minutes later they were hauled aboard, some three and a half hours after ditching. Tragically, Lt. Haynes and Sgt. Dennison were found to be dead. The survivors were wrapped in warm blankets and plied with hot rum before being taken to Great Yarmouth and then to a British Naval Hospital. Sgt. Johnson was found to have suffered a broken leg during the ditching. Two days later they were picked up by a 351st ship and flown back to Polebrook where Sgts. Johnson and Dunlap were transferred to ground duties and Sgt. Rawdon to C-47s. Lt. Kogelman continued to fly, completing 30 missions with the rank of captain. Lt. Shafer also flew again but was killed by German citizens when he parachuted from Lt. Dixey's ship on June 14, 1944.

FEBRUARY 22, 1944   MISSION NO. 83
Sixteen planes, led by Lt. Gaylord and Lt. Smith with Lt. Mahaffey as navigator and Captain Wallace as bombardier, flew the high box of the 94th Combat Wing. Another six planes flew in the high squadron of the low box. The high box did an excellent job of bombing the airfield at Bernberg, while the low box bombed Magdeburg as a target of opportunity when they found the primary target obscured by cloud. About 25 to 50 enemy fighters of various types were seen. They

lay in wait to pick off stragglers, but made an occasional attack through the formation. Flak at the target was negligible, but for some reason the return trip was made over the Ruhr Valley where an intense and accurate flak barrage was thrown up.

Lt. Pugh in 42-39857 was shot down by fighters over the target, but Lt. Ritsema's plane, 42-31612, fell victim to the Ruhr flak. Lt. Mears in 42-31882 was unable to land due to damaged landing gear. Mears pointed the plane towards the east. He and his crew bailed out over Norfolk. The plane crashed into the North Sea. Lt. Watson was forced to crash land 42-38023 at Framlingham. 42-38038, piloted by Lt. Winton, had been hit in the nose section by cannon fire which killed the navigator, Lt. John R. Jonaitis, and the bombardier, Lt. David J. Van de Walle. The plane crash landed at Wittering without hydraulics and brakes.

FEBRUARY 24, 1944   MISSION NO. 84
The Group took another crack at Schweinfurt. The bombing was excellent, with many direct hits on the buildings of the Deutsche Star ball bearing works. Sixteen planes attacked the target, led by Lt. Colonel Ball and Lt. Holsapple with Lt. Duncan and Lt. Maze as navigators and Lt. Behrendt as bombardier in the Pathfinder lead ship. About 25 FW 190s and Me 109s were encountered. Most of the attacks came while the formation was in the target area, pressed in from above and level head-on and from level and below the tail. Flak at the target was moderate and accurate.

Two planes failed to return from this mission. 42-3136, piloted by Lt. LeClerc, fell out of formation west of Osnabruck with number two engine smoking. The ship crash landed in Eastern Holland. Lt. Coughman's ship, 42-3517, went down about 50 miles west of Osnabruck.

FEBRUARY 25, 1944   MISSION NO. 85
Eleven planes flew this mission to Augsburg, Germany. They formed the lead and high squadrons of a composite high box led by Lt. Floden and Lt. Craven with Lt. Badger as navigator and Captain Watts as bombardier. Enemy aircraft opposition consisted of about 30 planes, including Me 109s, FW 190s and Me 110s and 210s. Most of the attacks were from above and head-on, often by formations of three or four fighters in line abreast. Intense accurate flak was encountered at the target and there was considerable flak at various points on the way in and out. However, all planes returned without casualties.

MARCH 2, 1944   MISSION NO. 86
Twenty-one planes flew a mission to Frankfurt, led by Major Ledoux and Lt. Peck with Lt. Barton as navigator in a Pathfinder ship. Bombing was through 10/10 cloud and observations of the results were impossible. Just before the I.P., about 15 Me 109s and FW 190s began persistent attacks, most of them in simulated escort formation from above and level. A second attack was made on the way back, just East of Lille, by about 10 fighters. Light to moderate accurate flak was encountered at the target and at various points along the route.

Lt. Seaman, in 42-31776, was flying Tail-end Charlie. Approximately 50 miles from the target, the plane was attacked by about 20 enemy fighters. This attack knocked out the number two engine and set number three on fire. Lt. Seaman put the plane into a dive towards some cloud cover, putting out the fire in number three engine on the way down. Oil from the damaged engines streamed down the belly of the plane and covered the ball turret. So that he could see, S/Sgt. Burchinall broke the glass in the turret, which had already been hit by a 20mm shell.

As the plane broke out of the clouds over Eastern France, it was immediately fired on by a battery of 20mm guns. The plane was hit again and again. To add to the troubles, two Me 109s started attacking. The tail gunner, S/Sgt. Allen, was seriously wounded. A 20mm shell passed through him from under his shoulder blade and came out under his collar bone. 7.7mm bullets hit his arm and leg, breaking both. Bleeding badly from his wounds, he bailed out and was picked up immediately and hospitalized. The same attack severed the control cables, leaving the pilot with virtually no control over a madly vibrating plane and only a hole in the wing where the number two engine had been. As the ball turret gunner climbed out of his turret to get more ammunition the turret hit the ground and tore up into the plane, throwing S/Sgt. Burchinall into the radio room. The plane had landed by itself! With the control cables shot away and no power it had landed in a large open field near Abbeville. The crew was soon captured, with the exception of Lt. Seaman, who managed to remain at large until the invasion of Europe.

MARCH 3, 1944 — MISSION NO. 87

The ordered target was Erkner, Germany. High cloud in the target area forced the formation to choose a last resort target. Bombs were dropped on Wilhelmshaven through solid cloud. No enemy aircraft were seen throughout the mission and flak was light and inaccurate. Sixteen planes completed the mission, led by Colonel Romig and Major Gilmore with Major Menees as navigator in a Pathfinder ship.

MARCH 4, 1944 — MISSION NO. 88

The Group took off for Berlin and climbed over 27,000 foot high cloud banks in an attempt to get there. A still higher mass of cloud loomed ahead, so they were forced to turn back. They bombed Bonn as a last resort target. Fifteen planes completed the mission, led by Lt. Cruthirds and Lt. McCluskey with Lt. Sullivan as navigator and Lt. Lee as bombardier. Bombing was done through heavy clouds and results were not clearly seen. However, calculations based on bombs away pictures indicated that bombs fell in the northwest corner of the town. There was no fighter opposition and flak was light and inaccurate.

MARCH 6, 1944 — MISSION NO. 89

The briefed target was Erkner, Germany. Because of clouds in this area, the Wing Leader picked a last resort target. It was Templin, a German town with a population of 6,300 located about 38 miles northeast of Berlin. Twenty planes flew the mission in the low box of the Combat Wing. They were led by Major Roper and Lt. McCluskey with Lt. Manthey as navigator and Lt. Behrendt as bombardier. From 100 to 150 enemy fighters were encountered between Hanover and the target. They included Me 110s and 410s and a few Me 109s. Most of those fighters flew in large formations, peeling off to attack at all levels and from all around the clock. Rockets were used from a distance, after which the enemy planes closed in with cannon. Meager to moderate flak was met at several points along the route, most of it quite accurate. In spite of the intensity of the opposition, all planes returned without casualties.

MARCH 8, 1944 — MISSION NO. 90

The target was Erkner again. This time it was hit squarely with a pattern of incendiaries covering the V.K.P. ball bearing factory area. Sixteen planes completed the mission, led by Colonel Lacey with Major Menees as navigator flying in a Pathfinder ship. About 25 enemy fighters were encountered between Berlin and Hanover. The majority of these were Me 109s with a few FW 190s and four Ju 87s. About 12 attacks were made, mostly from below to avoid the strong fighter escort. A few attacks were made head-on from above by Me 109s and there was one report that FW 189s attempted air-to-air bombing. Accurate flak was encountered at several points, but all planes returned safely and there were no casualties.

MARCH 9, 1944 — MISSION NO. 91

Bombs were dropped on Pathfinder smoke markers over the industrial area of Berlin. Fifteen planes completed the mission, led by Lt. Gaylord and Lt. Brooksby with Captain Schwartz as navigator and Captain Huff as bombardier. Throughout the long mission not a single enemy fighter was seen. An intense flak barrage was seen over Berlin, but the formation escaped damage and injury.

MARCH 11, 1944 — MISSION NO. 92

Twenty planes took off to bomb Munster, led by Lt. Floden with Lt. Sullivan as navigator in a Pathfinder ship. Bombing was unobserved because of solid cloud cover. No enemy fighters were seen and flak was light and inaccurate.

MARCH 13, 1944 — MISSION NO. 93

Twenty-one planes took off to bomb the aerodrome at Beauvoir, France, but because the target area was covered in cloud all but one squadron brought back their bombs. The low squadron bombed Poix Aerodrome with poor results. Group Leader for this mission was Captain Kelley with Lt. Grunow as copilot, Captain Matthews as navigator and Lt. Lyttle as bombardier. The only enemy planes seen were about five Me 109s, which did not attack. Flak was light, damaging two planes but inflicting no casualties.

MARCH 16, 1944 — MISSION NO. 94

Eleven planes completed a mission to Augsburg, led by Colonel Rogner with Captain Matthews as navigator in a Pathfinder ship. Bombing was done through clouds and the results unobserved. About

15 Me 109s and FW 190s were encountered. Most of the attacks were from the tail, but a few attacked from level and below. Inaccurate flak was encountered at several points on the route. All planes returned without casualties.

MARCH 18, 1944   MISSION NO. 95

Twenty-one planes attacked the aerodrome at Landsberg, Germany. Bombing results were good. The formation was led by Captain Harris and Lt. Brooksby, with Lt. Pullen as navigator and Captain Baird as bombardier. Enemy fighters started to attack just before the target and continued until about 20 minutes after bombs away. There was considerable flak at the target. Four planes failed to return from this mission.

The plane piloted by Lt. Neuberg, 42-38032, fell out of the formation with the right wing and number three engine on fire. Aircraft 42-37832, flown by Lt. Illies, had most of its vertical stabilizer shot away before exploding in mid-air. Lt. Martin's plane, 42-31966, had just turned after bombing the target and was heading west when it was attacked head-on by about 12 FW 190s. The oxygen tanks were hit, causing fires to break out. The right wing was knocked off by cannon fire. In addition, the pilot was hit in the right side of the face by a 20mm shell. With the loss of the wing, the plane immediately went into a tight spin, throwing the crew members to the roof of the plane. The copilot, Lt. Sinnott, tried to control the ship for some time but then decided it was time to abandon the plane at about 2,000 feet. He managed to get out the forward hatch, but unfortunately his parachute did not open. The only other crew member that was able to escape from the plane was Lt. DeRoever, the bombardier, who bailed out so low that he hit a tree as soon as he pulled the ripcord on his parachute.

Lt. Mears headed the badly damaged 42-37825 towards Switzerland. The story is told by T/Sgt. Richard Hobt. "My last mission, number 23 for me and number 22 for the rest of the crew started on the morning of March 18, 1944, with the usual early call at 0200 hours in the morning. After briefing we were delayed by weather and did not take off as I recall until about 1000 hours. We thought due to the long wait, that as in many other instances, the mission would be cancelled. The target was the airfield at Landsberg, Germany, which is approximately 20 miles due east of Munich, Germany. The reason for the raid was to disrupt the training of aircrews on the Me 410s and to destroy the facility. I do not recall any special problems or encounters with the enemy as we proceeded to the target area. The weather was very good, only about 4/10 cloud cover. My main concern was our bombing altitude, we were the lead aircraft, a brand new B-17G of the low squadron at approximately 18,000 feet. Our bomb run was good and we could observe our bombs hitting the hangars and runways.

"Almost immediately after the bomb run, the tail gunner called out, 'Enemy fighters at six o'clock low and climbing to our altitude.' The six aircraft were identified as FW 190s and upon gaining our altitude they proceeded from the six o'clock position level to ahead of our formation, turned and made a level head-on pass at 12 o'clock. The three aircraft in the lead element were hit with a heavy concentration of machine gun and 20mm cannon fire and were, I think, heavily damaged. As for our condition, we were struck in the nose, a 20mm shell exploding in the navigator's compartment, another 20mm shell exploded at the base of the pilot's control column. A large hole was blown in the fuselage on the left side just below the top turret, numbers one and two engines shot out and an oil fire started in number three. The pilot, stunned by the above mentioned shell, lost control of the aircraft and we were in a steep dive passing under our left wingman as he exploded. We fell from 18,000 feet to about 5,000 feet before the copilot and the pilot regained control.

"An assessment of our damage and loss of fuel made the return to England out of the question and we headed east towards the Swiss border. I was attempting to notify the base of our condition as we crossed Lake Constance. As we crossed the border we were intercepted by four Swiss fighters, later identified as Morane's. They escorted us to Dubendorf airfield outside of Zurich. Due to our damage we felt we could only attempt one pass. There were three other B-17s and twelve B-24s all trying to land at about the same time. We came in downwind and on contacting the ground, the landing gear collapsed. As luck would have it we all escaped injury and we were very glad to be in Switzerland and not Germany."

MARCH 19, 1944   MISSION NO. 96

Twenty-one planes completed the mission to the

secret weapon installation at Watten, France. The formation was led by Captain Clay and Lt. Emerson, with Lt. Pullen as navigator and Lt. Matthews as bombardier. The bomb pattern fell to the right of the target area. There was some accurate flak, but none of the planes were seriously damaged.

MARCH 20, 1944   MISSION NO. 97

Twenty-one planes took off for Frankfurt, led by Captain Nesmith and Lt. Gordon with Lt. Korf as navigator and Captain Luff as bombardier. Over France, the formation ran into clouds reaching above 28,000 feet. The mission was recalled without dropping bombs.

MARCH 22, 1944   MISSION NO. 98

Orianenburg, Germany was briefed as a visual target, but because of heavy cloud cover Berlin was bombed instead. Sixteen planes, led by Major Carraway with Captain Schwartz as navigator and Lt. Henry as bombardier in a Pathfinder ship, bombed through cloud on smoke markers. No enemy fighters were seen throughout the mission. The Berlin flak defenses threw up an intense barrage at the right altitude, but most of it was off for deflection.

Lt. Slosson flying as spare in 42-39849 was not seen to join the formation and did not return from the mission.

MARCH 23, 1944   MISSION NO. 99

The briefed target was Lippstadt, but cloud cover made visual bombing impossible. Instead, the 21 planes flying in the low box bombed Munster with unobserved results. The 14 planes flying in a composite high box jettisoned their bombs in open country northwest of Munster. There was very little enemy opposition. Only seven enemy fighters were seen, but they did not attack. The low box was led by Captain Lynch and Captain Holsapple, with Lt. Manthey as navigator and Lt. Behrendt as bombardier. The composite high box was led by Captain Gaylord and Lt. Gordon, with Lt. Korf as navigator and Captain Wallace as bombardier.

MARCH 24, 1944   MISSION NO. 100

Twenty-one planes took off to bomb Schweinfurt, led by Captain Harris and Lt. Dowling with Lt. Cleveland as navigator and Lt. Fireman as bombardier. All planes completed the mission. Bombing was through 10/10 cloud and results were unobserved. No enemy fighters ventured up through the clouds and the flak encountered at half a dozen points along the route was inaccurate. All planes returned without casualties.

MARCH 26, 1944   MISSION NO. 101

Eighteen planes, led by Captain Nesmith and Lt. Gordon with Lt. Schadegg as bombardier and Lt. Simons as navigator, flew to Watten. Bombs landed somewhat short of the briefed M.P.I. and only slight damage was done to this very difficult target. No enemy fighters were seen in the air. Very accurate flak at the target caused minor damage to six planes, but there were no losses or casualties.

MARCH 27, 1944   MISSION NO. 102

A highly successful mission to the airfield at Tours was flown by 30 planes in a high composite box and in a lead box. They were led by Colonel Ball and Captain Gaylord, with Captain Wallace as bombardier and Major Menees as navigator. Bombing was excellent. A direct hit on the workshops, which were the briefed M.P.I., by the bombs of the lead ship caused a violent explosion. Strike photos indicate that a fire was started and other damage included three large holes in the roof of the main hangar, the destruction of half the roof of another large hangar, half a large workshop, the complete destruction of the four small workshops which constituted the M.P.I. and five craters in the main highway from Tours. Incendiaries from the high composite group hit the main hangar and workshops and started fires in the barracks area. As usual on recent missions to France, there was no opposition from enemy aircraft. The only flak seen was a few inaccurate bursts at La Havre.

MARCH 29, 1944   MISSION NO. 103

Flying the high box of the Combat Wing, 18 planes led by Captain Cruthirds and Lt. McCafferty with Lt. Sullivan as navigator and Lt. Lee as bombardier, completed a mission to Brunswick. Bombing was by Pathfinder technique through cloud cover. Results were not observed, but black smoke was seen coming up from the target area. Just after bombs away about 10 Me 109s and FW 190s attacked. They concentrated for the most part on the tail of the high squadron while a few FWs fired rockets from a distance. Flak was encountered at several points along the route and at the target, where it was moderate and not very accurate. About eight bursts of rocket flak were seen in the area of the target. Two planes were damaged, but all returned without casualties.

APRIL 9, 1944   MISSION NO. 104

A long spell of bad weather kept the planes grounded for the first eight days of April. The order then came through for a long mission to the airfield at Rahmel, Poland. Eighteen ships flew the mission in the low box of the Combat Wing, and two in the high box of the Composite Wing. The low box was led by Lt. McCluskey and Lt. Dennis, with Lt. Manthey as navigator and Lt. Giswein as bombardier. The mission as a whole was quite successful. All bombs hit in the area of the aircraft assembly plant and hangars. The Luftwaffe came up to try to stop this one. About 50 to 75 fighters were encountered from the I.P. to the target and as far back as the Baltic Sea and again over the Danish Peninsula. The attacks were from all around the clock from both below and above. Moderate flak was thrown up at various points along the route. Eight planes were damaged, but all returned to base. One man was killed and three wounded on this mission.

APRIL 10, 1944   MISSION NO. 105

The Group went after another airfield, Melsbrook, near Brussells. Eighteen planes completed the mission, flying the lead box of the Combat Wing. They were led by Lt. Colonel Burns and Captain Harris, with Lt. Decker as bombardier and Lt. Cleveland as navigator. The bombing was excellent. Flak was accurate in the target area where eight planes were damaged. However, all planes returned without casualties.

APRIL 11, 1944   MISSION NO. 106

Two 18-ship boxes took off for the briefed target at Stettin. The high box was led by Major Roper and Captain Nesmith, with Lt. Korf as navigator and Captain Wallace as bombardier. The low box was led by Lt. Floden and Lt. McCafferty, with Lt. Badger as navigator and Lt. Trolinger as bombardier.

Cloud covered the primary target so the secondary, Arminswalde, was bombed by the high box with excellent results. The low box dropped their bombs on an unidentified target of opportunity causing no apparent damage.

A group of 15 to 25 fighters were kept at a respectful distance by the escort and only a few half-hearted attacks were made. There was a lot of flak in the region of Dummer Lake and in the Kiel area on the way back. Ten ships were damaged and the lead bombardier, Captain Wallace, received a serious arm injury.

APRIL 13, 1944   MISSION NO. 107

Sixteen planes, flying a high box, completed the mission to Schweinfurt. They were led by Captain Cruthirds and Lt. McCafferty, with Lt. Sullivan as navigator and Lt. Lee as bombardier. Bombing was good and fighter opposition stiff. About 50 to 100 Me 109s and FW 190s were encountered. They flew in simulated escort formation in groups of six to twenty, attacking from mostly head-on, firing 20mm cannon and rockets.

42-37827, piloted by Lt. Whitchurch, was hit by 20mm shells near the I.P. Part of the vertical stabilizer was shot away. Lt. Whitchurch dropped his plane out of formation, jettisoned his bombs and rejoined the formation. He flew over the target, then peeled off and was last seen apparently still under control and accompanied by P-51s. There was considerable flak at the target. Fifteen planes were damaged by flak and fighters.

APRIL 18, 1944   MISSION NO. 108

Sixteen planes completed the mission to Oranienburg, on the outskirts of Berlin. They flew the lead box of the Combat Wing led by Colonel Romig and Lt. Grunow, with Captain Matthews as navigator and Lt. Lyttle as bombardier in a PFF ship. At the target, the bombs fell into the smoke from previous bombing. There were no enemy fighters and very little flak en route. However, at the target the flak was intensive and accurate.

Lt. Apperson was flying 42-31955 as the lead of the low squadron. The squadron dropped their bombs successfully, but within seconds of the bomb bay doors closing, '955 received a very solid hit. A very loud whack was heard and the aircraft shuddered. However, Lt. Apperson was not duly concerned as he had received similar hits before with no really grievous damage. He checked around the crew and established that no one had been hurt. A second later the right waist gunner, Sgt. Larry Kuslack, reported that something was burning. Just as Lt. Apperson was telling him to find it and put it out, Sgt. Bailey, the ball turret gunner, said, "Look behind number three engine."

Looking from the right hand seat, his normal position when flying lead, Lt. Apperson saw that flames were roaring back from the wing where the number three engine had been blown away. Diving to clear the formation, he ordered the crew to bail out.

Checking that everyone was out, Lt. Apperson left via the bomb bay. Feeling weak from lack of oxygen, he did not delay in opening his parachute, the same chute he had used on December 31, 1943. The opening shock was severe and the cold intense, but he remained conscious. At about 15,000 feet Lt. Apperson began hearing loud cracks. At first he thought he was being fired at. Then, seeing another B-17 formation above him, he realized that it was the sound of flak shells passing him. Lt. Apperson landed gently, brushing through pine trees, touching down amongst the flak guns that had most probably shot him down. He and the rest of his crew were quickly captured except Sgt. Matthews, the tail gunner. He had bailed out successfully, but when his parachute opened, he slipped from the harness and fell to his death. Eight other ships received flak damage.

APRIL 19, 1944   MISSION NO. 109
Thirty planes completed the mission to Kassel, Germany in a low box led by Lt. Brooksby and Lt. Dawling with Lt. Banton as navigator and Lt. Arnold as bombardier, and a high box led by Lt. McClusky and Lt. Dennis with Lt. Duchesneau as bombardier and Lt. Gwyn as navigator. Bombs of the high group fell in a wooded area beyond the target. Four planes of the low group chose Limburg as a target of opportunity and did an excellent job of bombing the marshaling yards there. The only enemy planes seen were three or four fighters which did not attack and the only accurate flak was at the target where five ships were damaged.

APRIL 20, 1944   MISSION NO. 110
Two groups, one of 15 planes and one with 17 planes, completed the mission to the no-ball target near La Glacerie in the Pas de Calais area. The bombing by squadrons was not very successful, although one squadron hit another no-ball installation with fairly good results. No enemy fighters were seen, but there was intense accurate flak in the target area and 30 planes were damaged

APRIL 22, 1944   MISSION NO. 111
Fifteen planes led by Major Richardson completed a mission to the marshaling yards at Hamm, Germany. The bombing was fairly good. No enemy fighters were seen and flak was inaccurate. After these planes had taken off for Hamm, 42-31988, piloted by Major Wheeler, cracked up during takeoff for a practice flight. As the plane left the runway number two engine failed. The copilot accidentally feathered number one. This caused the plane to go into a steep bank and stall. The left wing tip struck the ground and the ship somersaulted across a hedge and crashed, immediately catching fire. Lt. C. B. Montgomery, copilot, Captain William Winter, Group bombardier, S/Sgt. A. T. Brooks, a clerk in group operations and T/Sgt. W. A. Manley, bombsight mechanic, were killed. Major Wheeler, Corporal P. L. Black, a clerk in group operations, T/Sgt. D. J. Cutler, bombsight mechanic, and T/Sgt. J. D. Corwile, the radio operator, were seriously injured.

APRIL 24, 1944   MISSION NO. 112
The target was the air equipment depot at Erding, Germany. Sixteen planes completed the mission in the lead box of the Combat Wing. They were led by Major Stewart and Lt. Floden, with Lt. Sullivan as navigator and Lt. Lee as bombardier. Bombs were dropped in a compact pattern across the briefed M.P.I. with direct hits on three hangars. About 25 enemy fighters were seen but no direct attacks were made on the formation. At the coast on the way out, there was some extremely accurate flak from a few batteries near Ostend. Nine ships were damaged. One of them, 42-97305, piloted by Lt. Evans, was so badly damaged that it had to be ditched in the Channel. All crew members were picked up by Air Sea Rescue.

APRIL 25, 1944   MISSION NO. 113
The airfield at Nancy, France was the briefed target, but no bombs were dropped because of heavy cloud over most of France. Eighteen planes flew the mission, led by Captain Davey and Lt. McCluskey with Lt. Manthey as navigator and Lt. Giswein as bombardier. There was no fighter opposition and only inaccurate flak.

When the ships returned from the mission, 42-97258, piloted by Lt. McLott, could not get the landing gear down. Lt. McLott then flew over the Wash where he jettisoned the bombs and the ball turret. Returning to Polebrook he then made a perfect belly landing on the grass in front of the control tower.

This was the second crash landing at the base because of landing gear failure. On March 31, 42-107046, a 511th ship, had to land on the grass. The problem was diagnosed to be inadequate hardness of a key in the landing gear motor shaft.

APRIL 26, 1944   MISSION NO. 114

Seventeen planes flew a mission to Brunswick, led by Captain Clay and Lt. Van Tassel with Lt. Cleveland as navigator and Lt. Arnold as bombardier. Bombing was through solid cloud. There was no fighter opposition and flak was light and inaccurate.

Back at Polebrook an unusual first was taking place. Lt. Zotollo, who had been slow-timing an engine in 42-37780, found that as he was preparing to land the right landing gear would not extend. After flying around to use up fuel, he decided to make a one-wheel landing, rather than the customary wheels up landing. In front of a large crowd of spectators, who always gathered when they heard of a possible crash landing, Lt. Zotollo accomplished the landing on the first approach. The only damage sustained was to the right wing tip and both propellers on the right wing. This successful landing was much publicized and became a standard within the 351st training procedures.

APRIL 27, 1944   MISSIONS NO. 115 and 116

Eighteen planes flew a mission to a no-ball installation near Beauvoir, France. They were led by Captain Cruthirds and Lt. Nall, with Lt. Sullivan as navigator and Lt. Lee as bombardier. Drift trouble interfered with the sighting and all bombs landed in open field. There was no fighter opposition and only meager flak.

Another mission was flown in the afternoon, a second trip to the airfield at Nancy. Sixteen planes completed the mission led by Lt. Colonel Ledoux and Captain Brooksby, with Lt. Cleveland navigating and Lt. Decker as bombardier. Bombs were dropped in the target area but definite assessment of results was impossible because of smoke and cloud. Again, no enemy fighters were seen and flak was light and inaccurate.

APRIL 28, 1944   MISSION NO. 117

Eighteen planes flew to the airfield at Avord, France. The Group formation was led by Lt. Floden and Lt. Olson, with Lt. Badger as navigator and Lt. Trollinger as bombardier. A heavy concentration of incendiaries fell on the barracks and workshops. There were no enemy fighters or flak.

APRIL 29, 1944   MISSION NO. 118

The final target of the month was Berlin. Seventeen planes completed the mission, led by Captain Kelley and Lt. Dennis with Lt. Gwyn and Lt. Volotta as navigators and Lt. Behrendt as bombardier. Bombs were dropped on the city through almost solid cloud cover. No enemy fighters were seen, but flak at the target was intense and accurate, inflicting minor damage to 12 ships.

MAY 1, 1944   MISSIONS NO. 119 and 120

The first target briefed for the month was a no-ball installation in the Pas de Calais area. Eighteen planes took off, led by Captain Clay and Captain Crews with Lt. Pullen as navigator and Lt. Arnold as bombardier. They completed the flight as scheduled, but no bombs were dropped because the target area was covered by cloud. There was no fighter opposition or flak.

The target ordered for the afternoon was the marshaling yards and locomotive workshops at Rheims, France. Eighteen planes completed this mission flying the low box of a composite wing. They were led by Major Fishburne and Captain Nesmith with Lt. Simmons navigating and Lt. Rufeisen as bombardier. The bombing looked good but the bombs fell in the smoke caused by the lead group. Once again there was no fighter opposition or flak.

MAY 4, 1944   MISSION NO. 121

Thirty-seven planes took off for Berlin, led by Lt. Colonel Ball and Lt. Grunow with Lt. Badger as navigator and Lt. Trollinger as bombardier. However, cloud and dense and persistent contrails made the formation of Wings impossible and the entire mission was called off.

MAY 7, 1944   MISSION NO. 122

Berlin was again briefed as the main target. Thirty-four planes completed the mission led by Colonel Romig, who flew as Combat Wing Commander, and Lt. Grunow with Lt. Trollinger as bombardier and Lt. Badger as navigator. Bombing was by Pathfinder technique through solid cloud cover. There was no fighter opposition but the Berlin flak was intense and accurate. One ship,

42-37714, piloted by Lt. Presley on his first mission, was hit and went down through the clouds towards the target.

MAY 8, 1944   MISSION NO. 123

Twenty-seven planes went back to Berlin again. They were led by Lt. Colonel Ball and Lt. Grunow, with Captain Matthews and Lt. Gwyn as navigators and Lt. Behrendt as bombardier. As on the previous day, the mission was flown over solid cloud and bombing results were unobserved. A few enemy fighters were seen, but they did not attack. There was the customary intense flak barrage over the big city.

MAY 9, 1944   MISSION NO. 124

The target was the marshaling yard and engine repair shops in the city of Luxembourg. The Group put up 18 planes led by Captain Brooksby and Lt. Pullen, with Lt. Cleveland as navigator and Lt. Decker as bombardier. The bombing was only fair with the main concentration of bombs falling about 650 feet short of the M.P.I. The only fighters seen were two Me 109s which made one ineffective pass at the low squadron. Flak was meager and inaccurate.

MAY 11, 1944   MISSION NO. 125

Thirty-six planes returned to finish the job at Luxembourg. They were led by Lt. Colonel Burns and Captain Gaylord with Lt. Korf as navigator and Lt. Fireman as bombardier. This time the bombing was excellent. The main concentration of bombs of the lead box fell on the M.P.I. There were no enemy fighters and no flak throughout the whole mission.

MAY 12, 1944   MISSION NO. 126

The I.G. Farbenindustrie plant at Merseburg, Germany was the chosen target. Eighteen planes completed the mission, led by Captain Cruthirds and Lt. Crowe with Lt. Sullivan as navigator and Lt. Lee as bombardier. Bombing was excellent. The main concentration of bombs fell in the center of the target. Only three enemy fighters were seen and these did not attack. The only flak encountered was moderate and inaccurate.

MAY 13, 1944   MISSION NO. 127

Politz was the briefed target, but because it was covered by cloud the formation bombed the briefed last resort target, a constructional engineering plant just north of the city of Stettin. Sixteen planes completed the mission, led by Lt. Colonel Ledoux and Lt. Maginn with Lt. Cleveland as navigator and Lt. Decker as bombardier. Bombing was only fair. About 50 to 75 German fighters were seen, but only one ineffective pass was made at the Group. There was very little flak except at the target where nine ships were damaged.

MAY 19, 1944   MISSIONS NO. 128 and 129

Eighteen planes made another trip to Berlin and a second box of 16 planes bombed Kiel. The group that bombed Berlin was led by Captain Brooksby and Lt. Fowler, with Lt. Cleveland navigating and Lt. Decker as bombardier. The other group was led by Captain Kelley and Captain Winton, with Lt. Manthey as navigator and Lt. Giswein as bombardier. At Berlin the bombs fell at the extreme northeast edge of the city. The bombs of the other group probably did heavy damage at Kiel, but strikes could not be accurately plotted because of cloud in the area. About 50 Me 109s and FW 190s were encountered by the group that went to Berlin, but they did not attack effectively. Flak on both missions was generally inaccurate.

MAY 20, 1944   MISSION NO. 130

Eleven planes flew the mission to the airfield at Villacoublay, France. During Wing assembly the Pathfinder ship with Major Roper, the mission leader, Lt. Grunow, copilot, Lt. Gwyn, navigator and Lt. Behrendt, bombardier, was forced to turn back. For some unknown reason a Sky Marker was set off. Acrid smoke filled the ship and during the confusion two crew members bailed out. Lt. Grunow salvoed the Sky Marker and the other bombs into a field near Peterborough and flew the ship back to base. Several crew members reported sick after inhaling the fumes.

The Deputy Leader assumed command and led the remaining planes to the target. The bombs fell in a compact pattern with heavy concentrations on the briefed M.P.I., doing heavy damage to seven hangars. The only enemy plane seen was in the process of being shot down by P-47s. The only flak encountered was at the target where it was moderate and accurate. Ten planes were damaged, but all returned without casualties.

MAY 22, 1944   MISSION NO. 131

A 12-plane box flew to Kiel, led by Captain Floden and Lt. Dixey with Lt. Badger as navigator and Lt. Trollinger as bombardier. The bombs fell in open fields northwest of Kiel, where the Pathfinder ship in the lead group bombed although the target could be seen. There were no fighters and very little flak.

MAY 23, 1944　　　　　　　　　**MISSION NO. 132**

Twenty-five planes flew a mission to the marshaling yards at Epinal, France. They were led by Major Roper and Lt. Maginn with Lt. Behrendt as bombardier and Lt. Volotta as navigator. Bombs of the lead group were heavily concentrated in the target area. The Group encountered no flak or fighters.

During Wing assembly, tragedy struck. Lt. Crowe, who was being checked out as a first pilot by Lt. Nelson and his crew in 42-97325, collided with a B-24 from the 458th Bomb Group. Both planes crashed near Eye, Suffolk. As the crippled B-17 went down T/Sgt. T. Popp, radio operator, S/Sgt. J. Duggan, left waist gunner, and S/Sgt. E. Hardin, ball turret gunner, although injured, bailed out. The other crew members were killed when the plane crashed into marshlands near the River Dove.

Later that evening, a second tragedy was averted. At about 2300 hours, Lt. C. M. Walker, who had been on a night practice mission in 42-30857, was making an approach for landing when fire suddenly broke out in the cockpit and around the upper turret. Smoke filled the cockpit, making a landing impossible. Instinctively opening the throttles, Lt. Walker climbed away from the base. However, before he could give the order to bail out, the crew managed to extinguish the fire. Sgt. R. G. Martin, the engineer, was badly cut and burned when an oxygen bottle exploded as he was fighting the fire.

MAY 24, 1944　　　　　　　　　**MISSION NO. 133**

Another mission was flown to Berlin by 18 planes. They were led by Captain Clay and Lt. Hatten, with Lt. Pullen as navigator and Lt. Arnold as bombardier. The bombs fell in a widely scattered pattern over the eastern edge of the city. No enemy fighters came close enough to be identified, but flak over Berlin was intense and accurate.

The lead ship, 42-38005, piloted by Captain Clay, abandoned the lead position because of a feathered engine shortly before the target. This ship was reported as flying with the low group of the Wing for a time after the target, but it finally left the formation altogether and was forced to crash land on the Danish island of Als. There were no injuries, but the crew was quickly captured by the occupying forces.

MAY 25, 1944　　　　　　　　　**MISSION NO. 134**

An entire combat wing of three 12-ship boxes took off for the marshaling yards at Metz, France. Major Stewart and Captain Cruthirds led, with Lt. Badger as navigator and Lt. Trollinger as bombardier. The bombing of all three boxes was excellent. No enemy planes were seen and there was very little flak.

MAY 27, 1944　　　　　　　　　**MISSION NO. 135**

Eighteen planes completed the mission to Ludwigshafen, Germany, led by Captain Dixey and Captain McCafferty with Lt. Roberts navigating and Lt. Gross as bombardier. Bombs were dropped in a compact pattern on the northeast end of the marshaling yards. About 50 to 75 Me 109s and FW 190s attacked the formation before the target. They came in from the nose in groups of two to three and sometimes as many as six. Six B-17s were shot down during this attack; Lt. Sengstock in 42-97157, Lt. Johnson in 42-102470, Lt. Evans in 42-102613, Lt. Myers in 42-97149, Lt. Hopkins in 42-31975 and Lt. Peters in 42-31899 who landed in Switzerland.

The severity of these attacks can be best described by Lt. Redmond flying 42-39914 of the 509th Squadron.

"On about the second pass, one of the German groups of three was aiming right at my ship. As I saw the fire commence from their guns, I pulled up about 15 feet. This was the most violent maneuver I could do because of the whiplash effect at the end of the squadron. My bombardier, Tony Wagner, reported later that just after the pull up, he saw about twenty 20mm cannon shells burst just under the ship. As these Germans made their pass, they paid dearly. Tony Wagner, bombardier and Wes Creech, top turret, and Sam Bell, ball turret, combined on the German leader and blew him up as he approached. His explosion blew his right wing man into the line of fire of Marty Strom, the navigator, who very promptly shot his tail off. I mean this literally; it looked like a sewing machine poking holes in a sheet of paper. The tail separated from the fuselage of the plane and both parts tumbled out of sight. Strom reported this to be the fanciest shooting done by the 8th Air Force.

"At a later time, after a number of brews at the Officers Club, he admitted that he really was shooting at the prop, but got the tail. However, the result was the same. As the third plane passed under us, the ball turret and tail gunner blasted him. Vern Palmer, the tail gunner, reported that he had shot the canopy off and the pilot was bailing out. This was of course, the way it looked, but what actually happened was that he had crippled the plane and the pilot jettisoned the canopy and bailed out."

Many ships sustained damage, including Lt. Anderson's 42-107077, which returned to Polebrook with a hole four feet by 18 inches in the vertical stabilizer. In addition, two 20mm cannon shells had exploded at the rear of number three engine, turning the right wing into a sieve.

MAY 28, 1944   MISSION NO. 136
Thirteen planes took off to bomb Dessau, Germany, led by Captain Holsapple and Captain Winton with Lt. Manthey as navigator and Lt. Duchesneau as bombardier.

At the rendezvous point another wing of B-17s was assembling, causing the 351st to make a 360 degree turn to get out of their way. Unfortunately this maneuver put them behind the other two squadrons they were to lead. Increasing speed by some 10 mph the formation climbed mostly on full power. Just as the target area was reached the 351st assumed the Wing lead again, in time to meet 75 to 100 fighters head-on. On the first pass they shot down 42-97472, flown by Lt. Anderson, Flight Officer Probasco in 42-39987, Lt. Condon in 42-31757, Lt. Miller in 42-97191 and damaged the number one engine on 42-31721, flown by Lt. McClelland. Feathering this propeller, Lt. McClelland went on to bomb the target. After bombs away, the number two engine failed causing the plane to drop behind the formation.

Fortunately, the escorting P-47s had cleared the sky of enemy fighters and were now shepherding stragglers, including '721. Heading for home, but losing height gradually, Lt. McClelland felt that he would make it back with the help of the escort. However, suddenly, number four engine failed. Despite throwing everything overboard including the ball turret and with number three engine at full power, the plane was losing height rapidly. Just west of Frankfurt they were down to 3,000 feet and dropping so Lt. McClelland gave the order to bail out. All jumped successfully, but all were quickly captured except Sgt. Cruse who was killed on the ground by German civilians.

MAY 29, 1944   MISSION NO. 137
Sixteen planes flew a mission to the Focke-Wolf assembly plant at Sarau, Germany. They were led by Major Fishburne and Captain Nesmith, with Lt. Korf and Lt. Maltby as navigators and Lt. Fireman as bombardier. Bombs were dropped in a concentrated pattern on the assembly buildings and machine shops. About 25 to 30 enemy fighters were seen between Sorau and Stettin, but they were not very aggressive. Flak at many points along the route damaged 11 ships.

At one point on the way, as heavy flak was being thrown up, Sgt. Ruschman, left waist gunner in Lt. Raser's ship, saw 42-39853, piloted by Lt. Neal, bracketed by 88mm fire. Lt. Neal had already lost an engine on the way in and now a burst of flak knocked out another. As the plane started to drop behind, Sgt. Ruschman watched with horror as a shell passed up through the ball turret and went on through the top of the plane, but without exploding. He was convinced that the ball turret gunner of '853 was a dead man. Fortunately, the gunner had moved out from the ball turret some time before. Oil leaking from the damaged engine had blown onto the turret, obscuring his vision.

With the plane losing speed and altitude, Lt. Neal turned for home. However, the load proved too much for the remaining two engines. One of them blew a cylinder on the way to the coast. Then the remaining good engine was knocked out by flak at the coast. With only eight cylinders of one engine working, Lt. Neal was forced to ditch. The plane floated for 20 minutes and the whole crew was picked up by Air Sea Rescue.

MAY 30, 1944   MISSION NO. 138
The aircraft assembly plant at Oschersleben, Germany was attacked by 16 planes. The Group was led by Captain Gaylord and Lt. Brooks, with Lt. Simmons as navigator and Lt. Fireman as bombardier. Bombs hit the main workshops and power house. About 25 enemy fighters attacked head-on, just after the target. The plane piloted by Lt. Hicks, 42-31725, hit the deck after this attack. Flak was light and inaccurate.

MAY 31, 1944   **MISSION NO. 139**

On this last day of May a mission was flown to Luxeuil, an airfield in South Eastern France. A 12-plane box was put up, led by Captain McCafferty and Captain Dixey with Lt. Roberts and Lt. Shaffer as navigators and Lt. Lee as bombardier. The incendiaries fell into the smoke caused by previous groups. There were no fighters or flak.

JUNE 2, 1944   **MISSION NO. 140**

The Group's first pre-invasion tactical bombing mission to a gun emplacement near Equihen, France, was an uneventful affair. Bombing was by Pathfinder technique through 10/10 cloud, unimpeded by flak or fighters. Seventeen planes completed the mission, led by Lt. Maginn and Lt. Brooks with Lt. Sullivan as navigator and Lt. Dunnigan as bombardier.

JUNE 3, 1944   **MISSION NO. 141**

Seventeen planes flew to another tactical target in France, a defended area near Dannes. Major Richardson led the mission in a Pathfinder ship. The only enemy opposition was some meager and inaccurate flak.

JUNE 4, 1944   **MISSION NO. 142**

Two boxes of 12 ships each were sent to a highway-railway overpass at Palaiseau, France. One box was led by Captain Nesmith and Lt. Nay, with Lt. Korf as navigator and Lt. Loiacono as bombardier. The other box was led by Captain Lowery and Captain Floden, with Lt. Badger as navigator and Lt. Lee as bombardier. Bombs fell in the target area and did some damage to the nearby marshaling yard. There were no enemy fighters and only moderate flak at the target.

JUNE 6, 1944   **MISSION NO. 143**

The target for the morning of D-Day was the city of Caen. Thirty-four planes bombed through cloud with unobserved results. Six planes brought their bombs back. No enemy fighters appeared to interfere with the operation and there was very little flak. Bombing was by individual six-plane elements.

JUNE 7, 1944   **MISSION NO. 144**

Fifteen planes led by Lt. Colonel Ball in a Pathfinder ship attacked a tactical target at Falaise, France using GH equipment with estimated accurate results. There was no fighter opposition and no accurate flak.

JUNE 8, 1944   **MISSION NO. 145**

Thirty-five planes, led by Lt. Colonel Ledoux and Captain Brooksby with Lt. Cleveland and Lt. Dover as navigators and Lt. Decker as bombardier, flew to Etampes, France. No bombs were dropped because of solid cloud over the target. There was no enemy opposition.

JUNE 10, 1944   **MISSION NO. 146**

Eighteen planes, led by Major Roper with Lt. Sullivan as navigator in a Pathfinder ship, flew a mission to Gael airfield in France. Visual bombing was carried out on the north side of the field, with fair to good results. No enemy fighters were seen and there was no accurate flak.

JUNE 11, 1944   **MISSION NO. 147**

Eighteen planes flew the mission to Bernay St. Martin airfield, France. They were led by Colonel Romig, with Major Menees as navigator in a Pathfinder ship. Bombing was unobserved, but using GH technique it was estimated that bombs hit yards north of the M.P.I. There was no enemy opposition.

JUNE 12, 1944   **MISSION NO. 148**

To bomb Cambrai/Niergnies airfield in France, three 12-ship boxes were flown. The formation was led by Major Fishburne and Captain Gaylord, with Lt. Simmons as navigator and Lt. Fireman as bombardier. Considerable damage was done to hangars and dispersal sheds. There were no enemy fighters and only light flak. This, however, was enough to damage 42-37845, piloted by Lt. Guthrey, who was forced to ditch in the Channel on the way back. Two of the crew, Sgt. Leo C. Hamilton, radio operator and Sgt. Norbert E. Berendsen died of exposure and drowning. The other crew members were picked up safely by Air Sea Rescue.

JUNE 14, 1944   **MISSION NO. 149**

Fifty-seven planes completed the mission to Le Bourget airfield in France. One complete Wing was led by Lt. Colonel Ball and Lt. Dennis, with Lt. Gwyn as navigator and Lt. Giswein as bombardier. The others flew in a Composite Wing, led by Major Roper and Captain Floden with Lt. Badger as navigator and Lt. Lee as bombardier. All but one of the groups bombed with good results and considerable damage was done to the hangars and workshops. About 25 to 30 enemy fighters were seen, but they did not attack. Accurate flak at the target and at Dieppe shot down three planes, Lt. Ludwig flying 42-102478, Lt. Dixey in 42-97066 and Lt. Williamson piloting 42-97798.

The plane piloted by Lt. Raser, 43-37705, had just dropped its bombs when a 155mm shell burst immediately below the open bomb bay doors. Damage to the plane was considerable. It was riddled with holes and two engines on the same wing were knocked out. Many of the control cables were severed and this, with the uneven thrust of the two engines, made control of the aircraft almost impossible.

However, Lt. Raser was able to keep the plane on an even keel by using some controls of the autopilot and the remaining controls. With the loss of power, however, he had to drop below the formation and put the plane into a gentle glide to maintain speed. The engineer, Sgt. Omer Theroux, thinking and acting quickly, cut off pieces of the trailing antenna. Using this wire he was able to connect enough of the broken control wires to enable Lt. Raser to now have full control of the plane.

Staying directly below the formation until they reached the English coast, Lt. Raser then headed for the emergency field at Tangmere. There they were ordered to circle the field once to let a fellow ship land first. He was on fire! However, Lt. Raser finally managed to land his plane successfully without further damage or injury to the crew.

JUNE 15, 1944   MISSION NO. 150
Thirty-seven planes, led by Lt. Colonel Ledoux and Captain Grunow with Lt. Whitehead as navigator and Lt. Robinson as bombardier, flew a mission to the marshaling yards at Angouleme, France. The bombing was good and there was no enemy opposition throughout this mission.

JUNE 17, 1944   MISSION NO. 151
Seventeen planes, led by Captain Nesmith flying in a Pathfinder ship, flew a mission to Monchy/Breton airfield, France. Bombing was through overcast skies using GH technique, with estimated good results. No enemy fighters were seen, but there was light and accurate flak at Ostend.

JUNE 18, 1944   MISSION NO. 152
Hamburg was the target for two 18-ship boxes, a lead and a low. Major Fishburne and Lt. Maginn piloted the lead ship of the lead box, with Lt. Gootee as navigator and Lt. Dunnigan as bombardier. Bombs were dropped using Pathfinder techniques. Bombs away photographs indicated probable hits in the dock area. A great explosion of orange flame was seen and black smoke billowed up to 7,000 feet. There was no fighter opposition, but intense accurate flak at the target wounded two men and damaged 11 planes.

JUNE 20, 1944   MISSIONS NO. 153 and 154
In the morning, two 18-ship boxes, a lead and a low, flew to Hamburg. The flights were led by Lt. Colonel Ball and Lt. Maginn, with Lt. Gootee as navigator and Lt. Dunnigan as bombardier. Bombing by both boxes was good, with heavy concentrations of bursts on the distillation plant of an oil refinery, oil storage and dock areas. The only German fighters seen were four FW 190s which were chased away by P-47s. As usual, there was intense accurate flak at the target.

The briefed target for the afternoon was the pilotless aircraft installation at Watten. However, because of solid cloud over this area, a landing ground at Ypres/Viamertinghe, Belgium, was chosen as a target of opportunity. Twelve planes completed this mission, led by Lt. Brooks and Lt. Hopkins with Lt. Simmons as navigator and Lt. Loiacono as bombardier. No fighters were seen and flak was meager.

JUNE 21, 1944   MISSION NO. 155
Thirty-eight planes went to Berlin. Brigadier General Lacey flew in the lead ship with Lt. Dennis as copilot, Captain Matthews and Lt. Washburn as navigators and Lt. Giswein as bombardier. The planes, flying lead and low boxes of the lead Combat Wing and one squadron of a Composite Wing, dropped a heavy concentration of bombs on the Friedrichstrasse Station. About 40 enemy planes were sighted, but they did not attack. Flak at the target was intense and fairly accurate.

Aircraft 42-97144 developed mechanical trouble which forced the pilot, Lt. Walters, to crash land in Sweden. The ship flown by Lt. Hibbard, 42-30499, was badly damaged by flak. Fearing that the plane would not make it back to base, the crew, with exception of the pilot, copilot and navigator, bailed out over Holland. Lt. Hibbard managed to reach England, landing his damaged ship at Beccles.

JUNE 22, 1944 **MISSION NO. 156**

The oil storage farm at Rouen, France was target for two 12-ship boxes. Major Roper and Captain McCluskey flew the lead ship, with Lt. Sullivan as navigator and Lt. Behrendt as bombardier. Bombs of the lead group did some damage to oil storage tanks and shipyard buildings and the low box dropped a heavy concentration in the target area. There were no enemy fighters, but moderate and accurate flak over the target damaged 14 ships and shot down one. 42-97202, piloted by Lt. Watkins, spiraled down and exploded near the target.

JUNE 23, 1944 **MISSION NO. 157**

Twenty-four planes, led by Lt. Olson and Captain Davey in a Pathfinder ship, bombed (with GH equipment) a no-ball installation. No fighters were seen and flak was light and inaccurate.

JUNE 24, 1944 **MISSION NO. 158**

The crews were briefed on two more no-balls, near Fleury and Crepy, France. Two 12-ship boxes flew the mission. One was led by Lt. Brooks and Lt. Lemley, with Lt. Maltby as navigator and Lt. Strosky as bombardier. The other was led by Lt. Hales and Captain Holsapple, with Lt. Boardman as navigator and Lt. McFarlane as bombardier. One of the groups dropped their bombs four miles northwest of their target. The other group bombed a target of opportunity, the marshaling yards at St. Pol, with fair results. There were no enemy fighters, but moderate accurate flak damaged nine ships.

JUNE 25, 1944 **MISSION NO. 159**

Toulouse airfield was attacked by a Combat Wing of three 12-ship boxes. Major Fishburne and Captain Gaylord led, with Lt. Simmons as navigator and Lt. Loiacono as bombardier. Some hits were scored on the main hangar, mostly by the incendiary bombs of the low box. Moderate flak was encountered.

JUNE 28, 1944 **MISSION NO. 160**

Twenty-two ships in two boxes completed the mission to Leon/Couvron airfield in France. One was led by Lt. Dennis and Lt. Summers, with Lt. Washburn as navigator and Lt. Robinson as bombardier. The other was led by Major Richardson and Lt. Hales, with Lt. Boardman as navigator and Lt. McFarlane as bombardier. Both groups hit the target, damaging a hangar, runways and six dispersal sheds. There were no enemy fighters and only light inaccurate flak.

JUNE 29, 1944 **MISSION NO. 161**

The last operation of the month was a mission to Leipzig. Eighteen planes completed the mission, led by Lt. Viste and Lt. Fowler with Lt. Gallagher as navigator and Lt. Pinner as bombardier. Bombing was unobserved because of solid cloud. About 30 enemy planes were seen but only six attacked. There was intense accurate flak at the target.

JULY 4, 1944 **MISSION NO. 162**

The first mission for this month was a trip to a tactical target, a bridge at Saumur. The target was not attacked because of cloud cover in the area. Two 12-ship boxes were put up. One was led by Lt. Brooks and Lt. Hopkins, with Lt. Korf as navigator and Lt. Dunnigan as bombardier. The other was led by Captain Floden and Lt. Hales, with Lt. Badger as navigator and Lt. Lee as bombardier. No enemy fighters were seen and there was only light inaccurate flak.

JULY 6, 1944 **MISSIONS NO. 163 and 164**

In the morning 35 planes were sent to a flying-bomb (V-1 Buzz Bomb) installation in France. There were led by Lt. Dennis and Lt. Summers, with Lt. Washburn as navigator and Lt. Robinson as bombardier. Bombing results were only fair. The only enemy opposition consisted of some meager flak. In the afternoon, 12 ships were sent to another no-ball target. They were led by Captain Gaylord and Lt. Zotollo, with Lt. Simmons as navigator and Lt. Loiacono as bombardier. No bombs were dropped because of a bomb release malfunction in the lead ship. There was no enemy opposition.

JULY 7, 1944 **MISSION NO. 165**

To attack an aircraft plant at Leipzig, the Group put up 34 planes led by Lt. Colonel Ball and Lt. Dennis, with Lt. Washburn as navigator and Lt. Robinson as bombardier. The lead box put a heavy concentration in the workshop area, with several direct hits on workshops, offices, stores building and a foundry. The bombs of the low box fell into the smoke and probably did heavy damage. There was no fighter opposition, but there was intense flak at the target which damaged 10 ships.

Just after takeoff for the mission, Lt. Wishnewsky and crew had a close call. The number four engine of 43-37534 caught fire and then number two had a runaway propeller. There was a heavy ground mist making it difficult for the pilot to see the runway.

After three attempts to land, Lt. Wishnewsky eventually brought the plane in on its belly, just missing the control tower and parked aircraft.

JULY 8, 1944 **MISSION NO. 166**

Two 12-ship boxes were sent to bomb more no-ball targets. One box, led by Lt. Viste and Lt. Mertzlufft with Lt. Gallagher as navigator and Lt. Pinner as bombardier, bombed a target of opportunity. This was an unused airfield at Abbeville. The other box, led by Captain McClusky and Lt. Caughlin with Lt. Gwyn as navigator and Captain Behrendt as bombardier, bombed their target with good results. There were no enemy fighters and very little flak.

JULY 9, 1944 **MISSION NO. 167**

Another no-ball! Only one 12-plane box flew the mission, led by Lt. Brooks and Lt. Hopkins with Lt. Korf as navigator and Lt. Hamel as bombardier. Bombs were not dropped because of cloud over the target. Fighter opposition, as usual, was nonexistent and flak at the target was light.

JULY 11, 1944 **MISSION NO. 168**

Two 18-ship boxes, led by Colonel Romig and Captain Floden with Lt. Badger as navigator and Captain Lyttle as bombardier, attacked Munich. Bombs were dropped on the smoke markers of the preceding Wing because the Pathfinder equipment in the lead ship went out of order on the bomb run. Results were unobserved. Once again no enemy fighters, but intense flak.

JULY 12, 1944 **MISSION NO. 169**

Two 18-ship boxes took off for Munich again. Lt. Garcia and Lt. Fowler flew the lead ship in one box, with Lt. Fagan as navigator and Lt. Palmer as bombardier. The other box was led by Lt. White and Lt. Auten, with Lt. Washburn as navigator and Lt. Robinson as bombardier. There were no enemy fighters, but there was intense accurate flak at the target.

On the bomb run, Lt. Irwin's plane, 42-38028, received a direct hit. This was described by the copilot, Lt. DeVan. "The sky was filled with flak, I saw a puff directly ahead and level. Then one exploded under the fuselage, setting the aircraft on fire and rendering all systems dead. Lt. Irwin had been knocked semi-unconscious, but I roused him and motioned for him to bail out. I then followed him out and going down on the parachute I could see the aircraft going down in flames."

Lt. Irwin explains the trouble he had in parachuting to safety. "After clearing the plane and feeling that I was falling normally, I attempted to snap the chute pack to the harness I was wearing and found that this started me tumbling and I could not snap the chute pack to the harness. I was forced to trail the pack at arms length above my head to stop the spinning and fall feet first again. After three unsuccessful attempts, I broke through the cloud level (approximately 4,000 feet above ground) and could see trees and ground coming up fast. I made a fourth attempt by jerking my pack down very fast and slapping it to my chest hard. One D-Ring connected and held. I was then able to connect the second snap, pull the chute release and float down to where the parachute hung in the top of the trees.

"A few minutes later, after I managed to swing myself to a tree trunk and was climbing down the tree, I was spotted by a three-man search team, headed by a German soldier, and captured. After being searched for weapons, etc. I was marched several miles to a small local military camp and was held there overnight. I realized shortly after reaching the ground and during the march, that my face, nose and ears were badly burned and that I had some gashes and cuts in the calf of one leg, apparently slight flak wounds, but was otherwise in a fair condition."

Sgt. Franklin, tail gunner, S/Sgt. Hughes, radio operator, and Sgt. Strawn, waist gunner, left by the rear door. Sgt. Miller and S/Sgt. Torok, the engineer and the ball turret gunner, although uninjured in the original blast, were unable to escape and were killed when the ship crashed on the banks of the river Isar, northeast of Munich. Sgt. Franklin was captured almost immediately. S/Sgt. Hughes managed to evade capture for three days and was picked up by the Germans close to the Swiss border. Sgt. Strawn, unfortunately landed in the river and was drowned. What happened to Lt. Herman and Flight Officer Pulliam is unknown, but it is possible that they were killed by the initial blast.

JULY 13, 1944 **MISSION NO. 170**

The third consecutive mission to Munich was completed by 18 planes. They were led by Major Roper and Captain Dennis, with Captain Sullivan as navigator and Lt. Robinson as bombardier. About 25 FW 190s and Me 109s were seen, but no attacks were made on the formation. Intense flak at the target knocked one plane, 42-31748, out of formation. The pilot, Lt. Aldrege, informed the Group Leader that his oxygen system was out and the plane went down through the clouds.

When the planes returned and started landing, heavy rain started to fall, cutting down visibility. 43-37674, flown by Lt. Guthrey, landed too far down the runway, could not stop, ran off the end of the runway, through a hedge and through the barbed wire entanglements marking the perimeter of the base. The plane was badly damaged, but no one was hurt. A few minutes later, Lt. Wishnewsky in 43-37780 did the same. This time when crashing through the barbed wire the number three engine was wrenched off. The plane caught fire and was damaged beyond repair before the flames could be extinguished. Again, fortunately, no crew members were hurt.

JULY 16, 1944 **MISSION NO. 171**
The briefed target was again Munich, but high cloud made it impossible to get there and Stuttgart was bombed instead. Thirty-six planes flew the mission, led by Lt. Colonel Vorhees and Captain Dennis with Lt. Washburn as navigator and Lt. Robinson as bombardier.

JULY 18, 1944 **MISSION NO. 172**
Thirty-six planes flew a mission to Peenemunde, led by Major Roper and Captain Holsapple with Lt. Gwyn as navigator and Captain Behrendt as bombardier. The two boxes both bombed with good results, scoring direct hits on the electrolytic hydrogen plant, the main steam and power plant and other buildings. There were no enemy fighters and the only flak was inaccurate.

JULY 19, 1944 **MISSION NO. 173**
An aircraft assembly plant at Augsburg was the target for three 12-ship boxes. They were led by Major Fishburne, Lt. Viste, Captain Cleveland and Lt. Decker. The lead box scored some hits at the north end of a hangar and the other two dropped in the smoke caused by the bombs from the lead box. Near Memmingen, six FW 190s made a single pass at the formation and succeeded in knocking out two planes, Lt. Chapman piloting 42-107077 and Lt. Konecheck flying 42-102949. Several other planes were damaged by intense accurate flak at the target.

The base was honored and mildly disrupted by a visit from Secretary of War Stimson, General Spaatz, General Doolittle and other high ranking officers. Mr. Stimson gave a speech to the combat crew members and others who were not flying at the time. The entire party then made an inspection tour of the base.

JULY 20, 1944 **MISSION NO. 174**
Two 12-ship boxes were sent to Leipzig/Kolleda airfield, led by Lt. Brooks, Lt. Hopkins, Lt. Korf, Lt. Hamel and Captain Floden, Lt. Leland, Lt. Badger and Lt. Lee. Bombing was through solid cloud cover. There were no German fighters and only moderate inaccurate flak.

JULY 21, 1944 **MISSION NO. 175**
The V.K.F. ball bearing plant at Schweinfurt was the target for two 12-ship boxes led by Major Roper, Lt. White, Lt. Washburn and Lt. Robinson. The lead box dropped a heavy concentration of bombs on the target, scoring hits on a heat treatment shop, two machine shops, administrative offices and store and packing departments. The low box overshot their target slightly, but still did a lot of damage. No enemy fighters were seen, but there was intense accurate flak at the target.

JULY 24, 1944 **MISSION NO. 176**
Twenty-six planes, led by Lt. Colonel Ball, Captain Gaylord, Lt. Korf and Lt. Loiacono, flew a mission to the German front line west of St. Lo. Visibility was poor and bombs had to be dropped some distance from the briefed target. There was some fairly accurate flak, but no fighters were seen.

JULY 25, 1944 **MISSION NO. 177**
Another mission to St. Lo. This time the bombing was accurate, just in front of the American sector. Thirty-nine planes completed the mission, led by Lt. Colonel Burns, Captain Floden, Lt. Boardman and Lt. Badger as navigators and Lt. Lee as bombardier.

JULY 28, 1944 **MISSION NO. 178**
Three 12-ship boxes flew the mission to Merseburg, led by Major Fishburne, Lt. Fowler, Captain Cleveland and Lt. Heck. Bombing results were unobserved. Ten or fifteen FW 190s and Me 109s made two passes at the formation and shot down

42-102952, piloted by Lt. Long. There was moderate to intense flak at the target.

JULY 29, 1944   **MISSION NO. 179**

Another mission to Merseburg and again bombs were dropped through solid cloud. The Wing of three 12-ship boxes was led by Lt. Colonel Burns, Captain McClusky, Lt. Washburn and Captain Behrendt. The only fighter opposition consisted of four Me 109s which made one pass at the formation. Intense accurate flak at the target hit 42-38146, piloted by Lt. Morton. It was knocked out of formation and exploded in mid-air.

The plane piloted by Lt. Hillebrand, 43-37705, was also hit by flak over the target. A succession of bursts set fire to the number one engine, knocked out the number two engine, blasted the plexiglass nose, mortally wounded the bombardier, Lt. Gumaer, and stunned the navigator, Lt. Tollerson. The bomb bay doors were damaged, taking considerable effort and time to close them. Lt. Hillebrand put the plane into a steep dive and extinguished the fire, but he was unable to feather the number two propeller.

With only his two starboard engines functioning, the bomb bay doors still open and wind blasting through the shattered nose, Lt. Hillebrand dropped his plane from 25,000 feet and pulled out of the dive at 1,000 feet. He was 550 miles within strongly defended German territory in a badly battered aircraft. One propeller was still windmilling, the bomb bay doors still refused to close, the navigator's maps had all blown out of the ship and the port side fuel tanks were leaking badly. There was also a seriously wounded bombardier on board. Lt. Hillebrand considered all these things, but still decided to take his plane home. He dropped the ship to treetop height and ordered the crew to jettison all equipment. S/Sgt. Schacht was putting up a good fight with the bomb bay doors, eventually getting them almost closed. The navigator, Lt. Tollerson, was busy trying to save the life of Lt. Gumaer with all the first aid he knew.

For 500 miles they flew on the deck through fire from rifles, machine guns and every piece of heavier armament the Germans were able to aim at them. A flak burst finally killed Lt. Gumaer and started a fire on the catwalk. Lt. Tollerson and S/Sgt. Schacht put out the blaze. Fuel was running low and Lt. Hillebrand was experimenting with engine settings to maintain sufficient airspeed and conserve fuel. When the Channel was in sight, the radio operator sent out an SOS. An Air Sea Rescue launch came out to meet the wounded ship, but it was not needed. Lt. Hillebrand set his plane down in a good landing at North Creake on the coast of England.

Two crew members were slightly injured when Lt. Stewart, in 42-31875, ran into a tree when his brakes failed after landing at Polebrook.

JULY 31, 1944   **MISSION NO. 180**

Thirty-six planes completed another mission to Munich. Led by Lt. Zotollo, Lt. Sherfey, Lt. Gootee and Lt. Dunnigan, they bombed by Pathfinder technique. No fighters were seen and flak was light and inaccurate.

AUGUST 1, 1944   **MISSION NO. 181**

The first target for this month was the airfield at Chateaudun, France. The 36 planes that attacked scored hits on the runways and perimeter tracks. No fighters were seen throughout the mission and flak was light and inaccurate. The mission was led by Major Fishburne and Captain Floden, with Captain Badger as navigator and Lt. McFarlane as bombardier.

AUGUST 3, 1944   **MISSION NO. 182**

Thirty-six planes flew to Saarbrucken, led by Lt. Colonel Burns and Lt. Viste with Captain Cleveland as navigator and Lt. Decker as bombardier. The bombing was good, with hits on the junction of the Metz-Trier railroad and hits on a viaduct and the marshaling yards. There were no attacks by enemy planes. Flak at the target was moderate and accurate. The plane piloted by Lt. Brackens, 42-97492, was hit in the number three engine just after bombs away. The crew bailed out before the plane went into a spin and exploded.

AUGUST 4, 1944   **MISSION NO. 183**

Twenty-four planes completed the mission to the airfield at Anklam, Germany. The Group was led by Major Carraway and Captain Holsapple, with Lt. Gwyn as navigator and Captain Behrendt as bombardier. Hits were scored on the main hangar and workshops. There was only meager flak en-route and no fighter opposition.

AUGUST 5, 1944   MISSION NO. 184

This next mission was an attack on the underground oil storage tanks at Nienburg, Germany. Three 12-ship boxes flew the mission, led by Major Fishburne and Captain Brooks with Lt. Thackerey as navigator and Lt. Hamel as bombardier. A good concentration of bombs was dropped on the target. Once again there was no fighter opposition and only light flak.

AUGUST 6, 1944   MISSION NO. 185

The Group was briefed to fly to Berlin as the 94th "A" Combat Wing, providing 39 aircraft including two PFF ships and three flying spares. The Combat Wing Commander was Lt. Colonel Robert W. Burns. The Lead Pilot was Captain Sterling L. McClusky, with Lt. Billy V. Gwyn as navigator and Captain Allan D. Behrendt as bombardier. The high group was led by Lt. Gerald D. Viste with Captain Logan, Lt. Gallagher and Lt. Pinner. The low group was led by Lt. Charles R. Woodrum with Lt. Rohrbacher, Lt. Tuerck and Lt. Carneal. The first planes took off at 0710 hours. Wing assembly was successfully made at 5,000 feet at the Kings Cliff buncher.

Departing the English coast at Felixstowe, the 94th "A" Combat Wing was in its proper position, seventh formation in the First Division. However, the proceeding formations overshot the last turn before the enemy coast, leaving the 94th "A" leading the Division from just before the enemy coast up to the target. By this time, the Group had 34 aircraft, 12 in the lead group and 11 each in the high and low boxes. Two ships had returned with mechanical difficulties after the flying spares had returned as planned.

The flight from the enemy coast to the I.P. passed without incident. However, the approach to the I.P. brought the formation over anti-aircraft artillery installations to the east of Berlin. At this point, 42-97211 in the lead box, piloted by Lt. Hibbard, and 42-97381, piloted by the low box leader, Lt. Woodrum, were hit by flak. Lt. Woodrum immediately lowered his wheels as signal for the deputy leader to take over and then pulled out of the formation. Lt. Hibbard salvoed his bombs, but remained with his formation.

The 94th "A" Combat Wing continued on its bombing run through continuous following flak. Bombing was visual with mixed results. The lead group's bombs covered the M.P.I. and the high group's bombs fell just short, but the low group's bombs were well over. After the bomb release, the formation, buffeted from the flak, made a ragged turn, especially the low group, which had borne the brunt of the accurate flak. At this point about twelve FW 190s and six Me 109s attacked. The attacks were very persistent, the fighters coming in from the rear through their own flak.

The low group was hit particularly hard, both by flak and fighters. The aircraft flown by Lts. Pattison, Barieau and Uttley, already damaged by flak, were shot down by fighters. Lt. Strange's ship was hit by flak over the target, caught fire and blew up. Lt. Boyd's aircraft, 42-107046, was attacked from the rear by FW 190s. The 20mm shells tore open the trailing edges of the wings and exploded on the upper turret, throwing S/Sgt. Karnes to the floor and blowing away his oxygen mask. The same burst also hit the ball turret, killing Sgt. Kearns. At this point Lt. Boyd ordered the crew to abandon the aircraft. Lt. Wassner, bombardier, and Lt. Marsden, navigator, immediately jumped from the front escape hatch. The tail and waist gunners exited from the rear door. S/Sgt. Thompson, the radio operator, was reaching for his parachute when the plane exploded, killing him and the two pilots, Lt. Boyd and Lt. Snyder. The explosion blew S/Sgt. Karnes clear of the plane, but with only one of his parachute snaps connected, which fortunately was sufficient to hold him when his parachute opened.

When Lt. Woodrum turned away from his lead position of the low group, his aircraft had just received a burst from an 88mm shell. It had hit the number four engine just behind the fire wall and the engine caught fire immediately. It was understood amongst the pilots that once this spot was hit, it would only take one and a half minutes for the fire to spread to the fuel tanks behind it. Lt. Woodrum immediately feathered the number four propeller and ordered his crew to prepare to bail out. On hearing this, the copilot, Lt. Rohrbacher, carried out the procedure that he and Lt. Woodrum had previously agreed, should such a situation as this arise. He gathered the forward crew members in the nose, ensured that they bailed out through the forward escape hatch and then followed them. Meanwhile Lt. Woodrum salvoed his bombs, only to find that four of the 500-pound bombs had hung up.

Woodrum put his ship into a sideslip from 23,000 feet down to 11,000 feet. The vacuum, created behind the fire wall in the number four engine by this sideslipping drop, extinguished the fire. After pulling the plane straight and level, Lt. Woodrum discovered that the rest of the crew had not bailed out with the copilot, navigators, bombardier and engineer. His violent maneuvers had, however, loosened the bombs, which fell out safely.

Lt. Woodrum then ordered Lt. Fish from the tail gunner position to act as copilot, the ball turret gunner to the tail gunner position and one of the waist gunners to the nose guns. Not knowing where he was, he dropped to 8,000 feet and took a heading of 31.5 degrees. Southeast of Muritz Lake he was picked up by two P-51s who told him to take a heading of 290 degrees, before fuel shortage forced them to leave him.

Just north of Hamburg another engine lost power and Lt. Woodrum found it necessary to put the plane into a shallow dive to maintain speed, but because he was still in enemy territory he forbade the crew to jettison any armament. From the time he dropped out of formation the ship had been fired on by series after series of flak guns, but crossing the mouth of the Elbe River at 4,000 feet, the flak reached an intensity which the crew believed the ship could not weather.

As they came over the North Sea, Woodrum took a heading of 270 degrees until just north of the Zuider Zee. He was then able to contact Air Sea Rescue who gave him a more southwesterly direction.

Lt. Woodrum considered trying to make a landing back at Polebrook. However, Lt. Fish, who had been trying to keep track of fuel consumption on the back of an envelope because the fuel gauges were smashed, reported that the fuel would not last that far. They then decided that they would try to land at Leiston. A safe landing was made, despite the fact that the emergency water supply was used to bring up the hydraulic pressure for the brakes.

Meanwhile, Lt. Petty landed his severely damaged aircraft, 42-31509, in Sweden.

AUGUST 8, 1944   MISSION NO. 186

Thirty-six planes flew a ground support mission to St. Sylvain, France. Clouds obscured the target area and it was decided to bring the bombs home. However, the lead box dropped its bombs accidentally along a secondary road. There were no enemy fighters, but moderate and very accurate flak was encountered. The Wing was led by Major Carraway and Captain Floden, with Captain Badger as navigator and Lt. McFarlane as bombardier.

AUGUST 9, 1944   MISSION NO. 187

Munich was the briefed target, but clouds up to 30,000 feet blocked the way. Bombs were dropped instead on the secondary target, Elsenborn Camp in Belgium. Five ships, separated from the rest of the Group at the turnback, bombed the marshaling yards at Luxembourg. Two 12-ship boxes were put up, one led by Lts. Hales, Moulton, Kinnucan and Kubetin the other led by Lts. Zotollo, Lawsen, Rowen and Loiacono. Just before the turn back Lt. Zotollo's plane, 44-6077, ran into icing conditions which froze the pitot tube. With the air speed indicator unusable, Lt. Zotollo handed over command to the deputy lead, Lt. Dingle.

Unfortunately just as this transfer of command and the change of positions of the planes began, the Wing started to turn back. By the time the turn had been completed in thick cloud, the formation had broken up. Breaking from the cloud Lt. Zotollo and Lt. Dingle were the only planes to be seen. Not only had they lost the Wing, but by now the three navigators, two in the lead and one in the deputy lead plane, were completely lost.

Setting a course towards the west, they hoped that a visual sighting would assist them to establish their position. Still formatting on the deputy lead ship, Lt. Zotollo's plane was racked by exploding flak. They were over the coast of Holland. One shell passed through the right wing, puncturing a fuel tank and igniting the gasoline. Putting the plane into a dive, Lt. Zotollo attempted to blow the fire out. To no avail, the flames spread. Leveling off, he gave the order to bail out. The whole crew escaped before the plane exploded. On landing, Sgts. Barton, West and Carter managed to evade capture and reach the Allied lines. The rest were quickly captured by the Germans.

Lt. Myl's plane, 42-107216, was damaged over the target and forced to ditch in the Channel. Before the crew could be picked up by Air Sea Rescue, Sgts. McClure and Rasmussen had died of exposure.

AUGUST 11, 1944 **MISSION NO. 188**

Twenty-seven planes bombed the radio station at Brest with good results. No enemy fighters were seen and flak was light. Lt. Colonel Burns and Lt. Viste led the wing, with Lt. Gallagher as navigator and Captain Lyttle as bombardier.

AUGUST 12, 1944

Shortly before midnight, 42-107005 was destroyed by fire. An armorer was checking the turrets on the ship when fire broke out around the upper turret. The ship was totally destroyed before fire appliances could get to the hard stand.

AUGUST 13, 1944 **MISSION NO. 189**

A ground support attack near Louviers, France, was the mission for three 12-ship boxes, led by Lt. Colonel Wood and Captain Brooks with Lt. Thackerey and Lt. Hamel. Bombs were dropped in the target area, hitting a road junction and the approach to a bridge over the Eure River. There was some accurate flak en route, but no enemy fighters.

AUGUST 14, 1944 **MISSION NO. 190**

Once again, cloud obscured the briefed target at Sindelfingen, Germany, so the secondary, Haguenau, France was bombed. Several hangars were hit. There was no enemy opposition. Three 12-ship boxes completed the mission and were led by Colonel Romig and Captain Floden with Major Menees as navigator and Lt. Branaman as bombardier.

AUGUST 16, 1944 **MISSION NO. 191**

Lt. Colonel Burns and Captain Brooks, with Lt. Thackerey as navigator and Lt. Hamel as bombardier, led a wing of 35 ships to the target at Schkeuckitz, Germany. There were probable hits on the flight hangar and other installations of the Siebel Flugzengwerke. There were no enemy fighters, but intense and accurate flak at the target damaged many planes and shot down 42-31702, piloted by Lt. Cartwright.

Just before bombs away, for some inexplicable reason, the low box drifted immediately underneath the rear elements of the high box. Lt. Dundas, bombardier in 44-6156 flown by Lt. McCall, noticed the lower formation just before he released the bombs. He called to the tail gunner, S/Sgt. Parker, to count the planes passing underneath and let him know when they had all gone. Somehow Sgt. Parker miscounted. Instead of the 21 he had thought he had seen, only 18 had gone. Lt. Dundas dropped the bombs. To his horror, he saw another element of B-17s appear below him. He watched the ninth, tenth and eleventh bombs, which were carrying fragmentation canisters, hit 43-37900 (flown by Lt. Kennedy), on the left wing. The plane plummeted down out of the formation.

Lt. Kennedy's first thought was that he had been hit by flak. The plane was in a dive into the heart of the anti-aircraft fire and practically out of control. There was additional damage from innumerable flak hits as the plane swept lower. After partially regaining control, Lt. Kennedy could see the extensive damage to the left wing. There was an enormous hole in the wing itself, the number two engine was dead and there was extensive damage to the entire trailing edge, including the loss of the left aileron and left flap, as well as the Tokyo tank and the oxygen system.

By the time that Lt. Kennedy had regained effective control, he was at about 1,500 feet and trying to quickly get away from the target area. Keeping the plane as low as possible to minimize exposure to further flak damage, he plotted a course back to England. Frequently he flew as low as fifty feet to avoid the flak. Finally, the Channel came in sight and then England. With many systems inoperative due to the extensive damage, the landing gear and braking system had to be operated manually for the landing at Polebrook.

Damage inspection showed that one bomb went between the front and rear spar, another just behind the rear spar and the third on the trailing edge.

During debriefing the incident caused much comment. Lt. Dundas, however, kept quiet throughout, before sheepishly sliding out from the back of the hall.

AUGUST 18, 1944 **MISSION NO. 192**

Thirty-six planes attacked a bridge at Namur, scoring hits on the bridge and its approaches. No fighters were seen, but accurate flak damaged four ships. The formation was led by Colonel Rogner and Captain Holsapple, with Major Matthews as navigator and Lt. Steitz as bombardier.

AUGUST 24, 1944 **MISSION NO. 193**

The armament works at Buchenwald, Germany

was successfully bombed by the low and high boxes, but the lead box dropped on the secondary target, the airfield at Nordhausen. About 20 to 30 enemy fighters were seen but they made no attacks on the Wing. Flak was moderate and fairly accurate. Leaders of the Wing were Major Richardson, Captain Logan, Lt. Fagan and Lt. Decker.

AUGUST 25, 1944   MISSIONS NO. 194 and 195

Thirty-four planes completed the mission to the secret weapon experimental site at Peenemunde. The Wing was led by Major Carraway and Lt. Hales, with Lt. Boardman as navigator and Lt. Branaman as bombardier.

In the afternoon, 11 planes bombed the oxygen plant at Henin-Leitard with fair results. There were no enemy fighters or flak throughout the mission. The Group was led by Major Richardson and Lt. Garcia, with Lt. Fagan as navigator and Lt. Palmer as bombardier.

A freak accident occurred after the planes landed from the first mission. Lt. Woodrum was taking 42-97381 back to its dispersal when the brakes failed. The plane struck an asphalt cooking machine being used by a maintenance crew on the runway. It then hit the tow-target aircraft which was a B-17E model, 42-9121, before it came to a stop. The tow-target aircraft had the left wing tip knocked off and '381 was badly damaged.

AUGUST 26, 1944   MISSION NO. 196

Twelve ships took off on a mission to Willebrocke, Belgium, but did not drop their bombs because of cloud cover in the target area. The Group leaders were Lts. Hales, Poston, Boardman and Branaman.

AUGUST 27, 1944   MISSION NO. 197

Berlin was the briefed target, but a cloud bank building up to 35,000 feet forced the formation to turn back at the Danish coast. Three 12-ship boxes were led by Major Fishburne and Lt. Wolcott, with Captain Cleveland as navigator and Lt. Smith as bombardier.

AUGUST 30, 1944   MISSION NO. 198

Thirty-four planes bombed Kiel using Pathfinder techniques through solid cloud. There was only light inaccurate flak and no enemy fighters. The formation was led by Lt. Colonel Wood and Captain Pryor, with Lt. Maltby as navigator and Lt. Schadegg as bombardier.

SEPTEMBER 5, 1944   MISSION NO. 199

Bombs were dropped using Pathfinder techniques through solid cloud cover on Ludwigshafen. It was impossible to observe the bomb strikes, but heavy black smoke was seen billowing up through the clouds after bombs away. There were no enemy fighters, but intense accurate flak was encountered at the target. One plane, 43-38139, piloted by Lt. Wright, was hit by flak over the target. It burst into flames and completely lost one wing before going down. Thirty-five planes flew this mission led by Major Fishburne and Captain McCluskey with Lt. Gulnac as navigator and Lt. Craig as bombardier.

SEPTEMBER 8, 1944   MISSION NO. 200

The second mission of the month was another attack on Ludwigshafen. Bombing results were unobserved because of smoke and haze in the target area. The only enemy opposition consisted of intense flak over the target.

The plane piloted by Lt. Shera, 42-31560, was forced down with one engine feathered, south of Saarbrucken.

Lt. Barker was forced to land 42-97193, with two badly damaged engines, near Paris. Lt. Barker and his crew were returned to Polebrook.

During Wing assembly for this mission Lt. Haba's plane, 42-31238, encountered icing problems and crashed in England near Market Deeping. All crew members with the exception of the tail gunner were killed.

SEPTEMBER 9, 1944   MISSION NO. 201

Ludwigshafen again was the target and again bombing had to be done through 10/10 cloud. The Pathfinder equipment went out of commission and bombs were dropped on the smoke markers of the wing ahead. The only thing resembling an enemy fighter was one twin-engine plane, possibly jet-propelled, but it did not attempt to attack. There was intense and fairly accurate flak at the target. Lt. Evan's plane, 44-6108, had an engine knocked out by flak and was forced to leave the formation and turn back to France. The plane was landed successfully and the crew returned to base. Thirty-five planes completed the mission, led by Major Stewart and Captain Hales with Lt. Boardman navigating and Lt. Branaman as bombardier.

SEPTEMBER 10, 1944 MISSION NO. 202

The bombing results of this mission to Gagenau, Germany were good. Bombs of the lead box scored one direct hit on a factory workshop and one salvo landed near a bridge across the river Murg. The low box pattern covered five large workshops of the Daimler-Benz factory. However, the high box dropped their bombs in woods near the target. Thirty-six planes flew this mission, led by Brigadier General Lacey flying as Combat Wing Air Commander and Group Leader. His pilot was Captain Pryor, with Major Matthews as navigator and Lt. Schadegg as bombardier.

SEPTEMBER 11, 1944 MISSION NO. 203

Thirty-six planes completed the mission at Lutzkendorf, but only the lead box was able to bomb this target. Clouds moving in over the area compelled the low and high boxes to bomb the secondary target, the B.M.W. Factory at Eisenach. Bombs hit the southeastern end of the factory area and hits were scored on the railway and in the town. No enemy fighters were seen, but there was moderate flak. Lt. Walker was forced to land 42-97216, which was badly damaged, at Brussels/Evere airfield. The crew returned to base. The Group was led by Major Carraway, Captain Auten, Lt. Gulnac and Lt. Steitz.

SEPTEMBER 12, 1944 MISSION NO. 204

The briefed primary target was Ruhland, but clouds in this area prevented bombing. The lead and low boxes bombed an unidentified target near Ruhland. The high box bombed the outskirts of the city of Plauen. Flak was light and inaccurate. The Luftwaffe came up in force northeast of Berlin. About 35 to 50 fighters were seen, mostly Me 109s and FW 190s and a few rocket firing Do 217s. They attacked in pairs or small groups from the tail. A few also dropped aerial bombs without noticeable results.

Six planes were shot down in the target area. They were Lt. Schoenian in 43-37986, Lt. Hennegan in 43-38123, Lt. Adams in 43-38089, Lt. Brown in 43-37850, Lt. Lopert in 42-97318 and Lt. Schmollinger in 44-8100. Lt. Hadley, in 44-6139, managed to make it back as far as Belgium where he crash landed. The Group was led by Major Fishburne, Captain Fowler, Captain Cleveland and Lt. Heck.

SEPTEMBER 17, 1944 MISSION NO. 205

Forty-one planes bombed enemy positions at Nijmegen just before the push for the bridge and the airborne landing at Arnhem. No enemy fighters were seen and flak was meager. Lt. Colonel Glawe led the mission, with Lt. Hales as pilot, Lts. Leisman and Boardman as navigators and Lt. Branaman as bombardier.

SEPTEMBER 19, 1944 MISSION NO. 206

The marshaling yards at Soest, Germany were the briefed target. Because of haze over the target, only the low box dropped their bombs, about one third of them hitting the M.P.I. The lead box bombed a target of opportunity at Emmerich. The high box brought their bombs back to base. Thirty-seven planes flew the mission, but due to very low ceiling over Polebrook when the formation returned, most of the planes were forced to land at other fields. Although flak was light, one plane 42-38153, piloted by Lt. Butler, was so badly damaged that it had to be ditched. The entire crew was picked up by Air Sea Rescue. Lt. Colonel Vorhees flew as Group Leader, with Captain McCluskey as his pilot, Lts. Curley and Maltby as navigators and Lt. Schadegg as bombardier.

SEPTEMBER 22, 1944 MISSION NO. 207

Kassel was bombed by Pathfinder techniques through 8/10 cloud, with unobserved results. Flak at the target was moderate and fairly accurate. Thirty-six planes completed the mission. Lt. Colonel Wood flew as Combat Wing Air Commander and Group Leader, with Lt. Eickhoff as his pilot, Lt. Gulnac as navigator and Lt. Steitz as bombardier.

SEPTEMBER 25, 1944 MISSION NO. 208

Again bombing had to be done through heavy cloud. This time the target was Frankfurt. No enemy fighters were encountered and at the target there was a moderate flak barrage. Major Richardson flew as the 94th Combat Wing Air Commander and Group Leader, with Captain Viste, Major Menees and Captain Lyttle.

SEPTEMBER 26, 1944 MISSION NO. 209

Only the low and high boxes attacked the briefed target, the marshaling yards at Osnabruck. The low box pattern hit the briefed M.P.I., but bombs of the high box fell in open fields 2,400 yards to the right. The lead box attacked the last resort target, the airfield at Rheine. Major Stewart led the Group, with Captain Hales as his pilot, Lt. Boardman as navigator and Lt. Branaman as bombardier.

SEPTEMBER 27, 1944   MISSION NO. 210

Cologne was attacked using Pathfinder markers. Observation of the results was impossible due to 9/10 cloud cover in the target area. No enemy fighters were seen although one crew reported that they saw 18 planes that might have been Me 163s, flying at about 40,000 feet over the target. Major Carraway was Combat Wing Air Commander and Group Leader, Lt. Woodrum his pilot, Lt. Lechner his navigator and Lt. Henry his bombardier.

Over the target a flak shell entered the ball turret of 42-98004, piloted by Captain Geiger, and exploded. The ball turret was blown completely away and a large hole blown in the right side of the fuselage. Sgt. Kurtz, the "Y" radio operator, and Sgt. Divil, the ball turret gunner, were blown out of the ship. Somehow the plane held together and Captain Geiger brought it back to base.

SEPTEMBER 28, 1944   MISSION NO. 211

The last mission of the month was an attack on Magdeburg. Bombs were dropped through solid cloud. No enemy fighters were seen but flak was moderate and quite accurate. Lt. Colonel Wood flew as Group Leader, with Lts. Eichhoff, Gulnac and Steitz. Lt. Barker's ship, 42-97926, lost three engines and had to crash land at Ypres on the way back from the target. The crew returned to Polebrook, although the plane was later scrapped.

OCTOBER 2, 1944   MISSION NO. 212

An ordnance depot at Kassel was bombed using Pathfinders with visual assistance. The deputy lead took over the lead position during the bomb run when the Pathfinder equipment in the lead ship went out of order, but at the last minute it was possible to do a visual sighting. Bombs of the lead squadron fell in the target area, but cloud prevented an accurate assessment.

The bombs of the low squadron were dropped on smoke markers of the lead and landed approximately one half mile short of the target. The high squadron bombed about one mile short. No enemy fighters were seen, but accurate, continuous, following flak at the target damaged 14 planes. Lt. Colonel Burns flew as Group Leader and 94th Combat Wing Air Commander. Lt. Wolcott flew as his pilot, Major Menees as navigator, Lt. Wayne Smith as bombardier, Lt. Lunan as Mickey operator and Lt. Coulam as tail gunner observer. Thirty-seven planes started on the mission, but because of mechanical difficulties, two were forced to return without bombing the target.

OCTOBER 3, 1944   MISSION NO. 213

The marshaling yards at Nuremburg were bombed through cloud with unobserved results. Again no enemy fighters were seen. Moderate flak over the target and over the battle line between Strasbourg and Metz damaged nine planes. One of them, 43-38518, piloted by Lt. Cregar, was damaged so severely that it left the formation shortly after the bomb run and was forced to land in occupied territory. Thirty-six planes bombed the target with 500-pound general purpose and incendiary bombs. The Group Leader, 94th Combat Wing Air Commander, was Lt. Colonel Glawe with Lt. Leland as his pilot, Lts. Cheswick and Goodman as navigators, Lt. Maxwell as bombardier, Lt. Schoen as Mickey operator and Lt. Duffey as tail gunner observer.

OCTOBER 5, 1944   MISSION NO. 214

This was an attack on the important marshaling yards at Cologne. The lead plane, piloted by Colonel Wood and Lt. Woodrum, was forced to turn back just off the enemy coast by mechanical difficulties. Pathfinder equipment in the deputy lead went out of commission, so the lead ship of the high squadron took over for the Pathfinder bombing of the target. The Mickey operator estimated that the bombs fell slightly south of the briefed M.P.I. No enemy fighters were seen. Flak at the target was intense and fairly accurate, but no planes were damaged.

Lt. Johnson and Lt. Hadley were forced to land at Brussels to refuel and returned to base the next day. The deputy lead ship that took over after the lead aborted was piloted by Lt. Anderson and Lt. Rice, with Lt. Morrissette as navigator, Lt. Tracewitz as bombardier and Lt. Trombley as Mickey operator.

OCTOBER 6, 1944   MISSION NO. 215

The synthetic oil refinery at Politz was the briefed target, but clouds made visual bombing impossible. The secondary target, Stargard airfield, was bombed instead. The bombs of the lead squadron fell in a long narrow pattern on the landing ground just short of the M.P.I., with a few bombs on the M.P.I. building. Bombs of the low squadron fell into the pattern of the lead, with the heaviest concentration slightly to the left of the M.P.I. Bombs of the high squadron fell short, but hit the control buildings and one hangar. This mission was definitely a milk run, no fighters, no flak!

Thirty-six planes completed the mission. Major Richardson flew as Group Leader and 94th Combat Wing Air Commander, with Captain Eickhoff as his pilot, Lts. Gulnac and Bury as navigators, Lt. Steitz as bombardier, Lt. Hoeldtke as Mickey operator and Lt. Penticoff as tail gunner observer.

OCTOBER 7, 1944   MISSION NO. 216

The group retuned to the synthetic oil plant at Politz, which this time was successfully bombed. The mission definitely was no milk run. Intense and accurate flak at the target shot down seven planes and damaged 24. The accuracy of the flak may have been because the Group was forced to make a 360 degree turn just before the bomb run.

The lead plane, 44-8222, piloted by Lt. Colonel Glawe and Lt. Bartzocas, left the formation with two engines feathered and a large hole and fuel leak in one wing. Lt. Colonel Glawe eventually landed in Sweden, together with Lt. McGuire in 43-37674, Flight Officer Fisher in 43-38426 and Lt. Evans in 42-97196.

Lt. Peterson in 42-31192 also headed for Sweden. The plane was hit by flak shortly after leaving the I.P. One engine was knocked out and fuel tanks were holed. Falling well behind the formation, they dropped their bombs on the target and headed north when a second engine cut out due to lack of fuel from the punctured tanks. The crew jettisoned all guns and ammunition as the plane lost altitude. Crossing Bornhalt Island, the ship was again damaged by flak and another engine was knocked out. Rapidly losing altitude, Lt. Peterson ordered the crew to prepare for ditching. Breaking through the overcast at 300 feet they saw that they were over land, but too low to jump. Lt. Peterson decided to attempt a crash landing in a small level field immediately ahead. Lining up the plane and preparing to set it down, he suddenly noticed several people in the field picking potatoes.

Desperately applying power to his remaining engine, he lifted the B-17 to miss them. However, he had lost a lot of the little room he had in the field. The plane overshot into a clump of trees, a large rock tearing off the right wing and the large trees wrecking the rest of the plane. The crash threw Sgts. Best and Jensen clear. Recovering their senses they dragged the rest of the crew out of the wreckage. Lt. Christenson and Sgt. Balko were still alive, but died in the hospital. The remaining crew members had been killed in the crash.

Lt. Merril's plane, 43-38171, left the formation on fire just after the target. All the crew bailed out successfully, as did Lt. Dargues' crew in 43-38527. In Flight Officer Stahl's crew, Sgt. Bob Baillio, ball turret gunner, and Sgt. Israel Goodman, tail gunner, were both killed and Sgt. Ray Huskey was seriously wounded. Sgt. Lester Canada, waist gunner on Lt. Ballard's crew, was also seriously wounded.

Forty-seven planes flew this mission, 12 of them forming the lead squadron of a composite group. Lt. Colonel Glawe flew as leader of the 351st Group, with Lt. Bartzocas as pilot, Lts. Levinson and Mendell as navigators, Lt. Clarke as Mickey operator and Lt. Pollyea as ball turret gunner observer. Major Stewart was the leader of the composite group, with Captain Geiger as pilot, Lts. Boardman and Luich as navigators, Lt. Branaman as bombardier, Lt. Schoen as Mickey operator and Lt. Zimmerman as tail gunner observer. Bombing was done visually, but an effective smoke screen made assessment of the results impossible.

OCTOBER 12, 1944

Colonel Burns assumed command of the Group, replacing Colonel Romig who returned to the United States.

Robert Wiygul Burns was born in Nettleton, Mississippi on December 8, 1916. He graduated from high school in Ecru, Mississippi in 1933 and from Mississippi State Teachers College in 1938 with a Bachelor of Science degree. He enlisted in the Army in 1939 as an aviation cadet and received his pilot wings and a commission as a Second Lieutenant in November 1939 at Kelly Field, Texas.

Assigned to the 7th Reconnaissance Squadron, Lt. Burns went to the Panama Canal Zone. In February 1942, he assumed command of Headquarters

Squadron, 6th Bombardment Group. He became Commander of the 74th Bombardment Squadron in Guatemala City, Guatemala, in June 1942.

He returned to the United States in November 1942 and was assigned as Deputy Commander of the 351st Bombardment Group at Geiger Field, Washington.

OCTOBER 14, 1944   MISSION NO. 217

The marshaling yards at Cologne were the target. Although bombs were dropped through 9/10 cloud, Mickey operators estimated that bombs fell within the M.P.I. area. No enemy aircraft opposition was encountered and flak was inaccurate. Thirty-six planes completed the mission, led by Major Carraway and Captain Eickhoff with Lts. Gulnac and Bury as navigators, Lt. Steitz as bombardier, Lt. Hoeldtke as Mickey operator and Lt. Penticoff as tail gunner observer.

OCTOBER 15, 1944   MISSION NO. 218

This next attack in the Cologne series was made visually, as the clouds in the target area had broken up to 4/10. However, the target was partially obscured by cloud and an effective smoke screen. Bombs of the lead squadron fell across a main autobahn one and one half miles northwest of the marshaling yards. The low squadron bombed by Pathfinder, their bombs falling on a railroad junction and industrial area one mile southeast of the primary target. The pattern of the high squadron fell on a main autobahn bridge across the Rhine, scoring a few hits on the bridge. The clearer weather made the flak much more lethal. Intense and sustained following fire damaged 22 ships, 12 of them seriously.

Lt. Muffett's plane, 42-97965, went in over the target with one engine feathered. He dropped his bombs and came out of the target with another engine knocked out and a third smoking. Lt. Muffet managed to nurse his crippled ship back to Belgium, where he made an emergency landing near Brussels.

Thirty-five planes attacked the target led by Major Davey and Captain Woodrum with Lts. Cosgrove and Morrissette as navigators, Lt. Homza as Mickey operator and Lt. Fish as tail gunner observer. Upon his return from the United States, Major Roper replaced Lt. Colonel Wood as the Commanding Officer of the 510th Squadron.

OCTOBER 17, 1944   MISSION NO. 219

Again, Cologne was bombed through clouds with unobserved results. A new staggered formation, used for the first time on this mission, appeared to be successful in confusing the flak gunners. There was moderate flak at the target, but it was widely scattered and only six of the 36 planes were damaged. The entire flight was made above 9/10 cloud and there was solid cloud at 8,000 feet over England when the planes returned. Lt. Colonel Ball flew this mission as Group Leader and 94th Combat Wing Air Commander, with Captain Leland as pilot, Lt. Cheswick and Lt. Talbot as navigators, Lt. Maxwell as bombardier, Lt. Schoen as Mickey operator and Lt. Molitor as tail gunner observer.

OCTOBER 18, 1944   MISSION NO. 220

Only 12 planes took part in this fourth successive mission to Cologne. They flew high squadron with the 384th Bomb Group. Bombing was through 9/10 cloud using GH. Photographs taken through a break in the clouds show a concentration of bombs hitting open fields more than 7,000 feet northwest of the target. The squadron was led by Captain Gibbons and Major Gorham, Lt. Love, Lt. Ralph, and Lt. Bell as the GH operator.

OCTOBER 19, 1944   MISSION NO. 221

The Heinrich Lonz factory at Mannhein was attacked by 36 planes. Bombing was through 10/10 cloud by Pathfinder methods with believed good results. The Group was led by Major Roper and Captain Viste, with Lt. Gallagher and Lt. Huntley as navigators, Lt. Smith as bombardier, Lt. Lunan as Mickey operator and Lt. Hammond as tail gunner observer.

OCTOBER 22, 1944   MISSION NO. 222

Heavy cloud again necessitated the use of Pathfinder equipment, this time over the industrial area of Hanover. The Luftwaffe was still standing down and flak was meager. The 36 planes of the Group were led by Colonel Burns and Captain Eickoff.

OCTOBER 25, 1944   MISSION NO. 223

The briefed target was the Rhenania-Ossag oil refinery at Hamburg. As usual, bombing was through solid cloud. PFF equipment worked well and heavy, black smoke was seen coming up through the cloud indicating that the bombing was successful. There was intense flak, but well below the formation's altitude and no planes were damaged. The Group was led by Major Richardson and Captain Woodrum, with Lts. Cosgrove and Ouder as navigators, Lt. Henry as bombardier, Lt. Homza as Mickey operator and Lt. Fish as tail gunner observer.

OCTOBER 26, 1944   MISSION NO. 224

The ordnance depot at Bielefield was bombed by 36 planes through 9/10 cloud. The Pathfinder equipment in the lead ship functioned poorly, forcing the Group to bomb on the smoke markers of the preceding group. The Group Leader was Major Stewart, with Captain Geiger as his pilot, Lts. Boardman and Cheswick as navigators, Lt. Branaman as bombardier, Lt. Schoen as Mickey operator and Lt. Molitor as tail gunner observer.

OCTOBER 28, 1944   MISSION NO. 225

Another marshaling yard was the target, this time at Munster. Bombing was through 9/10 cloud with some visual assistance. However, results could not be observed. Moderate and accurate flak at the target damaged 22 planes. Lt. Fultz landed 42-97651 at Wittering with the hydraulic system out and Lt. Stear, the bombardier, wounded. Lt. Tebbel's ship was seriously damaged by flak. When the oxygen system in the waist exploded, the tail gunner, S/Sgt. Lloyd Babin, bailed out and four other members of the crew, S/Sgt. Garrity, S/Sgt. Fisher, Sgt. Heaberlin and Sgt. Juul, were wounded. Thirty-six planes completed the mission led by Major Carraway and Captain Wolcott, with Lts. Glover and Kyser as navigators, Lt. Wayne Smith as bombardier, Lt. Lunan as Mickey operator and Lt. Hammond as tail gunner observer.

OCTOBER 30, 1944   MISSION NO. 226

The briefed primary was the oil refinery at Gelsenkirchen, but cloud made visual bombing impossible. The secondary, Munster's marshaling yard, was bombed by PFF instead. The 36 planes that completed this mission were led by Major Davey and Captain Gibbons, Lt. Love, Lt. Ralph, and Lt. Hoeldtke as Mickey operator.

NOVEMBER 4, 1944   MISSION NO. 227

The target for the whole First Division was the oil refinery at Harburg. The 351st Bomb Group's contribution was 36 planes. These took off at 0845 hours and flew over scattered clouds which increased to 10/10 over the target. The lead and high squadrons dropped their bombs on PFF smoke markers, but the smoke marker of the low squadron failed to go off. This squadron then bombed the last resort target, the airfield at Nordholz. The mission was uneventful with no enemy fighters and only light flak. Lt. Colonel Ball was the Group Leader, with Captain Pryor as pilot, Lts. Curley and Cosgrove as navigators, Captain Schadegg as bombardier, Lt. Trombley as Mickey operator and Lt. Edwards as tail gunner observer.

NOVEMBER 5, 1944   MISSION NO. 228

Thirty-six planes took off at 0745 hours for the marshaling yards at Frankfurt. Most of the route was flown over fairly solid cloud, but over the target there were a few breaks which made it possible to see the city from directly above. Therefore visual assistance was given to the Pathfinder bombing. Bombs fell up to two miles from the M.P.I., but did damage to the old city of Frankfurt. There were no enemy fighters and flak was relatively ineffective, causing damage to two planes. Squalls over England caused some trouble on return and the formation had to divert to Beccles. Major Gorham led the Group, with Captain Eickoff as pilot, Lts. Love and Martin as navigators, Lt. Steitz as bombardier, Lt. Lunan as Mickey operator and Lt. Adams as tail gunner observer.

NOVEMBER 6, 1944   MISSION NO. 229

The target for this group was the oil refinery at Hamburg. Three 12-ship squadrons took off, flying over 3/10 cloud which gradually increased to 5/10 over the target. Bomb strikes could not be plotted because of cloud and smoke. A moderate flak barrage at the target damaged seven planes. Major Richardson flew as Group Leader and 94th Combat Wing Air Commander. Lt. Weatherman was his pilot, with Lt. Lunan as Mickey operator and Lt. Johnson as tail gunner observer.

NOVEMBER 9, 1944   MISSION NO. 230

The entire 8th Air Force bombed fortifications in the battle line, as a prelude to a new offensive against Germany. The briefed target for the Group was a fortress in the Metz area. The lead and low squadrons dropped their bombs accidentally when one bomb fell prematurely from the lead ship. The high squadron bombed the last resort target at Saarbrucken. No enemy fighters were seen and flak was inaccurate, damaging only one plane. The Group was led by Captain Dennis and Captain

Gibbons, with Lt. Love, Lt. Ralph, and Flight Officer Dimick as GH operator.

NOVEMBER 16, 1944   MISSION NO. 231

Thirty-seven planes bombed the front line area near Eschweiler through smoke and haze. Polebrook was closed in due to weather when the planes returned and many of them were forced to land at other fields in England. Major Carraway led the Group, with Lt. D. S. Anderson as his pilot, Lts. Morrissette and Gourash as navigators, Captain Lyttle as bombardier, Lt. Trombley as Mickey operator and Lt. Rice as tail gunner observer.

NOVEMBER 21, 1944   MISSION NO. 232

Thirty-five planes took part in a concerted attack on the German's synthetic oil production. Just before the target, Merseburg, the formation ran into high clouds with bases down to 18,500 feet. The low squadron lost the rest of the formation in this cloud and bombed a target of opportunity, the railroad at Apolda, between Weimar and Naumberg. The lead and high squadrons bombed the primary target by Pathfinder methods with unobserved results. No enemy fighters were seen, but intense accurate flak at the target damaged 16 ships and shot one down, 43-37727, piloted by Lt. Loehndorf.

The plane piloted by Lt. Stahl was so badly damaged that he was forced to land at Brussels airfield. The Group Leader was Captain Geiger, with Lt. Poston as pilot, Lts. Boardman and Irwin as navigators, Lt. Maxwell as bombardier, Lt. Schoen as Mickey operator and Lt. Molitor as tail gunner observer.

NOVEMBER 23, 1944   MISSION NO. 233

Twelve planes flew as a screening force for the First Division's mission to Gelsenkirchen. The 12 planes dropped 349 cartons of chaff west of the Ruhr. There were no enemy aircraft or flak. Major Davey led the squadron, with Lt. Weatherman as pilot, Lts. Kyser and McCarthy as navigators, Lt. Schiffman as bombardier and Lt. Lunan as Mickey operator.

NOVEMBER 25, 1944   MISSION NO. 234

Thirty-five planes started out over 5/10 cloud which increased to 10/10 over the target, the oil refinery at Merseburg. Bombing was by Pathfinder techniques with unobserved results. Colonel Burns flew as Group Leader and 94th Combat Wing Air Commander. Captain Eickhoff flew as his pilot with Captain Gulnac and Lt. Tabb as navigators, Captain Lyttle as bombardier, Lt. Ohrel as Mickey operator and Lt. Penticoff as tail gunner observer.

NOVEMBER 26, 1944   MISSION NO. 235

The oil refinery at Misburg was the next target. The three squadrons found the target free of cloud, but had to bomb using Pathfinder methods because of haze and smoke screens. Intense accurate flak shot down one plane, 43-37571, piloted by Lt. Boettcher, and damaged six others. Lt. Gonske's plane was hit by flak just before the I.P. Two engines were knocked out and the navigator, Flight Officer Clark, was wounded. Lt. Gonske jettisoned his bombs, turned back and landed successfully in Belgium, where Flight Officer Clark was hospitalized and the rest of the crew ferried back to England. Major Roper was the Group Leader, with Captain Gibbons as pilot, Lts. Love and Martin as navigators, Lt. Ralph as bombardier, Lt. Ohrel as Mickey operator and Lt. Penticoff as tail gunner observer.

NOVEMBER 29, 1944   MISSION NO. 236

Along with the rest of the First Division, the Group went back to Misburg. Bombing was through solid cloud. Lt. Colonel Stewart flew as Group Leader and 94th Combat Wing Air Commander, with Lt. Poston as pilot, Lt. Irwin and Captain Boardman as navigators, Lt. Plant as bombardier, Lt. Schoen as Mickey operator and Lt. Molitor as tail gunner observer.

NOVEMBER 30, 1944   MISSION NO. 237

The last mission of the month was an attack on enemy fuel supplies at Bohlen. Only two squadrons, the lead and low, bombed the primary target. Bombs were dropped visually with Pathfinder assistance. A very effective smoke screen made the observation of strikes impossible. The high squadron bombed the last resort target at Rudolstadt. No enemy fighters were seen, but flak damaged eight planes.

One plane, piloted by Lt. Belmeyer, had to land in France. In another, the pilot, Lt. David W. Basehore, was severely hit in the head by flak. The plane was badly damaged, but the copilot, Lt. Johnson, brought it back and landed without brakes at Wittering. Lt. Basehore died approximately one hour after landing. The Group was led by Major Davey and Captain Logan, with Lts. Glover and Huntley as navigators, Lt. W. R. Smith as bombardier, Lt. Lunan as Mickey operator and Lt. Card as tail gunner observer.

DECEMBER 4, 1944   MISSION NO. 238

The Kassel marshaling yard was the target for the whole First Air Division. Three squadrons took off at 0740 hours, reached the target at 1300 hours, bombed using Pathfinder methods and returned to base at 1700 hours, flying above 10/10 cloud throughout the mission. The formation was led by Major Gorham, with Captain Eickhoff as pilot, Lts. Kelley and Tabb as navigators, Lt. Androkitis as bombardier, Lt. Ohrel as Mickey operator and Lt. Penticoff as tail gunner observer.

DECEMBER 5, 1944   MISSION NO. 239

Thirty-three planes bombed the Tegal Steel Works at Berlin with poor results. The only bursts that could be plotted appeared about five miles northeast of the briefed target. Flak at the target was meager, but accurate. Five ships were damaged and one, 43-38432, piloted by Captain Williamson, was hit by flak at the target just after bombs away. He fell out of formation under control and was forced to land in enemy territory. Lt. Colonel Ball flew as Group Leader and 94th Combat Wing Air Commander, with Captain Pryor as pilot, Lts. Curley and Allen as navigators, Lt. Henry as bombardier, Lt. Trombley as Mickey operator and Lt. Edwards as observer.

DECEMBER 9, 1944   MISSION NO. 240

The target for the Group was the airfield at Sindelfingen, near Stuttgart. Bomb strikes could not be accurately plotted because of 7/10 cloud over the target. A bomb release malfunction in the lead ship of the high squadron at the briefed target forced the squadron to bomb the last resort target, Grosselfingen. The results were unknown. Captain Geiger led the Group on this mission, with Captain Trapp as pilot, Lts. Talbot and Luich as navigators, Lt. McFarlane as bombardier, Lt. Hardaway as Mickey operator and Lt. Bullock as tail gunner.

DECEMBER 11, 1944   MISSION NO. 241

The target for the 351st together with the rest of the First Division "A" Force was the marshaling yards at Frankfurt. Bombing was by Pathfinder technique through solid cloud. The only flak was a few inaccurate bursts at the target. The main difficulty on this mission was caused by high cloud, in places rising to 30,000 feet, through which the formation had to return. Major Richardson flew as Group Leader and 94th Combat Wing Air Commander, with Major Korges as pilot, Lts. Kyser and Hecht as navigators, Lt. Schiffman as bombardier, Lt. Schoen as Mickey operator and Lt. Love as tail gunner observer.

The 351st also put up a screening force which dropped 226 cartons of chaff between 49 degrees 39' N - 08 degrees 05' E and 49 degrees 39' N - 08 degrees 09' E. This 12-ship formation was led by Captain Trapp and Lt. Bullock, with Lt. Luich as navigator, Lt. Hubbell as bombardier, Lt. Hardaway as Mickey operator and Lt. Molitor as tail gunner.

DECEMBER 12, 1944   MISSION NO. 242

The target for the Group, the synthetic oil plant at Merseberg, was covered by 10/10 cloud and haze and had to be bombed by Pathfinder methods. There was moderate flak at the target, but no ships were damaged. One ship, piloted by Lt. Barker, was forced to land at St. Trond because of mechanical difficulties. The formation of 36 planes was led by Captains Dennis and Eickhoff, with Lts. Kelley and Hill as navigators, Captain Steitz as bombardier, Lt. Ohrel as Mickey operator and Lt. Cook as tail gunner observer.

DECEMBER 15, 1944   MISSION NO. 243

The Group led the 94th Combat Wing to Kassel, bombing with 500-pound general purpose and M17 incendiaries using Pathfinder techniques. Lt. Colonel Burns flew as Group Leader and 94th Combat Wing Air Commander, with Captain Anderson as pilot, Captain Maltby and Lt. Morrissette as navigators, Captain Lyttle as bombardier, Lt. Trombley as Mickey operator and Lt. Edwards as observer.

DECEMBER 18, 1944   MISSION NO. 244

The briefed target was the marshaling yards at Cologne, but the mission had to be abandoned near the I.P. It was found to be impossible for the formation to climb above cloud layers which extended above 30,000 feet. The formation was led by Lt. Colonel Stewart, with Captain Poston as pilot, Captain Boardman and Lt. Nelson as navigators, Lt. Maxwell as bombardier, Lt. Schoen as Mickey operator and Lt. Molitor as observer.

DECEMBER 19, 1944   MISSION NO. 245

In support of ground forces, the Group attacked

a front line installation at Kall. Bombing was by GH methods with unobserved results. The mission was unhindered except by solid cloud and dense persistent contrails. A heavy fog closed in on the field before the planes returned and most of them were compelled to land at other bases. Major Korges led the Group, with Lt. Daugherty as pilot, Lts. Maggini and Huntley as navigators, Lt. Stump as bombardier, Lt. Schoen as Mickey operator and Lt. Stewart as tail gunner observer.

DECEMBER 24, 1944   MISSION NO. 246

The target assigned for Christmas Eve was Biblis airfield in Germany. Polebrook was still completely closed in by dense fog and most of the planes were scattered all over England. To fly the mission, they took off from wherever they happened to be. Sixteen planes flew in the high squadron and two in the lead squadron of a composite group that went to Biblis. The two planes in the lead squadron bombed the secondary target, Kaiserslautern. Four planes flew with the Deenethorpe group to bomb Koblenz and five planes, which were scheduled to fly with Deenethorpe, were unable to join the formation and flew with other groups instead. Three bombed Merzhausen airfield and two bombed the airfield at Giessen. Two more bombed Frankfurt/Main airfield with the 493rd Bomb Group. All bombing was done visually with apparently good results.

Twenty-six planes were also put up to fly a spoof mission to a point over the English Channel. When this last formation had taken off only two B-17s remained on the base! Fog still persisted and again the planes had to land elsewhere.

DECEMBER 27, 1944   MISSION NO. 247

Eventually the fog lifted and the planes were able to get back in time to take off for a mission to a railway bridge behind the front lines at Bullay. Bombing was excellent, with direct hits in the center of the bridge and several hits on the approaches and the marshaling yards. No enemy planes were seen, but flak at the target damaged six planes. The Group was led by Major Roper, with Captain Eickhoff as pilot, Lts. Bury and Malone as navigators, Lt. Reed as bombardier, Lt. Real as Mickey operator and Lt. Cook as observer.

DECEMBER 28, 1944   MISSION NO. 248

The marshaling yards at Rheinbach, Germany, was the briefed target, but cloud cover in this area compelled the Group to bomb the secondary target, the marshaling yards at Koblenz. Bombing was by Pathfinder technique with unobserved results. There were no enemy fighters and only meager inaccurate flak which did no damage. One plane, piloted by Lt. Buttel, was forced to land at Ghent because of mechanical difficulties. The Group was led by Lt. Colonel Carraway, with Captain Maginn as pilot, Lts. Cosgrove and Cornell as navigators, Lt. Henry as bombardier, Lt. Trombley as Mickey operator and Lts. Edwards and Macmillan as gunner observers.

DECEMBER 30, 1944   MISSION NO. 249

Thirty-six planes attacked the marshaling yard at Kaiserslautern using Pathfinder techniques. There were no enemy fighters and no flak. Major Geiger was the Group Leader, with Captain Trapp as pilot, Lt. Luich as navigator, Lt. Malerich as GH operator, Lt. McFarlane as bombardier, Lt. Schoen as Mickey operator and Lt. Holloway as tail gunner observer.

DECEMBER 31, 1944   MISSION NO. 250

A bombsight malfunction in the lead ship made it impossible to get an accurate sighting on the primary target, the Krefeld-Uerdingen marshaling yards. This prompted the lead and high squadrons to bomb a target of opportunity, Munchen-Gladbach. The low squadron bombed the primary target using GH with visual assistance. Their bombs fell across a road and railroad junction about three miles southeast of the city. One plane, unable to join the formation, flew with the 398th Group. Another plane had mechanical difficulties and bombed a target of opportunity at Grevenbraich. Moderate flak at the target damaged one plane. Major Korges led the Group, with Captain Logan as pilot, Lt. Glover as navigator, Lt. Peterson as GH navigator, Lt. W. R. Smith as bombardier, Lt. Hardaway as Mickey operator and Lt. Stewart as gunner observer.

Chapter Four

THE END IN SIGHT

1944 had seen some of the fiercest air battles the Group was to encounter. It was a year in which the Group had received a Distinguished Unit Citation for its actions on January 11, 1944. Two members of the 510th Squadron had posthumously received the Medal of Honor. 1945 opened with the German Ardennes offensive in full swing. In the air, however, the Allies had clear superiority over the Luftwaffe. The bomber formations were able to fly without opposition from enemy fighters, but they still had to brave formidable flak.

JANUARY 1, 1945   MISSION NO. 251

Bad weather at the briefed target, the oil storage plant at Derben, made bombing impossible. The secondary, Kassel, was bombed using Pathfinders. Bombs of the lead squadron hit short of the Kassel marshaling yards and the pattern of the low squadron hit in a residential section on the western edge of Kassel. There was no photo cover for the high squadron, but visual observations indicated that the bombing was good. Flak at the target damaged nine planes and Lt. Kasper landed at Brussels when one of his gunners was wounded by flak. Major Roper led this mission as 94th Combat Wing Air Commander. Captain Eickhoff flew as his pilot, with Captain Gulnac and Lt. Bury as navigators, Captain Steitz as bombardier, Lt. Real as Mickey operator and Lt. Miller as tail gunner observer.

JANUARY 2, 1945   MISSION NO. 252

The Group bombed the communications center at Mayen with excellent results. The only enemy opposition was some light flak that damaged four planes. The formation was led by Major Gorham with Captain Pryor as pilot, Lt. Cosgrove as navigator, Lt. Malerich as GH navigator, Lt. Trombley as Mickey operator and Lt. Edwards as gunner observer.

JANUARY 3, 1945   MISSION NO. 253

The briefed target was another communications center at Kalscheuren, but this target was obscured by cloud and Cologne was bombed instead. No enemy planes were seen and there was only scattered flak at the target. Lt. Colonel Stewart led the formation with Captain Poston as pilot, Captain Boardman and Lt. Talbott as navigators, Lt. Maxwell as bombardier, Lt. Schoen as Mickey operator and Lt. Steward as tail gunner observer.

JANUARY 5, 1945   MISSION NO. 254

Bad weather again prevented the bombing of the primary target, the landing ground at Eudenbach. The secondary, Koblenz marshaling yard, was bombed on the markers of the Pathfinder ship of the high squadron. Lt. Murray had trouble with one engine and was forced to land at Brussels. The Group was led by Major Korges, with Captain Weatherman as pilot, Lts. Kyser and Maginni as navigators, Lt. Schiffman as bombardier, Lt. Hardaway as Mickey operator and Lt. Lowe as tail gunner observer.

JANUARY 6, 1945   MISSION NO. 255

Using Pathfinder techniques, a bridge over the Rhine at Bonn was bombed by 38 planes. This was the secondary target, since high cloud prevented the bombing of the briefed primary, the Euskirchen rail center. The entire route was flown over seven to 10/10 clouds. Captain Dennis led the formation, with Captain Gibbons as pilot, Lt. Love as navigator, Lt. Snyder as GH navigator, Lt. Ralph as bombardier and Lt. Miller as gunner observer.

JANUARY 7, 1945   MISSION NO. 256

An attack using GH was carried out on the communications center at Bitburg. There was no enemy opposition, but snow flurries made landing difficult when the planes returned to base.

JANUARY 10, 1945   MISSION NO. 257

The landing ground at Euskirchen was attacked by 32 planes led by Major Hinkle with Captain Trapp as pilot, Lt. Luich as navigator, Lt. McFarlane as bombardier, Lt. Schoen as Mickey operator and Lt. Kniering as gunner observer. Light but accurate flak at the target damaged four ships. Adverse weather conditions broke up the high squadron, causing three planes to bomb with the 401st Bomb Group, one with the 303rd and one with aircraft of the Second Division.

During takeoff, 42-97381 had an unusual accident. As the ship started down the runway for takeoff, the front hatch came open and the nose gunner started slamming it in an effort to close it. The pilot heard the noise and thought it was coming from the number two engine. He cut his throttles and applied his brakes. The plane slid off the end of the runway and when it hit the soft ground it nosed over and then settled back on its tail. The plane was badly damaged and one gunner was slightly injured.

JANUARY 14, 1945   MISSION NO. 258

To attack Cologne the Group furnished the 94th "A" Group and the low squadron of the 94th "B" Group. The particular targets were two bridges. The lead squadron dropped their bombs in a residential section with some hits on a large train shed near the eastern approach to the bridge. The low squadron bombed the wrong bridge, but with good results, scoring a direct hit near the center of the span and another near the eastern shore. The high squadron dropped a good pattern on and around their bridge, while the "B" low squadron dropped on their target into the smoke of previous bombing. There were no enemy fighters, but intense accurate flak at the target damaged 22 planes.

Major Roper flew as Combat Wing Air Commander and "A" Group Leader, with Captain Eickhoff as pilot, Captain Gulnac and Lt. Volotta as navigators, Lt. Reed as bombardier, Lt. Real as Mickey operator and Lt. Adams as tail gunner observer.

JANUARY 17, 1945   MISSION NO. 259

The briefed target was the railway viaduct at Altenbeken, but adverse weather forced the Group to bomb railway workshops at Paderborn. Bombing was through 10/10 clouds with unobserved results. No enemy planes were seen and the only flak, which was meager and inaccurate, was en route.

Major Roper led the Group on this mission, with Captain Purcell as pilot, Lts. Bury and Harris as navigators, Lt. Reed as bombardier, Lt. Real as Mickey operator and Lt. Thomas as gunner observer.

Lt. Della-Cioppa was piloting 42-31384, *Buckeye Babe*, on her 108th mission. However this was not to be an easy mission for the crew, as told by Lt. Clark, the navigator. "This was not a long or hazardous mission in our opinion and we were overjoyed that we would get another milk run under our belts. We were assigned as an element leader in the lower left squadron of the Group, and had joined up with the Group with no problems at all. As we passed over the English coast one of the engines began throwing oil, but continued to run. Still feeling that this was an easy mission, we foolishly continued on our merry way. By the time we had crossed the French coast, the engine gave out and the propeller could not be feathered. Almost simultaneously another engine began to throw oil. Still thinking that we could make the mission without difficulty, and not wishing to be chewed out for aborting, we continued. Soon however this second engine threw out all its oil and could not be feathered. We were now forced to relinquish our leadership of the element. Just before we arrived over the target, the third engine started to throw oil, and by the time we had dropped our bombs had ceased to function. At this point we had to drop out of formation and request fighter support.

"We still had one engine running, but it simply was not enough to keep us flying on a level course. Particularly with the other three windmilling all the time. In spite of jettisoning everything we could she gradually lost height. We had P-51 fighter coverage until we lost them in a cloud bank at about 11,000 feet. We stayed in this cloud cover until we were down to about 5,000 feet. My calculations at this point were that we could make the Allied lines before we had to bail out or crash land, so we chose to ride her down. The crew concurred with this decision, and none bailed out despite being given the opportunity. Eventually it became obvious that we could not make it beyond the lines.

The pilots did a beautiful job, setting her down with wheels up in a large field in Holland. Just before landing we were fired upon by flak batteries stationed in all four corners of the field. Fortunately none of them hit us. The plane bounced a few times but there was no fire and not one member of the crew received a scratch. Immediately after disembarking from the aircraft we were surrounded by the German soldiers from the flak batteries. This rendered any thought of escape useless."

JANUARY 20, 1945   MISSION NO. 260

The synthetic oil plant at Sterkrade was bombed using Micro-H techniques. However, the Nijmegen beacon was improperly delayed and as a result the bombing was poor. Bombs-away photos indicated that bombs of the lead and low squadrons hit the southeast corner of Essen. The high squadron was unable to pick up any of the Micro-H beacons and bombed the secondary target, Rheine, by Pathfinders. Cloud cover of 9/10 and thick contrails made visual bombing impossible. Moderate and accurate flak at both targets damaged 23 planes. Group Leader on this mission was Major Roper, with Captain Pryor as pilot, Lts. Cosgrove and Wolz as navigators, Captain Lyttle as bombardier, Lt. Trombley as Mickey operator and Lt. Edwards as tail gunner observer.

JANUARY 21, 1945   MISSION NO. 261

Along with the rest of the First Division, the 351st bombed a tank depot at Aschaffenburg. In the target area, the GH equipment in the lead plane and the PFF equipment in the deputy lead of the lead squadron went out of commission. The high squadron took over the lead and bombed by Pathfinder with unobserved results. There were no enemy fighters and no flak. Lt. Colonel Stewart flew this mission as Group Leader and 94th Combat Wing Air Commander, with Captain Poston as pilot, Lt. Talbott as navigator, Lt. Plant as bombardier, Lt. Schoen as Mickey operator and Lt. Hollows as tail gunner observer.

JANUARY 22, 1945   MISSION NO. 262

Two squadrons flying with the 94th "B" Group made another trip to the synthetic oil plant at Sterkrade. The lead squadron bombed the primary target visually, hitting the southeast corner of the target area. The leader of the low squadron was unable to get his bombs away at the primary target. He led the squadron towards the secondary, the Rheine marshaling yards, but as the planes approached the target, the deputy lead ship was hit by flak, lost two engines and salvoed bombs to reduce weight. The rest of the squadron, with the exception of the leader, dropped at the same time, well short of the target.

Flak at both targets damaged 11 planes. Lt. Johnson and Lt. Whittaker were forced to land their damaged planes in Belgium. Lt. Goldsborough, in 44-6078, was seen straggling soon after bombing. With two engines out of commission, Lt. Goldsborough, struggling to maintain height and speed, made for the Allied lines in Holland. When he thought that he had reached the Allied lines, and at only 2,000 feet he gave the order to bail out. Unfortunately, Sgt. Shirts hesitated too long and was taken to his death with the aircraft. The rest of the crew landed between the lines. A patrol of Canadian soldiers came to their rescue, but before they could return to their own lines, all were captured by the Germans. Major Roper led the Group with Captain Weatherman, Lts. Kyser, LeFevre, Schiffman, Hardaway and Stewart.

JANUARY 28, 1945   MISSION NO. 263

Together with the rest of the First Division, the Group attacked the marshaling yards at Cologne. Up to the target there was solid cloud which cleared just past the target. Bombing was by Pathfinder methods, but the cameras were able to record the bomb patterns. Bombs of the lead squadron hit an industrial area one mile west northwest of the PFF aiming point. The center of the high squadron pattern fell 1,600 feet from the aiming point and the low squadron's hit two miles west of the target in a built up area of Cologne. Accurate flak over the target damaged 14 planes.

Major Roper led the Group, with Captain Eickoff as pilot, Major Matthews as navigator, Lt. Malerich as GH navigator, Captain Lyttle as bombardier, Lt. Real as Mickey operator and Lt. Bowen as tail gunner observer.

JANUARY 29, 1945   MISSION NO. 264

The marshaling yards at Siegen were attacked by 35 planes using Pathfinder techniques. There were no enemy fighters and no flak. The Group was led by Lt. Colonel Carraway, with Captain Gaylord as pilot, Lts. Morrissette and Fuller as navigators, Lt. Traczewitz as bombardier, Lt. Trombley as Mickey operator and Lt. Fish as gunner observer.

FEBRUARY 1, 1945   MISSION NO. 265

Together with the whole First Division, the Group went to Ludwigshafen and bombed by Pathfinder. Nothing showed up on the screens except clouds, but Mickey men thought that the bombs hit one or two miles north of the M.P.I. No enemy planes were seen and there was only meager flak which damaged one plane.

Major Roper led the Group, with Captain Trapp as pilot, Lt. Luich and Flight Officer Brandon as navigators, Captain McFarlane as bombardier, Lt. Schoen as Mickey operator and Lt. Steward as tail gunner observer.

The need for Lt. Blaney, in 43-37665 of the 510th Squadron, to abort with the failure of number one engine spoiled the record that M/Sgt. Seaborn O. Jones had established for maintenance. M/Sgt. Jones had been the crew chief on three 510th Squadron aircraft and this was the first abort that any of them had. 42-31560 had 60 missions when it was lost, 43-38465 had 40, and '665 had 63 until this mission. This total of 163 missions without an abort for mechanical reasons was a significant and noteworthy achievement for M/Sgt. Jones.

FEBRUARY 3, 1945   MISSION NO. 266

The 351st flew the "C" Group of the 94th Combat Wing to attack Berlin. The bombs of the lead squadron fell on the briefed M.P.I., which was a transportation area near the center of the city. The low squadron dropped on the edge of the target area, about one half mile east of the M.P.I. The bombs of the high squadron hit in and around the yards of the Gorlitzen passenger station. There were no enemy fighters and surprisingly enough, hardly any flak.

The Group Leader was Major Roper, with Lt. Coulam as pilot, Lts. Kyser and LeFevre as navigators, Lt. Schiffman as bombardier, Lt. Hardaway as Mickey operator and Lt. Holloway as gunner observer.

FEBRUARY 6, 1945   MISSION NO. 267

For the composite box, the Group provided the lead and low squadrons. With planes of the 401st Bomb Group flying the high box, the formation intended to bomb Lutzkendorf. However, reports from the Scouting Force indicated that there was solid cloud in that area, so a target of opportunity, Lutter, was bombed through 8/10 cloud. Lutter, a small village, was thoroughly blasted and a few bombs fell on the railway connecting Fulda with Gersfield.

Clouds were down to 200 feet over the base when the planes returned, making landing difficult. Observers in the control tower were horrified when two planes collided while trying to land. They were Lt. Ashton in 43-38080 and Lt. Vergen in 43-37595. All crew members were killed. Major Roper led this mission, with Captain Gibbons as pilot, Captain Gulnac and Lt. Madsen as navigators, Captain Steitz as bombardier, Lt. Real as Mickey operator and Lt. Franz as tail gunner observer.

FEBRUARY 7, 1945   MISSION NO. 268

Again Lutzkendorf was briefed as the primary target, but the Group was recalled before the planes had left the coast of England.

FEBRUARY 9, 1945   MISSION NO. 269

The mission to Lutzkendorf was finally completed by 35 planes flying with the 94th Combat Wing "A" Task Force. Bombs of the lead squadron fell 5,100 feet over and slightly to the left of the target, which was the synthetic oil plant of Wintershall A.G. The low squadron dropped in open fields 7,500 feet to the left of the target and the high dropped in a quarry 10,000 feet over. None of the bombs did any noticeable damage. There were no enemy fighters as usual, but accurate flak at the target damaged 10 planes. Most of the route was flown over solid cloud, but it broke up to about 4/10 at eleven degrees east and bombs were dropped visually.

Major Roper again led, with Captain D. Anderson as pilot, Lt. Morrissette and Flight Officer Phelps as navigators, Lt. Traczewitz as bombardier, Lt. Trombley as Mickey operator and Lt. Fish as tail gunner observer.

FEBRUARY 10, 1945   MISSION NO. 270

The 94th "A" Force, of which the Group provided 38 planes, was briefed to attack a road bridge over the Rhine at Wessel. However, this was covered by clouds up to 28,000 feet and the secondary target, a fuel depot at Dulmen, near Munster, was bombed instead. Bombing was by Micro-H technique, with bombs falling an estimated one mile northwest of the target. There were no fighters and no flak. The formation was led by Lt. Colonel Stewart, with Captain Poston as pilot, Lts. Talbot and Craig as navigators, Lt. Plant as bombardier, Lt. Hardaway as Mickey operator and Lt. Steward as tail gunner observer. The Group also provided a screening force of six planes.

FEBRUARY 14, 1945   MISSION NO. 271
The Group attacked Dresden by Pathfinder methods. The Mickey set in the lead plane was out of commission, so the lead plane of the low squadron took over. Photos which show some ground detail indicate that the main concentration of bombs fell in the middle of a thickly built-up area north of the river, near the railway station. There were no enemy fighters and no flak at the target.

Lt. Ash's plane, 43-38405, was hit by flak at Egmond on the Dutch coast. The plane went into a spin with smoke pouring from the cockpit, but the crew bailed out safely. Thirteen planes landed in friendly territory on the European Continent. Lt. Kirkland and his crew bailed out when 43-38650 ran out of fuel.

Major Richardson led the formation, with Captain Weatherman as pilot, Lts. Kyser and LeFevre as navigators, Lt. Schiffman as bombardier, Lt. Engfer as Mickey operator and Lt. Wolf as tail gunner observer.

FEBRUARY 15, 1945   MISSION NO. 272
Since many of the planes were still away from base, the Group could only furnish one squadron. They flew the high squadron of a composite group in the 94th "B" Combat Wing. The primary target was the synthetic oil plant at Bohlen, but because of cloud cover the secondary target, Dresden marshaling yards, was attacked instead. Bombs were dropped through solid cloud with unobserved results. There were no enemy fighters and only meager flak.

FEBRUARY 16, 1945   MISSION NO. 273
Again, only one squadron could be put into the air, this time to attack the Gelsenkirchen coking plant. Cloud cover of only 3/10 in the target area made visual bombing possible. Photos show the bombs falling into open fields near Dorsten, nine and a half miles north of the briefed target. Intense flak started up three minutes before bombs away and continued for six minutes after. 42-97687, piloted by Lt. Rossen, left the formation with one engine dead, but managed to land in Belgium. Weather over the base was closed in, allowing only one plane to land. The rest landed at other fields in England and on the European Continent.

FEBRUARY 19, 1945   MISSION NO. 274
Solid cloud at Gelsenkirchen forced the Group to bomb the secondary, the railway center at Munster, using Pathfinder methods. Photos show that the lead and low squadron patterns merged to form a heavy concentration of bursts on the southern junction of the yards. The pattern crossed the important shunting neck and the bridge at the railway junction of the towns Wesel and Dortmund-Hamm. Bombs of the high squadron fell in open fields 11,200 feet south of the briefed M.P.I. No enemy planes were seen, but accurate flak at the target damaged five planes. This mission was led by Lt. Colonel Stewart, with Captain Gibbons as pilot, Lts. Love and Malerich as navigators, Lt. Ralph as bombardier, Lt. Williams as Mickey operator and Lt. Bowen as tail gunner observer.

FEBRUARY 20, 1945   MISSION NO. 275
The 351st led the 94th Combat Wing to bomb Nurenburg. The bombs landed about a mile south of the briefed Pathfinder M.P.I. Accurate flak along the Rhine damaged seven ships. The formation was led by Colonel Burns as Air Commander, Captain Pryor as lead pilot, Major Menees and Flight Officer Phelps as navigators, Captain Steitz as bombardier, Lt. Trombley as Mickey operator and Lt. Holloway as tail gunner observer.

FEBRUARY 21, 1945   MISSION NO. 276
Nurenburg was again the target, this time for the whole 8th Air Force. The area was still covered by cloud and no ground detail showed up in the strike photos. There was no flak at the target, but accurate flak south of Koblenz and at the front lines damaged 19 planes. Lt. Colonel Stewart led the Group, with Captain Trapp as pilot, Lt. McFarlane and Flight Officer Eaton as navigators, Lt. Talbot as bombardier, Lt. Hardaway as Mickey operator and Lt. Galloway as tail gunner observer.

FEBRUARY 22, 1945   MISSION NO. 277
The long expected and hoped for break in the weather occurred, allowing the Group to bomb visually the marshaling yards at Salzwedel, Germany. Bombing was good. No flak was

seen, but for the first time recently the Luftwaffe was up in force. Although the formation was not attacked, about 25 FW 190s and Me 109s were seen engaged in dog fights with the escort fighters. The Group was led by Major Richardson, with Captain Weatherman as pilot, Lt. Kyser as navigator, Lt. Schiffman as bombardier, Lt. Krasner as Mickey operator and Lt. Belardine as tail gunner.

FEBRUARY 23, 1945   MISSION NO. 278

Once again solid cloud covered the briefed target at Eger, Czechoslovakia, forcing the Group to bomb the secondary, Plauen, instead. Bombing was through cloud, but results were estimated as good. Nine planes had to land on the European Continent to refuel. Major Gorham led the Group, with Captain Redman as pilot, Captain Gulnac and Lt. Madsen as navigators, Captain Steitz as bombardier, Lt. Real as Mickey operator and Lt. Montross as tail gunner.

FEBRUARY 24, 1945   MISSION NO. 279

Although a nominal stand down, the Group put up a 12-ship screening force for First Division groups attacking the Harburg Oil Refineries near the town of Hamburg. In addition, three flying spares were provided for the 401st Bomb Group, one completing the mission. The formation was led by Captain D. S. Anderson, with Lt. Patterson as copilot, Lt. Morrissette and Flight Officer Phelps as navigators, Lt. Trombley as Mickey operator and Lt. Fish as tail gunner observer.

FEBRUARY 25, 1945   MISSION NO. 280

The Group attacked the Munich marshaling yards, flying as "C" Group of the 94th "B" Combat Wing. No enemy fighters were seen, but 19 planes were damaged by accurate flak at the target. One plane, 43-37854, was badly hit and made for Switzerland. During the subsequent crash landing, the pilot, Lt. Abplanalp, was killed by a branch of a tree that smashed into the cockpit.

Just before bombs away 42-97843, piloted by Lt. Sandel, had the radio and two engines on the right side knocked out. Lt. Sandel managed to stay in formation and Lt. Rosenblatt dropped his bombs with the rest. Then the plane started losing height at about 800 feet a minute. The decision had to be made to head for Switzerland or back to friendly territory, the latter four times as far. Lt. Sandel chose France. By this time he was down to 4,000 feet, minus the ball turret and all guns and ammunition. He was making good progress and was within seven minutes of crossing the front lines when an FW 190 saw him and closed in for the kill. With no guns to defend themselves, the crew huddled in the waist while the FW 190 poured 20mm shells into the plane. Sgt. Dahlmand, the tail gunner, was hit in the arm and leg on the FW's first run. On its second run it turned the B-17's stabilizer and waist section into a sieve, but then the fighter appeared to run out of ammunition, because it flew away. One minute later, crossing the front lines north of Strasburg, a barrage of flak hit the ship, wounding Lt. Rosenblatt and Lt. Sandel, and puncturing the fuel tanks of numbers one and four engines. Lt. Clarac, the copilot, took over and found that only one engine was working properly. He spotted the Fighter Airfield at Lunneville and started to let down. With the hydraulic system out they would have no brakes, but the bombardier was so badly wounded that a crash landing was out of the question. However, the landing was successful and the plane stopped by using the hand pump.

The Group Leader was Captain Maginn, with Captain D. S. Anderson as pilot, Lts. Morrissette and Fuller as navigators, Lt. Traczewitz as bombardier, Lt. Trombley as Mickey operator and Lt. Fish as tail gunner observer.

FEBRUARY 26, 1945   MISSION NO. 281

The whole 8th Air Force joined in an all out attack on Berlin and the part played by the Group was uneventful. There were no fighters and only meager flak. Bombing was by Pathfinders through solid cloud. Lt. Colonel Stewart led the Group on this mission, with Captain Poston as pilot, Lt. Luich and Flight Officer Bateman as navigators, Lt. Plant as bombardier, Lt. Hardaway as Mickey operator and Lt. Belardine as tail gunner observer.

FEBRUARY 27, 1945   MISSION NO. 282

Bombs were dropped on the railway center at Leipzig through 10/10 cloud and results were not observed. There were no enemy aircraft and only light inaccurate flak. Major Korges was the Group leader, with Captain Trapp as pilot, Lts. Talbot and Fuller as navigators, Captain McFarlane as bombardier, Lt. Delaura as Mickey operator and Lt. Belardine as gunner observer.

This mission was the 100th for the 510th Squadron's 42-38038, *April Girl II*. The ship had never aborted for mechanical reasons. The only time it returned early was on June 24, 1944 when Lt. C. M. Walker could not find the formation. M/Sgt. Ralph P. Montavon had been the crew chief since the aircraft was assigned to the Squadron on January 14, 1944. The ship was named *April Girl II* to replace the original *April Girl* which was shot down on January 11, 1944 over Oschersleben. Captain Sterling L. McClusky had named the ships *April Girl* because he and his wife were expecting a baby in April 1944, which they confidently expected to be a girl. It was a boy!

FEBRUARY 28, 1945   **MISSION NO. 283**

The target for the last mission of the month was the marshaling yards at Soest. Bombs were dropped through solid cloud using GH techniques. It was estimated that the bombs fell slightly north of the briefed M.P.I. The Group was led by Lt. Colonel Ball, with Captain Gibbons as pilot, Lts. Love and Hubbell as navigators, Lt. Ralph as bombardier, Lt. Real as Mickey operator and Lt. Bowen as tail gunner observer. At the end of this month the 511th Squadron was made Lead Squadron. It had assigned to it all the Lead Crews, those who would be flying Lead and Deputy of the Lead Squadron, together with the Lead of the other squadrons on every mission. All PFF ships not already in the Squadron moved in and an equal number moved out. This left a total of 15 ships plus the Tow Target and GH Training planes assigned to the Squadron.

MARCH 1, 1945   **MISSION NO. 284**

The briefed primary target was the railway center at Goppingen, but cloud cover caused the Group to attack the secondary, the marshaling yards at Heilbronn. This was after making one blind run on the primary, but the GH equipment was out of commission and the Mickey in the lead ship was giving very weak returns. The Deputy Lead took over the Lead for the PFF run on the secondary. Captain Dennis led the Group, with Captain D. S. Anderson as pilot, Lt. Morrissette as navigator, Lt. Heiser as GH navigator, Lt. Traczewitz as bombardier, Lt. Trombley as Mickey operator and Lt. Fish as tail gunner observer.

MARCH 2, 1945   **MISSION NO. 285**

Bohlen was the briefed target, but the secondary, the marshaling yards at Chemnitz, was bombed instead. Photo coverage was incomplete because of cloud and haze, but the fall of smoke markers indicated that the main concentration of bombs fell in the central part of the city. Major Hinkle led the Group, with Captain Poston as pilot, Lt. Luich as navigator, Lt. Plant as bombardier, Lt. Hardaway as Mickey operator and Lt. Galloway as tailgunner observer.

The crews that were not flying the mission were joined for lunch by two P-51 Mustang pilots from the 368th Squadron of the 359th Fighter Group. After lunch the two P-51s took off and started to buzz the airfield. After a low level pass along the main runway from west to east they then returned at low level, straight for the control tower. Passing the tower to the left, the lead pilot flicked over the tree to the west of the briefing room. His wingman was unable to react in time. The P-51 smashed through the top of the tree, the right wing tore off and fell behind the Sergeant's Club. The rest of the plane crashed into the woods half a mile north. The wreckage caught fire and Lt. Merle G. Aunspaugh was killed. The shaken element leader landed and was immediately placed under arrest by Colonel Ball, who then rang the Commanding Officer of East Wretham and demanded that he collect his pilot and court martial him.

MARCH 4, 1945   **MISSION NO. 286**

The aircraft factory at Schwabmunchen was bombed through cloud using GH methods. The wing formation assembled over France with some difficulty because the buncher signals were weak and clouds were thicker and higher than forecasted. Lt. Colonel Stewart led the formation, with Captain Trapp as pilot, Lt. Luich as navigator, Lt. Delaura as Mickey operator and Lt. Belardine as tail gunner observer.

MARCH 5, 1945   **MISSION NO. 287**

The secondary target, the marshaling yards at Chemnitz, was attacked using PFF because cloud prevented the Group from bombing the primary, the synthetic oil plant at Ruhland. This mission was led by Major Richardson, with Captain Coulam as pilot, Lt. Glover as navigator, Lt. LeFevre as bombardier, Lt. Hardaway as Mickey operator and Lt. Schulte as tail gunner observer.

MARCH 6, 1945

There was a stand down this day and only practice missions were flown. At about 1200 hours a terrific roar of an airplane in a dive was heard. Then a P-51 came down through the overcast sky in a steep diving spin, crashing in a field near Barnwell. The pilot was killed.

MARCH 8, 1945   MISSION NO. 288

Once again the primary target, Bottrop, could not be bombed because of cloud cover. However, the secondary, the marshaling yards at Essen, were bombed instead. The entire route was flown over solid clouds and bombing results were unobserved, but Mickey operators thought that the bombs hit in the target area. The Group was led by Captain Pryor and Captain Gaylord, with Lt. Gootee as navigator, Captain Schadegg as bombardier, Lt. Trombley as Mickey operator, Lt. O'Brien as GH navigator and Lt. Love as tail gunner observer.

MARCH 9, 1945   MISSION NO. 289

At last the clouds relented, allowing the locomotive workshops at Kassel to be bombed visually. The main concentration of bombs fell slightly west of the M.P.I. There were no enemy fighters, but flak at the target was moderate to intense. Lt. Colonel Carraway led the Group, with Captain Anderson as pilot, Lt. Morrissette as navigator, Lt. Traczewitz as bombardier, Lt. O'Brien as GH navigator, Lt. Grondin as Mickey operator and Lt. Fish as tail gunner operator.

MARCH 10, 1945   MISSION NO. 290

Only the lead plane and two other planes in the lead squadron bombed the target, an overpass in the marshaling yards at Hagen. The other 33 planes bombed when a bomb release malfunction on the deputy lead ship caused the bombs to be released accidentally. These bombs are believed to have fallen in the southern part of Dortmund. Lt. Colonel Stewart led the Group, with Lt. Cutler as pilot, Lt. Tabb as navigator, Lt. Burr as bombardier, Lt. Swift as GH navigator, Lt. Wellins as Mickey operator and Lt. Belardine as tail gunner observer.

MARCH 11, 1945   MISSION NO. 291

The Group, along with the rest of the First Division, attacked the shipyards at Bremen. PFF methods were used to bomb through solid cloud. Mickey operators estimated that the bombs fell slightly east of the M.P.I. Fairly accurate flak damaged two planes, but as usual no enemy fighters were seen. Major Korges led the formation, with Captain Poston as pilot, Lt. Tabb as navigator, Lt. Burr as bombardier, Lt. Real as Mickey operator and Lt. Galloway as gunner observer.

MARCH 12, 1945   MISSION NO. 292

The port of Swinemund, which was being used to evacuate German troops from Russia to Norway, was bombed by PFF with unobserved results. However, photos taken over the target show a mushroom of black oily smoke rising 1,000 feet above the clouds. Brigadier General Lacey led this mission, with Captain Purcell as pilot, Major Matthews as navigator, Captain Steitz as bombardier, Lt. Real as Mickey operator and Lt. Schulte as tail gunner observer.

MARCH 14, 1945   MISSION NO. 293

The railway center at Lohne was bombed visually, although for the first part of the bomb run GH was used. Excellent results were achieved, although moderate accurate flak damaged two planes. The Group Leader was Lt. Colonel Stewart, with Captain Pryor as pilot, Lt. Gootee as navigator, Captain Schadegg as bombardier, Lt. O'Brien as GH navigator, Lt. Trombley as Mickey operator and Lt. Love as tail gunner observer.

MARCH 15, 1945   MISSION NO. 294

Because of ground haze when the Group bombed Oranienburg, the target had to be identified by triangulation of visual checkpoints. Bombs of the lead squadron dropped on and around the M.P.I. The high squadron bombs fell 17,000 feet short of the target. The low squadron's bombs fell into the smoke covering the target. Flak at the target and at several places along the route damaged five planes. The formation was led by Major Richardson who, on the completion of this mission, handed over command of the 509th Squadron to Major Korges. The pilot was Captain Anderson, with Lt. Morrissette as navigator, Lt. Traczewitz as bombardier, Lt. Trombley as Mickey operator and Lt. Fish as tail gunner observer.

MARCH 17, 1945   MISSION NO. 295

The secondary target, the Zeiss Optical Instrument factory, was attacked when the primary, the power station at Moblis, was obscured by cloud. The lead and high squadrons bombed by Pathfinders. The low squadron bombed on its own lead aircraft when a combination of cloud, a near collision with another formation, and mechanical difficulties of the lead plane caused this squadron to fall behind on the bomb run.

Captain Dennis led the Group, with Captain Poston as pilot, Lt. Love as navigator, Lt. Burr as bombardier, Lt. Hardaway as Mickey operator and Lt. Belardine as gunner observer.

MARCH 18, 1945   MISSION NO. 296

Although 3/10 cloud allowed the target at Berlin to be identified visually, bombs were dropped using Pathfinder techniques. The lead and low squadron bombs fell one and a quarter miles south of the M.P.I. and the high squadron's bombs fell three miles southeast of the M.P.I. A few jet-propelled fighters were seen, but the formation was not attacked. Moderate flak at the target damaged seven planes. The Group was led by Lt. Colonel Stewart, with Captain Pryor as pilot, Lt. Grondin as Mickey operator and Lt. Love as tail gunner observer.

MARCH 19, 1945   MISSION NO. 297

Again cloud prevented Moblis from being attacked, so the secondary target, the chemical and explosives plant at Plauen, was bombed instead. Pathfinder equipment failed in the lead ships of all three squadrons and bombing had to be done on the smoke markers of the deputy lead.

One plane, piloted by Lt. Kirkland, developed engine trouble and became separated from the formation. East of the front lines, three Me 262 jet-propelled fighters came up through the haze and made three passes at the bomber's tail. However, no damage was done to the plane and Lt. Kirkland was able to land safely at Stanstead. The Group was lead by Captain Maginn, with Captain Trapp as pilot, Lt. Talbott as navigator, Lt. Hunter as bombardier, Lt. DeLaura as Mickey operator and Lt. LeFevre as tail gunner observer.

MARCH 21, 1945   MISSION NO. 298

The weather was clear and the bombing fairly good when the Group attacked the airfield at Hopsten. Light flak damaged five planes, but as usual there were no fighters. Major Richardson led the formation, with Captain D. S. Anderson as pilot, Lt. Morrissette as navigator, Lt. Traczewitz as bombardier, Lt. Swift as GH navigator, Lt. Real as Mickey operator and Lt. Fish as tail gunner observer.

MARCH 22, 1945   MISSION NO. 299

To attack a headquarters building and camp at Barmingholten, the Group was able to fly through clear skies and bomb visually. However, the bombing of the lead squadron was so scattered that no major damage was done. The low and high squadron patterns fell on the M.P.I., covering the five main buildings and starting fires in at least two of them.

Lt. Colonel Stewart led the Group, with Captain Purcell as pilot, Lt. Bury as navigator, Lt. Stear as bombardier, Lt. Swift as GH navigator, Lt. Real as Mickey operator and Lt. Franz as tail gunner observer.

MARCH 23, 1945   MISSION NO. 300

The lead and low squadrons attacked the marshaling yards at Recklinghausen, and the high squadron bombed the marshaling yards at Westerholt. There were no enemy fighters, but flak damaged 19 planes. While the weather was clear, bombing was done in a variety of ways. The lead bombed visually, the low visually with initial help by GH, and the high by GH visual assist. A target identification error by the GH navigator resulted in the bombing of Westerholt by mistake. The low squadron had gyro trouble on the bomb run, forcing them to turn and have a second run at the target. The lead squadron bomb pattern fell in the target area. The low squadron pattern was loose and scattered, however, the high squadron did a good job at Westerholt.

The Group was led by Major Korges, with Captain Pryor as pilot, Lt. Gootee as navigator, Captain Schadegg as bombardier, Lt. Swift as GH navigator, Lt. Hardaway as Mickey operator and Lt. Love as tail gunner observer.

MARCH 24, 1945   MISSIONS NO. 301 and 302

In the morning three squadrons went to Vechte airfield. The weather was clear all the way and the bombing was good with 65 percent of the bombs hitting within 1,000 feet of the M.P.I. Group Leader was Major Gorham, with Captain Trapp as pilot, Lt. Talbott as navigator, Lt. Hunter as bombardier and Lt. Belardine as tail gunner observer.

In the afternoon, one squadron flew the lead of the 94th Combat Wing in an attack on the Twente-Enschade airfield in Holland. Meager flak damaged two planes. Bombing and weather were again good. Lt. Colonel Stewart led the squadron, with Captain Wilcox as pilot, Lt. Madsen as navigator, Lt. Austin as bombardier, Lt. Wellins as GH navigator, Lt. O'Brien as Mickey operator and Lt. Leibrock as tail gunner observer.

MARCH 25, 1945

This was a hectic day, despite the fact that the scheduled mission was scrubbed one hour after takeoff. During the preflight checks on 43-37665 the number three engine caught fire. The fire could not be put out by hand extinguishers, or blown out by the propeller. The ship, which was loaded with bombs, caught fire. The area was cleared and at 0400 hours the bomb load blew up. The plane in the next dispersal, 43-38435, was damaged beyond repair. The crew chiefs' shack at dispersal was wrecked when one of the engines from '665 was blown into it. In addition, 42-107124 and 44-6108 were damaged.

During the morning's attempted assembly, 43-38465 with Lt. Dahlborg's crew on board narrowly escaped a head-on collision with 43-39070. Lt. Dahlborg had to maneuver so violently that the bombs tore loose from the racks and fell through the bomb bay doors. The left wing tip of Lt. Dahlborg's ship passed between the left wing and horizontal stabilizer of '070. Fortunately no one was injured and both planes landed safely.

MARCH 26, 1945   MISSION NO. 303

Cloud cover made bombing of a flak battery at Zeitz impossible and the secondary, the Plauen cellulose plant, was bombed instead. There were no fighters and no flak. The only trouble was caused by the weather. Severe turbulence at altitude made assembly and flying the briefed course difficult, and bulging cumulus forced the formation off course several times. Bombing was fairly good. Lt. Colonel Ball led the Group, with Captain Anderson as pilot, Lt. Morrissette as navigator, Lt. Traczewitz as bombardier, Lt. DeLaura as Mickey operator and Lt. Fish as tail gunner observer.

MARCH 28, 1945   MISSION NO. 304

A return trip to Berlin was flown with the rest of the First Division. Flak at the target damaged six planes. The formation bombed using Pathfinder techniques. Captain Gaylord led the Group, with Captain Purcell as pilot, Lt. Bury as navigator, Lt. Stear as bombardier and Lt. Real as Mickey operator.

MARCH 30, 1945   MISSION NO. 305

Thirty-three planes bombed the ship building area of Bremen using Pathfinder methods. Flak at the target damaged 14 planes. Colonel Carter, the new Commanding Officer, led the Group on this mission. Captain Trapp was his pilot with Major Bounds as navigator, Lt. Hunter as bombardier, Lt. DeLaura as Mickey operator and Lt. R. LeFevre as tail gunner observer. Colonel Merlin I. Carter took over the command of the Group from Colonel Burns, who returned to the United States. Colonel Carter came from Des Moines, Iowa, and was a graduate of the University of Iowa. He was commissioned in the Officers' Reserve Corps on June 22, 1929, and began active duty in the Army Air Corps on June 28, 1929. He was promoted to the rank of Colonel on June 15, 1942. He received his primary flying training at March Field, California, and advanced flying training at Kelly Field, Texas. Carter was a qualified fighter pilot, twin-engine bomber pilot, and aerial observer, as well as a B-17 pilot. Colonel Carter served with the 16th Observer Squadron, Ft. Riley, Kansas, the 20th Pursuit Group, Barksdale, Louisiana, and the 18th Composite Group, Territory of Hawaii. He also held the posts of Squadron Commander at the A. C. Technical School, Chanute Field, Executive Officer at the Basic Training Center, Jefferson Barracks, Missouri, Commanding Officer of the New York Civilian School Area at Lynbrook, and Base Commander of 223 CCTS at Dyersburg, Tennessee. Before coming to England to take over command of the Group, Colonel Carter was Commanding Officer of the XXII Bomber Command.

MARCH 31, 1945   MISSION NO. 306

Three squadrons bombed the Halle marshaling yards through 10/10 cloud using Pathfinders. Mickey operators estimated that the bombs fell in the target area. The Group was led by Major Hinkle, with Captain Wilcox as pilot, Lt. Craig as navigator, Lt. Austin as bombardier, Lt. Wellins as Mickey operator and Lt. Belardine as tail gunner observer.

APRIL 2, 1945   MISSION NO. 307

The briefed target was the airfield at Rotenburg, but the planes were recalled before Wing assembly.

APRIL 4, 1945   MISSION NO. 308

The airfield at Rotenburg was again the briefed primary, but since this target was covered by clouds the Fassburg airfield was attacked instead. The Group took off at 0630 hours and assembled as the Lead Group of the 94th Combat Wing. The target was bombed visually but strikes were unobserved. The Air Commander was Lt. Colonel Stewart, with Captain D. S. Anderson as pilot, Lt. Morrissette as navigator, Lt. Traczewitz as bombardier, Lt. Grondin as Mickey operator and Lt. Fish as gunner observer.

APRIL 5, 1945   MISSION NO. 309
The ordnance depot at Ingolstadt was the target for the Group's 300th credited mission. The formation assembled with the rest of the Combat Wing over the European Continent, flying as 94th Combat Wing "C" Group. Cloud in the assembly area made it difficult to identify the other groups in the Wing, but from then on, the mission was a milk run. Bombing was through 5/10 cloud, from 14,000 feet, with good results. The Group was led by Major Gorham, with Captain Purcell as pilot, Lt. Bury as navigator, Lt. Stear as bombardier, Lt. Real as Mickey operator and Lt. Galloway as tail gunner observer.

APRIL 7, 1945   MISSION NO. 310
The Group flew as the 94th Combat Wing "B" Group to attack the marshaling yards at Luneburg. Bombs were dropped by PFF methods with visual assistance. The bursts were unobserved, but bombs away photos indicate that bombs fell on and around the briefed M.P.I. Lt. Colonel Stewart was the Air Commander, with Captain Robinson as pilot, Lt. Allen as navigator, Lt. Hall as bombardier, Lt. Grondin as Mickey operator and Lt. Bochert as tail gunner. In the afternoon General Lacey presented M/Sgt. Ralph P. Montavon with the Legion of Merit in recognition of his maintenance record on 42-38038, *April Girl II*. This was her 111th combat mission without a mechanical abort.

APRIL 8, 1945   MISSION NO. 311
Three squadrons forming the 94th Combat Wing "A" Group attacked the secondary, when the primary, the airfield at Zerbst, was found to be covered by cloud. Bombs were dropped through 5/10 cloud using PFF methods with visual assist. Bombs of the lead squadron fell into the target area, the railway yards and station at Halberstadt. The main concentration was on and around the assigned M.P.I. The pattern of the low squadron fell into the smoke of the lead's bombs. The bombs of the high squadron fell to the left of the target, into the western part of the city. Lt. Colonel Stewart was Group Leader, with Captain Trapp as pilot, Lt. Talbott as navigator, Lt. Hunter as bombardier, Lt. DeLaura as Mickey operator and Lt. LeFevre as tail gunner.

APRIL 9, 1945   MISSION NO. 312
The primary target for this mission, the airfield at Furstenfeldbruck, was successfully attacked by the Group flying as the 94th Combat Group "B" Group. Bombing was done visually by squadrons. The lead squadron hit the M.P.I., the low squadron's bombs fell into the smoke, and the high squadron also hit the briefed M.P.I. No enemy aircraft were seen, but moderate flak at the target damaged four planes. Two planes were forced to land on the European Continent because of mechanical difficulties.

Major Geiger led the Group, with Captain Wilcox as pilot, Lt. Madsen as navigator, Lt. Austin as bombardier, Lt. Wellins as Mickey operator and Lt. Belardine as tail gunner observer.

APRIL 10, 1945   MISSION NO. 313
Flying as 94th Combat Wing "C" Group, the planes bombed the hangar area of the airfield at Oranienburg. Bombs were dropped by squadrons. With sightings made visually, results were good. Ninety-five percent of the bombs of the lead and high squadrons fell within 1,000 feet of the M.P.I., but the pattern of the low squadron fell to the right of the M.P.I. Inaccurate flak at the target damaged one plane.

The Group was led by Captain Dennis, with Captain Maish as pilot, Lt. Gootee as navigator, Captain Schadegg as bombardier, Lt. Krasner as Mickey operator and Lt. Love as tail gunner observer.

APRIL 11, 1945   MISSION NO. 314
The underground oil storage depot at Freiham, Germany, was the target for the planes flying the 94th Combat Wing "A" Group. Bombing was by squadrons with individual sightings. All bombs fell within 2,000 feet of the assigned M.P.I. Moderate flak damaged two planes, but all returned safely.

The Air Commander was Colonel Carter, with Captain Purcell as pilot, Lt. Bury as navigator, Lt.

Stear as bombardier, Lt. Real as Mickey operator and Lt. Galloway as tail gunner observer.

APRIL 14, 1945   **MISSION NO. 315**

This first mission to France in many months was part of the drive by French ground forces to get the Germans out of their long held pocket at the mouth of the Gironde. The target was an old fort at Royan, which had been converted to a heavy gun position controlling the entrance to Bordeaux. The squadrons bombed individually with visual sightings. One hundred percent of the bombs of the lead and low squadrons fell within 1,000 feet of the M.P.I. The high squadron pattern fell short with most of the bombs falling in the water.

Lt. Colonel Carraway led the Group, with Captain Trapp as pilot, Lt. Talbott as navigator, Lt. Hunter as bombardier, Lt. DeLaura as Mickey operator and Lt. Belardine as tail gunner observer.

APRIL 15, 1945   **MISSION NO. 316**

For this mission the crews were briefed to circle at the I. P. and await instructions to bomb any one of six targets at the mouth of the Gironde River. After circling for about an hour and a half, the planes finally attacked a gun position. Bombing was done visually in six sections of six ships each. The Group Leader was Captain Maginn, with Captain Wilcox as pilot, Lt. Madsen as navigator, Lt. Austin as bombardier, Lt. Wellins as Mickey operator and Lt. Galloway as tail gunner observer. Such was the domination of the skies by the Allies, Brigadier General Lacey flew as 94th Air Commander in an unarmed plane. This was the *Black Bitch*, a totally black ship used by the 351st as an assembly ship, tow target, and "general hack". Originally, 42-39914 was assigned to the 509th Squadron in February 1944 and christened *Lucky Strike*. Returning from a mission on June 14, 1944 her right undercarriage leg collapsed, tearing right away from the wing. Put into the hangar, she was repaired and flew with the 509th until September 28, 1944 when she completed her 50th mission. She was then stripped of all turrets and armor plate, painted with automobile black and had smoke generators placed in her tail. With less weight she was about 15 mph faster and far more maneuverable. Once during Group assembly, Lt. Colonel Ball flew up through the clouds and met another group head-on. His way of escape was to "split S" down, which he did successfully.

APRIL 16, 1945   **MISSION NO. 317**

The Group bombed Regensburg marshaling yards, flying as the 94th Combat Wing "C" Group. Bombing was by squadrons and results were good. Major Korges led the Group, with Captain Maish as pilot, Lt. Gootee as navigator, Captain Schadegg as bombardier, Lt. Krasner as Mickey operator and Lt. Love as tail gunner.

APRIL 17, 1945   **MISSION NO. 318**

The Dresden marshaling yards were bombed by the Group, which was flying as the 94th Combat Wing "B" Group. The formation was forced to fly at only 20,500 feet because of dense cirrus haze. This haze necessitated bombing by Pathfinder methods. All bombs hit within the target area. Major Geiger led the Group, with Captain Trapp as pilot, Lt. Talbott as navigator, Lt. Hunter as bombardier, Lt. O'Brien as GH navigator, Lt. DeLaura as Mickey operator and Lt. LeFevre as tail gunner observer.

APRIL 18, 1945   **MISSION NO. 319**

Flying as 94th Combat Wing "C" Group, the Group successfully attacked the marshaling yards at Traunstein. Flak at the target damaged two planes. Major Gorham led the Group, with Captain Wilcox as pilot, Lt. Madsen as navigator, Lt. Austin as bombardier, Lt. Wellins as Mickey operator and Lt. Leibrock as tail gunner.

APRIL 20, 1945   **MISSION NO. 320**

The Group led the 94th Combat Wing to attack the marshaling yards at Brandenburg. GH techniques were used with moderate success. As usual, no enemy fighters were seen and flak was meager and inaccurate. This was the last German flak to be fired at the planes of the 351st Bombardment Group (H)! Group Leader for this last mission was Major Hinkle, with Captain Maish as pilot, Lt. Gootee as navigator, Captain Schadegg as bombardier, Lt. O'Brien as GH navigator, Lt. Krasner as Mickey operator and Lt. Galloway as tail gunner.

Chapter Five
HOME RUN

During the first week of May, most of the Group's personnel spent their time waiting for the war in Germany to end. Plans were made for observation tours over Belgium, Germany and France, to give ground personnel an opportunity to see the damage the bombing had done to the enemy. The first of these tours was flown on May 7, 1945. Fifty planes were loaded with ground personnel and flown over a route that included Liege, Aachen, Duisberg, Dusseldorf, Essen, Darmstadt, Cologne, Frankfurt and Karlsruhe. The same route was flown the next day. Schweinfurt was included in two later tours.

The official V-E Day, May 8, was celebrated by a meeting of all personnel in the main hangar. Captain Callahan, 511th Squadron S-2 Officer, directed a program that recalled high points in the history of the Group. The program also included a talk by Lt. Colonel Ball on one of the toughest missions, the attack on Schweinfurt on August 17, 1943, a talk by Colonel Carter and a prayer by Chaplain Kreutzer.

Immediately after V-E Day, work began on revival mission flights to pick up released prisoners of war. Four of these flights were made to a POW center at Linz, Austria. On May 10, thirty-eight planes picked up 1,050 French and Polish prisoners who were brought to France. Thirty-nine planes made the trip on May 11 and flew out 1,120 prisoners, of these 16 were Americans, 917 French, 147 British, 10 Polish, and 30 New Zealanders. On May 12, thirty-four planes picked up 985 French prisoners, 19 British and 5 Belgian. The last of these missions was flown on May 13 when thirty-two planes flew out 948 French prisoners, 12 Polish, 15 British and 2 South Africans.

On May 16 the Group was ordered to prepare for movement back to the United States. The base immediately plunged into a frenzy of packing, processing and celebrating. When the first shipment of ten planes took off for the United States on May 26, it was at last believed that the work in the ETO was at an end. The next shipment was scheduled and scrubbed several times, but eventually definite departure dates were set. June 5 and 6 were announced as the takeoff dates for the rest of the planes. Each carrying 20 men, they were to proceed to Bradley Field, Connecticut, by way of Valley in Wales, Meeks, Iceland and Goose Bay, Labrador. June 10 was set as the date for the rest of the Group personnel to leave for the United States by ship.

During the next two weeks, the Operations Office was a madhouse and the Duty Officers spent most of their time talking on four telephones at once. At last, after many rescinded orders, the rest of the planes got off the ground on June 9. This brought the total of Group personnel transported by air to 1,500 men.

First base on the "Home Run" was Valley Airfield in Wales. One plane did not even get to first base. This plane, 44-8639, piloted by Lt. Robinson, got lost in the soup over Wales. The pilot called for a QDM, but whether he received it or not will never be known. The plane and the charred remains of twenty bodies, some burned beyond recognition, were eventually found on a bleak hillside a few miles from Valley.

The rest of the planes landed safely, but with some difficulty in a ripping crosswind. After refueling, they took off the next morning for Meeks Field in Iceland. This dreary outpost of the Air Transport Command network did what it could to make the returning warriors comfortable. It provided them with good food and a bed to sleep in,

81

and then sped them on their way the next morning. One group of men had a slightly extended stay at Meeks. The plane piloted by Captain Wilcox blew a few pistons in number three engine shortly after takeoff and had to wait for an engine change.

Goose Bay, Labrador, was the next stop. Just after the planes landed, and some time before Captain Wilcox was due, the weather closed in. Captain Wilcox homed in at 5,000 feet, reached the cone of silence and looked around for the airfield. All he saw was soup. He let down a couple of thousand feet and still could not see anything. When he got down to 500 feet and still could see nothing but the top of an occasional tall tree protruding through the mist, Captain Wilcox began to sweat. Sgt. Speaker, the crew chief, began to pray, and Lt. Bateman, the navigator, began to put on his parachute. About that time the bombardier, who was crouched in the nose with a map, spotted a break in the mist and through it saw the end of a flare-lighted runway. Captain Wilcox saw it too. He racked his aircraft around and came in for a perfect downwind landing. Two days later, when the weather broke, he learned that Goose Bay Airfield was completely surrounded by high hills.

It was not until June 13 that the home plate was reached. Some of the men in the aircraft swore they could feel a difference in the atmosphere as soon as their navigators assured them that they were over America. A few of the planes landed for fuel at Bangor, Maine, before proceeding to their final destination, Bradley Field, Connecticut.

At Bradley Field, crews and passengers climbed out of their planes and stood on American soil. After sitting in the shade of their planes for an hour or so, trucks came out and hauled them and their gear into the hangar. There the Red Cross handed out paper cups of milk. For many of the men, it was the first drink of fresh milk they had tasted in two years.

The war-weary B-17s were left lined up on the runways. The men continued on by train to Camp Myles Standish, near Boston. There they waited another two days before being sent to their various reception centers. From there they were sent on 30 days rest and recuperation.

Meanwhile, back in England at Station 110, the ground echelon was readying itself to go home by ship. About 150 officers and men were detailed as a holding party to perform the pleasant task of handing the base back to the British. The remainder of the Group, 718 of them, traveled by truck over the familiar tree-lined road to Oundle, where they boarded a train for Glasgow.

The *Queen Elizabeth* sailed for New York at 1745 hours on June 24, loaded down with 15,000 returning soldiers. It docked four and a half days later at Pier 91, greeted by bands and WACS and WAVES and cheering civilians. Under the command of Major Edward Lehan, Group Ground Executive, the echelon was moved by train to Camp Kilmer, New Jersey, where they received initial processing. An advance party was sent to Sioux Falls Army Air Field. The rest were sent to their various reception centers, where they were sent home to rest for 30 days.

Members of the air echelon, now rested and recuperated, began to arrive at Sioux Falls about the middle of July. By the middle of August most of the Group personnel had reported in and many had already been assigned to other stations. Eventually by August 28, only a handful of men remained to carry out the last orders for the 351st Bomb Group (H). ON THAT DAY IT CEASED TO BE.

Chapter Six
GROUND PERSONNEL

Previous chapters of this book have focused on the flying personnel of the Group and the missions they flew. This was, of course, the primary reason for the Group's existence. However, to mount these missions a lot of effort was required by ground engineering crews, armament mechanics and other supporting units. This chapter describes some of this effort.

Polebrook, a typical 8th Army Air Force bomber base, was a flat grassy plain some four square miles in area. It was crisscrossed by concrete runways, encircled by a perimeter track and dotted around its edges by dispersal areas where the bombers were parked when not needed for their deadly missions. One mile to the north, blending with the woods and thickets of the countryside, were the barracks and mess halls of the maintenance crews and other supporting personnel. On the northern side of the field were the barracks and mess halls of the combat personnel. These were interspersed amongst workshops and administrative buildings, huddling behind three cavernous hangars. Amongst these administrative buildings was the Headquarters building. This was the hub of the station. Here were the offices of the Commanding Officer and his staff. This building also housed the Group Intelligence Section, known as the S-2 office.

The primary function of the Group Intelligence Section was to maintain a complete up-to-date file of photographs, maps and other related material of the enemy industrial areas, military installations, transportation facilities or any other facility that could be termed as essential to the enemy war effort. This material was stored, updated and made available for use by the combat crews for those missions selected by 8th Air Force Headquarters. The section was responsible for analyzing, interpreting and presenting this information to the combat crews prior to their departure on a mission. Interrogation of these same crews on their return played an important part in the accomplishment of a mission.

The S-2 office was located in a large room at the rear of the Headquarters building, with one wall completely covered by a sectional map of the area from west of the base to the Russian border and from Denmark down to southern France. The S-2 officers and non-commissioned officers occupied this room. To the right of this room was the map room in which all the maps and targets were stored. To the left was a room filled with models, posters and reading material. These all dealt with plane, ship and uniform identification of both Allied and enemy forces. The large wall map, over which a clear plastic sheet was fastened, was called the situation map. It pinpointed all German Air Force airfields, marked with large headed pins upon which the number and kind of enemy aircraft stationed at that field was inscribed. Locations of flak gun positions and their range were indicated by red grease pencil. This map was constantly being updated by information forwarded from 8th Air Force Headquarters.

The wheels of a mission began turning as soon as a field order was received from Headquarters through communications. At times a brief advanced field order came in with the bare essentials, but generally once it started to come off the TWX machine it continued at a steady pace. The base was instantly put on alert and the different sections began their preparations from the information furnished on the field order. Usually the field order started coming in at about 2000 to 2200 hours, giving the primary, secondary and last resort targets. From then on began the mad scramble to prepare all the material needed for the briefing and the mission. All targets had a designated letter and number code which identified it. Along with the target, the field order gave the number of planes requested, armament, takeoff time, weather and other pertinent information.

The target and route were marked on the situation map, and the S-2 officers then began putting together the picture that they would have to present to the combat crews at the briefing. In the map room the navigator kits were prepared. These kits contained maps covering the entire route and photographs of the target areas. The flight plan from the I.P. to the target was marked on the maps in white ink. This was done so that the navigator and bombardier, together with the pilots, could more easily identify landmarks along the way to the target. All this information was placed in a clear plastic enclosure to make up a four page folder so that each stage could be easily followed when needed. The entire package was then enclosed in a folder on which the last three digits of a plane's serial number had been marked. This enabled the navigator assigned to that plane to pick up his individual kit. These kits were passed out after briefing and had to be returned after interrogation.

The Squadron Operations office clerk on the 1200 to 2000 hour shift was given notice of an impending mission and then noted the time of breakfast and briefing for the lead crews. These crews had to be awakened first since they had to attend a special briefing. Shortly afterwards, the remaining personnel who would be taking part in the mission were awakened. Once or twice it was necessary to double back to rouse someone who had gone back to sleep and hurry him along.

The briefing took place in a large Quonset hut located on the line. It was set up like a small theater. All the crews flying that particular mission had to attend the briefing and the entire mission was then revealed to them by the briefing officers. The time of the briefing varied with the length of the mission, but usually took place between 0300 and 0800 hours. A large map, identical to that in the S-2 office, covered the wall at the back of the stage area. A red ribbon indicated the route to the target and back to the base. This map was covered by a curtain until drawn by an S-2 officer when revealing the mission for the day. It was upon this revelation that the oohs and aahs or curses were uttered by the crews, depending on the notoriety or easy reputation associated with that particular target. The S-2 officer then proceeded to describe the route, the importance of the target, the amount of flak to be expected, and the kinds and number of enemy aircraft to be on the lookout for. He also pointed out the landmarks to be used as navigational aids while on the bomb run from the I.P. to the target. Operations, Armament, Communications and Weather Officers then presented their respective sections of the briefing. After this the crews would cross the road to the supply room to pick up flight suits, gloves, parachutes, etc. Then they would get aboard the trucks that were to take them to the flight line.

After takeoff everyone tried to get some "sack time" before preparing for the bombers' return and the interrogation. A strike report was usually radioed back after the bombs were dropped, giving a preliminary visual assessment of the success or failure of the mission. The true picture came after the S-2 Photo Officer analyzed the prints from the aerial cameras.

The squadron aircraft maintenance effort to put an attacking force into the air began with the barracks' lights being snapped on and loud voices telling everyone to "hit the deck". Putting on damp, cold clothing in chilly winter air was an added misery during that time of the year. Then it was out to the waiting two-and-a-half ton truck. The men, sitting in two sleepy rows, were usually puffing on cigarettes. The truck took them to the field, going around the taxiway and stopping at intervals so that they could get off near their assigned aircraft. It normally took two mechanics to pre-flight a B-17, usually the crew chief or assistant crew chief and one other.

All four propellers had to be turned over by hand through several complete revolutions to ensure that the lower cylinders were empty of any oil that might have collected in them. This was known as "pulling the props through" and it had the added advantage of getting the blood circulating. Following this exercise the portable gasoline powered generator was started and plugged into the plane's electrical system. This indispensable little machine had a one cylinder, air cooled, two stroke engine. These "putt putts" as they were called were used any time power was needed inside a plane when its engines were not running.

The two mechanics then got up into the cockpit and started the engines. After the engines were warmed, checks were made of the magnetos, oil pressure, etc. Following this, full power was applied to each engine in turn to make sure that they could achieve 2,500 rpm. This alerted everyone for miles around that a mission was imminent. Following the pre-flight check, the crew chief was required to sign a form stating that the check had been completed. While the flight crew would make a similar check before they prepared to take off, it was important that any mechanical problem should be found while there was still time to make the necessary corrections.

After the pre-flight checks by the aircraft and engine maintenance crews, it was the turn of the radio mechanic to carry out his checks. The fuel tanks would then be "topped off", and the other consumables such as engine oil, oxygen, hydraulic fluids, etc., would be replenished as necessary.

The bombs were delivered to the planes on bomb trailers by the squadron ordnance men. The armorers would load the bombs into the bomb bays and the fuses would be screwed in after the bombs were secured to the racks. Fuses were inserted into the 2,000 pounders prior to loading because their length did not leave enough room in the bomb bay once they were on the shackles. As the work progressed, and if time permitted, the maintenance men would take turns to lie down or just take a break in the tent that usually stood by each hardstand. Most of the ground crews had fixed up these tents with wooden flooring and framing. Inside each tent were steel cots or bunks and a stove. Depending on their scrounging ability, there might also be coffee or tea and food. The coke that was supplied for the stoves can only be described as fire resistant. Victory over this noncombustible fuel could only be achieved by the cautious use of 100 octane gasoline. This gasoline had been saved when sediment or water had to be drained from B-17 fuel tanks.

Sometimes an oxygen leak, a hydraulic leak or an electrical malfunction would be found. Then there would a frantic burst of activity to effect the repair before the "start the engines" flare went up from the tower. Many crew chiefs had a fear of forgetting to fasten the gas tank filler caps tightly, so they used to get one man to physically check each cap after the first man had finished topping them up.

If the takeoff schedule allowed, the ground crews could take it in turns to go to breakfast. Oh! The delights of those powdered eggs baked into a lumpy mass, streaked with green and gold!

Fortunately, English bread was available in the mess. If Spam or canned sausage or even corned beef was available, a most nourishing sandwich could be made. During the two years that the Group was at Polebrook, many wondered when, if ever, the seasons changed since most of the time they were cold, wet and always hungry. However the rations were adequate, but more often than not poorly prepared by amateurs, since the all night working did not mesh too well with the traditional Army routine of breakfast, dinner and supper at set times. When working all night in the cold, the interval between supper and breakfast was an eternity to twenty-year-old stomachs.

The flight crews would arrive at their plane for the day approximately 30 to 45 minutes prior to takeoff. The receivers for the .50 caliber machine guns remained in the planes so that the gunners had only to bring the barrels and firing mechanisms to install and then check them. The bombardier would check the bomb bay and its contents. The flight engineer would confer with the crew chief and then do some checking of his own. Invariably one of the flight crew would go through the meaningless ritual of kicking the main tires or spinning the turbine wheel of one of the superchargers. This was meant to indicate some knowledge of the machine, but it never failed to amuse the ground crews.

All glass on the plane had to be as clean as possible. One morning one of the mechanics in the 509th BS was lying on top of the fuselage cleaning the cockpit windshields and was knocked off when the top turret gunner rotated his turret. This fall badly injured the mechanic, but his loss was felt even more so on subsequent missions, as ground crew replacements were almost nonexistent. It was however remarkable that so few accidents occurred with the frantic hustle and bustle of these last minute preparations, particularly since they were often in the dark and cold of first light.

The time for takeoff finally arrived. A flare would arc up into the sky and the engines would be started. Sometimes an engine would not start, usually because it had been over-primed. This was what was known as "crew chief heart attack time". The planes pulled off the hardstands according to their position in the formation. There was however, always the possibility that despite all the hard work and gallons of nervous sweat, that a red flare would be sent up from the tower, indicating that the mission had been scrubbed. This was always a great let down and caused despondency amongst the ground crews. If all was going well, the second flare, signaling that now was the time to taxi out, was sent up. The pilot would give thumbs up, the ground crewmen would pull the chocks and the big bird would waddle away. Some pilots would release the brakes too early, ride up onto the chocks, then give the signal to pull them away. With the tremendous weight on them, the chocks had to be pounded to pieces before they could be freed. An anxious pilot would be in the cockpit gassing the engines and cursing the man down by the wheel, while the equally anxious mechanic would be down in the propwash, the exhausts roaring in his ears, breaking his back to free the chock, and of course cursing the pilot.

After the big planes taxied off the hardstands and on to the outer perimeter, it was then a matter of waiting their turn to take off. When the third flare went up it was time for the lead plane to start moving, leaving behind a small cloud of blue smoke. Slowly at first, then gathering speed, with its tail wheel up, it passed the control tower. Moving towards the end of the runway one of the gunners might give the "V" sign to some of the ground crews watching the takeoff. As the plane became airborne and cleared the field boundaries, the reverberating echoes of its engines rocked the field. By then the second ship would be underway, then the third, until all the ships assigned to the mission had gone. Each thundering run was an epic of suspense, ending when the 30 tons of plane, bombs, fuel and men lifted from the earth and climbed away. By this time the first plane would be sweeping a huge circle around the field, waiting for the second and third plane to gradually move into position behind it, forming a triangular element of three. Now the whole horizon was speckled with the patterns of planes from other bases. The sky was filled with the sound of stately, shifting Fortresses as they found their places in the formation and eventually moved off into the distance.

While they waited for the planes to return from battle, the ground crewmen who were out early to get the planes ready, would go for breakfast. The other crewmen stayed out on the line. There they would straighten up the dispersal area or try to help out on a disabled plane in order to get it ready for the next day.

Most of the maintenance work was carried out on the hardstands, but any that could not be done there was transferred to the Sub-Depot. This was located in the J type hangar, with its attached workshops and offices. The work that was transferred were large jobs such as repair of severe battle damage, large component exchange or major overhauls. The Sub-Depot had advanced technical equipment, some of which had been made by Sub-Depot personnel.

Occasionally a ride was available, but more often than not it was necessary to walk back through the woods to the barracks area. The huts in this area were Quonsets with two rows of bunks on each side and an aisle down the center. At each end of the aisle there were double doors. The outside door could be opened while the inside door remained closed. This was so that no light would show to the outside. This precaution plus the drawn "blackout curtains" at each window in the hut made the area invisible to any enemy aircraft that might be flying over at night. Beside each bunk was a footlocker and above the foot locker was an area for hanging clothing. Each hut was heated by a small, round, pot-bellied stove, fueled with coke. It was colder than an iceberg at the ends of the huts, but fairly warm in the central area. Most of the card games and "bull sessions" took place on the bunks closest to the stove, especially in the winter. However, most personnel could not tell the English summer from the English winter.

One of the first signs to the ground crewmen waiting out at the hardstands that the returning planes were approaching the field was the movement of the crash trucks. One would drive to the end of the runway, another to the control tower. The approaching planes would shoot a red flare if they had dead crewmen on board or a green flare if they had wounded. This was to alert the medics, so that they would be prepared to get the wounded out of the planes and into the base hospital as soon as the plane landed. Those with dead or wounded aboard, or those with battle damage, would land early. Otherwise it would take about twenty minutes before all the planes had landed and were on their way to the dispersals.

Upon returning to base the crews poured into the briefing room for interrogation, picking up coffee and doughnuts or a shot or two of spirits. These they downed while being interrogated. There was one crew to a table with an S-2 officer doing the questioning. The information that this officer tried to record was sightings of any of our planes that were hit, number of parachutes if any, density and accuracy of the flak, number of enemy aircraft destroyed or damaged, and direction of enemy aircraft attacks and their effectiveness. Confirmation by other crew members usually helped to get a credit for a "kill". All these reports along with the photo analysis were sent on to Wing Headquarters and from there to Command. There the total picture of the mission was assembled and an assessment of the success or failure was made.

As soon as the engines stopped and the crews were off to be debriefed, the maintenance men were already clambering over the planes. Empty shell casings were swept out, battle damage was assessed and an estimate made of the time required to get the ship airworthy. The Engineering Officer would get a report on the battle damage and he would then make an estimate of how many ships would be available for the next mission.

The Engineering Officer then fed this information back to his Squadron Operations Office. These Operations Offices worked around the clock, broken into three shifts, 0800 to 1600 hours, 1600 to 2400 hours, and 2400 to 0800 hours. The Operations Office maintained a status board mounted on a wall which listed all the flying personnel assigned to the squadron together with their availability. They were listed as crews, but any position might require substitution due to illness, wounds, killed in action, or even if they had a weekend pass. Men who were nearing completion of their tour of duty would always come by and check the status board. Often they would ask the Operations Officer to assign them as a substitution so that they might complete the required number of missions more quickly.

The Squadron Operations Officer checked his status board very carefully and had a great deal to consider in making out the list of personnel who would participate in the next day's mission. Ground school sessions had to be attended by "stand down" personnel. These sessions included training such as Link Trainer, Gee and Radio, Codes, Mickey Trainer, Celestial Navigation, Gunnery Training, Dinghy Drill and much more that would increase the skills of the crews. Each Ground School schedule required at least 18 copies. These copies were posted in places on the base where everyone could be expected to find them, such as the Orderly Room, Group and Squadron Operations, each Enlisted Combat Personnel Barracks, each Officers' Barracks, the Officers' Club and the Mess Halls.

To the ground personnel, whether working on the flight line, in the bomb dumps or in the relative warmth of the Operations Offices, the work seemed unrelenting and unending. However, morale on the base was helped by motion picture shows and the American Red Cross. Polebrook was fortunate to have a Red Cross Club on the base in its own building, attractively decorated with dancing figures along the walls. Anyone attending the Club was served cakes, soft drinks or coffee. The Special Services Officers' tasks included arranging for movies to be shown, organizing shows, station dances, and in general ensuring that station life did not become too drab or monotonous.

The Chaplains were a strong influence. No one who watched the combat crews kneel to receive a final benediction before entering their plane ever doubted the value of those sincere, quiet men whose job included everything from running errands for pipe tobacco, to sitting beside a dying airman in the hospital or in a damaged B-17.

The Flight Surgeons played an important part in keeping up morale. Psychiatrists as well as physicians, they knew their combat crews well and were quick to spot signs of combat fatigue. Often this was cured by the simple solution of sending such individuals or crews to a rest home for a few days.

In these rest homes the men lazed, fished, read, or did whatever they pleased and usually came back refreshed and ready to go again.

Soon after the Group arrived in England, many of the men acquired bicycles. These they used to get to the neighborhood pubs and nearby towns. Many men were not used to riding bikes and much amusement was had by bystanders watching their antics. One fellow used to run into the barracks wall and shout "whoa" if he wanted to stop. Others claimed that their bikes got drunk on the way back from town and would run into hedges and ditches, this being the excuse for all the scratches and grazes. Stolen or borrowed bikes were a problem. Tracking them down kept one member of the 1061st M. P. Company employed full-time. The main responsibility of the M. P. Company was to maintain order on the base and guard the important installations. They also investigated accidents and checked passes at the main gate. The passes checked were mainly of G .I.'s boarding the famous bus that took personnel into Peterborough. There were four other guard posts around the field and at the bomb dump. Civilians were allowed to pass through the field if they had the correct pass. The first post notified the other post of cars or bikes coming through so that they could check that they did indeed go through. These civilians were permitted to pass through because of the hardship of having to go all the way around if they wanted to get to Hemington.

The American G .I. went on doing his job with his particular brand of American know-how, with a maximum adaptability and with a minimum of fuss. There was no glory in the anonymous but necessary job of packing a parachute or driving a truck or guarding a Fortress in the rain swept hours between midnight and dawn. Nobody handed out medals to the man who picked the sullen, slippery bombs out of the mud and hoisted them into the yawning bomb bays with equipment that had been known to slip and let a 1,000 pound bomb fall and crush a bomb loader's foot. Nobody complimented the weary eyed technicians in the photo labs, working frantically to get the strike photos of the day's mission processed in the minimum of time. Nobody wrote glamorous newspaper stories about the cooks, K. P.'s or the many clerks. All he got was to grumble about the lack of mail and the excess of mud. Sometimes he might go into town by bicycle or liberty bus to do a little pub-crawling. He might even have a date with a girl, and once in a while he married the girl. Occasionally he looked at the mud outside his Nissen hut and made plans to plant some grass or flowers there in the spring. But mostly he thought of home and what he would do when this wretched war was over.

Members of the 351st show two English children a B-17.
Group includes in rear: Gerald Swift, Ben Pitts, Thomas Hudson, L. Harrell, Kenneth Tait, Balthazar Silva, John Moen, Heber Stamps, Robert Whitman, Henry Forster, Paul Salva. Front: R. Belicki, William Riggs, Robert Hayes, Elias Vargas.

Chapter Seven
COMMANDING OFFICERS

351st BOMB GROUP COMMANDING OFFICERS

Colonel William Hatcher — November 24, 1942 – December 31, 1943
Colonel Eugene Romig — January 3, 1944 – October 12, 1944
Colonel Robert Burns — October 12, 1944 – March 30, 1945
Colonel Merlin Carter — March 30, 1945 –

508th SQUADRON (YB-)

Major Kieth Birlem — November 24, 1942 – May 7, 1943
Lt. Col. James Stewart — May 14, 1943 –

509th SQUADRON (RQ-)

Lt. Col. Elzia Ledoux — November 24, 1942 – July 1, 1944
Major Paul Fishburne — July 1, 1944 – September 25, 1944
Major Franklin Richardson — September 25, 1944 – March 25, 1945
Major Mortimore Korges — March 25, 1945 –

510th SQUADRON (TU-)

Captain William Forsythe — November 24, 1942 – May 14, 1943
Major John Blaylock — May 17, 1943 – December 31, 1943
Major Leonard Roper — January 4, 1944 – July 21, 1944
Lt. Col. Paul Wood — July 21, 1944 – October 15, 1944
Major Leonard Roper — October 15, 1944 – January 17, 1945
Major John Gorham — January 17, 1945 –

511th SQUADRON (DS-)

Lt. Col. Clinton Ball — November 24, 1942 – September 23, 1943
Captain Harry Morse — September 27, 1943 – October 1, 1943
Lt. Col. John Carraway — October 1, 1943 –

Chapter Eight

THE DUTY TO REMEMBER

The French have an expression: *"le devoir de mémoire."* It is *"the duty to remember"* – to remember those who served their country in war and those who gave their lives for liberty by keeping their stories alive for future generations.

This book was written because the authors also believe it is appropriate to remember the accomplishments and sacrifices of those who served their countries and, in particular, the men of the 351st Bomb Group. This chapter describes a few of the memorials that preserve their names and accomplishments.

Some memorials stand alone in a churchyard or next to a country road. Others are just one among many. Regardless of their location, they provide a place and an opportunity for people to pause and remember.

Polebrook Airfield – A memorial was placed at the east end of the old runway in 1981 as the Memorial Association began a series of projects to remember the accomplishments of those who served with the 351st Bomb Group during World War II.

National Museum of the Air Force – Memorials provide a place for gatherings such as the 2002 351st B.G. reunion. Veterans paused to give tribute to those who made the ultimate sacrifice and to renew old friendships forged in more difficult times.

Polebrook Airfield – Trees form a border between the memorial park and fields that were once busy runways. On the right past the marble bench dedicated to Major General Robert Burns, the arched roof of the old hangar can be seen.

ENGLAND

Polebrook Airfield
Northamptonshire

Today, a narrow country road along the eastern perimeter of what once was Polebrook Airfield takes visitors to the memorial. A row of trees separates the memorial park from fields that were once runways. A dark, triangular-shaped stone sits next to the trees.

Many visitors, like James Myl, are touched by what they see, "There was some special magic about this place. It was as if the Triangle J had been lifted from the tail section of a B-17 Flying Fortress, transformed into granite and marble and perfectly placed along one edge of what remains of the old runway. What combat flying activity had once made a noisy and dangerous area was now a quiet, restful place."

Representing the 351st Bomb Group Association, Myl made a special trip to England in 1991 for the memorial's tenth anniversary and to thank Miriam Rothschild Lane who provided the land for the park. Along with letters of gratitude from Chief of Staff General Merrill McPeek USAF and British Prime Minister John Major, Myl presented her a framed, hand-lettered parchment tribute.

George Cahill, President of the National Flag Foundation, and Clay Snedegar, President of the 351st Bomb Group Association, signed the document. Below crossed flags of England and the United States the tribute reads:

"During World War II, some 6,000 men and women of the 351st Heavy Bombardment Group, Eighth United States Army Air Force, served in England at Polebrook, an airbase hastily constructed on lands belonging to the Lane family of Ashton Wold.

"After the war, veterans of this group organized the 351st Bomb Group Association. One of its projects was to build a memorial at the old base. The Honorable Miriam Rothschild Lane donated a long term lease of four acres at Polebrook on which the Association erected the memorial.

"The Honorable Miriam Rothschild Lane gave to the Americans land at the end of their old main runway for the memorial. She generously provided that the Americans would have use of the land for 999 years for a token payment of 999 peppercorns, which frame this tribute."

The "Triangle J" taken from the tail of the Group's B-17s forms the basic design of the memorial. It is inscribed: "In memory of the 351st Bombardment Group (Heavy) Eighth United States Army Air Force, 311 group combat bombing missions were flown from this airfield over occupied Europe between 1943-1945, 175 B-17 Flying Fortresses and their crews were lost, 303 enemy aircraft were destroyed in aerial combat."

The 8th Air Force emblem is pictured above the inscription. Below it the group emblem is surrounded by the four squadron emblems. The triangular piece of granite rests on a rectangular platform depicting a Flying Fortress with the Triangle J on her tail, flanked by the dates 1943 and 1945.

Below the large J on the reverse side is written: "The 351st Bombardment Group (H) Reunion Association gratefully acknowledges the generous donation of the land for this memorial by the Lane family of Ashton Wold House, Ashton."

The memorial, cut from a seven ton block of black African granite, was crafted by Richard Morris of the Morris Granite and Marble Company of Denbigh, Wales, and dedicated on June 18, 1981.

All Saints' Church
Polebrook

A "Roll of Honor" is located in the village church that honors those of the Group who died during the war. Names of living and deceased veterans who served at Polebrook are also included. It is the work of Roy Handforth and Ken Harbour of the 351st Bomb Group Research Foundation.

Flags, photographs and other items are found in the church. A copy of the tribute to Miriam Rothschild Lane hangs next to plaques honoring Medal of Honor recipients 2nd Lt. Walter E. Truemper and S/Sgt. Archibald Mathies.

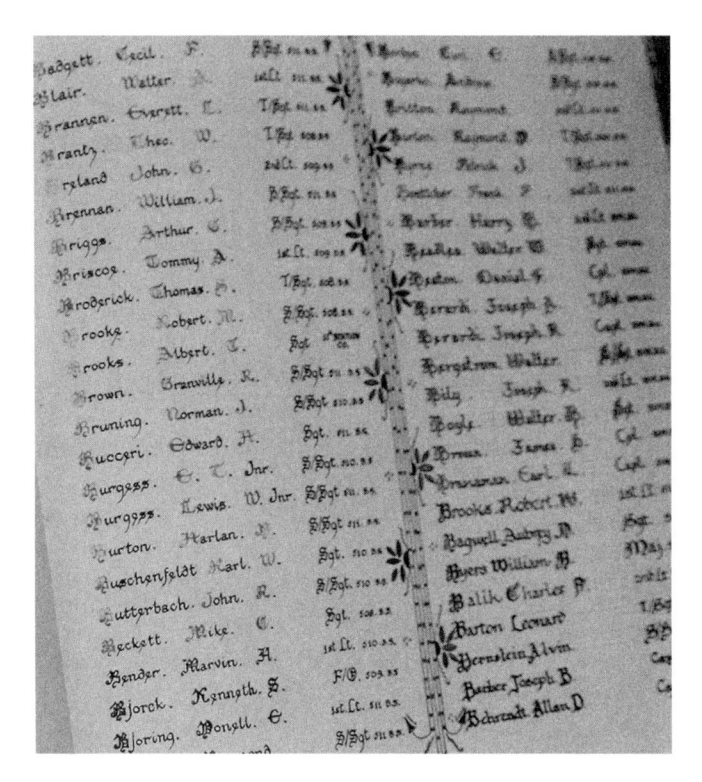

Roll of Honor – The names of many who served at Polebrook are remembered in this book at the village church.

Barmouth, Wales

The loss of aircraft and their crews during combat is difficult, but a loss after victory is even more so. Just one month following the war, on June 8, 1945, the Group lost 20 men when 44-8639 crashed into a hillside near Barmouth, Wales. All were on their way home.

Fifteen-year-old Matthew Rimmer and his mother, Jenny, researched the crash, had a stainless steel plaque created and placed it at the site on the 50th anniversary of the tragedy. The plaque lists the names of the 20 who died.

Barmouth – Twenty airmen on their way home perished on a hillside near this memorial created by Matthew Rimmer and his mother.

UNITED STATES

National Museum of the U.S. Air Force
Dayton, Ohio

On October 9, 1982 a memorial to the 351st Bomb Group was dedicated at the Air Force museum at Wright-Patterson AFB in Dayton, Ohio. This memorial, consisting of a bronze plaque shaded by a Linden tree, was suggested and coordinated by General James T. Stewart of the 508th Bomb Squadron.

On August 6, 2000, the memorial was upgraded with a triangular granite stone replicating the memorial at Polebrook. The marker's inscribed text is the same, but the placement and style of the unit patches and B-17 are different. The original plaque is displayed at the base of the memorial.

Dayton – A replica of the Polebrook Airfield Memorial is located in the Air Force Museum's Memorial Park.

Air Force Academy
Colorado Springs, Colorado

A bronze plaque was mounted on the Cemetery Wall through the efforts of Captain Dennis W. Farrell of the Air Force Academy at Colorado Springs and James Clements, former president of the 351st Bomb Group Association. It was dedicated on July 25, 1983.

The plaque is nearly identical to the bronze plaque at Dayton and can be found near the center of the wall. Above the names of the commanding officers and Medal of Honor recipients it reads, "In honor of those who served in the 351st Bombardment Group (H), 8th Air Force, Polebrook, England."

Air Force Academy – "In honor of those who served…"

Whiteman Air Force Base
Missouri

The 351st was reactivated in 1963 at Whiteman AFB as a Missile Wing with three missile squadrons, the 508th, 509th and 510th. George Catlett worked with Colonel Roger Smith, C.O. of the 351st, on a memorial at the base.

A granite slab presented to the reunion association following the dedication of the Polebrook Airfield memorial was incorporated into this memorial. A B-17G Bomber with a Triangle J on the vertical stabilizer was carved on the face of the slab with the inscription: "Presented by Morris Granite and Marble to the 351st Bomb Group Reunion Association on the occasion of the unveiling of their memorial June 18, 1981." A bronze plaque, part of the memorial, contains the emblems the bomb group and the missile wing.

The memorial at Whiteman was dedicated on October 9, 1983 and is located near the base's Community Activity Center. The 351st Missile Wing was deactivated in 1995.

Whiteman AFB – The granite slab presented to the Memorial Association in 1981 is seen in the upper left corner which gives this memorial a flag-like appearance. L to R: Junior Edwards, Howard Stickford, Fred Dundas, unknown.

Phillips Park
Aurora, Illinois

This hometown memorial is dedicated to Medal of Honor recipient 2nd Lt. Walter E. Truemper, the navigator aboard Ten Horsepower. He died Febuary 20, 1944 while trying to land the damaged plane in order to save the life of the severely wounded pilot.

Shaped from two colors of gray granite, the obelisk near the park's Victory gardens reads: "This monument, erected by the citizens of Aurora, is gratefully dedicated to Lt. Walter E. Truemper, USAAC, who's heroic sacrifice has written a most glorious page in Aurora's history."

Truemper was also remembered at Mather AFB, Sacramento, California in 1983 when Building 3750 was dedicated as "Truemper Hall." Mather closed in 1993 and is now the Sacramento Mather Airport. Truemper Way, a street on the airport, still pays tribute as do streets at Elmendorf AFB, Anchorage, Alaska and Lackland AFB, San Antonio, Texas.

Aurora, Illinios – A grateful hometown remembers the heroic efforts of Medal of Honor recipient Lt. Walter Truemper.

Library, Pennsylvania

Erected in 1944 by United Mine Workers of America Local 73 and District 5 and the friends and employees of the Pittsburgh Coal Company, this monument pays tribute to Medal of Honor recipient S/Sgt. Archibald Mathies and others whose lives were lost during wartime. Mathies was flight engineer and ball turret gunner aboard Ten Horsepower and died while trying to save the life of the wounded pilot.

Library, Pennsylvania – This memorial pays tribute to veterans of several wars, including Medal of Honor recipient S/Sgt. Archie Mathies.

On the tall center column of the memorial, below a carving of airmen's wings, it reads: "Archie Mathies, Staff Sergeant U. S. Army Air Corps, posthumously awarded the Congressional Medal of Honor for conspicuous gallantry, born June 3, 1916 at Stonehouse, Scotland, killed in action over enemy occupied Europe in the Flying Fortress MIZPAH February 20, 1944 - Greater love hath no man than this, that a man lay down his life for his friend."

A portrait of Mathies hangs in the Hall of Valor at the Air Force museum in Dayton, Ohio. Dormitories at Bolling AFB, Washington, D.C. and Ramstein AFB in Germany bear his name. On February 13, 1987, the Mathies NCO Academy was dedicated at RAF Upwood.

Mighty Eighth Air Force Museum
Pooler, Georgia

Another replica of the Polebrook Airfield memorial was placed in the Memorial Gardens at the Mighty Eighth Air Force Museum in 1997. This triangular shaped marker contains the same text that is on the face of the Polebrook memorial, but the unit patches and B-17 design are similar to those on the memorial in Dayton.

On the reverse side, below the large "J" on the monument's pedestal, the story of the 999 peppercorns is told: "Here is a replica of the Eighth Air Force, 351st Bomb Group (Triangle J) monument erected on one end of the main runway at Polebrook, England in 1981. That year, a 999 years lease was granted by the landowners on behalf of the English people. The lease was legally secured by payment of 999 peppercorns in recognition that the people of Great Britain owe the Americans a large debt of gratitude. Members of the 351st Bomb Group Association acknowledge with sincere appreciation this gift of land and the sentiments of the donors and the English people."

Mighty Eighth Museum – This memorial is a replica of the one at Polebrook Airfield. The four squadron patches are on the sides of the triangle. A large J on the reverse side evokes the Group's B-17 tail marking.

In July 2005, a statue of Benton Love was commissioned for the Mighty Eighth Air Force Museum to commemorate his courage and valor during WWII. Ben Love was lead navigator and flew 25 missions for the Group while he was stationed at Polebrook.

Simon Maxwell, a British sculptor, used photographs of Love, his uniform jacket, pants, hat and shirt to create this life-size tribute. The final bronzed statue was produced in the Morris Singer Art Foundry in the UK. It stands at the end of the reflecting pool in the memorial gardens facing the museum.

Mighty Eighth Museum – This life-sized bronze sculpture was created using photographs and clothing from one of the Group's lead navigators, Benton Love.

The dedication ceremony took place on June 15, 2007 with several hundred members of the 351st Bomb Group Memorial Association in attendance. The Group held its annual reunion at the museum.

BELGIUM

La Bruyère, Namur

After losing two engines in the target area, the *Katy Will* 44-6139 of the 511th was forced to land in a field near the front lines on September 12, 1944. The nine crewmembers safely returned to base, and the plane was later salvaged.

Fifty years later the citizens of La Bruyère recognized "all those who contributed to the liberation of our villages" and dedicated the memorial to the crew of 44-6139. Pilot Donald Hadley, copilot Tauno Maki, navigator Zebulon Hites and gunner Milton Griffin made a special trip to attend the event.

La Bruyère – Located near the field where a 511th crew made an emergency landing, this memorial thanks all those who assisted in the liberation of the surrounding communities.

FRANCE

Ban-sur-Meurthe-Clefcy, Lorraine

The *Queen of the Air* was downed by German fighters on the Ludwigshafen mission. Most of the crewmembers were killed; the radio operator, T/Sgt. William R. Stroh, evaded capture.

The memorial, located on a country road, is an irregular shaped stone with the face smoothed for the lettering. Below the "Red Devil" squadron patch of the 510th, the inscription translates: "In tribute to 8 American airmen shot down here in aerial combat on May 27, 1944 on board a U.S. Air Force B-17."

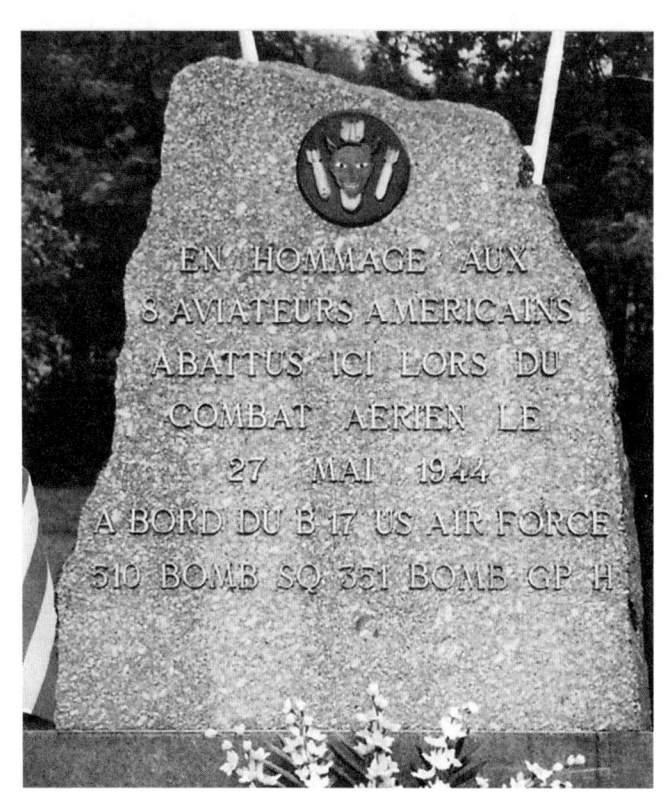

Ban-sur-Meurthe-Clefcy – This memorial next to a country road pays homage to a crew of the 510th lost during aerial combat over France.

Ploeren, Brittany

This metal plaque hanging inside the Ploeren Town Hall is unusual in that it contains a tribute to both German and American airmen.

The Concho Clipper was lost on the May 29, 1943 mission to St. Nazaire, and the plaque lists all ten crewmen between the patches for the 509th Squadron and the 351st Group. Also remembered is a young German fighter pilot, Horst Cuno, who died August 12, 1941.

At the dedication ceremony November 10, 2006, Charles Woehrle, the navigator and last remaining crewmember of *The Concho Clipper*, welcomed the fact that former enemies are now friends.

Ploeren – A plaque in the town hall pays tribute to airmen lost during the war.

Muzillac, Brittany

On the June 28, 1943 mission to St. Nazaire, Capt. R. W. Adams and the crew of *High Ball* were the first to fall out of formation, crashing on the outskirts of Muzillac. Four men were dead, and four more were captured. Townspeople were successful in helping the navigator and copilot return to England. The mayor persuaded the occupying forces to bury the dead in the parish cemetery with full military honors.

On June 30, 2007 dignitaries, school children, veterans and townspeople, including a few who aided the crew 64 years earlier, paid tribute to *High Ball's* crew. The event's organizers were André Franc, Michel Lereec and Bernard Le Lan. Mayor Jo Brohan reminded those gathered of "the duty to remember the dead, the suffering endured, and the challenge to build a lasting peace between all the people of the earth."

Following the ceremony, a card of thanks, signed by veterans of the 351st Bomb Group, their families and friends at the 2007 reunion, was presented to the mayor. Four veterans who signed the card had flown on the mission.

Muzillac – The churchyard of St. Therese Church provides an idyllic setting for this tribute to the crew of *High Ball*, 511th Squadron.

Belle-Île-en-Mer, Brittany

Mehitabel was also lost on the June 28, 1943 mission. Badly damaged by flak, Lt. Copeland determined they could not make it back to England and headed back toward the mainland. *Mehitabel* crashed on a small island and seven crewmen were captured.

In 1950, a monument in memory of the three airmen killed was erected at Bourdoulic by M. Raglois and financed with his personal funds. In 1994 the monument was moved a short distance to the entrance of the municipal airport where it remains today. In 2000, a plaque was added that bears the names of the three who died.

The inscription translates: "In memory of the three Allied airmen who fell in this place to defend our freedom on June 28, 1943. As you pass by, oh my brother, pause to meditate and pray."

Belle-Île-en-Mer – Frank Hanan, Merwyn Ranum and Edward Tuminiski are remembered on this memorial that invites the passer-by to meditate and pray: "Passant, ô mon Frère, Recueilles-toi et pries."

THE DUTY TO REMEMBER

Chapter Nine
351st B.G. MISSION LOG

MISSION	DATE	TARGET	NUMBER OF AIRCRAFT DISPATCHED	ATTACKED	LEADER
1	05-13-43	St. Omer, France	-	-	Recalled-Mission n/c
2	05-14-43	Courtrai, Belgium	18	16	Col. Hatcher
3	05-15-43	Emden	19	18	Maj. Wurzbach
4	05-19-43	Kiel	21	16	Col. Hatcher
5	05-21-43	Wilhelmshaven	19	12	Maj. Wurzbach
6	05-29-43	St. Nazaire, France	21	16	Col. Hatcher
7	06-11-43	Bremen	22	18	Maj. Burns
8	06-13-43	Bremen	21	14	Capt. Ball
9	06-15-43	Le Mans, France	-	-	Cloud-Rtnd. w/o bombing
10	06-22-43	Huls	21	16	Maj. Burns
11	06-23-43	Villacoublay, France	-	-	Recalled-Mission n/c
12	06-25-43	Nordenheim (Secondary)	20	17	Maj. Milton
13	06-26-43	Villacoublay, France	-	-	Cloud-Rtnd. w/o bombing
14	06-28-43	St. Nazaire, France	20	19	Maj. Milton
15	06-29-43	Triqueville, France	-	-	Cloud-Rtnd. w/o bombing
16	07-04-43	Le Mans, France	18	17	Maj. Ball
17	07-10-43	Villacoublay, France	-	-	Cloud-Rtnd. w/o bombing
18	07-14-43	Amiens A/F, France	20	18	Maj. Ball
19	07-17-43	Hannover	26	15	Maj. Ledoux
20	07-24-43	Heroya, Norway	21	21	Maj. Burns
21	07-25-43	Hamburg	20	17	Maj. Ball
22	07-26-43	Hamburg	24	15	Capt. Stewart
23	07-28-43	Kassel	-	-	Recalled
24	07-29-43	Kiel	20	17	Maj. Ledoux
25	07-30-43	Kassel	21	16	Capt. Stewart
26	08-12-43	Bochum (Secondary)	21	14	Maj. Milton
27	08-15-43	Flushing (Secondary)	19	18	Maj. Blaylock
28	08-16-43	Le Bourget, France	21	21	Maj. Blaylock
29	08-17-43	Schweinfurt	28	28	Col. Hatcher
30	08-19-43	Gilze-Rijen, Holland	9	7	Capt. Johnson
31	08-24-43	Villacoublay, France	22	16	Col. Hatcher
32	08-27-43	Watten, France	22	22	Maj. Ledoux
33	08-31-43	Amiens A/F (Secondary)	21	19	Maj. Blaylock
34	09-02-43	Conche, France	-	-	Recalled-Mission n/c
35	09-03-43	Romilly Sur Seine, France	19	17	Capt. Stewart
36	09-06-43	Offenburg (Secondary)	23	20	Col. Hatcher

Rtnd. w/o bombing = Returned without bombing
Mission n/c = Mission not credited
Note: Target locations are in Germany when no country is listed

MISSION	DATE	TARGET	NUMBER OF AIRCRAFT DISPATCHED	ATTACKED	LEADER
37	09-07-43	Brussels A/F, Belgium	19	18	Maj. Ball
38	09-09-43	Lille A/F, France	19	19	Lt. Col. Burns
39	09-15-43	Romilly Sur Seine, France	19	17	Maj. Stewart
40	09-16-43	Nantes, France	19	19	Maj. Ball
41	09-23-43	Nantes, France	19	17	Lt. Col. Burns
42	09-26-43	Meulan, France	-	-	Cloud-Rtnd. w/o bombing
43	09-27-43	Emden	19	17	Capt. Morse
44	10-02-43	Emden (H2X)	19	19	Capt. Stewart
45	10-04-43	Frankfurt	19	14	Maj. Blaylock
46	10-08-43	Bremen	21	14	Maj. Ledoux
47	10-09-43	Anklam	21	21	Lt. Col. Burns
48	10-10-43	Munster	18	9	Maj. Stewart
49	10-14-43	Schweinfurt	18	10	Maj. Blaylock
50	10-20-43	Duren, France	-	-	Cloud-Rtnd. w/o bombing
51	11-03-43	Wilhelmshaven (H2X)	25	25	Maj. Ball
52	11-05-43	Gelsenkirchen (H2X)	21	14	Capt. Carraway
53	11-07-43	Wesel (H2X)	21	19	Maj. Blaylock
54	11-16-43	Knaben	21	18	Maj. Ledoux
55	11-26-43	Bremen (H2X)	39	37	Maj. Blaylock
56	11-29-43	Bremen	-	-	Recalled-Mission n/c
57	12-01-43	Solingen (H2X)	40	35	Maj. Stewart
58	12-05-43	Paris, France	-	-	Cloud-Rtnd. w/o bombing
59	12-11-43	Emden	42	34	Capt. Oldham
60	12-13-43	Kiel (H2X)	23	19	Col. Lacey
61	12-16-43	Bremen	-	-	Recalled-Mission n/c
62	12-20-43	Bremen	37	27	Lts. Lynch & Gaylord
63	12-22-43	Osnabruck	-	-	Cloud-Rtnd. w/o bombing
64	12-24-43	No-ball, France	34	34	Lt. Col. Burns
65	12-30-43	Ludwigshafen (H2X)	38	36	Lts. Gaylord & Cruthirds
66	12-31-43	Cognac (Secondary)	34	34	Col. Hatcher
67	01-04-44	Kiel (H2X)	17	15	Maj. Stewart
68	01-05-44	Tours, France	18	16	Lt. Gaylord
69	01-07-44	Ludwigshafen (H2X)	18	7	Maj. Ledoux
70	01-11-44	Oschersleben/Konigslutter	23	22	Capt. Oldham
71	01-19-44	No-ball, France	10	10	Capt. Roper
72	01-21-44	No-ball, France	20	20	Lt. Kelley
73	01-24-44	Frankfurt	-	-	Recalled-Mission n/c
74	01-29-44	Frankfurt (H2X)	30	24	Maj. Ball
75	01-30-44	Brunswick (H2X)	29	28	Capt. Roper & Maj. Ledoux
76	02-03-44	Wilhelmshaven (H2X)	32	27	Maj. Stewart
77	02-04-44	Frankfurt (H2X)	28	23	Maj. Roper
78	02-05-44	Chateauroux, France	27	25	Col. Romig
79	02-06-44	Caen A/F (Secondary)	34	34	Maj. Ledoux
80	02-11-44	Frankfurt (H2X)	26	21	Lt. Col. Burns
81	02-20-44	Liepzig	39	34	Majs. Roper & Stewart
82	02-21-44	Achmer (Secondary)	32	28	Lt. Col. Cobb
83	02-22-44	Bernberg/Magdeberg	26	22	Lt. Gaylord
84	02-24-44	Schweinfurt	20	16	Lt. Col. Ball

MISSION	DATE	TARGET	NUMBER OF AIRCRAFT DISPATCHED	ATTACKED	LEADER
85	02-25-44	Augsburg	12	11	Lt. Floden
86	03-02-44	Frankfurt (H2X)	25	21	Maj. Ledoux
87	03-03-44	Wilhelmshaven (Sec) (H2X)	19	15	Maj. Gilmore
88	03-04-44	Bonn (Secondary) (H2X)	18	15	Lt. Cruthirds
89	03-06-44	Berlin	21	20	Maj. Roper
90	03-08-44	Berlin (H2X)	21	16	Brig. Gen. Lacey
91	03-09-44	Berlin	20	15	Lt. Gaylord
92	03-11-44	Munster (H2X)	20	19	Lt. Floden
93	03-13-44	Poix, France	21	7	Capt. Kelley
94	03-16-44	Augsburg (H2X)	20	11	Col. Rogner
95	03-18-44	Landsberg	21	21	Capt. Harris
96	03-19-44	Watten, France	21	21	Capt. Clay
97	03-20-44	Frankfurt	-	-	Cloud-Rtnd. w/o bombing
98	03-22-44	Orianenburg	19	16	Maj. Carraway
99	03-23-44	Munster (Secondary)	35	34	Capts. Lynch & Gaylord
100	03-24-44	Schweinfurt (H2X)	21	21	Capt. Harris
101	03-26-44	Watten, France	18	18	Capt. Nesmith
102	03-27-44	Tours, France	30	30	Capt. Richardson
103	03-29-44	Brunswick (H2X)	18	18	Capt. Cruthirds
104	04-09-44	Rahmela, Poland	25	20	Lt. McCluskey
105	04-10-44	Melsbroek, Belgium	19	18	Lt. Col. Burns
106	04-11-44	Arnimswalde (Secondary)	36	34	Maj. Roper
107	04-13-44	Schweinfurt	18	16	Capt. Cruthirds
108	04-18-44	Orianenburg	17	15	Col. Romig
109	04-19-44	Kassel	30	30	Lt. Brooksby
110	04-20-44	No-ball, France	36	32	
111	04-22-44	Hamm	19	15	Maj. Richardson
112	04-24-44	Erding	17	16	Maj. Stewart
113	04-25-44	Nancy, France	-	-	Cloud-Rtnd. w/o bombing
114	04-26-44	Brunswick	19	17	Capt. Clay
115	04-27-44	Nancy, France	18	16	Lt. Col. Ledoux
116	04-27-44	No-ball, France	18	18	Capt. Cruthirds
117	04-28-44	Avord A/F, France	18	18	Lt. Floden
118	04-29-44	Berlin (H2X)	18	17	Capt. Kelley
119	05-01-44	No-ball, France	-	-	Cloud-Rtnd. w/o bombing
120	05-01-44	Rheims, France	18	18	Maj. Fishburne
121	05-04-44	Berlin	-	-	Cloud-Rtnd. w/o bombing
122	05-07-44	Berlin (H2X)	35	34	Col. Romig
123	05-08-44	Berlin (H2X)	37	27	Lt. Col. Ball
124	05-09-44	Luxemburg	18	18	Capt. Brooksby
125	05-11-44	Luxemburg	36	36	Lt. Col. Burns
126	05-12-44	Merseburg	18	18	Capt. Cruthirds
127	05-13-44	Stettin (Secondary)	16	16	Lt. Col. Ledoux
128	05-19-44	Berlin (H2X)	38	34	Capt. Brooksby
129	05-19-44	Kiel	-	-	Capt. Kelley
130	05-20-44	Villacoublay, France	12	11	Maj. Roper
131	05-22-44	Kiel (H2X)	12	12	Capt. Floden
132	05-23-44	Epinal, France	26	25	Maj. Roper

Rtnd. w/o bombing = Returned without bombing
Mission n/c = Mission not credited
Note: Target locations are in Germany when no country is listed

MISSION	DATE	TARGET	NUMBER OF AIRCRAFT DISPATCHED	ATTACKED	LEADER
133	05-24-44	Berlin (H2X)	18	18	Capt. Clay
134	05-25-44	Metz, France	38	35	Maj. Stewart
135	05-27-44	Ludwigshafen	19	18	Capt. Dixey
136	05-28-44	Dessau	20	13	Capt. Holsapple
137	05-29-44	Sorau	18	16	Capt. Nesmith
138	05-30-44	Oschersleben	18	16	Capt. Gaylord
139	05-31-44	Luxeuil A/F, France	12	12	Capt. McCafferty
140	06-02-44	Equihen, France (H2X)	17	16	Lt. Maginn
141	06-03-44	Dannes, France (H2X)	17	17	Maj. Richardson
142	06-04-44	Palaiseau, France	24	24	Capt. Nesmith
143	06-06-44	Caen, France (H2X)	34	34	
144	06-07-44	Falaise, France	17	15	Lt. Col. Ball
145	06-08-44	Etampes, France	-	-	Cloud-Rtnd. w/o bombing
146	06-10-44	Gael A/F, France	18	17	Maj. Roper
147	06-11-44	Barnay/St. Martin, France	18	17	Col. Romig
148	06-12-44	Cambrai, France	36	35	Maj. Fishburne
149	06-14-44	Le Bourget, France	59	57	Lt. Col. Ball & Maj. Roper
150	06-15-44	Angouleme, France	38	37	Lt. Col. Ledoux
151	06-17-44	Monchy A/F, France(GH)	19	16	Capt. Nesmith
152	06-18-44	Hamburg (H2X)	36	36	Maj. Fishburne
153	06-20-44	Hamburg	36	36	Lt. Col. Ball
154	06-20-44	Ypres, Belgium (Secondary)	12	12	Lt. Brooks
155	06-21-44	Berlin	42	38	Brig. Gen. Lacey
156	06-22-44	Rouen, France	25	24	Maj. Roper
157	06-23-44	No-ball, France (GH)	24	24	Lt. Olsen
158	06-24-44	No-ball, France	25	24	Lt. Brooks
159	06-25-44	Toulouse A/F, France	38	35	Maj. Fishburne
160	06-28-44	Leon A/F, France	24	22	Lt. Dennis
161	06-29-44	Leipzig	18	17	Lt. Viste
162	07-04-44	Saumur, France	-	-	Cloud-Rtnd. w/o bombing
163	07-06-44	No-ball, France	38	35	Lt. Dennis
164	07-06-44	No-ball, France	-	-	Rtnd. w/o bombing
165	07-07-44	Leipzig	36	36	Lt. Col. Ball
166	07-08-44	No-ball, France	24	23	Capt. McCluskey
167	07-09-44	No-ball, France	-	-	Cloud-Rtnd. w/o bombing
168	07-11-44	Munich (H2X)	39	37	Col. Romig
169	07-12-44	Munich (H2X)	36	34	Lt. Garcia
170	07-13-44	Munich (H2X)	19	18	Maj. Roper
171	07-16-44	Stuttgart (Secondary) (H2X)	39	35	Lt. Col. Vorhees
172	07-18-44	Peenemunde	36	36	Maj. Roper
173	07-19-44	Augsburg	37	36	Maj. Fishburne
174	07-20-44	Leipzig	24	24	Lt. Brooks
175	07-21-44	Schweinfurt	24	24	Maj. Roper
176	07-24-44	St. Lo, France	39	26	Lt. Col. Ball
177	07-25-44	St. Lo, France	39	39	Lt. Col. Burns
178	07-28-44	Merseberg	37	35	Maj. Fishburne
179	07-29-44	Merseberg (H2X)	38	36	Lt. Col. Burns
180	07-31-44	Munich (H2X)	37	36	Lt. Zotollo

MISSION	DATE	TARGET	NUMBER OF AIRCRAFT		LEADER
			DISPATCHED	ATTACKED	
181	08-01-44	Chateaudun, France	36	36	Maj. Fishburne
182	08-03-44	Saarbrucken	36	36	Lt. Col. Burns
183	08-04-44	Anklam	24	24	Maj. Carraway
184	08-05-44	Nienburg	36	36	Maj. Fishburne
185	08-06-44	Berlin	37	34	Lt. Col. Burns
186	08-08-44	St. Sylvain, France	37	12	Maj. Carraway
187	08-09-44	Elsenborn (Secondary)	23	21	Lt. Hales
188	08-11-44	Brest, France	29	27	Lt. Col. Burns
189	08-13-44	Louvier, France	36	36	Lt. Col. Wood
190	08-14-44	Haguenau (Secondary)	36	36	Col. Romig
191	08-16-44	Schkeuditz	38	35	Lt. Col. Burns
192	08-18-44	Namur, France	36	36	Col. Rogner
193	08-24-44	Buchenwald	37	36	Maj. Richardson
194	08-25-44	Peenemunde	36	34	Maj. Carraway
195	08-25-44	Henin-Lietard	12	11	Maj. Richardson
196	08-26-44	Willebroeke, Belgium	-	-	Cloud-Rtnd. w/o bombing
197	08-27-44	Berlin	-	-	Recalled-Rtnd. w/o bombing
198	08-30-44	Kiel (H2X)	37	34	Lt. Col. Wood
199	09-05-44	Ludwigshafen	36	35	Maj. Fishburne
200	09-08-44	Ludwigshafen	37	36	Maj. Richardson
201	09-09-44	Ludwigshafen (H2X)	37	35	Maj. Stewart
202	09-10-44	Gagenau	36	36	Brig. Gen. Lacey
203	09-11-44	Lutzkendorf	37	36	Maj. Carraway
204	09-12-44	Plauen (Secondary)	37	35	Maj. Fishburne
205	09-17-44	Nijmegen, Holland	43	41	Lt. Col. Glawe
206	09-19-44	Soest	37	25	Lt. Col. Vorhees
207	09-22-44	Kassel	36	36	Lt. Col. Wood
208	09-25-44	Frankfurt (H2X)	36	35	Maj. Richardson
209	09-26-44	Osnabruck	36	36	Maj. Stewart
210	09-27-44	Cologne (H2X)	38	36	Maj. Carraway
211	09-28-44	Magdeburg	37	37	Lt. Col. Wood
212	10-02-44	Kassel	37	35	Lt. Col. Burns
213	10-03-44	Nurenburg (H2X)	37	36	Lt. Col. Glawe
214	10-05-44	Cologne (H2X)	38	35	Lt. Col. Wood
215	10-06-44	Stargard (Secondary)	37	36	Maj. Richardson
216	10-07-44	Politz	48	47	Lt. Col. Glawe
217	10-14-44	Cologne (H2X)	37	36	Maj. Carraway
218	10-15-44	Cologne (H2X)	37	35	Maj. Davey
219	10-17-44	Cologne (H2X)	36	36	Lt. Col. Ball
220	10-18-44	Cologne (GH)	12	12	Capt. Gibbons
221	10-19-44	Mannheim (H2X)	36	36	Maj. Roper
222	10-22-44	Hannover (H2X)	36	36	Lt. Col. Burns
223	10-25-44	Hamburg (H2X)	37	37	Maj. Richardson
224	10-26-44	Bielefeld (H2X)	36	36	Maj. Stewart
225	10-28-44	Munster (H2X)	36	36	Maj. Carraway
226	10-30-44	Munster (Secondary) (H2X)	38	36	Maj. Davey
227	11-04-44	Harburg (H2X)	36	36	Lt. Col. Ball
228	11-05-44	Frankfurt (H2X)	36	36	Maj. Gorham

Rtnd. w/o bombing = Returned without bombing
Mission n/c = Mission not credited
Note: Target locations are in Germany when no country is listed

MISSION	DATE	TARGET	NUMBER OF AIRCRAFT DISPATCHED	ATTACKED	LEADER
229	11-06-44	Hamburg (H2X)	37	36	Maj. Richardson
230	11-09-44	Metz, France	37	36	Capt. Dennis
231	11-16-44	Eschweiler (H2X)	38	37	Maj. Carraway
232	11-21-44	Merseberg (H2X)	36	35	Capt. Geiger
233	11-23-44	Screening Force	13	13	Maj. Davey
234	11-25-44	Merseberg (H2X)	38	35	Col. Romig
235	11-26-44	Misburg (H2X)	36	35	Maj. Roper
236	11-29-44	Misburg (H2X)	36	36	Lt. Col. Stewart
237	11-30-44	Bohlen	36	35	Maj. Davey
238	12-04-44	Kassel (H2X)	36	34	Maj. Gorham
239	12-05-44	Berlin	36	33	Lt. Col. Ball
240	12-09-44	Sindelfingen (H2X)	36	33	Capt. Geiger
241	12-11-44	Frankfurt & Screening (H2X)	39	24	Maj. Richardson
242	12-12-44	Merseberg (H2X)	36	36	Capt. Dennis
243	12-15-44	Kassel (H2X)	36	36	Lt. Col. Burns
244	12-18-44	Cologne	-	-	Recalled-Mission n/c
245	12-19-44	Kall (GH)	36	36	Maj. Korges
246	12-24-44	Biblis A/F	55	55	
247	12-27-44	Bullay	37	35	Maj. Roper
248	12-28-44	Koblenz (Secondary) (H2X)	36	36	Lt. Col. Carraway
249	12-30-44	Kaiserlauten (GH)	37	36	Maj. Geiger
250	12-31-44	Krefeld	38	35	Maj. Korges
251	01-01-45	Kassel (Secondary) (H2X)	36	35	Maj. Roper
252	01-02-45	Mayen	38	34	Maj. Gorham
253	01-03-45	Cologne (Secondary) (H2X)	38	35	Lt. Col. Stewart
254	01-05-45	Koblenz (Secondary) (H2X)	38	35	Maj. Korges
255	01-06-45	Bonn (Secondary) (H2X)	38	38	Capt. Dennis
256	01-07-45	Bitburg (GH)	38	37	
257	01-10-45	Euskirchen (GH)	37	32	Maj. Hinkle
258	01-14-45	Cologne	48	45	Maj. Roper
259	01-17-45	Paderborn (Secondary) (H2X)	36	36	Maj. Roper
260	01-20-45	Sterkrade (H2X)	36	34	Maj. Roper
261	01-21-45	Ascheffenburg (H2X)	36	32	Lt. Col. Stewart
262	01-22-45	Sterkrade (H2X)	36	14	Maj. Roper
263	01-28-45	Cologne (H2X)	36	36	Maj. Roper
264	01-29-45	Siegen (H2X)	38	35	Lt. Col. Carraway
265	02-01-45	Ludwigshafen (H2X)	37	34	Maj. Roper
266	02-03-45	Berlin	39	37	Maj. Roper
267	02-06-45	Lutter (Secondary)	28	25	Maj. Roper
268	02-07-45	Lutzkendorf	-	-	Recalled-Mission n/c
269	02-09-45	Lutzkendorf	38	35	Maj. Roper
270	02-10-45	Dulmen (Secondary) (GH)	44	38	Lt. Col. Stewart
271	02-14-45	Dresden (H2X)	37	34	Maj. Richardson
272	02-15-45	Dresden (Secondary) (H2X)	12	12	
273	02-16-45	Gelsenkirchen	12	12	
274	02-19-45	Munster (Secondary) (H2X)	36	36	Lt. Col. Stewart
275	02-20-45	Nurenburg (H2X)	37	36	Col. Burns
276	02-21-45	Nurenburg (H2X)	36	35	Lt. Col. Stewart

MISSION	DATE	TARGET	NUMBER OF AIRCRAFT DISPATCHED	ATTACKED	LEADER
277	02-22-45	Salzwedel	37	36	Maj. Richardson
278	02-23-45	Plauen (Secondary) (H2X)	37	36	Maj. Gorham
279	02-24-45	Screening Force	13	13	Capt. Anderson
280	02-25-45	Munich	36	33	Capt. Maginn
281	02-26-45	Berlin (H2X)	36	34	Lt. Col. Stewart
282	02-27-45	Leipzig (H2X)	30	30	Maj. Korges
283	02-28-45	Soest (GH)	36	36	Lt. Col. Ball
284	03-01-45	Heilbronn (Secondary) (H2X)	37	37	Capt. Dennis
285	03-02-45	Chemnitz (Secondary)	36	35	Maj. Hinkle
286	03-04-45	Schwabmunchen (H2X)	38	37	Maj. Richardson
287	03-05-45	Chemnitz (Secondary) (H2X)	37	35	Maj. Richardson
288	03-08-45	Essen (Secondary) (H2X)	38	36	Capt. Pryor
289	03-09-45	Kassel	36	35	Lt. Col. Carraway
290	03-10-45	Hagen (GH)	36	36	Lt. Col. Stewart
291	03-11-45	Bremen (H2X)	38	37	Maj. Korges
292	03-12-45	Swinemunde (H2X)	37	37	Brig. Gen. Lacey
293	03-14-45	Lohne	36	36	Lt. Col. Stewart
294	03-15-45	Oranienburg	37	35	Maj. Richardson
295	03-17-45	Molbis (H2X)	36	35	Capt. Dennis
296	03-18-45	Berlin (H2X)	36	36	Lt. Col. Stewart
297	03-19-45	Plauen (Secondary) (H2X)	36	34	Capt. Maginn
298	03-21-45	Hopsten	38	38	Maj. Richardson
299	03-22-45	Berningholten	38	38	Lt. Col. Stewart
300	03-23-45	Recklinghausen	38	38	Maj. Korges
301	03-24-45	Vechte A/F	36	34	Maj. Gorham
302	03-24-45	Twente A/F	13	13	Lt. Col. Stewart
303	03-26-45	Plauen (Secondary)	35	35	Lt. Col. Ball
304	03-28-45	Berlin (H2X)	37	37	Capt. Gaylord
305	03-30-45	Bremen (H2X)	35	33	Col. Carter
306	03-31-45	Halle (H2X)	38	34	Maj. Hinkle
307	04-02-45	Rotenburg	-	-	Recalled-Mission n/c
308	04-04-45	Fassburg (Secondary)	38	26	Lt. Col. Stewart
309	04-05-45	Ingolstadt	38	37	Maj. Gorham
310	04-07-45	Luneburg	38	38	Lt. Col. Stewart
311	04-08-45	Halberstadt (Secondary)	38	37	Lt. Col. Stewart
312	04-09-45	Furstenfeldbruck	38	36	Maj. Geiger
313	04-10-45	Orianenburg	36	36	Capt. Dennis
314	04-11-45	Freiham	36	36	Col. Carter
315	04-14-45	Royan, France	38	38	Lt. Col. Carraway
316	04-15-45	Gironde Estuary	38	38	Capt. Maginn
317	04-16-45	Regensberg	38	37	Maj. Korges
318	04-17-45	Dresden	38	38	Maj. Geiger
319	04-18-45	Traunstein	30	30	Maj. Gorham
320	04-20-45	Brandenberg	30	30	Maj. Hinkle

Missions Reported - 320
Missions Credited - 311

Rtnd. w/o bombing = Returned without bombing
Mission n/c = Mission not credited
Note: Target locations are in Germany when no country is listed

Chapter Ten
THEIR AIRCRAFT

YB-508th Squadron, RQ-509th Squadron, TU-510th Squadron, DS-511th Squadron. Officer listed was the last pilot to fly the aircraft. (Number of missions flown)

42-9121   THE BIG BITCH
April 15, 1943, used as Station "hack" and Target Tug, August 25, 1944 transferred to 447th Sub-Depot, salvaged May 29, 1945

42-3046 TU-X   OLD JACKSON
July 30, 1943, Lt. Maser, crash landed Sutton, scrapped (6)

42-3090 YB-N   T'AINT A BIRD
September 7, 1943, battle damaged, sent to Second Base Air Depot November 10, 1943, salvaged June 18, 1945 (13)

42-3093 TU-K   NOBODY'S DARLING
December 31, 1943, Lt. Chalmers, crash landed Burnham on Sea, scrapped (8)

42-3106 YB-M   DOUBLE TROUBLE
July 14, 1943, Lt. Peck, crash landed, scrapped (1)

42-3120 RQ-O   GREMLINS DELIGHT
June 18, 1944, returned to ZOI (24)

42-3136 DS-P   NO BALLS AT ALL
February 24, 1944, Lt. LeClerc, MIA (22)

42-3140 RQ-P   PATTY ANN II
December 1, 1943, Captain Harris, ditched (19)

42-3141 YB-A   HITLERS HEADACHE
April 1944, returned to ZOI (15)

42-3150 DS-Q   FOUL BALL
September 6, 1943, Lt. Norris, ditched (11)

42-3152 TU-A   SLEEPY LAGOON
October 9, 1943, F.O. Warring, MIA (17)

42-3173 DS-R   SPARE BALL
May 15, 1943, Lt. Meli, MIA (1)

42-3272 TU-M   CAPTAIN BILL
July 25, 1943, Lt. Boyd, MIA (10)

42-3495 TU-C
December 31, 1943, Lt. Saville, MIA (9)

42-3509 DS-Z   CRYSTAL BALL
January 30, 1944, Lt. Robertson, MIA (12)

42-3517 YB-O   HAPPY WARRIOR
February 24, 1944, Lt. Caughman, MIA (15)

42-3523 TU-M   APRIL GIRL
January 11, 1944, Lt. Procak, MIA (11)

42-3532 DS-O   LUCILLE BALL
November 5, 1943, Lt. Gaylord, crash landed Ipswich, scrapped (4)

42-3542 RQ-V   SHADY LADY II
July 1944, returned to ZOI (24)

42-3560 YB-H   SALTY DOG
November 26, 1943, Lt. Blaisdell, ditched (1)

42-5756 RQ-R   KAY L II
June 1944, returned to ZOI (19)

42-5807 DS-T   MINOR BALL
October 4, 1943, Lt. Nauman, MIA (10)

42-5812 DS-O   CANNON BALL
August 17, 1943, Lt. Pinkerton, MIA (9)

MIA = (Aircraft missing in action)

42-5814 YB-B
June 13, 1943, Lt. Forrest, ditched (1)

42-5815 RQ-Q   *STARDUST*
June 13, 1943, Lt. Jackson, MIA (1)

42-5823 YB-C   *ROUND TRIP*
June 1944, returned to ZOI (29)

42-5824 DS-S   *SCREW BALL*
April 10, 1944, returned to ZOI (34)

42-6096 DS-W   *ONDA BALL*
October 14, 1943, Lt. Crismond, MIA (4)

42-6151 YB-M
August 1944, transferred to 490th B.G. (26)

42-29491 RQ
May 7, 1943, Lt. Snipes, collided with 42-29865 over Polebrook

42-29603 DS-R   *SPIT BALL*
October 9, 1943, Lt. Maser, MIA (15)

42-29630 RQ-S   *PICCADILLY COMMANDO*
December 31, 1943, Lt. Smith, MIA (30)

42-29654 YB-B   *DOTTIE J*
May 1944, returned to ZOI (16)

42-29684 RQ-T   *EAGER EAGLE*
September 6, 1943, Captain Hathaway, ditched (16)

42-29701 TU-B   *IN THE MOOD*
May 19, 1943, Lt. Mansfield, MIA (1)

42-29716 YB-H   *FAST WOMAN*
August 27, 1943, Lt. Suit, MIA (9)

42-29726 RQ-Q   *POISONALITY*
July 30, 1943, Lt. Maginnis, crash landed, Leiston, scrapped (3)

42-29749 RQ-Z   *BELLE OF THE BAYOUS*
May 1944, returned to ZOI (37)

42-29762 TU-D   *COUP DE GRACE*
April 1944, returned to ZOI (41)

42-29812 RQ-U   *LUCIFER JR*
April 1944, returned to ZOI (30)

42-29817 YB-D   *ARGONAUT II*
June 28, 1943, Lt. King, MIA (7)

42-29821 YB-F   *ARGONAUT*
                        then VOX POP II
January 7, 1944, Lt. Anderson, crashed Sutton Bridge (21)

42-29825 DS-Z   *MAJOR BALL*
September 15, 1943, Major Stewart, crash landed Polebrook, scrapped (9)

42-29826 YB-H
June 22, 1943, Lt. Turgeon, MIA (3)

42-29831 TU-H   *THE INVADER*
April 16, 1944, returned to ZOI (40)

42-29835 DS-Y   *PISTOL BALL*
July 18, 1944, returned to ZOI (35)

42-29838 RQ-U   *THE CONCHO CLIPPER*
May 29, 1943, Lt. Russell, MIA (4)

42-29839 TU-C   *CHEROKEE GIRL*
August 17, 1943, Lt. Hansen, MIA (13)

42-29841 RQ-V   *SHADY LADY*
September 6, 1943, Lt. Spika, crash landed New Romney, scrapped (15)

42-29843 TU-D
June 28, 1943, Lt. Moss, MIA (7)

42-29847 DS-T   *HIGH BALL*
June 28, 1943, Lt. Adams, MIA (4)

42-29848 TU-F   *AMATOL*
May 28, 1944, returned to ZOI (27)

42-29849 DS-U   *LINDA BALL*
March 6, 1944, transferred to 3rd Bomb Division (34)

42-29850 TU-G   *GREMLIN'S CASTLE*
July 15, 1944, returned to ZOI (28)

42-29851 YB-J   *ARGONAUT III*
October 10, 1943, Lt. Argiropulos, abandoned over Norfolk (28)

42-29852 DS-V   *FIREBALL*
November 3, 1943, Lt. Nardi, MIA (18)

42-29858 YB-G   *MURDER INCORPORATED then CENSORED*
February 21, 1944, Lt. Evans, crash landed near Oundle, scrapped (29)

42-29859 TU-H   *THE ANNIHILATOR*
May 14, 1943, Captain Forsyth, MIA (1)

42-29860 RQ-W   *SNOOZIN SUSAN*
July 21, 1944, returned to ZOI (37)

42-29861 RQ-X   *BUCKSHOT*
January 11, 1944, Lt. Cannon, MIA (31)

42-29862 YB-H
May 14, 1943, Lt. McCoy, MIA (1)

42-29863 RQ-Y   *AINT IT GRUESOME then KENTUCKY BABE*
February 11, 1944, Captain Carson, MIA (43)

42-29865 YB
May 7, 1943, Major Birlem, collided with 42-29491 over Polebrook

42-29868 YB-K   *THE VENUS*
October 9, 1943, Lt. Turley, MIA (23)

42-29872 DS-W   *SNOW BALL*
July 17, 1943, Lt. Peters, ditched (6)

42-29874 TU-J   *EL CONQUISTADOR*
August 12, 1943, Lt. Garcia, crash landed Leiston, scrapped (10)

42-29877 DS-X   *SPEED BALL*
December 31, 1943, Lt. Jones, MIA (24)

42-29882 YB-L   *SHARON ANN*
July 18, 1944, returned to ZOI (38)

42-29887 TU-K   *MEHITABEL*
June 28, 1943, Lt. Copeland, MIA (7)

42-29925 TU-L   *THE DUCHESS*
June 7, 1944, returned to ZOI (39)

42-29948 TU-B   *JENNIE*
December 31, 1943, Lt. Wells, MIA (30)

42-30499 RQ-Q   *MY PRINCESS*
August 1, 1944, salvaged at 2nd Secondary Air Depot (46)

42-30780 RQ-T   *EAGER EAGLE II*
January 11, 1944, Lt. Myers, MIA (10)

42-30785 YB-H
October 4, 1943, Lt. Reed, MIA (1)

42-30790 DS-Q   *CUE BALL*
October 9, 1943, Captain Morse, MIA (2)

42-30857 TU-J   *MY DEVOTION*
December 17, 1944, returned to ZOI (34)

42-30866 YB-S   *PISTOL PACKIN MAMA*
February 21, 1944, Lt. Kogelman, ditched (5)

42-30867 TU-N
October 9, 1943, Lt. Christman, MIA (2)

42-30994 YB-T   *OLE DAD*
July 15, 1944, transferred to 486th B.G., salvaged May 29, 1945 (27)

42-31162 DS-V   *VICTORY BALL*
December 30, 1943, Lt. Parsons, MIA (8)

42-31179 DS-B   *STINKY WEATHER*
December 31, 1943, Lt. Putman, MIA (2)

42-31192 YB-R
October 7, 1944, Lt. Peterson, crash landed Sweden (41)

42-31238 DS-A   *DEVIL'S BALL*
September 8, 1944, Lt. Haba, crashed Market Deeping (64)

42-31384 RQ-T   *BUCKEYE BABE*
January 17, 1945, Lt. Della Cioppa, MIA (103)

42-31481 TU-B
January 11, 1944, Lt. Case, MIA (1)

42-31509 TU-V   *TWINKEL TOES*
August 6, 1944, Lt. Petty, landed in Sweden (41)

42-31560 TU-A
September 8, 1944, Lt. Shera, MIA (60)

MIA = (Aircraft missing in action)

42-31612 TU-B
February 22, 1944, Lt. Ritzema, MIA (8)

42-31694 DS-V
February 11, 1944, Lt. Turbyne, crash landed and burned Southend (3)

42-31702 YB-A
August 16, 1944, Lt. Cartwright, MIA (47)

42-31711 YB-F
May 6, 1945, transferred to First Base Air Depot (87)

42-31714 DS-R/TU-R   SKY BALL
May 17, 1945, damaged by fire, scrapped (60)

42-31721 TU-S   BLACK MAGIC
May 28, 1944, Lt. McClelland, MIA (35)

42-31725 RQ-L   LI'L GINNY
May 30, 1944, Lt. Hicks, MIA (34)

42-31748 DS-V
July 13, 1944, Lt. Aldrege, MIA (41)

42-31757 YB-G   ROUND TRIP
May 28, 1944, Lt. Condon, MIA (23)

42-31763 TU-A   TEN HORSEPOWER
February 20, 1944, Lt. Nelson, crashed near Glatton (6)

42-31776 YB-H   MAGGIES DRAWERS
March 2, 1944, Lt. Seaman, MIA (1)

42-31875 DS-P
July 29, 1944, Lt. Stewart, crash landed Polebrook, scrapped (26)

42-31879 YB-Q   THE SHARK
September 1944, returned to ZOI (53)

42-31882 DS-F
February 22, 1944, Lt. Mears, abandoned over England (3)

42-31899 TU-B   CHATTERBOX
May 27, 1944, Lt. Peters, landed in Switzerland (18)

42-31955 YB-K
April 18, 1944, Lt. Apperson, MIA (14)

42-31966 DS-X
March 18, 1944, Lt. Martin, MIA (5)

42-31975 TU-O   QUEEN OF THE AIR
May 27, 1944, Lt. Hopkins, MIA (28)

42-31988 TU-C   THE BLONDE BOMBER
April 22, 1944, Major Wheeler, crashed on takeoff Polebrook (3)

42-37714 TU-T   RONCHI
May 7, 1944, Lt. Pressley, MIA (18)

42-37731 TU-A
December 31, 1943, Major Blaylock, MIA (12)

42-37774 YB-N
December 31, 1943, Lt. Apperson, abandoned over Bassingbourne (6)

42-37780 DS-G   GOLDEN BALL
July 17, 1944, transferred to 487th B.G. (26)

42-37817 TU-A   ARISTOCRAP
November 26, 1943, Lt. Castle, MIA (2)

42-37825 DS-Q   SUPER BALL
March 18, 1944, Lt. Mears, landed in Switzerland (26)

42-37827 YB-J
April 13, 1944, Lt. Whitchurch, MIA (24)

42-37832 RQ-N   CASA DE EMBRIAGOS
March 18, 1944, Lt. Illies, MIA (15)

42-37845 RQ-F   WILDFIRE
June 12, 1944, Lt. Guthrey, ditched (55)

42-37847 DS-R
December 1, 1943, Lt. Plant, MIA (3)

42-38005 RQ-G   STORMY WEATHER
May 24, 1944, Captain Clay, MIA (24)

42-38023 YB-H   YANKEE REBEL
February 22, 1944, Lt. Watson, crash landed Framlingham, scrapped (10)

42-38028 TU-Q   PAPPY'S PRIDE
July 12, 1944, Lt. Irwin, MIA (36)

42-38032 RQ-X
March 18, 1944, Lt. Neuberg, MIA (17)

42-38038 TU-R/P   APRIL GIRL II
June 13, 1945, returned to ZOI (111)

42-38146 YB-D
July 29, 1944, Lt. Morton, MIA (37)

42-38153 DS-F   BEDLAM BALL
September 19, 1944, Lt. Butler, ditched (49)

42-39760 RQ-M
July 27, 1944, salvaged (30)

42-39761 DS-D   FIREBALL II
January 11, 1944, Lt. White, MIA (13)

42-39778 DS-A   LUCKY BALL
December 22, 1943, Lt. Maginn, ditched (2)

42-39780 TU-S   LITTLE TWINK
December 30, 1943, Lt. Adiamak, crash landed Hawkinge, scrapped (4)

42-39823 TU-O   IRON ASS
December 31, 1943, Lt. Bender, MIA (8)

42-39834 DS-F   CANNON BALL
January 30, 1944, Lt. Mears, crash landed Polebrook, scrapped (14)

42-39835 TU-N   WANTTA SPAR
July 1944, transferred to 388th B.G. (16)

42-39839 DS-D
November 26, 1943, Lt. Lemley, crash landed Marham, transferred to 8th AF HQ November 28, 1943, returned to ZOI March 30, 1947 (1)

42-39848 DS-C   ARCHI BALL
July 1944, declared War Weary, salvaged July 27, 1944 (27)

42-39849 YB-K
March 22, 1944, Lt. Slosson, MIA (23)

42-39853 TU-P   PAPA'S PASSION
May 29, 1944, Lt. Neal, ditched (23)

42-39857 DS-H   BELLE OF THE BALL
February 22, 1944, Lt. Pugh, MIA (16)

42-39905 YB-C
January 11, 1944, Lt. Garner, MIA (2)

42-39914 RQ-S   LUCKY STRIKE
                   then THE BLACK BITCH
June 13, 1945, returned to ZOI (51)

42-39987 DS-D   PIN BALL
May 28, 1944, F.O. Probesco, MIA (31)

42-97066 YB-O
June 14, 1944, Lt. Dixey, MIA (22)

42-97144 RQ-R
June 21, 1944, Lt. Walters, crash landed Sweden (30)

42-97149 RQ-X
May 27, 1944, Lt. Myers, MIA (13)

42-97157 YB-N   MR. MALFUNCTION
May 27, 1944, Lt. Sengstock, MIA (20)

42-97169 RQ-N   MY GAL II
June 1945, returned to ZOI (106)

42-97191 DS-X   SILVER BALL
May 28, 1944, Lt. Miller, MIA (16)

42-97193 RQ-P/L/O STAR DUSTER
June 14, 1945, returned to ZOI (81)

42-97196 TU-M   BOBBIE ANNE
October 7, 1944, Lt. Evans, landed in Sweden (53)

42-97202 RQ-Z
June 22, 1944, Lt. Watkins, MIA (32)

42-97216 RQ-U/TU-U "2 AND 6"
May 8, 1945, scrapped after fire damage (79)

42-97252 TU-K   DEVIL'S MISTRESS
June 11, 1945, returned to ZOI (103)

42-97258 YB-P   SILVER METEOR
May 31, 1945, returned to ZOI (84)

42-97305 YB-L
April 24, 1944, Lt. Evans, ditched (5)

42-97318 DS-S   DINAH MIGHT
September 12, 1944, Lt. Lopert, MIA (47)

MIA = (Aircraft missing in action)

42-97325 YB-H
May 23, 1944, Lt. Crowe, collided with B-24 near Eye, Suffolk (17)

42-97349 YB-B   SILVER DOLLAR
May 31, 1945, returned to ZOI (120)

42-97381 DS-U   LINDA BALL II
May 26, 1945, returned to ZOI (66)

42-97472 DS-H
May 28, 1944, Lt. Anderson, MIA (23)

42-97492 DS-B   SLOW BALL
August 3, 1944, Lt. Brackens, MIA (49)

42-97600 -Y
August 20, 1944, transferred to 401st B.G., MIA November 21, 1944

42-97601 -Z   GYPSY GAL
July 19, 1944, MIA with 457th B.G.

42-97636 -L
August 8, 1944, crash landed with 401st B.G.

42-97638
October 7, 1944, MIA with 457th B.G.

42-97649
August 1944, transferred to 457th B.G.

42-97651 TU-Y/DS-Y
May 1945, transferred to 305th B.G. (34)

42-97687 YB-Z/DS-Z
May 1945, transferred to 305th B.G. (31)

42-97701 RQ-B/DS-B   NADINE L
May 1945, transferred to 305th B.G. (51)

42-97798 YB-H
June 14, 1944, Lt. Williamson, MIA (10)

42-97843 YB-C   HOT ROCK
May 28, 1945, returned to ZOI (57)

42-97926 RQ-X   FAST BABY
September 28, 1944, Lt. Barker, crash landed Ypres, Belgium, scrapped (50)

42-97947 -U
August 20, 1944, transferred to 401st B.G.

42-97951 -C
September 17, 1944, MIA with 457th B.G.

42-97965 TU-Z/YB-Z
October 15, 1944, Lt. Muffett, crash landed Belgium, scrapped (16)

42-98004 YB-H
September 27, 1944, Captain Geiger, battle damage, scrapped (25)

42-102470 YB-J
May 27, 1944, Lt. Johnson, MIA (9)

42-102478 TU-O
June 14, 1944, Lt. Ludwig, MIA (3)

42-102576 TU-C   EASTER BUNNY
December 9, 1944, Lt. Haskins, crash landed Polebrook, scrapped (65)

42-102613 YB-C
May 27, 1944, Lt. Evans, MIA (10)

42-102676 DS-P/TU-P   *17 AND MISS LEDD*
May 23, 1945, returned to ZOI (31)

42-102949 YB-G
July 19, 1944, Lt. Konecheck, MIA (22)

42-102952 DS-H
July 28, 1944, Lt. Long, MIA (28)

42-102955 TU-P/RQ-L   CHATTERBOX II
May 29, 1945, returned to ZOI (72)

42-102971 YB-J
August 6, 1944, Lt. Pattison, MIA (26)

42-107005 DS-Q   LUCILLE BALL II
August 12, 1944, burned on hardstand (23)

42-107046 DS-Z   SCREW BALL
August 6, 1944, Lt. Boyd, MIA (21)

42-107077 TU-D   SHOO SHOO BABY
July 19, 1944, Lt. Chapman, MIA (31)

42-107124 TU-F   *MOLLIE MULE*
June 11, 1945, returned to ZOI (85)

42-107216 DS-Y   *THUNDERBALL*
August 9, 1944, Lt. Myl, ditched (34)

43-37512 TU-S   *TRADE WINDS*
May 26, 1945, returned to ZOI (119)

43-37515 TU-L   *JOHN SILVER*
June 11, 1945, returned to ZOI (95)

43-37524 DS-D   *QUEEN OF THE BALL*
December 9, 1944, Lt. Ashton, abandoned on the Continent, scrapped (63)

43-37533 DS-G
August 6, 1944, Lt. Strange, MIA (4)

43-37534 YB-L
July 7, 1944, Lt. Wishnewsky, crash landed Polebrook, scrapped (13)

43-37557 YB-K   *HUBBA HUBBA*
August 6, 1944, Lt. Barrieau, MIA (30)

43-37571 DS-X   *DOTTIES TAXI*
November 26, 1944, Lt. Boettcher, MIA (59)

43-37595 RQ-O   *VERGEN'S VIRGINS*
February 6, 1945, Lt. Vergen, collided with 43-38080 over Polebrook (70)

43-37665 TU-N   *LASSIE COME HOME*
March 25, 1945, exploded on base (89)

43-37674 RQ-F
October 7, 1944, Lt. McGuire, landed in Sweden (31)

43-37676 RQ-L   *FLAK MAGIC*
December 12, 1944, Lt. Barker, crash landed St. Trond, Belgium, captured (60)

43-37696 RQ-Z   *TRANSIT BELLE*
May 26, 1945, returned to ZOI (105)

43-37705 TU-T/DS-F/TU-V   *THE LITTLE ONE*
May 24, 1945, returned to ZOI (72)

43-37727 YB-N
November 21, 1944, Lt. Loehndorf, MIA (46)

43-37780 YB-O
July 12, 1944, Lt. Wishnewsky crash landed Polebrook, scrapped (6)

43-37850 YB-G   *UMBRIGO*
September 12, 1944, Lt. Brown, MIA (25)

43-37854 RQ-V   *TORCHY TESS*
February 25, 1945, Lt. Abplanalp, crash landed in Switzerland (53)

43-37862 TU-G   *FEARLESS FOSDICK*
June 1945, returned to ZOI (81)

43-37900 YB-H
March 30, 1945, Lt. Marschek, abandoned on the Continent, scrapped (80)

43-37920 DS-L
August 6, 1944, Lt. Uttley, MIA (6)

43-37956 YB-L
May 26, 1945, returned to ZOI (79)

43-37957 TU-D
June 1945, returned to ZOI (46)

43-37964 RQ-M   *DOZEY DOATES*
April 9, 1945, Lt. Northrup, abandoned on the Continent (95)

43-37978 YB-J
May 31, 1945, returned to ZOI (48)

43-37986 DS-H
September 12, 1944, Lt. Schoenian, MIA (10)

43-38070 DS-G
May 26, 1945, returned to ZOI (56)

43-38080 DS-Q
February 6, 1945, Lt. Ashton, collided with 43-37595 over Polebrook (34)

43-38089 DS-P
September 12, 1944, Lt. Adams, MIA (13)

43-38116 RQ-Q   *CLASSIE CHASSIS*
March 2, 1945, scrapped, battle damage (50)

43-38123 TU-V   *BABY BUTCH*
September 12, 1944, Lt. Hennegan, MIA (9)

MIA = (Aircraft missing in action)

43-38130 YB-K   TEXAS BELLE
May 31, 1945, returned to ZOI (70)

43-38139 YB-D
September 5, 1944, Lt. Wright, MIA (11)

43-38171 DS-Y
October 7, 1944, Lt. Merrill, crash landed in Sweden (21)

43-38277 YB-O
June 1945, returned to ZOI (59)

43-38405 YB-D
February 14, 1945, Lt. Ash, MIA (27)

43-38426 DS-B
October 7, 1944, F.O. Fisher, landed in Sweden (7)

43-38428 DS-A/RQ-A
June 1945, returned to ZOI (78)

43-38432 RQ-P
December 5, 1944, Captain Williamson, MIA (19)

43-38435 DS-H/TU-O GLORY BOUND
March 25, 1945, damaged in explosion of 43-37665, scrapped (68)

43-38461 TU-T
February 26, 1945, Lt. Gottschalk, abandoned on the Continent, scrapped (49)

43-38465 TU-A   FAVORITE LADY
June 8, 1945, returned to ZOI (81)

43-38518 DS-N
October 3, 1944, Lt. Cregar, MIA (4)

43-38527 DS-C
October 7, 1944, Lt. Dargue, MIA (3)

43-38567 YB-G
December 28, 1944, Lt. Buttel, crash landed Belgium, scrapped (24)

43-38585 DS-K
December 31, 1944, Lt. Armstrong, crash landed Polebrook, scrapped (30)

43-38591 RQ-U   MYASSISDRAGGIN
April 9, 1945, Lt. Hampton, abandoned on the Continent (54)

43-38592 DS-N/RQ-B
May 23, 1945, returned to ZOI (64)

43-38640 RQ-C   ANNIE MARIE
July 7, 1945, returned to ZOI (75)

43-38650 DS-M   MERRIE CHRISTIE
February 14, 1945, Lt. Kirkland, crash landed in France, scrapped (36)

43-38666 RQ-T/YB-H
June 1945, returned to ZOI (49)

43-38691 DS-B
June 1945, returned to ZOI (29)

43-38694 DS-C/TU-D BIGAS BIRD
June 1945, returned to ZOI (66)

43-38753 YB-C   LUCKY JEWELL
June 1945, returned to ZOI (70)

43-38799 YB-Q   HEAVEN CAN WAIT
May 1945, returned to ZOI (62)

43-38813 YB-M/YB-U
May 1945, returned to ZOI (39)

43-38872 DS-G
May 1945, transferred to 384th B.G. (10)

43-38920 RQ-O   MORT'S ORPHANS
June 1945, returned to ZOI (37)

43-38954 YB-G   THE INVICTUS
June 1945, returned to ZOI (53)

43-39001 TU-M   COUP DE GRACE II
June 8, 1945, returned to ZOI (62)

43-39020 TU-C   WAR HAWK
May 24, 1945, returned to ZOI (40)

43-39156 TU-T
May 24, 1945, returned to ZOI (33)

44-6077 RQ-W
August 9, 1944, Lt. Zotollo, MIA (27)

44-6078 RQ-G   HARD HEARTED MAMA
January 22, 1945, Lt. Goldsborough, MIA (55)

44-6082 TU-B   WISCONSIN BEAUTY
June 1945, returned to ZOI (85)

44-6108 RQ-Y/YB-Y   BLACK WIDOW
June 1945, returned to ZOI (95)

44-6139 DS-K
September 12, 1944, Lt. Hadley, crash landed Belgium, scrapped (30)

44-6156 RQ-R   LITTLE CHAPEL
May 26, 1945, returned to ZOI (89)

44-6565 DS-Q/TU-Q
May 23, 1945, returned to ZOI (28)

44-6566 RQ-F
June 1945, returned to ZOI (63)

44-6579 DS-J/YB-X   MARTHA
June 1945, returned to ZOI (56)

44-6610 TU-B   FEED 'EM
May 24, 1945, returned to ZOI (52)

44-6802 DS-X
June 4, 1945, transferred to 94th C.W. (19)

44-6907 RQ-P
May 1945, returned to ZOI (28)

44-6952 RQ-H
May 1945, returned to ZOI (15)

44-8045 DS-L   THE PATHFINDER
June 1945, transferred to 305th B.G. (54)

44-8079 DS-V   JANET
June 1945, transferred to 305th B.G. (32)

44-8100 DS-B
September 12, 1944, Lt. Schmollinger, MIA (12)

44-8222 YB-A
October 7, 1944, Lt. Bartzocas, landed in Sweden (4)

44-8280 TU-H   L'LLE BOY
May 13, 1945, damaged in taxiing accident, scrapped (73)

44-8358 DS-A   LITTLE RUNT
May 1945, transferred to 305th B.G. (27)

44-8374 DS-U
May 1945, transferred to 305th B.G. (23)

44-8376 DS-F
May 1945, transferred to 305th B.G. (33)

44-8410 YB-A   MISS GLAMOUR PANTS
May 25, 1945, returned to ZOI (68)

44-8412 YB-H   LIL LADY
May 26, 1945, returned to ZOI (29)

44-8455 DS-O/M
June 1945, transferred to 305th B.G. (14)

44-8468 TU-J/DS-J
June 1945, transferred to 305th B.G. (22)

44-8617 RQ-G
June 1945, returned to ZOI (38)

44-8664 DS-D
May 1945, transferred to 305th B.G. (19)

44-8774 DS-Z
May 1945, transferred to 305th B.G. (12)

44-8780 DS-H
May 1945, transferred to 305th B.G. (13)

44-8842 DS-N
May 1945, transferred to 305th B.G. (3)

44-8846 DS-M   HALF PINT
May 1945, transferred to 305th B.G. (6)

44-8867 DS-P
May 1945, transferred to 305th B.G. (7)

MIA = (Aircraft missing in action)

Chapter Eleven
ALL GAVE SOME, SOME GAVE ALL

MAY 7, 1943
508th
Major Keith G. Birlem, 1st Lt. Harry L. Bartholomew, 1st Lt. Courtland H. Young, 2nd Lt. Henry G. Summers, 2nd Lt. Clarence B. Yunt, T/Sgt. Thomas S. Broderick, S/Sgt. Oscar R. Tipton, S/Sgt. Walter D. Lappage, S/Sgt. Robert M. Brooke, S/Sgt. Paul R. Fennell (All killed).

509th
1st Lt. Roy Snipes, 1st Lt. Rupert L. Torrey, 2nd Lt. George F. Cotherman, T/Sgt. Harold J. Wellnitz, S/Sgt. Irving L. Berger, S/Sgt. Edward G. Cihlar, S/Sgt. Harry J. Kelley, S/Sgt. Maurice R. Marquis, S/Sgt. Charles E. Chadbourne (All killed).

MAY 14, 1943
508th
1st Lt. Clifford J. McCoy (POW), 2nd Lt. Charles J. Nickels (POW), 2nd Lt. L. Carlisle (POW), 2nd Lt. Jerry C. Scollard (POW), T/Sgt. Peter R. Brasic (POW), T/Sgt. Cecil F. Bazar (POW), S/Sgt. Cleman N. Smith (POW), S/Sgt. Robert H. Hilton (KIA), S/Sgt. George G. Osborne (POW), S/Sgt. William G. Lafferty (POW).

510th
Captain William R. Forsythe (POW), 1st Lt. R. C. Stewart (POW), 2nd Lt. James T. McDonald (POW), 2nd Lt. Robert V. Ostheimer (POW), Sgt. Francis M. Daly (POW), T/Sgt. Wilton A. Wixom (POW), S/Sgt. Leroy D. Donaldson (KIA), S/Sgt. Albert L. Jensen (KIA), Sgt. Thomas P. Culkin (POW), S/Sgt. Ralph C. Tarr (POW).

MAY 15, 1943
511th
1st Lt. Joseph A. Meli Jr. (KIA), 2nd Lt. Robert P. Cooper (KIA), 2nd Lt. Jack Howell (KIA), 2nd Lt. Howard E. Lewis (KIA), T/Sgt. Dewey K. Bishop (KIA), S/Sgt. Melvin E. Hugo (KIA), S/Sgt. Stanford W. Henry (KIA), S/Sgt. Charles D. Summers (KIA), S/Sgt. Louis M. Hilscher (KIA), S/Sgt. Bernard A. Guenzig (KIA).

MAY 19, 1943
510th
2nd Lt. Robert W. Mansfield (POW), 2nd Lt. Leonard D. Jasinek (KIA), 2nd Lt. Alec S. White (POW), 2nd Lt. David F. Nash (POW), T/Sgt. Elmer L. Peterson (KIA), S/Sgt. Charles E. Anchors (MIA), S/Sgt. Louis S. Strumolo (MIA), Sgt. Thomas V. Higgins (MIA), S/Sgt. Clifford Coyle (MIA), T/Sgt. Willard A. Backman (MIA).

511th
T/Sgt. Lewis T. Baker (KIA).

MAY 26, 1943
320th Service Squadron
M/Sgt. William T. Funderburk (Killed in a jeep accident).

MAY 29, 1943
509th
1st Lt. Colonel J. Russell Jr. (POW), 1st Lt. Charles B. Woehrle (POW), 2nd Lt. Roy P. Stealey (POW), F.O. Leo Grikstas (POW), T/Sgt. James F. Welk (KIA), T/Sgt. Wayne I. Baldwin (KIA), S/Sgt. Charles T. Eaton (POW), S/Sgt. Nahannie Bader (KIA), S/Sgt. Maurice A. McLaughlin (POW), S/Sgt. Frederick D. Williams Jr. (POW).

JUNE 11, 1943
510th
S/Sgt. Walfred Putaansuu (KIA).

511th
2nd Lt. Frederick L. Angel (KIA).

JUNE 13, 1943
508th
T/Sgt. Harry C. Rosebuck (MIA), S/Sgt. Joseph H. Hayes (MIA).

509th
1st Lt. Robert W. Jackson (POW), F.O. Chester L. Lott (POW), 2nd Lt. Herman M. Lindsey (POW), 2nd Lt. Charles Noetzel (KIA), T/Sgt. John E. Adams (POW), S/Sgt. Wallis L. Patton (POW), Sgt. Roy Johnson (KIA), Sgt. William E. Whittaker (POW), S/Sgt. Edward H. Berry (KIA), Sgt. Floyd W. Viles (POW).

JUNE 22, 1943
508th
2nd Lt. Leo P. Turgeon (POW), 2nd Lt. Burton W. Caruso (POW), 2nd Lt. Charles R. Bryant Jr. (POW), 2nd Lt. John R. Turney (POW), T/Sgt. John W. Cabaniss (POW), S/Sgt. Lawrence J. Ferns (POW), Sgt. Edward Knower (POW), Sgt. Video Pacciotti (POW), S/Sgt. Fred L. Aye (POW), S/Sgt. Leasure B. McGinnis (POW).

510th
Cpl. John C. Jett (Natural death).

511th
Sgt. Stanley J. Myszka (KIA).

JUNE 28, 1943
508th
2nd Lt. William C. King (MIA), 2nd Lt. Lloyd J. Gullickson (MIA), 2nd Lt. Sidney H. Lang (MIA), 2nd Lt. Russel E. McDonald (POW), T/Sgt. Charles F. Armstrong Jr. (MIA), T/Sgt. Leroy E. Birkley (POW), S/Sgt. Jack F. Sanderson (POW), S/Sgt. Earnest S. Taylor (POW), Sgt. Bradley E. Learned (MIA), Sgt. Reid Q. Merry (MIA), S/Sgt. Waino J. McKeen (KIA).

510th
2nd Lt. Derward R. Copeland (POW), 2nd Lt. Donald L. Parker (POW), 2nd Lt. Ralph S. Reback (POW), 2nd Lt. William C. Shanley (POW), S/Sgt. Frank W. Hanan (KIA), S/Sgt. John J. Castello (POW), S/Sgt. Edward R. Tuminiski (KIA), Sgt. Robert L. Wood (POW), Sgt. Merwyn A. Ranum (KIA), T/Sgt. Vincent P. Klanka (POW).

511th
1st Lt. John M. Moss (POW), 2nd Lt. Leonard Bigelow (POW), 2nd Lt. Jack R. Mason (MIA), 2nd Lt. Aaron Lazerson (MIA), T/Sgt. Joseph J. Beal (KIA), T/Sgt. Burt L. Almy (POW), S/Sgt. John A. Kennedy (KIA), S/Sgt. Theodore E. Malish (MIA), S/Sgt. Emery K. Criswell (POW), S/Sgt. Lonnie Owens (MIA).

1st Lt. Robert W. Adams (POW), 2nd Lt. Joseph P. Normile (Escaped), 2nd Lt. Roy L. Sage (POW), F.O. George H. Gloudeman (Escaped), T/Sgt. Everett L. Brannen (KIA), S/Sgt. Donald F. Capper (POW), S/Sgt. William W. Claggett (POW), S/Sgt. Joseph S. Wolfe (KIA), S/Sgt. Dragie J. Yareff (KIA), T/Sgt. Ermyle E. Young (KIA).

JULY 17, 1943
511th
2nd Lt. Fred M. Wattles Jr. (KIA).

JULY 25, 1943
510th
1st Lt. Edwin S. Boyd (POW), 2nd Lt. Joseph C. Perkins (KIA), 2nd Lt. Delbert P. Ray (POW), 2nd Lt. Eldon M. Tolman (POW), T/Sgt. Eddie E. Hamlin (POW), S/Sgt. Charles D. Cavanaugh (POW), S/Sgt. Joseph W. Keen (KIA), S/Sgt. Roy L. Weatherford (KIA), Sgt. Albert T. Garrison (KIA), Sgt. John A. Lewis (KIA).

JULY 29, 1943
1119th Quartermaster Company,
304th Service Group
Pvt. Bethando R. Giannetti (Killed in aircraft accident).

508th
2nd Lt. Robert J. Roessler (KIA).

JULY 31, 1943
509th
T/Sgt. Jimmy E. McCurdy (Died of wounds).

AUGUST 12, 1943
510th
S/Sgt. Edward W. Henninger (KIA).

AUGUST 17, 1943
510th
1st Lt. Helmuth F. Hansen (POW), F.O. J. Z. Comfort (POW), 1st Lt. Dale P. Van Brunt (POW), 2nd Lt. John W. Dytman (POW), S/Sgt. Tuite H. Ambrose (KIA), T/Sgt. Adam G. Gazek Jr. (POW), T/Sgt. Donald G. Boss (POW), S/Sgt. Elwin C. Smith (POW), S/Sgt. Paul Hennesey (POW), S/Sgt. August F. Warden (POW).

511th

1st Lt. Max A. Pinkerton (POW), F.O. Herbert F. Berreau (KIA), 2nd Lt. Charles R. Rosewall (POW), 2nd Lt. Lee A. Santi (POW), S/Sgt. Clifton A. Langseth (POW), T/Sgt. Paul J. Gallipeo (POW), S/Sgt. Joseph T. Roman (POW), S/Sgt. Clifford D. Hall (POW), S/Sgt. Howard J. Licht (POW), T/Sgt. Howard W. Marvin (POW).

AUGUST 27, 1943
508th

1st Lt. William J. Suit (KIA), 2nd Lt. James F. Grayson (KIA), 2nd Lt. Bennie H. Bell Jr. (POW), 2nd Lt. Myron L. Johnson (POW), T/Sgt. Alexander B. Noe (POW), T/Sgt. Bertil E. Erickson (Escaped), S/Sgt. Joseph M. May (POW), S/Sgt. Louis A. Lochen (POW), S/Sgt. Lionel D. Mount (KIA).

SEPTEMBER 17, 1943
508th

Cpl. Lester C. Kroeger (Killed in bus accident).

OCTOBER 4, 1943
508th

1st Lt. Theodore W. Reed Jr. (KIA), 2nd Lt. William P. Bourland (POW), Capt. Lawrence P. Stover (POW), 1st Lt. Alex A. Feldstein (KIA), T/Sgt. Donald K. Browne (POW), T/Sgt. Edward A. Spencer (POW), Sgt. Donald S. Ford (POW), S/Sgt. Thaddeus C. Wallace (POW), S/Sgt. Frank Fontana Jr. (KIA), Sgt. John P. Hagan (POW).

511th

1st Lt. Daniel D. Nauman (MIA), 2nd Lt. William R. Keister (MIA), 1st Lt. Walter A. Blair (MIA), S/Sgt. Mario Suozzo (KIA), T/Sgt. Robert F. Martin (MIA), T/Sgt. Roy A. Rush (MIA), S/Sgt. Lewis W. Burgess Jr. (KIA), S/Sgt. Willard O. Hunter (MIA), S/Sgt. Ralph G. Robeson (MIA), S/Sgt. William R. Rowsley (MIA).

OCTOBER 9, 1943
508th

1st Lt. Joseph H. Turley (MIA), 1st Lt. Frank E. Williams (POW), 2nd Lt. Robert W. Coe (MIA), 2nd Lt. Abraham Silverman (KIA), T/Sgt. Theodore P. Curis (POW), T/Sgt. Theodore W. Brantz (KIA), S/Sgt. Raymond A. Hammond (MIA), S/Sgt. Nelson O. Harmon (MIA), Sgt. Alvin L. Jeanes (KIA), S/Sgt. William E. Trask (MIA).

F.O. William H. Warring (POW), 2nd Lt. Howard A. Davis (POW), 2nd Lt. Max Polin (POW), Sgt. David E. Hennis (POW), S/Sgt. Gordon L. Schmitt (POW), S/Sgt. Thomas H. Klimp (POW), S/Sgt. James I. Quillin (POW), Sgt. Virgil V. Summers (POW), Sgt. Victor V. Vlha (POW), S/Sgt. Wyndell H. Killough (KIA).

510th

1st Lt. Lloyd A. Christman (POW), 1st Lt. James D. Laird (POW), 2nd Lt. Eldred E. Hancy (POW), 1st Lt. John J. Hemm (POW), T/Sgt. Commodore I. Sharp (POW), T/Sgt. David D. Pressel (KIA), S/Sgt. James D. White (POW), S/Sgt. William D. Klink (POW), S/Sgt. John R. Butterbach (KIA), S/Sgt. Edmond J. Blais (KIA).

511th

1st Lt. Howard G. Maser (POW), 2nd Lt. Donald L. L'Abbee (POW), 2nd Lt. Morris S. Eagle (POW), Sgt. Howard J. Ferguson (POW), S/Sgt. Everrett L. Sanford (POW), T/Sgt. Paul M. Walsh (POW), S/Sgt. William R. McGee (POW), T/Sgt. Harold R. Crum (POW), S/Sgt. Kenneth W Gorsuch (KIA), S/Sgt. Malvern H. Morgan Jr. (POW).

Capt. Harry B. Morse Jr. (POW), 1st Lt. George V. Nicolescu (POW), Capt. Charles M. Shaw (POW), 1st Lt. Benjamin C. Fincher Jr. (POW), S/Sgt. William J. Doubledee (POW), T/Sgt. George R. Lee (POW), S/Sgt. Joseph E. Hill (POW), T/Sgt. Carl Pettus (POW), S/Sgt. James H. Vander Laan (POW), Sgt. Torrido Marci (POW), S/Sgt. Richard H. Getchell (POW).

OCTOBER 14, 1943
511th

1st Lt. Oliver W. Crismon (POW), 2nd Lt. Malcolm Higgins (POW), 2nd Lt. Walter Moriarity (POW), 2nd Lt. James D. Billett (POW), T/Sgt. Theodore N. Bievi (POW), T/Sgt. Hardy Jones (POW), S/Sgt. Harvey Miller (POW), S/Sgt. Granville R. Brown (KIA), S/Sgt. Ernest W. Chambers (POW), S/Sgt. William C. Pickett Jr. (POW).

NOVEMBER 3, 1943
511th

1st Lt. Elmer J. Nardi (KIA), 2nd Lt. Harold Bergman (KIA), 2nd Lt. Orlyn E. Master (POW), Lt. Bradley E. Squires (POW), T/Sgt. Frank Swica (KIA), T/Sgt. Ganusheau S. Wade (POW), S/Sgt. John J. Yarush

(POW), S/Sgt. Donald D. Happold (POW), S/Sgt. Harlan D. Burton (KIA), S/Sgt. Henry Gates (POW).

NOVEMBER 5, 1943
511th
S/Sgt. George C. Osborn (KIA), Sgt. Edward Lupinski (KIA).

NOVEMBER 26, 1943
508th
2nd Lt. Orville L. Castle (KIA), 2nd Lt. Leon Anderson (KIA), 2nd Lt. Marion R. Cessna (POW), 2nd Lt. Kenneth D. Williams (POW), Sgt. Clinton D. Logan (POW), Sgt. Mike C. Beckett (KIA), Sgt. Lawton Wilkes (Killed as POW), Sgt. Robert L. Cheek Jr. (POW), Sgt. Francis J. Bousquet (POW), S/Sgt. George W. Bond (POW).

511th
S/Sgt. Charles A. Foubert (MIA).

DECEMBER 1, 1943
509th
Capt. Eugene P. Harris (MIA), 2nd Lt. James O'Donoghue (KIA), 1st Lt. Tommy A. Briscoe (KIA), S/Sgt. John J. McLain (KIA), T/Sgt. Charles Tigue (MIA), S/Sgt. Harold R. Mellott (KIA), S/Sgt. Mitchell D. Miles (KIA).

511th
2nd Lt. James M. Plant (POW), 1st Lt. Frederick Smith (POW), 2nd Lt. F. Larson (POW), 2nd Lt. W. Dillard (POW), Sgt. T. F. Harkins (POW), T/Sgt. B. L. Hunter (POW), Sgt. Jakey F. Hobbs (POW), Sgt. J. R. Rowe (POW), Sgt. P. C. O'Neill (POW), S/Sgt. J. W. Hill (POW).

DECEMBER 20, 1943
510th
2nd Lt. Frank A. Gardiner (POW), S/Sgt. Duane E. Albro (POW).

DECEMBER 22, 1943
511th
2nd Lt. James D. McMorrow (MIA), S/Sgt. Docite Nadeau (MIA), S/Sgt. Clarence A. Rowlinson (MIA), Sgt. Edward H. Bucceri (MIA), Sgt. Albert R. Meyer (KIA).

DECEMBER 30, 1943
508th
1st Lt. Roy A. Parsons (POW), 2nd Lt. Henry C. Foster (POW), 2nd Lt. Erwin N. Cooper (KIA), 2nd Lt. Fred W. Ahlheim (POW), S/Sgt. Lloyd W. Wallace (POW), Sgt. Casper J. Maggio (KIA), S/Sgt. Robert B. Mitchell (POW), Sgt. Gene H. Munson (KIA), Sgt. Fred A. Bogar (KIA), Sgt. John J. West (POW).

510th
2nd Lt. Leighton K. Zeiner (KIA), S/Sgt. John G. Bone (KIA), S/Sgt. Dominick N. Ciarfaglia (KIA), S/Sgt. Charles T. Ellman (KIA), Sgt. Grady Fuqua (KIA).

DECEMBER 31, 1943
508th
1st Lt. Willis D. Smith (POW), 2nd Lt. Harlan B. Bixby (POW), 2nd Lt. Richard W. Speers (POW), 1st Lt. William W. White (POW), S/Sgt. John L. Norris (POW), S/Sgt. Stephen J. Badnar (POW), Sgt. Carl W. Linblad (POW), S/Sgt. Clarence J. Begin (POW), S/Sgt. Norman J. St. Peter (POW), S/Sgt. Charles A. Knothe (POW), Sgt. Alton A. Walker (POW) (511th).

510th
1st Lt. Homer B. Wells (POW), 2nd Lt. Frederick G. Pugsley (POW), 2nd Lt. Arnold J. Kline (POW), S/Sgt. Warren G. Maney (POW), S/Sgt. Kenneth D. Cook (POW), T/Sgt. Fred H. Wright (POW), S/Sgt. Charles M. Brown (POW), Sgt. Glenn L. Gienau (POW), Sgt. Earnest G. Balsis (POW), Sgt. Newlin R. Happersett (POW).

1st Lt. Marvin H. Bender (POW), 2nd Lt. William J. Grupp (POW), 2nd Lt. Harold O. Freeman (Escaped), 2nd Lt. Robert B. Wilcox (Escaped), S/Sgt. Francis E. Anderson (Escaped), Sgt. Francis W. Rollins (POW), S/Sgt. Harold F. Long (POW), Sgt. Veikko J. Koski (POW), S/Sgt. Levi H. Collins (POW), S/Sgt. Lawrence R. Anderson (POW).

1st Lt. Ralph M. Saville (Escaped), 2nd Lt. William E. Playford (Escaped), 1st Lt. Raymond E. Light Jr. (POW), 2nd Lt. Alphonse J. Elsaesser (POW), T/Sgt. Gilbert L. Morris (Escaped), T/Sgt. George R. Leonard (Escaped), S/Sgt. George F. Kelley Jr. (Escaped), Sgt. Sidney C. Pulver (POW), S/Sgt. John R. Myrick (Escaped), S/Sgt. Irvin Gassaway (Escaped).

Major John R. Blaylock (KIA), Col. William A. Hatcher Jr. (POW), Capt. Jack E. Danby (POW), 2nd

Lt. James A. Taylor (KIA), Capt. John W. Smith (POW), S/Sgt. William S. Maupin Jr. (POW), T/Sgt. Edward C. Kase (POW), T/Sgt. Adam J. Fischer (POW), T/Sgt. Roger Blaser (POW), S/Sgt. Joseph R. Quiles (POW), Capt. Edward C. Boykin Jr. (KIA).

511th
1st Lt. Albert E. Jones (MIA), 2nd Lt. Kenneth L. Vaughan (POW), 2nd Lt. Alfred L. Dearborn (MIA), 2nd Lt. Charles A. Bronako (POW), S/Sgt. David H. Van Dyke (MIA), S/Sgt. William J. Brennan (KIA), S/Sgt. Casimir Pavlic (MIA), Sgt. Michael T. Morey (KIA), Sgt. Carl Q. Bekken (KIA), Sgt. Raymond F. Bittner (MIA).

2nd Lt. Warren L. Putman (KIA), F.O. Thomas A. Irvine (KIA), 2nd Lt. Irving J. Shwayder (Escaped), 2nd Lt. Jack R. Wood (POW), Sgt. Ray E. Pratre (KIA), S/Sgt. Wesley F. Greene (POW), Sgt. John J. Gilson (POW), Sgt. Robert O. Diehl (POW), Sgt. Albert R. Custer (KIA), Sgt. Jack D. McKinney (POW).

JANUARY 7, 1944
511th
1st Lt. Harvey J. Anderson (KIA), 2nd Lt. Douglas E. Webb (KIA), 2nd Lt. William H. Udick (KIA), S/Sgt. Richard J. Allen (KIA), S/Sgt. Frank H. McNamara (KIA), S/Sgt. Leonard Edwards (KIA).

JANUARY 11, 1944
508th
1st Lt. Thomas D. Garner (POW), 2nd Lt. Edward R. Hodgson (POW), 2nd Lt. Tony Diprima (POW), 2nd Lt. Albert F. La Shier (POW), S/Sgt. Victor B. Pyles (POW), S/Sgt. Bruce W. Warden (POW), Sgt. Keith S. Cummins (POW), Sgt. William O. Hefferman Jr. (POW), Sgt. Erwin G. Huggett (KIA), S/Sgt. Ralph C. Foster (KIA).

509th
1st Lt. Harold C. Cannon (POW), 2nd Lt. John E. May (POW), 2nd Lt. George M. Farrell (POW), 2nd Lt. Robert H. Wood (POW), T/Sgt. James B. Ball (POW), T/Sgt. Paul Kallas (POW), S/Sgt. Richard W. Emmick (POW), S/Sgt. Wayne A. Kittilson (POW), S/Sgt. Manuel Trujillo (POW), S/Sgt. Robert Broadsky (POW).

2nd Lt. William H. Myers (KIA), 2nd Lt. John B. Hart Jr. (KIA), 2nd Lt. William F. Carmichael (POW), 2nd Lt. Arthur M. Jones Jr. (MIA), T/Sgt. Clyde M. Caudle (MIA), T/Sgt. Lavern W. Sherman (KIA), Sgt. William N. Bloshko (POW), Sgt. Herbert H. Bivens (POW), Sgt. John S. Ricci (KIA), Sgt. James W. Mansfield (KIA).

510th
1st Lt. George J. Procak (POW), 2nd Lt. George B. Neely (POW), 2nd Lt. Jerrold S. Trumbower (POW), 2nd Lt. James P. Keating (POW), S/Sgt. John J. Cipriano (POW), T/Sgt. Saul E. Susman (POW), Sgt. Peter J. Goinvic (POW), Sgt. Eugene R. Chelstowski (POW), S/Sgt. Otis L. Williams (POW), S/Sgt. E. T. Burgess Jr. (KIA).

1st Lt. Richard J. Case (POW), 1st Lt. George E. Smith (POW), 2nd Lt. Edward P. Jackson (POW), 1st Lt. David L. Steed (POW), T/Sgt. Donald L. Hansen (POW), Sgt. James Wiersma (POW), S/Sgt. Harry G. Simmons Jr. (POW), S/Sgt. Harold J. Peters (POW), S/Sgt. David W. Flanzbaum (POW), S/Sgt. Raymond E. Howard (KIA).

511th
2nd Lt. Thompson E. White (POW), 2nd Lt. Valleau Wilkie Jr. (POW), 2nd Lt. Fred Warren Jr. (POW), T/Sgt. Peter A. Soderling (POW), Sgt. Clyde L. Mellen (POW), S/Sgt. Harry D. Dratz (Escaped), Sgt. Norman Elkin (Escaped), Sgt. John E. Watson (POW), Sgt. Walter R. Snyder (Escaped), Sgt. Hyman A. Hitow (POW).

JANUARY 29, 1944
508th
T/Sgt. James T. McQuaid (Killed when exiting the A/C to close front hatch and ran into the propeller).

JANUARY 30, 1944
511th
1st Lt. Charles E. Robertson (POW), 2nd Lt. Robert P. Robbins (POW), 2nd Lt. Milton J. Kaplan (POW), F.O. Earl E. Holmes (POW), T/Sgt. Henry L. James (POW), T/Sgt. William R. Delaney (POW), S/Sgt. Norris R. Stewart (POW), S/Sgt. Emil F. Ambrose (POW), Sgt. Lloyde M. Gabriel (POW), S/Sgt. Earl W. Winburn (POW).

FEBRUARY 3, 1944
510th
T/Sgt. Vernon R. Schnuelle (KIA).

FEBRUARY 11, 1944
508th
Sgt. Stanley A. Sokolowski (Escaped).

509th

Capt. John P. Carson Jr. (POW), 2nd Lt. Merlyn Rutherford (Escaped), 2nd Lt. Henry M. Heldmann (Escaped), 2nd Lt. William H. Spinning (Escaped), T/Sgt. Joseph R. Haywood (Escaped), T/Sgt. John Landers (Escaped), S/Sgt. Richard C. Howard (KIA), S/Sgt. James W. Riley (POW).

FEBRUARY 12, 1944
511th

2nd Lt. John A. McCall (Died of wounds).

FEBRUARY 20, 1944
510th

2nd Lt. Clarence R. Nelson (KIA), F.O. Ronald Bartley (KIA), 2nd Lt. Walter E. Truemper (KIA), 2nd Lt. Joseph R. Martin (POW), S/Sgt. Archie Mathies (KIA).

FEBRUARY 21, 1944
508th

2nd Lt. William J. Armour (MIA), S/Sgt. Wesley Locke (MIA), S/Sgt. William F. Speiser (MIA), 2nd Lt. Carey D. Haynes (KIA), S/Sgt. Gilbert L. Denison (KIA).

509th

T/Sgt. Norman F. Ballard (KIA).

FEBRUARY 22, 1944
510th

2nd Lt. William H. Ritzema (POW), 2nd Lt. Paul Straw (POW), 2nd Lt. Robert V. Shuss (POW), 2nd Lt. Lorin A. Wolfe (POW), S/Sgt. Richard H. Stewart (POW), Sgt. Frank J. De Marco (KIA), Sgt. John Zundel (POW), Sgt. Octavio A. Duran (POW), Sgt. William H. Leach (POW), Sgt. Donald C. Pearson (POW), 2nd Lt. John R. Jonaitis (KIA), 2nd Lt. David J. Van de Walle (KIA).

511th

2nd Lt. John H. Pugh (POW), 2nd Lt. Robert M. Hart (POW), 2nd Lt. William J. Schmitz (POW), 2nd Lt Richard J. Gilbert (POW), Sgt. Ralph D. Priode (POW), Sgt. John W. Sauer (POW), Sgt. Nicholas Mustacchia (POW), S/Sgt. Adam W. Quinn (POW), Sgt. Isaac G. Guest (POW), Sgt. Carter Gibson (POW).

FEBRUARY 24, 1944
508th

1st Lt. Richard B. Caughman (Returned), 2nd Lt. John V. Boehm (POW), 1st Lt. John B. Avel (Escaped), 1st Lt. Richard E. S. Perkins (POW), S/Sgt. Eugene C. Strassburger (KIA), T/Sgt. John C. Mattilia (Returned), S/Sgt. Howard M. Langer (POW), S/Sgt. Eugene A. Colburn (Returned), S/Sgt. Paul B. Young (Returned), Sgt. James W. McGinty (Escaped).

511th

2nd Lt. Walter B. LeClerc (POW), 2nd Lt. James W. Ellis (POW), 2nd Lt. George T. Kilduff (POW), 2nd Lt. Arthur W. Starratt (POW), S/Sgt. Ralph A. Grooms (POW), S/Sgt. Bruce M. Stone (POW), Sgt. Archie L. Stinebaugh (POW), Sgt. John L. Taylor (POW), Sgt. Howard W. Kramer (POW), Sgt. Harold H. Hay (POW).

MARCH 2, 1944
508th

1st Lt. Robert A. Seaman (Escaped), 2nd Lt. Don D. Fowler (POW), 2nd Lt. Stanley R. Danheiser (POW), 2nd Lt. John R. Griffith (POW), T/Sgt. William W. Nolan (POW), T/Sgt. William J. Pappas (POW), S/Sgt. Charlie S. Fouzie (POW), S/Sgt. Henry J. Annucci (POW), S/Sgt. Clifford H. Allen (POW), S/Sgt. Frank E. Burchinal Jr. (POW), S/Sgt. Carthal B. Carver (KIA).

MARCH 6, 1944
511th

Sgt. Robert K. Wood (KIA).

MARCH 18, 1944
509th

1st Lt. Walter R. Illies (KIA), 2nd Lt. John G. Breland (KIA), 2nd Lt. Richard Perle (POW), 2nd Lt. Robert W. Casper (POW), T/Sgt. Robert D. Vaughn (KIA), T/Sgt. Albert J. Jacques (KIA), S/Sgt. William H. Brown (POW), S/Sgt. Robbie R. Alexander (KIA), S/Sgt. Arthur C. Briggs (KIA), S/Sgt. Merle W. Thompson (POW), S/Sgt. Garland M. Childers (KIA).

1st Lt. Raymond E. Neuberg (POW), 2nd Lt. Robert E. Swenson (KIA), 2nd Lt. Charles L. Finkelstein (KIA), 2nd Lt. William A. Manley (KIA), T/Sgt. Earl R. Sharp (POW), T/Sgt. Ira Houk (POW), S/Sgt. David W. Eckes (KIA), S/Sgt. Lewis A. Lowans (KIA), S/Sgt. Robert Workman (POW), S/Sgt. Neal M. Quigley (POW).

511th

2nd Lt. Paul Martin (KIA), 2nd Lt. John H. Sinnott (KIA), 2nd Lt. Guy A. Lightfoot Jr. (KIA), 2nd Lt.

Frederick R. DeRoever (POW), M/Sgt. George A. Lesko (KIA), S/Sgt. Michael Vargo (KIA), Sgt. Charles Glebus (KIA), Sgt. Charles E. Meyer (KIA), Sgt. Sterling B. Vermillion (KIA), Sgt. Fred C. Saucedo (KIA).

1st Lt. George W. Mears, 1st Lt. Russell E. Ward, 1st Lt. James D. Mahaffey, 1st Lt. Richard L. David, T/Sgt. Samuel R. Simms, T/Sgt. Richard D. Hobt, S/Sgt. Earl R. Echstenkamper, S/Sgt. John B. Lucas Jr., S/Sgt. Caleb B. Hurst, Sgt. Frank L. Selover (The crew landed in Switzerland; all interned).

MARCH 22, 1944
508th
2nd Lt. Wyman C. Slosson (KIA), 2nd Lt. David A. Smithline (POW), 2nd Lt. Joseph W. Daugherty (POW), 2nd Lt. James P. Higgins (POW), S/Sgt. James R. Green (POW), S/Sgt. Edward T. DeMattos (POW), Sgt. Verlyn G. Brown (POW), Sgt. Emette Highland (POW), Sgt. Ronald W. Power (POW), Sgt. Warren M. Beahr (POW).

APRIL 11, 1944
510th
S/Sgt. Claude L. Atkins Jr. (KIA)

APRIL 13, 1944
509th
2nd Lt. Gilbert W. Whitchurch (POW), 2nd Lt. Eugene Sylvester (POW), 2nd Lt. Newton C. Wilbur (POW), 2nd Lt. Richard M. Cox (KIA), S/Sgt. Frederick W. Gowen (POW), Sgt. Andrew Boyarko Jr. (POW), Sgt. Frederick R. Vester (POW), Sgt. Maurice W. Turner (POW), Sgt. Donal F. Luse Jr. (POW), Sgt. Robert Mondragon (POW).

APRIL 18, 1944
508th
1st Lt. Edward B. Apperson (POW), 2nd Lt. John P. Ledyard (POW), 1st Lt. William E. Connors Jr. (POW), 2nd Lt. Hal Marsh (POW), T/Sgt. David R. Gaitskill (POW), T/Sgt. Donald E. Johnson (POW), T/Sgt. Laurence J. Kulsluch (POW), S/Sgt. Bernard L. Mandella (POW), S/Sgt. Raymond E. Bailey (POW), S/Sgt. Charles E. Matthews (KIA).

APRIL 22, 1944
351st HQ
Capt. William A. Winter

510th
2nd Lt. Chester B. Montgomery

511th
T/Sgt. William S. Manley

11th Station Complement
Sgt. Albert T. Brooks
(All killed in aircraft crash while on practice mission).

MAY 7, 1944
510th
2nd Lt. Robert G. Presley (POW), 2nd Lt. Nixon C. Stamper (POW), 2nd Lt. James W. Simpson (POW), 2nd Lt. Herbert J. Mosebach (POW), S/Sgt. Ernest E. Cocco (POW), S/Sgt. Robert W. Kleeman (POW), Sgt. Kenneth L. Mellon (POW), Sgt. Alex Warcola (POW), Sgt. Fred J. Van Sant (POW), Sgt. Isaac W. Robertson (POW).

MAY 23, 1944
508th
1st Lt. Peter E. Crowe (KIA), 1st Lt. Norris N. Nelson (KIA), 2nd Lt. Robert A. Russeth (KIA), 1st Lt. Frank Rubin (KIA), T/Sgt. Gerald W. Fiebelkorn (KIA), S/Sgt. Frank T. Lopez (KIA).

MAY 24, 1944
509th
Capt. Robert B. Clay (POW), 1st Lt. Frank Hatten (POW), 1st Lt. Marshall R. Pullen (POW), 1st Lt. George W. Arnold (POW), T/Sgt. Charles B. Hilcott (POW), T/Sgt. Frank W. Belsinger (POW), S/Sgt. Daniel H. Surprise (POW), S/Sgt. Franklin L. Travis (POW), S/Sgt. Michael De'Marie (POW), 1st Lt. James H. Wimmer (POW).

MAY 27, 1944
508th
1st Lt. Edgar F. Sengstock (POW), 2nd Lt. Harold D. Emerson (KIA), 2nd Lt. Robert E. Fitzpatrick (POW), 2nd Lt. Wilfred W. Kirby (POW), S/Sgt. Robert J. Sahulcik (POW), S/Sgt. Ralph T. Green (POW), S/Sgt. Robert W. Wenzloff (KIA), S/Sgt. John M. Kilby (POW), S/Sgt. Oliver R. Weatherholt (POW).

1st Lt. Gosta Johnson (POW), 2nd Lt. Herbert C. Neumann (POW), 2nd Lt. Robert A. Schmidt (POW), 2nd Lt. Samuel Rosenberg (POW), T/Sgt. John Anderson (POW), S/Sgt. Joseph R. Smith (POW), S/Sgt. Edward V. Kolling (POW), S/Sgt. Johnnie A. De Hart (POW), S/Sgt. Richard S. Drews (POW).

1st Lt. Howard R. Evans (POW), 2nd Lt. James J. Duffy (POW), 2nd Lt. Joseph P. Norton

(KIA), 1st Lt. Roger W. Peterson (POW), S/Sgt. Donald G. Kopf (KIA), S/Sgt. Glen E. Joiner (MIA), T/Sgt. Ronald C. Pope (MIA), Sgt. Jack W. Honsowetz (MIA), S/Sgt. Stephen Kovacs (KIA).

509th
1st Lt. Tedfred E. Myers (POW), 2nd Lt. Clarence A. Butrum (POW), 2nd Lt. Henry M. Roszyk (POW), 2nd Lt. Vernon N. Naas (POW), T/Sgt. Walter C. Stanford (POW), T/Sgt. Edwin S. Draper (POW), S/Sgt. Woodrow W. Blackburn (POW), S/Sgt. William J. Mansmann (POW), S/Sgt. Avon Roysden (POW), S/Sgt. John M. Denton (POW).

510th
1st Lt. Horace E. Hopkins (KIA), 2nd Lt. Everett M. Hale (KIA), 2nd Lt. Carl W. Habecker (KIA), T/Sgt. Dwight E. Suddock (POW), T/Sgt. Richard J. Atwood (KIA), T/Sgt. William R. Stroh (Returned), S/Sgt. Avondel L. Willhite (KIA), T/Sgt. Lyle A. Norquist (KIA), S/Sgt. Samuel A. Snyder (KIA), S/Sgt. Norman J. Bruning (KIA).

1st Lt. Harold M. Peters, 2nd Lt. Honor G. Windes, 1st Lt. Richard G. Miller, 1st Lt. Ferris S. Martin, T/Sgt. William O. Konkell, T/Sgt. Vee L. Taylor, S/Sgt. Willie Vandeberg, S/Sgt. Raymond J. King, S/Sgt. Walter T. Gilliam, S/Sgt. Reed L. Moulton (All interned, landed in Switzerland).

MAY 28, 1944
508th
2nd Lt. William J. Condon (KIA), 2nd Lt. Joseph P. Kolceski (KIA), 2nd Lt. Laddie J. Zindar (KIA), 2nd Lt. Edwin S. Onken (POW), Sgt. John J. Jackson (POW), S/Sgt. William H. Morris (POW), Sgt. Charles G. Jenkins (KIA), Sgt. Harry M. Norris (KIA), S/Sgt. Junny O. Jackson (KIA).

510th
2nd Lt. Charles F. Anderson (POW), F.O. Robert L. McFetridge (POW), 2nd Lt. Robert E. Ryan (POW), 2nd Lt. William H. Baird (POW), Sgt. Neal W. William (POW), S/Sgt. Casper Vecchione (POW), S/Sgt. Bernard J. Matzke (POW), Sgt. George P. Nitzberg (POW), Sgt. Edward E. Vanhorn (POW).

1st Lt. Clyde McClelland (POW), 1st Lt. Richard E. Francis (POW), 1st Lt. John B. Duncan (POW), 1st Lt. George F. Kiely (POW), T/Sgt. Louis E. Poole (POW), T/Sgt. Leonard J. Kriesky (POW), S/Sgt. Junior H. Edwards (POW), S/Sgt. Nathan L. William (POW), S/Sgt. Leroy D. Cruse (KIA).

511th
2nd Lt. Carl F. Miller (KIA), 2nd Lt. Maurice G. Fikes (POW), 2nd Lt. Russell A. Brown (POW), S/Sgt. Ernest A. Lemcke (POW), T/Sgt. Frank Avry (POW), T/Sgt. James D. McCann (POW), Sgt. Albert L. Lien (POW), Sgt. Anthony J. Bushlow (POW), S/Sgt. Isador P. Kaplowitz (KIA), S/Sgt. George A. Stafford (POW).

F.O. Robert E. L. Probasco (POW), 2nd Lt. Stephen B. Lewellyn (POW), 2nd Lt. William P. Bragg (POW), 2nd Lt. Bruno Branch (POW), S/Sgt. Herman T. Ulreich (POW), S/Sgt. Arlie W. Moore (KIA), Sgt. Raymond G. Seaman (KIA), Sgt. Edward J. Frankowski (POW), Sgt. Norman W. Ringstmeyer (KIA), Sgt. James D. Singleton (POW).

MAY 30, 1944
509th
2nd Lt. Crawford E. Hicks (POW), 2nd Lt. Eugene J. Bianco (POW), 2nd Lt. Hardy A. Mitchener (POW), 2nd Lt. Lester L. Kunz (KIA), S/Sgt. Francis E. Young (POW), S/Sgt. Ulis C. Briggs (POW), Sgt. Lowell A. Reid (POW), Sgt. Marvin R. Allen (POW), Sgt. Stephen N. Vasilik (POW), Sgt. Kenneth E. Geldermann (POW).

JUNE 12, 1944
509th
Sgt. Norbert E. Berendsen (KIA), Sgt. Leo C. Hamilton (KIA).

JUNE 14, 1944
508th
1st Lt. Joseph R. Dixey Jr. (Returned), Capt. James R. Lowery Jr. (Returned), 2nd Lt. Robert C. Shafer (Died of wounds as POW), 1st Lt. Thomas E. Trolinger (POW), T/Sgt. Robert E. McCullough (POW), S/Sgt. Donald L. Kemohah (POW), S/Sgt. Joe Barnes (POW), Sgt. Arthur B. Gross (POW), T/Sgt. Donald V. Henderson (KIA), S/Sgt. John W. Offutt (POW).

510th
1st Lt. Augustus J. Cesarini (KIA), 2nd Lt. Frank G. Ludwig (POW), 2nd Lt. George B. Reineke (POW), S/Sgt. Frederick J. Hale (Escaped), Sgt. Tuttle E. Pardue Jr. (POW), S/Sgt. George Walter (POW), S/Sgt. Robert C. Lageman (POW), Sgt. Fred W. Nicklas (POW), Sgt. Joe C. Gholston (POW), Sgt. John J. Kulak (POW).

2nd Lt. George L. Williamson Jr. (POW), 2ndLt. Roland A. Cadoret (POW), 2nd Lt. Ashley A. Thornburg (POW), 2nd Lt. William L. Clanton (POW), S/Sgt. Eugene L. Leavitt (POW), S/Sgt. Robert G. Whitman (POW), S/Sgt. Walter R. Subora (POW), Sgt. Joseph H. La Rocco (POW), Sgt. Robert G. Mautz (POW), Sgt. Charles K. Hock (POW).

JUNE 21, 1944
509th
2nd Lt. Jerry C. Walters, 2nd Lt. Lester R. Driggers, 2nd Lt. John Kowalski, 2nd Lt. George Black, S/Sgt. Lewis S. Freedman, S/Sgt. William A. Oliver, Sgt. Leon T. Sanford, Sgt. Martin J. O'Malley, Sgt. Theodore E. Duggan, Sgt. Michael Marchese (All interned, landed Sweden).

2nd Lt. Douglas F. Raymond (POW), S/Sgt. James H. Harris (POW), S/Sgt. Donald G. Miles (POW), Sgt. Levi M. Pratt (POW), Sgt. Hopper E. Biddle (POW), Sgt. David M. Harman (POW), Sgt. Verlyn T. Kveen (POW).

JUNE 22, 1944
509th
1st Lt. Robert T. Watkins (POW), 2nd Lt. Frank D. Williams (POW), 2nd Lt. Douglas J. Sier (POW), 2nd Lt. Ralph E. Hoover (POW), T/Sgt. Earl H. Louiso (POW), T/Sgt. Isadore Traschen (Returned), S/Sgt. Leonard E. Kleinjan (POW), S/Sgt. Thomas F. LaGrua (Returned), S/Sgt. Ralph L. Futhey (Returned).

JULY 12, 1944
510th
2nd Lt. Samuel F. Irwin (POW), 2nd Lt. Brian L. DeVan (POW), F.O. Eugene T. Pulliam (KIA), 2nd Lt. Samuel W. Herman (KIA), S/Sgt. Zolton P. Torok (KIA), S/Sgt. Ira W. Hughes (POW), Sgt. David R. Strawn (KIA), Sgt. Charles R. Miller (KIA), Sgt. Dick L. Franklin (POW).

JULY 13, 1944
511th
2nd Lt. Cleo D. Aldrege (POW), 2nd Lt. Donovan L. Hart (POW), 2nd Lt. Stanley B. Cressey (POW), 2nd Lt. Glenn C. Ballantyne (POW), Sgt. Frank B. Knapp (POW), S/Sgt. Thomas T. Marshall Jr. (POW), Sgt. Don H. Gristmasher (POW), Sgt. Carl A. Irwin (POW), Sgt. Arthur B. Bevier (POW).

JULY 19, 1944
508th
1st Lt. Herbert C. Konecheck (KIA), 2nd Lt. Barrett A. Levinsky (KIA), 2nd Lt. Joseph C. DiFranks (KIA), Sgt. Kenneth W. Landstrom (POW), S/Sgt. Charles L. Wiles (POW), S/Sgt. Guerine P. Lostocco (KIA), Sgt. Philip W. Hersey (KIA), S/Sgt. James C. Ocamb (KIA), S/Sgt. Max S. Hainert (KIA).

510th
2nd Lt. Richard G. Chapman (POW), 2nd Lt. William C. Arther Jr. (KIA), 2nd Lt. Lewis A. Page Jr. (POW), S/Sgt. Kenneth L. Graham (POW), S/Sgt. Earl H. Russell (POW), Sgt. Albert E. Binsfield (POW), Sgt. Harry C. Hoff (KIA), Sgt. James T. Laverty Jr. (KIA), Sgt. Oscar D. Kemp (KIA).

JULY 28, 1944
508th
Sgt. Gleen C. Owen (KIA).

511th
1st Lt. William P. Long (POW), 2nd Lt. Benjamin E. Upshaw (POW), 2nd Lt. Peter Mandros Jr. (KIA), F.O. Charles C. Gratiot (KIA), T/Sgt. Jack C. Hurley (POW), T/Sgt. Donald G. Skoglund (POW), Sgt. Carmelo J. Frontino (POW), S/Sgt. Frank Gozy (POW), S/Sgt. James H. Howarth (POW).

JULY 29, 1944
510th
2nd Lt. Thomas V. Gumaer (KIA).

511th
2nd Lt. John M. Morton (KIA), 2nd Lt. Warren J. Bragdon (KIA), 2nd Lt. William J. Fuerth (KIA), 2nd Lt. McCaleb D. Taylor (KIA), T/Sgt. James E. Ellis (KIA), S/Sgt. Maurice J. Franzblau (KIA), Sgt. Clarence B. McGuire (KIA), Sgt. Fenton D. Strohmeyer (KIA), Sgt. Guido Signoretti (KIA).

AUGUST 3, 1944
511th
1st Lt. Ralph S. Brackens (POW), 2nd Lt. William M. Beals (POW), 2nd Lt. Daniel W. Moseley (POW), 2nd Lt. George O. Cobb (POW), S/Sgt. William F. Williamson (POW), S/Sgt. Billy M. Hardesty (POW), Sgt. George A. McCrary (POW), Sgt. Robert F. Mattice (POW), S/Sgt. James O. Atkins (POW).

AUGUST 6, 1944
508th

1st Lt. Paul F. Pattison (POW), 2nd Lt. Francis H. Parker (POW), 1st Lt. Leonard B. Roberts (KIA), 2nd Lt. Roland H. Chamberlain (KIA), T/Sgt. Clyde U. Bullock (POW), S/Sgt. Winfred O. Riemer (POW), Sgt. John R. Smith (POW), Sgt. Frank L. Espinoza (POW), Sgt. Clarence A. Bessanson (POW).

2nd Lt. William M. Petty Jr., 2nd Lt. James B. Coman, F.O. Floyd L. Buzzi, 2nd Lt. Donald W. Becker, S/Sgt. Thomas Dimbro, S/Sgt. Lawrence A. Prater, Sgt. Edward Leikam, Sgt. Vincent J. Doyle, Sgt. Parry J. Boogard (All interned, landed Sweden).

511th

2nd Lt. William M. Boyd Jr. (KIA), 2nd Lt. Chester J. Snyder (KIA), 2nd Lt. Arthur K. Marsden (POW), 2nd Lt. Donald R. Wassner (POW), S/Sgt. William F. Kames (POW), S/Sgt. Max K. Thompson Jr. (KIA), Sgt. Edward W. Handel (POW), Sgt. Malcolm L. Keams (KIA), Sgt. Edward E. Gavin (POW).

1st Lt. Wilson R. Strange (KIA), 2nd Lt. George J. Pappas (POW), F.O. Frank E. Booth (KIA), F.O. Otis G. Smith (POW), T/Sgt. Kenneth F. Barlow (POW), S/Sgt. Ross J. Morell (POW), Sgt. Edward J. Prokop (KIA), Sgt. Lionel S. Zeigler (POW), Sgt. Donald B. Killoran (POW).

1st Lt. George W. Uttley Jr. (KIA), 2nd Lt. Charles W. Hayes (KIA), 2nd Lt. Milton A. Sheir (POW), 2nd Lt. James Ralston Jr. (KIA), S/Sgt. Cecil F. Badgett (KIA), S/Sgt. Alvin Bernstein (POW), Sgt. William T. Saunders (KIA), Sgt. Joe Garza (KIA), Sgt. Marion C. Coverdale (KIA).

2nd Lt. Jerome E. Barieau Jr. (POW), 2nd Lt. Donald C. Wilson (POW), 1st Lt. Walter A. Wall (POW), F.O. Morris H. Clifton (POW), S/Sgt. George L. Weaver (POW), S/Sgt. Harry F. Wilson (POW), T/Sgt. Kenneth C. Law (KIA), Sgt. Albert A. Levy Jr. (POW), Sgt. John Mazur (POW).

2nd Lt. William G. Rohrbacher (POW), 1st Lt. Paul A. Tuerck (POW), 2nd Lt. Virgil E. Carneal Jr. (POW), 2nd Lt. Ellis C. Thompkins (POW), Sgt. Nicholas Marcinizyn (POW), F.O. Vernon E. Smith (POW).

AUGUST 9, 1944
511th

1st Lt. Anthony J. Zotollo (POW), 1st Lt. Robert L. Lawsen (POW), 1st Lt. John E. Rowan (POW), 1st Lt. Joseph Loiacono (POW), T/Sgt. Leonard L. Barton (Returned), T/Sgt. Edwin West (Returned), S/Sgt. Louis L. Cohen (POW), Sgt. Bernard F. Calderbank (POW), S/Sgt. Henry J. Fiengo (POW), S/Sgt. Claudius E. Carter (Returned), 1st Lt. Wayne W. Livesay (POW), S/Sgt. Clair L. Miller (POW).

T/Sgt. Lester W. McClure (MIA), S/Sgt. Merton H. Rasmussen (MIA).

AUGUST 16, 1944
508th

2nd Lt. Edgar D. Cartwright (POW), 2nd Lt. Robert C. Schwartz (KIA), F.O. Joseph T. Gerhardt (POW), 2nd Lt. William R. Chauncey Jr. (KIA), S/Sgt. Eugene D. Moss (POW), S/Sgt. Garlan R. Gillespie (POW), Sgt. Raymond F. Newbauer (POW), Sgt. George R. Greenmyre (POW), Sgt. George W. Light (POW).

SEPTEMBER 5, 1944
508th

1st Lt. William G. Wright (KIA), 2nd Lt. Robert A. Swanson (KIA), 2nd Lt. John S. Swanson (KIA), 2nd Lt. Rollins O. Mahony Jr. (POW), S/Sgt. Andrew H. Bender (KIA), Sgt. Leory O. Thomas (KIA), Sgt. Dick O. Hopper (KIA), Sgt. George F. Anello (POW), Sgt. Lewis L. Cain (KIA).

510th

2nd Lt. George W. Shera Jr. (POW), 2nd Lt. Leroy A. Swetnam (POW), F.O. Stephen G. Loverds (POW), F.O. Richard M. Mason (POW), S/Sgt. Dewey A. Cooper Jr. (KIA), S/Sgt. Wallace J. Van Wirt (KIA), Sgt. Robert W. Hagans (POW), Sgt. Edward C. Jancsak (KIA), Sgt. Don W. Freeman (Returned).

511th

2nd Lt. John C. Haba (KIA), 2nd Lt. Clinton M. Cavett (KIA), 2nd Lt. Eugene J. Hooks (KIA), 2nd Lt. Robert A. McGlohon (KIA), S/Sgt. Ernest J. Clinton (KIA), S/Sgt. James S. Singleton (KIA), Sgt. Roy A. Morrison (KIA), Sgt. Raymond T. McCloskey (KIA).

SEPTEMBER 12, 1944
510th

1st Lt. Edward J. Hennegan (POW), 2nd Lt. George H. Avaritt (POW), 2nd Lt. Walter M. Culbert (POW), 2nd Lt. Eugene C. Saur (POW), Sgt. Karl W. Buschenfeldt (Died of wounds in POW Camp), S/Sgt. James C. Waters (POW), S/Sgt. John H.

Strick (POW), Sgt. Emmett F. Bennett (POW), S/Sgt. Clair I. Carl (KIA).

511th
2nd Lt. Charles C. Schoenian (POW), 2nd Lt. Lovick C. Miller (POW), 2nd Lt. Robert D. Munn (POW), 2nd Lt. John M. Watson (POW), Sgt. Robert F. Beavers (POW), Sgt. Jesse J. Austin Jr. (KIA), Sgt. Joseph C. Lohneis (KIA), Sgt. Anthony R. Cappdona (KIA), Sgt. William W. Anderson (POW).

2nd Lt. Claude T. Adams (POW), 2nd Lt. George R. Holden (POW), 2nd Lt. Anthony J. Nardone (POW), 2nd Lt. Carl M. Kennedy (POW), S/Sgt. Robert M. Hayes (POW), S/Sgt. Herbert O. Goldstein (POW), Sgt. Anthony P. Salerno (POW), Sgt. Charles P. Belmonte (POW), S/Sgt. Gus Siciliano Jr. (POW).

2nd Lt. James R. Brown (POW), 2nd Lt. Andrew C. Hess (KIA), 2nd Lt. Ernest G. Ornett (POW), 2nd Lt. John Rasko (POW), Sgt. Lawrence R. Wester (POW), Sgt. Louis Katko (KIA), Sgt. Leon H. Cinq-Mars (KIA), Sgt. Ralph J. DeDomenico (KIA), S/Sgt. William H. Wilmut (KIA).

2nd Lt. Robert C. Lopert (POW), 2nd Lt. Darwin R. Nichols (KIA), 2nd Lt. Fred R. Dahl Jr. (KIA), 2nd Lt. Charles L. Surges (POW), Sgt. Albert M. Sandlin (POW), Sgt. Alton W. Dreyer (POW), Sgt. Jesse Coa (POW), Sgt. Paul Pomeraux (POW), Sgt. Lawrence F. Goodman (POW).

2nd Lt. William F. Schmollinger (POW), 2nd Lt. Allen M. Meyers (POW), 2nd Lt. Charles I. Mason (POW), 2nd Lt. Melvin W. Steffes (POW), Sgt. Albert R. Preston Jr. (POW), Sgt. William M. Ohde Jr. (POW), Sgt. Fred H. Dingler (POW), Sgt. Ermilo P. Flores (POW), Sgt. Marvin F. Ketcherside (POW).

SEPTEMBER 27, 1944
508th
Sgt. Kenneth D. Divil (KIA).

509th
Sgt. Dwight L. Gryder (Died of wounds).

511th
Sgt. John J. Kurtz (POW).

OCTOBER 3, 1944
508th
S/Sgt. Edward J. Karolewics (KIA).

511th
1st Lt. Charles E. Cregar Jr. (POW), 2nd Lt. Sanford N. Groendyke (POW), F.O. James D. Timmie Jr. (POW), 1st Lt. John F. Dwyer (KIA), T/Sgt. Edward L. Huth (POW), S/Sgt. Elwood A. Zigenfus (POW), S/Sgt. Cecil C. McWhorter (POW), S/Sgt. Charles E. Weller (POW), S/Sgt. Thomas W. Richardson (POW).

OCTOBER 7, 1944
508th
Sgt. Bob A. Baillio (KIA).

509th
1st Lt. Einer Petersen (KIA), 2nd Lt. Duane A. Wilson (KIA), 2nd Lt. Benjamin F. Christensen (KIA), F.O. William F. Rooney (KIA), Sgt. Louis R. Candelaria (KIA), Sgt. Lawrence E. Jensen (Returned), Sgt. Robert W. Crawford (KIA), Sgt. J. K. Blake Jr. (KIA), Sgt. Lloyd G. Best (Returned).

1st Lt. Arthur Bartzocas, Lt. Col. Benoid E. Glawe, 1st Lt. Seymore R. Levinson, 2nd Lt. Lloyd H. Kline, T/Sgt. Louis W. Walters, T/Sgt. Joseph Massara, S/Sgt. Paul E. Waxler, 1st Lt. Thomas W. Clarke, 2nd Lt. Albert Pollyea, 2nd Lt. Carlton E. Mendell (All interned, landed in Sweden).

2nd Lt. David R. McGuire, 2nd Lt. Alfred K. Simpson Jr., 2nd Lt. Carl J. Thompson, 2nd Lt. George R. Storms, Sgt. Andrew Messaros, Sgt. Mason G. Austin, Sgt. Raleigh A. Bohl, Sgt. Richard E. Smith, Sgt. Clyde P. Hughes (All interned, landed in Sweden).

510th
2nd Lt. Vernon B. Evans, 2nd Lt. Edward W. Holub, 2nd Lt. Harry Margolis, S/Sgt. John M. Cox, S/Sgt. Douglas T. Gerard, T/Sgt. Joseph R. Milani, Sgt. Martin A. Mills, Sgt. Robert L. Glynn Jr., Sgt. William Bell (All interned, landed in Sweden).

511th
F.O. Allen M. Fisher, F.O. Thomas M. Carnegie, F.O. Anthony Cannizzaro, 2nd Lt. Robert C. Wagoner, S/Sgt. Thomas W. Brink, Sgt. Charles A. Stevens, Sgt. Lester L. Kern, Sgt. Joseph A. Chickola, Sgt. Jack A. Tucker (All interned, landed in Sweden).

1st Lt. Danforth N. Merrill (POW), 2nd Lt. Robert V. Ayette (POW), 2nd Lt. Michael F. O'Shea Jr. (POW), 1st Lt. William H. Custard Jr. (POW), Sgt. Eugene G. Edmonds (POW), T/Sgt. James W. Williams

(POW), Sgt. Claude M. Chaffin (POW), Sgt. Thomas A. Veltry (POW), T/Sgt. Ralph W. Choquette (POW).

1st Lt. Donald S. Dargue (POW), 2nd Lt. Harold P. Anderson (POW), 2nd Lt. George P. LeCheminant (POW), 2nd Lt. Raymond M. Brooks (POW), S/Sgt. Edward R. Asmus Jr. (KIA), S/Sgt. William L. Birch (POW), Sgt. Leo J. Collins (POW), Sgt. Francis J. Cawetzka (POW), Sgt. George A. Dingee Jr. (POW), S/Sgt. Alexander Hormerte (POW).

OCTOBER 28, 1944
509th
S/Sgt. Lloyd D. Babin (POW).

NOVEMBER 9, 1944
510th
Sgt. Albert S. Altman (KIA).

NOVEMBER 21, 1944
508th
2nd Lt. Warren E. Loehndorf (KIA), F.O. John J. Simcich (KIA), F.O. Jordan Ivanoff (KIA), 2nd Lt. Stanley N. Kemp (POW), Sgt. Leland C. Potter (POW), Sgt. Bernard S. Townsend (POW), Sgt. Harold L. Dillon (POW), Sgt. Evan D. Olsen (POW), Sgt. Basil W. Albright (POW).

NOVEMBER 26, 1944
511th
2nd Lt. Frank P. Boettcher (KIA), F.O. Edward L. Walota (KIA), 2nd Lt. Leonard U. Mitchell (POW), 2nd Lt. Robert L. Francis (POW), M/Sgt. Buford Wilhoit (POW), Sgt. Robert E. Wombold (POW), Sgt. Robert S. Jarois (POW), Sgt. Robert B. Westcoff (POW), Sgt. Richard J. Cook (POW).

NOVEMBER 30, 1944
509th
1st Lt. David W. Basehore (KIA).

DECEMBER 5, 1944
511th
Capt. Henry F. Williamson Jr. (POW), 2nd Lt. Andrew L. Cadwell Jr. (POW), 2nd Lt. Andrew A. Gourash (POW), F.O. Joseph R. Bredar (POW), S/Sgt. Robert W. Shepard (POW), S/Sgt. Arthur F. Eterson (POW), S/Sgt. Harold A. Bishop (POW), Sgt. John L. Coble (POW), Sgt. Dallas M. Smith (POW).

JANUARY 17, 1945
509th
2nd Lt. Marius N. Della-Cioppa (POW), 2nd Lt. Dell J. Harvey (POW), 2nd Lt. Spurgeon W. Clark Jr. (POW), Sgt. Walter J. Saltys (POW), Sgt. Richard M. Smith (POW), S/Sgt. Edward Venezia (POW), Sgt. Herman R. Fancher (POW), S/Sgt. George F. Shearer Jr. (POW), Sgt. James E. Fager (POW).

JANUARY 22, 1945
509th
1st Lt. Richard H. Goldsborough (POW), 2nd Lt. Charles F. Balik (POW), F.O. John Romanishin (POW), Sgt. George F. Shirts (KIA), T/Sgt. Carl F. Miller (POW), T/Sgt. Thomas F. Kennedy Jr. (POW), S/Sgt. Ramsey P. Fendall (POW), S/Sgt. John M. Kalapp (POW), Sgt. Jack T. Rushing (POW).

JANUARY 28, 1945
510th
Cpl. William H. Spicer (Killed - struck by jeep).

FEBRUARY 6, 1945
509th
2nd Lt. Reinhold W. Vergen (KIA), F.O. Robert E. Sollers (KIA), F.O. Stanley L. Dietel (KIA), Sgt. Francis T. Leonard (KIA), Sgt. Emerald G. Cutting (KIA), Sgt. Albert B. Cantrelle (KIA), Sgt. Joseph E. Ventress (KIA), Sgt. Philip M. Singleton (KIA), S/Sgt. Robert L. Wheatley (KIA).

511th
1st Lt. Edward R. Ashton (KIA), F.O. George Y. Bowman (KIA), 2nd Lt. Donald A. Cornell (KIA), 2nd Lt. John F. McNeill (KIA), S/Sgt. John P. Folks (KIA), T/Sgt. James S. Allman (KIA), Sgt. John Y. Nelson (KIA), S/Sgt. Bruce S. Cook (KIA), Sgt. Harold R. Wieland (KIA), Sgt. John C. Connelly (KIA).

FEBRUARY 14, 1945
508th
1st Lt. Curtis E. Ash (POW), 2nd Lt. Ned Benedict (POW), 1st Lt. Robert W. Hays (KIA), Sgt. Arthur A. Nicholas (POW), T/Sgt. Robert B. Pierce (POW), S/Sgt. Ward E. Brady (POW), Sgt. Kenneth Graser (POW), Sgt. John R. Norbo (POW), Sgt. Louis D. Anderson (POW).

FEBRUARY 25, 1945
509th
2nd Lt. Charles R. Abplanalp (KIA), 2nd Lt. Harold V. Gividen (Interned), 2nd Lt. George F. Brown (Interned), Sgt. Ernest C. Ogden (Interned), Sgt. Clinton O. Norby (Interned), Sgt. Paul Levinson (Interned), Sgt. Herbert Berlin (Interned), Sgt. John D. Genetti (Interned), Sgt. Gene C. Bullock (Interned).

MARCH 12, 1945
510th
S/Sgt. Harry Charm (KIA).

JUNE 8, 1945
509th
1st Lt. Joseph C. Robinson, Capt. Joseph A. Glover Jr., 1st Lt. Howard B. Hibbard, 1st Lt. Richard E. Higley, M/Sgt. John Q. Montgomery, T/Sgt. Paul Lucyk, S/Sgt. Robert E. Smith, S/Sgt. Santo A. Caruso, S/Sgt. Teed O. Smith, Sgt. Boyd P. Dobbs, Sgt. Edwin R. Birtwell, Sgt. Sheldon R. Coons Jr., Sgt. Camille F. Devaney, Cpl. Calvert G. P'Poole, T/Sgt. Lester A.F. Rhein, Sgt. David I. Rapoport, T/Sgt. Max Marksheid, Sgt. John D. Leasure, T/Sgt. Morris Lizewski, T/Sgt. Kenneth W. Craumer. (All killed on the flight home to the United States. The B-17 crashed near Barmouth, Wales).

June 8, 1945: Remains of Lt. Joseph Robinson's aircraft on a Welsh hillside near Barmouth. (S. Evans)

Chapter Twelve
GROUP PERSONNEL

Abbogast / Bailey

A

Last	First	Rank	Unit	Status
Abbogast	Billy B.	Sgt.	508th	
Abel	Clayton S.	S/Sgt.	509th	
Aberman	Hyman	Cpl.	201st	Finance Sect.
Aplanalp	Charles R.	2nd Lt.	509th	KIA 2/25/45
Abraham	Walter A.	PFC	2098	Avn. F/F Pltn.
Abrams	Ted E.	2nd Lt.	11th	St. Comp.
Abromeit	Edward F.	T/Sgt.	510th	
Accordini	Lawrence F.	S/Sgt.	509th	
Acheychek	Walter A.	Sgt.	509th	
Achilles	James M.	Cpl.	508th	
Ackerman	Edwin C.	Sgt.	351st	HQ
Ackerman	Richard M.	T/Sgt.	509th	
Acree	John D.	Sgt.	508th	
Acree	Walter M. Jr.	F.O.	511th	
Acunto	Vincent S.	1st Lt.	509th	
Adam	Van T.	S/Sgt.	510th	
Adamczyk	Frank P.	S/Sgt.	510th	
Adamiak	Joseph R.	1st Lt.	511th	
Adams	Andrew Jr.	S/Sgt.	510th	
Adams	Calvin H.	Sgt.	508th	
Adams	Charles	Cpl.	511th	
Adams	Claude T.	2nd Lt.	511th	POW 9/12/44
Adams	Clifford B.	1st Lt.	509th	
Adams	Donald L.	S/Sgt.	447th	Sub-Depot
Adams	George F.	1st Lt.	510th	
Adams	Jack	Cpl.	854th	Chemical Co.
Adams	John E.	T/Sgt.	509th	POW 6/13/43
Adams	Joseph P.	Cpl.	447th	Sub-Depot
Adams	Joseph S. Jr.	S/Sgt.	509th	
Adams	Lionel E.	Sgt.	447th	Sub-Depot
Adams	Richard J.	S/Sgt.	508th	
Adams	Robert L.	1st Lt.	511th	
Adams	Robert W.	1st Lt.	511th	POW 11/21/44
Adams	Victor C.	Cpl.	510th	
Adams	Winfield H.	Cpl.	1629th	
Adkins	Lester V.	S/Sgt.	511th	
Adkins	Norman B.	Sgt.	509th	
Adler	Homer H.	S/Sgt.	447th	Sub-Depot
Adomo	Bernard N.	Cpl.	509th	
Ahem	George E.	S/Sgt.	508th	
Ahlheim	Fred W.	2nd Lt.	510th	
Ahumada	Camilo V.	Cpl.	447th	Sub-Depot
Akers	Harold E.	1st Lt.	508th	
Akins	Arren A.	Maj.	351st	HQ
Akins	Frederick A.	Sgt.	447th	Sub-Depot
Albrecht	Raymond J.	Sgt.	511th	
Albright	Basil W.	Sgt.	508th	POW 11/21/44
Albro	Duane E.	S/Sgt.	510th	POW 12/20/43
Alcorn	Edward B.	Cpl.	510th	
Alderson	Jack E.	T/Sgt.	508th	
Aldrege	Cleo D.	2nd Lt.	511th	POW 7/13/44
Alexander	Charles C.	PFC	510th	
Alexander	James H.	T/Sgt.	508th	
Alexander	Lester J.	T/Sgt.	510th	
Akire	Robbie R.	S/Sgt.	509th	KIA 3/18/44
Allan	Maurice M.	PFC	510th	
Allavie	Albert L.	2nd Lt.	509th	
Allen	John E.	2nd Lt.	511th	
Allen	Albert W.	1st Lt.	510th	
Allen	Clifford H.	S/Sgt.	510th	
Allen	Francis A.	Cpl.	508th	POW 3/2/44
Allen	Marvin R.	Sgt.	509th	
Allen	Mason S.	Cpl.	509th	POW 6/30/44
Allen	Melvin H.	S/Sgt.	510th	
Allen	Raymond W.	Sgt.	511th	
Alley	Richard J.	Cpl.	509th	KIA 1/7/44
Allison	David L.	2nd Lt.	509th	
Allman	Pachal E.	Sgt.	511th	
Alloway	James S.	T/Sgt.	511th	KIA 2/6/45
Almy	Charles E.	Sgt.	508th	
Alsop	Jack L	F.O.	511th	
Altman	Burt L.	T/Sgt.	511th	POW 6/28/43
Alvarado	Delbert L.	Sgt.	510th	
Alverson	Albert S.	Sgt.	508th	KIA 11/9/44
Amabilo	Philip R.	PFC	11th	St. Comp.
Ambrose	George E.	PFC	1061st	MP Company
Ambrose	Elmo R.	Cpl.	11th	St. Comp.
Amenrud	Emil F.	S/Sgt.	511th	POW 1/30/44
Amick	Tuite M.	T/Sgt.	510th	KIA 8/17/43
Ammerman	Wallace A.	PFC	511th	
Amos	Frederick F.	S/Sgt.	2098th	Avn. F/F Pltn.
Amundson	Robert M.	Cpl.	508th	
Anchors	Charles W.	S/Sgt.	511th	
Ande	Robert R.	F.O.	509th	
Anderson	Charles E.	S/Sgt.	510th	MIA 6/19/43
Anderson	Ralph F. Jr.	2nd Lt.	510th	
Anderson	Charles F.	Cpl.	510th	POW 6/28/44
Anderson	Clifford	1st Lt.	508th	
Anderson	Duane S.	Capt.	511th	
Anderson	Edward E.	S/Sgt.	508th	
Anderson	Elmer A.	1st Lt.	509th	
Anderson	Francis E.	S/Sgt.	508th	
Anderson	George P.	S/Sgt.	510th	
Anderson	Harold P.	2nd Lt.	511th	POW 10/7/44
Anderson	Harvey J.	1st Lt.	511th	KIA 1/7/44
Anderson	Ivan E.	Sgt.	509th	
Anderson	James L.	F.O.	509th	
Anderson	Jerry D.	Sgt.	509th	POW 6/27/44
Anderson	John	T/Sgt.	508th	
Anderson	Joseph W.	1st Lt.	511th	
Anderson	Lawrence R.	S/Sgt.	510th	POW 12/31/43
Anderson	Leon E.	2nd Lt.	508th	KIA 11/26/44
Anderson	Louis D.	PFC	508th	POW 2/14/45
Anderson	Myron C.	T/Sgt.	511th	
Anderson	Paul G.	Maj.	508th	
Anderson	Robert G.	Sgt.	509th	
Anderson	Sven V.	S/Sgt.	510th	
Anderson	Thomas P.	S/Sgt.	511th	
Anderson	William W.	Sgt.	511th	POW 9/12/44
Andreoni	Alex	1st Lt.	510th	
Androkitis	John	S/Sgt.	508th	
Anello	George F.	Cpl.	509th	POW 9/5/44
Anez	Joseph L.	Sgt.	509th	
Angel	Frederick L.	2nd Lt.	511th	KIA 6/11/43
Angelini	Joseph S.	Capt.	510th	
Angell	Richard P.	F.O.	510th	
Anger	Albert	S/Sgt.	511th	
Angerame	Francis	PFC	1206th	QM Company
Anglen	Roy E.	PFC	1206th	QM Company
Anker	Norman H.	T/Sgt.	509th	POW 3/2/44
Annuci	Henry J.	Sgt.	508th	
Aryan	Lester D.	S/Sgt.	510th	
Aossey	Mike J.	S/Sgt.	511th	
Aparson	Robert G.	Sgt.	508th	
Apicella	Joseph R.	2nd Lt.	510th	
Appelman	Herman	T/Sgt.	508th	
Apperson	Edward B.	1st Lt.	508th	POW 4/18/44
Appleford	Donald J.	S/Sgt.	510th	
Applegate	Vincent F.	PFC	1206th	QM Company
Arasin	John C.	T/Sgt.	508th	
Arbetello	Anthony J.	Pvt.	11th	St. Comp.
Arceneaux	Richard L.	2nd Lt.	511th	
Archer	James J.	Sgt.	509th	
Arcia	Fred	Cpl.	511th	
Arens	Gerald W.	Cpl.	509th	
Argiropolus	Theodore	1st Lt.	508th	
Arkwright	William R.	T/Sgt.	509th	
Armiling	S.	Cpl.	509th	
Amistead	Richard H.	Sgt.	508th	
Armour	William J.	2nd Lt.	508th	MIA 2/22/44
Armstrong	Charles D.	S/Sgt.	511th	
Armstrong	Edward H.	T/Sgt.	508th	KIA 6/28/43
Armstrong	Charles S.	S/Sgt.	509th	
Armstrong	Clyde W.	2nd Lt.	511th	
Armstrong	Harry T.	Maj.	508th	
Arnold	Joseph L.	S/Sgt.	508th	
Arnold	Melvin T.	T/Sgt.	509th	POW 6/24/44
Arrendondo	George W.	1st Lt.	509th	
Arsenault	Robert A.	S/Sgt.	511th	
Arsenhault	Rudolpho	PFC	447th	Sub-Depot
Arther	Ohezine D.	T/Sgt.	351st	HQ
	Joseph C.	PFC	508th	
	William C. Jr.	2nd Lt.	510th	KIA 7/19/44

Last	First	Rank	Unit	Status
Arthur	Francis W.	M/Sgt.	511th	
Artney	Charles T.	Sgt.	508th	POW 2/14/45
Asdell	Frederick T.	2nd Lt.	509th	
Ash	Curtis E.	1st Lt.	508th	KIA 2/6/45
Ashton	Edward R.	1st Lt.	511th	KIA 10/7/44
Asmus	Edward R. Jr.	S/Sgt.	511th	St. Comp.
Aston	Eugene L.	Pvt.	11th	KIA 4/11/44
Atkins	Claude L. Jr.	S/Sgt.	510th	POW 8/3/44
Atkins	James O.	S/Sgt.	511th	MP Company
Atkinson	James R.	Sgt.	1061st	
Attanasio	Richard S. Jr.	S/Sgt.	510th	
Attaway	Vincent M.	S/Sgt.	509th	QM Company
Atwood	Alton A.	Cpl.	1206th	
Atwood	Elliot	T/Sgt.	511th	KIA 5/27/44
Augustin	Richard J.	T/Sgt.	510th	
Austin	Oswald E.	F.O.	508th	Finance Sect.
Austin	Eddie F.	Cpl.	201st	
Austin	Jack P.	1st Sgt.	511th	KIA 9/12/44
Austin	Jesse J. Jr.	Sgt.	511th	Int'd 10/7/44
Austin	Mason G.	Sgt.	509th	St. Comp.
Auten	Matt S.	Sgt.	11th	
Autenreith	Renford H.	Capt.	508th	
Avaritt	Charles H.	S/Sgt.	510th	
Avery	Herbert D.	2nd Lt.	508th	POW 9/12/44
Avignone	George H.	2nd Lt.	508th	
Avison	John B.	Sgt.	511th	
Avry	Joseph A.	S/Sgt.	508th	
Axtell	Richard M.	2nd Lt.	511th	POW 5/28/44
Aye	Frank H.	T/Sgt.	510th	
Ayers	George F.	Sgt.	508th	POW 6/22/43
Ayette	Fred L.	S/Sgt.	447th	Sub-Depot
	James W.	Sgt.	511th	POW 10/7/44
	Robert V.	2nd Lt.	508th	

B

Last	First	Rank	Unit	Status
Babin	Lloyd D.	S/Sgt.	509th	POW 10/28/44
Backman	Willard A.	T/Sgt.	510th	MIA 5/19/43
Bacon	Robert R.	2nd Lt.	510th	
Badal	John	S/Sgt.	508th	
Bader	Alvin G.	S/Sgt.	509th	
Bader	Nahannie	Capt.	508th	
Badger	William D. Jr.	S/Sgt.	511th	
Badgett	Cecil F.	Sgt.	508th	KIA 8/6/44
Badnar	Stephen J.	S/Sgt.	511th	POW 12/31/43
Bado	Nicholas M.	Sgt.	510th	
Bagwell	Aubrey D.	Cpl.	508th	
Bailey	Bowman R.	S/Sgt.	508th	
Bailey	Byron L.	T/Sgt.	510th	
Bailey	Edward	S/Sgt.	509th	
Bailey	James M. Jr.	S/Sgt.	511th	
Bailey	Lilburn R.	Cpl.	508th	
Bailey	Raymond E.	S/Sgt.	510th	POW 4/18/44

Last Name	First Name	Rank	Unit	Notes
Bailey	Robert T.	M/Sgt.	509th	
Bailey	William H.	S/Sgt.	509th	
Baillio	Bob A.	Sgt.	508th	KIA 10/7/44
Baim	Leslie S.	S/Sgt.	509th	
Bainco	Eugene J.	2nd Lt.	509th	
Baird	Archer M.	Capt.	510th	
Baird	Edward R. Jr.	Sgt.	510th	
Baird	Philip W. G. Jr.	F.O.	510th	POW 5/28/44
Baird	William H.	2nd Lt.	510th	
Baker	Boyd E.	S/Sgt.	511th	
Baker	Harold L.	Sgt.	508th	
Baker	Lewis T.	T/Sgt.	511th	KIA 5/19/43
Baker	Lowell E.	S/Sgt.	510th	
Baker	William V.	Sgt.	508th	
Bakkar	Harm	Sgt.	508th	
Bakkar	Horton	T/Sgt.	510th	
Baldwin	Kenneth D.	T/Sgt.	509th	
Baldwin	Roland N.	1st Lt.	509th	
Baldwin	Wayne L.	T/Sgt.	509th	KIA 5/29/43
Balfour	James N.	2nd Lt.	509th	
Balik	Charles F.	2nd Lt.	508th	
Balkovich	Michael J.	Capt.	508th	
Ball	Clinton F.	Lt. Col.	351st	HQ
Ball	James B.	T/Sgt.	509th	POW 1/11/44
Ballard	Clair C.	2nd Lt.	509th	
Ballard	Cleo C.	T/Sgt.	509th	
Ballard	D. H.	Pvt.	11th	St. Comp.
Ballard	Norman F.	T/Sgt.	509th	KIA 2/21/44
Ballard	Ralph T.	1st Lt.	508th	
Ballentyne	Glenn C.	2nd Lt.	511th	POW 7/13/44
Balliott	William R.	1st Lt.	509th	
Balmer	Frederick J.	Cpl.	511th	
Balser	William L. Jr.	F.O.	508th	
Balsis	Ernest G.	S/Sgt.	510th	
Baltz	Robert A.	Sgt.	508th	
Baltz	Robert J.	2nd Lt.	509th	POW 12/31/43
Banas	Andzy J.	Pvt.	508th	
Banda	Emiel A.	2nd Lt.	508th	
Bandy	Allen J.	S/Sgt.	508th	
Banks	Donald E.	T/Sgt.	510th	
Banks	Hartley B.	2nd Lt.	508th	
Banton	Herbert L.	PFC	510th	
Barbaham	Moye B.	1st Lt.	447th	Sub-Depot
Barbeaux	Aloysius	Sgt.	511th	
Barber	Duward C.	PFC	447th	Sub-Depot
Barber	Harry B.	T/Sgt.	510th	
Barber	Joseph G.	Capt.	1629th	Ord. S&M Co.
Barber	Samuel S.	PFC	1629th	Ord. S&M Co.
Barbiero	Anthony S.	T/Sgt.	511th	
Barcelona	Lester D.	Sgt.	510th	
Barclay	Charles J.	T/Sgt.	508th	
Bardeen	Morton	T/Sgt.		
Barel				
Barg	Bartram B.	Cpl.	511th	
Barieau	Jerome E. Jr.	1st Lt.	511th	POW 8/6/44
Barker	James R.	Sgt.	509th	
Barker	Roy A.	S/Sgt.	508th	
Barker	Will G.	S/Sgt.	510th	POW 8/6/44
Bartlett	Maurice D.	T/Sgt.	508th	
Barlow	Kenneth F.	1st Lt.	511th	
Barnard	Morris L.	S/Sgt.	511th	POW 6/14/44
Barnes	Carl E.	S/Sgt.	510th	
Barnes	Ernest L.	T/Sgt.	509th	
Barnes	George A.	S/Sgt.	508th	
Barnes	Joe	Sgt.	509th	
Barnes	John W.	PFC	511th	
Barnes	William E.	S/Sgt.	447th	Sub-Depot
Barnett	John F.	2nd Lt.	509th	
Barnfeld	Arnold A.	1st Lt.	510th	
Barnhart	Allen J.	1st Lt.	508th	
Barnhart	Arthur L.	T/Sgt.	510th	
Barnhart	Joseph H.	2nd Lt.	511th	KIA 3/22/44
Baron	Eugene A.	T/Sgt.	511th	KIA 6/28/43
Barr	Chester R.	PFC	854th	POW 8/3/44
Barr	Robert A.	1st Lt.	1061st	Chemical Co.
Barrett	Ernest F.	Sgt.	511th	
Barrie	Warren J.	Cpl.	509th	
Barrows	Elmer A.	Sgt.	509th	
Barstow	Richard H.	Sgt.	508th	
Barszcz	Benedict J.	Sgt.	508th	
Bartel	Edward A.	Sgt.	511th	POW 9/12/44
Bartholomew	Alvin L.	Sgt.	511th	
Bartholomew	Harry L.	PFC	508th	
Bartlett	Maurice D.	Cpl.	1206th	QM Company
Bartley	Harold E.	S/Sgt.	447th	Sub-Depot
Bartley	Ronald E.	S/Sgt.	508th	Int'd 8/6/44
Bartog	Joseph	2nd Lt.	508th	
Barton	Charles D.	Sgt.	508th	KIA 11/26/43
Barton	Leonard L.	Capt.	511th	
Bartzocas	Arthur	M/Sgt.	508th	
Basar	Walter F.	M/Sgt.	510th	
Basehore	David W.	Cpl.	510th	HQ
Bass	James E.	S/Sgt.	511th	
Bass	James S.	S/Sgt.	508th	
Bass	Willie C.	PFC	351st	St. Comp.
Bassford	Theodore A.	2nd Lt.	11th	POW 12/31/43
Basta	Dominic J.	Sgt.	508th	
Bastone	John R.	Cpl.	1629th	
Bately	William W.	PFC	511th	
Bateman	William L. Jr.	1st Lt.	1629th	
Bates	Leslie E.	Pvt.	510th.	St. Comp.
Bates	Wesley R.	S/Sgt.	11th	
Batinchok	George P.	Sgt.	510th	
Batley	William W.	PFC	508th	KIA 12/31/43
Baty	William C.	Cpl.	447th	Sub-Depot
Baucon	Joseph	Cpl.	511th	
Bauer	Carl J.	1st Lt.	511th	
Bauer	Donald P.	Sgt.	509th	
Bauer	Irving J.	S/Sgt.	508th	Killed 2/26/43
Bauer	Joseph W.	T/Sgt.	510th	
Baugher	Robert B.	PFC	510th	
Baxley	David H.	S/Sgt.	508th	
Baxter	Charles E.	T/Sgt.	510th	
Bay	Robert J.	S/Sgt.	510th	
Baylerian	George M.	T/Sgt.	510th	
Baynes	John H.	T/Sgt.	508th	POW 5/14/43
Bazar	Cecil F.	T/Sgt.	510th	
Beadle	Charles J.	S/Sgt.	509th	
Beadles	Wallace J.	Sgt.	510th	
Beadman	William J.	S/Sgt.	508th	KIA 3/22/44
Beahr	Warren M.	Sgt.	511th	
Beal	David R.	Sgt.	510th	
Beal	Joseph J.	Sgt.	508th	KIA 6/28/43
Beals	William M.	2nd Lt.	511th	POW 8/3/44
Beam	Frank	PFC	854th	Chemical Co.
Beanham	George W.	PFC	1061st	MP Company
Beard	Vernon C.	1st Lt.	511th	
Beard	Wayne A.	Sgt.	509th	
Beatch	Daniel	Cpl.	509th	
Beaton	Daniel F.	Cpl.	509th	
Beattie	Frederick W.	Sgt.	508th	
Beatty	Elmer	Sgt.	511th	
Beavers	Robert F.	Sgt.	511th	POW 9/12/44
Bechtol	Charles D.	PFC	508th	
Beck	George	Pvt.	1206th	QM Company
Beck	Harley H.	Cpl.	508th	
Beck	R. A.	S/Sgt.	510th	
Beck	Rayvon	F.O.	510th	
Becker	Donald W.	Cpl.	510th	KIA 2/20/44
Beckett	Mike C.	2nd Lt.	508th	
Beckman	Wallace G.	Sgt.	508th	
Beckstein	George	Capt.	511th	
Becoste	G. D.	M/Sgt.	508th	Int'd 10/7/44
Bedard	Roland F.	M/Sgt.	510th	
Bedell	Louis J.	Cpl.	509th	
Beech	William E.	S/Sgt.	509th	KIA 11/30/44
Beene	Doyle W.	S/Sgt.	511th	
Beer	Howard R.	PFC	1206th	QM Company
Begin	Clarence J.	2nd Lt.	508th	
Behling	Benjamin J.	S/Sgt.	1629th	Ord. S&M Co.
Behn	Wilbur W.	PFC	510th	
Behrendt	Allen D.	1st Lt.	1629th	
Beigner	G.	Capt.	510th	
Beiler	Morris	PFC	11th	St. Comp.
Beitzel	Harry M.	T/Sgt.	510th	
Bekken	Carl Q.	Sgt.	509th	
Belardine	Michael J.	1st Lt.	509th	KIA 12/31/43
Belcher	Clarence L.	Cpl.	509th	
Belcher	Jack D.	Cpl.	11th	St. Comp.
Bek	Robert	2nd Lt.	508th	
Belk	Bennie H. Jr.	2nd Lt.	508th	POW 8/27/43
Bell	G. L.	Sgt.	509th	
Bell	John A.	T/Sgt.	509th	
Bell	John B.	PFC	511th	
Bell	Orland H.	S/Sgt.	510th	
Bell	Robert V.	M/Sgt.	508th	
Bell	Samuel N.	Sgt.	509th	
Bellows	William	Sgt.	510th	Int'd 10/7/44
Belmeyer	Allen R.	2nd Lt.	510th	
Belmonte	John I.	1st Lt.	510th	
Belot	Charles P.	Sgt.	510th	POW 9/12/44
Belote	Howard C.	1st Lt.	511th	
Belser	Ivy L.	1st Lt.	508th	
Belsinger	William L. Jr.	F.O.	511th	
Bender	Frank W.	T/Sgt.	509th	POW 5/24/44
Bender	Andrew H.	S/Sgt.	508th	KIA 9/5/44
Bendle	Marvin H.	1st Lt.	510th	POW 12/31/43
Benedetti	Aubrey E.	Sgt.	508th	
Benedict	Joseph J.	Sgt.	11th	St. Comp.
Benedict	David M.	Cpl.	447th	Sub-Depot
Benedict	Ned	2nd Lt.	508th	
Benevich	Wilbur S.	1st Lt.	510th	
Benfante	Lucian J.	S/Sgt.	511th	
Benger	J. L.	Pvt.	1206th	QM Company
Benjamin	Jesse R.	Sgt.	351st	HQ
Benner	Lawrence P.	2nd Lt.	511th	
Bennett	Gordon H.	Sgt.	201st	Finance Sect.
Bennett	Charles E.	1st Lt.	508th	
Bennett	Charles W.	Cpl.	11th	St. Comp.
Bennett	Donald C.	1st Lt.	510th	POW 9/12/44
Bennett	Emmett F.	Sgt.	510th	
Benson	Harry A.	S/Sgt.	509th	
Benson	Jack W.	Sgt.	509th	
Bent	Lyle J.	S/Sgt.	510th	
Bentley	Kenneth L.	S/Sgt.	509th	
Benton	Roland	S/Sgt.	509th	
Berardi	Harry L.	T/Sgt.	510th	
Berardi	John V.	Sgt.	252nd	Medical Disp.
Berendsen	Marvin R.	S/Sgt.	510th	
Berg	Joseph A.	1st Lt.	509th	
Berger	Joseph R.	S/Sgt.	509th	KIA 6/12/44
Berger	Norbert E.	Sgt.	509th	
Berger	Walter O.	PFC	854th	Chemical Co.
Bergin	Billie L.	1st Lt.	510th	
Bergin	Edward W.	S/Sgt.	509th	KIA 5/7/43
Bergman	Irving L.	S/Sgt.	508th	
Bergman	Robert E.	Sgt.	511th	
Bergstrom	Harold E.	2nd Lt.	511th	KIA 11/3/43
	Walter	S/Sgt.	508th	

Beringer / Branch

Surname	First Name	Rank	Unit	Notes
Beringer	John F.	1st Lt.	508th	
Berkenpas	Naphi	1st Lt.	508th	POW 6/28/43
Berkow	Benjamin L.	1st Lt.	508th	KIA 5/7/43
Berkowitz	George	Sgt.	509th	
Berlick	Carl	Sgt.	1629th	Ord. S&M Co.
Berlin	Herbert	Sgt.	509th	Int'd 2/25/45
Berndt	John G.	Sgt.	509th	
Bernfeld	Arnold A.	2nd Lt.	510th	Killed 6/8/45
Bernhart	Joseph H.	S/Sgt.	511th	Killed 5/15/43
Bernstein	Alvin	F.O.	508th	
Berreau	Herbert F.	Sgt.	511th	POW 8/6/44
Bereth	Victor	Sgt.	511th	POW 8/17/43
Berry	Edward H.	S/Sgt.	509th	Killed 2/26/43
Berry	Henry K.	S/Sgt.	510th	
Berth	George H.	Cpl.	510th	
Bertolas	Tulio I.	Cpl.	508th	
Besch	Raymond J.	T/Sgt.	511th	
Besher	Jack M.	Sgt.	509th	
Bessanson	Clarence A.	Sgt.	508th	POW 8/6/44
Bessoir	William A.	S/Sgt.	508th	St. Comp.
Best	Charles H.	2nd Lt.	11th	
Best	Lloyd G.	Sgt.	510th	Int'd 10/7/44
Beuchiet	Willie J.	Sgt.	509th	
Beucler	Eugene J.	2nd Lt.	510th	POW 5/30/44
Beveridge	Frederick J.	Cpl.	509th	
Bevier	Arthur J.	1st Lt.	508th	
Bevington	Arthur B.	Sgt.	511th	POW 6/21/44
Beyer	Lawrence C.	Sgt.	508th	
Beyer	Clarence A. G.	Cpl.	508th	POW 7/13/44
Bianco	Gilbert L.	S/Sgt.	510th	
Bickner	Vincent	Cpl.	509th	
Biddle	Hopper E.	1st Lt.	511th	HQ
Biel	Walter T.	2nd Lt.	351st	
Bien	Warren L.	1st Lt.	447th	
Bienick	Michael A.	Spec. 4	511th	
Bierley	Verner W.	Cpl.	511th	
Biever	Theodore N.	Sgt.	511th	MP Company
Bigelow	Gilbert O.	T/Sgt.	1061st	POW 6/28/43
Bigelow	Leonard	1st Lt.	511th	
Bigham	Harvey H.	2nd Lt.	510th	POW 10/14/43
Bijak	J. L.	T/Sgt.	509th	
Bijaer	Ralph	Cpl.	511th	St. Comp.
Bianko	Clarence M.	Cpl.	447th	Sub-Depot
Blecky	Richard P.	T/Sgt.	508th	
Billett	James D.	2nd Lt.	511th	POW 10/14/43
Billin	Jack	Sgt.	511th	
Billings	Tyre N.	PFC	508th	
Bills	Linden A.	Sgt.	1061st	MP Company
Bilson	John J.	Sgt.	508th	
Bily	Joseph R.	2nd Lt.	511th	POW 7/19/44
Binsfield	Albert E.	S/Sgt.	510th	POW 11/21/44
Birch	William L.	S/Sgt.	511th	
Bird	John F.	1st Lt.	509th	
Birkelback	Gilbert W.	T/Sgt.	508th	
Birkley	Leroy E.	T/Sgt.	508th	POW 6/28/43
Birlem	Keith G.	Maj.	508th	KIA 5/7/43
Birtles	Alva A.	S/Sgt.	511th	
Birtwell	Edwin R.	Sgt.	509th	Killed 6/8/45
Bishop	Dewey K.	Sgt.	509th	
Bishop	Harold A.	T/Sgt.	511th	Killed 5/15/43
Bishop	James	S/Sgt.	511th	
Bishop	Richard E.	Lt.	511th	Killed 2/26/43
Bistine	Morris C.	T/Sgt.	509th	
Bitner	John E.	T/Sgt.	510th	
Bittner	Raymond F.	Sgt.	511th	MIA 12/31/43
Bittner	Robert L.	T/Sgt.	510th	
Bivens	Herbert H.	Sgt.	509th	POW 1/11/44
Bixby	Harlan B.	2nd Lt.	508th	POW 12/31/43
Bizniek	Michael A.	S/Sgt.	351st	HQ
Bjerke	Loren L.	Sgt.	509th	
Bjorck	Kenneth S.	F.O.	511th	
Bjoring	Donnell E.	1st Lt.	511th	HQ
Blachowicz	Anthony J.	Sgt.	351st	
Black	Donald W.	Sgt.	508th	
Black	George	2nd Lt.	509th	Int'd 6/21/44
Black	Junior L.	Sgt.	510th	
Black	Porter L.	Cpl.	11th	St. Comp.
Black	Roy L.	T/Sgt.	511th	
Black	Warren P.	PFC	447th	Sub-Depot
Blackburn	Sanford	Cpl.	510th	
Blackburn	Woodrow W.	S/Sgt.	509th	
Blackford	Carl L.	1st Lt.	511th	
Blackman	Rae E.	Cpl.	508th	
Blackwell	Joseph K.	2nd Lt.	509th	St. Comp.
Blades	Lewis F.	PFC	510th	MIA 10/4/43
Blaich	Walter A.	1st Lt.	511th	KIA 10/9/43
Blair	Edmond J.	S/Sgt.	510th	
Blaisdell	Lawrence H.	1st Lt.	508th	
Blake	J. K. Jr.	Sgt.	509th	KIA 10/7/44
Blakesley	Charles W.	Cpl.	447th	Sub-Depot
Blancett	Lloyd D.	1st Lt.	509th	
Blanchard	Charles A.	M/Sgt.	509th	
Blanck	Rubin	T/Sgt.	511th	
Bland	Anderson	PFC	1061st	
Blaney	James E.	1st Lt.	511th	POW 12/31/43
Blank	Allen C.	2nd Lt.	510th	
Blank	William C.	2nd Lt.	508th	
Blankenbeckl	John R.	T/Sgt.	510th	
Blankenship	J. D.	PFC	509th	
Blankenship	Willard	Sgt.	511th	
Blaser	Roger	T/Sgt.	510th	
Blasko	Michael	PFC	508th	
Blaylock	John R.	Maj.	510th	KIA 12/31/43
Bledsoe	Russell M.	Sgt.	1629th	Ord. S&M Co.
Bleile	Harry C.	F.O.	511th	
Bleser	William L. Jr.	F.O.	508th	MP Company
Blevins	David H.	PFC	1061st	Sub-Depot
Blickensderf	Wayne	1st Lt.	447th	HQ
Blitz	Louis	Cpl.	351st	
Bloguszewski	Frank J.	2nd Lt.	351st	POW 1/11/44
Bloshko	William N.	Cpl.	509th	QM Company
Bluford	John R.	S/Sgt.	509th	
Blume	Otto	S/Sgt.	508th	
Bluxome	John D.	Capt.	510th	
Blythe	Roger H.	S/Sgt.	508th	
Boardman	Lester W.	S/Sgt.	511th	
Bochek	Raymond	1st Lt.	509th	
Bocher	Jack M.	Sgt.	508th	
Bochert	Gustave A.	T/Sgt.	508th	
Bockman	Clarence W.	Sgt.	511th	
Bodek	Stanley A.	Sgt.	509th	
Bodell	Louis J.	Sgt.	1629th	Ord. S&M Co.
Boden	Thelbert A.	S/Sgt.	508th	
Bodi	James R.	2nd Lt.	508th	POW 2/24/44
Bodnar	Stephen J.	2nd Lt.	511th	KIA 11/26/44
Boehm	John V.	Sgt.	509th	
Boettcher	Frank P.	T/Sgt.	509th	Int'd 10/7/44
Boetter	James W.	Sgt.	508th	KIA 12/30/43
Bogar	Fred A.	S/Sgt.	509th	
Boggs	Calvin E.	T/Sgt.	509th	
Bogle	Lloyd W.	S/Sgt.	1629th	Ord. S&M Co.
Bogue	William W.	Cpl.	508th	
Bohl	Raleigh A.	M/Sgt.	508th	HQ
Bohn	Roy A.	PFC	1061st	MP Company
Bohney	Wayne A.	T/Sgt.	511th	POW 11/26/43
Bohm	Richard G.	2nd Lt.	508th	
Boisineau	William E.	S/Sgt.	508th	
Boland	Gerard T.	T/Sgt.	510th	KIA 12/30/43
Bolbotowski	Lawrence	S/Sgt.	508th	
Boles	Chester H.	Cpl.	509th	
Bolick	Robert B.	M/Sgt.	510th	
Bolinder	Lester G.	PFC	510th	
Bologna	Carleton R.	T/Sgt.	508th	
Bolton	Joseph M.	T/Sgt.	508th	Int'd 8/6/44
Bonanno	Cecil T.	F.O.	509th	
Bond	Joseph	S/Sgt.	508th	
Bondeson	George W.	S/Sgt.	510th	
Bone	John P.	1st Lt.	508th	
Bonnett	Maurice E.	S/Sgt.	509th	
Bonsell	Carroll G.	Sgt.	511th	
Bonvai	Donald S.	Sgt.	509th	
Boogard	Stephen J.	Sgt.	509th	
Booker	Parry J.	Sgt.	508th	
	John D.	Sgt.	510th	
Boone	Louis E.	T/Sgt.	511th	
Booth	Frank E.	F.O.	511th	KIA 8/6/44
Booth	Roy W.	M/Sgt.	510th	
Borchert	Martin J.	1st Lt.	510th	
Borden	Carl E.	S/Sgt.	509th	
Borer	Malcolm J.	PFC	509th	
Bosch	Raymond J.	S/Sgt.	508th	POW 8/17/43
Boss	Donald G.	T/Sgt.	510th	
Boston	Bernard C.	T/Sgt.	510th	
Botkin	Harold V.	Sgt.	509th	
Boucher	Arthur W.	Cpl.	447th	Sub-Depot
Boucher	Richard E.	1st Lt.	508th	
Bounds	William F.	Maj.	511th	
Boundy	Charles G.	S/Sgt.	511th	
Bourdeau	Russell H.	Sgt.	510th	
Bourdeaux	Philip J.	2nd Lt.	509th	POW 10/4/43
Bourland	Willie L. Sr.	PFC	508th	
Bourne	Francis J.	Sgt.	511th	
Bousquet	Andrew	S/Sgt.	511th	
Bovan	Dozier E. Jr.	Sgt.	509th	
Bowen	Robert	2nd Lt.	1629th	Ord. S&M Co.
Bowen	Robert E.	S/Sgt.	508th	
Bowers	Michael G.	PFC	509th	
Bowles	Mitchell H.	T/Sgt.	511th	
Bowles	Robert W.	Col.	351st	HQ
Bowman	Thomas L.	Sgt.	1206th	QM Company
Bowser	George Y.	F.O.	511th	KIA 2/6/45
Boyarko	Paul E. Jr.	2nd Lt.	508th	POW 4/13/44
Boyce	Andrew Jr.	2nd Lt.	509th	Sub-Depot
Boyd	Rush A.	Cpl.	447th	POW 7/25/43
Boyd	Edwin S.	1st Lt.	510th	
Boykin	Marion F.	S/Sgt.	509th	KIA 8/6/44
Boyle	William M. Jr.	2nd Lt.	511th	KIA 12/31/43
Braathen	Edward C. Jr.	Capt.	508th	
Brackens	Walter B.	T/Sgt.	509th	POW 8/3/44
Braden	Finn W.	1st Lt.	511th	
Bradic	Ralph S.	1st Lt.	509th	
Bradley	Merle S.	S/Sgt.	509th	
Bradley	George	Sgt.	509th	
Bradshaw	Benedict J.	S/Sgt.	447th	Sub-Depot
Brady	James D.	Capt.	510th	
Brady	Masten C.	Cpl.	1061st	MP Company
Braem	James J.	T/Sgt.	509th	POW 2/14/45
Bragdon	Ward E.	S/Sgt.	508th	
Bragg	Robert W.	Sgt.	510th	
Braley	Warren J.	2nd Lt.	511th	KIA 7/29/44
Branaman	William P.	2nd Lt.	511th	POW 5/28/44
Branch	M. P.	PFC	1061st	MP Company
	Earl L.	1st Lt.	508th	
	Bruno	2nd Lt.	511th	POW 5/28/44

Surname	Given	Rank	Unit	Notes
Brandes	V. J.	PFC	1629th	Ord. S&M Co.
Brandon	John H.	1st Lt.	511th	
Brandt	Daniel J.	S/Sgt.	447th	Sub-Depot
Branham	James A.	T/Sgt.	511th	KIA 6/28/43
Brannen	Everett L.	T/Sgt.	508th	KIA 10/9/43
Brantz	Theodore W.	M/Sgt.	447th	Sub-Depot
Brashier	Twyman D.	T/Sgt.	508th	POW 5/14/43
Brasic	Peter R.	T/Sgt.	509th	
Braun	Foster J.	Cpl.	510th	
Brazi	Robert	S/Sgt.	510th	
Breallion	Richard	F.O.	511th	POW 12/5/44
Bredar	Joseph R.	T/Sgt.	509th	
Breeding	Bill F.	T/Sgt.	509th	
Breedlove	George R.	T/Sgt.	510th	
Breemalkamp	Henry S.	2nd Lt.	508th	
Breitbarth	Theodore C.	T/Sgt.	509th	KIA 3/18/44
Breland	John G.	2nd Lt.	511th	
Brendle	Leroy G.	Cpl.	11th	St. Comp.
Breniak	Alexander J.	PFC	508th	
Brennan	Joseph G.	T/Sgt.	509th	
Brennan	Richard F.	1st Lt.	511th	KIA 12/31/43
Brennan	William J.	S/Sgt.	508th	
Brenner	George	Cpl.	1206th	QM Company
Brenner	Harold C.	Sgt.	510th	
Brenner	Seymour	PFC	511th	
Brereton	John D.	2nd Lt.	509th	
Bressan	Renato	Cpl.	508th	
Brewbaker	George L.	Maj.	11th	St. Comp.
Brewlak	Alexander J.	PFC	11th	St. Comp.
Brickman	Raoul D.	T/Sgt.	508th	
Brickner	Charles F.	Cpl.	11th	St. Comp.
Briggs	Arthur C.	S/Sgt.	509th	KIA 5/18/44
Briggs	Donald V.	S/Sgt.	511th	
Briggs	Ulis C.	Sgt.	509th	POW 5/30/44
Bright	Kenneth S.	Sgt.	509th	
Brill	Sylvester C.	M/Sgt.	511th	
Brillon	Richard J.	S/Sgt.	510th	
Brink	Thomas W.	S/Sgt.	511th	Int'd 10/7/44
Briscoe	Tommy A.	1st Lt.	509th	KIA 12/1/43
Brittain	Charles E.	2nd Lt.	509th	
Brittan	William D.	S/Sgt.	508th	
Britton	Raymond J.	1st Lt.	511th	
Broadmeadow	Edward T. Jr.	S/Sgt.	508th	
Broadwater	Archibald	Sgt.	447th	Sub-Depot
Brock	Luther F.	Sgt.	510th	
Brockman	Richard C.	Cpl.	447th	Sub-Depot
Brod	William E.	S/Sgt.	510th	
Broderick	Thomas S.	T/Sgt.	508th	KIA 5/7/43
Broderick	William	PFC	510th	
Brodsky	Robert	S/Sgt.	509th	POW 1/11/44
Brody	John J.	Sgt.	509th	
Brogdon	John C. Jr.	Capt.	1206th	QM Company
Brolan	John R.	Cpl.	509th	
Bromberg	Raymond C.	S/Sgt.	511th	
Bromley	Charles W.	2nd Lt.	510th	
Bronako	Charles A.	2nd Lt.	511th	
Broniak	Alexander J.	Cpl.	11th	St. Comp.
Brooke	Robert M.	S/Sgt.	508th	KIA 5/7/43
Brooks	Albert T.	Sgt.	11th	St. Comp. KIA 4/22/44
Brooks	Edwin	Cpl.	509th	
Brooks	Elton M.	PFC	509th	
Brooks	Raymond M.	2nd Lt.	511th	POW 10/7/44
Brooks	Richard H.	Capt.	511th	
Brooks	Robert W.	1st Lt.	510th	
Brooks	Sherman E.	Spec. 4	511th	MIA 12/22/43
Brooksby	Walter H.	Sgt.	511th	
Brosek	Marvin A.	Capt.	509th	
Brots	J. L.	S/Sgt.	1061st	MP Company
Broucher	Frederick J.	1st Lt.	511th	
Brown	Richard E.	2nd Lt.	508th	
Brown	Benjamin C.	Pvt.	511th	
Brown	Charles M.	S/Sgt.	510th	POW 12/31/43
Brown	Charles R.	Sgt.	447th	Sub-Depot
Brown	Clarence D. Jr.	PFC	509th	
Brown	Donald R.	Sgt.	508th	
Brown	Fred	Pvt.	509th	
Brown	Fred S.	Cpl.	510th	
Brown	George F.	2nd Lt.	509th	Int'd 2/25/45
Brown	Gerald M.	S/Sgt.	509th	
Brown	Granville R.	Sgt.	511th	KIA 10/14/43
Brown	Harold H.	Spec. 4	1629th	Ord. S&M Co.
Brown	Harry M.	2nd Lt.	511th	
Brown	Hayden L.	T/Sgt.	447th	Sub-Depot
Brown	Howard L.	1st Lt.	511th	
Brown	James M.	T/Sgt.	510th	
Brown	James R.	Cpl.	1206th	
Brown	Jeff C.	M/Sgt.	511th	POW 9/12/44
Brown	John F.	Sgt.	508th	
Brown	Julius V.	Sgt.	510th	
Brown	Oscar F.	M/Sgt.	509th	POW 5/28/44
Brown	Paul C.	Sgt.	509th	POW 3/22/44
Brown	R. A.	PFC	1629th	Ord. S&M Co.
Brown	Robert S.	S/Sgt.	508th	
Brown	Roger B.	T/Sgt.	511th	
Brown	Ronald A.	Cpl.	1061st	MP Company
Brown	Russell A.	M/Sgt.	511th	POW 5/28/44
Brown	Verlyn G.	Sgt.	509th	POW 3/22/44
Brown	William C.	Sgt.	11th	St. Comp.
Brown	William H.	T/Sgt.	509th	POW 3/18/44
Browne	Donald K.	S/Sgt.	508th	POW 10/4/43
Brownell	Charles C.	S/Sgt.	511th	
Brownell	John	S/Sgt.	511th	
Brubacher	John	Sgt.	510th	
Bruce	Glenn	Cpl.	509th	
Bruce	Preston L.	S/Sgt.	511th	
Brumbelow	Roy D.	2nd Lt.	510th	St. Comp.
Brunger	George D.	2nd Lt.	510th	
Bruning	Norman J.	F.O.	508th	KIA 5/27/44
Brunner	Robert E.	2nd Lt.	509th	
Bryant	Charles R. Jr.	S/Sgt.	508th	POW 6/22/43
Bryant	Keith M.	Sgt.	511th	
Bryant	Robert	Cpl.	509th	
Bryant	William K.	PFC	508th	
Bucceri	Edward H.	2nd Lt.	511th	
Buchanan	Charlie C.	Capt.	508th	MIA 12/22/43
Bucheit	Willie J.	Sgt.	511th	
Bucholz	Henry A.	Pvt.	508th	
Budke	Gerald F.	Sgt.	509th	
Budney	Vincent H. J.	Sgt.	447th	Sub-Depot
Buffett	Leo C.	S/Sgt.	508th	
Bugdanowitz	Robert	Sgt.	351st	
Bukow	Robert C.	T/Sgt.	509th	HQ
Bullock	Clyde U.	1st Lt.	508th	
Bullock	Gene C.	T/Sgt.	509th	POW 8/6/44
Bullock	Virgil M.	Sgt.	509th	Int'd 2/25/45
Bulski	Adolph F.	1st Lt.	508th	
Bumgartner	Thomas P.	Cpl.	508th	
Bunescu	August	2nd Lt.	509th	
Bunnell	Jerry A.	S/Sgt.	508th	
Buntin	Paul F.	Capt.	511th	
Burch	Cedric W.	Sgt.	508th	POW 3/2/44
Burchinal	Frank E. Jr.	Cpl.	509th	
Burd	Rufinus C.	S/Sgt.	508th	Sub-Depot
Burden	Archie E.	S/Sgt.	447th	
Burg	Walter C.	PFC	508th	
Burgess	E. T.	1st Lt.	510th	KIA 1/11/44
Burgess	James H.	PFC	447th	Sub-Depot
Burgess	Lewis W. Jr.	2nd Lt.	511th	KIA 10/4/43
Burish	Gordon F.	Sgt.	447th	Sub-Depot
Burke	Adelberg	Sgt.	510th	Killed 2/26/43
Burke	Norman P.	T/Sgt.	509th	
Burkett	Kent R.	S/Sgt.	508th	
Burks	Hubert C.	1st Lt.	511th	
Burks	James	Sgt.	509th	
Burleson	Robert L.	2nd Lt.	510th	HQ
Burlow	George E.	Spec. 5	511th	
Burman	Herbert W.	M/Sgt.	510th	
Burnett	Robert J.	2nd Lt.	510th	Sub-Depot
Burnham	Prentis E.	PFC	508th	St. Comp.
Burns	P. A.	Sgt.	508th	
Burns	Robert W.	Col.	351st	
Burress	Malcolm S.	1st Lt.	511th	
Burrier	James H.	Cpl.	447th	Sub-Depot
Burrough	William D.	PFC	11th	St. Comp.
Burroughs	Rudolph E.	Cpl.	508th	
Burton	James E.	S/Sgt.	509th	
Burton	Harlan D.	S/Sgt.	511th	KIA 11/3/43
Burton	James H.	M/Sgt.	447th	Sub-Depot
Burton	Raymond D.	T/Sgt.	509th	
Bury	Thomas E.	S/Sgt.	508th	
Busby	John W.	1st Lt.	511th	POW 9/12/44
Buschenfeldt	Samuel J.	M/Sgt.	510th	
Buschenfield	Karl W. Jr.	Sgt.	509th	
Buselmyer	Donald A.	2nd Lt.	509th	POW 5/28/44
Bushlow	Harold W.	Sgt.	511th	Ord. S&M Co.
Busse	Anthony J.	S/Sgt.	1629th	St. Comp.
Bussman	Walter I.	PFC	11th	
Butenschoen	C. B.	S/Sgt.	508th	
Butler	Joseph A.	2nd Lt.	510th	
Butler	Donald J.	Pvt.	508th	
Butler	Huber M.	T/Sgt.	511th	
Butrum	Raymond T.	1st Lt.	509th	St. Comp.
Buttall	Clarence A.	2nd Lt.	509th	HQ
Buttel	Cedric G.	S/Sgt.	509th	
Butterbach	Robert W.	1st Lt.	508th	St. Comp.
Buttermore	John R.	S/Sgt.	510th	Int'd 8/6/44
Buttner	John	Cpl.	11th	Ord. S&M Co.
Butzlare	Francis S.	T/Sgt.	508th	Chem. Co.
Butzler	Arthur J.	S/Sgt.	351st	QM Company
Buxton	Bernard C.	S/Sgt.	508th	
Buzzi	William T.	1st Lt.	11th	
Byers	Floyd L.	F.O.	508th	POW 6/22/43
Byers	H. L.	PFC	1629th	Ord. S&M Co.
Byrd	William B.	1st Lt.	508th	HQ
Byron	Eugene D.	S/Sgt.	854th	POW 6/14/44
Byme	August A.	S/Sgt.	511th	POW 12/5/44
Bymes	Patrick J.	T/Sgt.	1206th	
Bzoskie	Raymond V.	PFC	510th	
C				
Cabaniss	Francis B.	1st Lt.	511th	KIA 9/5/44
Cabrera	Orville M.	2nd Lt.		POW 8/9/44
Cacace	John W.	T/Sgt.	508th	
Cackowsky	Trini F.	T/Sgt.	508th	
Cadel	Salvatore R.	1st Lt.	511th	
Cadenhead	Raymond J.	Spec. 5	1629th	
Cadoret	Leonard	M/Sgt.	351st	
Cadreau	Lloyd L.	2nd Lt.	509th	
Cadwell	John A.	M/Sgt.	510th	
Cafarella	Andrew L. Jr.	2nd Lt.	511th	
Cagle	Robert A.	T/Sgt.	509th	
Cain	Henderson	1st Lt.	508th	
Calderbank	Lewis L.	Sgt.	508th	
Caldwell	Bernard F.	Sgt.	511th	
Caldwell	Joseph C.	T/Sgt.	508th	

137

Callahan / Claggett

Last Name	First Name	Rank	Unit	Notes
Callahan	James W.	M/Sgt.	510th	
Callahan	Stephen R.	Capt.	511th	
Callaway	Albert L.	1st Lt.	351st	HQ
Callicott	Maurice G.	Spec. 4	511th	
Calvin	Eugene R.	S/Sgt.	1629th	Ord. S&M Co.
Camel	Marvin G.	S/Sgt.	509th	
Cameron	William O.	Pvt.	511th	
Cameron	John A.	PFC	1061st	MP Company
Camm	Lyman B.	PFC	510th	
Camp	Clement G.	S/Sgt.	509th	
Company	Clifford O.	T/Sgt.	510th	
Campbell	Herbert J.	Cpl.	508th	
Campbell	Hugh C.	S/Sgt.	510th	
Campbell	James V.	S/Sgt.	509th	
Campbell	Julius E.	S/Sgt.	510th	
Campbell	Parley R.	S/Sgt.	509th	
Campbell	William R.	S/Sgt.	511th	
Campisi	Vito F.	PFC	511th	
Canada	Lester N.	S/Sgt.	508th	
Candelaria	Louis R.	Sgt.	509th	KIA 10/7/44
Canetzka	Frank J.	Sgt.	511th	
Cannerelli	John J.	F.O.	510th	
Cannizzaro	Anthony	Pvt.	511th	Int'd 10/7/44
Cannizzo	Joseph	F.O.	510th	
Cannon	Charles F.	S/Sgt.	509th	
Cannon	Charles N.	S/Sgt.	509th	
Cannon	Harold C.	1st Lt.	509th	POW 1/11/44
Cannon	Meredith W.	T/Sgt.	511th	
Canons	Joseph C.	1st Lt.	509th	
Cantrell	Hugh C.	PFC	509th	
Cantrell	Lloyd L. Jr.	1st Lt.	509th	
Cantrelle	Albert B.	Sgt.	510th	KIA 2/6/45
Capobianco	Frederick J.	T/Sgt.	509th	
Caporale	Michael R.	F.O.	510th	
Cappaccio	Paul R.	PFC	508th	
Cappona	Anthony P.	Sgt.	511th	KIA 9/12/44
Capper	Donald F.	S/Sgt.	509th	POW 6/28/43
Capps	Edwin A.	F.O.	508th	
Carbone	Anthony R.	1st Lt.	509th	
Card	Robert G.	S/Sgt.	511th	
Cardamona	Thomas V.	S/Sgt.	508th	
Cariens	Leo F.	Sgt.	508th	
Carl	Clair I.	S/Sgt.	510th	
Carlberg	Stanley T.	Sgt.	509th	
Carle	Richard D.	1st Lt.	510th	
Carlin	William H.	Cpl.	447th	
Carlo	Carmine	Pvt.	508th	Sub-Depot
Carlotta	Michael Jr.	2nd Lt.	511th	
Carlson	Charles E. Jr.	S/Sgt.	509th	
Carlson	Dale L.	S/Sgt.	511th	
Carlson	Donald J.	T/Sgt.	508th	
Carlson	Eric G.	2nd Lt.	508th	
Carlson	Norman W.	Pvt.	1629th	Ord. S&M Co.
Carlyle	Barney W.	PFC	509th	
Carman	Herbert W.	PFC	1629th	Sub-Depot
Carmichael	Charles E.	S/Sgt.	447th	
Carmichael	William F.	2nd Lt.	509th	POW 1/11/44
Carneal	Virgil E. Jr.	2nd Lt.	511th	POW 8/6/44
Carnegie	Thomas M. III	F.O.	511th	Int'd 10/7/44
Carney	Francis J.	Sgt.	508th	
Carney	Joseph S.	Sgt.	508th	
Carney	William A.	S/Sgt.	511th	
Carr	William P.	PFC	1629th	Ord. S&M Co.
Carr	John H.	M/Sgt.	511th	
Carr	Mahlon L.	PFC	508th	
Carranza	Joseph F.	Cpl.	510th	
Carraway	John B.	Lt. Col.	510th	
Carroll	Leo J.	1st Lt.	511th	
Carroll	Marvin W.	Pvt.	509th	
Carroll	Silas E. Jr.	Sgt.	1206th	QM Company
Carson	Charles W.	PFC	447th	Sub-Depot
Carson	Clarence L.	1st Lt.	511th	
Carson	John P. Jr.	Capt.	508th	
Carswell	Bryce J.	Sgt.	509th	POW 2/11/44
Carswell	Sam F.	Cpl.	510th	
Carter	Claudius E.	S/Sgt.	511th	
Carter	Merlin I.	Col.	351st	HQ
Carter	Oliver R.	T/Sgt.	508th	
Carter	William A.	Sgt.	511th	
Cartwright	Edgar D.	2nd Lt.	508th	POW 9/16/44
Cartwright	H. W.	S/Sgt.	508th	
Caruso	Burton W.	2nd Lt.	509th	POW 6/22/43
Caruso	Santo A.	S/Sgt.	508th	Killed 6/8/45
Carver	Carthal B.	S/Sgt.	508th	KIA 3/2/44
Canwile	John D.	T/Sgt.	510th	
Case	Clyde W.	S/Sgt.	351st	
Case	Richard J.	S/Sgt.	509th	HQ
Casey	Donald R.	S/Sgt.	510th	POW 3/18/44
Casey	Patrick K.	PFC	511th	
Casper	Robert W.	S/Sgt.	509th	
Cassella	Robert D.	2nd Lt.	508th	
Castellani	William	Sgt.	1629th	Ord. S&M Co.
Caster	A. R.	Sgt.	511th	
Castle	Orville L.	2nd Lt.	508th	
Casto	Leo W.	Pvt.	511th	KIA 11/26/43
Catalini	Vincent L.	Capt.	509th	
Cater	Ernest J.	2nd Lt.	351st	HQ
Catlett	George M.	Sgt.	510th	
Catlett	William H.	Sgt.	508th	
Cator	Ralph A.	M/Sgt.	511th	
Catterall	Calvin	S/Sgt.	508th	
Caudill	Carroll C.	Cpl.	509th	
Caudle	Clyde M.	T/Sgt.	509th	MIA 1/11/44
Caughlan	Eugene C.	1st Lt.	510th	
Caughman	Richard D.	1st Lt.	508th	
Cauthen	John K.	S/Sgt.	509th	
Cavanaugh	Carl F.	Spec. 5	854th	Chemical Co.
Cavanaugh	Charles D.	S/Sgt.	510th	POW 7/25/43
Cavett	Frank W.	2nd Lt.	511th	KIA 9/8/44
Cawetzka	Clinton M.	2nd Lt.	509th	POW 10/7/44
Cebrzynski	Francis J.	F.O.	511th	
Cebulak	Frank Z.	Sgt.	508th	
Cecicco	Joseph S.	S/Sgt.	508th	Sub-Depot
Cefoia	Albert J.	S/Sgt.	447th	
Cehoda	Anthony J.	PFC	1629th	Ord. S&M Co.
Celentano	Joseph P.	PFC	511th	
Cella	Vincent P.	Cpl.	11th	St. Comp.
Celler	William P.	Sgt.	11th	St. Comp.
Genons	Irving	S/Sgt.	509th	
Centola	Joseph C.	1st Lt.	509th	
Centola	J. L.	Pvt.	11th	St. Comp.
Cenrackio	Ralph Q.	PFC	510th	
Cerasini	Armond J.	S/Sgt.	854th	Chemical Co.
Cervantes	John F.	Sgt.	509th	
Cesarini	Frank O.	Sgt.	510th	
Ceska	Augustus J.	1st Lt.	510th	KIA 6/14/44
Cessna	Paul T.	Sgt.	510th	
Chaapel	Marion R.	2nd Lt.	508th	POW 11/26/43
Chacon	Robert R.	Sgt.	509th	
Chacon	Alejandro J.	S/Sgt.	511th	
Chadbourne	Arturo C.	Sgt.	509th	
Chaffin	Charles E.	S/Sgt.	509th	Killed 5/7/43
Chagnon	Claude M.	S/Sgt.	511th	POW 10/7/44
Chalas	Harry J.	Cpl.	1629th	Ord. S&M Co.
Chalby	John R.	2nd Lt.	510th	
Chalmers	Leo A.	1st Lt.	351st	HQ
Chamberlain	Robert P.	1st Lt.	510th	
Chamberlain	Fred J.	2nd Lt.	508th	KIA 8/6/44
Chamberlin	Roland H.	2nd Lt.	510th	
Chambers	Clarence J.	S/Sgt.	511th	POW 10/14/43
Chambers	Ernest W.	S/Sgt.	509th	
Chambers	Harry K.	2nd Lt.	508th	
Chambers	Henry M.	PFC	11th	
Chambers	Herman W.	S/Sgt.	1061st	MP Company
Chance	Cleary C.	Cpl.	1061st	MP Company
Chandler	Floyd	Cpl.	447th	Sub-Depot
Chandler	James	Sgt.	508th	
Chandler	Walton W.	PFC	508th	
Chaney	Wess C.	2nd Lt.	1061st	MP Company
Chaney	Don M.	S/Sgt.	508th	
Chaney	Robert M.	Sgt.	509th	
Chapin	Ralph W.	Cpl.	508th	
Chaplinski	John	T/Sgt.	509th	
Chaplow	Leroy H.	Cpl.	508th	
Chapman	H. B.	Maj.	511th	
Chapman	Jack A.	PFC	509th	
Chapman	James R.	1st Lt.	508th	POW 7/19/44
Chapman	Richard G.	2nd Lt.	510th	
Chappel	Jerome J.	S/Sgt.	511th	KIA 3/12/45
Charm	Harry	S/Sgt.	510th	
Charyn	Milton	Cpl.	511th	
Chase	Frank A.	T/Sgt.	509th	
Chase	Robert	Cpl.	508th	KIA 8/16/44
Chauncey	William R. Jr.	2nd Lt.	508th	POW 11/26/43
Cheek	Robert L. Jr.	Sgt.	508th	POW 1/11/44
Chelstowski	Eugene R.	Sgt.	510th	
Chenoweth	Stewart C.	2nd Lt.	511th	
Chere	G. A.	Cpl.	1629th	Ord. S&M Co.
Cheswick	Richard R.	1st Lt.	508th	
Chewning	Edward C. Jr.	1st Lt.	508th	Int'd 10/7/44
Chickola	Joseph A.	Sgt.	511th	KIA 3/18/44
Childers	Garland M.	S/Sgt.	509th	
Childers	Woodrow W.	PFC	1061st	MP Company
Chiler	Joseph H.	S/Sgt.	508th	
Chiodo	Thomas F.	Sgt.	509th	
Chmielewski	Edward C.	Sgt.	508th	
Chmura	M.	S/Sgt.	508th	
Choquette	Bennie J.	T/Sgt.	509th	
Christensen	Bruno J.	S/Sgt.	508th	
Christensen	Ralph W.	T/Sgt.	511th	POW 10/7/44
Christensen	Benjamin F.	2nd Lt.	509th	KIA 10/7/44
Christiansen	Harold A.	M/Sgt.	508th	
Christiansen	Paul W.	1st Lt.	508th	
Christie	Charles N.	T/Sgt.	508th	
Christie	Christian O.	Spec. 5	854th	Chemical Co.
Christman	Joseph F.	S/Sgt.	510th	
Christopher	Lewis J.	Sgt.	508th	
Christophers	Lloyd A.	1st Lt.	447th	
Chubb	James A.	2nd Lt.	510th	
Church	William R.	2nd Lt.	508th	
Church	Richard G.	M/Sgt.	510th	
Churchill	John B.	2nd Lt.	508th	
Ciarcia	John W.	PFC	11th	
Ciarfaglia	Conrad P.	Cpl.	510th	
Cieslak	Tony	S/Sgt.	510th	KIA 12/30/43
Cieslik	Dominick N.	Cpl.	510th	
Cieslinski	Thaddeus G.	Cpl.	508th	Sub-Depot
Cihlar	William F.	Sgt.	447th	
Cina	Benjamin R.	PFC	252nd	Medical Disp.
Cinq-Mars	John S.	S/Sgt.	509th	Killed 5/7/43
Cipriano	Edward G.	Cpl.	11th	St. Comp.
Ciraulo	Nicholas A.	Cpl.	510th	KIA 9/12/44
Civizzio	Leon H.	Sgt.	511th	POW 1/11/44
Clagett	John J.	S/Sgt.	510th	
Claggett	Samuel J.	Sgt.	252nd	
	Rocco F.	1st Lt.	510th	
	Albert L.	T/Sgt.	351st	
	Lawrence G.	S/Sgt.	509th	
		1st Lt.	509th	HQ

Claggett / Crane

Last Name	First Name	Rank	Unit	Notes
Claggett	William W.	S/Sgt.	511th	POW 6/28/43
Claire	Joseph C.	Pvt.	11th	St. Comp.
Clancy	Charles M.	Sgt.	510th	
Clanton	Earnest E.	Pvt.	1206th	QM Company
Clapp	William L.	2nd Lt.	510th	POW 6/14/44
Clarac	Harold A.	S/Sgt.	508th	
Clark	Edward H. L.	1st Lt.	508th	
Clark	Charles H.	Sgt.	11th	St. Comp.
Clark	Donald L.	F.O.	510th	
Clark	Douglas W.	2nd Lt.	508th	
Clark	James T.	Cpl.	1061st	MP Company
Clark	Johnny E.	2nd Lt.	511th	
Clark	Spurgeon W. Jr.	2nd Lt.	509th	POW 1/17/45
Clark	Vernon A.	S/Sgt.	511th	
Clark	Virgil L.	S/Sgt.	510th	
Clark	William S.	Sgt.	509th	
Clarke	James H.	1st Lt.	201st	Finance Sect.
Clarke	Thomas W.	1st Lt.	509th	Int'd 10/7/44
Claveau	Troy V.	Pvt.	510th	
Clay	Robert E.	T/Sgt.	508th	
Clay	Bolba A.	S/Sgt.	509th	POW 5/24/44
Clay	Robert B.	Capt.	11th	St. Comp.
Clayburn	Clyde W.	PFC	510th	
Clayton	John M.	PFC	508th	
Cleary	John P.	Cpl.	1061st	MP Company
Clegg	Oliver L.	Cpl.	510th	Sub-Depot
Clemence	John A.	Sgt.	447th	
Clemens	Charles J.	2nd Lt.	510th	
Clements	James S.	S/Sgt.	509th	
Clendenning	Wesley J.	2nd Lt.	509th	Ord. S&M Co.
Cleveland	Careleton A.	PFC	1629th	
Cleveland	Joe I.	T/Sgt.	509th	
Click	Orville R.	PFC	11th	St. Comp.
Clifton	James R.	PFC	11th	St. Comp.
Clifton	Luther R.	F.O.	511th	POW 8/6/44
Clifton	Morris H.	PFC	508th	
Climer	Curvis E.	Cpl.	508th	
Cline	James T.	S/Sgt.	511th	KIA 9/8/44
Clinton	Ernest J.	S/Sgt.	509th	
Clinton	William H.	Sgt.	1206th	QM Company
Clise	Jack M.	Sgt.	511th	POW 9/12/44
Cliver	William A.	Cpl.	11th	St. Comp.
Clodfelter	David O.	PFC	854th	Chemical Co.
Cloos	Drexil H.	PFC	11th	St. Comp.
Cluett	Gregory S.	F.O.	11th	St. Comp.
Clupper	Fred L.	Sgt.	351st	
Coa	Jesse	Sgt.	508th	
Coan	Francis M.	Cpl.	1206th	QM Company
Coaten	William C.	PFC	511th	POW 8/3/44
Coates	Charles M. Jr.	PFC	11th	
Coates	Donald	PFC	11th	
Cobb	George O.	2nd Lt.	511th	
Cobb	Roy J.	Cpl.	511th	
Cobb	Thomas A.	S/Sgt.	508th	
Coble	John L.	Sgt.	511th	
Coburn	Dillon B.	T/Sgt.	509th	
Cocco	Ernest E.	S/Sgt.	510th	
Coculto	Joseph R.	T/Sgt.	510th	
Code	Orrin J. Jr.	2nd Lt.	510th	
Coe	Robert W.	2nd Lt.	508th	
Coff	Earl G.	PFC	510th	
Coffey	Daniel M.	S/Sgt.	508th	
Coffman	Henry	F.O.	508th	
Cohen	William I.	2nd Lt.	508th	
Cohen	Henry D.	S/Sgt.	511th	KIA 5/28/44
Coile	Louis L.	Sgt.	511th	
Colbert	Henry P.	Pvt.	508th	
Colbert	Isom	PFC	508th	
Colbum	William E. Jr.	1st Lt.	508th	KIA 2/6/45
Colbum	Eugene A.	S/Sgt.	509th	
Colbum	Roland H.	Sgt.	447th	
Cole	Bernard E.	1st Lt.	511th	POW 4/18/44
Cole	Boyd W.	S/Sgt.	511th	
Cole	Darrell V. Jr.	1st Lt.	508th	
Cole	Max S.	Sgt.	511th	
Cole	Willie L.	S/Sgt.	509th	
Coleman	Clyde W.	T/Sgt.	510th	
Coleman	Ermin E. Jr.	Sgt.	509th	
Coleman	Ludie M. Jr.	Cpl.	510th	
Colky	Albert	2nd Lt.	508th	
Collar	Clifton C.	Sgt.	509th	
Collette	John W.	F.O.	511th	POW 12/31/43
Collier	G. R.	Pvt.	510th	
Collier	Harry J.	PFC	11th	St. Comp.
Collier	R. J.	Cpl.	1061st	MP Company
Collins	Burl T.	2nd Lt.	509th	POW 11/26/44
Collins	Duluth C.	Sgt.	508th	Sub-Depot
Collins	Elmo Jr.	1st Lt.	510th	
Collins	Eugene I.	Pvt.	351st	
Collins	Jerry G.	Sgt.	509th	Killed 6/8/45
Collins	Johnnie N.	Spec. 5	1061st	HQ
Collins	Joseph A.	Sgt.	510th	KIA 9/8/44
Collins	Kenneth W.	Sgt.	508th	KIA 12/30/43
Collins	Leo J.	S/Sgt.	1061st	MP Company
Collins	Levi H.	PFC	447th	KIA 5/15/43
Collins	Melvin J.	S/Sgt.	510th	
Collins	Wallace E.	1st Lt.	511th	
Colodny	Eugene T.	S/Sgt.	509th	
Colona	Tony	Cpl.	1061st	
Colowski	Chester J.	S/Sgt.	510th	POW 6/28/43
Cols	R. F.	2nd Lt.	510th	
Colvin	Clifford K.	F.O.	511th	
Coman	James B.	2nd Lt.	508th	Int'd 8/6/44
Comfort	J. Z.	F.O.	510th	POW 5/17/43
Compa	Adrian K.	2nd Lt.	510th	
Comperchio	John J.	S/Sgt.	509th	
Comstock	Frederick O.	2nd Lt.	509th	
Condin	Robert L.	Sgt.	508th	
Condon	Robert W.	1st Lt.	508th	
Condon	William J.	2nd Lt.	508th	
Conley	James L.	Cpl.	508th	
Conley	Leo W.	T/Sgt.	511th	
Conley	Joseph R.	S/Sgt.	508th	
Conley	Ralph M.	S/Sgt.	508th	
Conley	Ralph P.	S/Sgt.	508th	
Conn	Robert	Pvt.	511th	
Connel	H. E.	Sgt.	508th	
Connelly	William I.	F.O.	508th	
Connelly	Henry D.	Sgt.	508th	
Conner	John C.	Sgt.	511th	
Connors	Harold W.	Pvt.	508th	
Conrad	William E. Jr.	1st Lt.	508th	
Conrad	Joseph	S/Sgt.	509th	
Conroy	Theron W.	Sgt.	508th	
Consoli	Neil P.	1st Lt.	511th	
Contioso	Samuel S.	2nd Lt.	508th	
Cook	Ralph T.	Sgt.	511th	
Cook	Bruce S.	Sgt.	509th	
Cook	Byron F.	T/Sgt.	509th	
Cook	Charles E.	T/Sgt.	509th	
Cook	David C.	T/Sgt.	509th	
Cook	John R.	S/Sgt.	508th	
Cook	Kenneth D.	S/Sgt.	510th	POW 12/31/43
Cook	Leo W.	1st Lt.	510th	
Cook	P. A.	F.O.	511th	HQ
Cook	Richard J.	Sgt.	351st	
Cook	Wardon E.	S/Sgt.	511th	POW 11/26/44
Cook	William L.	S/Sgt.	447th	Sub-Depot
Cook	Joseph Y.	1st Lt.	508th	
Cooley	Roland E. Jr.	2nd Lt.	509th	
Coon	Edward L.	Sgt.	508th	
Cooney	Nicholas J.	Sgt.	510th	
Coons	Sheldon R. Jr.	Pvt.	351st	
Cooper	Dewey A. Jr.	Sgt.	509th	Killed 6/8/45
Cooper	Erwin N.	2nd Lt.	508th	KIA 9/8/44
Cooper	Robert A.	Cpl.	1061st	KIA 12/30/43
Cooper	Robert P.	2nd Lt.	508th	MP Company
Cooper	Thomas L.	1st Lt.	510th	KIA 5/15/43
Copeland	Derward R.	1st Lt.	509th	
Copobianco	Frederick J.	T/Sgt.	510th	POW 6/28/43
Copt	Marcel M.	S/Sgt.	511th	
Corcoran	Thomas J.	S/Sgt.	509th	
Corcoran	William V.	T/Sgt.	511th	
Cordel	Junior	Pvt.	511th	
Cordell	Gardner L.	PFC	510th	
Corder	Delbert E.	PFC	511th	
Cordery	Henry C.	T/Sgt.	509th	
Core	Elmer E.	S/Sgt.	510th	
Corigliano	Frank A.	Cpl.	510th	
Corish	Arthur R.	Cpl.	508th	KIA 2/6/45
Cornell	Donald A.	2nd Lt.	511th	
Cornell	William I.	Sgt.	508th	
Cornett	John F.	Cpl.	508th	Sub-Depot
Cornish	Clarence C.	S/Sgt.	447th	
Cortez	Ramiro G.	Sgt.	511th	
Cosgrove	William P.	1st Lt.	511th	
Costello	John J.	S/Sgt.	508th	POW 6/28/43
Costello	Patrick J.	2nd Lt.	508th	Killed 5/7/43
Cotherman	George F.	2nd Lt.	509th	
Cotterman	Jack W.	S/Sgt.	510th	
Cotton	Curties L.	T/Sgt.	509th	
Cottrell	Charles R.	Cpl.	508th	KIA 8/6/44
Coulam	John R.	Capt.	511th	
Counts	John T.	2nd Lt.	510th	
Court	George W.	Sgt.	1629th	Ord. S&M Co.
Courtney	Claude C. Jr.	Cpl.	508th	
Courtney	Elwood B.	S/Sgt.	508th	
Coverdale	Marion C.	Sgt.	511th	
Covert	Franklin E.	S/Sgt.	510th	
Covert	Paul T.	S/Sgt.	511th	
Covey	William J.	S/Sgt.	510th	
Coward	John L.	Sgt.	508th	
Cowdin	James D. R.	Cpl.	447th	Sub-Depot
Cowell	John B.	S/Sgt.	508th	
Cowings	R. P.	PFC	508th	
Cowley	Ralph P. Jr.	T/Sgt.	508th	Int'd 10/7/44
Cox	John M.	S/Sgt.	510th	
Cox	Kenneth N.	S/Sgt.	509th	KIA 4/13/44
Cox	Richard M.	2nd Lt.	509th	
Cox	Trimadge A.	PFC	1061st	MP Company
Coyle	William B.	2nd Lt.	510th	
Coyle	William R.	S/Sgt.	508th	
Coyle	Clifford H.	S/Sgt.	510th	MIA 5/19/43
Cozzolino	John N.	Sgt.	508th	
Crabb	Joseph N.	Sgt.	508th	
Craig	Nicholas	Capt.	351st	HQ
Craig	Kenneth M.	1st Lt.	508th	
Craig	Edward W.	Maj.	510th	HQ
Craig	Fletcher M.	PFC	1061st	MP Company
Crallo	Herndon K.	Sgt.	509th	
Cram	Jesse E.	1st Lt.	511th	
Cramer	Roy A.	Cpl.	510th	
Cramer	Paul	Pvt.	447th	Sub-Depot
Crandall	Marvin L.	Sgt.	509th	
Crandall	Vincent R.	1st Lt.	509th	
Crandall	William L.	S/Sgt.	509th	
Crandall	Donald G.	S/Sgt.	510th	
Crandall	Robert G.	F.O.	509th	
Crane	Charles L.	Sgt.	508th	

Crane / Decicco

Last Name	First Name	Rank	Unit	Notes
Crane	Ralph M.	T/Sgt.	510th	
Crane	Verne W.	S/Sgt.	511th	
Craumer	Kenneth W.	T/Sgt.	509th	Killed 6/8/45
Craven	James D.	1st Lt.	508th	
Craven	Linden W.	Cpl.	508th	
Craver	Charles M.	S/Sgt.	509th	
Craver	Robert E.	Pvt.	11th	St. Comp.
Cravin	William F.	1st Lt.	511th	Sub-Depot
Crawford	Donald J.	T/Sgt.	447th	
Crawford	Leslie D.	1st Lt.	508th	
Crawford	Raymond P.	Cpl.	511th	
Crawford	Robert W.	Sgt.	509th	KIA 10/7/44
Cray		Cpl.	509th	
Creach	David C.	S/Sgt.	510th	
Creech	Wesley J.	S/Sgt.	509th	
Creek	Douglas W.	T/Sgt.	508th	
Cregar	Charles E.	1st Lt.	511th	POW 10/3/44
Crennan	Joseph M.	1st Lt.	511th	
Crenshaw	W. H.	Sgt.	1061st	
Cressey	Stanley B.	PFC	511th	MP Company
Crews	Archie E.	2nd Lt.	509th	
Crews	Oscar L.	1st Lt.	508th	
Crews	Robert W.	Capt.	511th	
Criqui	Joseph E.	1st Lt.	510th	POW 10/14/43
Crismon	Oliver W.	S/Sgt.	511th	POW 6/28/43
Criswell	Emery K.	S/Sgt.	510th	
Crittenden	John B.	T/Sgt.	509th	
Crivello	William R.	S/Sgt.	510th	
Crockett	J.C.	PFC	11th	St. Comp.
Crockett	William	1st Lt.	510th	
Crone	Robert G.	S/Sgt.	511th	
Croney	Henry A.	Sgt.	509th	
Cronin	James J.	1st Lt.	511th	POW 10/9/43
Crosby	Robert T.	Sgt.	509th	
Crouch	Charles T.	Sgt.	508th	
Crouch	Wesley	Sgt.	106/1st	
Crowder	Morris	T/Sgt.	510th	Sub-Depot
Crowe	Peter E.	1st Lt.	447th	KIA 5/28/44
Crowell	Frank A.	Sgt.	508th	
Crowell	Gene H.	2nd Lt.	509th	
Croydon	Theodore	1st Lt.	510th	St. Comp.
Crum	Charles J.	S/Sgt.	510th	
Crum	Harold R.	T/Sgt.	511th	POW 10/9/43
Crumley	Warner	M/Sgt.	509th	
Crumley	Jack F.	Cpl.	510th	
Crump	Robert E.	S/Sgt.	508th	
Crump	Herbert B.	Sgt.	508th	
Cruse	Sherman	Cpl.	106/1st	
Crutcher	Leroy D.	S/Sgt.	510th	
Cruthirds	John W.	1st Lt.	508th	
Cue	Leslie S.	Capt.	508th	
	Bertrum G.	S/Sgt.	511th	
Culbert	Walter M.	2nd Lt.	510th	
Culkin	Thomas P.	Sgt.	510th	POW 9/12/44
Cullen	J. J. J.	2nd Lt.	11th	POW 5/14/43
Culver	Alfred B.	S/Sgt.	511th	St. Comp.
Culver	S. C.	Sgt.	510th	
Cummins	George W.	S/Sgt.	510th	
Cummins	Keith S.	Sgt.	508th	
Cumpata	Frank G.	2nd Lt.	509th	POW 1/11/44
Cunningham	John	Pvt.	11th	St. Comp.
Cunningham	Paul H.	Pvt.	11th	St. Comp.
Cunningham	Thomas W.	PFC	11th	St. Comp.
Cunningham	William J.	1st Lt.	509th	
Cupit	Otis R.	S/Sgt.	1629th	Ord. S&M Co.
Cupp	Clarence F.	M/Sgt.	510th	
Curcio	Dominick E.	T/Sgt.	511th	
Curis	Theodore P.	T/Sgt.	508th	POW 10/9/43
Curley	John F.	1st Lt.	511th	
Curley	Leo A.	1st Lt.	351st	HQ
Curran	John R.	Sgt.	509th	
Currie	Gail G. Jr.	2nd Lt.	508th	
Curry	James J.	Cpl.	511th	
Curry	James R.	Sgt.	509th	
Curse	Joseph R.	Sgt.	511th	
Curtis	Leroy D.	Sgt.	510th	
Cushman	Billy S.	S/Sgt.	508th	
Custard	Aaron D.	2nd Lt.	510th	
Custer	William H. Jr.	1st Lt.	511th	POW 10/7/44
Cutforth	Albert R.	S/Sgt.	511th	KIA 12/31/43
Cutler	Stanley E. Jr.	2nd Lt.	510th	
Cutler	Donald J.	2nd Lt.	509th	
Cutting	Joseph C.	Sgt.	511th	
Cuvar	Robert L.	Pvt.	510th	
Czachorowsky	Emerald G.	Capt.	509th	KIA 2/6/45
Czarzasty	Joseph J.	Sgt.	510th	
Cznakiel	Edmond M.	Sgt.	508th	
	Bert J.	Cpl.	511th	

D

Last Name	First Name	Rank	Unit	Notes
D'Amore	John J.	PFC	11th	St. Comp.
D'Angelo	John V.	Cpl.	508th	
D'Azze	Jack E.	S/Sgt.	508th	
Dahl	Fred R. Jr.	2nd Lt.	511th	KIA 9/12/44
Dahl	Gordon W.	PFC	509th	
Dahlborg	William	S/Sgt.	509th	
Dahlman	Edwin J.	Cpl.	11th	
Daigle	Lucien	1st Lt.	508th	
Daigle	Reginald	Sgt.	509th	
Daily	Frank E.	Spec. 4	1629th	Ord. S&M Co.
DalPorto	Bernard Jr.	S/Sgt.	1629th	Ord. S&M Co.
Daley	Joseph J.	Capt.	447th	Sub-Depot
Dalidowicz	Stanley P.	Cpl.	509th	
Daloiso	Ralph	S/Sgt.	511th	
Dalton	John L. Jr.	F.O.	509th	
Daly	Francis M.	Pvt.	510th	POW 5/14/43
Daly	William J.	T/Sgt.	11th	St. Comp.
Damos	Paul G.	Capt.	510th	
Danby	Jack E.	2nd Lt.	508th	POW 12/31/43
Danheiser	Stanley R.	Sgt.	509th	
Daniel	Jack H.	T/Sgt.	509th	
Daniels	George	S/Sgt.	447th	Sub-Depot
Daniels	James N.	Pvt.	508th	
Daniels	Willard L.	PFC	11th	St. Comp.
Danielson	Robert B.	1st Lt.	511th	St. Comp.
Daniul	Walter	S/Sgt.	508th	Ord. S&M Co.
Dank	Joseph T.	Cpl.	510th	
Danshaw	John W.	Spec. 5	11th	St. Comp.
Dansie	Westley M.	S/Sgt.	11th	St. Comp.
Dantzler	Charles N.	T/Sgt.	510th	
Darban	Charles	Sgt.	509th	
Dargis	William P.	M/Sgt.	508th	
Dargue	Donald S.	1st Lt.	511th	POW 10/7/44
Darley	Richard J.	2nd Lt.	509th	
Daring	Lewis E.	Sgt.	511th	
Darrel	John	Sgt.	510th	
Darty	Earnley C.	Sgt.	509th	
Dascher	Jefferson A.	M/Sgt.	508th	St. Comp.
Daubert	John A.	PFC	11th	
Daugher	Robert B.	PFC	510th	
Daugherty	Charles E. Jr.	Capt.	509th	POW 3/22/44
Daugherty	Joseph W.	2nd Lt.	508th	
Daughtry	Ennis L.	Sgt.	511th	
Dauzat	Paul	Pvt.	508th	
Davault	Dean W.	S/Sgt.	508th	
Davey	Kenneth W.	Capt.	510th	
David	Edward F.	Sgt.	509th	Sub-Depot
David	James C.	Capt.	447th	Int'd 3/18/44
Davies	Richard L.	1st Lt.	511th	
Davis	John H.	Pvt.	510th	Sub-Depot
Davis	Andrew L.	Cpl.	447th	
Davis	Burton K.	1st Lt.	511th	
Davis	Clarence V.	Spec. 5	854th	Chemical Co.
Davis	Cleo H.	T/Sgt.	510th	
Davis	Earl B.	T/Sgt.	508th	
Davis	Edwin C.	PFC	509th	
Davis	Edwin L. Jr.	S/Sgt.	510th	
Davis	Emerson	Cpl.	509th	
Davis	Gore O.	T/Sgt.	509th	
Davis	Homer O.	PFC	11th	
Davis	Horace F.	PFC	508th	POW 10/9/43
Davis	Howard A.	2nd Lt.	508th	
Davis	James W.	T/Sgt.	508th	
Davis	King E.	Pvt.	1206th	QM Company
Davis	Leoland J. Jr.	T/Sgt.	508th	
Davis	Lynn C.	Cpl.	509th	
Davis	Perry	PFC	854th	Chemical Co.
Davis	Richard L.	1st Lt.	511th	
Davis	Samuel A.	M/Sgt.	511th	
Davis	W. B.	PFC	509th	
Davis	Willard E.	S/Sgt.	509th	
Davison	William E.	S/Sgt.	511th	
Davison	Lowell A.	S/Sgt.	510th	
Davison	William O.	T/Sgt.	1629th	Ord. S&M Co.
Dawsey	James R.	Cpl.	510th	
Dawson	Malcolm H.	T/Sgt.	509th	
Dawson	Robert C.	Cpl.	508th	
Dawson	Samuel J.	Sgt.	508th	
Day	Thomas A.	1st Lt.	509th	
Day	Ernest W.	T/Sgt.	854th	Chemical Co.
Day	Jack F.	S/Sgt.	447th	Sub-Depot
Day	William A.	1st Lt.	509th	
DeBlanc	William L.	Sgt.	508th	
DeBlock	Wilbur A.	S/Sgt.	510th	
DeBoer	Nicholas	Sgt.	510th	
DeBolt	Dale C.	Sgt.	11th	St. Comp.
DeBruce	Wayne S.	T/Sgt.	447th	Sub-Depot
DeCecco	Joseph T.	Cpl.	509th	
DeClue	Ernest E.	PFC	511th	
DeCresce	Charles H.	S/Sgt.	510th	
DeDemonico	Isadore C.	Sgt.	509th	
DeGennaro	Ralph J.	Sgt.	511th	KIA 9/12/44
DeGraff	Louis D.	Sgt.	510th	
DeGroodt	John W.	S/Sgt.	509th	
Deguglielmo	Donald E.	Sgt.	509th	
DeHart	Anthony F.	S/Sgt.	447th	Sub-Depot
DeLaura	Johnnie A.	S/Sgt.	508th	POW 5/27/44
DeLeon	John V.	1st Lt.	510th	
DeMarco	Jacinto M.	PFC	509th	
DeMarie	Lorenzo B.	PFC	854th	Chemical Co.
DeMattos	Frank J.	Sgt.	510th	
DeMore	Michael	S/Sgt.	509th	
DePaulo	Edward T.	S/Sgt.	508th	POW 3/22/44
DeVan	Louis	Cpl.	252nd	Medical Disp.
Deal	Vincent J.	Sgt.	509th	
Deal	Brian L.	2nd Lt.	511th	
Deal	Edgar J.	2nd Lt.	11th	St. Comp.
Dean	James F.	Capt.	508th	
Dean	Joe M.	Pvt.	509th	
Dean	Frank J.	T/Sgt.	11th	St. Comp.
Dear	William L.	1st Lt.	511th	
Dearborn	Nick P.	PFC	509th	
Dearth	Alfred L.	2nd Lt.	511th	MIA 12/31/43
Deaver	Edwin K.	T/Sgt.	508th	
Debnar	James W.	PFC	508th	
Decicco	Albert J.	S/Sgt.	447th	Sub-Depot

Decker / Dunnigan

Surname	First Name	Rank	Unit	Notes
Decker	George M.	1st Lt.	509th	
Decker	Harold F.	PFC	447th	Sub-Depot
Deckleman	Henry F.	Cpl.	510th	
Dee	John B.	1st Lt.	11th	St. Comp.
Deene	Doyle W.	Cpl.	510th	
Deering	L. D.	PFC	509th	
Deery	William N.	2nd Lt.	511th	
Deiman	Arthur L.	Sgt.	508th	POW 1/30/44
Del Conte	Albert A.	T/Sgt.	510th	
Del Conte	G. C.	T/Sgt.	510th	
Delaney	James J.	S/Sgt.	508th	
Delaney	William R.	T/Sgt.	511th	
Delbo	Isidore D.	Pvt.	510th	
Delk	Aubrey M.	M/Sgt.	511th	
Delker	Elmer S.	2nd Lt.	509th	
Della-Cioppa	Marius N.	2nd Lt.	511th	
Demerritt	George H.	S/Sgt.	508th	KIA 2/21/44
Demos	Paul C.	S/Sgt.	509th	
Demoss	C. H.	PFC	510th	
Dempsey	Charles A.	M/Sgt.	508th	Medical Disp.
Denenkamp	Carl J.	Sgt.	1206th	QM Company
Dengel	Edward H. Jr.	1st Lt.	508th	
Denilson	Austin V.	2nd Lt.	511th	
Denison	Gilbert L.	S/Sgt.	508th	
Dennen	Cornelius E.	Sgt.	509th	
Denney	Aaron	PFC	511th	
Dennis	Edwin E.	Cpl.	252nd	
Dennis	Lee H.	Maj.	510th	
Denniston	Paul H.	Sgt.	509th	
Denny	Robert E.	Spec. 4	1629th	
Denton	John M.	S/Sgt.	509th	POW 5/27/44
Derby	George J.	S/Sgt.	510th	
Deroever	Frederick R.	PFC	447th	Sub-Depot
Derosa	Frank J.	S/Sgt.	511th	
Derrick	Walter C.	T/Sgt.	1206th	QM Company
Desmong	Paul E.	Sgt.	511th	
Detner	Byron J.	T/Sgt.	510th	
Detro	Lester D.	2nd Lt.	510th	
Deupree	James Y.	Sgt.	508th	
Deutsch	Charles E.	Sgt.	509th	Killed 6/8/45
Devaney	Camille F.	Sgt.	854th	Chemical Co.
Dever	Paul P.	P/O	509th	
Devilin	Gerard P.	S/Sgt.	510th	
Devore	Louis	Cpl.	252nd	Medical Disp.
Devries	Ray M.	Sgt.	1629th	
Di Pascale	Angelo J.	T/Sgt.	510th	
Diaz	Ignacio Z	PFC	508th	
DiChiera	Salvador P.	S/Sgt.	854th	Chemical Co.
Dick	Kenneth F.	T/Sgt.	508th	
Dickens	Enoch D.	Sgt.	509th	
Dickerson	Carl L.	S/Sgt.	508th	
Dickerson	Houston R.	S/Sgt.	447th	Sub-Depot
Dickman	Ralph L.	S/Sgt.	511th	
Dickmann	Joseph A.	1st Lt.	509th	
Didier	Albert F.	S/Sgt.	252nd	Medical Disp.
Dido	Robert J.	F.O.	508th	
Diehl	Robert O.	F.O.	510th	
Dietel	Stanley L.	Sgt.	511th	
Dietrich	Augustus P.	Cpl.	11th	POW 12/31/43
Dietrich	Douglas S.	S/Sgt.	509th	KIA 2/6/45
Dietrich	Dexter L.	2nd Lt.	510th	St. Comp.
DiFranks	Edward P.	S/Sgt.	510th	
Diffenbaugh	Joseph C.	S/Sgt.	508th	KIA 7/19/44
Dillard	Blase J.	S/Sgt.	510th	
Dillard	Raymond G.	PFC	509th	
Dillavon	W. W.	2nd Lt.	447th	
Dillenbeck	Jewel W.	Cpl.	511th	POW 12/1/43
Diller	George J.	S/Sgt.	508th	
Dillon	Francisco H.	S/Sgt.	510th	
Dillon	Merle L.	Sgt.	508th	
Dillow	Harold L.	S/Sgt.	508th	POW 11/21/44
Ditz	Ray T.	T/Sgt.	511th	
Dimbro	Harold E.	PFC	510th	
Dingee	Orrin D.	T/Sgt.	509th	
Dingle	Thomas	S/Sgt.	508th	Int'd 8/6/44
Dingler	George A.	Sgt.	511th	POW 10/7/44
Dinkins	Lawrence J.	Cpl.	511th	
Dinning	Fred H.	1st Lt.	854th	POW 9/12/44
Dinning	Joseph W.	Sgt.	510th	Chemical Co.
Dinsmore	Richard G.	PFC	508th	
Diprima	Warringer D.	Capt.	510th	
Disbrow	Tony	2nd Lt.	508th	POW 1/11/44
Disney	Arthur	S/Sgt.	509th	
Divil	William C.	1st Lt.	511th	KIA 9/27/44
Dixey	Kenneth D.	Sgt.	508th	
Dixon	Joseph R.	1st Lt.	510th	
Dixon	Celestial	S/Sgt.	509th	
Dixon	Charles F.	S/Sgt.	854th	Chemical Co.
Dobbins	Robert L.	Pvt.	511th	
Dobbs	Warren C.	Sgt.	508th	
Dmichowski	John	Sgt.	510th	
Dobrowolski	Kenneth G.	PFC	509th	Killed 6/8/45
Dochod	Boyd P.	S/Sgt.	508th	
Doeppin g	Thaddeus J.	S/Sgt.	511th	St. Comp.
Docimo	Joseph W.	2nd Lt.	11th	
Dockter	Orest J.	1st Lt.	510th	
Dodge	Gerhard C.	T/Sgt.	351st	HQ
Dodge	Gardner A.	S/Sgt.	351st	HQ
Doepping	H. F.	M/Sgt.	510th	
Doerr	Gordon N.	PFC	509th	HQ
Doerr	Gerald J.	Cpl.	351st	
Dohla	W. J.	S/Sgt.	508th	
Dohm	William E.	2nd Lt.	509th	
Dohun	Daniel C.	2nd Lt.	511th	
Doka	Andrew Z.	1st Lt.	508th	
Dolan	William J.	S/Sgt.	511th	
Dolanc	Victor E.	Sgt.	509th	
Doll	Morpert C.	PFC	252nd	Medical Disp.
Domine	Fred P.	Sgt.	508th	
Domonkos	Alador	Cpl.	510th	
Donadio	Rick	T/Sgt.	509th	KIA 5/14/43
Donahay	Joseph L.	S/Sgt.	510th	
Donaldson	Dexter L.	S/Sgt.	510th	
Donaldson	Leroy D.	S/Sgt.	508th	
Donaldson	William E.	Sgt.	509th	Sub-Depot
Donart	Jack P.	S/Sgt.	510th	
Donatelli	Raymond G.	PFC	447th	
Dondy	Jewel W.	2nd Lt.	511th	
Donelan	Walter L.	Cpl.	508th	
Donilon	Austin V.	S/Sgt.	510th	
Donnelly	Edward F.	Sgt.	508th	
Donnelly	Frank R.	S/Sgt.	511th	
Donnelly	Leon W. Jr.	T/Sgt.	510th	
Donovan	James	Cpl.	1206th	QM Company
Doran	Edward B.	1st Lt.	1629th	Ord. S&M Co.
Dorfler	Warren L.	Sgt.	511th	
Dornick	Frank G.	Cpl.	510th	
Dorsey	Donald S.	S/Sgt.	508th	
Dortch	William P.	T/Sgt.	511th	
Doty	Herbert J.	Sgt.	508th	POW 10/9/43
Doubledee	William J.	M/Sgt.	511th	
Doucet	Paul L.	M/Sgt.	508th	
Doucett	Philip L.	Sgt.	510th	
Douglas	James W.	Cpl.	508th	
Douglass	Richard G.	PFC	509th	
Dovon	J. M.	S/Sgt.	511th	
Dower	Frank A. Jr.	1st Lt.	508th	Int'd 8/6/44
Dowling	Carl T.	Pvt.	509th	
Downdy	A. E.	Capt.	509th	
Downing	John L. Jr.	Cpl.	508th	MP Company
Doyle	Charles L.	S/Sgt.	510th	
Doyle	Clayton L.	2nd Lt.	509th	
Doyle	John J.	S/Sgt.	511th	
Dragg	Lawrence J.	Sgt.	508th	Ord. S&M Co.
Drake	Vincent E.	2nd Lt.	511th	POW 5/27/44
Drake	William P.	S/Sgt.	509th	
Draper	Guthrey W.	Sgt.	1061st	
Dreeger	Paul F.	1st Lt.	511th	
Drew	Ray V.	PFC	1629th	
Drew	Edwin S.	T/Sgt.	509th	POW 5/27/44
Drewman	Elsmer W.	2nd Lt.	510th	
Drews	Francis E.	M/Sgt.	509th	
Dreyer	George C.	PFC	508th	POW 9/12/44
Dreyer	W. J.	Cpl.	351st	
Drifmeyer	Raymond W.	Cpl.	1206th	QM Company
Driggers	Lester R.	2nd Lt.	509th	Int'd 6/21/44
Dropp	Michael G.	Cpl.	447th	Sub-Depot
Drought	Donald B.	1st Lt.	508th	
Drozdowski	Chester V.	PFC	1206th	QM Company
Druback	Edward J.	S/Sgt.	1206th	QM Company
Drummond	William A.	Pvt.	351st	HQ
Drury	Stanley G.	T/Sgt.	510th	
DuPre	Frederick A.	1st Sgt.	509th	
Dubose	Jackson L.	T/Sgt.	511th	
Ducharme	Herve W.	PFC	1206th	QM Company
Duchesneau	John R.	2nd Lt.	510th	
Dudas	Michael M	1st Lt.	509th	
Dudek	George F.	PFC	508th	
Dudley	Charles F. III	2nd Lt.	510th	
Dudley	George J.	T/Sgt.	509th	POW 5/27/44
Dufault	Maurice L.	T/Sgt.	508th	
Duff	Earl	PFC	11th	St. Comp.
Duffy	Alexander J.	S/Sgt.	510th	
Duffy	Gerard R.	T/Sgt.	508th	
Duffy	James J.	2nd Lt.	508th	
Duffy	John J.	1st Lt.	508th	
Duffy	Welford E.	1st Lt.	447th	Sub-Depot
Dugan	Steven	S/Sgt.	508th	
Duggan	Joseph T.	S/Sgt.	509th	
Duggan	Laurel L.	Sgt.	508th	
Duke	Theodore E.	S/Sgt.	509th	Int'd 6/21/44
Dullin	Phillip A.	S/Sgt.	511th	
Dumas	L.	T/Sgt.	11th	St. Comp.
Dumas	Bernard C.	T/Sgt.	510th	St. Comp.
Dumas	Jennings C.	2nd Lt.	509th	
Dunaway	Richard C.	Cpl.	11th	
Dunbar	George F.	T/Sgt.	447th	Sub-Depot
Duncan	Harley G.	2nd Lt.	508th	
Dundas	Bernard P.	Sgt.	511th	
Dunham	John B.	1st Lt.	510th	POW 5/28/44
Dunkelburger	Frederick B.	2nd Lt.	509th	
Dunlap	Dennis E.	S/Sgt.	511th	
Dunlap	Robert S.	PFC	252nd	Medical Disp.
Dunlap	Clyde A.	T/Sgt.	508th	
Dunlop	Oscar E.	PFC	510th	
Dunmire	Raymond W.	T/Sgt.	447th	Sub-Depot
Dunn	John P.	S/Sgt.	510th	
Dunn	Hershel A.	M/Sgt.	509th	
Dunn	Charles R.	S/Sgt.	509th	
Dunn	David E. Jr.	1st Lt.	508th	
Dunn	Floyd L.	Sgt.	511th	
Dunn	James	1st Lt.	854th	Chemical Co.
Dunn	J. W.	Spec. 5	508th	
Dunn	Philip H.	S/Sgt.	509th	
Dunnahoe	George E.	Sgt.	511th	
Dunnigan	John J. E.	1st Lt.	508th	

Dupont / Ferguson

Last Name	First Name	Rank	Unit	Notes
Dupont	Harold A.	S/Sgt.	509th	
Dupre	Frederick A.	1st Lt.	509th	
Dupuis	Norman A.	Sgt.	11th	St. Comp.
Duran	Octavio A.	Sgt.	510th	POW 2/22/44
Durbin	Alphonsus J.	1st Lt.	508th	
Durbo	I. D.	Pvt.	510th	
Durham	Jack	Cpl.	509th	
Durivage	Roland A.	S/Sgt.	1629th	Ord. S&M Co.
Durkin	John P.	T/Sgt.	509th	
Durst	Charles R.	S/Sgt.	508th	
Dustin	Richard M.	S/Sgt.	510th	
Dutty	James E.	S/Sgt.	508th	
Duval	Robert L.	T/Sgt.	510th	
Duvall	Harold E.	T/Sgt.	509th	
Duvall	R. R.	Cpl.	509th	
Dwyer	John F.	1st Lt.	511th	KIA 10/3/44
Dye	Thomas B.	T/Sgt.	511th	
Dyer	George E.	2nd Lt.	511th	
Dyer	William H.	Cpl.	509th	
Dym	Irving	PFC	1206th	QM Company
Dytman	John W.	2nd Lt.	510th	POW 8/17/43

E

Last Name	First Name	Rank	Unit	Notes
Eacrett	Harold J.	S/Sgt.	509th	
Eagan	Frank J.	T/Sgt.	511th	
Eagle	Morris S.	2nd Lt.	511th	POW 10/9/43
Eaglefeather	Gilbert	S/Sgt.	509th	
Eaheart	Karl F. Jr.	Sgt.	508th	
Eames	Michael J.	Cpl.	854th	Chemical Co.
Earls	Woodrow W.	PFC	509th	
Earp	Ordell G.	S/Sgt.	351st	
Eason	Henry	Sgt.	447th	
Easterling	Edwin	S/Sgt.	11th	Sub-Depot
Eastlund	Arnold	Sgt.	511th	St. Comp.
Eaton	Edgar H.	2nd Lt.	1629th	Int'd 3/18/44
Eaton	Carl F.	M/Sgt.	508th	
Eaton	Charles T.	S/Sgt.	509th	KIA 3/18/44
Eaton	Donald H.	2nd Lt.	510th	
Eaton	Merril H.	Sgt.	508th	
Eaver	C. F.	Pvt.	11th	St. Comp.
Eaves	Leon R.	PFC	511th	
Echstenkamper	Earl R.	S/Sgt.	508th	POW 10/7/44
Eck	Arthur W.	T/Sgt.	511th	
Eckert	James C.	Cpl.	1629th	
Eckersell	James T.	S/Sgt.	508th	
Eckes	David W.	S/Sgt.	509th	
Eckman	Claude D.	M/Sgt.	510th	
Economu	Angelo	Cpl.	508th	
Eddy	Harry L.	1st Lt.	11th	St. Comp.
Edelman	Stanley	1st Lt.	511th	
Edmonds	Eugene G.	Sgt.	511th	
Edwards	Donovan	T/Sgt.	511th	
Edwards	George A.	Capt.	510th	
Edwards	Harold W.	1st Lt.	508th	
Edwards	Harry W.	Sgt.	511th	
Edwards	J. R.	S/Sgt.	508th	
Edwards	Junior H.	S/Sgt.	510th	
Edwards	Leonard	1st Lt.	511th	
Edwards	Lewis W.	PFC	511th	
Edwards	William L.	S/Sgt.	509th	
Effisino	X. I.	Sgt.	508th	
Effron	Raphael A.	S/Sgt.	508th	
Eichamer	Jesse	Cpl.	511th	
Eichin	George	Capt.	510th	
Eickhoff	Albert M.	Sgt.	508th	
Eimermann	John T.	2nd Lt.	511th	
Einsmann	Paul W.	Capt.	510th	
Eisenhart	Phillip H.	Sgt.	510th	
Ekas	Clyde E.	T/Sgt.	508th	
Ekberg	Virden S.	T/Sgt.	511th	
Ekblad	John O.	Sgt.	510th	
Ekensteen	Carl A.	Capt.	508th	
Elder	Ralph R.	F.O.	511th	
Eldred	Robert D.	T/Sgt.	509th	
Elder	Clifford E.	Cpl.	351st	
Elias	Hyman	PFC	510th	HQ
Elkin	Norman E.	2nd Lt.	510th	St. Comp.
Elkin	Samuel	PFC	510th	
Elkins	William W.	Sgt.	510th	
Ellersick	Russell R.	PFC	508th	
Elliot	Lloyd L.	Cpl.	511th	
Elliott	James E.	Sgt.	1629th	Ord. S&M Co.
Elliott	Russell C.	T/Sgt.	511th	
Elliott	William T.	T/Sgt.	510th	
Elliott	Y.	S/Sgt.	510th	
Ellis	James E.	2nd Lt.	511th	POW 2/24/44
Ellis	James M.	T/Sgt.	508th	
Ellis	Melvin R.	T/Sgt.	1206th	HQ
Ellis	Raymond N.	Cpl.	351st	
Ellman	Charles T.	S/Sgt.	510th	
Elmore	D. S.	S/Sgt.	509th	
Elsaesser	Alphonse J.	2nd Lt.	510th	POW 12/31/43
Elsloo	John H.	1st Lt.	511th	
Elsmore	Floyd B.	S/Sgt.	508th	
Embree	Hoy D.	S/Sgt.	511th	
Emerson	Harold D.	2nd Lt.	508th	KIA 5/27/44
Emerson	John S.	1st Lt.	509th	
Emigh	James K.	T/Sgt.	511th	
Emmick	Richard W.	T/Sgt.	509th	
Emmke	George A.	S/Sgt.	510th	
Enders	Elwyn G.	S/Sgt.	508th	
Engfer	Otto E.	T/Sgt.	509th	
England	Carl J.	1st Lt.	510th	
Engle	James M.	Cpl.	511th	
Englert	Harry D. Jr.	PFC	511th	

Last Name	First Name	Rank	Unit	Notes
Englert	Robert B.	Sgt.	510th	
Engles	Irving C.	T/Sgt.	508th	
Engles	Wayland D.	Sgt.	511th	
English	William M.	Cpl.	252nd	Medical Disp.
Enockson	Stanley H.	Sgt.	508th	
Enos	Frederick C. Jr.	S/Sgt.	1206th	QM Company
Enstein	Wilbert	PFC	508th	
Epley	Paul L.	Sgt.	508th	
Epstein	Burt A.	Sgt.	508th	
Erickson	Bertel W.	T/Sgt.	11th	St. Comp.
Erickson	Hilding W.	Cpl.	508th	
Ericsson	Bertel E.	Capt.	510th	
Ernst	John W.	Sgt.	508th	
Ernst	Wilmar F.	2nd Lt.	510th	
Erskine	Dalmar H.	Capt.	509th	
Erwin	Woodrow	Sgt.	508th	Killed 2/26/43
Espinoza	Frank L.	Sgt.	509th	POW 8/6/44
Espriu	Edmund F.	PFC	511th	POW 12/5/44
Eterson	Arthur F.	T/Sgt.	510th	
Ethen	Wallace R.	S/Sgt.	511th	
Ethridge	Eugene	T/Sgt.	510th	
Etzweiler	Edward W.	Cpl.	351st	HQ
Eubanks	William L.	PFC	510th	
Eustler	Bernard C.	Sgt.	510th	
Evanoika	Joseph F.	T/Sgt.	508th	
Evans	Billie E.	1st Lt.	511th	
Evans	Ferrell H.	2nd Lt.	509th	
Evans	Hershel	M/Sgt.	509th	
Evans	Howard R.	1st Lt.	508th	
Evans	Ivan D.	PFC	1629th	Ord. S&M Co.
Evans	Robert L.	S/Sgt.	510th	
Evans	Vernon B.	2nd Lt.	510th	
Evans	William T.	Pvt.	510th	
Evanson	Arthur P.	Sgt.	1206th	QM Company
Even	William P.	Sgt.	509th	
Everett	Garland L.	PFC	1629th	Ord. S&M Co.
Evitts	Forest	S/Sgt.	1206th	QM Company

F

Last Name	First Name	Rank	Unit	Notes
Faber	Merlin F.	Cpl.	1629th	Ord. S&M Co.
Fabien	Joseph J.	PFC	11th	St. Comp.
Fabiszewski	Joseph P.	S/Sgt.	11th	St. Comp.
Fabrick	John M.	1st Lt.	351st	HQ
Fagan	George J.	1st Lt.	508th	POW 1/17/45
Fager	James E.	Sgt.	509th	
Fagersten	David H.	T/Sgt.	511th	
Fagg	George A.	T/Sgt.	511th	
Fail	J. L.	S/Sgt.	508th	
Fainstein	Bernard	2nd Lt.	509th	
Fairchild	Joe E.	M/Sgt.	510th	
Falcey	Edward J.	S/Sgt.	509th	
Fales	Addison	Cpl.	509th	
Fales	John T.	1st Lt.	509th	
Falk	Arthur A.	T/Sgt.	509th	
Fallhaber	W. J.	T/Sgt.	510th	
Fall	James L. Jr.	T/Sgt.	508th	
Fallon	Donald J.	S/Sgt.	511th	
Faltisek	Emil W. Jr.	2nd Lt.	510th	POW 1/17/45
Famariss	Richard A.	S/Sgt.	509th	
Fancher	Herman R.	Pvt.	508th	
Fanning	Louie	PFC	509th	HQ
Fanning	Paul T.	S/Sgt.	351st	
Farina	Arnold M.	S/Sgt.	508th	
Farinha	Aldo A.	Sgt.	510th	
Farley	Hugh R.	Sgt.	508th	
Farmer	James L.	Sgt.	508th	HQ
Farmer	Robert P.	Cpl.	509th	POW 1/11/44
Farr	Howard T.	S/Sgt.	510th	
Farrell	Burl L.	1st Lt.	508th	
Farrell	Dale M.	2nd Lt.	510th	
Farrell	Bernard A.	M/Sgt.	511th	
Farris	Philip L.	S/Sgt.	510th	
Farthing	Louis	Cpl.	510th	Sub-Depot
Fashingbauer	Ruben R.	PFC	447th	
Fassler	William J.	T/Sgt.	509th	
Fastow	Clyde D.	Sgt.	510th	HQ
Fauks	Eugene H.	Sgt.	351st	
Faulhaber	Tony	PFC	1629th	Ord. S&M Co.
Faulkner	Andrew T.	Maj.	508th	St. Comp.
Fausette	Jack H.	S/Sgt.	11th	
Favatella	David L.	Sgt.	510th	
Fawbush	Kenneth E.	S/Sgt.	510th	
Fawbush	James L.	T/Sgt.	508th	
Fawcett	M. P.	Pvt.	511th	
Fay	John F.	S/Sgt.	510th	
Feaman	Joseph J.	Sgt.	1206th	QM Company
Fearson	Otto H.	1st Lt.	511th	
Feasler	George	Cpl.	509th	
Fedelen	Merle L.	PFC	508th	
Fedor	Thomas	T/Sgt.	11th	St. Comp.
Feeney	Edwin C.	Sgt.	508th	
Feeney	Bernard	Sgt.	509th	
Fegan	Harry E.	2nd Lt.	510th	
Feinstein	Alex A.	S/Sgt.	508th	KIA 10/4/43
Feldmiller	Donald P.	1st Lt.	1629th	Ord. S&M Co.
Feldstein	Ramsey P.	Cpl.	509th	POW 1/22/45
Felten	Paul R.	Sgt.	508th	Killed 5/7/43
Fendall	Albert C.	S/Sgt.	511th	
Fennell	Charles E.	Cpl.	1629th	Ord. S&M Co.
Ferguson	Howard J.	Sgt.	511th	POW 10/9/43
Ferguson				
Ferguson				

Ferguson / Fuller

Last	First	Rank	Unit	Notes
Ferguson	James C.	Cpl.	11th	St. Comp.
Ferguson	Lloyd R.	S/Sgt.	509th	
Ferguson	Maurice P.	Pvt.	510th	
Fernbach	Ferdinand J.	1st Lt.	508th	POW 6/22/43
Ferns	William A.	2nd Lt.	509th	
Ferrell	William S.	M/Sgt.	447th	Sub-Depot
Ferrier	Joseph L.	Cpl.	511th	
Ferry	James	Sgt.	509th	
Fetters	Richard C.	PFC	508th	
Fidler	Richard	S/Sgt.	509th	
Fie	William W.	S/Sgt.	447th	Sub-Depot
Fiebelkorn	Gerald W.	T/Sgt.	508th	KIA 5/23/44
Fields	James H.	S/Sgt.	510th	
Fiengo	Henry J.	S/Sgt.	511th	POW 8/9/44
Fiering	Leroy D.	Sgt.	447th	Sub-Depot
Fifield	Shirley S.	Sgt.	447th	Sub-Depot
Figg	George A.	Pvt.	511th	
Fig	Kenneth C.	Sgt.	508th	
Fikes	Maurice G.	2nd Lt.	511th	
Filipowski	John J.	Spec. 5	854th	Chemical Co.
Filla	Lawrence P.	S/Sgt.	511th	
Fillipi	Frank J.	Sgt.	510th	
Finch	Jackson B.	T/Sgt.	509th	
Fincher	Benjamin C.	S/Sgt.	510th	POW 10/9/43
Fineberg	Sidney T.	1st Lt.	1629th	Ord. S&M Co.
Fink	Charles E. Jr.	S/Sgt.	511th	
Finklestein	Richard	Spec. 5	508th	
Finklestein	Charles L.	2nd Lt.	1206th	QM Company
Finlay	John D.	Maj.	509th	KIA 3/18/44
Finley	Bruce V.	2nd Lt.	11th	St. Comp.
Finley	Louis F.	Sgt.	510th	
Finley	Robert C.	T/Sgt.	509th	
Finn	Charles E.	S/Sgt.	508th	
Finn	William N.	2nd Lt.	508th	
Finnan	Fred L.	T/Sgt.	510th	
Finnegan	Patrick J.	1st Lt.	511th	
Finnell	Benjamin J.	2nd Lt.	510th	
Finnell	Kay R.	S/Sgt.	511th	
Finns	Richard H.	S/Sgt.	508th	
Fireman	Harry	1st Lt.	511th	
Firestein	Walter	Cpl.	511th	
Firtin	John L.	2nd Lt.	509th	POW 12/31/43
Fischer	Adam J.	T/Sgt.	510th	
Fischer	Edwin G.	T/Sgt.	509th	
Fischer	Jerome F.	1st Lt.	508th	
Fish	Donald L.	1st Lt.	511th	
Fishburne	Paul L.	Maj.	511th	Int'd 10/7/44
Fisher	Allen M.	F.O.	508th	
Fisher	Byron W.	2nd Lt.	511th	HQ
Fisher	Harward L.	Capt.	351st	
Fisher	Lamont C.	S/Sgt.	509th	

Last	First	Rank	Unit	Notes
Fisher	Milford M.	S/Sgt.	511th	
Fisher	Rossie B.	Pvt.	511th	
Fisher	Vernon E.	Sgt.	511th	
Fishback	Woody W.	1st Lt.	510th	
Fitch	Walter M.	M/Sgt.	509th	
Fitchen	Nathan P.	Sgt.	11th	St. Comp.
Fitzgerald	William	1st Lt.	508th	
Fitzgerald	John H.	T/Sgt.	509th	
Fitzpatrick	Owen J.	1st Lt.	511th	
Fitzpatrick	Joseph F.	S/Sgt.	509th	
Fitzwater	Robert E.	2nd Lt.	508th	
Fixa	George E. Jr.	PFC	509th	
Fladland	Richard F.	Sgt.	510th	
Flammer	Gorman L.	2nd Lt.	510th	
Flanagan	George R.	Sgt.	511th	HQ
Flanagan	John J.	Pvt.	351st	
Flanagan	Matthew A.	S/Sgt.	510th	
Flanzbaum	Robert R.	Sgt.	510th	POW 1/11/44
Flatow	David W.	S/Sgt.	511th	
Fleener	Gilbert	Sgt.	11th	St. Comp.
Fleischer	Delmer L.	PFC	11th	St. Comp.
Fleischer	Herbert L.	1st Lt.	508th	
Fleming	Robert D.	Sgt.	510th	
Fleming	Frank J.	S/Sgt.	511th	Sub-Depot
Fleming	Leroy D.	Sgt.	447th	
Fletcher	Seldon R.	Capt.	508th	
Flette	David A.	2nd Lt.	510th	
Flint	Stanley C.	Sgt.	11th	St. Comp.
Flint	Donald T.	T/Sgt.	508th	
Floden	Harold F.	Capt.	510th	St. Comp.
Floden	Donald E.	Capt.	508th	
Florentino	Delmar L.	PFC	11th	
Flores	Ranjel	PFC	510th	POW 9/12/44
Floresta	Emilio P.	Sgt.	1061st	
Flotte	John G. Jr.	S/Sgt.	508th	
Floun	Stanley C.	Sgt.	511th	Sub-Depot
Floumoy	Herschel R.	T/Sgt.	447th	HQ
Flowers	Patrick W.	1st Lt.	351st	QM Company
Flowers	Earnest E.	PFC	1206th	Sub-Depot
Fly	Hulon C.	T/Sgt.	447th	
Flynn	Paul L.	1st Lt.	509th	
Foard	William	2nd Lt.	511th	
Foeler	Robert S. Jr.	1st Lt.	854th	Chemical Co.
Foley	Clyde W.	Cpl.	511th	
Foley	James S.	S/Sgt.	509th	
Folgate	John F.	1st Lt.	510th	
Folks	Delbert M.	1st Lt.	508th	
Fong	John P.	S/Sgt.	511th	KIA 2/6/45
Fontaine	James K.	2nd Lt.	511th	
Fontana	Robert Y.	F.O.	509th	
Fontana	Frank Jr.	S/Sgt.	508th	POW 10/4/43
Frank	Malvin A.	S/Sgt.	509th	

Last	First	Rank	Unit	Notes
Ford	Donald S.	Sgt.	508th	POW 10/4/43
Ford	Jay R.	Pvt.	508th	
Ford	John P.	1st Lt.	510th	
Fore	John G.	1st Lt.	447th	Sub-Depot
Foreman	Stanley D.	M/Sgt.	509th	
Forest	Willard T.	Sgt.	508th	
Forget	William E.	S/Sgt.	510th	
Forit	Floren F.	Sgt.	509th	
Forno	Anthony P.	T/Sgt.	511th	
Forrest	Albert H.	1st Lt.	509th	
Forrester	Allan B.	S/Sgt.	447th	Sub-Depot
Forrester	Cecil O.	2nd Lt.	447th	Sub-Depot
Forrstrom	William	PFC	508th	
Forsaith	Wayne	S/Sgt.	509th	
Forshey	Ralph M.	Sgt.	1206th	QM Company
Forsmann	Robert F.	M/Sgt.	510th	
Forster	John B.	2nd Lt.	510th	
Forsythe	Henry	Sgt.	510th	
Forsythe	Charles	S/Sgt.	510th	
Fort	William R.	Capt.	510th	
Fortin	James D.	2nd Lt.	511th	St. Comp.
Fortin	John L.	S/Sgt.	509th	
Fortner	Joseph Jr.	PFC	1629th	Ord. S&M Co.
Fortner	Donald C.	Cpl.	508th	
Foshay	Vernon R.	Cpl.	351st	
Foster	Louis A. Jr.	PFC	509th	HQ
Foster	Emery	Pvt.	510th	
Foster	Henry C.	2nd Lt.	510th	
Foster	Jim H.	S/Sgt.	510th	
Foster	Orphus	Sgt.	509th	
Foubert	Paul F.	Capt.	508th	
Foust	Ralph C.	PFC	508th	
Fouzie	Charles A.	S/Sgt.	511th	MIA 11/26/43
Foward	William A.	Cpl.	1061st	MP Company
Fowler	Charles S.	S/Sgt.	508th	
Fowler	Donald W.	Sgt.	511th	POW 3/2/44
Fowler	Clyde W.	Sgt.	509th	
Fowler	Don D.	2nd Lt.	508th	
Fowler	Eli S.	1st Lt.	509th	
Fox	George F.	Cpl.	510th	
Fox	John T.	Sgt.	511th	
Foy	Robert L.	S/Sgt.	854th	Chemical Co.
Fraioli	Lebron O.	Spec. 5	511th	
Francis	Ralph N.	S/Sgt.	509th	
Francis	Franklin P.	1st Lt.	511th	
Francum	Frank P.	1st Lt.	508th	
Frandes	Richard E.	1st Lt.	509th	
Frank	Robert L.	2nd Lt.	510th	
Frank	William R.	Sgt.	510th	
Frank	Ray W.	PFC	1061st	MP Company
Frank	Vincent J.	Pvt.	11th	St. Comp.
Frank	Henry F. Jr.	Sgt.	509th	

Last	First	Rank	Unit	Notes
Frank	Philip A.	F.O.	511th	
Frankart	Louis F.	M/Sgt.	508th	
Frankel	David	Cpl.	510th	
Franklin	Dick L.	Sgt.	510th	
Franklin	James R.	PFC	11th	St. Comp.
Frankovich	John A.	S/Sgt.	510th	
Frankowski	Edward J.	Sgt.	511th	
Franks	Harold H.	Sgt.	509th	
Franks	Wallace B.	T/Sgt.	509th	
Franson	Walter M.	M/Sgt.	511th	
Franson	Dean F.	T/Sgt.	511th	
Franz	Glen W.	1st Lt.	511th	
Franz	Richard B.	T/Sgt.	509th	
Franzblau	William J.	S/Sgt.	511th	KIA 7/29/44
Franzen	Maurice J.	2nd Lt.	509th	
Frasher	Victor	Capt.	508th	
Freedman	James H.	S/Sgt.	509th	
Freeman	Lewis B.	S/Sgt.	510th	
Freeman	Don W.	M/Sgt.	509th	
Freeman	Floyd D.	2nd Lt.	510th	
Freeman	Harold O.	Capt.	351st	
Freeman	John W.	Cpl.	351st	
Freisman	Rendall	1st Lt.	509th	HQ
Freyherr	Richard H.	Sgt.	511th	HQ
Friday	Frank J.	Sgt.	447th	Sub-Depot
Friden	Joseph B.	PFC	510th	
Fridy	Richard A.	Capt.	854th	Chemical Co.
Friedland	Robert W.	Capt.	854th	Chemical Co.
Friedlander	Harold M.	2nd Lt.	509th	
Friend	Herbert D.	1st Lt.	510th	
Friess	Walter E.	PFC	854th	Chemical Co.
Frisbee	Charles L.	Spec. 5	11th	St. Comp.
Frischknecht	William J.	Sgt.	510th	
Frischolz	Paul	Sgt.	508th	
Fritch	Joseph V.	Capt.	510th	
Fritts	Bertrand W.	S/Sgt.	509th	
Fritz	Roy Jr.	Cpl.	509th	
Fritzsinger	Donald L.	Sgt.	508th	
Fromme	Jack E.	T/Sgt.	509th	
Frontino	Byron C.	1st Lt.	508th	
Fruchter	Carmelo J.	Sgt.	511th	
Fry	Philip H.	2nd Lt.	509th	POW 7/28/44
Fry	George F.	PFC	509th	
Fry	Jack D.	PFC	509th	
Fuerth	Robert E.	2nd Lt.	511th	
Fulks	William J.	T/Sgt.	510th	KIA 7/29/44
Fuller	Raeford W.	Capt.	508th	
Fuller	Charles A.	1st Lt.	511th	
Fuller	Frank D.	Cpl.	1629th	Ord. S&M Co.
Fuller	Jack	S/Sgt.	510th	
Fuller	James G.	Pvt.	511th	
Fuller	Kermit J.			

143

Fuller / Goodman

Fuller	Robert D.	S/Sgt.	508th		Gardner	Robert H.	2nd Lt.	509th		Gerard	Douglas T.	S/Sgt.	510th	Int'd 10/7/44	Giuffre	Anthony R.	Cpl.	511th	
Fullin	Angelo	T/Sgt.	511th		Gargala	Walter S.	S/Sgt.	509th		Gere	Duane O.	S/Sgt.	511th	POW 8/16/44	Givens	James C. T.	Spec. 5	854th	Chemical Co.
Fulmer	Hoyt J.	PFC	508th		Garland	James R.	S/Sgt.	508th		Gerhardt	Joseph T.	F.O.	508th		Givens	Lloyd C.	Cpl.	510th	Int'd 2/25/45
Fulton	James K.	S/Sgt.	508th		Garneau	Robert P.	Pvt.	11th	St. Comp.	Gerke	Carl A.	Cpl.	510th		Gividen	Harold V.	2nd Lt.	509th	
Fultz	Irvin R.	1st Lt.	510th		Garner	Joseph P.	2nd Lt.	510th		Germain	Jerome P.	S/Sgt.	509th		Gladding	Donald K.	2nd Lt.	509th	
Funchess	Jack S.	Sgt.	508th		Garner	Thomas D.	1st Lt.	508th	POW 1/11/44	Geroda	J. P.	Pvt.	1629th	Ord. S&M Co.	Glass	George T.	PFC	1206th	QM Company
Funderbunk	Van R.	S/Sgt.	509th		Garrard	Harold A.	Pvt.	1206th	QM Company	Gerry	William E.	Sgt.	508th		Glavin	Lester J.	Sgt.	447th	Sub-Depot
Funderburk	William T.	M/Sgt.	1206th QM Co.	KIA 5/26/43	Garrett	Evert L.	S/Sgt.	509th		Gershon	Jack	Pvt.	508th		Glawe	Benoid E.	Lt. Col.	351st	HQInt'd 10/7/44
Funicello	Joseph J.	T/Sgt.	510th		Garrett	Richard P.	PFC	508th		Gerski	William P.	S/Sgt.	511th		Glazier	Frederick R.	Capt.	511th	
Fuqua	Grady	Sgt.	510th	KIA 12/30/43	Garrett	Samuel R.	T/Sgt.	510th		Gerstner	Edward W.	Spec. 4	854th	Chemical Co.	Glazier	Maurice	PFC	11th	St. Comp.
Fuquay	Jolly E.	S/Sgt.	510th		Garrison	Albert T.	Sgt.	508th		Gertz	Harold G.	Cpl.	508th		Glebus	Charles	Sgt.	511th	KIA 3/18/44
Furst	Morton	T/Sgt.	508th		Garrity	Thomas J.	S/Sgt.	510th		Getchell	Richard H.	S/Sgt.	511th	POW 10/9/43	Gleich	Daniel G.	M/Sgt.	511th	
Futcher	Charles W.	1st Lt.	508th		Garrow	Edward L.	S/Sgt.	509th	Sub-Depot	Gettys	John C.	Sgt.	1061st	POW 6/14/44	Glendenning	Orville L.	M/Sgt.	510th	
Futhey	Ralph L.	S/Sgt.	509th		Garske	Eugene F.	Cpl.	447th		Gholston	Joe C.	Sgt.	510th		Glenn	William A.	T/Sgt.	509th	
Fyler	Leonard C.	T/Sgt.	508th		Garst	George L.	Sgt.	511th		Giannetti	Bethando R.	Pvt.	1206th QM Co.	Killed 7/29/43	Glick	George A.	S/Sgt.	510th	
					Garvey	Kieran A.	Sgt.	508th		Gianoto	John J.	S/Sgt.	509th		Gloudeman	George H.	F.O.	511th	
G					Garvie	Robert S. III	Sgt.	510th		Giarusso	John A.	T/Sgt.	510th		Glover	Henry R. Jr.	Sgt.	510th	
Gable	Clark	1st Lt.	508th		Garza	Joe	Sgt.	511th	KIA 8/6/44	Gibb	Robert D.	Capt.	509th		Glover	Joseph A. Jr.	S/Sgt.	509th	Killed 6/8/45
Gable	Kenneth D.	S/Sgt.	510th		Garza	Matias R. Jr.	Cpl.	509th		Gibbons	James M.	Capt.	510th		Glover	Stuart A. Jr.	Sgt.	508th	Int'd 10/7/44
Gabriel	Lloyd M.	Sgt.	511th	POW 1/30/44	Gasner	Edwin L.	Sgt.	510th		Gibbs	John C.	Sgt.	508th		Glynn	Robert L. Jr.	Sgt.	351st	HQ
Gabriel	Samuel J.	M/Sgt.	511th		Gasparovich	Andrew R.	Sgt.	509th		Gibbs	Maynard V.	M/Sgt.	509th		Gnup	Edward	PFC	508th	
Gach	Walter J.	PFC	11th	St. Comp.	Gassaway	Irvin	T/Sgt.	510th		Gibson	Carter	Sgt.	511th	POW 2/22/44	Goble	Delbert D.	S/Sgt.	510th	
Gacthall	R. H.	S/Sgt.	508th		Gassman	Charles W.	Pvt.	511th		Gibson	Edward W.	Sgt.	1061st	MP Company	Goble	John H.	Cpl.	511th	Medical Disp.
Gaddis	Raymond W.	S/Sgt.	510th		Gates	Clifford O.	Cpl.	510th		Gibson	James M.	Sgt.	447th	Sub-Depot	Goder	Orrin H.	2nd Lt.	252nd	
Gaddy	Harry B.	T/Sgt.	511th		Gates	Donald R.	Sgt.	511th		Gibson	Neal R.	Cpl.	509th		Godlewski	Raymond	S/Sgt.	509th	POW 1/11/44
Gaestel	Joseph	1st Lt.	511th		Gates	Henry C.	S/Sgt.	511th	POW 11/3/43	Gibson	Norman F.	S/Sgt.	510th		Godsey	Charles W.	1st Sgt.	510th	St. Comp.
Gaiat	Leon S.	S/Sgt.	1061st	MP Company	Gates	Richard J.	PFC	511th		Giddings	Walter B.	Sgt.	509th		Godsey	Dallas L.	Sgt.	510th	POW 1/22/45
Gainer	James	PFC	511th		Gattens	James H.	M/Sgt.	508th		Gienau	Charles M.	M/Sgt.	509th		Goebbel	William A.	T/Sgt.	509th	POW 9/12/44
Gaitskill	David R.	T/Sgt.	508th	POW 4/18/44	Gaum	Roy E.	1st Sgt.	510th		Gierowski	Glenn L.	Sgt.	509th		Goetz	Charles	M/Sgt.	509th	
Galas	Benjamin P.	Cpl.	508th		Gavin	Edward E.	Sgt.	511th	POW8/6/44	Gil	Edward	Sgt.	510th	POW 12/31/43	Goff	Earl G.	PFC	252nd	Medical Disp.
Galbreath	Robert A.	S/Sgt.	509th		Gavral	Vincent	Sgt.	508th		Gilbert	Arthur	PFC	1061st	MP Company	Goforth	George T.	F.O.	510th	
Galietta	Anthony J.	Sgt.	509th		Gay	Jasper D.	1st Lt.	509th		Gildhouse	Richard J.	2nd Lt.	511th	POW 2/22/44	Goinvic	Peter J.	Sgt.	510th	POW 1/11/44
Gallagher	Thomas J.	1st Lt.	509th		Gaylord	Donald A.	Capt.	351st		Gilleland	Clifford M.	PFC	508th		Goldberg	Murray L.	T/Sgt.	11th	St. Comp.
Gallipeo	Robert E.	2nd Lt.	509th	POW 8/17/43	Gazek	Adam G. Jr.	T/Sgt.	510th	Sub-Depot	Gillen	William H.	2nd Lt.	1061st		Goldberg	Leo F.	2nd Lt.	508th	
Gallmore	Paul J.	T/Sgt.	511th		Gecewicz	Steve J.	Sgt.	447th	Sub-Depot	Gillespie	Jack E.	Capt.	447th		Goldcamp	Richard M.	T/Sgt.	509th	POW 1/22/45
Galloway	Joseph H.	1st Sgt.	511th		Gee	Lloyd G.	Pvt.	511th	Finance Sect.	Gilliam	Garlan R.	1st Lt.	510th		Goldsborough	Herbert O.	1st Sgt.	511th	POW 9/12/44
Gambal	Vincent	Sgt.	508th		Gee	Ray F.	Sgt.	201st		Gilliland	Walter T.	S/Sgt.	510th	Int'd 5/27/44	Goldstein	Herman	S/Sgt.	508th	
Gandrud	Charles L.	1st Lt.	509th		Gegner	Lionel	Cpl.	510th		Gilman	George R.	S/Sgt.	509th		Goldstein	John J.	S/Sgt.	511th	
Ganey	Edward J.	Sgt.	509th		Geiger	Jerome H.	Maj.	508th		Gilmore	Meredith M.	2nd Lt.	508th		Goldthorpe	Chester J.	S/Sgt.	510th	
Gant	James S.	Cpl.	11th	St. Comp.	Geiger	Warren N.	Cpl.	447th		Gilmore	Edward S.	T/Sgt.	509th	POW 12/31/43	Golomski	Katrino	Sgt.	509th	
Gantt	John W.	PFC	1061st	MP Company	Geiselman	Ralph J.	Sgt.	511th		Gilson	William A.	Sgt.	511th		Gomez	Albert J.	1st Lt.	511th	
Ganus	Andrew M.	S/Sgt.	511th		Geist	Andrew P. Jr.	Sgt.	510th		Gingery	Lee E.	T/Sgt.	510th		Gonella	Edwin J.	Sgt.	510th	Sub-Depot
Garbindo	Julian J.	S/Sgt.	510th		Gelches	Thomas Jr.	PFC	11th	St. Comp.	Ginsberg	Samuel L.	Cpl.	511th		Gonske	Gerald F.	Cpl.	447th	Sub-Depot
Garcia	Carlos L.	PFC	11th	St. Comp.	Gelderman	Kenneth E.	Cpl.	447th	Sub-Depot	Giordano	John J.	T/Sgt.	508th		Gonyea	Jose L.	PFC	1061st	MP Company
Garcia	Eldridge D.	Cpl.	447th	Sub-Depot	Geller	Irving	1st Lt.	510th		Giorgino	Angelo	S/Sgt.	508th		Gonzalez	Lewis	Sgt.	509th	
Garcia	Jose A.	Capt.	510th		Gelsleichter	Robert L.	T/Sgt.	509th		Giovannini	Silvio	Cpl.	510th		Gooch	Justus R.	1st Sgt.	511th	POW 1/22/45
Garcia	Leo	Cpl.	11th	St. Comp.	Genetti	Robert D.	1st Lt.	509th	Int'd 2/25/45	Gipple	Robert C.	2nd Lt.	508th		Good	Kenneth W.	Sgt.	510th	POW 9/12/44
Garcia	Richard	1st Lt.	509th		Gengel	Edward H.	2nd Lt.	511th		Gipson	James M.	T/Sgt.	509th		Goodenough	Arnold W.	1st Sgt.	511th	
Gardner	Frank A.	2nd Lt.	510th	POW 12/20/43	Genone	Joseph C.	1st Lt.	509th		Girard	Arthur E.	Cpl.	508th		Goodman	Israel J.	S/Sgt.	508th	
Gardner	D. J.	S/Sgt.	509th		Geraghty	John J. Jr.	Sgt.	11th	St. Comp.	Girardin	Robert L.	2nd Lt.	511th		Goodman	Lawrence F.	Sgt.	511th	
Gardner	Edwin G.	Cpl.	447th	Sub-Depot	Geraghty	Wiliam H.	PFC	509th		Giswein	Manuel H.	1st Lt.	510th		Goodman	Stanley J.	1st Sgt.	508th	POW 9/12/44

Goodman / Hallman

Surname	First	Rank	Unit	Notes
Goodman	Walter F.	T/Sgt.	508th	
Goodrich	John W.	2nd Lt.	508th	
Goodson	Roger W.	T/Sgt.	11th	
Goodwin	Jack	PFC	511th	St. Comp.
Goodwin	R. E.	Pvt.	511th	
Goottee	Norman L.	1st Lt.	511th	
Gordon	David L.	Sgt.	508th	
Gordon	Forrest B.	S/Sgt.	510th	
Gordon	Harper A.	1st Lt.	511th	KIA 10/9/43
Goree	Lewis G.	PFC	511th	Sub-Depot
Gorham	Edward F.	T/Sgt.	509th	
Gorham	John D. Jr.	Maj.	510th	
Gorr	Gottfried L.	1st Lt.	511th	
Gorski	Walter P.	Sgt.	508th	
Gorsuch	Kenneth W.	S/Sgt.	511th	POW 12/5/44
Gossett	Charles W.	S/Sgt.	447th	
Gossman	Robert W.	F.O.	508th	
Gottschalk	William H.	1st Lt.	510th	
Gough	William W.	T/Sgt.	510th	
Gould	D. E.	Cpl.	509th	
Gourash	Andrew A.	2nd Lt.	511th	POW 4/13/44
Gouveia	Raymond G.	Sgt.	509th	
Gover	Walter L.	M/Sgt.	510th	
Govreau	Louis J.	1st Lt.	508th	
Gowan	Fred A.	Cpl.	509th	
Gowan	Frederick W.	S/Sgt.	509th	POW 7/28/944
Gower	Francis M.	2nd Lt.	510th	
Gozy	Frank	Sgt.	511th	
Grabowski	Henry J.	S/Sgt.	510th	St. Comp.
Gracey	Harry R.	Sgt.	11th	
Graddy	Thomas B.	PFC	510th	
Graff	Eugene L.	T/Sgt.	509th	
Graff	Harry L.	S/Sgt.	510th	St. Comp.
Graham	Earl G.	PFC	508th	
Graham	James L.	2nd Lt.	509th	
Graham	Kenneth L.	Sgt.	510th	POW 7/19/44
Graham	Lawrence C.	S/Sgt.	510th	
Graham	Marion L.	Sgt.	11th	St. Comp.
Graham	Maxwell L.	Sgt.	508th	
Graham	Robert H.	S/Sgt.	509th	
Graham	Thomas H.	Sgt.	508th	
Graham	William C.	S/Sgt.	510th	
Graham	William J.	Cpl.	1206th	QM Company
Graham	William W.	T/Sgt.	510th	
Granata	Salvatore R.	Sgt.	508th	
Grande	Steven S.	Pvt.	11th	St. Comp.
Graney	Andrew K.	S/Sgt.	509th	
Grant	Richard S.	S/Sgt.	511th	
Grantham	Albert L.	Sgt.	511th	
Grantham	Claud H.	Pvt.	11th	St. Comp.
Graser	Kenneth	Sgt.	508th	POW 2/14/45
Grassnehr	Donald W.	Sgt.	511th	

Surname	First	Rank	Unit	Notes
Gratiot	Charles C.	F.O.	511th	KIA 7/28/44
Gravert	Elvin L.	Cpl.	11th	St. Comp.
Gray	Cyrus R.	Pvt. 1	11th	St. Comp.
Gray	Francis W.	1st Lt.	510th	
Gray	William E.	Sgt.	509th	
Gray	Woodrow W.	PFC	351st	HQ
Grayson	James F.	2nd Lt.	508th	KIA 8/27/43
Greaves	Harold	S/Sgt.	509th	
Green	Berle	PFC	508th	
Green	Clarence G.	Sgt.	508th	POW 3/22/44
Green	James R.	S/Sgt.	508th	
Green	Jesse H.	2nd Lt.	511th	
Green	Lawrence E.	Sgt.	510th	
Green	Orville G.	S/Sgt.	508th	
Green	Ralph T.	S/Sgt.	508th	POW 5/27/44
Green	Robert C.	Pvt.	508th	
Green	Thomas E.	2nd Lt.	510th	St. Comp.
Greenawald	William M. Jr.	Sgt.	11th	
Greenberg	Louis E.	Sgt.	509th	
Greenberg	David L.	Cpl.	509th	
Greenberg	George G.	T/Sgt.	1629th	Ord. S&M Co.
Greene	Meyer B.	Sgt.	511th	HQ
Greene	Arlow E.	Sgt.	1061st	MP Company
Greene	John W.	PFC	1206th	QM Company
Greene	Murray	S/Sgt.	11th	St. Comp.
Greene	Orville G.	S/Sgt.	508th	
Greene	Wesley F.	Sgt.	511th	POW 8/16/44
Greenmyre	George R.	T/Sgt.	508th	
Greenwold	Charles E.	1st Lt.	509th	
Greenwood	John E.	2nd Lt.	509th	
Greenwood	Lowell E.	2nd Lt.	509th	
Gregory	Ted W.	S/Sgt.	509th	
Gregory	Adolph	PFC	509th	
Geiss	Umberto	S/Sgt.	1629th	Ord. S&M Co.
Grella	Morie E.	PFC	510th	
Grennan	Daniel B.	T/Sgt.	509th	
Griffin	Don R.	Sgt.	511th	POW 2/22/44
Griffin	Donald T.	1st Lt.	447th	Sub-Depot
Griffin	Milton L.	S/Sgt.	351st	HQ
Griffin	Spencer F.	S/Sgt.	508th	
Griffin	Warren R.	Cpl.	509th	
Griffith	Charles F.	S/Sgt.	1629th	Ord. S&M Co.
Griffith	John R.	Cpl.	510th	
Griffiths	David K.	2nd Lt.	508th	MIA 6/28/43
Griggs	Charles C.	Capt.	510th	
Grigsby	Howard B.	T/Sgt.	508th	POW 3/2/44
Grigsby	William D.	1st Lt.	508th	
Grikstas	Leo	PFC	1629th	Ord. S&M Co.
Grim	Lester F.	F.O.	509th	KIA 7/29/44
Grimm	Harry F.	PFC	508th	POW 5/29/43
Griskiewicz	Walter C.	S/Sgt.	511th	St. Comp.

Surname	First	Rank	Unit	Notes
Grissom	Lawrence C.	Sgt.	510th	
Grissom	V. F. Jr.	1st Lt.	510th	
Gristmacher	Don H.	Sgt.	511th	POW 7/13/44
Grittner	Leo A.	Sgt.	447th	Sub-Depot
Grizzard	Richard A.	S/Sgt.	1061st	MP Company
Groce	Lawrence J.	PFC	511th	POW 10/3/44
Groendyke	Sanford N.	2nd Lt.	1061st	MP Company
Grogan	James T.	PFC	511th	
Grogan	Terrell V.	PFC	11th	St. Comp.
Grondin	Paul E.	1st Lt.	511th	POW 2/24/44
Groomer	Logan G.	S/Sgt.	508th	POW 6/14/44
Grooms	Ralph A.	S/Sgt.	510th	
Gross	Arthur B.	Sgt.	508th	
Gross	George W.	1st Lt.	509th	
Gross	Nathan H.	1st Lt.	510th	
Gross	Wallace H.	T/Sgt.	510th	
Grossman	Arthur J.	PFC	509th	
Groth	Robert C.	F.O.	510th	
Grothe	Delford L.	PFC	510th	
Grubb	Hoyle E.	Cpl.	511th	
Gruchocinski	Mitchell K.	1st Lt.	1061st	MP Company
Grundish	Wayne A.	2nd Lt.	11th	St. Comp.
Grundman	Otto W.	Sgt.	511th	
Grunow	Albert E.	Capt.	510th	
Grupp	William J.	2nd Lt.	510th	
Gryder	Dwight L.	Sgt.	509th	POW 12/31/43
Guadino	Anthony	PFC	1629th	POW 9/27/44
Guagenti	Samuel	Sgt.	510th	Ord. S&M Co.
Guard	Oakland B.	Cpl.	509th	
Guarino	Ben C.	Sgt.	509th	
Guckes	Phillip F.	T/Sgt.	508th	
Gue	Galen B.	S/Sgt.	510th	
Guenther	Richard C.	S/Sgt.	509th	
Guenzig	Bernard A.	S/Sgt.	1629th	Ord. S&M Co.
Guerra	Johnnie R.	PFC	510th	
Guerrero	Tomas T.	T/Sgt.	509th	
Guest	Isaac E.	Sgt.	511th	POW 2/22/44
Guest	Joseph P.	S/Sgt.	447th	Sub-Depot
Gugar	Donald A.	M/Sgt.	351st	HQ
Guida	Bartholomew F.	Cpl.	508th	
Guidie	Edward C.	Cpl.	509th	
Guill	Robert L.	S/Sgt.	509th	
Guingrich	Lawrence C.	S/Sgt.	510th	
Gullickson	Lloyd L.	2nd Lt.	508th	MIA 6/28/43
Gulnac	John R.	Capt.	510th	
Gumaer	Thomas V.	2nd Lt.	510th	KIA 7/29/44
Gunster	Robert	T/Sgt.	510th	
Gunther	Jere A.	2nd Lt.	508th	
Gurbindo	Julian J.	PFC	511th	
Gurke	Samuel	S/Sgt.	351st	HQ
Gumari	Francis T.	Cpl.	511th	
Gusen	C.	Sgt.	510th	

Surname	First	Rank	Unit	Notes
Guthrey	Verner B.	1st Lt.	509th	
Guthrie	R.	S/Sgt.	508th	
Gwyn	Allen H.	2nd Lt.	509th	
Gwyn	Billy, B.	2nd Lt.	510th	
Gwyn	Billy V.	2nd Lt.	510th	

H

Surname	First	Rank	Unit	Notes
Haag	Robert K.	PFC	508th	
Haba	John C.	2nd Lt.	511th	KIA 9/8/44
Habecker	Carl W.	2nd Lt.	511th	KIA 5/27/44
Haddock	James W.	PFC	510th	
Hadley	Donald E.	1st Lt.	511th	
Haft	Harold W.	1st Lt.	510th	
Hagan	Bartholomew R.	S/Sgt.	508th	
Hagan	Hubert D.	Cpl.	509th	
Hagan	John P.	Sgt.	508th	POW 10/4/43
Hagans	Samuel E. Jr.	PFC	509th	
Hagbo	Robert W.	Sgt.	510th	POW 9/8/44
Haggard	Magnus A.	S/Sgt.	510th	
Haggard	Irwin L.	PFC	1206th	QM Company
Haggard	Willie L.	PFC	1206th	QM Company
Haggerty	Winston N.	T/Sgt.	510th	
Hago	Frank J.	S/Sgt.	447th	Sub-Depot
Hahn	S.	Cpl.	447th	Sub-Depot
Hain	Julien V.	Pvt.	1061st	MP Company
Hainert	Jack D.	Sgt.	510th	KIA 7/19/44
Haines	Max S.	Sgt.	510th	
Haislip	Fred C.	PFC	509th	
Hakeos	Samuel T.	S/Sgt.	510th	
Halbrook	Ray F.	PFC	11th	St. Comp.
Haldeman	Clarence R.	S/Sgt.	508th	
Halder	Clarence E.	S/Sgt.	510th	
Hale	Arvil E.	Sgt.	511th	
Hale	Everett M.	S/Sgt.	509th	
Hale	Frederick J.	2nd Lt.	511th	KIA 5/27/44
Hales	Kenneth	S/Sgt.	511th	
Halford	Kenneth C.	Capt.	508th	
Hall	Hollis H. Jr.	2nd Lt.	510th	
Hall	Clarence H.	PFC	11th	St. Comp.
Hall	Clifford D.	S/Sgt.	511th	POW 8/17/43
Hall	Edward F.	PFC	511th	
Hall	Hugh D.	T/Sgt.	509th	
Hall	Jack	M/Sgt.	447th	Sub-Depot
Hall	John L.	1st Lt.	508th	
Hall	Oscar R.	Sgt.	510th	
Haller	Raymond E.	1st Lt.	509th	
Haller	William D.	T/Sgt.	511th	
Halligan	Benjamin F.	1st Lt.	509th	
Hallman	Frederick B.	T. S/Sgt.	511th	
Hallman	William	Cpl.	510th	
	John P.	T/Sgt.		

145

Hallowa / Hemm

Surname	First	Rank	Unit	Notes
Hallowa	Roy A.	1st Lt.	508th	
Halonen	John A.	Sgt.	351st	HQ
Halpin	Robert H.	1st Lt.	509th	
Halstead	Cecil E.	T/Sgt.	11th	St. Comp.
Halstead	Kenneth G.	T/Sgt.	511th	
Hatom	John F.	2nd Lt.	510th	
Haluska	Emil G.	Sgt.	509th	
Ham	Numa R.	Maj.	447th	Sub-Depot
Hamby	James L.	PFC	1061st	MP Company
Hamel	Henry	2nd Lt.	511th	
Hames	Allen G.	Cpl.	1061st	MP Company
Hamilton	James B.	2nd Lt.	508th	
Hamilton	Leo C.	Sgt.	509th	KIA 6/12/44
Hamilton	Willard L.	Sgt.	511th	
Hamilton	William S.	S/Sgt.	508th	
Hamit	Lawrence K.	T/Sgt.	510th	
Hamlin	Eddie E.	S/Sgt.	508th	POW 7/25/43
Hamlin	Harry F. Jr.	S/Sgt.	511th	
Hamm	Wayne H.	Sgt.	508th	
Hammack	Charles E.	T/Sgt.	509th	
Hammaker	Robert S.	1st Lt.	510th	
Hammet	Charles D.	S/Sgt.	509th	
Hammond	Clinton W.	1st Lt.	511th	
Hammond	Douglas	Sgt.	510th	
Hammond	John F.	Cpl.	447th	Sub-Depot
Hammond	Raymond A.	S/Sgt.	508th	KIA 10/9/43
Hammond	Robert B.	S/Sgt.	510th	
Hampton	Roy L.	S/Sgt.	1629th	Ord. S&M Co.
Hanan	Warren Y.	1st Lt.	509th	
Hanchett	Frank W.	Sgt.	510th	KIA 6/28/43
Hancock	Rufus J.	S/Sgt.	509th	
Hancock	Elmo C.	Cpl.	511th	
Hancock	Frank	Spec. 5	252nd	Medical Disp.
Hancock	Paul	S/Sgt.	351st	HQ
Hancy	Walter B.	Cpl.	510th	POW 10/9/43
Handel	Eldred E.	2nd Lt.	510th	POW 8/6/44
Handley	Edward W.	Sgt.	511th	
Handley	Charles G.	S/Sgt.	508th	
Handschuh	William T.	Cpl.	447th	Sub-Depot
Handy	Bernard	Spec. 5	11th	St. Comp.
Handy	Ernest J.	1st Lt.	510th	
Haney	James J.	T/Sgt.	509th	
Hango	Virgil J.	Sgt.	510th	
Hanham	Stephen	Cpl.	447th	Sub-Depot
Hankinson	G. D.	Sgt.	511th	
Hanks	John C.	T/Sgt.	511th	
Hanley	Clifton J.	Sgt.	510th	
Hann	James E.	S/Sgt.	509th	
Hanna	H. T.	Pvt.	510th	
Hanna	Deane M.	S/Sgt.	510th	
Hanna	Henry T.	PFC	510th	
Hannigan	William P.	Cpl.	508th	

Surname	First	Rank	Unit	Notes
Hanning	George J.	Spec. 5	252nd	Medical Disp.
Hansen	Donald L.	T/Sgt.	510th	POW 1/11/44
Hansen	George K.	2nd Lt.	510th	
Hansen	Glen W.	S/Sgt.	511th	POW 8/17/43
Hansen	Helmuth F.	1st Lt.	510th	
Hansen	Jess P. Jr.	1st Lt.	509th	
Hansen	Robert	Sgt.	508th	
Hanson	Sylvester N.	2nd Lt.	509th	
Hanson	Vance A.	1st Lt.	508th	
Hanson	Elmer L.	T/Sgt.	510th	
Hanson	Ernest T.	PFC	11th	St. Comp.
Hanson	Floyd N.	Sgt.	510th	
Hanson	Martin M.	Sgt.	509th	
Hanson	William R.	T/Sgt.	447th	Sub-Depot
Hansowitz	Jack W.	Pvt.	508th	
Hansevack	Emil L.	S/Sgt.	509th	
Haggland	Stanley E.	S/Sgt.	508th	
Hapel	William S.	PFC	510th	
Happersett	Newlin R.	Sgt.	510th	POW 12/31/43
Happold	Donald D.	Sgt.	511th	
Harber	Walter H.	T/Sgt.	447th	
Harbison	Charles	Sgt.	509th	Sub-Depot
Hardaway	Horace E.	1st Lt.	510th	
Harden	Edwin G.	Sgt.	509th	
Hardesty	Billy M.	S/Sgt.	511th	POW 8/3/44
Hardman	Harper	S/Sgt.	447th	Sub-Depot
Hardy	Edward H.	PFC	1061st	MP Company
Hare	Arthur S.	PFC	854th	Chemical Co.
Harison	William M.	S/Sgt.	511th	
Harker	Joseph E.	2nd Lt.	509th	
Harker	Orris W.	S/Sgt.	1206th	QM Company
Harkins	Charles J. Jr.	1st Lt.	508th	
Harkins	James C.	2nd Lt.	510th	
Harley	Thomas F.	2nd Lt.	511th	KIA 12/1/43
Harm	Wayne N.	Sgt.	509th	
Harman	David M.	Sgt.	509th	POW 6/21/44
Harman	Morris V.	1st Lt.	508th	
Harman	Wesley G.	M/Sgt.	511th	
Harmon	William H.	S/Sgt.	11th	St. Comp.
Harmon	John N.	S/Sgt.	508th	
Harnevious	Nelson O.	Cpl.	510th	KIA 10/9/43
Harney	Lewis	S/Sgt.	511th	St. Comp.
Harnowicz	Paul	Cpl.	508th	
Harp	John R.	Cpl.	509th	
Harp	Fred O.	T/Sgt.	510th	
Harpster	Frederick M.	1st Lt.	508th	
Harrell	John J.	2nd Lt.	509th	
Harrell	William H.	Sgt.	509th	
Harrell	Elisha T.	S/Sgt.	510th	
Harrington	James N.	PFC	11th	St. Comp.
Harrington	Robert J.			

Surname	First	Rank	Unit	Notes
Harrington	Robert M.	S/Sgt.	509th	
Harris	Austin C.	Pvt.	11th	St. Comp.
Harris	Charles E.	Cpl.	508th	
Harris	Charles M.	2nd Lt.	510th	
Harris	Douglas L.	1st Lt.	509th	
Harris	Eugene P.	Capt.	509th	KIA 12/1/43
Harris	Frederick F.	Sgt.	509th	
Harris	James H.	1st Lt.	508th	POW 6/21/44
Harrison	Charles H.	S/Sgt.	510th	
Harrison	F.	T/Sgt.	510th	
Harrison	Fred	Sgt.	508th	
Harrison	John R.	S/Sgt.	511th	
Harriss	Donald C.	S/Sgt.	510th	
Harrod	John H.	T/Sgt.	509th	
Harryman	Milburn E.	T/Sgt.	511th	
Hart	Chester E.	S/Sgt.	11th	St. Comp.
Hart	David E.	Sgt.	510th	
Hart	Donovan L.	2nd Lt.	511th	POW 7/13/44
Hart	George A.	PFC	508th	
Hart	H.	Sgt.	447th	Sub-Depot
Hart	James H.	Sgt.	509th	
Hart	John B. Jr.	2nd Lt.	509th	KIA 1/11/44
Hart	John H.	1st Lt.	511th	
Hart	Robert M.	2nd Lt.	511th	POW 2/22/44
Hartmann	William Jr.	Sgt.	508th	
Hartnett	Alexander	S/Sgt.	509th	
Hartwell	Eugene M.	Capt.	351st	HQ
Harty	Arthur L.	S/Sgt.	511th	
Hartz	Charles W.	Cpl.	510th	
Harvard	George W.	S/Sgt.	509th	
Harvey	Augustus R.	PFC	1206th	QM Company
Harvey	Dell J.	2nd Lt.	509th	POW 1/17/45
Harward	William A.	T/Sgt.	508th	
Haselden	Donald L.	2nd Lt.	509th	
Hashberger	Charles W.	T/Sgt.	510th	
Haskell	Harold E.	Capt.	508th	
Haskins	Ray F.	S/Sgt.	510th	
Haskins	Elvin L.	Cpl.	508th	
Hassler	Willis R.	1st Lt.	509th	
Hastings	Paul H.	PFC	510th	
Hastings	Carleton F.	Sgt.	508th	
Hasty	Donald E.	Sgt.	447th	Sub-Depot
Hatcher	William D.	Cpl.	508th	
Hatcher	Robert L.	S/Sgt.	510th	
Hathaway	William A.	2nd Lt.	351st HQ	POW 12/31/43
Hathaway	Fred C.	Col.	508th	
Hatten	Richard E.	2nd Lt.	509th	
Hauck	Frank	1st Lt.	447th	POW 5/24/44
Hauck	Donald R.	1st Lt.	509th	
Hawkins	Martin L.	2nd Lt.	508th	
Hawkins	Harold H.	Sgt.	509th	
	Kenneth M.	M/Sgt.	509th	

Surname	First	Rank	Unit	Notes
Hawley	Thomas A.	T/Sgt.	511th	POW 2/24/44
Hay	Harold H.	Sgt.	511th	
Haycock	Elvis L.	Cpl.	510th	
Hayden	Lynn M.	PFC	11th	St. Comp.
Hayes	Charles H.	T/Sgt.	510th	
Hayes	Charles W.	2nd Lt.	511th	KIA 8/6/44
Hayes	Clement E.	Capt.	510th	
Hayes	Jack H.	PFC	1061st	MP Company
Hayes	Joseph H.	S/Sgt.	508th	MIA 6/13/43
Hayes	Robert J.	Sgt.	511th	
Hayes	Robert M.	S/Sgt.	511th	POW 9/12/44
Hayman	William E.	M/Sgt.	447th	Sub-Depot
Haynes	Clifford B.	S/Sgt.	511th	
Haynes	Carey D.	2nd Lt.	508th	KIA 2/21/44
Haynes	Sidney P.	Sgt.	510th	
Haynes	Winfield S. Jr.	T/Sgt.	510th	
Hays	Hubert G.	S/Sgt.	509th	
Hays	John B.	2nd Lt.	508th	
Haywood	Robert W.	1st Lt.	508th	KIA 2/14/45
Hazen	Joseph R.	T/Sgt.	509th	
Heaberlin	Willard H.	S/Sgt.	511th	
Heacox	Lorain F.	Sgt.	508th	
Heard	Ralph E.	2nd Lt.	510th	
Heard	Calvin J.	S/Sgt.	509th	
Heard	Joseph J.	2nd Lt.	509th	
Hearn	William S.	T/Sgt.	509th	
Heart	William P.	1st Lt.	508th	
Heath	K. F.	Sgt.	511th	
Heaton	Vernie P. Jr.	S/Sgt.	510th	
Hecht	Joseph F.	Sgt.	509th	
Hecht	Arnold S.	1st Lt.	510th	
Hechtman	William R.	S/Sgt.	509th	
Heck	John O.	2nd Lt.	508th	
Heckart	John W.	S/Sgt.	510th	
Hedden	Hurley F.	PFC	11th	St. Comp.
Hedrick	Daniel T.	1st Lt.	509th	
Hedrick	Burley	Sgt.	510th	
Hefferman	Carrol A.	2nd Lt.	447th	Sub-Depot
Heffner	William O. Jr.	Cpl.	509th	
Hefka	Joseph	Sgt.	508th	
Hegner	William	1st Lt.	510th	POW 1/11/44
Heidorn	Edward A.	Sgt.	509th	
Heinrich	George C.	Pvt.	508th	
Held	Oscar	2nd Lt.	510th	
Heldmann	Earl C.	S/Sgt.	447th	
Heller	Henry M.	2nd Lt.	509th	HQ
Helman	David M.	1st Lt.	511th	
Helton	Herman	2nd Lt.	508th	
Helton	Hubert E.	1st Lt.	509th	
Hemm	L. T.	Cpl.	508th	
Hemm	John J.	1st Lt.	510th	POW 10/9/43
	Wilfred O.	PFC	510th	

Hempel / Hosley

Last	First	Rank	Unit	Notes	Last	First	Rank	Unit	Notes	Last	First	Rank	Unit	Notes
Hempel	Gottfried E.	Sgt.	508th		Hess	Andrew C.	2nd Lt.	511th	KIA 9/12/44	Holmes	Earl E.	F.O.	511th	POW 1/30/44
Hempel	William J.	Sgt.	511th		Hesseltine	Fred J.	T/Sgt.	511th		Holmes	William H.	T/Sgt.	508th	
Henderson	Donald V.	2nd Lt.	508th		Hester	Richard C.	PFC	509th	Sub-Depot	Holmstadt	Thorsten H.	Sgt.	508th	
Henderson	Edward E.	T/Sgt.	509th	KIA 6/14/44	Heustess	Charles B.	Cpl.	447th	Medical Disp.	Holsapple	Harry B.	Capt.	510th	
Henderson	Edward T.	PFC	509th	Sub-Depot	Heyden	Carl F.	Cpl.	252nd		Holsen	Roland G.	S/Sgt.	508th	
Henderson	J. B.	S/Sgt.	447th		Heyob	Elmer W.	2nd Lt.	509th		Holt	Lawrence T.	S/Sgt.	11th	St. Comp.
Henderson	Wayne	PFC	509th		Hibbard	Howard R.	1st Lt.	509th	Killed 6/8/45	Holtman	Eugene F.	2nd Lt.	511th	
Hendrick	Wydell S	T/Sgt.	11th	St. Comp.	Hibbard	John W.	Pvt.	1629th	Ord. S&M Co.	Holton	Wallace A.	S/Sgt.	508th	
Hendrick	Burley	Cpl.	447th	Sub-Depot	Hickel	James L.	1st Lt.	510th		Holtzman	Harry T.	S/Sgt.	510th	Int'd 10/7/44
Hendrick	Harry	PFC	508th		Hickle		S/Sgt.	508th		Holub	Edward W.	2nd Lt.	509th	
Hendrickson	Melvin R.	Cpl.	510th		Hickman	Willis C.	T/Sgt.	510th		Homser	George E.	Sgt.	511th	
Hendrickson	Wilford	S/Sgt.	511th		Hicks	Crawford E.	2nd Lt.	509th		Homstad	Floyd F.	1st Lt.	509th	
Hendrickson	Wilfred E.	T/Sgt.	511th		Hicks	Hilton W.	Cpl.	11th	St. Comp.	Homza	George J.	1st Lt.	511th	
Hendrix	John F.	Sgt.	1206th	QM Company	Higgenbotham	Walter	T/Sgt.	447th	Sub-Depot	Honig	Harold D.	Cpl.	11th	MIA 5/27/44
Henkel	Walter D.	S/Sgt.	509th		Higgins	Herbert W.	Sgt.	447th	Sub-Depot	Honsowetz	Jack W.	Sgt.	508th	
Henley	James E.	S/Sgt.	508th		Higgins	Hubert D.	S/Sgt.	510th		Hood	Ray A.	Sgt.	509th	St. Comp.
Henley	Stacey Q.	2nd Lt.	508th		Higgins	James P.	2nd Lt.	508th	POW 3/22/44	Hoodnick	Frank J.	PFC	11th	
Hennegan	Howard L.	S/Sgt.	508th		Higgins	Malcolm H.	S/Sgt.	508th	POW 10/14/43	Hooks	Eugene E.	2nd Lt.	511th	KIA 9/8/44
Henneforth	Edward J.	2nd Lt.	510th	POW 9/12/44	Highfill	Thomas V.	S/Sgt.	510th	MIA 5/19/43	Hooper	Edward P. Jr.	S/Sgt.	508th	
Hennessey	Paul	S/Sgt.	510th	POW 8/17/43	Highland	Jack G.	Sgt.	11th	St. Comp.	Hoorsch	Phillip M.	S/Sgt.	509th	
Henning	Frank H.	PFC	854th	Chemical Co.	Higley	Emette	Sgt.	508th		Hoover	Gary L.	Sgt.	511th	
Henninger	Edward W.	S/Sgt.	510th	KIA 8/12/43	Hilcott	Richard E.	1st Lt.	509th	Killed 6/8/45	Hoover	Henry L.	T/Sgt.	1206th	QM Company
Hennings	Detlef F.	PFC	854th	Chemical Co.	Hildebrandt	Charles B.	T/Sgt.	509th	POW 5/24/44	Hoover	Ralph E.	PFC	1061st	MP Company
Hennings	Maxwalton A.	S/Sgt.	509th		Hildebrandt	Samuel H.	Sgt.	1206th	QM Company	Hopkins	Francis J.	PFC	509th	POW 6/22/44
Hennis	David E.	Sgt.	508th		Hildenbrand	James B.	PFC	854th	Chemical Co.	Hopkins	Horace E.	2nd Lt.	511th	
Henrickson	Kenneth D.	S/Sgt.	508th		Hildenbrand	Rudolph	S/Sgt.	511th		Hopper	Dick O.	1st Lt.	510th	KIA 5/27/44
Henry	Charles F.	1st Lt.	511th		Hildreth	John W.	Cpl.	508th	Sub-Depot	Hopper	James C.	Sgt.	508th	
Henry	Howard C.	PFC	854th	Chemical Co.	Hill	James E.	PFC	854th	Chemical Co.	Hopper	Jewel G.	T/Sgt.	511th	KIA 9/5/44
Henry	Stanford W.	S/Sgt.	510th		Hill	John B.	T/Sgt.	447th	Sub-Depot	Horan	Joseph P.	Spec. 5	854th	Chemical Co.
Henry	Stephen J.	S/Sgt.	511th	KIA 5/15/43	Hill	John W.	S/Sgt.	509th		Horan	Thomas W.	1st Lt.	447th	Sub-Depot
Hepburn	William S.	S/Sgt.	510th		Hill	Joseph E.	S/Sgt.	11th	St. Comp.	Horan	William K.	2nd Lt.	508th	
Heppert	Paul A.	Cpl.	447th	Sub-Depot	Hill	Leslie C.	Sgt.	511th		Hord	Cletus T.	Cpl.	511th	St. Comp.
Hereford	Roscoe W.	Sgt.	509th		Hill	Muary	2nd Lt.	511th		Horgan	Russell V.	1st Lt.	510th	
Herlich	Richard W.	T/Sgt.	510th	KIA 7/12/44	Hill	Ora L.	S/Sgt.	511th	POW 10/9/43	Horkay	Clyde W.	PFC	508th	Sub-Depot
Herline	Robert C.	PFC	351st	HQ	Hill	Robert W.	T/Sgt.	508th		Horne	Paul L.	Pvt.	511th	St. Comp.
Herman	Edward T.	Pvt.	509th		Hill	Stanley J.	T/Sgt.	511th		Horne	Carl W.	Sgt.	447th	POW 10/7/44
Herman	Elmer T. Jr.	Sgt.	508th		Hill	Wayne F.	Cpl.	511th		Hornick	George Jr.	2nd Lt.	511th	
Herman	Merle A.	1st Lt.	511th	MP Company	Hill	William E.	S/Sgt.	351st		Hornick	Alexander	1st Lt.	854th	Chemical Co.
Herman	Samuel W.	2nd Lt.	510th	KIA 7/19/44	Hillard	Dallas G.	2nd Lt.	511th		Hormerte	John A.	2nd Lt.	447th	Sub-Depot
Herman	Sol	PFC	351st	HQ	Hillebrand	Mahlon A.	1st Lt.	510th		Horn	Russell V.	Sgt.	508th	St. Comp.
Hermann	Louis V.	Pvt.	509th		Hilliard	James H.	S/Sgt.	511th		Horn	Clyde W.	PFC	511th	
Herr	Leroy M.	Sgt.	1061st		Hilliard	Robert K.	T/Sgt.	508th		Horne	Paul L.	Pvt.	511th	
Herrick	Jackson L.	T/Sgt.	508th		Hillway	Charles A.	2nd Lt.	351st		Hornick	Carl W.	Sgt.	447th	
Herring	James H.	2nd Lt.	511th		Hilscher	Louis M.	S/Sgt.	511th	KIA 5/15/43	Hornick	George Jr.	2nd Lt.	511th	POW 10/7/44
Herring	Wayland	Sgt.	510th		Hilton	Max T.	2nd Lt.	508th	KIA 5/14/43	Horns	Frederick F.	1st Lt.	1629th	Ord. S&M Co.
Hersey	Donald W.	1st Lt.	508th		Himes	Robert H.	Pvt.	1629th	Ord. S&M Co.	Hornsby	John A. Jr.	S/Sgt.	509th	
Hersey	Douglas S.	Sgt.	510th		Hingle	Lafayette N.	2nd Lt.	509th		Horowitz	Norman B.	2nd Lt.	511th	
Hersey	Philip W.	Sgt.	508th	KIA 7/19/44	Hinkel	Edward C.	Cpl.	509th		Horsey	Kenneth E.	T/Sgt.	11th	St. Comp.
Hertzberg	Abraham	1st Lt.	511th		Hinkle	Charles W.	Lt. Col.	351st	HQ	Horstman	Vernon G.	1st Lt.	351st	HQ
Herzich	John J.	Cpl.	351st	HQ	Hinkle	Carl C. Jr.	Cpl.	509th		Horton	Clarence J.	S/Sgt.	510th	
Herzog	Robert J.	Capt.	510th		Hirsch	Ollie B.	2nd Lt.	447th	Sub-Depot	Horton	Mortimore	1st Lt.	508th	
						Paul	1st Lt.	2098th	Avn. F/F Pltn.	Horwarth	Zoltan T.	S/Sgt.	510th	
										Hoskins	John W.	Pvt.	1206th	
										Hosley	Edwin J.	S/Sgt.	509th	

Hoster / Jewell

Last Name	First Name	Rank	Unit	Notes
Hoster	John H.	Sgt.	508th	
Hotchkin	George W.	1st Lt.	511th	
Hottensen	Donald L.	S/Sgt.	508th	
Houck	George D.	Pvt.	1206th	Medical Disp.
Houck	John R.	Capt.	509th	QM Company
Hough	Martin L.	M/Sgt.	509th	
Hough	Richard G.	2nd Lt.	510th	POW 3/18/44
Houk	Ira	T/Sgt.	509th	
Hoult	Ressie H.	Cpl.	510th	St. Comp.
Houns	William R.	S/Sgt.	510th	
House	William H.	Sgt.	11th	
Houser	Elmer J.	1st Lt.	510th	
Houtchens	Burnice L.	F.O.	509th	
Hovey	Walter C.	S/Sgt.	508th	
Howard	Charles B.	Sgt.	509th	
Howard	Charles M.	S/Sgt.	508th	
Howard	Joseph	S/Sgt.	509th	
Howard	Raymond E.	S/Sgt.	509th	KIA 2/11/44
Howard	Richard C.	Cpl.	511th	
Howard	Robert T.	S/Sgt.	508th	POW 7/28/44
Howarth	William H.	Cpl.	447th	
Howarth	James H.	1st Lt.	854th	Chemical Co.
Howe	Zolton	Sgt.	511th	
Howell	William C.	2nd Lt.	1629th	Ord. S&M Co.
Howell	Jack	2nd Lt.	508th	
Howell	Melvin D.	1st Lt.	511th	KIA 5/15/43
Howes	Thomas	F.O.	511th	
Howes	George P.	S/Sgt.	510th	
Howett	Robert L.	S/Sgt.	508th	
Howin	Carl M.	Cpl.	508th	Sub-Depot
Hoydn	Raymond J.	S/Sgt.	511th	
Hrycay	Walter	Sgt.	11th	St. Comp.
Hubbard	John D.	1st Lt.	511th	
Hubbell	Charles H.	F.O.	511th	
Huber	Fritz A.	S/Sgt.	510th	KIA 1/11/44
Hubinger	Charles J.	S/Sgt.	508th	
Huckle	Charles J.	PFC	1061st	MP Company
Hudkins	Richard W.	Sgt.	509th	Int'd 10/7/44
Hudson	Albert W.	Sgt.	509th	
Hudson	Thomas B.	M/Sgt.	510th	POW 7/12/44
Huesing	Irvin C.	2nd Lt.	351st	HQ
Huff	Donald Y.	Sgt.	511th	
Huff	Gene L.	1st Lt.	511th	
Huff	Paschel M.	T/Sgt.	511th	
Huffman	Alfred O.	Sgt.	508th	
Huggett	Erwin G.	S/Sgt.	511th	
Huggins	David E.	PFC	1061st	
Hughes	Albert L.	Sgt.	509th	
Hughes	Clyde P.	1st Lt.	509th	
Hughes	Francis E.	Sgt.	509th	
Hughes	Gary L.	T/Sgt.	509th	
Hughes	Ira W.	S/Sgt.	510th	POW 7/12/44
Hughes	Jack C.	Sgt.	508th	
Hughes	Joseph E.	1st Lt.	508th	
Hughes	Philip H.	Sgt.	511th	
Hughes	Philip L.	Pvt.	511th	
Hughes	Robert L.	PFC	1061st	MP Company
Hugo	Victor E.	Sgt.	510th	
Hull	Wilburn L.	S/Sgt.	510th	KIA 5/15/43
Hull	Melvin E.	1st Lt.	511th	
Hullender	Charles	Sgt.	508th	
Hulme	Clyde E.	S/Sgt.	510th	
Hulme	Ivey B.	Sgt.	351st	HQ
Huls	Marcus W.	Sgt.	508th	
Hulse	Kenneth L.	T/Sgt.	508th	
Humphrey	Phillip G.	F.O.	509th	
Huneke	Lewis H.	Sgt.	509th	
Hunt	Edgar A.	S/Sgt.	509th	
Hunt	Leolan E.	1st Lt.	510th	
Hunter	B. L.	T/Sgt.	511th	POW 12/1/43
Hunter	Byron D.	T/Sgt.	509th	
Hunter	Clarence L.	1st Lt.	510th	
Hunter	Dean L.	Sgt.	508th	
Hunter	Lloyd T.	1st Lt.	508th	MIA 10/4/43
Hunter	Maurice D.	T/Sgt.	510th	
Hunter	Robert E.	S/Sgt.	511th	Sub-Depot
Hunter	Willard O.	S/Sgt.	509th	
Hunting	Robert H.	Sgt.	511th	
Huntingdon	Ralph C.	T/Sgt.	508th	Sub-Depot
Huntingdon	Verlan G.	Cpl.	447th	
Huntley	Elver F.	1st Lt.	508th	POW 7/28/44
Huppert	Paul C.	Spec. 4	509th	
Hurlbutt	Carl R.	Sgt.	447th	
Hurley	Jack C.	T/Sgt.	511th	Chemical Co.
Hurley	Robert G.	1st Lt.	510th	
Hurst	Adrian M.	Spec. 5	854th	Chemical Co.
Hurst	Caleb B.	S/Sgt.	511th	Int'd 3/18/44
Hurst	James L.	Sgt.	509th	
Hurst	Junior	Cpl.	508th	
Hurst	Phillip	PFC	11th	St. Comp.
Huskey	Richard R.	Cpl.	11th	St. Comp.
Huss	Ray	S/Sgt.	508th	Ord. S&M Co.
Hutcherson	Joseph S.	Pvt.	1629th	
Hutchings	Robert A.	Sgt.	510th	
Hutchings	Alba A.	T/Sgt.	508th	
Hutchison	Thomas C.	Sgt.	854th	Chemical Co.
Huth	Edwin B.	Sgt.	511th	POW 10/3/44
Hutton	Edward L.	T/Sgt.	509th	
Huxton	Richard H.	Sgt.	447th	Sub-Depot
Hyde	W. D.	1st Lt.	508th	Sub-Depot
Hyde	Roy E.	Sgt.	508th	
Hygren	Walter J.	T/Sgt.	508th	
	William E.	T/Sgt.		
Hynes	Walter J.	Cpl.	509th	
Hypes	Virgil V.	Spec. 5	351st	HQ
Iannini	Anthony J.	Pvt.	511th	
Iannone	Nicholas J.	Pvt.	447th	
Ieivent	Danial	Sgt.	510th	Sub-Depot
Illies	Walter R.	1st Lt.	509th	
Imhoff	Robert H.	S/Sgt.	508th	KIA 3/18/44
Imler	Bruce F.	T/Sgt.	508th	
Incivilito	Joseph P.	S/Sgt.	447th	Sub-Depot
Infante	Edward	Sgt.	509th	
Ingber	Phillip H.	S/Sgt.	508th	
Ingison	Walter C.	T/Sgt.	508th	
Ingold	Rex H.	PFC	1061st	MP Company
Ingraham	Eugene S.	S/Sgt.	510th	
Ingram	Eppy V.	Cpl.	11th	St. Comp.
Ireland	Edward L. Jr.	T/Sgt.	511th	
Irish	Henry P.	Sgt.	11th	St. Comp.
Irish	Russell C.	1st Lt.	1206th	QM Company
Irle	Robert F.	S/Sgt.	510th	
Irvine	Thomas A.	2nd Lt.	511th	KIA 12/31/43
Irving	Robert D.	T/Sgt.	510th	
Irwin	Carl A.	Sgt.	511th	POW 7/13/44
Irwin	Irl A.	1st Lt.	508th	
Isaacson	Samuel F.	2nd Lt.	510th	POW 7/12/44
Iso	Gerald	T/Sgt.	510th	
Isoardi	A. K.	Pvt.	509th	
Israel	Joseph J.	2nd Lt.	508th	
Italiano	Alvin	2nd Lt.	510th	
Ivanoff	F. J.	Cpl.	509th	
Iverson	Jordan	F.O.	508th	
Iverson	Alvin L.	2nd Lt.	854th	Chemical Co.
Ives	Arnold S.	Sgt.	511th	
Iwanowski	George R. Jr.	1st Lt.	11th	St. Comp.
	Walter M.	2nd Lt.		
Jablonski	Albert F.	S/Sgt.	509th	
Jacen	Joseph C.	PFC	1206th	QM Company
Jackson	Andrew A.	S/Sgt.	511th	
Jackson	Bobby L.	S/Sgt.	510th	
Jackson	Charles L.	Cpl.	508th	
Jackson	Edward P.	2nd Lt.	510th	POW 1/11/44
Jackson	George C.	2nd Lt.	508th	
Jackson	George G.	Sgt.	510th	
Jackson	Harvey F.	Sgt.	510th	
Jackson	Jack	T/Sgt.	509th	
Jackson	James J.	Pvt.	508th	
Jackson	John J.	Sgt.	11th	St. Comp.
Jackson	Junny O.	S/Sgt.	508th	POW 5/28/44
Jackson	Kenneth R.	PFC	508th	KIA 5/28/44
Jackson	Robert C.	S/Sgt.	510th	POW 6/13/43
Jackson	Robert W.	1st Lt.	509th	
Jackson	Roy V.	Spec. 5	854th	Chemical Co.
Jackson	William B.	Cpl.	509th	
Jacobs	Melvin C.	S/Sgt.	511th	
Jacobs	Ralph D.	M/Sgt.	510th	
Jacobs	Willis D.	S/Sgt.	351st	HQ
Jacobs	Willis H.	Sgt.	509th	
Jacobson	David L.	Sgt.	509th	
Jacobus	Edward F.	1st Lt.	509th	
Jacoby	Robert C.	Cpl.	511th	POW 1/30/44
James	Herman J.	1st Lt.	509th	
James	Cecil G.	Sgt.	509th	
James	Gerald E.	S/Sgt.	509th	
James	Glenn J.	S/Sgt.	511th	
James	Henry L.	T/Sgt.	510th	
James	John H.	Sgt.	508th	
James	Roy L.	1st Lt.	510th	
James	Thomas P.	T/Sgt.	509th	
Jamison	James A.	S/Sgt.	508th	Sub-Depot
Jancsak	Edward C.	Cpl.	447th	
Janesko	Robert T.	S/Sgt.	510th	KIA 9/8/44
Jankowski	Daltaus J.	T/Sgt.	509th	
Janoaitis	Millard G.	1st Lt.	508th	
Jantz	Eugene R.	T/Sgt.	510th	
Jaquemart	Albert J.	S/Sgt.	508th	
Jaques	Robert S.	T/Sgt.	509th	KIA 3/18/44
Jarois	George J.	Sgt.	511th	POW 11/26/44
Jaros	Stanley Jr.	Sgt.	510th	
Jasick	Leonard D.	T/Sgt.	509th	
Jasinek	Robert C.	2nd Lt.	510th	KIA 5/19/43
Jason	Harold G.	2nd Lt.	508th	
Jasper	Charles W.	2nd Lt.	510th	
Jatho	Vince R.	Sgt.	509th	
Javoric	David B.	Pvt.	509th	
Jay	Weston O.	Cpl.	854th	Chemical Co.
Jayne	George J.	2nd Lt.	511th	Sub-Depot
Jazuk	Alvin L.	Cpl.	447th	
Jeanes	Joseph C.	Sgt.	508th	Ord. S&M Co.
Jeger	Charles G.	PFC	1629th	
Jenkins	George D.	Sgt.	508th	KIA 5/28/44
Jenkins	Albert L.	2nd Lt.	351st	HQ
Jensen	Donald L.	S/Sgt.	510th	KIA 5/14/43
Jensen	Lawrence E.	Sgt.	509th	Int'd 10/7/44
Jensen	Richard A.	Cpl.	509th	
Jeremiah	Benjamin T.	1st Lt.	854th	Chemical Co.
Jernigan	Kenneth R.	T/Sgt.	511th	
Jester	John H.	Pvt.	351st	HQ
Jett	John C.	Cpl.	510th	Died 6/22/43
Jewell	Thomas	S/Sgt.	508th	

Jilcott / Kendall

Last	First	Rank	Unit	Notes
Jilcott	Charles B.	T/Sgt.	509th	
Jillson	John S.	1st Lt.	510th	
Jiminez	Jose A.	S/Sgt.	510th	
Jizmejian	Varsted G.	1st Lt.	11th	St. Comp.
Jobes	Robert E.	Sgt.	510th	
Jochem	Raymond R.	Cpl.	509th	
Jockell	Kenneth P.	S/Sgt.	510th	
John	Arthur H.	T/Sgt.	511th	
Johnson	Aaron E.	S/Sgt.	508th	
Johnson	Arthur M.	2nd Lt.	508th	
Johnson	Byron L.	2nd Lt.	508th	
Johnson	Carl E.	S/Sgt.	510th	
Johnson	Charles R. Sr.	Sgt.	510th	
Johnson	Chester	Spec. 5	854th	Chemical Co.
Johnson	Daniel A.	S/Sgt.	510th	
Johnson	David R.	Cpl.	510th	
Johnson	Donald E.	T/Sgt.	508th	POW 4/18/44
Johnson	Elmer G.	1st Lt.	510th	
Johnson	Frank W.	S/Sgt.	510th	
Johnson	Franklin D.	Sgt.	511th	
Johnson	Gosta	1st Lt.	508th	POW 5/27/44
Johnson	Grant D.	S/Sgt.	510th	
Johnson	Guinn R.	PFC	510th	
Johnson	H. R.	S/Sgt.	510th	
Johnson	Harold C.	T/Sgt.	511th	
Johnson	Harold W.	Sgt.	447th	Sub-Depot
Johnson	Harvey E.	S/Sgt.	510th	
Johnson	Henry C.	PFC	510th	
Johnson	Henry D.	Lt. Col.	447th	Sub-Depot
Johnson	Hugo R.	T/Sgt.	510th	
Johnson	James W.	Sgt.	508th	
Johnson	Jess E.	Sgt.	509th	POW 8/27/43
Johnson	Kendall D.	S/Sgt.	511th	
Johnson	Maurice A.	PFC	509th	
Johnson	Myron L.	2nd Lt.	508th	
Johnson	Norman B.	S/Sgt.	508th	
Johnson	Norman P.	S/Sgt.	509th	
Johnson	Paul V.	Sgt.	1629th	Ord. S&M Co.
Johnson	Peter B.	Sgt.	510th	
Johnson	Ralph S.	S/Sgt.	509th	KIA 6/13/43
Johnson	Robert H.	1st Lt.	508th	
Johnson	Robert J.	Sgt.	508th	
Johnson	Robert L.	S/Sgt.	511th	
Johnson	Roger S.	1st Lt.	509th	
Johnson	Roy	Sgt.	510th	
Johnson	Sheldon E.	Sgt.	447th	Sub-Depot
Johnson	Thomas N.	Cpl.	508th	
Johnson	Van L.	Sgt.	508th	
Johnson	Walter	S/Sgt.	511th	
Johnson	Walter S.	Sgt.	510th	
Johnson	Wesley R.	2nd Lt.	509th	
Johnson	Wilburn N.	PFC	1061st	MP Company
Johnson	William A.	Sgt.	509th	
Johnston	Harry D. Jr.	1st Lt.	509th	
Johnston	James E.	1st Lt.	510th	
Johnston	Jesse E.	S/Sgt.	511th	
Johnston	John W.	Cpl.	447th	Sub-Depot
Johnstone	Fred	Sgt.	510th	
Joiner	Glen E.	S/Sgt.	508th	MIA 5/27/44
Jonaitis	John R.	2nd Lt.	510th	KIA 2/22/44
Johncaitis	Baltrus J. Jr.	1st Lt.	508th	
Joncas	Maurice E.	1st Lt.	509th	MIA 12/31/43
Jones	Albert E.	2nd Lt.	511th	MIA 1/11/44
Jones	Alfred F.	S/Sgt.	511th	Medical Disp.
Jones	Allen P.	Sgt.	510th	
Jones	Arthur M. Jr.	2nd Lt.	509th	QM Company
Jones	Arthur R.	Spec. 5	252nd	Chemical Co.
Jones	Bob	PFC	1206th	MP Company
Jones	Carrol W.	Pvt.	854th	
Jones	Charlie M.	Sgt.	1061st	
Jones	Gordon A.	T/Sgt.	509th	
Jones	Hardy	Sgt.	511th	
Jones	Harold B.	2nd Lt.	510th	
Jones	Harold L.	Cpl.	508th	
Jones	Herbert T.	S/Sgt.	509th	
Jones	James R.	PFC	510th	
Jones	Jeter P. Jr.	Sgt.	509th	
Jones	John H.	S/Sgt.	508th	
Jones	Lawrence	Cpl.	510th	
Jones	Marvin L.	T/Sgt.	508th	
Jones	Oscar V.	M/Sgt.	510th	
Jones	P. W.	F.O.	511th	
Jones	Robert G.	2nd Lt.	508th	
Jones	Robert J.	Capt.	252nd	Medical Disp.
Jones	Samuel L.	Sgt.	1629th	Ord. S&M Co.
Jones	Seaborn O.	PFC	508th	
Jones	Thompson W.	S/Sgt.	11th	St. Comp.
Jones	William W.	2nd Lt.	510th	
Joorfetz	Robert C.	Capt.	508th	
Jordan	Martin M. Jr.	Sgt.	854th	Chemical Co.
Jordan	Marvin G.	PFC	508th	
Jordan	William T.	Cpl.	510th	
Jordan	Raymond F.	F.O.	511th	
Joseph	Don R.	T/Sgt.	509th	
Joyce	Francis E.	Sgt.	511th	KIA 9/12/44
Joyce	John D.	Sgt.	511th	
Julian	Salvatore	Sgt.	509th	
Julien	Frank J.	S/Sgt.	510th	
Jurczak	Andrew	Capt.	351st	HQ
Jurena	Julius J.	Pvt.	509th	
Justice	Cecil	PFC	510th	
Jutho	Charles	2nd Lt.	508th	
Juul	Edward N.	Sgt.	509th	QM Company

K

Last	First	Rank	Unit	Notes
Kabakoff	Alfred B.	F.O.	508th	
Kable	Kelvin D.	1st Lt.	508th	
Kaczka	Theodore	S/Sgt.	510th	
Kaczor	Louis	PFC	509th	
Kaczorek	Joseph E.	1st Lt.	1206th	QM Company
Kafer	Walter E.	Sgt.	509th	
Kailey	Paul G.	Sgt.	509th	
Kaiserlik	Russell J.	Sgt.	447th	Sub-Depot
Kalapp	John M.	S/Sgt.	509th	POW 1/22/45
Kale	Henry F.	1st Lt.	508th	
Kalichinsky	Ralph F.	PFC	1061st	MP Company
Kalis	Albert J.	S/Sgt.	510th	
Kalita	John C.	Cpl.	510th	
Kallas	Paul	T/Sgt.	509th	POW 1/11/44
Kalley	Vernon D.	Cpl.	509th	
Kalway	Richard F.	S/Sgt.	11th	St. Comp.
Kane	Jerome H.	Sgt.	510th	
Kane	John J.	S/Sgt.	508th	
Kanes	Joseph	T/Sgt.	509th	
Kaochele	Paul R.	S/Sgt.	509th	
Kaplan	Albert	Sgt.	510th	
Kaplan	Alex	PFC	11th	St. Comp.
Kaplan	Milton J.	F.O.	508th	
Kaplan	Sidney D.	2nd Lt.	511th	POW 1/30/44
Kaplowitz	Isador P.	PFC	508th	
Karagiannis	Martin	S/Sgt.	511th	KIA 5/28/44
Karg	James J.	1st Lt.	511th	
Karke	J.	Cpl.	508th	
Karnes	James N.	Cpl.	510th	
Karnes	William F.	S/Sgt.	511th	POW 8/6/44
Karniewski	Walter L.	Cpl.	508th	
Karolewicz	Edward J.	S/Sgt.	510th	KIA 10/3/44
Kary	Jones J.	Cpl.	508th	
Kasala	Victor A.	PFC	854th	Chemical Co.
Kasalia	Charles	S/Sgt.	508th	
Kase	Edward C.	S/Sgt.	11th	St. Comp.
Kaschelo	Paul R.	T/Sgt.	510th	POW 12/31/43
Kasper	George F.	S/Sgt.	510th	
Kasper	Robert R.	S/Sgt.	508th	
Kather	Alfred C.	1st Lt.	511th	
Katko	Louis	Cpl.	510th	
Kaufman	Kenneth G.	F.O.	511th	
Kaufman	Nathan	Sgt.	509th	
Kavinsky	Irving	Sgt.	511th	
Kaylor	Donn G.	S/Sgt.	508th	
Keane	Joseph P.	Capt.	351st	HQ
Kearney	James M.	S/Sgt.	509th	
Kearney	John P.	T/Sgt.	509th	
Kearney	Joseph F.	Sgt.	1206th	QM Company
Kearns	Malcolm M.	Sgt.	511th	POW 8/6/44
Keasler	William E.	Cpl.	508th	POW 1/11/44
Keating	James P.	2nd Lt.	510th	
Keck	Robert A.	T/Sgt.	510th	
Keefe	Ernest J.	T/Sgt.	510th	
Keegan	Thomas J.	2nd Lt.	509th	
Keeler	DeWitt C.	2nd Lt.	510th	
Keeler	Jack C.	Sgt.	509th	
Keeler	Kenneth W.	Cpl.	447th	Sub-Depot
Keen	Vern J.	S/Sgt.	510th	KIA 7/25/43
Keener	Joseph W.	PFC	1206th	QM Company
Keese	Allen	1st Lt.	509th	
Keese	Alwyn I.	T/Sgt.	508th	
Kehoe	Merlin C. Jr.	S/Sgt.	511th	
Keister	George R.	2nd Lt.	511th	MIA 10/4/43
Keith	William R.	T/Sgt.	508th	
Keith	Donald L.	S/Sgt.	511th	
Kelcher	William F.	2nd Lt.	508th	
Kelder	John J.	Sgt.	511th	
Kelleher	Daniel F.	Cpl.	510th	
Keller	Harold D.	1st Lt.	508th	
Keller	John W.	1st Lt.	510th	Killed 5/7/43
Keller	Stanley R.	Capt.	509th	
Kelley	Bernard J.	S/Sgt.	510th	
Kelley	Frederic S.	Cpl.	351st	
Kelley	George F. Jr.	Sgt.	509th	Chemical Co.
Kelley	Harold G.	S/Sgt.	854th	
Kelley	Harry J.	S/Sgt.	509th	
Kelley	Paul B.	PFC	508th	
Kelley	Raymond O.	1st Lt.	510th	
Kelley	Vernon D.	Sgt.	509th	
Kelley	Robert C.	S/Sgt.	509th	
Kellner	Richard P.	S/Sgt.	511th	HQ
Kellogg	John J.	PFC	1061st	MP Company
Kellsher	Bernard J.	1st Lt.	1629th	Ord. S&M Co.
Kelly	Charles M.	Pvt.	508th	POW 6/14/44
Kelly	Harold T.	S/Sgt.	508th	
Kelly	James J.	Sgt.	510th	KIA 7/19/44
Kelly	John H.	2nd Lt.	508th	
Kelly	John M. Jr.	T/Sgt.	510th	
Kelly	Mills P.	PFC	511th	
Kelt	Robert D.	S/Sgt.	1061st	
Kemohah	Paul	S/Sgt.	854th	Chemical Co.
Kemp	Donald L.	Sgt.	508th	
Kemp	Arthur L.	PFC		
Kempe	Oscar D.			
Kemplin	Stanley N.			
Kendall	E. J. Volney A. J.			

Kengott / Kubetin

Surname	First	Rank	Unit	Status
Kengott	Robert A.	PFC	447th	Sub-Depot
Keniston	Martin M.	M/Sgt.	508th	
Kennair	James J.	PFC	252nd	Medical Disp.
Kennard	Wesley M.	S/Sgt.	511th	
Kennedy	Albert L.	1st. Lt.	510th	
Kennedy	Carl M.	2nd Lt.	511th	
Kennedy	Fred A.	1st Lt.	508th	
Kennedy	Frederic T. Jr.	1st Lt.	508th	
Kennedy	Herbert L.	Sgt.	351st	HQ
Kennedy	John A.	S/Sgt.	511th	KIA 6/28/43
Kennedy	John W. Jr.	S/Sgt.	508th	
Kennedy	Thomas F. Jr.	T/Sgt.	509th	POW 1/22/45
Kennedy	Thomas M.	S/Sgt.	510th	
Kennelly	David	Sgt.	508th	
Kenney	Lawrence E.	PFC	509th	
Kenney	Winston K.	Sgt.	510th	
Kenny	William F.	1st Lt.	510th	
Kensey	John R.	1st Lt.	510th	
Kent	William H. Jr.	T/Sgt.	509th	
Kenyon	Frederick C.	S/Sgt.	508th	
Kepler	Vern J.	Cpl.	447th	Sub-Depot
Keplinger	Virgil H.	Pvt.	351st	HQ
Kerchin	Joseph F.	M/Sgt.	447th	Sub-Depot
Kern	Charles W.	Lt.	511th	
Kern	Jack P.	1st Lt.	508th	Int'd 10/7/44
Kerr	Lester L.	Sgt.	511th	
Kerr	Vernon L.	T/Sgt.	510th	
Kessler	Samuel	Sgt.	509th	
Kessler	Willie I.	PFC	510th	
Kestenbaum	Martin E.	1st Lt.	510th	
Kesterson	J. D.	Pvt.	1061st	MP Company
Ketcherside	Marvin F.	Sgt.	511th	POW 9/12/44
Ketelsen	Arthur W.	2nd Lt.	510th	
Ketney	C. P.	Sgt.	508th	
Kettinger	Kenneth P.	PFC	510th	POW 5/28/44
Kevorkian	Gerard O.	1st Lt.	1629th	Ord. S&M Co.
Kewin	George R.	Sgt.	510th	
Kicmol	Edward M.	Sgt.	508th	
Kidder	George D.	Cpl.	511th	St. Comp.
Kidder	Ira N.	Sgt.	508th	POW 5/27/44
Kidwell	Preston B.	F.O.	511th	
Kiegler	Stanley H.	Sgt.	508th	
Kiely	George F.	1st Lt.	510th	
Kiem	Frederick R.	Cpl.	1629th	Avn.F/F Pltn.
Kiewit	Edson L.	S/Sgt.	510th	
Kihm	John W.	1st Lt.	508th	
Kilby	John M.	S/Sgt.	508th	
Killduff	George T.	2nd Lt.	511th	
Killian	Joseph P.	1st Lt.	508th	
Killinger	John A.	1st Lt.	510th	
Killons	Robert W.	S/Sgt.	2098th	Avn. F/F Pltn.
Killoran	Donald B.	Sgt.	511th	POW 8/6/44
Killough	Wyndell H.	S/Sgt.	508th	KIA 10/9/43
Killpack	Edward S.	S/SGt.	508th	
Kilmer	Jonas	Cpl.	447th	Sub-Depot
Kimble	Arthur	M/Sgt.	511th	
Kimmel	Ivan G.	S/Sgt.	508th	
Kimmons	Robert W.	Cpl.	11th	St. Comp.
Kimp	T. H.	S/Sgt.	508th	
Kinannon	Harold W.	Cpl.	2098th	Avn. F/F Pltn.
Kinard	Wesley	2nd Lt.	511th	
King	Charles P.	S/Sgt.	508th	
King	David M.	Pvt.	11th	St. Comp.
King	Greene A.	2nd Lt.	510th	
King	Herbert R.	1st Lt.	509th	
King	James	Cpl.	351st	HQ
King	James G.	Pvt.	1206th	QM Company
King	John B.	1st Lt.	510th	
King	John W.	T/Sgt.	511th	
King	Raymond J.	1st. Lt.	509th	
King	Raymond V.	S/Sgt.	510th	
King	Robert E.	Sgt.	508th	
King	Sumner A. Jr.	T/Sgt.	510th	
King	William C.	Sgt.	510th	
Kinnamon	Baynard	2nd Lt.	508th	MIA 6/28/43
Kinne	Darrell H.	Sgt.	447th	Sub-Depot
Kinnear	Walter D.	Sgt.	510th	
Kinney	Glen R.	Cpl.	11th	St. Comp.
Kinnucan	Rex E.	1st Lt.	508th	
Kinsella	Richard V.	T/Sgt.	509th	
Kinsey	Chester L.	Sgt.	508th	
Kinsora	Robert C.	S/Sgt.	509th	
Kinter	Herbert M.	Sgt.	11th	St. Comp.
Kinz	Lester L.	2nd Lt.	509th	
Kinzel	John C.	1st Lt.	509th	
Kirby	Richard J.	Cpl.	511th	
Kirby	Francis X.	T/Sgt.	508th	POW 5/27/44
Kirk	Wilfred W.	2nd Lt.	510th	
Kirk	Mitchell A.	Cpl.	509th	
Kirk	Paul G.	Sgt.	509th	
Kirka	Stanley J.	Sgt.	508th	
Kirker	Harry J.	S/Sgt.	510th	
Kirkland	John C.	2nd Lt.	508th	
Kirkland	John R.	1st Lt.	509th	
Kirkland	Paul B.	Cpl.	509th	
Kirkwood	Donald E.	Sgt.	510th	
Kirshner	Leonard M.	Sgt.	509th	
Kiser	Arthur E. Jr.	2nd Lt.	510th	
Kistner	Harold E. Jr.	S/Sgt.	508th	
Kitchen	James D.	Sgt.	509th	
Kitko	Joseph D.	S/Sgt.	509th	POW 1/11/44
Kittilson	Wayne A.	S/Sgt.	509th	
Kitzmiller	Lloyd	Sgt.	509th	
Klaar	George	2nd Lt.	509th	
Klag	Stanley D.	S/Sgt.	510th	
Klanka	Vincent P.	S/Sgt.	508th	POW 6/28/43
Klassen	Lester M.	S/Sgt.	508th	
Kleeman	Robert W.	Cpl.	510th	POW 5/7/44
Kleinjan	Leonard E.	M/Sgt.	509th	POW 6/22/44
Kleinman	Isaac E.	S/Sgt.	510th	
Klemenc	Anthony	Cpl.	511th	
Klepper	Walter	Sgt.	508th	
Kligman	Edward	2nd Lt.	508th	
Klimp	Thomas H.	S/Sgt.	510th	POW 10/9/43
Klinc	William D.	Cpl.	510th	POW 10/9/43
Kline	Arnold J.	2nd Lt.	510th	POW 12/31/43
Kline	Lloyd H.	1st Lt.	509th	Int'd 10/7/44
Klingens	H. B.	PFC	509th	
Klink	William D.	S/Sgt.	510th	
Klodzynski	Ralph J.	Sgt.	510th	
Kloster	Wilfred G.	S/Sgt.	509th	
Klyve	Stanley S.	S/Sgt.	511th	
Knabo	Walter L.	Sgt.	509th	
Knaphus	Torkief M.	T/Sgt.	510th	
Knapp	Frank B.	Sgt.	511th	POW 7/13/44
Knapp	Richard P.	1st Lt.	509th	
Kneuppel	Donald E.	1st Lt.	510th	
Knezek	Arthur C.	Sgt.	508th	
Knie	John W.	Sgt.	509th	
Kniering	William C.	PFC	508th	
Knight	Raleigh G.	1st Lt.	509th	
Knothe	Charles R.	S/Sgt.	508th	POW 12/31/43
Knower	Edward	Sgt.	508th	POW 6/22/43
Knowles	Albert C.	Sgt.	509th	
Knowles	Henry F.	Cpl.	11th	St. Comp.
Knowles	Thomas C.	S/Sgt.	509th	
Knox	Nicholas J.	2nd Lt.	11th	St. Comp.
Knudtson	Elwood A.	S/Sgt.	508th	
Koch	Howard E.	2nd Lt.	510th	
Kocsis	Albert	Cpl.	509th	
Koency	Harvey R.	T/Sgt.	508th	POW 5/27/44
Koerper	Walter C.	2nd Lt.	510th	St. Comp.
Koether	Paul C.	Maj.	1206th	QM Company
Koffend	Joseph	1st Lt.	511th	
Kofoed	Lawrence L.	1st Lt.	508th	
Kogelman	Albert M.	Sgt.	508th	
Kohlbeck	James F.	Capt.	509th	
Kohler	Robert H.	1st Lt.	508th	KIA 5/28/44
Kohorst	Paul P.	2nd Lt.	510th	POW 5/27/44
Kolakowski	Joseph	Pvt.	1206th	QM Company
Kolar	Donald V.	1st Lt.	508th	
Kolb	Brice F.	T/Sgt.	511th	
Kolb	Darwin C.	S/Sgt.	508th	
Kolceski	Joseph P.	2nd Lt.	508th	
Kolessar	Thomas A.	S/Sgt.	509th	
Kolling	Edward V.	Sgt.	508th	
Koltko	Walter	S/Sgt.	510th	
Kombol	John J.	S/Sgt.	509th	
Komisarek	Louis E.	S/Sgt.	508th	
Kondelka	George C.	S/Sgt.	509th	KIA 7/19/44
Konecheck	Herbert C.	1st Lt.	510th	
Konfala	John S.	Sgt.	511th	Sub-Depot
Kongott	Robert A.	Cpl.	447th	Int'd 5/27/44
Konkell	William O.	T/Sgt.	510th	KIA 5/27/44
Kopf	Donald G.	S/Sgt.	508th	
Korf	Leonard L.	1st Lt.	511th	
Korges	Mortimore L.	Maj.	509th	
Kornell	Eugene M.	Sgt.	351st	HQ
Koryn	Joseph M.	T/Sgt.	511th	
Kosch	William	Sgt.	511th	
Koscielny	Leonard S.	S/Sgt.	510th	
Koski	Veikko J.	Sgt.	510th	POW 12/31/43
Koslev	Lawrence	Sgt.	509th	
Koss	Gordon C.	S/Sgt.	508th	KIA 5/27/44
Koss	S. J.	Sgt.	510th	Int'd 6/21/44
Kostyshak	Peter	Cpl.	511th	
Koszarek	Andrew J.	PFC	1206th	QM Company
Kotash	George C.	Capt.	510th	
Koudelka	Stephen	Sgt.	509th	
Kovacs	John	S/Sgt.	508th	POW 2/24/44
Kowalski	A. C.	2nd Lt.	509th	
Kozak	Howard W.	2nd Lt.	508th	
Kraft	Herbert L.	Sgt.	511th	
Kramer	Harry D.	1st Lt.	511th	
Krasner	Wendell A.	Sgt.	511th	
Kratz	Harold J.	Cpl.	510th	
Kratz	Harry F.	T/Sgt.	511th	
Krause	Elmer W.	Sgt.	508th	
Krause	Verle B.	1st Lt.	508th	St. Comp.
Kreeger	Karl H.	S/Sgt.	510th	Sub-Depot
Kries	Theodore	Cpl.	509th	POW 5/28/44
Krinkel	Victor F.	Sgt.	510th	
Krentzel	Robert L.	Capt.	11th	Killed 9/17/43
Kreutzer	Franklin B.	2nd Lt.	509th	Ord. S&M Co.
Krier	Leonard J.	T/Sgt.	447th	
Kriesher	Elmer W.	T/Sgt.	510th	
Kriesky	Lester C.	S/Sgt.	508th	
Kroeger	William E.	1st Lt.	510th	
Kroeger	John	Cpl.	508th	
Krogher	Fred A.	S/Sgt.	1629th	
Kronchenko	Albert F.	1st Lt.	511th	
Kronlein	George F.	Sgt.	509th	
Krueger	Jack B.	T/Sgt.	447th	
Krueger	Stephen	S/Sgt.	510th	
Krueger	Jack	Cpl.	510th	
Krul	Henry	S/Sgt.	509th	
Krunstock	Alexander H.	PFC	508th	
Kruso		1st Lt.		
Kubetin				

Kubiatowski / Leonard

Surname	First	Rank	Unit	Notes
Kubiatowski	Alfred B.	Cpl.	509th	
Kucksar	Thomas A.	1st Lt.	511th	
Kucsmas	Michael	S/Sgt.	509th	
Kudulis	Adolph T.	M/Sgt.	510th	
Kuehn	Leo A.	Cpl.	510th	
Kuelther	John J.	S/Sgt.	511th	
Kufik	Wallace	S/Sgt.	508th	
Kuhens	Eldon L.	Pvt.	11th	St. Comp.
Kuhns	Adam R.	T/Sgt.	508th	
Kulak	John J.	Sgt.	510th	POW 6/14/44
Kulapp	John M.	Sgt.	509th	
Kulasinski	Andrew J.	Cpl.	1206th	QM Company
Kulich	George	T/Sgt.	508th	
Kulick	Edward	Cpl.	508th	
Kulik	George	Cpl.	510th	
Kulsluch	Lawrence J.	S/Sgt.	508th	POW 4/18/44
Kultek	Edward	Sgt.	447th	
Kunes	Joseph	S/Sgt.	11th	Sub-Depot
Kungl	John J.	PFC	510th	St. Comp.
Kunkle	John A.	Cpl.	511th	
Kunz	Lester L.	2nd Lt.	509th	KIA 5/30/44
Kunz	Raymond J.	1st Lt.	508th	
Kupersmith	Rudolph R.	2nd Lt.	447th	Sub-Depot
Kuraner	Irving G.	Sgt.	510th	
Kurek	Edward A.	Cpl.	509th	
Kuret	Frank J.	Sgt.	447th	Sub-Depot
Kurkiewicz	W. S.	M/Sgt.	11th	St. Comp.
Kurland	Murray W.	S/Sgt.	508th	
Kurtz	John J.	Sgt.	509th	POW 9/27/44
Kurtze	Verlyn T.	1st Lt.	511th	
Kuskie	Lewis A.	1st Lt.	510th	
Kuss	Thomas C.	1st Lt.	509th	
Kuzera	Joseph S.	PFC	1629th	Ord. S&M Co.
Kuzler	Edmund F.	Sgt.	508th	
Kuzmich	Bernard C.	Sgt.	510th	POW 6/21/44
Kveen	William	M/Sgt.	447th	
Kysar	Verlyn T.	Sgt.	509th	
Kyser	Lewis A.	1st Lt.	511th	
	Thomas C.	1st Lt.	509th	

L

Surname	First	Rank	Unit	Notes
L'Abbee	Donald	2nd Lt.	511th	POW 10/9/43
La Flure	John S.	Sgt.	854th	Chemical Co.
La Rocco	Joseph H.	Sgt.	510th	POW 6/14/44
LaFave	Robert J.	2nd Lt.	511th	
LaGrua	Thomas F.	S/Sgt.	509th	
LaJeunesse	Roger J. Jr.	Sgt.	509th	
LaShier	Albert F.	2nd Lt.	508th	
Laborie	Emile W.	PFC	1061st	MP Company
Labrado	Luis G.	Cpl.	509th	
Lacey	Robert E.	1st Lt.	511th	
Lachance	William H.	M/Sgt.	351st	HQ
Lack	Denson W.	S/Sgt.	11th	St. Comp.

Surname	First	Rank	Unit	Notes
Lacroix	Ovide B.	T/Sgt.	509th	Avn. F/F Pltn.
Lacroix	William E.	PFC	2098th	St. Comp.
Lacy	Kenneth J.	Sgt.	11th	
Ladshaw	David J.	S/Sgt.	510th	
Lafauci	Paul	Sgt.	511th	
Lafferty	William G.	S/Sgt.	508th	Killed 5/7/43
Lafon	Edward B.	M/Sgt.	11th	St. Comp.
Lageman	Robert C.	2nd Lt.	447th	Sub-Depot
Lager	Charles E.	Sgt.	510th	POW 6/14/44
Lagerhausen	Walter W. Jr.	T/Sgt.	509th	
Lagrun	Thomas F.	Cpl.	11th	St. Comp.
Laha	John T.	2nd Lt.	508th	
Lahr	J.	S/Sgt.	509th	POW 10/9/43
Laird	James D.	Sgt.	508th	
Laird	Royden C.	S/Sgt.	510th	
Lake	William H.	1st Lt.	508th	
Lamb	Charles M.	S/Sgt.	447th	
Lamb	Everett E.	F.O.	508th	
Lamb	John E.	Cpl.	510th	
Lamb	Maurice C.	PFC	509th	
Lambert	William Jr.	1st Lt.	508th	
Lammon	Edward L.	Sgt.	509th	
Lamont	James E.	1st Lt.	511th	
Lance	Theodore S.	PFC	509th	
Lance	Thomas T.	Sgt.	510th	
Landay	Philip I.	Sgt.	508th	
Landers	John R.	T/Sgt.	508th	
Landino	Patrick M.	2nd Lt.	511th	
Landis	Clarence E.	Cpl.	508th	
Landscoot	Morris C.	Spec. 5	854th	Chemical Co.
Landstrom	Kenneth W.	S/Sgt.	508th	POW 7/19/44
Landuyt	Omer A.	Cpl.	11th	St. Comp.
Lane	John L.	Sgt.	351st	HQ
Lane	William H.	Cpl.	447th	Sub-Depot
Laney	William C.	2nd Lt.	510th	
Lang	Sidney H.	2nd Lt.	508th	MIA 6/28/43
Langdon	Robert H.	1st Lt.	511th	
Lange	Arthur E.	Cpl.	508th	
Lange	Clyde E.	S/Sgt.	511th	
Lange	Henry	Cpl.	1061st	MP Company
Langenbahn	Charles J.	PFC	854th	Chemical Co.
Langer	Howard M.	S/Sgt.	508th	
Langers	Larry E.	S/Sgt.	509th	
Langille	Frederick A.	2nd Lt.	511th	POW 10/7/44
Langione	Canzio M.	Sgt.	510th	
Langley	Chester L.	PFC	854th	Chemical Co.
Langley	Maurice S.	S/Sgt.	511th	
Langseth	Clifton A.	Cpl.	11th	St. Comp.
Langstaff	Joseph	S/Sgt.	508th	POW 8/17/43
Lanius	John St. P.	Sgt.	511th	
Lannon	James E.	PFC	201st	Finance Sect.
Lannon	William J.	Cpl.	447th	Sub-Depot

Surname	First	Rank	Unit	Notes
Lantrip	Roy G.	Sgt.	511th	
Lanum	George M.	Cpl.	509th	
Lanzclatta	Gerado	S/Sgt.	351st	
Lanplant	William	Pvt.	11th	
Lappage	P. F.	Sgt.	511th	
Larsen	Walter D.	S/Sgt.	508th	
Lafon	Frederick H.	M/Sgt.	447th	St. Comp.
Larson	Robert L.	2nd Lt.	511th	
Larson	Donald J.	T/Sgt.	510th	Sub-Depot
Larson	Everett B.	Cpl.	447th	Sub-Depot
Larson	F.	2nd Lt.	508th	
Larson	Laurel E.	S/Sgt.	511th	POW 12/1/43
Larson	Leonard G.	Sgt.	2098th	Avn. F/F Pltn.
Larson	Leonard W.	S/Sgt.	508th	
Lassman	William H.	F.O.	447th	Sub-Depot
Lathe	Raymond L.	Sgt.	508th	
Latimer	Bernard J.	Sgt.	510th	
Latzke	Frederick L.	T/Sgt.	509th	
Lau	Albert F.	PFC	508th	
Laughlin	Raymond A.	Sgt.	509th	
Laun	Joseph P.	S/Sgt.	509th	
Laurenzo	Carl A.	PFC	201st	Finance Sect.
Laux	William A. Jr.	Sgt.	11th	St. Comp.
Laverty	James T. Jr.	Sgt.	510th	KIA 7/19/44
Law	Frederick W.	T/Sgt.	509th	
Lawhon	Kenneth C.	Sgt.	511th	
Lawing	Arthur W.	Cpl.	854th	Chemical Co.
Lawler	Harry C.	Sgt.	447th	Sub-Depot
Lawler	Thomas M.	T/Sgt.	509th	
Lawsen	Vernon P.	1st Lt.	510th	POW 8/9/44
Lawson	Robert L.	Sgt.	511th	
Lawson	George C. Jr.	T/Sgt.	510th	
Lawson	Jackson A.	Sgt.	509th	
Lawson	John F.	Sgt.	510th	
Lazar	L. V.	S/Sgt.	447th	Sub-Depot
Lazar	Stentford R.	Cpl.	11th	
Lazelle	Alexander	Pvt.	510th	
Lazerson	Joseph J.	2nd Lt.	509th	
Lemanzyk	LeBaron M.	1st Lt.	509th	
Lemcke	Aaron	2nd Lt.	511th	MIA 6/28/43
LeBlanc	Bernard M.	S/Sgt.	11th	St. Comp.
LeCheminant	Wilbur A. Jr.	S/Sgt.	508th	
LeClerc	George P.	2nd Lt.	509th	
LeFave	Walter B.	2nd Lt.	510th	
LeFevre	Lawrence C.	Sgt.	854th	Chemical Co.
LePage	Edward J.	S/Sgt.	508th	
Lea	Bertrand E.	PFC	11th	St. Comp.
Lea	John B.	Pvt.	447th	Sub-Depot
Leach	Robert K.	Sgt.	508th	POW 2/22/44
Leal	William H.	S/Sgt.	511th	
Leale	Philip F.	Sgt.	510th	
	Leslie P.	F.O.	510th	

Surname	First	Rank	Unit	Notes
Leamon	Wilbur L.	Sgt.	510th	
Leapley	Richard L.	Sgt.	509th	
Lear	Eugene W.	S/Sgt.	509th	MIA 6/28/43
Learned	Bradley E.	Sgt.	508th	
Leary	Wayne A.	S/Sgt.	508th	
Leasure	Harry	Sgt.	11th	St. Comp.
Leasure	John D.	Sgt.	509th	Killed 6/8/45
Leavitt	Eugene L.	S/Sgt.	510th	POW 6/14/44
Leavitt	John H. Jr.	1st Lt.	511th	
Leber	Gail W.	1st Lt.	11th	St. Comp.
Lechner	James R.	S/Sgt.	511th	
Ledoux	Elzia Lt.	Col.	509th	
Ledyard	John P.	2nd Lt.	508th	POW 4/18/44
Lee	Duward	Sgt.	509th	
Lee	George R.	T/Sgt.	511th	
Lee	James M.	Sgt.	508th	
Lee	Ralph E.	S/Sgt.	511th	
Leeds	Robert E.	Capt.	508th	
Leedy	Leonard	Capt.	11th	St. Comp.
Leep	John	PFC	508th	
Lees	William H. Jr.	S/SGt.	1629th	Ord. S&M Co.
Leewer	Paul A.	Sgt.	509th	
Lefebvre	William G.	1st Lt.	508th	
Legandre	Albert H.	M/Sgt.	511th	
Legut	Lawrence R.	S/Sgt.	508th	
Lehan	Emanuel J.	Sgt.	447th	Sub-Depot
Leibrock	Edward J.	Maj.	351st	HQ
Leigh	Arthur R.	2nd Lt.	511th	
Leigh	Daniel	1st Lt.	509th	
Leikam	Robert W.	Cpl.	510th	Int'd 8/6/44
Leiman	Edward	Capt.	508th	
Leimbeck	Leroy J.	T/Sgt.	11th	St. Comp.
Leinkuehler	Robert E.	PFC	508th	
Leipzig	Irving R.	1st Lt.	854th	Chemical Co.
Leisman	John S.	Spec. 5	508th	
Leivent	Gilbert A.	1st Lt.	511th	
Leland	Daniel	2nd Lt.	509th	
Lelionis	Lloyd	Sgt.	510th	
Lemcke	Anthony	Capt.	508th	
Lemley	Alex L.	T/Sgt.	508th	
Lemley	Ernest A.	S/Sgt.	511th	POW 5/28/44
Lemon	Clarence P.	1st Lt.	511th	
Lendino	Edwin B. Jr.	S/Sgt.	510th	
Lenhart	Viron E.	2nd Lt.	854th	Chemical Co.
Lenz	Patrick M.	PFC	508th	
Lenze	Glen A.	Sgt.	11th	St. Comp.
Leonard	John H.	Sgt.	447th	Sub-Depot
Leonard	Thomas B.	1st Lt.	508th	
Leonard	Dale R.	S/Sgt.	511th	
Leonard	Francis	Sgt.	510th	KIA 2/6/45
Leonard	George R.	T. Sgt.	509th	
Leonard	James L.	S/Sgt.	510th	

Last Name	First Name	Rank	Unit	Notes
Leonard	Wayne D.	Cpl.	508th	
Leone	Eugene F.	2nd Lt.	509th	
Leppert	Charles F.	1st Lt.	351st	HQ
Leritz	Leonard L.	S/Sgt.	11th	St. Comp.
Lesch	Oscar W.	1st Lt.	511th	
Lesko	George A.	PFC	1061st	MP Company
Leslie	Herman W.	M/Sgt.	511th	KIA 3/18/44
Lesperance	Russell J.	1st Lt.	509th	
Letterman	Stewart R.	Cpl.	511th	
Levin	Abraham	2nd Lt.	510th	
Levin	Leon P.	1st Lt.	508th	
Levine	Bernard	T/Sgt.	11th	St. Comp.
Levine	Murray J.	PFC	447th	
Levine	Philip	Sgt.	510th	Sub-Depot
Levine	Walter	2nd Lt.	11th	St. Comp.
Levine	Paul	Sgt.	509th	Int'd 2/25/45
Levinson	Seymour R.	1st Lt.	509th	Int'd 10/7/44
Levitt	Marvin	Cpl.	511th	
Levy	Albert A. Jr.	Sgt.	252nd	Medical Disp.
Lewellen	Charles H.	Capt.	511th	POW 5/28/44
Lewellyn	Stephen B.	2nd Lt.	510th	
Lewellyn	Thomas S.	T/Sgt.	509th	
Lewers	David D.	Sgt.	508th	
Lewey	William H.	S/Sgt.	854th	Chemical Co.
Lewis	Howard E.	2nd Lt.	1206th	QM Company
Lewis	John A.	Sgt.	509th	
Lewis	Lloyd L.	1st Lt.	447th	Sub-Depot
Lewis	Luin B.	T/Sgt.	511th	
Lewis	Merton H.	M/Sgt.	201st	
Lewis	Oliver	Cpl.	509th	
Lewis	Richard E.	Spec. 5	854th	Chemical Co.
Lewis	Roy A.	Sgt.	1206th	QM Company
Lewis	Vernon L.	F.O.	509th	
Lewis	William A.	Capt.	447th	Sub-Depot
Leyva	George A.	S/Sgt.	511th	
Leyva	Harold W.	S/Sgt.	510th	
Licht	Howard J.	Sgt.	511th	POW 8/17/43
Lidowicz	Stanley P. D.	Sgt.	510th	
Lien	Albert L.	S/Agt.	511th	POW 5/28/44
Light	George W.	Sgt.	508th	
Light	Raymond E. Jr.	2nd Lt.	510th	POW 12/31/43
Lightfoot	Guy A. Jr.	2nd Lt.	511th	
Lightner	Robert N.	S/Sgt.	447th	
Likens	Charles T.	S/Sgt.	511th	
Liles	Everett	M/Sgt.	510th	
Lilletherup	Ben W.	S/Sgt.	508th	
Lilley	Charles W. Jr.	Cpl.	509th	
Lilley	Melvin F.	Cpl.	510th	
Lillien	Richard A.	1st Lt.	511th	
Limbach	Austin B.	2nd Lt.	508th	
Linblad	Carl W.	Sgt.	508th	POW 12/31/43
Linden	William J.	T/Sgt.	508th	
Lindgren	Cyrus G.	2nd Lt.	511th	
Lindquist	Richard H.	Sgt.	510th	
Lindsay	Edward E.	T/Sgt.	510th	
Lindsey	Coy W.	Sgt.	447th	
Lindsey	Emory H.	S/Sgt.	509th	
Lindsey	Herman M.	2nd Lt.	509th	
Lindsey	Larry J.	PFC	509th	
Lineberger	Walter M.	S/Sgt.	509th	
Linehan	Kelly A.	T/Sgt.	1206th	QM Company
Linford	Edward T.	2nd Lt.	509th	
Linn	William R.	1st Lt.	508th	
Linnehan	Claude T.	Sgt.	510th	
Linquist	William F. Jr.	Sgt.	509th	
Lintner	Allyn A.	1st Lt.	509th	
Lipski	Harlan	PFC	509th	
Liptak	Boleslau	2nd Lt.	511th	
Lister	Mliis	S/Sgt.	508th	
Litchfield	Benjamin F. Jr.	Cpl.	510th	
Litsinger	Gerald W.	S/Sgt.	511th	
Littell	David W.	1st Lt.	508th	
Little	George C.	Cpl.	510th	
Littlefield	Dwain N.	T/Sgt.	510th	
Littler	Allen W.	Sgt.	509th	
Livesay	E. L.	S/Sgt.	508th	
Livingston	Wayne W.	1st Lt.	511th	
Lizewski	Robert W.	S/Sgt.	511th	
Lloyd	Morris	T/Sgt.	509th	Killed 6/8/45
LoPresto	Ernest C. Jr.	Sgt.	447th	Sub-Depot
Lochen	Angelo	Cpl.	510th	POW 8/27/43
Lockamy	Louis A.	Sgt.	508th	St. Comp.
Lockard	William L.	S/Sgt.	11th	
Locke	Chester C.	S/Sgt.	509th	MIA 2/21/44
Lodge	Wesley F.	S/Sgt.	508th	
Loe	Joseph	Capt.	511th	
Loeb	Lazard L.	1st Lt.	509th	
Loehndorf	Warren	2nd Lt.	510th	KIA 11/21/44
Loftus	John L.	S/Sgt.	447th	Sub-Depot
Logan	Clinton D.	Sgt.	508th	POW 11/26/43
Logan	William R.	Capt.	509th	
Lohneis	Joseph C.	S/Sgt.	509th	KIA 9/12/44
Loiacono	Joseph	1st Lt.	511th	POW 8/9/44
Lomen	Arnold J.	1st Lt.	508th	
London	Leonard H.	PFC	1206th	QM Company
Long	Clyde	S/Sgt.	510th	POW 12/31/43
Long	Harold F.	Sgt.	508th	
Long	Patsy	S/Sgt.	509th	
Long	Preston Q.	Sgt.	509th	
Long	Richard J.	2nd Lt.	508th	
Long	Verl P.	S/Sgt.	511th	
Long	William P.	1st Lt.	508th	POW 7/28/44
Longa	William	1st Lt.	510th	
Lonneman	Aloyius A.	Sgt.	510th	
Lopatin	Sol S.	T/Sgt.	351st	HQ
Lopert	Robert C.	2nd Lt.	511th	POW 9/12/44
Lopez	Frank T.	Sgt.	508th	
Lopresti	William B.	S/Sgt.	509th	
Lord	Donald J.	S/Sgt.	509th	Sub-Depot
Lord	Robert C.	1st Lt.	509th	
Lorenz	William F.	Cpl.	11th	St. Comp.
Loritz		Sgt.	447th	Sub-Depot
Lormon	LeRoy J.	PFC	508th	St. Comp.
Los	Bruno J.	PFC	11th	
Lostocco	Guerine P.	S/Sgt.	508th	KIA 7/19/44
Lotka	Raymond J.	S/Sgt.	509th	
Lott	Chester L.	F.O.	509th	KIA 6/13/43
Louiso	Earl H.	T/Sgt.	509th	POW 6/22/44
Lounsbury	Harold E. Jr.	S/Sgt.	511th	
Love	Benton F. Jr.	1st Lt.	508th	
Love	Howard S.	1st Lt.	510th	
Lovelace	Walter W.	S/Sgt.	509th	
Loverds	Basil L.	T/Sgt.	510th	POW 9/8/44
Lovett	Stephen G.	F.O.	510th	
Lowans	Paul A.	2nd Lt.	510th	KIA 3/18/44
Lowery	Lewis A.	Sgt.	509th	St. Comp.
Lowery	George E.	S/Sgt.	11th	
Lowry	James R.	Capt.	508th	
Loyd	Harold A.	T/Sgt.	509th	
Lozano	Ernest C. Jr.	S/Sgt.	511th	St. Comp.
Luberda	Frank C.	Cpl.	508th	Sub-Depot
Lubozynski	Andrew D.	Sgt.	510th	
Luby	Frank K.	1st Lt.	854th	Chemical Co.
Lucas	Edmund J.	Spec. 5	252nd	Medical Disp.
Lucas	Andrew F.	Cpl.	11th	St. Comp.
Lucas	Cecil C.	Pvt.	508th	
Luce	Frank R.	T/Sgt.	509th	
Luck	John B.	S/Sgt.	511th	Int'd 3/18/44
Lucyk	Henry A.	Cpl.	508th	
Ludwig	Paul	T/Sgt.	509th	Killed 6/8/45
Ludwig	Frank G.	2nd Lt.	510th	POW 6/14/44
Ludwig	Henry Jr.	S/Sgt.	509th	St. Comp.
Luedecker	Roger W.	T/Sgt.	511th	
Luich	Warren A.	1st Lt.	509th	
Luise	Albert W.	1st Lt.	510th	
Lukaszuk	Ralph J.	S/Sgt.	11th	
Lukkason	Edward P.	S/Sgt.	509th	St. Comp.
Lum	Joseph L.	1st Lt.	447th	Sub-Depot
Lunan	Peter C.	Cpl.	447th	Sub-Depot
Lund	James S.	1st Lt.	509th	
Lundeen	Thurston R.	2nd Lt.	508th	
	Lawrence G.	S/Sgt.	508th	
Lundgren	Earl	Sgt.	447th	Sub-Depot
Lungmus	William R.	Cpl.	447th	Sub-Depot
Lunsford	Gail C.	S/Sgt.	508th	
Lupinski	Edward R.	Sgt.	511th	KIA 11/5/43
Luse	Donal F. Jr.	Sgt.	509th	POW 4/13/44
Luter	Lloyd V.	Sgt.	508th	
Lush	Robert R.	Cpl.	511th	
Luvison	Herman L.	S/Sgt.	510th	
Lybolt	Walter S. Jr.	2nd Lt.	508th	
Lyday	Joseph H.	Maj.	351st	HQ
Lydy	George W.	Sgt.	447th	Sub-Depot
Lykins	Danvil	T/Sgt.	509th	POW 2/11/44
Lynch	David E.	S/Sgt.	509th	
Lynch	H. J.	Sgt.	509th	
Lynch	Nicholas M.	1st Lt.	510th	
Lynes	William H.	PFC	11th	St. Comp.
Lyons	Daniel J.	M/Sgt.	510th	
Lyons	Hershal W.	2nd Lt.	351st	HQ
Lyttle	William B.	Capt.	510th	

M

Last Name	First Name	Rank	Unit	Notes
Mabrey	William C.	1st Lt.	511th	
MacAlinden	R. J.	S/Sgt.	510th	
MacInnes	Carlton A.	Cpl.	1206th	QM Company
MacIntire	F. L.	T/Sgt.	508th	
MacKonagle	John H. Jr.	2nd Lt.	11th	St. Comp.
MacLachlan	John	2nd Lt.	509th	
MacLean	Donald E.	S/Sgt.	11th	St. Comp.
MacRath	William H.	Cpl.	201st	Finance Sect.
MacVeigh	William J.	PFC	511th	
Maccagnon	Angelo D.	Sgt.	447th	Sub-Depot
Macey	William B.	1st Sgt.	510th	
Machnik	John S.	Cpl.	1206th	QM Company
Mack	John C. Jr.	S/Sgt.	11th	St. Comp.
Madaras	Andrew J.	Cpl.	2098th	Avn. F/F Pltn.
Madden	Keith W.	F.O.	510th	
Maddux	Billy J.	1st Sgt.	509th	
Madeiros	W.	2nd Lt.	511th	
Madel	W. S.	Pvt.	508th	
Madsen	Rowland X.	1st Sgt.	511th	
Maffey	Ercole A.	S/Sgt.	511th	
Magee	James D.	S/Sgt.	508th	
Magelitz	Phillip R.	PFC	11th	St. Comp.
Maggiaro	Nick	1st Lt.	509th	
Maggini	Albert A.	1st Lt.	509th	
Maggio	Casper J.	Sgt.	508th	KIA 12/30/43
Maggiore	Salvatore J.	S/Sgt.	510th	
Maginn	Lewis J.	Capt.	511th	
Maginnis	Carlton A.	Spec. 5	1629th	Ord. S&M Co.
Maginnis	James J.	1st Lt.	510th	
Magness	Carl W.	2nd Lt.	509th	
Magnuson	Charles H.	Cpl.		

Last Name	First Name	Rank	Unit	Notes
Maguire	John F.	T/Sgt.	508th	
Maguire	Robert J.	S/Sgt.	854th	Chemical Co.
Mahaffey	James D.	1st Lt.	511th	Int'd 3/18/44
Mahan	Bryan C.	T/Sgt.	511th	
Mahas	Theodore G.	S/Sgt.	510th	
Mahin	John L.	1st Lt.	508th	
Mahkovtz	Louis M.	S/Sgt.	509th	
Mahnke	Ralph E.	1st Lt.	510th	
Mahoney	T.	Cpl.	511th	
Mahony	Rollins O. Jr.	2nd Lt.	508th	POW 9/5/44
Maiden	Richard A.	PFC	854th	Chemical Co.
Maiditch	Abe J.	M/Sgt.	11th	
Maidment	Eugene L.	Sgt.	11th	St. Comp.
Maish	Jay H.	Capt.	511th	St. Comp.
Majerus	Lester C.	Sgt.	511th	
Majors	Charles J.	S/Sgt.	509th	
Maki	Sulo I.	S/Sgt.	511th	
Maki	Tauno W.	1st Lt.	511th	
Maksimik	Walter I.	Spec. 5	11th	St. Comp.
Malamed	John	T/Sgt.	351st	HQ
Malcolm	Paul	T/Sgt.	351st	
Malemed	George D.	T/Sgt.	509th	
Malin	Sam E.	Pvt.	511th	
Malinowski	Ralph A.	T/Sgt.	511th	
Malish	Thaddeus T.	Cpl.	351st	
Malone	Theodore E.	S/Sgt.	511th	MIA 6/28/43
Malone	Lucius F. Jr.	1st Lt.	510th	HQ
Maloney	Oscar B.	S/Sgt.	508th	
Maloney	John F.	Sgt.	511th	
Maloney	Joseph A.	T/Sgt.	511th	
Maloney	Joseph M.	Sgt.	510th	
Maltby	Edward B.	Capt.	11th	
Maly	Edward	Sgt.	509th	
Mamerick	H.	PFC	508th	
Manchester	Andrew W.	T/Sgt.	511th	
Mancke	Wilbur W.	S/Sgt.	509th	
Mandella	Bernard L.	S/Sgt.	508th	POW 4/18/44
Mandros	Peter Jr.	2nd Lt.	511th	KIA 7/28/44
Maney	Warren G.	S/Sgt.	510th	POW 12/31/43
Mangino	Alfred N.	1st Lt.	11th	St. Comp.
Mangnanti	Michael	M/Sgt.	509th	
Mangus	Peter N.	T/Sgt.	508th	
Mangus	Warren E.	PFC	511th	St. Comp.
Manley	William A.	2nd Lt.	509th	KIA 3/18/44
Manley	William S.	S/Sgt.	511th	Killed 4/22/44
Mann	Ernest E.	PFC	351st	HQ
Mann	J. T. W.	T/Sgt.	510th	
Manning	R. L.	Spec. 5	11th	St. Comp.
Manning	George J.	Cpl.	252nd	Medical Disp.
Manning	Paul T.	PFC	509th	
Manning	William L.	S/Sgt.	511th	
Manos	Basil E.	Sgt.	510th	
Mansell	Raymond F.	T/Sgt.	510th	
Mansfield	James W.	S/Sgt.	509th	KIA 1/11/44
Mansfield	Robert W.	1st Lt.	510th	
Mansmann	William J.	1st Lt.	509th	POW 5/27/44
Manthey	Miles E.	1st Lt.	510th	
Mar	Haley	M/Sgt.	508th	
Marabella	Vincent M.	S/Sgt.	510th	
Marcellina	Andrew N.	Sgt.	509th	
Marchant	Vernal W.	Sgt.	510th	
Marchese	Dominick S.	Sgt.	508th	
Marchese	Michael	Sgt.	1206th	QM Company
Marcial	Torrido	S/Sgt.	509th	Int'd 2/21/44
Marcinizyn	Nicholas	S/Sgt.	511th	POW 10/9/43
Marcou	Leonard G.	Pvt.	511th	POW 8/6/44
Mardis	James W.	S/Sgt.	1206th	QM Company
Marez	Ernest T.	Cpl.	508th	
Margolis	Arthur	Sgt.	509th	
Margolis	Harry	2nd Lt.	509th	
Marino	Salvatore A.	Cpl.	510th	Int'd 10/7/44
Marison	William H.	S/Sgt.	509th	
Marke	John	Sgt.	508th	
Markert	Augustus F.	M/Sgt.	508th	
Markiewicz	Daniel J.	S/Sgt.	509th	
Markins	C. E.	S/Sgt.	510th	
Marks	Joseph T.	S/Sgt.	511th	
Marks	Louis S.	2nd Lt.	509th	
Marksberry	Hiram J.	Sgt.	511th	
Markshied	Max	T/Sgt.	509th	Killed 6/8/45
Markut	Frank A.	S/Sgt.	509th	
Marley	Johnie H.	PFC	1061st	MP Company
Marnierski	Stanley E.	T/Sgt.	511th	
Marquardt	Lloyd B.	1st Lt.	509th	
Marquis	Maurice R.	2nd Lt.	510th	Killed 5/7/43
Marrek	Frank	S/Sgt.	511th	
Marriott	Elmer R.	Cpl.	447th	Sub-Depot
Marriott	Kenneth M.	2nd Lt.	509th	
Marriott	Robert G.	S/Sgt.	511th	
Mars	William A.	1st Lt.	510th	
Marschak	Howard J.	2nd Lt.	508th	
Marsden	Arthur K.	2nd Lt.	511th	
Marsey	Donald W.	1st Lt.	510th	POW 3/18/44
Marsh	Hal	PFC	508th	St. Comp.
Marshall	Clarence E.	2nd Lt.	11th	
Marshall	Herbert H.	M/Sgt.	509th	
Marshall	Maurice W.	S/Sgt.	511th	POW 7/13/44
Marshall	Royce	T/Sgt.	510th	
Marshall	Samuel B. Jr.	S/Sgt.	510th	
Martens	Thomas T.	S/Sgt.	511th	
Mattila	Gregory N.	1st Lt.	508th	
Martin	Anthony A.	2nd Lt.	509th	
Martin	Bernard J.	1st Lt.	1206th	QM Company
Martin	Callie L.	Sgt.	509th	
Martin	Ferris S.	T/Sgt.	510th	Int'd 5/27/44
Martin	H. J.	S/Sgt.	508th	
Martin	Harold G.	T/Sgt.	510th	Sub-Depot
Martin	Howard V.	S/Sgt.	447th	
Martin	Jack R.	1st Lt.	511th	
Martin	James S.	1st Lt.	508th	
Martin	John M.	T/Sgt.	510th	
Martin	John W.	2nd Lt.	508th	
Martin	Joseph R.	2nd Lt.	510th	POW 2/20/44
Martin	Lyle S.	S/Sgt.	447th	Sub-Depot
Martin	Marlin	Sgt.	508th	
Martin	Paul	2nd Lt.	511th	KIA 3/18/44
Martin	Paul W.	T/Sgt.	508th	
Martin	Robert E.	T/Sgt.	510th	
Martin	Robert F.	T/Sgt.	511th	MIA 10/4/43
Martin	Warren H.	Sgt.	508th	
Martin	William E.	2nd Lt.	509th	
Martin	William H.	Cpl.	2098th	Avn. F/F Pltn.
Martin	William L.	S/Sgt.	510th	
Martinez	Zarin	2nd Lt.	509th	
Marutz	Joe A.	Sgt.	508th	
Marvin	William H.	M/Sgt.	511th	
Maschling	Howard W.	T/Sgt.	508th	POW 8/17/43
Maser	Vincent E.	Spec. 4	11th	St. Comp.
Masling	Howard G.	1st Lt.	511th	POW 10/9/43
Mason	Millard S.	T/Sgt.	508th	
Mason	Charles I.	2nd Lt.	511th	
Mason	Jack R.	2nd Lt.	508th	POW 9/12/44
Massara	Richard M.	F.O.	511th	MIA 6/28/43
Masse	Joseph	S/Sgt.	510th	POW 9/8/44
Master	Daniel J.	S/Sgt.	509th	
Matherly	Orlyn E.	S/Sgt.	510th	Int'd 10/7/44
Mathes	Carl W.	2nd Lt.	508th	POW 11/3/43
Mathieu	Vaden A.	S/Sgt.	511th	
Mathis	Archie	S/Sgt.	510th	KIA 2/20/44
Matlock	Louis J.	1st Lt.	1629th	Ord. S&M Co.
Matney	J. W.	Pvt.	351st	HQ
Matre	Edgar L.	S/Sgt.	510th	
Mattern	Charles S.	S/Sgt.	508th	
Matthews	Howard J.	1st Lt.	510th	
Matthews	Paul E.	Sgt.	447th	Sub-Depot
Matthews	Charles E.	S/Sgt.	508th	KIA 3/18/44
Matthews	Jack R.	PFC	1206th	QM Company
Mattice	Nelson E.	Capt.	11th	
Mattila	Richard H.	S/Sgt.	509th	
Mattix	Richard R.	T/Sgt.	510th	
Mattson	Vernon A.	2nd Lt.	509th	
Maturo	Dominic A.	1st Lt.	511th	POW 8/3/44
Matzke	Bernard J.	1st Lt.	510th	POW 5/28/44
Maupin	William S.	S/Sgt.	510th	POW 12/31/43
Mautz	Robert G.	Sgt.	510th	
Mawhorter	William L.	T/Sgt.	511th	
Maxwell	Earl B.	1st Lt.	508th	
Maxwell	Linville O.	2nd Lt.	11th	St. Comp.
May	Arthur F.	S/Sgt.	508th	
May	Earl W.	Sgt.	508th	
May	George H.	T/Sgt.	511th	
May	John E.	2nd Lt.	509th	POW 1/11/44
Mayarka	Joseph M.	S/Sgt.	508th	POW 8/27/43
Mayotte	Frank	Sgt.	511th	
Maze	Arthur J.	Capt.	509th	
Mazur	Charles L.	Sgt.	508th	POW 8/6/44
McAdama	John	Sgt.	511th	
McAfee	James C.	S/Sgt.	511th	
McAlinden	Frederick V.	1st Lt.	509th	
McAllister	Robert J.	S/Sgt.	510th	
McAngus	Joseph	Cpl.	511th	
McArrow	William	Sgt.	511th	
McArthur	E. L.	Sgt.	447th	Sub-Depot
McBee	Wilbur I.	T/Sgt.	511th	
McBride	Ralph W.	Cpl.	1206th	QM Company
McBryan	Chester E.	S/Sgt.	447th	Sub-Depot
McCafferty	Francis T.	PFC	854th	Chemical Co.
McCall	Daniel E.	Capt.	508th	
McCall	Clarence E.	Cpl.	510th	
McCall	John A.	2nd Lt.	511th	POW 2/12/44
McCandless	Kenneth R.	1st Lt.	509th	
McCann	Richard C.	2nd Lt.	510th	
McCann	James D.	2nd Lt.	511th	POW 5/28/44
McCarrity	Robert R.	Cpl.	510th	
McCarthy	Joseph M.	S/Sgt.	508th	
McCarthy	Fred R.	PFC	11th	St. Comp.
McCarthy	James A.	Cpl.	509th	
McCarthy	Philip J.	2nd Lt.	509th	
McCarthy	Richard D.	2nd Lt.	511th	
McCarty	William P.	Sgt.	1629th	Ord. S&M Co.
McClain	Owen H.	F.O.	510th	
McClean	Don E.	S/Sgt.	511th	
McClelland	Norman L.	2nd Lt.	508th	
McClenny	Samuel H.	2nd Lt.	510th	POW 5/28/44
McClintock	Clyde W.	1st Lt.	510th	
McCloskey	Jacob R.	2nd Lt.	509th	
McClure	Irving R.	Sgt.	511th	
McClusky	Raymond T.	T/Sgt.	511th	KIA 9/8/44
McConaghy	Lester W.	Capt.	510th	MIA 8/9/44
McConnell	Sterling L.	S/Sgt.	511th	
McConnell	Leo R.	PFC	1206th	
McConnell	Billie G. E.	S/Sgt.	510th	
McConnell	Harold G.	S/Sgt.	508th	
McConnell	Russell M.	2nd Lt.	511th	QM Company

Last Name	First Name	Rank	Unit	Notes
McCorkle	Donald A.	S/Sgt.	509th	
McCormick	Francis W.	PFC	509th	
McCormick	N. W.	2nd Lt.	11th	St. Comp.
McCoy	Clifford J.	1st Lt.	508th	
McCoy	Francis J.	Sgt.	510th	
McCracken	Raymond J.	T/Sgt.	508th	
McCrary	Earl F.	T/Sgt.	511th	
McCrary	George A.	Sgt.	511th	POW 8/3/44
McCrary	Wendell C.	T/Sgt.	511th	
McCubbin	Phillip J.	Cpl.	11th	St. Comp.
McCulloch	Robert L.	1st Lt.	511th	
McCullough	Jimmy E.	T/Sgt.	508th	
McCurdy	Howard S.	T/Sgt.	509th	POW 7/31/43
McCutcheon	Henry A.	Capt.	351st	HQ
McDaniel	Taduise	Cpl.	1629th	Ord. S&M Co.
McDaniel	James E.	PFC	511th	
McDermott	Reginald F.	S/Sgt.	508th	
McDermott	John F.	1st Lt.	510th	
McDevitt	Allen G.	Sgt.	510th	
McDonald	Alvin B.	2nd Lt.	511th	
McDonald	James E.	Sgt.	1061st	MP Company
McDonald	James T.	T/Sgt.	509th	
McDonald	John R.	2nd Lt.	510th	
McDonald	Russell E.	PFC	11th	St. Comp.
McDonald	Edward H.	2nd Lt.	508th	POW 6/28/43
McDonnell	Charles V.	Sgt.	509th	
McDougall	William E.	S/Sgt.	511th	
McDowell	Robert K.	PFC	11th	St. Comp.
McElrath	Robert W.	Pvt.	11th	St. Comp.
McElree	Daniel L.	S/Sgt.	511th	
McElvain	Frank C.	S/Sgt.	511th	
McFadden	Clyde C.	Cpl.	508th	
McFarland	John R.	PFC	510th	
McFarland	Robert N.	2nd Lt.	510th	
McFarland	William J.	1st Lt.	351st	
McFarlane	Charles E.	Sgt.	508th	
McFetridge	Robert L.	S/Sgt.	511th	
McGarrity	Robert L.	Capt.	508th	
McGarry	Joseph E.	F.O.	510th	
McGarry	James B.	T/Sgt.	508th	
McGaughran	James S.	2nd Lt.	510th	
McGee	James R.	S/Sgt.	509th	
McGee	Jack B.	T/Sgt.	511th	
McGee	Jesse B.	M/Sgt.	508th	
McGee	Joseph P.	PFC	511th	
McGee	Richard W.	1st Lt.	510th	
McGee	Robert L.	1st Lt.	508th	
McGee	William R.	2nd Lt.	511th	POW 10/9/43
McGhan	George N.	2nd Lt.	509th	
McGhan	Robert E.	2nd Lt.	510th	
McGilvray	Gaylon W.	S/Sgt.	511th	

Last Name	First Name	Rank	Unit	Notes
McGinn	William C. Jr.	S/Sgt.	447th	Sub-Depot
McGinnis	B. E.	1st Lt.	508th	
McGinnis	John L.	Sgt.	510th	
McGinnis	Leisure B.	S/Sgt.	508th	POW 6/22/43
McGinty	James W.	Sgt.	508th	
McGlohon	Robert A.	2nd Lt.	511th	KIA 9/8/44
McGorkle	Donald A.	Sgt.	509th	
McGorry	Henry J.	1st Lt.	11th	St. Comp.
McGowan	William J.	S/Sgt.	508th	KIA 7/29/44
McGuire	Clarence B.	Sgt.	511th	
McGuire	David R.	2nd Lt.	509th	
McInnes	Daniel L.	2nd Lt.	508th	
McInroe	Harold F.	PFC	1061st	MP Company
McIntosh	Allen	Cpl.	510th	
McIntyre	Walter C.	F.O.	510th	
McIntyre	Andrew J.	1st Lt.	508th	
McIntyre	George P.	1st Lt.	510th	
McIntyre	John H.	S/Sgt.	508th	
McJunkins	Thomas S.	Pvt.	11th	St. Comp.
McKee	Tracy C.	Sgt.	509th	
McKee	Adrian J.	S/Sgt.	510th	
McKee	D. T.	2nd Lt.	510th	
McKeehan	Patrick J.	Pvt.	11th	St. Comp.
McKeen	Charles V.	Sgt.	509th	
McKendry	Waino J.	Sgt.	508th	KIA 6/28/43
McKenzie	James C.	Sgt.	509th	
McKenzie	Bruce H.	1st Lt.	511th	
McKenzie	Charles W. D.	Sgt.	11th	St. Comp.
McKey	Max D.	Cpl.	510th	
McKinney	Robbie B.	Spec. 4	854th	Chemical Co.
McKinney	Jack D.	Sgt.	511th	POW 12/31/43
McKinney	Joseph R.	Capt.	11th	St. Comp.
McKinnon	Junior H.	Sgt.	509th	
McKinzie	Walter H.	1st Lt.	510th	
McKwain	James R.	Sgt.	508th	
McLain	Frank C.	S/Sgt.	511th	
McLain	Frederick E.	Sgt.	447th	Sub-Depot
McLarty	John J.	S/Sgt.	509th	KIA 12/1/43
McLaughlin	Norman E.	2nd Lt.	508th	
McLaughlin	Herbert G.	Pvt.	854th	Chemical Co.
McLaughlin	Kenneth D.	S/Sgt.	509th	POW 5/29/43
McLaughlin	Maurice A.	Cpl.	509th	
McLaughlin	Ray P.	1st Lt.	510th	
McLean	Stuart B.	1st Lt.	509th	
McLean	William E.	1st Lt.	351st	HQ
McLean	Harlan E.	2nd Lt.	509th	
McLott	Maurice	Sgt.	508th	
McMaghan	Sam H.	PFC	447th	Sub-Depot
McMahon	Donald W.	S/Sgt.	509th	
McMerrill	J. B.	2nd Lt.	510th	
	William J.	S/Sgt.	511th	
	Dale H.	Pvt.	510th	

Last Name	First Name	Rank	Unit	Notes
McMillan	Glen E.	1st Lt.	511th	
McMillan	Glenn E.	Cpl.	508th	
McMorrow	James D.	2nd Lt.	511th	MIA 12/22/43
McMullen	Thomas P.	2nd Lt.	511th	
McMullin	Dale E.	Sgt.	511th	
McNair	John A.	S/Sgt.	509th	
McNamara	Frank H.	2nd Lt.	511th	KIA 1/7/44
McNamara	John N.	1st Lt.	11th	
McNamara	William G.	S/Sgt.	508th	St. Comp.
McNeely	Carl F.	Sgt.	508th	
McNeight	Ira B.	1st Lt.	447th	Sub-Depot
McNeil	Verner H.	S/Sgt.	509th	
McNeill	Donald F.	Sgt.	510th	
McNeill	James D.	S/Sgt.	510th	KIA 2/6/45
McNeill	James T.	2nd Lt.	511th	
McNemey	John F.	Cpl.	1629th	Ord. S&M Co.
McNew	Lewis L.	S/Sgt.	509th	
McPherson	Neville D.	2nd Lt.	510th	
McQuaid	Loren M.	Cpl.	510th	Killed 1/29/44
McTask	Kenneth D.	T/Sgt.	508th	
McTighe	James T.	Sgt.	510th	HQ
McVaugh	John	1st Lt.	351st	
McWhorter	Henry J.	T/Sgt.	511th	
McWilliam	Charles P.	S/Sgt.	508th	
Meador	Cecil C.	S/Sgt.	511th	
Meadows	Norman D.	Sgt.	510th	
Meadows	Ray B.	S/Sgt.	508th	
Mears	John R.	Capt.	511th	Int'd 3/18/44
Medeiros	Julian C.	1st Lt.	508th	
Medick	George W.	1st Lt.	509th	
Meek	William	2nd Lt.	510th	
Meeres	Mark	Sgt.	511th	
Meffert	William O.	Cpl.	1629th	Ord. S&M Co.
Megelsh	T. V.	Pvt.	511th	
Meggers	Andrew	Cpl.	11th	St. Comp.
Meidinger	Donald B.	S/Sgt.	509th	
Meighen	August J.	Sgt.	508th	
Meiselman	William M.	S/Sgt.	447th	Sub-Depot
Melendez	Leonard	Sgt.	509th	KIA 12/1/43
Meli	George I.	Pvt.	854th	Chemical Co.
Mellen	Joseph A.	1st Lt.	509th	POW 1/11/44
Mellgren	Clyde L.	Sgt.	510th	
Mellon	Pat L.	2nd Lt.	508th	
Mellott	Kenneth L.	Sgt.	510th	POW 5/7/44
Menconi	Harold R.	S/Sgt.	509th	KIA 12/11/43
Mendell	Donald	Sgt.	509th	
Mendez	Carlton E.	2nd Lt.	509th	
Mendolis	Homer J.	Spec. 5	351st	
Menees	Frank N.	Maj.	351st	HQ
Menendez	Ralph W.	PFC	508th	
	George	Sgt.	510th	

Last Name	First Name	Rank	Unit	Notes
Mercer	James L.	2nd Lt.	508th	
Meredith	Arthur J.	T/Sgt.	511th	
Meredith	Guy O.	S/Sgt.	510th	
Mernagh	John J.	T/Sgt.	508th	
Merrell	Orval E.	S/Sgt.	508th	
Merrifield	William R.	PFC	510th	
Merrill	Calvin	1st Lt.	511th	POW 10/7/44
Merrill	Danforth N.	Sgt.	511th	
Merriman	Kenneth W.	Cpl.	510th	
Merritt	Harold J.	PFC	508th	
Merritt	John J.	PFC	508th	
Merry	Robert	S/Sgt.	509th	
Mertzluft	Reid Q.	S/Sgt.	508th	MIA 6/28/43
Messaros	Daniel J.	1st Lt.	509th	Int'd 10/7/44
Messner	Andrew	Sgt.	509th	
Metzger	Paul	S/Sgt.	510th	
Metzger	Eugene V.	Cpl.	509th	
Meurrier	Howard A.	S/Sgt.	510th	
Mevilas	Fred R.	S/Sgt.	511th	
Meyer	Joseph E.	Spec. 4	1629th	Ord. S&M Co.
Meyer	Albert R.	Sgt.	511th	KIA 12/22/43
Meyer	Charles E.	Sgt.	511th	KIA 3/18/44
Meyere	Eugene F.	1st Lt.	510th	
Meyers	Joseph	Pvt.	510th	
Meyers	Earl H.	S/Sgt.	510th	
Miars	Lynn L.	2nd Lt.	508th	
Michael	Deane M.	Sgt.	510th	
Michajla	Phillip J.	Sgt.	509th	
Michand	Edward C. Jr.	Sgt.	508th	
Michaud	L.	1st Lt.	511th	
Michel	Raymond L.	1st Lt.	509th	
Michel	John F.	Sgt.	508th	
Midkiff	Norman K.	T/Sgt.	511th	
Miele	Ray E.	Sgt.	511th	
Mihuc	R.	Sgt.	508th	
Mika	George A.	1st Lt.	511th	
Mikulicz	John P.	2nd Lt.	508th	
Milani	Joseph A.	M/Sgt.	351st	HQ
Milanowski	Joseph R.	T/Sgt.	510th	Int'd 10/7/44
Mile	Frank P.	T/Sgt.	511th	
Miles	William J.	S/Sgt.	511th	
Miles	Alfred	PFC	511th	
Miles	Donald G.	S/Sgt.	509th	POW 6/21/44
Miles	George L.	Sgt.	510th	
Miles	James E.	Sgt.	510th	
Miley	Mitchell D.	S/Sgt.	509th	KIA 12/1/43
Miles	Thomas R.	1st Lt.	508th	
Miley	Roy M.	S/Sgt.	508th	
Miller	Allan H.	S/Sgt.	508th	
Miller	Armandus P.	Sgt.	509th	
Miller	Carl F.	2nd Lt.	511th	
Miller	Carl F.	1st Lt.	511th	KIA 5/28/44

Surname	Given	Rank	Unit	Notes	Surname	Given	Rank	Unit	Notes	Surname	Given	Rank	Unit	Notes
Miller	Charles B.	T/Sgt.	447th	Sub-Depot	Minton	Albert N.	2nd Lt.	509th		Moore	Carl W.	T/Sgt.	510th	
Miller	Charles R.	Sgt.	510th	KIA 7/12/44	Mintzer	Edward H.	Sgt.	447th	Sub-Depot	Moore	Clifford L.	PFC	11th	
Miller	Clair L.	S/Sgt.	511th	MP Company	Misenheimer	Charles M.	S/Sgt.	509th		Moore	Darrel F.	S/Sgt.	508th	
Miller	Collette G.	Cpl.	1061st		Mishkin	Herbert M.	F.O.	511th		Moore	Frank W.	Sgt.	511th	St. Comp.
Miller	Donald M.	T/Sgt.	510th		Mitcham	Fred I.	Cpl.	1061st	MP Company	Moore	George	Sgt.	508th	
Miller	Edward M.	2nd Lt.	508th		Mitchell	Robert B.	S/Sgt.	508th	POW 12/30/43	Moore	Gordon B. Jr.	S/Sgt.	508th	
Miller	Floyd A.	Sgt.	510th		Mitchell	Anthony J.	PFC	11th	St. Comp.	Moore	Willis A.	1st Lt.	508th	
Miller	Forrest B.	Cpl.	447th	Sub-Depot	Mitchell	Arnold L.	S/Sgt.	509th		Moore	Zane G.	S/Sgt.	510th	
Miller	George M.	1st Lt.	508th		Mitchell	Austin G.	S/Sgt.	447th	Sub-Depot	Moorman	Manford D.	T/Sgt.	509th	
Miller	Glenn B.	Sgt.	447th	Sub-Depot	Mitchell	Charles F.	Sgt.	510th		Morales	P.A.	Cpl.	509th	
Miller	Harold	Cpl.	510th		Mitchell	Leo J.	Cpl.	509th	HQ	Moran	Joseph P.	1st Lt.	509th	
Miller	Harold D.	T/Sgt.	511th		Mitchell	Leonard U.	2nd Lt.	511th		Morasca	John J. Jr.	1st Lt.	508th	
Miller	Harvey M.	S/Sgt.	511th	POW 10/14/43	Mitchell	Stanley C.	Sgt.	351st	HQ	Mordecai	Clifford R.	2nd Lt.	511th	
Miller	Henry F.	T/Sgt.	509th		Mitchener	Hardy A.	2nd Lt.	509th	POW 5/30/44	Moreland	Edward B.	T/Sgt.	508th	
Miller	Henry O.	Sgt.	508th		Mittle	George A.	S/Sgt.	509th		Morell	Ross J.	S/Sgt.	509th	
Miller	John M.	S/Sgt.	508th		Mo	W.H.	T/Sgt.	508th		Morello	Nicholas J.	Sgt.	509th	
Miller	John Z.	1st Lt.	508th		Mobley	Troy D.	Cpl.	2098th	Avn. F/F Pltn.	Morey	Michael T.	Sgt.	511th	KIA 12/31/43
Miller	Junior W.	1st Lt.	511th		Moccia	Alfred J.	1st Lt.	508th		Morgan	Francis L.	S/Sgt.	509th	
Miller	Lee M.	1st Lt.	510th		Moen	John	M/Sgt.	511th		Morgan	James B.	S/Sgt.	511th	POW 10/9/43
Miller	Leslie	S/Sgt.	508th		Moetzel	Charles	2nd Lt.	509th	HQ	Morgan	Malvern H. Jr.	S/Sgt.	509th	
Miller	Lovick C.	2nd Lt.	510th		Mogensen	Charles	Sgt.	510th		Morgan	William P.	Cpl.	511th	
Miller	Mahlon S. Jr.	S/Sgt.	511th		Mokol	Emanuel	S/Sgt.	508th		Morgan	William M. III	S/Sgt.	511th	
Miller	Mark P.	1st Lt.	508th		Molaschi	William T.	2nd Lt.	509th		Morgenbesser	Sidney	M/Sgt.	447th	Sub-Depot
Miller	Norman O.	1st Lt.	511th		Molik	Arthur E.	T/Sgt.	508th		Moriarity	Walter	2nd Lt.	511th	POW 10/14/43
Miller	Paul B.	1st Lt.	510th		Molitor	Charles T.	S/Sgt.	511th		Morin	Alfred R.	Sgt.	1629th	Ord. S&M Co.
Miller	Raymond E.	2nd Lt.	508th		Mollenschlae	Franklin J.	2nd Lt.	508th		Morley	Carl J.	T/Sgt.	508th	
Miller	Richard G.	1st Lt.	510th	Int'd 5/27/44	Mollohan	Junior	Sgt.	510th		Morphew	James H. E.	S/Sgt.	509th	
Miller	Robert B.	Capt.	509th		Monaghan	Bernard W.	S/Sgt.	447th	Sub-Depot	Morrell	Ross J.	S/Sgt.	511th	POW 8/6/44
Miller	Robert H.	F.O.	510th		Monaghan	John B.	Sgt.	510th		Morris	Claude R.	T/Sgt.	509th	
Miller	Warren H.	Sgt.	510th		Monagin	Richard V.	Sgt.	447th	Sub-Depot	Morris	Gilbert L.	T/Sgt.	511th	
Miller	Wayne W.	Cpl.	351st	HQ	Monahan	Frank J.	S/Sgt.	508th		Morris	Henry	2nd Lt.	510th	
Miller	Whitney B.	1st Lt.	508th		Moncreif	Robert R.	S/Sgt.	509th		Morris	Joseph D.	PFC	511th	
Milinor	Thomas W.	Cpl.	11th	St. Comp.	Monday	Monroe C.	S/Sgt.	508th		Morris	Kenneth A.	S/Sgt.	510th	
Mills	David W.	2nd Lt.	510th		Mondragon	Robert	T/Sgt.	509th	POW 4/13/44	Morris	William A.	2nd Lt.	509th	
Mills	Donald O.	PFC	447th	Sub-Depot	Money	Arthur P. Jr.	2nd Lt.	508th		Morrisette	William H.	Sgt.	508th	
Mills	E. J.	Pvt.	11th	St. Comp.	Moniston	Martin M.	Sgt.	511th		Morrison	Milton	1st Lt.	511th	
Mills	Earl T.	Cpl.	508th		Monroe	Guy	Pvt.	1061st	MP Company	Morrison	Roy A.	S/Sgt.	511th	KIA 9/8/44
Mills	George L.	1st Lt.	509th		Monroe	Ronald E.	Cpl.	11th	St. Comp.	Morrison	Roy S.	Spec. 5	854th	Chemical Co.
Mills	Hulan C.	S/Sgt.	508th		Montagno	Michael J.	1st Lt.	509th		Morrissey	William C.	S/Sgt.	508th	
Mills	James T.	T/Sgt.	509th		Montalbano	Joseph	S/Sgt.	511th		Morrow	Joseph F.	F.O.	510th	
Mills	Martin A.	Sgt.	510th	Int'd 10/7/44	Montali	Louis J.	Sgt.	11th	St. Comp.	Morrow	Harold M.	T/Sgt.	511th	POW 10/4/43
Mills	Reuben	Sgt.	511th		Montalvo	R.	M/Sgt.	510th		Morse	John A.	Capt.	1061st	
Mills	Robert E.	T/Sgt.	447th	Sub-Depot	Montavon	Ralph P.	PFC	11th	St. Comp.	Mortensen	Harry B. Jr.	S/Sgt.	509th	KIA 7/29/44
Mills	William F.	S/Sgt.	508th		Montgomery	Aubrey L.	2nd Lt.	510th		Morton	William	S/Sgt.	508th	
Milton	Theodore R.	Maj.	351st	HQ	Montgomery	Chester B.	M/Sgt.	509th	Killed 6/8/45	Morton	Donald I.	Sgt.	510th	
Milton	Troy C.	Cpl.	447th	Sub-Depot	Montgomery	John Q.	1st Lt.	511th		Morton	Chester D.	2nd Lt.	508th	
Milutinovich	Marco S.	M/Sgt.	351st	HQ	Montross	William P.	1st Lt.	508th		Morton	John M.	S/Sgt.	509th	HQ
Mingos	William B.	T/Sgt.	510th		Moon	Frank K.Jr.	1st Lt.	509th		Morton	Robert E.	Sgt.	511th	POW 5/7/44
Minjares	Miguel A.	S/Sgt.	509th		Mooney	Harry P.	2nd Lt.	508th		Morton	Thomas J.	Sgt.	508th	
Minkin	Ralph	Cpl.	447th	Sub-Depot	Moore	Alfred A.	T/Sgt.	509th		Mosebach	William T.	2nd Lt.	509th	
Minor	Jerry A.	S/Sgt.	508th		Moore	Amos I.	2nd Lt.	510th		Moseley	Herbert J.	T/Sgt.	510th	
Mintich	George	T/Sgt.	511th		Moore	Arlie W.	S/Sgt.	511th	KIA 5/28/44					

Surname	Given	Rank	Unit	Notes
Moser	David J.	T/Sgt.	511th	
Moskosky	Michael	PFC	447th	POW 8/16/44
Moss	Eugene D.	S/Sgt.	508th	POW 6/28/43
Moss	John M.	1st Lt.	511th	
Motola	Frank P.	Sgt.	509th	
Motter	Edward T.	2nd Lt.	509th	Int'd 5/27/44
Moulton	Reed L.	S/Sgt.	510th	
Moulton	Richard B.	Capt.	508th	
Mount	John W. T. Jr.	S/Sgt.	509th	
Mount	Lionel D.	S/Sgt.	508th	KIA 8/27/43
Mouradian	James H.	Capt.	252nd	Medical Disp.
Moyer	Frank N.	1st Lt.	511th	
Mroz	Stanley	Sgt.	510th	
Mudd	Thomas L.	Sgt.	509th	
Muegge	Paul A.	M/Sgt.	511th	
Mueller	Arthur L.	Cpl.	508th	
Mueller	John B.	1st Lt.	510th	
Muerrier	Raymond H.	1st Lt.	509th	
Muesing	Fred R.	1st Lt.	511th	HQ
Muffett	Irving C.	S/Sgt.	351st	
Muhleman	Winfield F.	1st Lt.	508th	
Muirhead	Frank L.	1st Lt.	510th	
Mulcahy	Dewey	PFC	1061st	MP Company
Mullen	Henry L.	S/Sgt.	510th	
Mundth	Raphael D.	2nd Lt.	509th	
Munn	Donald	2nd Lt.	511th	
Munoth	Robert D.	2nd Lt.	508th	POW 9/12/44
Munson	Donald	2nd Lt.	511th	
Munson	Francis W.	S/Sgt.	508th	St. Comp.
Murewski	Gene H.	Sgt.	508th	KIA 12/30/43
Murfl	Donald S.	S/Sgt.	509th	
Murphy	Anselm S.	PFC	1061st	MP Company
Murphy	Clarence J.	S/Sgt.	510th	St. Comp.
Murphy	John J.	Sgt.	11th	
Murphy	Samuel F.	Cpl.	510th	
Murray	Terrence J.	2nd Lt.	509th	
Murray	Willand L.	T/Sgt.	510th	
Murray	William J.	Sgt.	508th	
Murray	Archie E.	Sgt.	509th	
Murray	Francis A.	T/Sgt.	1629th	Ord. S&M Co.
Murray	Gordon J.	Sgt.	509th	
Murray	James G.	2nd Lt.	508th	
Murray	James W.	Cpl.	11th	St. Comp.
Murrell	John P.	Sgt.	1061st	MP Company
Murryn	Robert G.	1st Lt.	508th	
Murryn	Robert H.	S/Sgt.	509th	
Murray	Robert J.	S/Sgt.	511th	
Murray	Thomas J. Jr.	Sgt.	509th	
Murray	William J. Jr.	T/Sgt.	509th	
Murrell	Billy J.	T/Sgt.	510th	
Murryn	John S.	S/Sgt.	510th	
Musser	Charles J.	2nd Lt.	510th	

Mustacchia - Olsen

Surname	First	Rank	Unit	Notes
Mustacchia	Nicholas	Sgt.	511th	POW 2/22/44
Muth	Jack D.	Sgt.	510th	
Myer	Albert R.	Sgt.	511th	
Myers	Alfred L.	S/Sgt.	509th	
Myers	Allen M.	2nd Lt.	511th	POW 9/12/44
Myers	Dorsey D.	T/Sgt.	511th	
Myers	Herbert L.	Spec. 5	1629th	Ord. S&M Co.
Myers	Tedfred E.	1st Lt.	509th	POW 5/27/44
Myers	William H.	2nd Lt.	509th	KIA 1/11/44
Myl	James A.	1st Lt.	510th	KIA 12/31/43
Myrick	John R.	T/Sgt.	510th	
Myszka	Stanley J.	Sgt.	511th	KIA 6/22/43

N

Surname	First	Rank	Unit	Notes
Naas	Vernon N.	2nd Lt.	509th	
Nachreiner	Reginald	T/Sgt.	510th	
Nacy	Joseph	PFC	11th	St. Comp.
Nadeau	Docite	S/Sgt.	511th	MIA 12/22/43
Nagle	Raymond E.	S/Sgt.	511th	
Nairn	Edward P.	2nd Lt.	508th	
Nall	John L.	1st Lt.	511th	
Nalley	Vincent A.	1st Lt.	511th	
Nappe	Frank	S/Sgt.	511th	
Nardi	Elmer J.	1st Lt.	511th	KIA 11/3/43
Nardone	Anthony J.	2nd Lt.	511th	POW 9/12/44
Nascara	Joseph M.	T/Sgt.	509th	
Nash	David F.	2nd Lt.	510th	POW 5/19/43
Nass	Vernon N.	2nd Lt.	509th	
Nasta	Dominick J.	Sgt.	508th	
Natanblut	Noah	S/Sgt.	447th	Sub-Depot
Nauman	Daniel D.	Capt.	511th	
Nauman	Henry A.	1st Lt.	511th	HQ
Navarra	Arthur	T/Sgt.	509th	Sub-Depot
Nay	George W.	S/Sgt.	508th	
Naylor	Benjamin F.	Cpl.	511th	St. Comp.
Neagle	Richard H.	T/Sgt.	351st	
Neal	Maurice J.	Cpl.	447th	
Neal	Alfred D.	1st Lt.	510th	
Nearman	William A.	S/Sgt.	511th	POW 1/11/44
Neaton	Gilbert S.	Cpl.	509th	
Nebbiai	Joseph F.	Sgt.	510th	
Necastro	Joseph J.	Sgt.	510th	
Needham	Harry C.	T/Sgt.	509th	
Neeler	Francis M.	1st Lt.	510th	
Neely	John F.	Sgt.	509th	
Neff	George B.	2nd Lt.	510th	
Nehr	Richard R.	S/Sgt.	510th	
Neibuhr	Elwood	S/Sgt.	508th	
Neil	Vernon D.	M/Sgt.	511th	
Neithing	Lloyd H.	T/Sgt.	509th	
Nelson	Eugene L.	Sgt.	508th	
Nelson	Anton L.	T/Sgt.	510th	
Nelson	Bernard F.	2nd Lt.	511th	
Nelson	Clarence R.	2nd Lt.	510th	
Nelson	Elmer T. Jr.	1st Lt.	508th	
Nelson	Frederick B.	S/Sgt.	508th	
Nelson	Glenn L.	S/Sgt.	511th	
Nelson	Jesse E.	F.O.	509th	
Nelson	Joe	S/Sgt.	510th	
Nelson	John Y.	Sgt.	511th	KIA 2/6/45
Nelson	Kermit A.	Cpl.	508th	
Nelson	Norris N.	1st Lt.	508th	KIA 5/23/44
Nelson	Robert A.	2nd Lt.	511th	
Nelson	Russell	T/Sgt.	509th	
Nesmith	Thomas T. G.	T/Sgt.	509th	
Nesh		Pvt.	508th	
Nesmith	Joseph F.	Capt.	511th	
Ness	Charles S.	2nd Lt.	510th	
Nething	Eugene L.	S/Sgt.	508th	
Neuberg	Raymond E.	1st Lt.	509th	POW 3/18/44
Neuhardt	Charles P.	PFC	1206th	QM Company
Neumann	Herbert C.	2nd Lt.	508th	POW 5/27/44
Neusted	Leslie J.	Cpl.	351st	
Nevilas	Joseph E.	Sgt.	509th	
Newbauer	Raymond F.	Sgt.	1629th	Ord. S&M Co.
Newby	Charles E.	S/Sgt.	508th	POW 8/16/44
Newcomb	Grant R.	1st Lt.	510th	
Newell	James P.	2nd Lt.	509th	
Newham	Gregory G.	S/Sgt.	510th	
Newhard	George N.	S/Sgt.	508th	
Newman	Floyd L.	2nd Lt.	509th	
Newman	Lloyd E.	Cpl.	511th	
Newsom	Peter J.	Cpl.	447th	
Newson	Bud J.	PFC	351st	
Newth	Franklin A.	S/Sgt.	510th	
Newton	Burle L.	2nd Lt.	508th	HQ
Nibert	Clark L.	Cpl.	509th	
Nicholas	Hugh D.	S/Sgt.	447th	Sub-Depot
Nichols	Arthur A.	Sgt.	508th	POW 2/14/45
Nichols	Darwin R.	2nd Lt.	511th	KIA 9/12/44
Nickeloff	William C.	Maj.	509th	
Nickels	William G.	1st Lt.	511th	
Nickerson	John E.	S/Sgt.	508th	
Nickerson	Charles J.	2nd Lt.	510th	
Nicklas	George M.	Sgt.	509th	POW 5/14/43
Nicolescu	Richard J.	Sgt.	510th	
Nipper	Fred W.	1st Lt.	511th	POW 6/14/44
Nitzberg	George V.	Sgt.	509th	POW 10/9/43
Nixdorf	Monroe	Cpl.	509th	
Nocefera	George P.	Sgt.	510th	POW 5/28/44
Nocera	Edward C.	Sgt.	509th	
Noe	Samuel C.	S/Sgt.	511th	
	Sebastian	S/Sgt.	508th	
	Alexander B.	T/Sgt.	508th	POW 8/27/43

Surname	First	Rank	Unit	Notes
Noetzel	Charles	2nd Lt.	509th	KIA 6/13/43
Nolan	Chester T.	Pvt.	11th	St. Comp.
Nolan	Walter J.	S/Sgt.	508th	POW 3/2/44
Nolan	William W.	T/Sgt.	11th	St. Comp.
Noonan	James F. Jr.	Cpl.	351st	
Nooney	H. P.	2nd Lt.	508th	HQ
Norbo	John R.	Sgt.	509th	
Norby	Clinton O.	Sgt.	508th	
Norden	Eldon C.	Cpl.	509th	
Nordone	Anthony J.	2nd Lt.	511th	
Norin	Alfred R.	Spec 4	1629th	Ord. S&M Co.
Normand	Alvin J.	T/Sgt.	509th	
Normile	Joseph P.	2nd Lt.	511th	KIA 5/27/44
Norquist	Lyle A	T/Sgt.	510th	
Norris	Clarence F.	1st Lt.	511th	
Norris	Clarence H.	1st Lt.	509th	
Norris	Donald M.	Capt.	511th	
Norris	Harry M.	Sgt.	508th	
Norris	John L.	S/Sgt.	509th	POW 12/31/43
Norris	Kenneth E.	S/Sgt.	351st	HQ
Norse	Lynn W.	S/Sgt.	509th	
Northcott	Max A.	T/Sgt.	509th	
Northern	Marvin O.	S/Sgt.	508th	
Northrup	Joseph P.	1st Lt.	510th	
Norton	Chester S.	2nd Lt.	508th	KIA 5/27/44
Nosak	Edward J.	T/Sgt.	509th	
Noschang	Thomas	S/Sgt.	510th	
Notargiacomo	Frank P.	S/Sgt.	508th	
Notola	Carlisle L.	2nd Lt.	509th	POW 5/14/43
Nottingham	Arthur	Maj.	508th	
Novaco	Nicholas	1st Lt.	351st	
Novack	Charles G.	Cpl.	509th	
Novak	Stephen H.	Sgt.	1629th	Ord. S&M Co.
Novitski	Louis J.	Sgt.	510th	
Nowakowski	Adolph A.	1st Lt.	509th	
Nowack	Carl M.	Cpl.	508th	
Nowlin	Dominic	Sgt.	510th	
Nuccio	Homer W.	Sgt.	509th	
Nulton	Paul E.	1st Lt.	511th	
Nuoffer	Milton	Cpl.	510th	
Nussbaum	Cedric G.	Sgt.	508th	
Nuttall	William E.	S/Sgt.	351st	
Nygren		T/Sgt.	508th	

O

Surname	First	Rank	Unit	Notes
O'Banion	Lowell A.	Sgt.	511th	
O'Brian	John H.	PFC	854th	Chemical Co.
O'Brien	Charles J.	2nd Lt.	508th	
O'Brien	Kenneth E.	S/Sgt.	509th	
O'Brien	Robert L.	S/Sgt.	509th	
O'Brien	William P.	1st Lt.	511th	
O'Bryant	John D.	S/Sgt.	508th	
O'Connell	Daniel L.	2nd Lt.	508th	
O'Connell	Edward J.	Cpl.	1629th	Ord. S&M Co.
O'Connell	Richard F.	S/Sgt.	1206th	QM Company
O'Connell	William J.	S/Sgt.	511th	
O'Connor	James K.	2nd Lt.	511th	
O'Connor	John G.	Cpl.	509th	
O'Dell	Carl S.	S/Sgt.	510th	
O'Dell	Clarence W.	Cpl.	201st	Finance Sect.
O'Donel	Wendell F.	PFC	510th	
O'Donnell	Kenneth B.	Sgt.	510th	
O'Donoghue	James J.	2nd Lt.	509th	KIA 12/1/43
O'Fearna	John H.	PFC	509th	
O'Hanlon	George E.	Sgt.	510th	
O'Hearn	Robert W.	S/Sgt.	510th	
O'Keefe	Lawrence J.	Sgt.	510th	
O'Lear	Stephen C.	Sgt.	509th	Sub-Depot
O'Leary	Edward J.	Sgt.	447th	
O'Leary	Joseph H.	PFC	11th	
O'Loughlin	William P.	T/Sgt.	509th	
O'Malley	Robert V.	S/Sgt.	351st	
O'Neill	Martin J.	Sgt.	509th	
O'Neill	John J.	S/Sgt.	509th	
O'Neill	John R.	Sgt.	510th	
O'Shea	Paul C.	Sgt.	511th	KIA 12/1/43
O'Shea	James R.	S/Sgt.	510th	
O'Toole	Michael F. Jr.	2nd Lt.	511th	POW 10/7/44
Oakes	Terrance S.	Cpl.	509th	
Ober	Thomas H.	1st Lt.	510th	
Oberhau	Daniel D.	Sgt.	1061st	MP Company
Ocamb	Frederick A.	Cpl.	509th	
Occulto	James C.	Sgt.	510th	KIA 7/19/44
Ochmanek	Joseph R.	T/Sgt.	510th	
Odell	Edwin J.	S/Sgt.	511th	
Odgers	Clarence W. Jr.	Cpl.	201st	Finance Sect.
Odom	Richard H.	PFC	508th	
Oen	James E.	S/Sgt.	1629th	Ord. S&M Co.
Offutt	Daniel A.	1st Lt.	510th	
Ogden	John W.	S/Sgt.	508th	POW 6/14/44
Ohde	Ernest C.	Sgt.	509th	Int'd 2/25/45
Ohr	William M. Jr.	Sgt.	511th	POW 9/12/44
Ohrel	Edward	M/Sgt.	511th	
Oldham	Charles G.	1st Lt.	511th	
Olivari	Orville	Capt.	508th	
Oliver	William E.	S/Sgt.	509th	
Oliver	John W.	Sgt.	509th	
Oliver	Kenneth A.	S/Sgt.	1206th	QM Company
Oliver	Oswell O.	S/Sgt.	1629th	Int'd 6/21/44
Oliveri	William A.	S/Sgt.	1061st	MP Company
Olivo	L. M.	Cpl.	508th	
Olsen	August A.	Sgt.	11th	St. Comp.
Olsen	Harry A.	1st Lt.	510th	
	Harry C. R.	1st Lt.		

Olsen / Pettus

Olsen	Robert W.	PFC	510th		Pagliaccio	Dominico A.	Sgt.	511th		Penticoff	Robert B.	1st Lt.	510th	
Olsen	Rodney A.	Sgt.	11th	St. Comp.	Paid	Richard I.	PFC	854th	Chemical Co.	Pentley	John V.	Spec. 4	252nd	Medical Disp.
Olson	Alvin S.	T/Sgt.	509th		Pakema	Andrew	Pvt.	11th		Peryra	Manuel O.	M/Sgt.	510th	
Olson	Edwin L.	Capt.	508th	POW 11/21/44	Pakey	Wilbur N.	Cpl.	511th		Perez	Benjamin J.	Sgt.	1061st	MP Company
Olson	Evan D.	Sgt.	511th		Palmer	David H.	1st Lt.	510th		Perez	Charles	PFC	511th	
Olson	Henry O.	Sgt.	510th		Palmer	George R.	Cpl.	11th		Perez	Stanley N.	S/Sgt.	508th	
Olson	Wendell D.	1st Lt.	508th	POW 5/28/44	Palmer	Henry D.	Cpl.	510th		Perkins	Ernest H.	PFC	447th	Sub-Depot
Olvera	Joseph L.	T/Sgt.	509th	Sub-Depot	Palmer	Howard A.	Sgt.	351st		Perkins	James H.	PFC	447th	Sub-Depot
Omer	Albert C.	T/Sgt.	509th		Palmer	Louis	1st Lt.	509th	HQ	Perkins	Joseph C.	2nd Lt.	510th	KIA 7/25/43
Omohundro	Jack H.	1st Lt.	509th		Palmer	Richard E.	T/Sgt.	509th		Perkins	Richard E.S.	1st Lt.	510th	POW 2/24/44
Onken	Edwin S.	2nd Lt.	508th		Palmer	Vernon M.	Sgt.	511th		Perkins	Ward J.	Sgt.	508th	
Opphile	Creyle G.	Cpl.	508th	POW 5/28/44	Palmer	William T. Jr.	T/Sgt.	510th		Perle	Richard	2nd Lt.	509th	POW 3/18/44
Orban	Charles W.	M/Sgt.	447th	Sub-Depot	Palonder	John R.	Cpl.	508th		Perlman	Norman N.	PFC	510th	
Orband	Daniel G.	Cpl.	508th		Panansky	Benjamin	PFC	510th	POW 8/6/44	Perriman	Edwin F.	Pvt.	511th	
Orff	Leslie B.	PFC	510th	Sub-Depot	Pancratz	Jack K.	T/Sgt.	509th	POW 6/13/43	Perry	Edward C.	Sgt.	510th	
Orndorff	William H.	2nd Lt.	447th		Pancucci	Daniel L.	PFC	510th		Perry	Eugene J.	T/Sgt.	510th	
Ornett	Ernest G.	2nd Lt.	508th	POW 9/12/44	Pansy	James W.	2098th	Avn. F/F Pltn.		Perry	Harry U.	1st Lt.	509th	
Orosz	Peter A.	Cpl.	511th	HQ	Papen	Henry D.	S/Sgt.	11th	St. Comp.	Perry	Kenneth E.	S/Sgt.	509th	
Orzechowski	Joseph H.	T/Sgt.	351st	Sub-Depot	Papenbrock	Leo E.	Sgt.	510th	KIA 12/31/43	Pershing	Raymond E.	Cpl.	508th	
Osborn	George C.	S/Sgt.	447th	KIA 11/5/43	Pappas	George J.	Sgt.	11th	St. Comp.	Persich	Reginald E.	PFC	508th	
Osborne	George G.	T/Sgt.	508th	POW 5/14/43	Pappas	William J.	2nd Lt.	511th		Petereit	Frank E. Jr.	S/Sgt.	508th	
Osbourne	Oliver W.	Sgt.	508th		Paquer	Robert E.	T/Sgt.	447th	Sub-Depot	Peters	William J.	S/Sgt.	511th	
Oslund	John W.	2nd Lt.	511th		Paquette	Philip E.	2nd Lt.	509th		Peters	Bernard E.	T/Sgt.	508th	
Osteen	D.	S/Sgt.	351st	HQ	Paquin	Joseph J.	PFC	447th	Sub-Depot	Peters	Earl J.	Sgt.	509th	
Ostheimer	Robert V.	2nd Lt.	510th	POW 5/14/43	Parchman	Robert	Pvt.	511th		Peters	Edmund P.	2nd Lt.	510th	
Otis	Wilbur V.	T/Sgt.	511th		Pardue	Tuttle E. Jr.	Sgt.	510th	Killed 2/26/43	Peters	Harold J.	S/Sgt.	509th	POW 1/11/44
Otte	Maximilian R.	S/Sgt.	510th		Parent	Vernon P.	Sgt.	509th	POW 6/14/44	Peters	Harold M.	1st Sgt.	510th	
Ottensen	D. L.	Sgt.	508th		Parish	Joseph C.	S/Sgt.	351st	HQ	Peters	Otto L.	Cpl.	508th	
Otto	John J.	Cpl.	511th		Parish	William R.	Cpl.	510th		Peters	Ray L.	T/Sgt.	511th	
Ouder	Melvin L.	1st Lt.	508th		Park	Robert S.	F.O.	511th		Peters	William E. Jr.	2nd Lt.	511th	
Ovehile	G. G.	Cpl.	1206th	QM Company	Parker	Dixie S.	S/Sgt.	509th		Peterson	Alex	PFC	508th	
Overholt	Orval O.	1st Lt.	508th		Parker	Donald L.	2nd Lt.	510th	POW 6/28/43	Peterson	Arlie E.	1st Lt.	510th	
Overmyer	John T.	F.O.	509th		Parker	Francis H.	PFC	508th	POW 8/6/44	Peterson	Arthur F.	S/Sgt.	511th	
Overton	Edward T.	Sgt.	508th	KIA 7/28/44	Parker	James B.	Sgt.	510th		Peterson	Einer	1st Lt.	509th	KIA 10/7/44
Overton	Richard L.	Sgt.	511th	MIA 6/28/43	Parker	Joseph E.	1st Sgt.	511th		Peterson	Elmer L.	T/Sgt.	510th	KIA 5/19/43
Owen	Glenn C.	Sgt.	508th		Parker	Paul	Pvt.	510th		Peterson	Fred O.	S/Sgt.	511th	
Owens	Lonnie	S/Sgt.	511th		Parker	R. P.	Cpl.	508th		Peterson	John P.	S/Sgt.	508th	
Owens	Vernon C.	T/Sgt.	510th		Parker	Walter B.	T/Sgt.	510th		Peterson	Lester N.	Pvt.	509th	
Owens	William R.	M/Sgt.	509th		Parker	Walter H.	Sgt.	508th		Peterson	Robert F.	T/Sgt.	510th	
Owers	Albert	Capt.	508th		Parkerson	Francis J.	Sgt.	510th		Peterson	Roger N.	1st Sgt.	508th	
Owre	Jesse C.	1st Lt.	510th		Parks	Donald L.	PFC	511th		Peterson	Roger W.	1st Sgt.	508th	POW 5/27/44
Oxley	Fred E.	Sgt.	508th		Parnell	Robert S.	Capt.	508th		Peterson	Roy H.	S/Sgt.	509th	St. Comp.
P					Parsells	Raymond	M. T/Sgt.	511th	MP Company	Peterson	Theodore B.	1st Sgt.	510th	
P'Pool	Calvert G.	Cpl.	509th	Killed 6/8/45	Parsons	Cecil E.	M/Sgt.	511th		Peterson	Thomas C.	1st Sgt.	508th	
Pacciotti	Video	Sgt.	508th	POW 6/22/43	Parsons	John L.	S/Sgt.	1061st		Peterson	Thomas G. Jr.	Sgt.	1061st	MP Company
Pack	Charles C.	Sgt.	510th		Parsons	Johnnie H.	T/Sgt.	508th		Peterson	Vernon J.	Sgt.	508th	
Pack	William T.	T/Sgt.	511th		Parsons	Roy A.	1st Lt.	508th	POW 12/30/43	Peterson	Anthony J.	Sgt.	447th	Sub-Depot
Padilla	Joseph C.	Sgt.	511th		Parten	Theron D.	1st Lt.	508th		Petrowski	Alex E.	T/Sgt.	11th	
Padula	Alberic A.	Cpl.	511th	POW 7/19/44	Pasqua	James B.	S/Sgt.	511th		Petrowsky	Frank E.	T/Sgt.	508th	St. Comp.
Page	Lewis A. Jr.	2nd Lt.	510th		Passwater	Ernest	Lt.	1206th	Killed 2/26/43	Petrucci	William H.	S/Sgt.	509th	
Page	Omar H.	S/Sgt.	510th		Patch	Wesley A.	Sgt.	511th	QM Company	Pettibone	Harold H.	T/Sgt.	510th	
										Pettigrew	Carl	T/Sgt.	511th	POW 10/9/43
										Pettus				

157

Last Name	First Name	Rank	Unit	Notes
Petty	William M. Jr.	2nd Lt.	508th	
Pevey	John L.	Cpl.	509th	
Pfeiffer	Harold H.	PFC	508th	
Pfleging	Kenneth J.	T/Sgt.	509th	Int'd 8/6/44
Phares	Arthur L.	Sgt.	508th	
Phelps	Leon R.	2nd Lt.	511th	
Phelps	William C.	Sgt.	510th	
Phillips	Charles J.	Pvt.	509th	
Phillips	Davis N.	S/Sgt.	447th	Sub-Depot
Phillips	Delmar H.	Sgt.	509th	Sub-Depot
Phillips	Edwin P.	Cpl.	1061st	MP Company
Phillips	Elmer L.	T/Sgt.	509th	HQ
Phillips	James A.	PFC	351st	
Phillips	James F.	Sgt.	511th	
Phillips	Vernon A.	1st Lt.	511th	
Phillips	Vondus Z	Pvt.	11th	St. Comp.
Piamam	Francis L.	S/Sgt.	509th	
Picard	Leo J.	T/Sgt.	508th	
Pickelsimer	Charles J.	S/Sgt.	509th	POW 10/14/43
Pickett	William C. Jr.	S/Sgt.	511th	
Pickler	Isadore	1st Lt.	510th	
Piech	Edward C.	2nd Lt.	509th	
Pierce	George A.	T/Sgt.	508th	Sub-Depot
Pierce	Harvey C.	Sgt.	447th	
Pierce	James M.	S/Sgt.	509th	
Pierce	Robert B.	T/Sgt.	508th	POW 2/14/45
Pierson	Roscoe M.	S/Sgt.	508th	
Pike	Charles M.	S/Sgt.	511th	
Pilcher	Gerald L.	T/Sgt.	510th	
Pillsbury	Warren D.	M/Sgt.	510th	
Pimental	William P.	Sgt.	510th	
Pine	Clem J.	S/Sgt.	511th	
Pink	Raymond J.	PFC	854th	Chemical Co.
Pinkerton	Max A.	1st Lt.	511th	POW 8/17/43
Pinner	Clay J.	1st Lt.	509th	
Pinner	Joseph C.	2nd Lt.	509th	St. Comp.
Pinta	Arthur L.	Sgt.	11th	
Piscotta	Paul J.	Cpl.	510th	
Pisman	Francis L.	T/Sgt.	508th	Chemical Co.
Pitrowski	Mike A.	PFC	854th	St. Comp.
Pitts	Ben W.	PFC	11th	
Plant	James M.	2nd Lt.	510th	
Plaskey	Edmund	Cpl.	508th	
Plaut	George H.	1st Lt.	511th	
Playford	William E.	2nd Lt.	511th	
Pleasant	Vernice J.	Sgt.	509th	
Plouf	Richard L.	Cpl.	11th	
Plouffe	John B.	T/Sgt.	510th	
Plourde	Isaac	PFC	854th	Chemical Co.
Plumley	Robert L.	S/Sgt.	510th	
Poach	Steven	PFC	447th	Sub-Depot
Podany	George A.	Cpl.	508th	
Podolak	William J.	Cpl.	511th	
Podoske	Jack N.	1st Lt.	509th	
Poeschl	Rudolph J. Jr.	S/Sgt.	508th	
Poff	Eldridge O.	Sgt.	447th	Sub-Depot
Pokorny	Joe M.	PFC	509th	
Polgroszek	Edward	Sgt.	510th	
Policheno	Nick M.	PFC	1629th	Ord. S&M Co.
Polin	Max	2nd Lt.	511th	POW 10/9/43
Polk	Cecil E.	Sgt.	510th	KIA 10/9/43
Pollock	William E.	S/Sgt.	11th	St. Comp.
Pollyea	Albert	2nd Lt.	511th	POW 9/12/44
Polnow	Fred T.	Sgt.	509th	
Polocia	J.	1st Lt.	854th	Chemical Co.
Poltrone	Joseph F.	Sgt.	11th	St. Comp.
Pomerantz	Ralph	2nd Lt.	508th	
Pomeraux	Paul	Sgt.	511th	
Ponder	Robert E.	S/Sgt.	510th	
Ponehal	Anthony J.	T/Sgt.	509th	
Poole	John F.	Capt.	11th	St. Comp.
Poole	Louis E.	PFC	508th	
Poor	Roger L.	Sgt.	509th	
Pope	Ronald C.	T/Sgt.	447th	
Popelka	James C.	M/Sgt.	510th	Sub-Depot
Popes	Edward R.	Sgt.	509th	
Popp	Harlan E.	1st Lt.	511th	
Poppe	Theodore W.	T/Sgt.	508th	
Porche	Edward R.	S/Sgt.	511th	St. Comp.
Port	Ensley L.	M/Sgt.	11th	
Porter	Stanley F.	T/Sgt.	511th	
Posey	John D.	1st Lt.	510th	
Posti	Leonard A.	T/Sgt.	447th	
Poston	Paul J.	Capt.	1629th	Ord. S&M Co.
Potter	Evan A.	2nd Lt.	509th	
Potter	Ian L.	Sgt.	508th	
Potter	Leland C.	Sgt.	509th	POW 11/21/44
Poucher	Robert K.	1st Lt.	509th	
Povlotsky	Loys H.	S/Sgt.	509th	
Powell	Philip	S/Sgt.	511th	
Powell	Beverly B.	PFC	508th	
Powell	Frank W.	Cpl.	1206th	QM Company
Powell	Harvey W.	PFC	511th	
Powell	Orville P.	T/Sgt.	351st	HQ
Powell	Paul E.	Sgt.	11th	St. Comp.
Power	William M.	1st Lt.	508th	
Power	William R.	2nd Lt.	511th	
Power	Ronald W.	2nd Lt.	509th	
Powers	William E.	S/Sgt.	511th	
Powers	William M.	Sgt.	510th	
Powers	M. G.	S/Sgt.	510th	
Powers	Paul Z.	PFC	509th	
Powers	Ralph F.	Cpl.	508th	
Powers	Richard C.	Cpl.	511th	
Prater	A. R.	1st Lt.	508th	HQ
Prater	Lawrence A.	S/Sgt.	447th	Sub-Depot
Pratre	Ray E.	Sgt.	508th	Int'd 8/6/44
Pratt	Levi M.	PFC	509th	KIA 12/31/43
Preisser	Richard H.	1st Lt.	510th	
Presley	Robert G.	2nd Lt.	510th	POW 5/7/44
Pressel	David D.	T/Sgt.	510th	KIA 10/9/43
Pressman	William G.	S/Sgt.	11th	St. Comp.
Preston	Albert R. Jr.	S/Sgt.	511th	POW 9/12/44
Preston	J. C.	2nd Lt.	509th	
Preston	Robert E.	1st Lt.	854th	Chemical Co.
Prewitt	William A.	Sgt.	11th	St. Comp.
Prewitt	Arthur J.	Cpl.	508th	
Prezlomski	Ora G.	S/Sgt.	510th	
Price	Harold	T/Sgt.	509th	
Price	Chester L.	Pvt.	11th	St. Comp.
Price	Edgar L.	S/Sgt.	508th	
Price	Felix	PFC	509th	
Price	Robert H.	Cpl.	447th	Sub-Depot
Price	Warren A.	Sgt.	510th	
Price	Woodrow W.	T/Sgt.	447th	
Primm	John R.	S/Sgt.	508th	Sub-Depot
Primmer	Harry W.	T/Sgt.	509th	
Priode	Ralph D.	Sgt.	510th	
Prior	Richard O.	T/Sgt.	511th	
Priore	Anthony J.	Spec. 5	11th	St. Comp.
Pritchard	Perry J.	S/Sgt.	508th	POW 5/28/44
Probasco	Robert E. L.	F.O.	511th	POW 1/11/44
Procak	George J.	1st Lt.	510th	
Prochniak	Steven A.	S/Sgt.	447th	Sub-Depot
Prociak	Myron J.	T/Sgt.	510th	
Proctor	David	2nd Lt.	508th	
Proebstal	David F.	PFC	1629th	Ord. S&M Co.
Prokop	Edward J.	Sgt.	511th	KIA 8/6/44
Prosek	John L.	Sgt.	1061st	MP Company
Proulx	Albert A.	T/Sgt.	509th	
Provenzale	Peter	Sgt.	510th	
Provenzano	Vincent	2nd Lt.	511th	
Pruitt	Edward E.	Sgt.	508th	
Prusak	Frank W.	S/Sgt.	510th	
Pryor	Clifford T.	Capt.	508th	
Przybylko	Alex J.	PFC	511th	
Pudney	Chester S.	Spec. 5	11th	St. Comp.
Pudsby	Norman C.	PFC	1061st	
Puduto	Danti A.	T/Sgt.	511th	
Pugh	John H.	Sgt.	509th	
Pugh	Robert J.	2nd Lt.	511th	
Pugsley	Frederick G.	2nd Lt.	508th	
Puhowsky	William A.	S/Sgt.	510th	POW 12/31/43
Pulaski	Eugene C.	Sgt.	509th	
Pullen	Marshall R.	1st Lt.	509th	POW 5/24/44
Pulliam	Eugene T.	F.O.	510th	KIA 7/12/44
Pulver	Sidney C.	Sgt.	510th	POW 12/31/43
Purcell	James M.	Capt.	511th	
Purdum	John H. Jr.	Cpl.	447th	Sub-Depot
Purpura	James G.	Cpl.	2098th	Avn. F/F Pltn.
Purvis	Paul L.	1st Lt.	508th	
Putaansuu	Walfred	S/Sgt.	510th	KIA 6/11/43
Putman	John P.	Sgt.	351st	HQ
Putman	Lewis T.	S/Sgt.	447th	Sub-Depot
Putnam	Warren L.	2nd Lt.	511th	KIA 12/31/43
Pyles	Victor B.	S/Sgt.	508th	POW 1/11/44

Q

Last Name	First Name	Rank	Unit	Notes
Quarles	Robert C.	S/Sgt.	508th	
Queen	Benjamin	S/Sgt.	510th	
Quenneville	Ernest J.	Sgt.	11th	St. Comp.
Quick	Vincent R.	Cpl.	447th	Sub-Depot
Quigley	Neal M.	S/Sgt.	509th	
Quiles	Joseph R.	S/Sgt.	510th	
Quillin	James I.	PFC	508th	
Quimby	Norman C.	Cpl.	1061st	MP Company
Quinn	Adam W.	S/Sgt.	511th	
Quinn	Fred B.	2nd Lt.	508th	
Quinn	John H.	S/Sgt.	509th	
Quinn	Paul V.	1st Lt.	509th	

R

Last Name	First Name	Rank	Unit	Notes
Rackett	John W. Jr.	Cpl.	447th	Sub-Depot
Radcliff	Carl G.	Sgt.	508th	
Radcliffe	Cyril W.	Sgt.	510th	
Rader	Daniel L.	1st Lt.	509th	
Rader	Fred I.	PFC	509th	
Radiske	Robert F.	Cpl.	510th	
Railey	Lilburn R. Jr.	Pvt.	509th	
Rainier	Harry L.	S/Sgt.	509th	
Rajala	Raymond H.	S/Sgt.	511th	
Rakovec	Frank W.	S/Sgt.	510th	
Ralph	Frederick S.	Capt.	511th	KIA 8/6/44
Ralston	James Jr.	2nd Lt.	508th	
Ramas	A.	Pvt.	510th	
Ramey	Enos	Sgt.	510th	
Ramirez	Manuel G.	Cpl.	509th	
Ramsaur	Jacob A.	PFC	509th	
Ramsey	Allen S.	Cpl.	351st	HQ
Ramsey	Luther L.	Pvt.	11th	St. Comp.
Ramsey	Robert P.	S/Sgt.	351st	HQ
Ramsey	Samuel C.	S/Sgt.	511th	
Randall	William S.	Capt.	510th	
Randayko	Robert H.	1st Lt.	511th	
Ranella	Walter J.	M/Sgt.	508th	
	Joseph A.	PFC	510th	
		Sgt.	509th	

Surname	First	Rank	Unit	Notes	Surname	First	Rank	Unit	Notes	Surname	First	Rank	Unit	Notes
Ranjel	Florentino	PFC	510th		Reidl	Laurence E.	Spec. 4	1629th	Ord. S&M Co.	Robles	Joseph J.	T/Sgt.	510th	
Rankin	Walter W. Jr.	S/Sgt.	511th		Reilly	James A.	T/Sgt.	511th		Robyn	A.	T/Sgt.	511th	
Ransom	Warren A.	1st Lt.	510th		Reilly	James C.	Capt.	508th		Rodgers	Edward	1st Lt.	510th	
Ranum	Merwyn A.	Sgt.	510th	KIA 6/28/43	Reilly	Paul C.	S/Sgt.	510th		Rodgers	William H.	T/Sgt.	508th	
Rapaport	David I.	Sgt.	509th	Killed 6/8/45	Reimer	William P.	T/Sgt.	511th		Rodig	Albert F.	S/Sgt.	510th	
Raser	William R.	1st Lt.	510th		Reineke	Winfred O.	S/Sgt.	508th		Rodness	Dale M.	S/Sgt.	508th	
Rasko	John	2nd Lt.	511th	POW 9/12/44	Reiner	George B.	2nd Lt.	510th		Rodriguez	William III	S/Sgt.	508th	
Rasmussen	Merton H.	S/Sgt.	511th	MIA 8/6/44	Reiseman	Max A.	Cpl.	201st	Finance Sect.	Roe	Roderick J.	F.O.	509th	
Rasmussen	Raymond J.	1st Lt.	509th		Reish	Manning M.	T/Sgt.	509th	KIA 6/14/44	Roebuck	Harry S.	Sgt.	508th	
Ratcliffe	William R.	S/Sgt.	508th		Reising	George D.	2nd Lt.	509th		Roebuck	Voyd	Sgt.	510th	
Rauch	John C.	Sgt.	510th		Reitzammer	Frank H.	1st Lt.	508th		Roehlk	John L.	1st Lt.	509th	
Rauf	Ben F.	S/Sgt.	510th		Relfsteck	Edward A.	Sgt.	447th	Sub-Depot	Roesal	Charles J.	S/Sgt.	508th	KIA 7/29/43
Rauhut	Arthur C.	S/Sgt.	508th		Remeis	Robert L.	1st Lt.	510th		Roessler	Robert J.	2nd Lt.	508th	
Rawdon	Joseph W.	S/Sgt.	447th	Sub-Depot	Remore	Henry J.	1st Lt.	509th		Rogers	Bryant	Sgt.	509th	
Ray	Delbert P.	1st Lt.	509th		Renaud	Anthony J.	PFC	351st	HQ	Rogers	Carroll F.	Sgt.	447th	Sub-Depot
Ray	Jack A.	Sgt.	511th		Renick	Fidelis E.	PFC	509th		Rogers	Eugene	S/Sgt.	510th	
Ray	Joseph R.	Cpl.	509th		Renner	Clarence G.	PFC	511th		Rogers	Henry E.	Spec. 4	854th	Chemical Co.
Read	Matthew B.	Sgt.	351st		Renniger	Walter F.	Sgt.	511th		Rogers	James G.	1st Lt.	511th	
Reagan	Robert	PFC	447th		Reppard	Argonne F.	2nd Lt.	1061st		Rogers	Michael O.	PFC	508th	
Reagen	John G.	Capt.	11th		Reppert	Darwin D.	1st Lt.	509th		Rogge	Orvis M.	S/Sgt.	509th	
Real	Douglas F.	2nd Lt.	447th	POW 6/28/43	Reschetar	Miles M.	T/Sgt.	510th		Rogge	Walter B.	T/Sgt.	509th	
Reback	Lawrence A.	T/Sgt.	509th	St. Comp.	Resnik	Joseph W.	M/Sgt.	509th		Rogos	William H.	T/Sgt.	508th	
Rebich	Ralph W.	Cpl.	511th		Resse	John J.	S/Sgt.	511th		Rohde	Aurellio M.	Sgt.	510th	
Rebo	Orin C.	Sgt.	11th	St. Comp.	Reuce	Arville L.	PFC	509th		Rohr	Albert	2nd Lt.	508th	
Recor	Clyde E.	Cpl.	510th		Rex	Calvin	Cpl.	509th		Rohrbacher	Carl W.	2nd Lt.	509th	
Redman	Frank P. III	Sgt.	1206th	QM Company	Reynolds	Joseph F.	Sgt.	510th		Rohrbaugh	Robert M.	2nd Lt.	510th	POW 8/6/44
Redman	Robert P.	1st Lt.	511th		Reynolds	Jack C.	S/Sgt.	508th		Rohweder	John	1st Lt.	508th	
Redmann	Robert E.	2nd Lt.	510th	POW 6/28/43	Reynolds	Sam B.	T/Sgt.	510th		Roiseman	Keith G.	2nd Lt.	511th	
Redmond	James J.	1st Lt.	509th	St. Comp.	Reznik	Elliot	2nd Lt.	509th		Roland	Delbert C.	2nd Lt.	508th	
Redo	Ewald E.	Cpl.	11th		Rhein	Lester A.	T/Sgt.	509th	Killed 6/8/45	Roland	Gordon E.	S/Sgt.	511th	
Redus	Hubert B.	Sgt.	510th		Rhoden	Aubrey L.	S/Sgt.	510th		Rolfe	Glen W.	S/Sgt.	508th	
Reece	Calvin	Cpl.	510th		Rhodes	Charles N.	Capt.	508th		Rollins	Manning M.	T/Sgt.	509th	
Reed	Alan B.	1st Lt.	509th		Rhodes	Earl G.	Sgt.	11th	St. Comp.	Rollman	L. P.	Pvt.	11th	St. Comp.
Reed	Francis E.	S/Sgt.	509th		Rhodes	Wilmer C.	Sgt.	510th		Roman	Vincent	F.O.	509th	POW 1/22/45
Reed	John W.	S/Sgt.	510th		Riccardi	Angelo M.	S/Sgt.	509th		Romanelli	Kenneth L.	Sgt.	351st	HQ
Reed	Odie A.	T/Sgt.	511th		Ricci	Gaeton M.	Cpl.	1206th	QM Company	Romanishin	B. A.	Cpl.	1206th	QM Company
Reed	Rodney S.	T/Sgt.	510th		Ricci	John S.	Sgt.	509th	KIA 1/11/44	Romanski	Adam S.	Cpl.	447th	Sub-Depot
Redmond	Theodore W.	1st Lt.	508th	KIA 10/4/43	Rice	Mark O.	1st Lt.	511th		Romanski	Albin J.	M/Sgt.	351st	HQ
Reed	Troy D.	Cpl.	1629th	Ord. S&M Co.	Rice	William E.	2nd Lt.	510th		Romecki	Frank J.	PFC	508th	POW 12/31/43
Reeder	Daniel J.	S/Sgt.	509th		Richards	Charles K.	Sgt.	509th		Romero	Tomas	T/Sgt.	510th	
Reese	Earl E.	S/Sgt.	511th		Richards	George H.	Sgt.	510th		Romig	Eugene A.	Spec. 5	2098th	Avn. F/F Pltn.
Regrut	Pershing G.	Cpl.	351st	HQ	Richards	James R.	Cpl.	2098th	Avn. F/F Pltn.	Rooney	Harry P.	Capt.	509th	POW 8/17/43
Rehm	Stephen	T/Sgt.	1629th	Ord. S&M Co.	Richardson	Thomas B.	Capt.	351st	HQ	Rooney	Joseph T.	T/Sgt.	511th	
Reid	Ernest O. Jr.	2nd Lt.	509th	MP Company	Richardson	Franklin A.	Maj.	509th		Root	Walter S.	Cpl.	508th	
Reid	Hollis E.	PFC	1061st		Richardson	John W.	1st Lt.	511th		Roper	Peter	Pvt.	11th	St. Comp.
Reid	Lowell A.	Sgt.	509th	POW 5/30/44	Richardson	Robert H.	Cpl.	351st	HQ					
Reidinger	August J.	Sgt.	510th		Richardson	Thomas W.	Sgt.	511th	POW 10/3/44					
					Richey	Joe R.	2nd Lt.	509th						
					Rickenbacker	Robert C.	S/Sgt.	511th	POW 2/11/44					
					Rickett	John A.	Sgt.	508th						
					Riddle	Vance T.	T/Sgt.	510th						

Roper / Schmid

Surname	Given	Rank	Unit	Notes
Roper	Bernard G.	S/Sgt.	509th	
Roper	Leonard B.	Maj.	510th	
Roper	Richard J.	1st Lt.	508th	
Rosaly	Manuel H.	T/Sgt.	510th	
Rosberger	Sydney	Lt.	509th	
Rose	Benton W.	2nd Lt.	508th	
Rose	Joe W.	Cpl.	11th	St. Comp.
Rosebuck	Harry C.	T/Sgt.	508th	MIA 6/13/43
Rosen	James P.	T/Sgt.	510th	
Rosenberg	Earl D.	PFC	510th	
Rosenberg	Samuel	2nd Lt.	508th	POW 5/27/44
Rosenberger	David H.	Cpl.	854th	Chemical Co.
Rosenblatt	Norman	2nd Lt.	511th	
Rosenfield	Leonard	Pvt.	509th	
Rosenthal	Arthur L.	2nd Lt.	511th	
Roser	Carl G.	Cpl.	447th	Sub-Depot
Rosewall	Charles R.	2nd Lt.	511th	POW 8/17/43
Ross	Chester F.	S/Sgt.	508th	
Ross	John K.	S/Sgt.	511th	
Ross	Joseph	Cpl.	1206th	QM Company
Ross	Max L.	T/Sgt.	508th	
Ross	Paul C.	1st Lt.	510th	
Rossen	Henry R.	T/Sgt.	511th	Killed 6/8/45
Rossi	Silvio A.	T/Sgt.	511th	
Rossman	Charles F.	M/Sgt.	511th	POW 5/27/44
Rosynai	William A.	2nd Lt.	509th	Ord. S&M Co.
Roszyk	Henry M.	2nd Lt.	511th	
Roth	Sidney	PFC	1629th	
Rothschild	Norton L.	1st Lt.	509th	
Roussin	Joseph L.	Sgt.	1061st	MP Company
Routson	Walter E.	T/Sgt.	510th	POW 8/9/44
Row	Roderick J.	2nd Lt.	510th	POW 12/1/43
Rowan	John E.	1st Lt.	511th	St. Comp.
Rowe	J. R.	Sgt.	11th	St. Comp.
Rowe	Joe W.	Cpl.	511th	MIA 12/22/43
Rowe	William A.	S/Sgt.	511th	MIA 10/4/43
Rowland	Harold D.	Sgt.	447th	Sub-Depot
Rowland	William E.	T/Sgt.	509th	POW 5/27/44
Rowling	Carl D.	PFC	510th	St. Comp.
Rowlinson	Clarence A.	S/Sgt.	508th	
Rowsley	William R.	S/Sgt.	510th	
Royle	Thomas N.	Cpl.	511th	
Roysden	Avon	S/Sgt.	509th	
Roznaviak	Emil E.	PFC	510th	
Rozzell	George M.	Cpl.	509th	
Rubel	Abe II	1st Lt.	508th	KIA 5/23/44
Rubin	Frank	Cpl.	510th	
Rubinstein	Samuel L.	1st Lt.	510th	
Rucker	David H.	S/Sgt.	510th	
Rude	Francis R.	2nd Lt.	511th	
Rudisill	Donald B.	Cpl.	509th	
Rudy	Rupert A.	Sgt.	509th	
Rueb	Sherman L.	Sgt.	510th	
Ruefestein	Samuel L.	Cpl.	508th	
Rufeisen	Wallace J.	2nd Lt.	511th	
Rugel	Joseph Jr.	Sgt.	509th	
Ruhf	Ben F.	S/Sgt.	510th	
Ruis	Percy A.	PFC	11th	
Ruiz	A.	PFC	447th	
Rule	Albert F.	S/Sgt.	511th	
Rumage	Charles J.	S/Sgt.	510th	
Rumbaugh	Robert H.	S/Sgt.	511th	
Runnels	Harold H.	PFC	11th	
Ruoti	Vincent	Sgt.	11th	
Ruppert	Russell W.	T/Sgt.	1206th	QM Company
Rusanowsky	Peter P.	S/Sgt.	511th	
Ruschman	Elmer F.	T/Sgt.	510th	
Ruschmyer	Harold W.	T/Sgt.	511th	
Rush	Roy A.	Sgt.	509th	
Rushing	Jack T.	Sgt.	509th	POW 1/22/45
Rusicki	Valentine B.	2nd Lt.	511th	
Rusmisel	D. S.	PFC	11th	St. Comp.
Russell	Andrew J.	Maj.	509th	POW 5/29/43
Russell	Colonel J. Jr.	1st Lt.	11th	
Russell	Donald A.	T/Sgt.	510th	POW 7/19/44
Russell	Earl H.	2nd Lt.	508th	
Russell	Glenn D.	Sgt.	509th	
Russell	Melvin A.	Sgt.	511th	
Russeth	William M.	2nd Lt.	508th	KIA 5/23/44
Russler	Robert A.	Sgt.	447th	Sub-Depot
Russman	Fay C.	Sgt.	252nd	
Russo	Robert M.	Cpl.	508th	
Russo	Antonio R.	PFC	11th	St. Comp.
Ruth	Joseph F.	Sgt.	511th	
Ruth	David	2nd Lt.	509th	
Rutherford	L.	Cpl.	1206th	QM Company
Rutledge	Merlyn I.	2nd Lt.	509th	
Rutledge	Foster H.	Cpl.	447th	HQ
Rutter	Joseph E.	2nd Lt.	351st	
Ruwdun	Walter A.	PFC	510th	
Ruwe	Joseph W.	Sgt.	511th	
Ryan	Theodore E.	Cpl.	11th	St. Comp.
Ryan	Donald T.	2nd Lt.	509th	
Ryan	Edward J.	S/Sgt.	508th	
Ryan	Francis J.	S/Sgt.	510th	
Ryan	Joseph W.	T/Sgt.	510th	
Ryan	Robert E.	Sgt.	510th	POW 5/28/44
Ryan	Thomas M.	2nd Lt.	508th	
Rybaczewski	Teddy	1st Lt.	511th	
Ryerson	Douglas T.	Sgt.	508th	
Rymer	Herman K.	S/Sgt.	509th	

S

Surname	Given	Rank	Unit	Notes
Sabato	Albert C.	Cpl.	351st	HQ
Sabia	Michael J.	2nd Lt.	510th	
Sabourine	Joseph F.	Cpl.	510th	
Sado	John S.	Sgt.	510th	
Sadowski	Peter	S/Sgt.	447th	Sub-Depot
Sage	Lyle G.	Cpl.	511th	POW 6/28/43
Sage	Roy L.	2nd Lt.	511th	
Sahlstrom	Evert V.	2nd Lt.	509th	
Sahulcik	Robert J.	S/Sgt.	510th	
Sain	Randall R.	S/Sgt.	508th	POW 5/27/44
Saiva	Paul W.	T/Sgt.	508th	
Saker	Edward P.	Cpl.	511th	
Saks	Raymond L.	1st Lt.	510th	
Salb	Richard M.	2nd Lt.	508th	
Saldi	Frank J.	T/Sgt.	511th	
Saldis	Charles J.	S/Sgt.	511th	
Salerno	Anthony P.	S/Sgt.	447th	POW 9/12/44
Sall	Leon	Sgt.	11th	St. Comp.
Sallee	John L.	Cpl.	511th	
Salsman	Calvin	Sgt.	511th	
Salter	Jesse S.	PFC	508th	
Saltman	David B.	Cpl.	510th	
Saltsman	Robert H.	T/Sgt.	511th	
Saltys	Walter J.	2nd Lt.	509th	
Salva	Paul F.	Sgt.	509th	POW 1/17/45
Sameichios	E.	PFC	509th	
Samek	Frank J.	Sgt.	510th	
Samko	George Jr.	Cpl.	447th	Sub-Depot
Samson	Amos D.	S/Sgt.	508th	
San	Socie Robert	Sgt.	508th	Medical Disp.
Sanchez	Joe M.	T/Sgt.	511th	
Sanchez	Wallace A.	Capt.	509th	
Sandel	Robert A.	1st Lt.	508th	
Sander	William A.	Sgt.	510th	
Sanders	Boyd W.	Sgt.	510th	
Sanders	Lester H.	PFC	447th	Sub-Depot
Sanders	R. F.	PFC	11th	St. Comp.
Sanderson	Jack F.	S/Sgt.	508th	POW 6/28/43
Sanderson	Leroy F.	Capt.	11th	St. Comp.
Sandlin	Albert M.	Sgt.	508th	POW 9/12/44
Sanford	Everett L.	S/Sgt.	511th	POW 10/9/43
Sanford	Leon T.	Sgt.	509th	Int'd 6/21/44
Sanford	Robert O. Jr.	Sgt.	509th	
Santi	Lee A.	2nd Lt.	511th	POW 8/17/43
Santoya	Gilbert F.	Cpl.	1629th	Ord. S&M Co.
Sardone	Salvatore	PFC	11th	St. Comp.
Sarica	Dominick P.	Cpl.	508th	
Sarra	Marion	T/Sgt.	11th	St. Comp.
Sarver	Richard H.	Sgt.	508th	
Sass	Max L.	S/Sgt.	508th	
Saucedo	Fred C.	Sgt.	511th	KIA 3/18/44
Sauer	Emmett B.	S/Sgt.	511th	
Sauer	Eugene C.	2nd Lt.	510th	POW 9/12/44
Sauer	John W.	Sgt.	511th	POW 2/22/44
Sauer	Nicholas J.	T/Sgt.	509th	
Saunders	William T.	Sgt.	511th	KIA 8/6/44
Savage	Richard J.	S/Sgt.	1629th	Ord. S&M Co.
Saville	Ralph M.	1st Lt.	510th	
Sawyer	William L.	Pvt.	510th	
Saxon	Robert W.	S/Sgt.	509th	
Scaffadi	Alfred	T/Sgt.	510th	
Scanlan	Joseph W.	Maj.	201st	Finance Sect.
Scanlon	Michael J.	PFC	447th	Sub-Depot
Scanlon	Thomas M.	1st Lt.	511th	
Scarlett	Jack C.	1st Lt.	510th	
Scarlett	Ralph L. Jr.	Sgt.	508th	
Scerrati	George T.	S/Sgt.	509th	
Schacht	Warren E.	T/Sgt.	510th	
Schade	Herman A.	S/Sgt.	11th	St. Comp.
Schadegg	John J.	Capt.	511th	
Schaeffer	Ned H.	Sgt.	11th	St. Comp.
Schaeffer	Richard	S/Sgt.	509th	
Schafer	Robert	Maj.	11th	St. Comp.
Schaffer	William	2nd Lt.	508th	
Schappaugh	Earl P.	S/Sgt.	510th	
Schauer	Walter A.	PFC	508th	
Scheahen	John J.	Pvt.	510th	
Schechtman	Joseph	Cpl.	11th	St. Comp.
Scheidel	Norman	Pvt.	510th	
Schemper	Raymond G.	Pvt.	1629th	Ord. S&M Co.
Schenck	J. Hall	1st Lt.	508th	
Schenian	Charles C.	2nd Lt.	511th	
Schenk	Ficklin A.	Capt.	447th	Sub-Depot
Schepper	Raymond B.	PFC	511th	
Schick	Frederick G.	S/Sgt.	11th	St. Comp.
Schiffler	Robert A.	Capt.	510th	
Schiffman	Arnold	1st Lt.	509th	
Schilling	Frederick W.	Sgt.	508th	
Schillo	Wesley D.	PFC	511th	
Schimpf	Thomas J.	1st Lt.	447th	Sub-Depot
Schindele	Dale C.	Capt.	511th	
Schippert	George A.	PFC	854th	Chemical Co.
Schissel	Victor R.	S/Sgt.	511th	
Schitter	Wilfred S.	Sgt.	11th	St. Comp.
Schlaak	Ottmar F.	Capt.	510th	
Schlader	Robert L.	S/Sgt.	510th	
Schleis	Joseph E.	Cpl.	11th	St. Comp.
Schleitwiler	Norman W.	S/Sgt.	854th	Chemical Co.
Schleth	Martin J.	Sgt.	1629th	Ord. S&M Co.
Schlstrom	Evert V.	Cpl.	509th	
Schmbel	Harry K.	S/Sgt.	509th	
Schmid	Frank X.	S/Sgt.	509th	

Schmidt / Silcox

Last	First	Rank	Unit	Notes
Schmidt	George R.	Cpl.	447th	Sub-Depot
Schmidt	Harold C.	1st Lt.	508th	
Schmidt	Louis	Cpl.	510th	
Schmidt	Robert A.	2nd Lt.	508th	POW 5/27/44
Schmidt	Robert G.	Sgt.	510th	
Schmidt	Stephen G.	S/Sgt.	508th	
Schmitter	Gordon L.	S/Sgt.	508th	
Schmitz	George E.	Cpl.	509th	
Schmitz	William J.	2nd Lt.	511th	POW 2/22/44
Schmollinger	William F.	2nd Lt.	511th	POW 9/12/44
Schnacht	Warren E.	Pvt.	510th	
Schnackenberg	Martin J.	S/Sgt.	447th	Sub-Depot
Schneider	Allen R.	1st Lt.	508th	
Schneider	Herbert	1st Lt.	509th	
Schneider	Ludwig G.	S/Sgt.	1206th	QM Company
Schneider	Robert F.	S/Sgt.	511th	
Schneider	Robert H.	Capt.	508th	
Schneider	Victor W.	Sgt.	1206th	QM Company
Schneider	William C.	Sgt.	509th	
Schneider	William R.	S/Sgt.	511th	
Schnell	Duane W.	S/Sgt.	508th	
Schnell	Earl D.	S/Sgt.	510th	KIA 2/3/44
Schnuelle	Vernon R.	T/Sgt.	510th	
Schnur	Howard L.	1st Lt.	508th	
Schoen	Arthur	1st Lt.	510th	
Schoenian	Charles C.	2nd Lt.	511th	POW 9/12/44
Schofield	Giles R.	2nd Lt.	510th	
Schohan	Benjamin	1st Lt.	2098th	Avn. F/F Pltn.
Schoonmaker	Elmer L.	M/Sgt.	511th	
Schoonover	Grover C.	T/Sgt.	509th	
Schouck	Ernest L.	Sgt.	509th	
Schrader	Paul A.	PFC	351st	HQ
Schrader	Verne	S/Sgt.	508th	
Schrankel	John W.	S/Sgt.	511th	St. Comp.
Schrock	Edwin O.	S/Sgt.	11th	
Schroeder	Ernest A.	Cpl.	1061st	MP Company
Schroeder	Ralph E.	Sgt.	1629th	Ord. S&M Co.
Schubel	Harry S.	Cpl.	509th	
Schubert	Lester D.	Cpl.	447th	Sub-Depot
Schuch	Johnie	Sgt.	511th	
Schuele	Frederick D.	Cpl.	201st	Finance Sect.
Schuler	Leonard L.	T/Sgt.	511th	
Schulman	George L.	1st Lt.	11th	St. Comp.
Schulman	Irvin	2nd Lt.	447th	Sub-Depot
Schultz	Harold A.	Cpl.	511th	
Schultz	Edward H.	Cpl.	252nd	Medical Disp.
Schulz	Peter J.	T/Sgt.	510th	
Schulz	Arthur H.	1st Lt.		
Schulz	George J.	Cpl.	447th	Sub-Depot
Schuman	Robert A.	Cpl.	252nd	Medical Disp.
Schurfield	Warren F.	Sgt.	510th	

Last	First	Rank	Unit	Notes
Schuyler	Hugh F.	S/Sgt.	508th	
Schwabe	Raymond T.	T/Sgt.	508th	
Schwan	William C.	Sgt.	11th	St. Comp.
Schwartz	Bertram S.	T/Sgt.	510th	
Schwartz	Jack L.	T/Sgt.	11th	St. Comp.
Schwartz	Milton	1st Lt.	511th	
Schwartz	Ralph H.	2nd Lt.	511th	
Schwartz	Raymond T.	T/Sgt.	508th	
Schwartz	Robert C.	2nd Lt.	508th	KIA 8/16/44
Schwartzberg	Harry	S/Sgt.	511th	
Schwartzenberg	Oscar C.	2nd Lt.	510th	
Schweiger	Marvin I.	Sgt.	11th	St. Comp.
Scileppi	James G.	PFC	508th	
Scillavou	G. J.	1st Lt.	508th	
Scodel	Alvin	2nd Lt.	508th	POW 5/14/43
Scollard	Jerry C.	2nd Lt.	509th	
Scott	Crewdson D.	S/Sgt.	511th	
Scott	Elmer C.	S/Sgt.	509th	
Scott	Glenn M.	S/Sgt.	508th	
Scott	Harold B.	T/Sgt.	511th	
Scott	James E.	S/Sgt.	511th	
Scott	John L.	Maj.	351st	HQ
Scott	Joseph A.	Cpl.	447th	Sub-Depot
Scott	Lavern R.	Spec. 5	511th	
Scott	Wallace R.	T/Sgt.	508th	Sub-Depot
Scozzafava	William J.	Sgt.	447th	
Scruggs	Kenneth A.	2nd Lt.	510th	
Seagraves	William L.	Cpl.	351st	HQ
Seale	Jack W.	1st Lt.	511th	
Seale	Garland T.	Cpl.	11th	St. Comp.
Seaman	Jasper C.	S/Sgt.	11th	
Seaman	Raymond G.	Sgt.	511th	KIA 5/28/44
Seaton	Robert A.	1st Lt.	508th	
Secrest	James S.	Capt.	508th	
Sedlacek	Wendell	2nd Lt.	509th	
Sedlak	Zdenek	S/Sgt.	508th	
See	Gilbert S.	S/Sgt.	509th	
Seeds	Gilbert F.	Cpl.	511th	
Seeger	Harry E.	T/Sgt.	508th	Sub-Depot
Seelbach	Robert J.	S/Sgt.	447th	
Seely	Verner	2nd Lt.	508th	
Sefinch	Louis F.	S/Sgt.	508th	
Segasser	Verner	S/Sgt.	510th	
Seger	Marshall J.	Pvt.	509th	
Seibert	Arthur W.	S/Sgt.	510th	
Seibert	Harold A.	S/Sgt.	1061st	MP Company
Seibert	James F.	2nd Lt.	509th	
Seidell	Robert E.	S/Sgt.	508th	
Sellers	Frank	2nd Lt.	511th	
Sellers	William A.	S/Sgt.	508th	
Selnick	Jacob S.	T/Sgt.	509th	

Last	First	Rank	Unit	Notes
Selover	Frank L.	S/Sgt.	511th	HQ
Seltzer	John L.	Maj.	351st	Chemical Co.
Semenchuk	Eugene	PFC	854th	
Senger	Robert J.	1st Lt.	447th	Sub-Depot
Sengstock	Edgar F.	1st Lt.	508th	POW 5/27/44
Senk	Leon	T/Sgt.	509th	
Senn	Warren R.	S/Sgt.	508th	
Sestak	Stanley J.	Cpl.	510th	
Severtson	Conrad I.	Sgt.	508th	Sub-Depot
Sevier	Oscar W.	Cpl.	11th	St. Comp.
Sevold	Leo O.	Cpl.	447th	Sub-Depot
Sewell	Robert E.	S/Sgt.	508th	
Sexter	Donald F.	S/Sgt.	11th	St. Comp.
Sexton	Arthur D.	1st Lt.	509th	
Sexton	Elisha J.	Sgt.	511th	
Seymour	Robert J.	2nd Lt.	11th	St. Comp.
Shadduck	Johnny D.	S/Sgt.	11th	
Shadoan	Louis M.	S/Sgt.	510th	
Shaeffer	Richard	S/Sgt.	509th	
Shafer	Robert C.	2nd Lt.	508th	POW 6/14/44
Shaffer	Verl R.	Maj.	511th	
Shalenko	John	T/Sgt.	509th	
Shamaley	Lee J.	Cpl.	351st	HQ
Shames	Joseph P.	1st Lt.	511th	
Shanks	John	PFC	510th	
Stanley	Charles W.	2nd Lt.	510th	POW 6/28/43
Stanley	William C.	2nd Lt.	509th	
Shapiro	Morrey H.	Sgt.	11th	
Shapurka	Thomas	Pvt.	510th	
Sharkey	John C.	Cpl.	351st	HQ
Sharp	Commodore I.	T/Sgt.	510th	POW 10/9/43
Sharp	Earl R.	S/Sgt.	509th	
Sharp	Elmer F.	Sgt.	11th	St. Comp.
Sharry	Fred A.	Pvt.	508th	
Shattuck	James H.	1st Lt.	510th	
Shaver	Donald L.	2nd Lt.	508th	POW 10/9/43
Shaver	Benjamin O.	1st Lt.	508th	
Shaw	James N.	Capt.	511th	St. Comp.
Shaw	Charles M.	2nd Lt.	508th	
Shaw	Leonard M.	Sgt.	11th	St. Comp.
Shaw	Vernon W.	Cpl.	508th	St. Comp.
Sheans	Wiley W.	S/Sgt.	511th	
Shearer	Leo E.	Sgt.	509th	
Shearer	George F. Jr.	S/Sgt.	1206th	POW 1/17/45 QM Company
Shearer	Joseph E.	S/Sgt.	11th	St. Comp.
Shebasta	Ross	Cpl.	1206th	QM Company
Sheets	Robert J.	Cpl.	510th	
Sheets	Charlie R.	1st Lt.	511th	POW 8/6/44
Sheir	Douglas L.	2nd Lt.	510th	
Shelden	Milton A.	S/Sgt.	447th	Sub-Depot
Shelton	Tom N.	T/Sgt.	509th	

Last	First	Rank	Unit	Notes
Shenk	Luther M.	S/Sgt.	511th	
Sheperd	James R.	M/Sgt.	509th	
Sheperd	Robert W.	Sgt.	511th	POW 12/5/44
Shepherd	Clarence R.	Sgt.	510th	
Shepherd	Walter J.	1st Lt.	511th	
Shepherd	George W. Jr.	2nd Lt.	510th	POW 9/8/44
Shera	Rubin	S/Sgt.	509th	
Sherer	Robert C.	1st Lt.	510th	
Sherfy	Paul F.	S/Sgt.	508th	
Sheridan	Clyde F.	Cpl.	511th	
Sherman	Lavern W.	T/Sgt.	509th	KIA 1/11/44
Sherman	Milton	1st Lt.	511th	
Sherrell	Donald E.	T/Sgt.	509th	
Sherril	Hickory C.	Sgt.	511th	
Sherrill	Edgar J.	S/Sgt.	447th	Sub-Depot
Sherrondy	Louis G.	Sgt.	508th	
Sherwood	Edward J.	S/Sgt.	510th	
Shields	Charles L.	S/Sgt.	510th	
Shields	Horace H.	S/Sgt.	511th	
Shimsky	Jack	Cpl.	2098th	Avn. F/F Pltn.
Shindeldecker	Donald D.	S/Sgt.	508th	
Shinlay	Paul A.	T/Sgt.	509th	
Shipman	Doyle E. Jr.	PFC	1061st	MP Company
Shiraldi	Frank J.	S/Sgt.	511th	
Shircel	Cyril F.	Sgt.	509th	
Shirley	Gaines A.	PFC	1206th	QM Company
Shirley	Orval J.	1st Lt.	511th	
Shirts	George F.	Sgt.	509th	KIA 1/22/45
Shlauter	Edward A.	S/Sgt.	509th	
Shone	Benjamin F.	Cpl.	511th	
Shortsleeves	Gerald H.	M/Sgt.	509th	
Shouck	Ernest	Sgt.	508th	
Shrewsbury	George H.	Sgt.	511th	
Shrom	David R.	S/Sgt.	508th	Sub-Depot
Shults	Clellan R.	Pvt.	447th	
Shumake	George C.	1st Lt.	508th	POW 2/22/44
Shuss	Robert V.	2nd Lt.	510th	
Shwayder	Irving J.	2nd Lt.	511th	Medical Disp.
Siano	James V.	Sgt.	252nd	
Sianowick	Theodore E.	S/Sgt.	509th	
Sichel	Stanley H.	1st Lt.	508th	
Siciliano	Gus Jr.	S/Sgt.	511th	POW 9/12/44
Sidorick	Nicholas S.	Sgt.	511th	
Sie	Edward J.	Spec. 5	1061st	MP Company
Siebert	James F.	Sgt.	1061st	MP Company
Siegel	Clyde L.	T/Sgt.	510th	
Siegelman	Joseph	Cpl.	509th	
Sier	Douglas J.	2nd Lt.	351st	HQ
Signorelli	Joseph V.	T/Sgt.	511th	KIA 7/29/44
Signoretti	Guido	Sgt.	511th	
Sigur	James P.	PFC	511th	
Silcox	Frank W.	Pvt.	511th	

Silva / Spooner

Last Name	First Name	Rank	Unit	Notes
Silva	Balthazar M.	S/Sgt.	447th	Sub-Depot
Silver	Samuel	S/Sgt.	508th	
Silver	William C. Jr.	2nd Lt.	510th	
Silverman	Abraham	Sgt.	508th	KIA 10/9/43
Silverman	Samuel M.	Sgt.	509th	
Silvia	Stanley I.	PFC	511th	
Silvio	Antone	F.O.	1206th	QM Company
Simcich	Victor V.	Pvt.	508th	KIA 11/21/44
Simmons	John J.	Pvt.	11th	St. Comp.
Simmons	Andrew L.	Pvt.	1206th	QM Company
Simmons	Arnold J.	PFC	11th	St. Comp.
Simmons	Clarence M.	2nd Lt.	510th	
Simmons	Clyde R.	S/Sgt.	510th	POW 1/11/44
Simmons	Harry G.	1st Lt.	511th	
Simmons	Max C.	S/Sgt.	508th	Killed 2/26/43
Simmons	William E.	T/Sgt.	509th	
Simms	Alvin	S/Sgt.	511th	Int'd 3/18/44
Simms	Samuel R.	1st Lt.	509th	
Simon	Edwin J.	2nd Lt.	510th	
Simon	James G.	1st Lt.	1206th	QM Company
Simon	Richard B.	S/Sgt.	509th	
Simonetta	Carlo J.	PFC	1061st	
Simons	Charles H.	Sgt.	508th	MP Company
Simons	Chester W.	T/Sgt.	510th	
Simons	Louis J.	S/Sgt.	509th	
Simons	William C.	1st Lt.	509th	Int'd 10/7/44
Simonsma	Johnson W.	2nd Lt.	510th	Avn. F/F Pltn.
Simpson	Alfred K. Jr.	2nd Lt.	2098th	
Simpson	James W.	Sgt.	510th	
Simpson	Lonnie T.	1st Lt.	511th	
Sinewskii	Nicholas	Sgt.	509th	
Singletary	Alva B.	PFC	11th	St. Comp.
Singletary	Hugh L.	PFC	1206th	QM Company
Singleton	James D.	Pvt.	511th	POW 5/28/44
Singleton	James S.	S/Sgt.	511th	KIA 9/8/44
Singleton	Phillip M.	1st Lt.	509th	KIA 2/6/45
Singleton	William	1st Lt.	511th	
Sinnott	John H.	PFC	511th	KIA 3/18/44
Sinreich	Frank J.	2nd Lt.	509th	St. Comp.
Sipher	John A.	1st Lt.	11th	St. Comp.
Sisk	Melvin D.	Pvt.	1061st	MP Company
Skalsky	Leo	S/Sgt.	509th	
Skarzinski	Joe G.	S/Sgt.	508th	
Skeen	Vernon C.	S/Sgt.	510th	
Skene	George J.	2nd Lt.	508th	
Skerker	William	1st Lt.	11th	
Skiles	Daniel A.	PFC	11th	St. Comp.
Skinner	Edwin D.	2nd Lt.	508th	St. Comp.
Skinner	George W.	S/Sgt.	511th	
Skinner	Stanley M.	PFC	509th	
Skinner	Walter C.	T/Sgt.	510th	
Skinner	William G.	M/Sgt.	447th	Sub-Depot
Skinner	Winfield F.	PFC	11th	St. Comp.
Skoglund	Donald G.	S/Sgt.	511th	
Skow	Woodrow H.	Cpl.	447th	Sub-Depot
Slack	Bob B.	S/Sgt.	509th	
Slater	Charles E.	S/Sgt.	511th	
Slater	Henry G. Jr.	1st Lt.	511th	
Slater	William C. Jr.	T/Sgt.	510th	
Slick	Fred R.	F.O.	511th	
Slick	Galen	PFC	1061st	MP Cmpany
Siger	Harry L.	Sgt.	509th	
Siloette	C. I.	Sgt.	509th	
Sloan	Guthrie T.	S/Sgt.	509th	
Sloan	Jack W.	Cpl.	510th	
Sloboda	Andrew	S/Sgt.	509th	
Sloboda	Joseph W.	2nd Lt.	509th	KIA 3/22/44
Slossen	Wyman C.	2nd Lt.	508th	Ord. S&M Co.
Small	Arnold J.	Cpl.	1629th	
Smallwood	Jack L.	S/Sgt.	509th	
Smart	James E.	S/St.	510th	
Smetana	Adolph J.	Capt.	511th	
Smick	Paul W.	1st Lt.	511th	POW 5/14/43
Smigiera	Teddy A.	F.O.	509th	POW 12/5/44
Smiljanic	Emil R.	Maj.	511th	HQ
Smith	Arthur J.	S/Sgt.	510th	
Smith	Charles D.	T/Sgt.	511th	
Smith	Cleman N.	Sgt.	351st	POW 8/17/43
Smith	Dallas M.	S/Sgt.	511th	
Smith	David D. Jr.	1st Lt.	509th	St. Comp.
Smith	Donald W.	1st Lt.	510th	POW 12/31/43
Smith	Earl J.	F.O.	509th	POW 1/11/44
Smith	Edward B.	Sgt.	511th	
Smith	Edwin C.	Cpl.	1206th	QM Company
Smith	Eugene R.	1st Lt.	509th	
Smith	Forbes M.	S/Sgt.	511th	Chemical Co.
Smith	Frederick A.	Spec. 5	854th	Sub-Depot
Smith	George E.	T/Sgt.	447th	POW 8/6/44
Smith	Harold R.	2nd Lt.	511th	Ord. S&M Co.
Smith	Howard C.	Cpl.	1629th	
Smith	Howard F.	S/Sgt.	511th	POW 12/31/43
Smith	Howard G.	Capt.	510th	POW 5/27/44
Smith	James C.	S/Sgt.	508th	
Smith	John J.	1st Lt.	509th	
Smith	John M. Jr.	1st Lt.	511th	
Smith	John R.	Sgt.	447th	Sub-Depot
Smith	John S.	Sgt.	511th	
Smith	John T.	Sgt.	447th	
Smith	John W.	Sgt.	511th	
Smith	Joseph R.	Sgt.	447th	
Smith	Leroy C.	Sgt.	447th	
Smith	Leslie E.	Sgt.	511th	
Smith	Luther	Sgt.	509th	
Smith	Mart G. Jr.	T/Sgt.	511th	
Smith	Mike	1st Lt.	1629th	Ord. S&M Co.
Smith	Otis G.	S/Sgt.	511th	POW 8/6/44
Smith	Paul J.	F.O.	511th	
Smith	Paul M.	T/Sgt.	508th	
Smith	Raymond L.	S/Sgt.	509th	
Smith	Raymond M.	S/Sgt.	511th	
Smith	Richard E.	S/Sgt.	509th	
Smith	Richard M.	Sgt.	509th	Int'd 10/7/44
Smith	Robert E.	S/Sgt.	509th	POW 1/17/45
Smith	Robert E.	1st Lt.	510th	Killed 6/8/45
Smith	Robert L. Jr.	S/Sgt.	509th	
Smith	Roy N.	Cpl.	11th	St. Comp.
Smith	Teed O.	S/Sgt.	509th	Killed 6/8/45
Smith	Vernis	Sgt.	509th	
Smith	Vernon E.	F.O.	509th	
Smith	Vincent F.	S/Sgt.	511th	POW 8/6/44
Smith	Walter E.	T/Sgt.	510th	
Smith	Wayne R.	1st Lt.	509th	
Smith	William A.	Cpl.	508th	
Smith	William A.	S/Sgt.	509th	
Smith	William M.	S/Sgt.	511th	
Smith	William R.	Capt.	511th	
Smith	Willis D.	1st Lt.	508th	POW 12/31/43
Smithline	David A.	2nd Lt.	508th	POW 3/22/44
Smithson	James H.	PFC	1629th	Ord. S&M Co.
Smolek	Alfred J.	S/Sgt.	511th	
Smouse	Lester J.	S/Sgt.	509th	
Smyanski	Edward J.	1st Lt.	510th	
Smyrski	Walter J.	Sgt.	509th	
Smyth	James D.	T/Sgt.	511th	
Snare	K.	Cpl.	508th	St. Comp.
Snedegar	Clay B.	Capt.	511th	
Snell	Charles R.	S/Sgt.	509th	
Snider	Charles H.	PFC	2098th	Avn. F/F Pltn.
Sninchak	John W.	T/Sgt.	510th	Killed 5/7/43
Snipes	Roy O.	1st Lt.	509th	
Snow	Wiley W.	Sgt.	511th	
Snowball	Jack W.	S/Sgt.	510th	KIA 5/27/44
Snyder	Chester J.	S/Sgt.	509th	
Snyder	David M.	2nd Lt.	510th	KIA 8/6/44
Snyder	Forest A.	T/Sgt.	511th	
Snyder	Franklin Jr.	PFC	509th	
Snyder	John V.	Cpl.	11th	St. Comp.
Snyder	Norman S.	Capt.	1629th	Ord. S&M Co.
Snyder	Samuel A.	S/Sgt.	510th	Killed 1/28/45
Snyder	Walter R.	Sgt.	510th	
Sockany	William L.	S/Sgt.	508th	MIA 2/21/44
Soden	Thelbert A.	Sgt.	508th	
Sodering	Peter A.	M/Sgt.	351st	
Sofness	Harold E.	T/Sgt.	511th	HQ
Sokol	George	Sgt.	511th	
Sokolowski	Stanley A.	T/Sgt.	508th	
Sokolski	Arthur F.	Cpl.	511th	
Soles	Carl E.	S/Sgt.	511th	Avn. F/F Pltn.
Solis	Jess A.	Spec. 5	2098th	KIA 2/6/45
Soller	Robert E.	F.O.	509th	
Sollers	Robert B.	S/Sgt.	511th	
Solomon	Arthur	Sgt.	508th	
Solover	F. L.	Pvt.	11th	St. Comp.
Soltys	John	Sgt.	509th	
Soltys	Walter J.	Sgt.	509th	
Sommer	Fred J.	Cpl.	11th	St. Comp.
Sommer	Robert E.	F.O.	510th	
Sondeno	Joseph O.	S/Sgt.	510th	Sub-Depot
Sones	Lee W.	1st Lt.	509th	
Songer	George A.	S/Sgt.	508th	
Sorge	Marlowe B.	S/Sgt.	510th	
Sorosiak	Aloyisus F.	PFC	447th	
Sosnowski	Harry R.	M/Sgt.	510th	
Soto	Wenseslao A.	S/Sgt.	510th	
Soucy	Herman J.	Cpl.	1629th	Ord. S&M Co.
Souder	Frederick J.	S/Sgt.	509th	
Southcott	Walter J.	Capt.	510th	
Sowell	Alonzo J.	1st Lt.	511th	
Sowell	Thomas R.	Sgt.	508th	Killed 2/26/43
Spader	Herman J.	PFC	511th	
Spangler	George A.	T/Sgt.	509th	
Sparby	Arnold S.	PFC	11th	
Sparzak	H. E.	Sgt.	510th	
Spaulding	Frank S.	T/Sgt.	511th	
Speak	Howard	S/Sgt.	508th	MIA 2/21/44
Speaker	John R.	1st Lt.	508th	
Spears	Billy R.	1st Lt.	509th	
Speer	Edward A.	Sgt.	511th	
Speers	Jack L.	T/Sgt.	508th	POW 10/4/43
Speiser	Morrie J.	2nd Lt.	509th	
Spence	William H.	Cpl.	1629th	Ord. S&M Co.
Spence	Douglas J.	Capt.	510th	Killed 1/28/45
Spencer	John A.	1st Lt.	510th	
Spencer	Robert M.	T/Sgt.	409th	
Spencer	Bruce A.	2nd Lt.	509th	
Speruzzi	William H.	M/Sgt.	351st	
Spicer	Marshall C.	T/Sgt.	511th	
Spierline	Felix	PFC	508th	
Spika	Irchel E.	1st Lt.	509th	
Spiller	Samuel H.			
Spinning				
Spivey				
Spoerri				
Spoonemore				
Spooner				

Spooner / Swiontek

Last Name	First Name	Rank	Unit	Notes
Spooner	William H.	Sgt.	447th	Sub-Depot
Sporrey	Warren H.	2nd Lt.	509th	
Spradley	Russell F.	T/Sgt.	511th	
Sprecher	Gordon A.	1st Lt.	508th	
Sprenger	Gerald W.	S/Sgt.	510th	
Sprott	James H.	S/Sgt.	509th	
Squires	Bradley E.	2nd Lt.	511th	POW 11/3/43
Sroczynski	Peter A.	Sgt.	447th	Sub-Depot
Sroka	Adam K.	Sgt.	511th	
St. Amant	John S.	Sgt.	511th	
St. Clair	Frank M.	Cpl.	511th	
St. Jean	Francis V.	PFC	11th	St. Comp.
St. Peter	Norman J.	S/Sgt.	509th	POW 12/31/43
St. Thomas	Edward L.	Sgt.	511th	St. Comp.
Stachniewicz	Walter	Sgt.	508th	
Stackhouse	Carl B.	1st Lt.	511th	
Stadelman	Victor A.	Sgt.	351st	HQ
Straehely	Alfred	T/Sgt.	509th	
Stafford	George A.	S/Sgt.	511th	POW 5/28/44
Stahl	Carl	1st Lt.	508th	
Stahl	Charles D.	PFC	1061st	MP Company
Staley	Harold W.	T/Sgt.	11th	St. Comp.
Stallings	Luther E. Jr.	Sgt.	509th	
Stamper	Nixon C.	2nd Lt.	510th	POW 5/7/44
Stamps	George M.	1st Lt.	511th	
Stancl	Heber T.	M/Sgt.	511th	
Standefer	George J.	PFC	509th	St. Comp.
Stanek	William S.	T/Sgt.	511th	
Stanford	Stanley V.	S/Sgt.	510th	
Stanley	Walter C.	T/Sgt.	508th	
Stanowick	James E.	Capt.	11th	
Stanzel	Theodore N.	S/Sgt.	509th	
Stark	Arno E.	2nd Lt.	511th	POW 2/24/44
Stark	Fred	PFC	11th	St. Comp.
Starks	Leland R.	PFC	509th	
Starr	Oscar B. Jr.	2nd Lt.	511th	
Starr	Roy P.	2nd Lt.	509th	POW 5/29/43
Starratt	Eldon L.	1st Lt.	511th	
Startwood	Harold D.	S/Sgt.	510th	
Starzynski	David L.	1st Lt.	351st	HQ
Stauff	Earl A.	Sgt.	510th	
Stealey	Michael	S/Sgt.	510th	
Stear	Michael W.	1st Lt.	510th	
Stecker	Richard C.	2nd Lt.	509th	
Steed	Daniel H.	F.O.	511th	
Steele	Melvin W.	2nd Lt.	511th	POW 9/12/44
Steele	Patrick P.	S/Sgt.	509th	

Last Name	First Name	Rank	Unit	Notes
Steiferman	Johnnie F.	Sgt.	351st	HQ
Steinbach	George L.	2nd Lt.	510th	
Steiner	Leander C.	Cpl.	1629th	Ord. S&M Co.
Steiner	Sidney B.	1st Lt.	508th	
Steir	John M.	PFC	508th	
Steitz	Warren C.	Capt.	351st	HQ
Stelley	Charles H.	Cpl.	510th	
Stennett	Frank A.	1st Lt.	511th	
Stentiford	Nolan L.	2nd Lt.	510th	
Stentiford	Archibald D.	T/Sgt.	510th	
Stephen	Melroy R.	S/Sgt.	510th	
Stephen	Richard C.	PFC	11th	St. Comp.
Stephens	Avery G.	S/Sgt.	510th	
Stephens	Charles J.	PFC	120th	QM Company
Stephens	Edward B.	Sgt.	509th	
Stephens	Franklin E.	PFC	351st	HQ
Stephens	James L.	Pvt.	510th	
Stephenson	Kenneth L.	T/Sgt.	509th	
Stepp	Norman J.	1st Lt.	509th	
Sterling	William A.	M/Sgt.	509th	
Sterling	Allen E.	2nd Lt.	509th	Int'd 10/7/44
Stern	Adrian J.	Sgt.	511th	
Sterns	Edward J.	Cpl.	509th	
Stetler	Francis E.	T/Sgt.	511th	POW 10/4/43
Stevens	Morris	Sgt.	508th	
Stevens	George R.	2nd Lt.	510th	
Stevens	Jack G.	Sgt.	447th	Sub-Depot
Stevens	Charles A.	Capt.	511th	Int'd 10/7/44
Stevens	Charles E.	S/Sgt.	509th	
Stevenson	Charles N.	2nd Lt.	509th	
Stevenson	Daniel F.	2nd Lt.	510th	
Steward	Ernest E.	1st Lt.	508th	
Stewart	Glenn M.	1st Lt.	511th	
Stewart	Jacob F.	T/Sgt.	508th	
Stewart	Joseph L.	Sgt.	511th	
Stewart	Thad C.	Cpl.	510th	
Stewart	Vernal A.	Lt. Col.	508th	
Stewart	R.C.	S/Sgt.	511th	
Stewart	Richard H.	S/Sgt.	510th	POW 5/14/43
Stickford	Stanley M.	2nd Lt.	509th	POW 2/22/44
Stickney	William J.	PFC	511th	
Stiever	Howard D.	Sgt.	510th	
Stiller	Herbert L.	Cpl.	509th	
Stilley	Anthony J.	PFC	511th	
	John C.	Sgt.	508th	
	Frederick A.	T/Sgt.	510th	

Last Name	First Name	Rank	Unit	Notes
Stilwell	John W.	F.O.	510th	
Stine	Henry A.	T/Sgt.	508th	
Stinebaugh	Archie L.	Sgt.	511th	POW 2/24/44
Stinett	Clarence W.	PFC	509th	
Stinson	Nolan L. Jr.	2nd Lt.	510th	
Stobaugh	Frank C.	Sgt.	509th	
Stockman	Walter	Capt.	510th	
Stoker	Ernest C.	PFC	508th	
Stokke	Ross H.	1st Lt.	509th	
Stolicker	Donald C.	Pvt.	511th	
Stone	Bruce M.	S/Sgt.	511th	
Stone	Francis M.	1st Lt.	509th	
Stone	John L.	S/Sgt.	510th	
Stoneback	Walter J.	T/Sgt.	510th	
Stormer	William H.	Sgt.	510th	
Storms	George R.	T/Sgt.	509th	
Stottlemeyer	Victor H.	2nd Lt.	509th	Int'd 10/7/44
Stout	George W.	Cpl.	511th	
Stout	Gordon	Cpl.	511th	
Stovel	George R.	T/Sgt.	508th	
Stover	Lawrence P.	1st Lt.	509th	
Strange	Paul D.	Capt.	508th	POW 10/4/43
Strassburger	Wilson R.	1st Lt.	511th	KIA 8/6/44
Stratakis	Eugene C.	S/Sgt.	508th	KIA 2/24/44
Stratton	Stylianos L.	2nd Lt.	510th	
Straub	Robert B.	Capt.	509th	HQ
Strautman	Philip T.	Capt.	252nd	Medical Disp.
Straw	Everett L.	S/Sgt.	509th	
Straw	Ezekial A.	2nd Lt.	508th	
Strawn	Paul D.	2nd Lt.	509th	POW 2/22/44
Streetman	David R.	Sgt.	510th	
Strick	Sinclair	S/Sgt.	510th	
Stricklan	John H.	1st Lt.	510th	KIA 7/12/44
Strickland	Percie B.	1st Lt.	509th	
Strickland	Whittie A.	Cpl.	1629th	Ord. S&M Co.
Stroh	William W.	Sgt.	510th	HQ
Strohmeyer	William R.	T/Sgt.	511th	
Strom	Fenton D.	Sgt.	510th	MIA 5/19/43
Strosky	Martin L.	2nd Lt.	509th	
Strouse	Samuel	1st Lt.	511th	
Strozza	James W.	Sgt.	509th	
Strumolo	Joseph	Cpl.	510th	
Stryker	Louis S.	Lt. Col.	508th	
Stuart	Roy T.	S/Sgt.	511th	
Stuart	Dale C.	1st Lt.	510th	
Stuart	Raymond C.	S/Sgt.	509th	
Stubblefield	Virgil R.	S/Sgt.	510th	Finance Sect.
Stuemke	Jack H.	Sgt.	201st	
Stull	Elmer A.	S/Sgt.	509th	
Stump	Nelson E.	Sgt.	508th	
Stump	Donald H.	1st Lt.	511th	
	Virgil R.	S/Sgt.	510th	

Last Name	First Name	Rank	Unit	Notes
Sturgel	Mark P.	Cpl.	508th	
Sturtevant	Gordon W.	Sgt.	510th	
Stussy	Henry W.	PFC	1629th	Ord. S&M Co.
Subora	Walter R.	S/Sgt.	510th	
Such	Stephen P.	Cpl.	11th	St. Comp.
Sucharewicz	J. P.	T/Sgt.	510th	
Suddock	Dwight E.	Sgt.	1061st	MP Company
Suddreth	James M.	Cpl.	508th	
Sugg	Charles H.	1st Lt.	509th	
Suit	William J.	1st Lt.	508th	KIA 8/27/43
Sukup	Arthur J.	Sgt.	509th	
Sulak	Clement J.	Sgt.	509th	
Sullivan	Edward L.	Capt.	510th	KIA 5/15/43
Sullivan	George L. Jr.	1st Lt.	508th	Killed 5/7/43
Sullivan	Joseph W.	Cpl.	510th	
Sullivan	Noel P.	F.O.	511th	
Summers	Odie W.	S/Sgt.	510th	
Summers	Charles D.	S/Sgt.	511th	KIA 5/15/43
Summers	Charlie M.	1st Lt.	510th	
Summers	Henry G.	2nd Lt.	508th	
Summers	James F.	S/Sgt.	510th	
Sumstrom	Robert B.	Sgt.	509th	
Suozzo	Virgil V.	Sgt.	508th	POW 10/9/43
Surges	Russell R.	S/Sgt.	447th	Sub-Depot
Surprise	Mario	T/Sgt.	511th	KIA 10/4/43
Surratt	Charles L.	2nd Lt.	511th	POW 9/12/44
Susman	Daniel H.	S/Sgt.	509th	POW 5/24/44
Suttle	Hubert L.	T/Sgt.	508th	
Sutton	Saul E.	Sgt.	510th	POW 1/11/44
Sutton	Lewis E.	Sgt.	508th	
Swaim	Richard X.	Capt.	509th	
Swain	Robert	PFC	1629th	Ord. S&M Co.
Swaner	Roland C.	S/Sgt.	508th	
Swanger	Kenneth L.	Sgt.	11th	St. Comp.
Swangin	Thomas J.	Sgt.	510th	
Swanson	Marion L.	T/Sgt.	511th	
Swarthout	Robert A.	2nd Lt.	508th	
Swarts	Walter F.	S/Sgt.	509th	
Swartwood	John S. L.	Sgt.	511th	
Swayze	Walter W.	Pvt.	510th	
Sweeney	Joseph A.	Capt.	511th	
Sweet	Alan D.	Cpl.	351st	HQ
Swenson	John S.	2nd Lt.	508th	KIA 9/5/44
Swenson	Robert E.	2nd Lt.	509th	KIA 3/18/44
Swetnam	Leroy A.	2nd Lt.	510th	KIA 9/8/44
Swica	Frank	T/Sgt.	511th	KIA 11/3/43
Swift	Gerald W.	M/Sgt.	511th	
Swift	Howard J.	1st Lt.	511th	
Swillen	William E.	Cpl.	1061st	MP Company
Swilley	Johney M.	PFC	11th	St. Comp.
Swiontek	Stanley S.	S/Sgt.	511th	

Swistak / Turitz

Last	First	Rank	Unit	Notes		Last	First	Rank	Unit	Notes		Last	First	Rank	Unit	Notes
Swistak	Joseph M.	T/Sgt.	508th			Tellerson	James C.	2nd Lt.	510th			Towers	Paul Z.	S/Sgt.	508th	
Sylvester	Eugene	2nd Lt.	509th	POW 4/13/44		Temkin	Samuel	M/Sgt.	1206th	QM Company		Townley	James P.	Capt.	351st	
Syskle	Harvey L.	S/Sgt.	511th			Tenney	Reed W.	S/Sgt.	510th	St. Comp.		Townsend	Bernard S.	Sgt.	508th	POW 11/21/44
Szabo	Robert J.	Sgt.	510th			Tenorio	Esenuel K.	T/Sgt.	11th	Sub-Depot		Townsend	Isaac	Sgt.	447th	Sub-Depot
Szoke	Frank J.	Sgt.	511th			Terflinger	George L.	PFC	447th			Towsley	William R.	S/Sgt.	511th	
Szumowski	Edward	Cpl.	511th	St. Comp.		Tertizzi	Alfred	Cpl.	511th			Tracy	Clair E.	2nd Lt.	508th	
Szunycoh	Frank M.	Cpl.	11th			Terni	Clarence A.	S/Sgt.	1629th			Tracy	Robert E.	S/Sgt.	510th	
Szwarc	Joseph J.	S/Sgt.	509th			Terrill	Morton N.	Sgt.	511th			Traczewitz	Gerald E.	1st Lt.	511th	
Szymanski	Edward J.	2nd Lt.	509th			Terry	Lawrence C.	2nd Lt.	511th			Trapolind	Sylvester L.	1st Lt.	508th	
						Terry	Walter E.	T/Sgt.	508th			Trapp	Norman A.	Capt.	511th	
T						Tessler	Stanley J.	S/Sgt.	511th			Traschen	Isadore	T/Sgt.	509th	
Tabb	William H.	1st Lt.	511th			Tetreault	Charles A.	Sgt.	510th			Trask	William E.	S/Sgt.	508th	MIA 10/9/43
Taddonio	Anthony	Sgt.	510th			Thackery	Logan W.	S/Sgt.	447th	Sub-Depot		Travis	Franklin L.	S/Sgt.	509th	
Tafoya	Andres J.	Cpl.	508th	Ord. S&M Co.		Thackston	Richard D.	1st Lt.	511th			Trego	John E.	S/Sgt.	510th	
Taggart	Earl E.	S/Sgt.	508th	St. Comp.		Thanasides	Ernest	2nd Lt.	508th			Trice	Troupe L.	Capt.	351st	HQ
Tait	Kenneth C.	Sgt.	1629th	Ord. S&M Co.		Tharrington	Clarence C.	T/Sgt.	511th			Tricker	Kenneth E.	T/Sgt.	510th	
Talbott	David	Sgt.	508th	POW 5/14/43		Thayer	Harvey C.	T/Sgt.	508th			Trimble	Ray L.	Sgt.	510th	
Tallent	John C.	1st Lt.	510th	St. Comp.		Theis	Richard C.	Sgt.	508th			Triplett	William T.	S/Sgt.	508th	
	R. L.	Sgt.	11th			Therac	Arthur J.	Lt.	508th			Triplit	Frank C.	1st Lt.	508th	MP Company
Talley	Emery L.	PFC	509th			Theroux	Omer L.	PFC	510th			Triwush	Henry	2nd Lt.	509th	
Talsky	Valerian C.	S/Sgt.	508th	Ord. S&M Co.		Theuret	Bobby G.	Sgt.	508th			Troiano	John J.	1st Lt.	510th	
Taney	Bert H.	S/Sgt.	1629th	Ord. S&M Co.		Theys	James A.	1st Lt.	509th			Troklus	Emil G.	T/Sgt.	509th	
Tanner	William J.	T/Sgt.	511th			Thibeau	Arthur J.	Pvt.	509th			Trolinger	Thomas E.	1st Lt.	508th	POW 6/14/44
Tarr	Ralph C.	2nd Lt.	508th			Thibodeau	Lewis C.	S/Sgt.	510th			Trombley	Joseph C.	Cpl.	509th	
Tate	Arthur H.	1st Lt.	510th	St. Comp.		Thilen	Arthur	F.O.	511th			Trombley	Raymond J.	1st Lt.	509th	
Tatro	John F.	Cpl.	11th			Thoman	Robert S.	2nd Lt.	508th			Trombly	Harvey H.	1st Lt.	511th	
Tattan	Mark H.	M/Sgt.	509th			Thomas	Charles F.	1st Lt.	351st	HQ		Troughtman	Albert M.	2nd Lt.	351st	HQ
Taylor	Daldon	T/Sgt.	508th			Thomas	Donald S.	1st Lt.	511th			Trout	Bennette W.	Sgt.	351st	HQ
Taylor	Earnest S.	Cpl.	447th	Sub-Depot		Thomas	Edmund W.	Maj.	511th			Troutman	Hansen D.	F.O.	510th	
Taylor	Frederick F.	S/Sgt.	508th	POW 6/28/43		Thomas	Everett C.	T/Sgt.	510th	MP Company		Truemper	John J.	F.O.	508th	
Taylor	James A.	1st Lt.	509th			Thomas	Frealon E.	Sgt.	1061st			Truempel	Walter E.	2nd Lt	510th	KIA 2/20/44
Taylor	Jimmie R.	2nd Lt.	510th	KIA 12/31/43			G. B.	Sgt.	511th			Trujillo	Manuel	S/Sgt.	509th	POW 1/11/44
Teace	Joe	Sgt.	510th			Thomas	Harvey E.	S/Sgt.	510th			Trujillo	Saturino L.	S/Sgt.	509th	
Taylor	John D.	PFC	511th			Thomas	Hubert E.	Cpl.	508th	Killed 5/7/43		Trull	Byron H.	PFC	1061st	
Taylor	John L.	Sgt.	509th	St. Comp.		Thomas	J. L.	Cpl.	508th			Trumbower	Jerrold S.	2nd Lt.	510th	MP Company
Taylor	Max T.	1st Lt.	511th			Thomas	James D.	Sgt.	510th			Truss	Oscar D.	S/Sgt.	447th	POW 1/11/44
Taylor	McCaleb D.	2nd Lt.	511th	POW 2/24/44		Thomas	Jesse D.	Sgt.	447th	Sub-Depot		Tryon	Chester	S/Sgt.	509th	Sub-Depot
Taylor	Nelson W.	S/Sgt.	447th	Sub-Depot		Thomas	John W.	Pvt.	508th	KIA 9/5/44		Tucker	Jack A.	Sgt.	511th	
Taylor	Robert E.	Sgt.	511th			Thomas	Leroy O.	Sgt.	510th			Tucker	James M.	S/Sgt.	509th	Int'd 10/7/44
Teachey	Robert K.	Sgt.	447th	Sub-Depot		Thomas	Otis F.	1st Lt.	511th			Tucker	John W.	PFC	1061st	MP Company
Teague	Stanley D.	2nd Lt.	509th	Int'd 5/27/44		Thomas	Wendel G.	1st Lt.	510th	POW 7/25/43		Tucker	Richard J.	2nd Lt.	510th	POW 1/11/44
Tebbel	Vee L.	T/Sgt.	510th			Thomas	Wilbur J.	M/Sgt.	1206th	QM Company		Tucker	Theodore L.	S/Sgt.	447th	Sub-Depot
Teegarden	Walter H.	PFC	508th			Thomasco	Francis F.	2nd Lt.	511th			Tuerck	Wiliam B.	S/Sgt.	509th	
Teel	William F.	PFC	11th	St. Comp.		Thompkins	Ellis C.	S/Sgt.	509th			Tuminski	Paul A.	Sgt.	511th	
Tell	William R.	Sgt.	11th	St. Comp.		Thompson	Allyn G.	Cpl.	447th	POW 8/6/44		Tunsford	Edward R.	2nd Lt.	510th	KIA 2/20/44
	Willard D.	T/Sgt.	511th			Thompson	Berton S.	Capt.	11th	St. Comp.		Tupper	Gail C.	S/Sgt.	508th	
Taylor	Arthur L.	Sgt.	509th	Int'd 10/7/44		Thompson	Carl J.	S/Sgt.	508th	St. Comp.		Turbeville	Edwin C.	Cpl.	510th	
Taylor	John R.	1st Lt.	510th	KIA 7/29/44		Thompson	Dale E.	2nd Lt.	510th	KIA 7/12/44		Turbyne	Lewis	Pvt.	511th	
Taylor	James E.	Sgt.	508th			Thompson	David W.	S/Sgt.	508th			Turen	Frank W.	1st Lt.	511th	KIA 6/28/43
Taylor	William E.	S/Sgt.	509th			Thompson	Harlan P.	2nd Lt.	509th	Killed 5/7/43		Turgeon	Nathan	1st Lt.	201st	Finance Sect.
Taylor	Walter V.	PFC	1206th	QM Company		Thompson	John F.	1st Lt.	510th			Turitz	Leo P.	2nd Lt.	508th	POW 6/22/43
						Thompson	John G.	1st Lt.	511th	QM Company			Philip	T/Sgt.	509th	

Last Name	First Name	Rank	Unit	Notes
Turley	George H.	S/Sgt.	510th	
Turley	Joseph H.	1st Lt.	508th	MIA 10/9/43
Turnbull	George W.	1st Lt.	1629th	Ord. S&M Co.
Turnbull	Robert J.	F.O.	509th	
Turner	Mack D.	Pvt.	11th	St. Comp.
Turner	Maurice W.	S/Sgt.	509th	
Turner	Morris G.	1st Lt.	511th	
Turney	John R.	2nd Lt.	508th	POW 6/22/43
Turok	Michael Jr.	PFC	509th	
Tussey	Frank G.	Cpl.	1061st	MP Company
Tuttle	Delbert E.	Pvt.	509th	
Tuttle	Keith E.	Pvt.	510th	
Tuttle	Martin R.	S/Sgt.	509th	
Twarog	Stanley W.	Cpl.	508th	
Twilley	George R. III	2nd Lt.	509th	
Tyler	Roscoe S.	T/Sgt.	510th	
Tyl	Walter	Pvt.	11th	St. Comp.
Tynan	John T.	Capt.	508th	
U				
Udell	Beauford	S/Sgt.	509th	
Udey	Charles R.	S/Sgt.	351st	HQ
Udick	William H.	2nd Lt.	511th	KIA 1/7/44
Udino	Anthony G.	Pvt.	2098th	Avn. F/F Pltn.
Udom	Frank K. Jr.	Sgt.	509th	
Uhl	George R.	Cpl.	510th	
Ullom	Max E.	2nd Lt.	509th	
Ulreich	Herman T.	S/Sgt.	511th	POW 5/28/44
Ulrich	William E.	2nd Lt.	509th	
Underhill	Donald B.	1st Lt.	508th	
Underwood	Roland L.	PFC	510th	
Underwood	Robert E.	S/Sgt.	509th	
Underwood	Robert M.	F.O.	509th	POW 7/28/44
Upshaw	Ben E.	2nd Lt.	510th	
Upton	Oran B.	S/Sgt.	510th	
Urbanek	Frank P.	T/Sgt.	510th	
Uribe	Joe	Cpl.	11th	St. Comp.
Usherwood	John E.	S/Sgt.	511th	
Uttley	George W. Jr.	1st Lt.	511th	KIA 8/6/44
V				
Vagias	Louis	2nd Lt.	510th	
Vahanian	Paul	T/Sgt.	511th	
Valencia	Mike F.	Pvt.	510th	
Valento	Joseph S.	Sgt.	510th	
Valenzuela	Arthur Jr.	Sgt.	509th	
Valerius	Frederick A.	S/Sgt.	510th	
Valotta	Alexander	1st Lt.	510th	
Van Beynum	Robert H.	Capt.	510th	
Van Brunt	Dale P.	1st Lt.	510th	POW 8/17/43
Van De Walle	David J.	2nd Lt.	510th	KIA 2/22/44
Van DeMark	Augustus B.	Pvt.	11th	St. Comp.
Van Dyke	David H.	S/Sgt.	511th	MIA 12/31/43
Van Hoover	Lester E.	Sgt.	447th	Sub-Depot
Van Hoozen	Benjamin D.	Sgt.	1206th	QM Company
Van Horn	Edward P. E.	Sgt.	510th	POW 5/28/44
Van Horn	Ralph C.	S/Sgt.	511th	
Van Sandt	James L.	1st Lt.	508th	
Van Sandt	William S.	S/Sgt.	509th	
Van Sant	Fred J.	Sgt.	510th	POW 5/7/44
Van Tassel	Newman	1st Lt.	509th	
VanEveren	Wallace J.	S/Sgt.	510th	KIA 9/8/44
VanHousen	Nathaniel M.	Sgt.	509th	
Vance	John C.	Sgt.	510th	
Vance	Edwin C.	Sgt.	509th	
Vandeberg	Orie D.	S/Sgt.	508th	
Vandemark	Willie	Pvt.	510th	Int'd 5/27/44
Vandergriff	Augustus B.	Pvt.	11th	St. Comp.
Vanderlaan	George C.	S/Sgt.	11th	St. Comp.
Vanderpool	James H.	S/Sgt.	511th	POW 10/9/43
Vanderpool	Earl C.	Cpl.	511th	
Vandever	Sidney J.	PFC	1629th	Ord. S&M Co.
Vann	Edward A.	Cpl.	509th	
Varaldi	James F.	S/Sgt.	854th	Chemical Co.
Varga	Thomas J.	Sgt.	511th	
Vargas	Elias H.	2nd Lt.	351st	KIA 3/18/44 HQ
Vargo	Michael	Capt.	508th	
Vasak	Otto R.	Sgt.	509th	POW 5/30/44
Vasconcellos	Gerald A.	Sgt.	11th	
Vasilik	Stephen N.	2nd Lt.	11th	
Vatella	Tony F.	PFC	508th	
Vaughan	Edgar A. Jr.	2nd Lt.	509th	
Vaughan	Freeman L.	S/Sgt.	447th	
Vaughan	Kenneth L.	2nd Lt.	508th	
Vaughn	Louis S.	PFC	511th	POW 12/31/43
Vaughn	Clyde W.	Sgt.	11th	St. Comp.
Vaughn	Joseph C.	2nd Lt.	508th	
Vaughn	Robert D.	T/Sgt.	509th	
Vaux	Richard W.	Sgt.	509th	KIA 3/18/44
Vavrock	Oakley K.	PFC	1061st	MP Company
Veazey	Caspar	Cpl.	1061st	MP Company
Vecchione	Jose A.	S/Sgt.	510th	POW 5/28/44
Velasquez	William C.	Cpl.	509th	
Veleba	Thomas A.	T/Sgt.	509th	POW 10/7/44
Veltry	Edward	Sgt.	509th	POW 1/17/45
Venezia	Joseph E.	Sgt.	509th	KIA 2/6/45
Ventress	Reinhold W.	1st Lt.	508th	KIA 2/6/45
Vergen	Elroy H.	Sgt.	509th	
Verhein	Sterling B.	Sgt.	511th	KIA 3/18/44
Vermillion	A. J.	Sgt.	509th	
Verson	Hector Jr.	T/Sgt.	508th	
Verstaeten	Keefer R.	Sgt.	510th	
Vest				
Vester	Frederick R.	S/Sgt.	509th	POW 4/13/44
Vicino	Charles F.	S/Sgt.	447th	Sub-Depot
Vidulich	Anthony	PFC	1206th	QM Company
Viles	Floyd W.	S/Sgt.	509th	POW 6/13/43
Vinsant	Thurlan W.	Sgt.	11th	St. Comp.
Vinson	Andreade J.	1st Lt.	509th	
Viola	Patrick	PFC	509th	
Visca	Dominick R.	Spec. 5	1206th	QM Company
Viste	Gerald D.	Capt.	509th	
Viviyal	Ross A.	S/Sgt.	511th	
Viviyan	James E.	Sgt.	510th	
Vlha	Patrick A.	S/Sgt.	509th	
Vogt	Victor V.	Sgt.	510th	
Volante	Verner E.	T/Sgt.	508th	
Volk	James D.	Spec. 5	511th	
Volotta	Raymond E.	Lt. Col.	11th	HQ
Von Flotow	Alexander	T/Sgt.	351st	HQ
Vorhees	Eugene H.	1st Lt.	508th	
Vorhies	William D.	Cpl.	511th	
Voss	Walter W.	T/Sgt.	508th	
Voxx	Howard M.	1st Lt.	508th	POW 11/3/43
Voyer	Joseph G.	PFC	1629th	Ord. S&M Co.
Voyles	Emerson E.	Sgt.	511th	Sub-Depot
Vukonich	Matt W.	S/Sgt.	509th	
W				
Wade	Ganusheau	T/Sgt.	511th	
Wade	James R.	S/Sgt.	508th	
Wadsworth	Lewis E.	Cpl.	447th	Sub-Depot
Wagers	Johnnie L.	2nd Lt.	351st	HQ
Wagers	Michael J.	S/Sgt.	447th	Sub-Depot
Wagner	Anthony F.	2nd Lt.	508th	
Wagner	Clyde E.	1st Lt.	509th	
Wagner	Roger W.	Sgt.	509th	
Wagoner	Robert C.	2nd Lt.	511th	Int'd 10/7/44
Waite	Harold G.	S/Sgt.	509th	
Walaszek	Stanley A.	1st Lt.	510th	
Walbrecht	A. L.	Cpl.	510th	
Walby	Charles T.	2nd Lt.	509th	
Waldron	Ronald A.	Sgt.	511th	POW 12/31/43
Walker	Alton A.	Spec. 5	508th	
Walker	Charles E.	S/Sgt.	1061st	MP Company
Walker	Charles M.	Cpl.	1629th	Ord. S&M Co.
Walker	Collis G.	Pvt.	11th	St. Comp.
Walker	Dale W.	PFC	351st	HQ
Walker	Durward E.	S/Sgt.	511th	
Walker	Earl L.	Pvt.	508th	
Walker	Everett	S/Sgt.	510th	
Walker	F. W.	S/Sgt.	510th	
Walker	Fred M.	Pvt.	510th	
Walker	Frederick W.	S/Sgt.	510th	
Walker	George T.	1st Lt.	509th	
Walker	H. F.	Cpl.	447th	Sub-Depot
Walker	Herbert C.	S/Sgt.	447th	Sub-Depot
Walker	Ira	Cpl.	510th	
Walker	Marvin L.	Sgt.	1629th	Ord. S&M Co.
Walker	Marvin R.	1st Lt.	509th	
Walker	Paul A.	F.O.	511th	
Walker	Thomas B.	1st Lt.	509th	POW 8/6/44
Walko	Richard	Sgt.	509th	Sub-Depot
Wall	Carl J.	M/Sgt.	508th	
Wall	Lavern D.	S/Sgt.	510th	POW 12/31/43
Wall	Richie M.	Cpl.	508th	
Wall	Robert J.	T/Sgt.	508th	POW 10/4/43
Wallace	Walter A.	1st Lt.	511th	
Wallace	Bertram E. Jr.	Cpl.	447th	Sub-Depot
Wallace	Harvey H. Jr.	S/Sgt.	511th	
Wallace	Lloyd W.	S/Sgt.	508th	
Walline	Robert T.	T/Sgt.	508th	St. Comp.
Wallon	Thaddeus C.	S/Sgt.	508th	
Wally	Leonard H.	S/Sgt.	508th	
Walota	Wendell K. B.	2nd Lt.	11th	
Walsh	Edward L.	2nd Lt.	511th	KIA 11/26/44
Walsh	Michael J.	F.O.	252nd	Medical Disp.
Walsh	Paul M.	Cpl.	511th	POW 10/9/43
Walsh	Thomas W.	T/Sgt.	509th	
Walter	William J.	2nd Lt.	510th	
Walter	George	2nd Lt.	511th	
Walter	John D.	2nd Lt.	510th	
Walters	Norman C.	2nd Lt.	509th	Int'd 6/21/44
Walters	Jerry C.	T/Sgt.	509th	Int'd 10/7/44
Walton	Louis W.	S/Sgt.	511th	
Wanda	Sam S.	F.O.	509th	
Wandetowski	Roger	T/Sgt.	511th	POW 5/7/44
Warcola	Vincent M.	Sgt.	510th	
Ward	Alex	S/Sgt.	510th	St. Comp.
Ward	Archie L.	Sgt.	11th	
Ward	Bernick G.	Cpl.	510th	Sub-Depot
Ward	Charles C. Jr.	Pvt.	447th	
Ward	Earl E.	1st Lt.	511th	Int'd 3/18/44
Warden	Russell E.	S/Sgt.	510th	POW 8/17/43
Warden	August F.	Sgt.	508th	POW 1/11/44
Ware	Bruce W.	F.O.	509th	
Wargacki	Merl H.	2nd Lt.	510th	
Warne	Stanley	F.O.	447th	Sub-Depot
Warner	Thurman R.	Sgt.	511th	
Warner	Howard B.	S/Sgt.	510th	
Warner	Lewis C.	Cpl.	447th	
Warner	Stewart M.	S/Sgt.	511th	
Warren	William O. III	2nd Lt.	510th	
Warren	Allen S. Jr.	Sgt.	508th	
Warren	Charles R. Jr.	S/Sgt.	510th	

Surname	Given	Rank	Unit	Notes
Warren	E. E.	M/Sgt.	510th	
Warren	Fred Jr.	2nd Lt.	511th	POW 1/11/44
Warren	Robert M. Jr.	1st Lt.	509th	
Warring	William H.	F.O.	508th	POW 10/9/43
Warth	Franklin C.	2nd Lt.	508th	
Waserman	Joseph	Cpl.	447th	Sub-Depot
Washburn	William F.	1st Lt.	510th	
Wasinger	Edward E.	T/Sgt.	511th	
Wasko	Theodore	S/Sgt.	508th	
Wasserman	Joseph	PFC	447th	Sub-Depot
Wassner	Donald R.	2nd Lt.	511th	POW 8/6/44
Waswick	Donald G.	1st Lt.	508th	
Waszkiewicz	Mearl C.	Sgt.	508th	
Waterbeck	Edward A.	S/Sgt.	509th	
Waterman	Walter M.	S/Sgt.	508th	
Waters	Fred B.	PFC	11th	St. Comp.
Waters	James C.	S/Sgt.	510th	POW 9/12/44
Watkins	Waitman R.	T/Sgt.	510th	
Watkins	Charles H.	S/Sgt.	510th	
Watson	Robert T.	Sgt.	509th	POW 6/22/44
Watson	Dexter E.	1st Lt.	508th	
Watson	Edmund J.	2nd Lt.	509th	
Watson	John B.	1st Lt.	509th	
Watson	John E.	T/Sgt.	511th	
Watson	John H.	Sgt.	510th	
Watson	John M.	Sgt.	510th	
Watson	Melvin S.	2nd Lt.	510th	
Wattles	William R.	Sgt.	508th	
Watts	Fred J.	M/Sgt.	511th	
Waxler	Ernest I.	Capt.	508th	
Way	Paul E.	S/Sgt.	509th	
Wayt	Fred T.	Sgt.	509th	
Weatherby	Francis H.	Cpl.	511th	
Weatherford	Francis E.	1st Lt.	508th	
Weatherholt	Roy L.	S/Sgt.	510th	KIA 7/17/43
Weatherman	Oliver R.	S/Sgt.	508th	KIA 7/25/43
Weaver	Vernon R.	Capt.	509th	POW 5/27/44
Weaver	Earl F.	Sgt.	509th	Int'd 10/7/44
Weaver	Edward M.	1st Lt.	854th	Chemical Co.
Weaver	George L.	S/Sgt.	511th	
Webb	H. R.	1st Lt.	11th	St. Comp.
Webb	William R.	S/Sgt.	509th	KIA 1/7/44
Webb	Douglas E.	2nd Lt.	511th	
Webb	Wade	PFC	2098th	Avn. F/F Pltn.
Webber	Robert L.	S/Sgt.	511th	
Weber	Francis M.	PFC	510th	
Weber	John T.	1st Lt.	509th	
Weber	Joseph B.	Sgt.	447th	Sub-Depot
Webster	Edward F.	Cpl.	508th	
Webster	John A.	S/Sgt.	508th	
Webster	Paul H.	Sgt.	11th	
Weedn	Ollie E.	T/Sgt.	11th	St. Comp.

Surname	Given	Rank	Unit	Notes
Weeks	John M. Jr.	1st Lt.	508th	
Wefel	Walther J. Jr.	1st Lt.	509th	
Wehner	Raymond H.	F.O.	510th	
Weida	Beecher L.	Sgt.	511th	
Weidman	Grant H.	2nd Lt.	511th	
Weiland	Robert K.	Sgt.	508th	
Weikel	Paul W.	Capt.	510th	
Weiland	Harold R.	Sgt.	511th	KIA 2/6/45
Weiner	Morris	PFC	511th	
Weir	Clifford O.	S/Sgt.	510th	
Weis	Richard J.	2nd Lt.	508th	
Weisman	Samuel G.	S/Sgt.	511th	
Weiss	Samuel	Cpl.	447th	Sub-Depot
Weisschnur	Elmer J.	F.O.	510th	
Wejta	William J.	1st Lt.	508th	
Welch	Eugene E.	T/Sgt.	509th	
Welch	Harvey W.	1st Lt.	508th	
Welch	John G.	PFC	508th	
Welcome	Francis E.	T/Sgt.	509th	
Welk	James F.	2nd Lt.	508th	KIA 5/29/43
Welk	Robert	Pvt.	511th	
Wellbeloved	John R.	1st Sgt.	510th	
Wellbeloved	Robert S.	1st Lt.	508th	
Weller	Ira	1st Lt.	509th	POW 10/3/44
Wellins	Harold J.	T/Sgt.	511th	Killed 5/7/43
Wellnitz	D. H.	Cpl.	11th	
Wells	Donald R.	Sgt.	509th	
Wells	Homer B.	1st Sgt.	511th	
Wells	Thomas N.	S/Sgt.	510th	POW 12/31/43
Welsh	E. E.	1st Lt.	509th	
Welsh	M. J.	S/Sgt.	508th	
Wendall	Charles A.	2nd Lt.	509th	
Wendt	Stanley	Sgt.	511th	
Wenzloff	Robert W.	S/Sgt.	508th	KIA 5/27/44
Werner	Regis A.	Pvt.	11th	St. Comp.
Werth	Frederick M.	2nd Lt.	252nd	Medical Disp.
Werts	Francis C.	S/Sgt.	510th	
Wertz	John R. Jr.	T/Sgt.	11th	St. Comp.
Wertz	William R.	Cpl.	509th	
Weskienicz	Edward A.	S/Sgt.	509th	
Wesley	Robert P.	Sgt.	508th	
Wessel	Lawrence F.	Cpl.	510th	
Wesson	Francis B.	Sgt.	508th	
West	Edwin	T/Sgt.	511th	
West	John J.	Sgt.	508th	
Westbrook	Frank P.	M/Sgt.	510th	POW 12/30/43
Westcott	Robert B.	Sgt.	511th	
Wester	Lawrence R.	Sgt.	511th	POW 9/12/44
Westercamp	Virgil J.	1st Lt.	510th	
Westfall	Russell J.	Cpl.	351st	HQ
Westhafer	Alva R.	2nd Lt.	509th	

Surname	Given	Rank	Unit	Notes
Weston	J. P.	S/Sgt.	508th	
Westrich	Edward G.	Cpl.	511th	
Wetherington	Louis L.	F.O.	508th	
Wetherington	Milton G.	T/Sgt.	509th	
Whalen	Robert G.	1st Lt.	511th	
Whatley	Philemon J.	Sgt.	510th	
Whatton	John J.	Cpl.	1206th	QM Company
Wheatley	Robert L.	S/Sgt.	509th	KIA 2/6/45
Wheeler	David W.	Capt.	11th	St. Comp.
Wheelock	Robert E.	Cpl.	510th	
Whestley	Robert L.	S/Sgt.	509th	
Whetstone	John B.	Sgt.	509th	
Whisler	Kenneth E.	PFC	11th	St. Comp.
Whisnant	Walter J.	Capt.	1061st	MP Company
Whitaker	George E.	1st Lt.	509th	
Whitaker	James	2nd Lt.	510th	
Whitaker	Walter W. Jr.	Sgt.	508th	
Whitbred	Andrew A.	T/Sgt.	509th	POW 4/13/44
Whitchurch	Gilbert W.	2nd Lt.	509th	POW 5/19/43
White	Alec S.	Pvt.	1629th	Ord. S&M Co.
White	Delbert E.	S/Sgt.	1629th	Ord. S&M Co.
White	Donald J.	1st Lt.	11th	St. Comp.
White	Donald W.	2nd Lt.	510th	
White	Elmer R.	Capt.	511th	
White	James D.	Sgt.	509th	
White	John R.	Cpl.	510th	
White	Lee C.	Sgt.	509th	
White	Lee R.	Cpl.	511th	
White	Norman J.	S/Sgt.	510th	
White	Paul D.	T/Sgt.	508th	
White	Roy B.	S/Sgt.	509th	
White	Thomas M.	Sgt.	447th	Sub-Depot
Whitehead	Thompson E.	2nd Lt.	511th	POW 1/11/44
Whitestone	William W.	2nd Lt.	508th	POW 12/31/43
Whitman	Woodrow W.	Cpl.	509th	
Whitman	George I.	1st Lt.	511th	
Whitney	Robert P.	S/Sgt.	508th	
Whittaker	Robert	S/Sgt.	509th	
Whittaker	Robert G.	S/Sgt.	510th	
Whittaker	Eugene	Cpl.	447th	Sub-Depot
Whitten	Donald A.	1st Lt.	510th	
Whitten	William E.	Sgt.	509th	POW 6/14/44
Wick	William T.	S/Sgt.	508th	POW 6/13/43
Widmier	Charles E.	Sgt.	508th	
Weiland	William R.	2nd Lt.	511th	
Wiencek	William W.	2nd Lt.	508th	
Wiersma	Russell E.	Pvt.	11th	
Wiese	Robert K.	Sgt.	508th	
Wiger	Henry J.	Sgt.	511th	POW 1/11/44
	James	S/Sgt.	510th	
	Wilfred A.	1st Lt.	508th	
	Oscar R.	F.O.	509th	

Surname	Given	Rank	Unit	Notes
Wigfield	Arol F.	M/Sgt.	510th	
Wiggs	Eldon M.	S/Sgt.	509th	
Wigington	James T.	Cpl.	511th	
Wilber	Ralph E.	S/Sgt.	447th	Sub-Depot
Wilbright	Thayne S.	PFC	447th	Sub-Depot
Wilbur	Claude M. Jr.	2nd Lt.	510th	
Wilbur	Newton C.	2nd Lt.	509th	POW 4/13/44
Wilburn	Richard E.	S/Sgt.	509th	
Wilcox	Frank H.	Capt.	511th	
Wilcox	Robert B.	2nd Lt.	510th	
Wile	William B.	Sgt.	509th	
Wiles	W. J.	S/Sgt.	511th	
Wiley	Charles L.	S/Sgt.	510th	POW 7/19/44
Wilhelm	R. M.	S/Sgt.	508th	
Wilhoit	Donald C.	M/Sgt.	511th	
Wilkes	Roy V.	PFC	11th	St. Comp.
Wilkie	Buford	M/Sgt.	511th	POW 11/26/44
Wilkins	Lawton H.	Sgt.	508th	POW 11/26/43
Will	Vallean Jr.	2nd Lt.	511th	St. Comp.
Will	William A.	Capt.	11th	
Willard	Harrison Jr.	F.O.	509th	
Willard	Leslie	PFC	11th	St. Comp.
Wilbright	Ralph L.	1st Lt.	511th	
Willhite	Robert A.	1st Lt.	1206th	QM Company
William	Thayne S.	S/Sgt.	11th	St. Comp.
Williams	Avondale L.	2nd Lt.	510th	KIA 5/27/44
Williams	W. A.	S/Sgt.	511th	
Williams	Clinton A.	2nd Lt.	510th	
Williams	Frank D.	Sgt.	509th	POW 6/22/44
Williams	Frank E.	Sgt.	508th	POW 10/9/43
Williams	Frederick R.	1st Lt.	509th	
Williams	Howard C.	Sgt.	510th	
Williams	Jack	Pvt.	447th	Sub-Depot
Williams	James M.	T/Sgt.	510th	
Williams	James W.	S/Sgt.	511th	POW 10/7/44
Williams	Kenneth D.	2nd Lt.	508th	POW 11/26/43
Williams	Louis G.	S/Sgt.	509th	
Williams	Nathan L.	Sgt.	510th	
Williams	Neal W.	S/Sgt.	510th	POW 5/28/44
Williams	Otis C.	Cpl.	511th	POW 1/11/44
Williams	Reginald R.	T/Sgt.	508th	
Williams	Richard L.	1st Lt.	510th	
Williams	Reuben L.	T/Sgt.	509th	
Williams	Warren J.	S/Sgt.	351st	HQ
Williams	George L. Jr.	2nd Lt.	508th	POW 6/14/44
Williamson	Henry F. Jr.	Capt.	510th	
Williamson	James H.	Sgt.	511th	
Williamson	John R.	S/Sgt.	511th	POW 8/3/44
Williamson	William F.	S/Sgt.	447th	Sub-Depot
Willis	Charles E.	S/Sgt.	510th	
Willis	Clinton	S/Sgt.	508th	
Willis	Owen L.	M/Sgt.	511th	

Wills / Zundel

Surname	First	Rank	Unit	Notes
Wills	Edward J.	PFC	447th	Sub-Depot
Wilmoth	Charles E.	T/Sgt.	510th	KIA 9/12/44
Wilmut	William H.	Sgt.	511th	
Wilsher	Louis M.	S/Sgt.	511th	
Wilson	Albert W.	Cpl.	11th	St. Comp.
Wilson	Boyd C.	Cpl.	1061st	MP Company
Wilson	Carl B.	1st Lt.	511th	
Wilson	Courtney G.	T/Sgt.	509th	
Wilson	Deck F.	PFC	11th	St. Comp.
Wilson	Donald C.	2nd Lt.	511th	POW 8/6/44
Wilson	Duane A.	2nd Lt.	509th	KIA 10/7/44
Wilson	Graham S.	S/Sgt.	511th	POW 8/6/44
Wilson	Harry F.	S/Sgt.	509th	
Wilson	J.C.	S/Sgt.	508th	
Wilson	John E.	S/Sgt.	510th	
Wilson	Kenneth N.	Sgt.	509th	
Wilson	Rayford R.	2nd Lt.	508th	
Wilson	Richard R.	Sgt.	11th	
Wilson	Robert J.	Capt.	510th	
Wilson	Thelbert R.	S/Sgt.	508th	
Wilson	Robert C.	S/Sgt.	509th	POW 5/24/44
Wimmer	James H.	1st Sgt.	511th	POW 1/30/44
Winburn	Earl W	S/Sgt.	511th	
Winchester	Leslye G.	T/Sgt.	508th	
Windbiel	George A.	S/Sgt.	510th	Int'd 5/27/44
Windes	Honor G.	2nd Lt.	510th	
Wingard	Charles S.	T/Sgt.	508th	
Winker	Lewis H.	S/Sgt.	509th	
Winkle	J.C.	Sgt.	509th	
Winslow	William H.	Capt.	511th	Killed 4/22/44
Winter	William A.	T/Sgt.	511th	HQ
Winterbauer	Harry L.	Cpl.	351st	
Winterfield	Herbert L.	S/Sgt.	511th	
Winters	Albert S.	2nd Lt.	510th	
Winton	Bruce F.	S/Sgt.	508th	
Winton	John W.	Cpl.	1061st	MP Company
Wipper	Fred J.	1st Lt.	508th	
Wisdom	Charles	1st Lt.	509th	
Wishnewsky	Peter P.	T/Sgt.	511th	St. Comp.
Witherspoon	Joseph P.	Sgt.	11th	
Witkiewicz	Joseph J.	Cpl.	509th	
Witowski	Mitchell P.	T/Sgt.	510th	POW 5/14/43
Witt	Jack J.	S/Sgt.	510th	St. Comp.
Witzke	George F.	T/Sgt.	509th	POW 5/29/43
Wixom	Wilton A.	S/Sgt.	510th	Finance Sect.
Wlostowski	Chester	1st Lt.	509th	
Woehrle	Charles B.	2nd Lt.	508th	
Wohleder	John M.	T/Sgt.	201st	
Wojtkiewicz	Raymond W.	Capt.	509th	
Wolcott	Charles E.	2nd Lt.	509th	
Wolf	Robert A.	S/Sgt.	511th	
Wolfe	Buddie			

Surname	First	Rank	Unit	Notes
Wolfe	Joseph S.	S/Sgt.	511th	KIA 6/28/43
Wolfe	Lorin A.	2nd Lt.	510th	POW 2/22/44
Wolfschohl	Clarence	Cpl.	511th	
Wollan	Wendell R.	1st Lt.	508th	
Wollenschlaeger	Franklin J.	1st Lt.	511th	
Wolosin	Andrew J.	Cpl.	1061st	MP Company
Wolschlaeger	Randolph J.	S/Sgt.	11th	St. Comp.
Wolverton	Edward H.	Cpl.	511th	
Wolz	Orvil L.	1st Lt.	511th	POW 11/26/44
Womble	Conrad G.	2nd Lt.	508th	
Wombold	Robert E.	Sgt.	509th	
Wood	Arthur L.	Sgt.	511th	
Wood	Jack C.	2nd Lt.	510th	
Wood	Jack R.	PFC	510th	
Wood	Lester L.	Col.	509th	
Wood	Maurice R.	Sgt.	509th	POW 1/11/44
Wood	Paul D. Lt.	S/Sgt.	509th	KIA 6/3/44
Wood	Robert G.	2nd Lt.	510th	POW 6/28/43
Wood	Robert H.	Sgt.	511th	Sub-Depot
Wood	Robert K.	Sgt.	447th	St. Comp.
Wood	Robert L.	Spec. 5	854th	Chemical Co.
Wood	Stanley A.	1st Lt.	508th	
Wood	William R.	1st Lt.	508th	
Woodard	Robert R.	F.O.	511th	
Woodard	Toy W.	S/Sgt.	511th	KIA 6/28/43
Woodbeck	Clarence R.	S/Sgt.	511th	POW 11/3/43
Woodbury	Richard E.	F.O.	511th	Sub-Depot
Woodhave	Theodore	T/Sgt.	447th	
Wooding	Roy L.	PFC	511th	
Woodrum	Charles R.	Cpl.	508th	
Woods	Homer C.	M/Sgt.	510th	
Woods	Lawrence M.	2nd Lt.	508th	
Woods	Raymond E.	S/Sgt.	510th	
Woodward	Arthur Q. Jr.	PFC	1061st	MP Company
Woodward	Ashton E.	Pvt.	508th	
Woodward	Edward E.	1st Lt.	508th	Killed 5/7/43
Woodward	Malcolm E.	1st Lt.	508th	KIA 6/28/43
Wooley	Phillip E.	Cpl.	511th	
Woolf	William H. Jr.	Pvt.	509th	
Woolridge	Lawrence W.	Sgt.	508th	St. Comp.
Wooten	Joseph W.	M/Sgt.	510th	Sub-Depot
Wordsworth	Edward D.	Capt.	509th	
Workman	Armand W.	Sgt.	351st	HQ
Workman	Fred O. Jr.	PFC	508th	
Works	John R.	S/Sgt.	510th	
Worrell	Robert	1st Sgt.	509th	Finance Sect.
Worthington	Raymond J. Jr.	1st Lt.	201st	
Wozniak	Dale E.	M/Sgt.	511th	POW 3/18/44
Wrenn	Woodrow W.	S/Sgt.	509th	
Wright	Andy	PFC	447th	
Wright	Clay J.	Cpl.	1206th	QM Company
Wright	Edman L.	Cpl.	11th	St. Comp.
	John A. III	1st Lt.	508th	Sub-Depot
	Clarence B.	2nd Lt.	508th	Killed 5/7/43

Surname	First	Rank	Unit	Notes
Wright	Fred H.	T/Sgt.	510th	POW 12/31/43
Wright	Jack E.	Sgt.	510th	
Wright	Kenneth S.	Sgt.	510th	KIA 9/5/44
Wright	William G.	1st Lt.	508th	
Wrisberg	John H.	1st Lt.	510th	
Wroblewski	Joseph	Cpl.	509th	
Wroblewski	Meiszylaw A.	S/Sgt.	510th	
Wuestschoefer	Clarence W.	Cpl.	508th	
Wurfl	Anselm S.	PFC	1061st	MP Company
Wyatt	Jack E.	S/Sgt.	508th	
Wyatt	Thomas H.	Sgt.	511th	
Wyker	Chester	1st Lt.	447th	Sub-Depot
Wylie	George C.	Sgt.	509th	
Wyrouck	Samuel H.	2nd Lt.	508th	
Wyzykowski	Adolph L.	PFC	510th	

Y

Surname	First	Rank	Unit	Notes
Yacench	Steve	Sgt.	447th	Sub-Depot
Yakiff	David	Sgt.	509th	
Yale	D. W.	Pvt.	508th	
Yanny	Lawrence A.	Spec. 5	854th	Chemical Co.
Yarcuske	Peter P.	1st Lt.	508th	
Yarcusko	Bernard B.	1st Lt.	508th	
Yardley	William A.	F.O.	511th	
Yareff	Dragie J.	S/Sgt.	511th	KIA 6/28/43
Yarush	John J.	S/Sgt.	511th	POW 11/3/43
Yates	Warren G.	S/Sgt.	511th	
Yazenski	Frank R.	M/Sgt.	447th	Sub-Depot
Yeager	Benjamin G.	Pvt.	511th	
Yerks	Arthur W.	Cpl.	508th	
Yingling	Arthur E.	S/Sgt.	510th	
Yoakam	Stanley E.	Cpl.	508th	
Yonally	Edward E.	S/Sgt.	510th	
Yonker	Herber S.	Cpl.	511th	
York	Loyd C.	PFC	1061st	MP Company
Young	Clifford J.	Pvt.	508th	
Young	Courtland H.	1st Lt.	508th	Killed 5/7/43
Young	Donald J.	1st Lt.	508th	KIA 6/28/43
Young	Ermyle E.	T/Sgt.	511th	
Young	Francis E.	S/Sgt.	509th	
Young	James G.	S/Sgt.	509th	
Young	Kenneth C.	PFC	351st	HQ
Young	Paul B.	S/Sgt.	508th	
Young	Robert W.	S/Sgt.	510th	
Young	Thomas J.	S/Sgt.	509th	Finance Sect.
Young	William M.	T/Sgt.	511th	
Youngberg	Raymond L.	S/Sgt.	509th	
Younge	Ernest W.	PFC	447th	Sub-Depot
Yule	Donald W.	Cpl.	508th	
Yunck	John A. III	1st Lt.	509th	
Yunt	Clarence B.	2nd Lt.	508th	

Surname	First	Rank	Unit	Notes
Yuritz	Philip	S/Sgt.	509th	
Yurkus	Leon D.	S/Sgt.	511th	

Z

Surname	First	Rank	Unit	Notes
Zaborsky	Henry	1st Lt.	511th	
Zacharzewski	Aloysius A.	S/Sgt.	11th	St. Comp.
Zachow	Herman H.	Pvt.	511th	
Zaitlen	Leo A.	S/Sgt.	509th	
Zajec	Rudolph B.	S/Sgt.	508th	
Zarin	Martin	2nd Lt.	509th	
Zarli	Frank C.	T/Sgt.	509th	
Zeigler	Lionel S.	Sgt.	511th	POW 8/6/44
Zeigler	Stanley H.	Sgt.	509th	
Zeiner	Leighton K.	2nd Lt.	510th	KIA 12/30/43
Zeitler	Seymour	T/Sgt.	510th	Sub-Depot
Zelaski	Eugene I.	Sgt.	447th	
Zelenitz	Frank A.	S/Sgt.	510th	
Zenor	Frank A.	S/Sgt.	509th	
Zenor	John W.	1st Lt.	509th	
Zibas	Peter J.	T/Sgt.	510th	
Zigenfus	Elwood A.	S/Sgt.	511th	POW 10/3/44
Zimmerman	Donald	T/Sgt.	509th	
Zimmerman	Harold A.	S/Sgt.	509th	
Zimmerman	John W.	2nd Lt.	511th	
Zindar	William B.	1st Lt.	508th	KIA 5/28/44
Zmolek	Laddie J.	2nd Lt.	508th	
Zombol	Alfred J.	S/Sgt.	511th	POW 8/9/44
Zotollo	Anthony J.	1st Lt.	509th	
Zubatch	Paul	S/Sgt.	510th	Sub-Depot
Zuchegno	Albert V.	Sgt.	447th	POW 10/3/44
Zundel	John H.	Sgt.	510th	

SPECIFICATIONS
B-17F

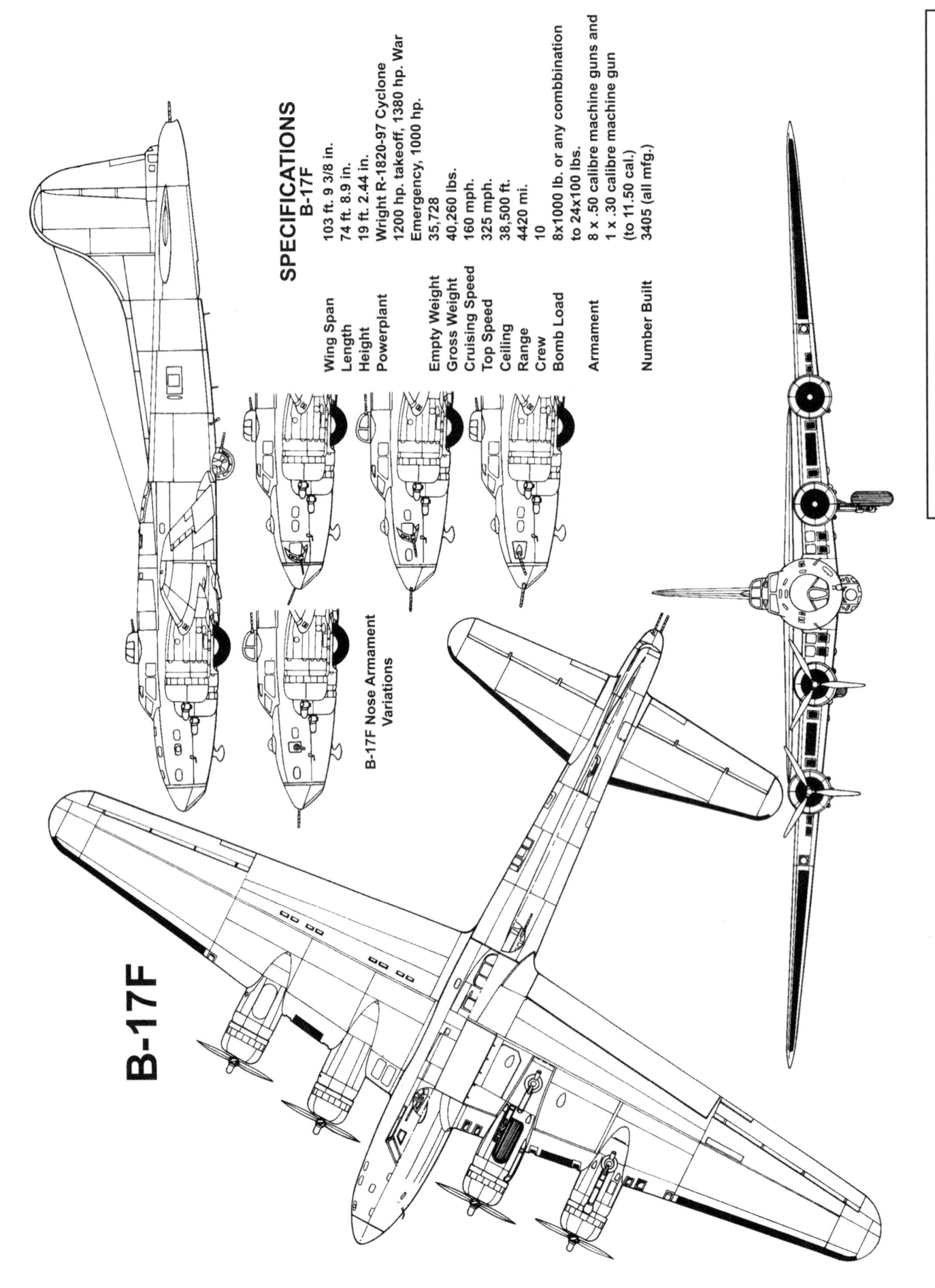

Wing Span	103 ft. 9 3/8 in.
Length	74 ft. 8.9 in.
Height	19 ft. 2.44 in.
Powerplant	Wright R-1820-97 Cyclone 1200 hp. takeoff, 1380 hp. War Emergency, 1000 hp.
Empty Weight	35,728
Gross Weight	40,260 lbs.
Cruising Speed	160 mph.
Top Speed	325 mph.
Ceiling	38,500 ft.
Range	4420 mi.
Crew	10
Bomb Load	8x1000 lb. or any combinnation to 24x100 lbs.
Armament	8 x .50 calibre machine guns and 1 x .30 calibre machine gun (to 11.50 cal.)
Number Built	3405 (all mfg.)

B-17F Nose Armament Variations

B-17F

B-17 line art provided by Squadron Signal Publications, all rights reserved.

B-17G

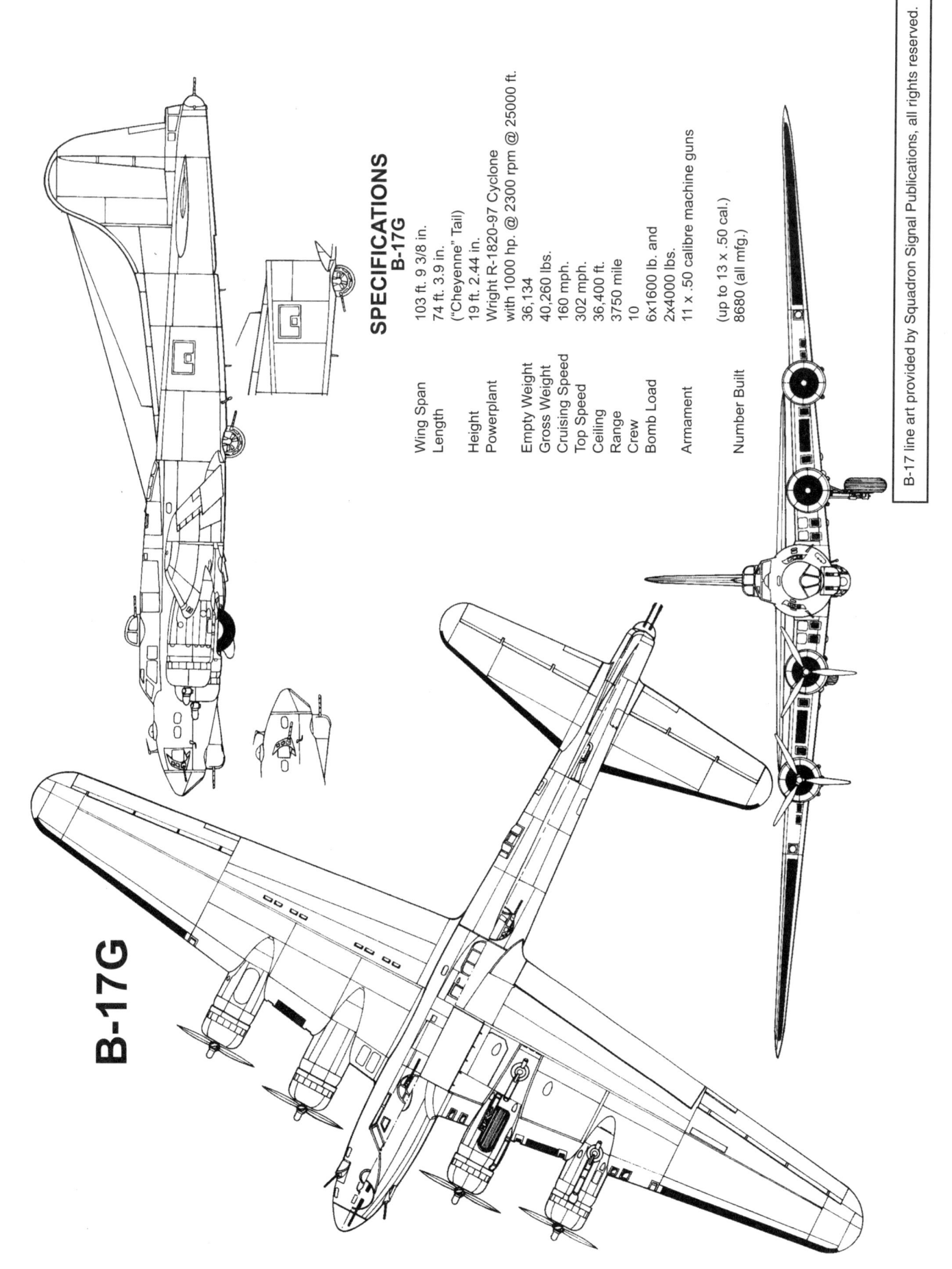

SPECIFICATIONS
B-17G

Wing Span	103 ft. 9 3/8 in.
Length	74 ft. 3.9 in. ("Cheyenne" Tail)
Height	19 ft. 2.44 in.
Powerplant	Wright R-1820-97 Cyclone with 1000 hp. @ 2300 rpm @ 25000 ft.
Empty Weight	36,134
Gross Weight	40,260 lbs.
Cruising Speed	160 mph.
Top Speed	302 mph.
Ceiling	36,400 ft.
Range	3750 mile
Crew	10
Bomb Load	6x1600 lb. and 2x4000 lbs.
Armament	11 x .50 calibre machine guns (up to 13 x .50 cal.)
Number Built	8680 (all mfg.)

B-17 line art provided by Squadron Signal Publications, all rights reserved.

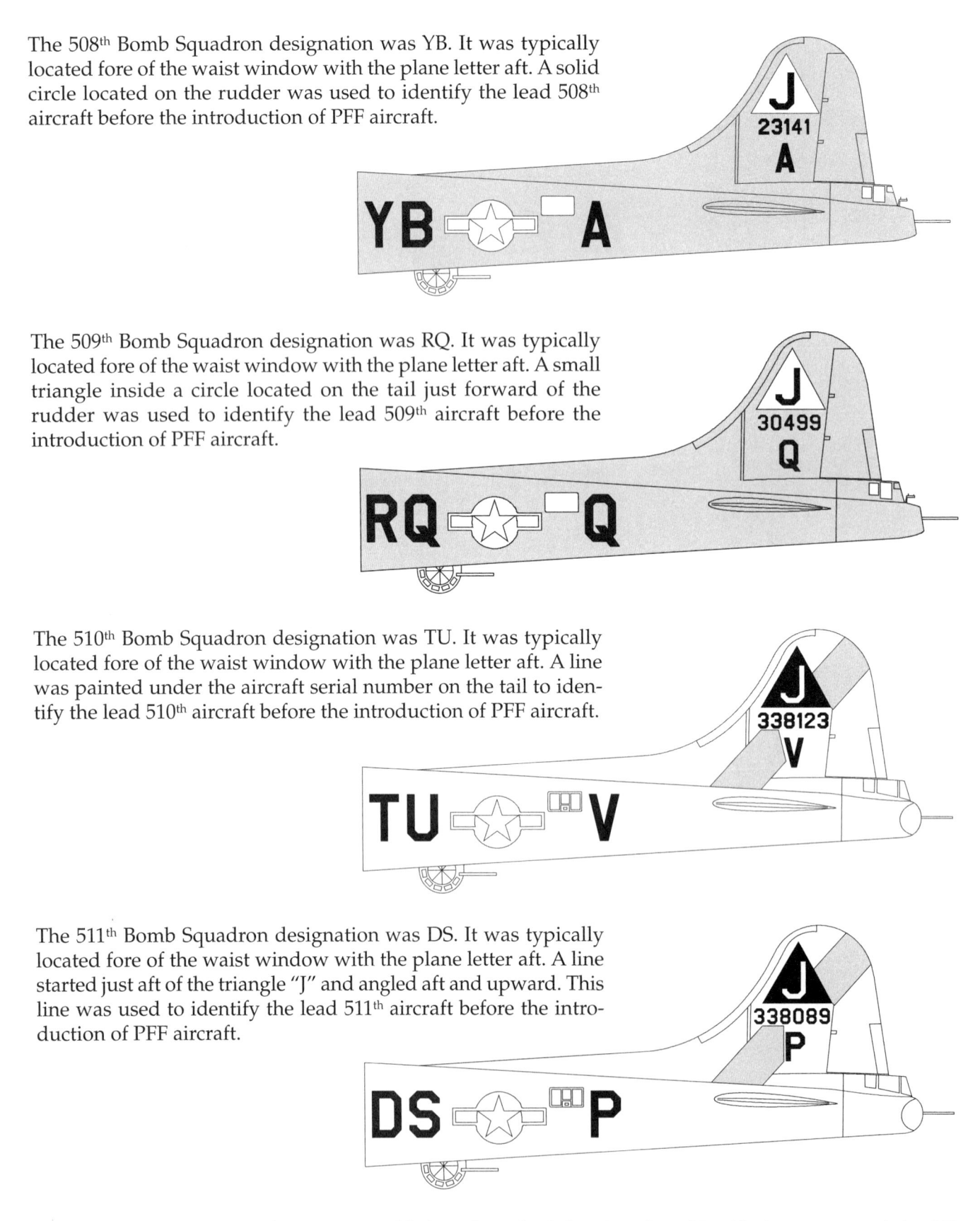

The 508th Bomb Squadron designation was YB. It was typically located fore of the waist window with the plane letter aft. A solid circle located on the rudder was used to identify the lead 508th aircraft before the introduction of PFF aircraft.

The 509th Bomb Squadron designation was RQ. It was typically located fore of the waist window with the plane letter aft. A small triangle inside a circle located on the tail just forward of the rudder was used to identify the lead 509th aircraft before the introduction of PFF aircraft.

The 510th Bomb Squadron designation was TU. It was typically located fore of the waist window with the plane letter aft. A line was painted under the aircraft serial number on the tail to identify the lead 510th aircraft before the introduction of PFF aircraft.

The 511th Bomb Squadron designation was DS. It was typically located fore of the waist window with the plane letter aft. A line started just aft of the triangle "J" and angled aft and upward. This line was used to identify the lead 511th aircraft before the introduction of PFF aircraft.

In mid 1944 a red diagonal stripe was added to the tail of the aircraft to identify it as a part of the 94th Combat Wing. The 508th and 509th aircraft above have an olive drab exterior with the early style tail turret. The 510th and 511th aircraft are bare aluminum with the diagonal stripe and the new Cheyenne tail turret.

The triangles on the tail of the B-17 were painted white with a black "J" when used on the olive drab camouflaged aircraft. The natural (aluminum) aircraft had a black triangle with a white "J" painted inside the triangle.

Eighth Air Force First Division

FEB 1943		**101 PCBW** 91 B.G. 306 B.G.	**102 PCBW** 303 B.G. 305 B.G.	
JUNE 1943		**101 PCBW** 91 B.G. 351 B.G. 381 B.G.	**102 PCBW** 305 B.G. 306 B.G. 92 B.G.	**103 PCBW** 303 B.G. 379 B.G. 384 B.G.
SEPT 1943		**1 CBW** 91 B.G. 351 B.G. 381 B.G.	**40 CBW** 305 B.G. 306 B.G. 92 B.G.	**41 CBW** 303 B.G. 379 B.G. 384 B.G.
NOV 1943	**92 CBW** 351 B.G. 401 B.G.	**1 CBW** 91 B.G. 381 B.G.		
DEC 1943	**94 CBW** 351 B.G. 401 B.G.			
JAN 1944	**94 CBW** 351 B.G. 401 B.G. 457 B.G.			
APR 1944		**1 CBW** 91 B.G. 381 B.G. 398 B.G.		

94 CBW   **1 CBW**

40 CBW   **41 CBW**

When the 351st arrived in England with four other bomb groups in May and June of 1943, the 101st and 102nd Provisional Combat Bomb Wings (PCBW) were reorganized, and the 103rd PCBW was added. In September 1943, the PCBWs were designated as the 1st, 40th and 41st Combat Bomb Wings (CBW). In November, the 1st Combat Wing was split, and the 351st joined with the 401st to form the 92nd CBW. One month later, this new wing became the 94th CBW. In January 1944, the 457th B.G. joined the 94th CBW. With the addition of the 398th B.G. in April 1944, the First Division had its full complement of four wings, each with three bomb groups.

By the end of the war, the Eighth Air Force was divided into three divisions with each division having a geometric symbol for identification. The First Division, which included the 351st, used a triangle. The Second used a circle, and the Third used squares. In August 1944, an additional symbol was added to identify the wings. A diagonal stripe was added to identify the groups in the 94th CBW. The 1st CBW used a vertical stripe, while the 40th CBW used a horizontal stripe. The 41st CBW used a wide border around their triangle.

B-17 Crew Positions

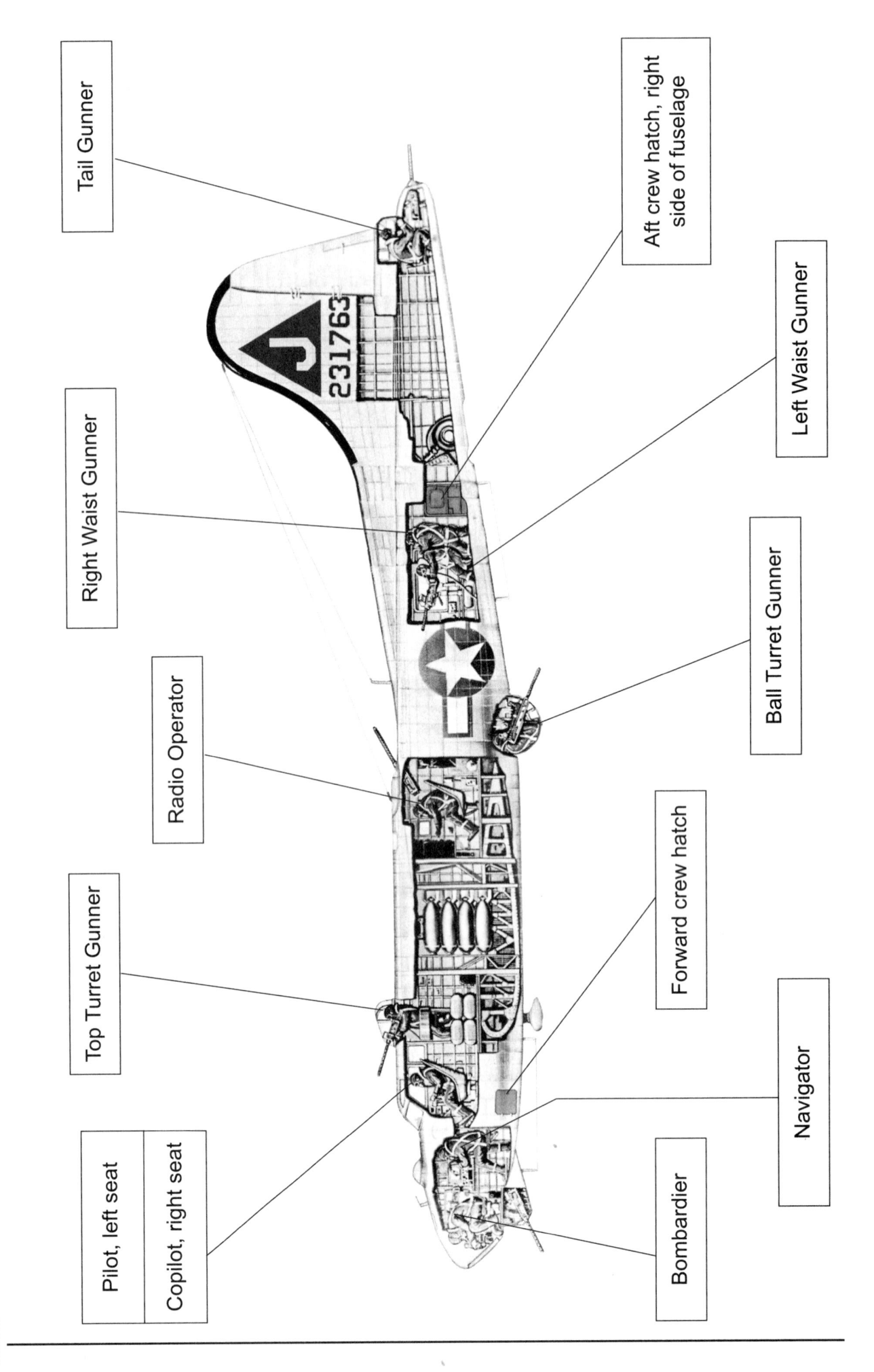

- Tail Gunner
- Aft crew hatch, right side of fuselage
- Right Waist Gunner
- Left Waist Gunner
- Radio Operator
- Ball Turret Gunner
- Top Turret Gunner
- Forward crew hatch
- Pilot, left seat
- Copilot, right seat
- Bombardier
- Navigator

GROUP PHOTOS

Lt. Anthony Zotollo. (E. West)

Fall 1944: Hunter Field, Georgia. Rear: Sgt. Michael Montagno, Sgt. William Morse, Sgt. Robert Smith, Sgt. Wallace Hoffman, Sgt. Elmer Phillips, Sgt. John Resnik. Front: 2nd Lt. James Gattens, 2nd Lt. Edward Szymanski, F.O. Preston Kidwell. (L. Gattens)

Front: Frank Cebrzynski, Tulio Bertolas. Rear: William Keasler, Kent Burkett, Alvin Bartholomew. (A. Bartholomew)

November 25, 1943: The 351st celebrates its first anniversary. L to R: Lt. Col. Robert Bowles, Maj. James Stewart, Col. William Hatcher, Maj. Leonard Roper, Lt. Col. Robert Burns, Maj. John Blaylock and Maj. Clinton Ball. (F. Richardson)

November 25, 1944: The 351st celebrates its second anniversary. L to R: Maj. James Stewart, Maj. Clinton Ball, Maj. Franklin Richardson, Lt. Col. Robert Burns, Maj. Leonard Roper, Lt. Col. Robert Bowles and Maj. John Carraway. (F. Richardson)

August 22, 1943: 509th crew. Rear: S/Sgt. Angelo Riccardi, Lt. James Maginnis P, Lt. George Wylie B, Lt. Roy Peterson CP, Lt. George Hornick N, Sgt. Daniel Reader. Front: Sgt. William Glenn, Sgt. Joseph Keane, Sgt. Raymond Rajala. (F. Richardson)

September 9, 1943: Captain John Carraway and crew, 511th Sqn. (F. Richardson)

June 1943. Rear: Lt. Robert Spika P, Lt. Lloyd Marquardt N, Lt. Floyd Homstad CP, Lt. Francis Stone B, Sgt. William Franz RW, Sgt. Edward Woodward LW.
Front: Sgt. Anker RO, Sgt. Neville McNerny TT, Sgt. Leo Skalsky BT, Sgt. Harvey Welsh TG. (F. Richardson)

September 6, 1943: Capt. Richard Hathaway and crew after Air Sea Rescue. (F. Richardson)

July 17, 1943: Lt. William Peters and crew after Air Sea Rescue. (F. Richardson)

October 22, 1943: Capt. Richard Hathaway with replacement aircraft. (F. Richardson)

September 18, 1943: 509th crew. Rear: Lt. Eugene Harris P, Lt. Merle Braden CP, Sgt. Harold Mellott WG, S/Sgt. Mitchell Miles TG, Lt. Edward Jacobson B, Lt. Tommy Briscoe N. Front: S/Sgt. Paul Lucyk WG, T/Sgt. Charles Tigue TT, S/Sgt. Richard Smith BT, T/Sgt. Alvin Olsen RO. (F. Richardson)

October 15, 1943: 510th crew. Rear: F.O. Robert Groth CP, Lt. Douglas Sheets B, T/Sgt. Peter Zibas TT, T/Sgt. Ralph Crane RO, Lt. Benjamin Schohan N, Capt. Jose Garcia P. Front: S/Sgt. Seymour Zeitler LW, S/Sgt. Arthur Farrell TG, T/Sgt. Tomas Romero BT, T/Sgt. Harry Bent RW. (F. Richardson)

September 22, 1943: 509th crew. Rear: Sgt. Tim Touchin TG, Sgt. Alonzo Sowell WG, Sgt. Charles Majors BT, Sgt. Robert Geilscheichter WG, Sgt. Roscoe Tyler TT, Sgt. Lloyd Blancett RO. Front: Lt. Robert Saltsman N, Lt. James Strouse P, Lt. Alva Westhafer CP. (F. Richardson)

511th crew. L to R: William Dean, Nicholas Sidorick, Mills Kelly, Carl Wilson P, Stewart Chenoweth, Alfred Terlizzi. (F. Richardson)

511th crew. Rear: Capt. Harry Morse P, Lt. George Nicolescu CP, S/Sgt. Joseph Hill TT, S/Sgt. Summers WG, T/Sgt. George Lee RO, S/Sgt. William Doubledee WG, Lt. Walter Blair B, Lt. Charles Shaw N. Front: S/Sgt. James Vander Laan BT, S/Sgt. Torrido Marcial TG. (C. Ball)

Lt. David Litsinger and crew, 511th Sqn. (C. Ball)

511th crew. Rear: Lt. Elmer Nardi P, Lt. Bradley Squires B, T/Sgt. Ganusheau Wade RO, T/Sgt. Frank Swica TT, S/Sgt. Donald Happold WG, S/Sgt. Henry Gates TG, Lt. Orlyn Master N, Lt. Harold Bergman CP. Front: Sgt. John Yarush WG, S/Sgt. Ralph Robeson WG, S/Sgt. Harlan Burton BT. (C. Ball)

Lt. Joseph Nesmith and crew, 511th Sqn. (C. Ball)

Lt. David Heller and crew, 511th Sqn. (C. Ball)

February 21, 1944: Lead crew. L to R: Lt. Marshall Pullen N, Capt. Robert Clay P, Lt. Col. Cobb, Air Commander, Capt. Archer Baird B. (F. Richardson)

April 10, 1944: Lead crew. L to R: unknown, Capt. Douglas Harris P, Lt. Col. Robert Burns, Air Commander, Lt. George Decker B, Lt. Carleton Cleveland N, Lt. George Mills TG. (F. Richardson)

Rear: Lt. Milton Sherman, Lt. Jack Doyle, Sgt. Norman Michelle, Sgt. Arthur Meredith, Lt. Donald Huff, Lt. Schwarts. Front: Sgt. Verl Long, Sgt. David Fagersten, unknown, Sgt. William Dolan. (C. Ball)

Lt. George Mears and crew, 511th Sqn. (C. Ball)

Lt. George Mears and crew interned in Switzerland. (J. Mahaffey)

July 8, 1944: Lead crew. L to R: Capt. Sterling McCluskey P, Lt. Billy Gwyn N, Capt. Allen Behrendt B, Lt. Eugene Caughlan P. (F. Richardson)

September 8, 1944: Lead crew. L to R: Maj. Franklin Richardson, Air Commander, Capt. Carleton Cleveland N, Lt. Fagan N, Lt. Thomas Clarke MO, Lt. Arthur Bartzocas P, Lt. Clinton Hammond TG. (F. Richardson)

September 25, 1944: Lead crew. Rear: Capt. Gerald Viste P, Capt. William Lyttle B, Lt. Thomas Gallagher N, Maj. Franklin Richardson, Air Commander. Front: unknown, Maj. Ralph Menees N, Lt. Thomas Clarke MO. (F. Richardson)

October 6, 1944: Lead crew. Rear: Maj. Franklin Richardson, Air Commander, Capt. John Eickhoff P, Lt. Donald Hoeldtke MO, Lt. Warren Steitz B. Front: Lt. Robert Penticoff TG, Lt. John Gulnac N, Lt. John Bury N. (F. Richardson)

Autumn 1944: 509th crew. L to R: Lt. John Coulam CP, Lt. Joseph Glover N, Lt. Charles Wolcott P, Lt. Smith B, Lt. James Lunan MO. (F. Richardson)

October 7, 1944: Lead crew. Rear: Maj. James Stewart, Air Commander, Lt. Lester Boardman N, Capt. Jerome Geiger P, Lt. Earl Brannaman B. Front: Lt. Albert Luich N, Lt. William Zimmerman TG, Lt. Arthur Schoen MO. (A. Schoen)

October 1944: Lead crew. Rear: Lt. Benton Love B, Lt. Charles Henry N, Maj. Franklin Richardson, Air Commander, unknown. Front: Lt. Donald Fish TG, Capt. Charles Woodrum P, Lt. George Homza MO. (F. Richardson)

December 11, 1944: Lead crew. Rear: Lt. Benton Love TG, Maj. Franklin Richardson, Air Commander, Maj. Mortimore Korges P, Lt. Arthur Schoen MO. Front: Lt. Thomas Kyser N, Lt. Arnold Schiffman B, Lt. Arnold Hecht N. (F. Richardson)

November 6, 1944: Lead crew. Rear: Maj. Franklin Richardson, Air Commander, Lt. Vernon Weatherman P, Lt. Benton Love, Lt. Robert Johnson. Front: Lt. James Lunan MO, Lt. Thomas Kyser N, Lt. Arnold Schiffman B. (F. Richardson)

January 3, 1945: Lead crew. Rear: Capt. Lester Boardman N, Lt. Arthur Schoen MO, Lt. Earl Maxwell B, Lt. John Talbott N. Front: Lt. Col. James Stewart, Air Commander, Capt. Evan Poston P, Lt. R. C. Stewart TG. (A. Schoen)

509th crew. Rear: Sgt. Larry Doyle, Lt. Ken Marriott, Lt. Archie Crews, Lt. Clint Hammond, Lt. Herman Helman. Front: Sgt. Irving Geller, Sgt. Robert Crawford, Sgt. Albert Proulx, Sgt. Harold Lowery. (F. Richardson)

Lt. Col. Elzia LeDoux, Col. Eugene Romig, Lt. Col. Robert Bowles. (F. Richardson)

March 5, 1945: Lead crew. Rear: Maj. Franklin Richardson, Air Commander, Capt. John Coulam P, Lt. Harold Schulte TG. Front: Lt. Horace Hardaway MO, Lt. Joseph Glover N, Lt. Edward LeFevre N, Lt. Smith B. (F. Richardson)

509th Lead crew. L to R: Lt. Louis Palmer, Capt. Eli Fowler, Lt. George Fagan, Lt. Richard Garcia. (F. Richardson)

Clark Gable filming, June 1943. (C. Stackhouse)

November 10, 1943: Awards Ceremony. L to R: Col. William Hatcher, Capt. William Winter, Lt. Joseph Shames. (F. Richardson)

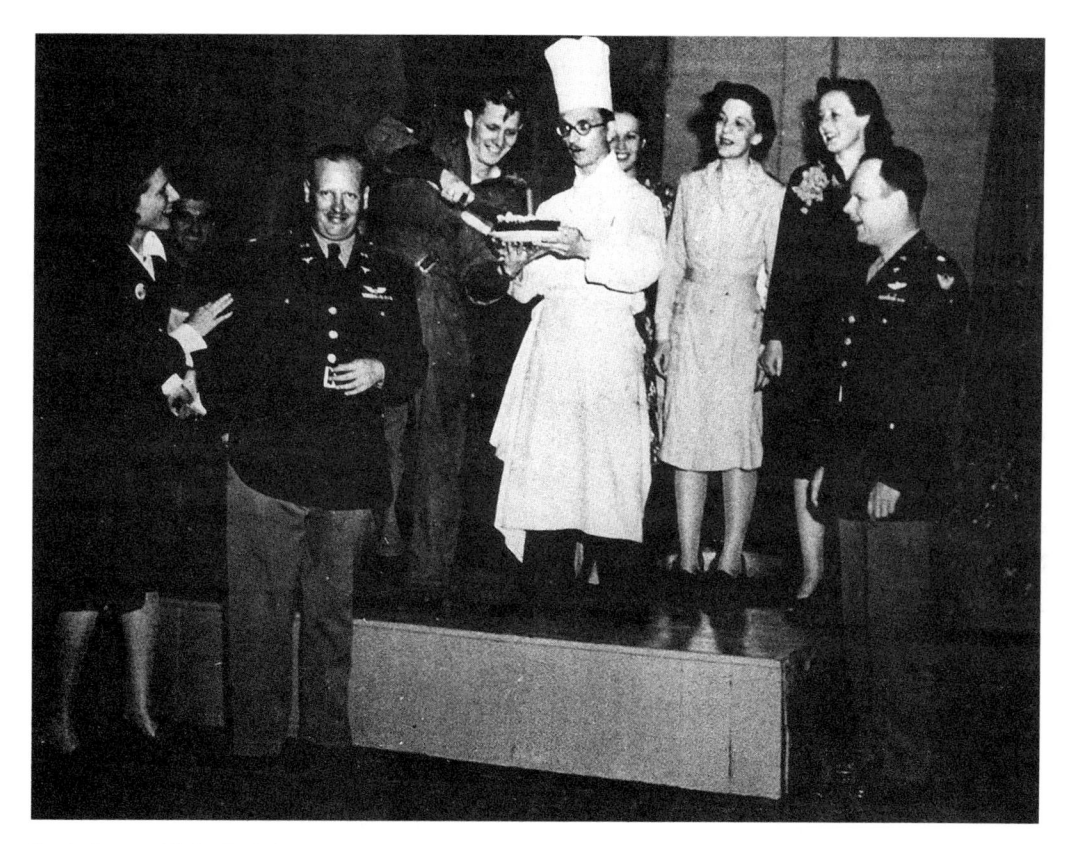

Red Cross Club, Polebrook. (Robinson)

July 12, 1943: Col. Hatcher presents the Air Medal to Lt. Col. Theodore Milton. (F. Richardson)

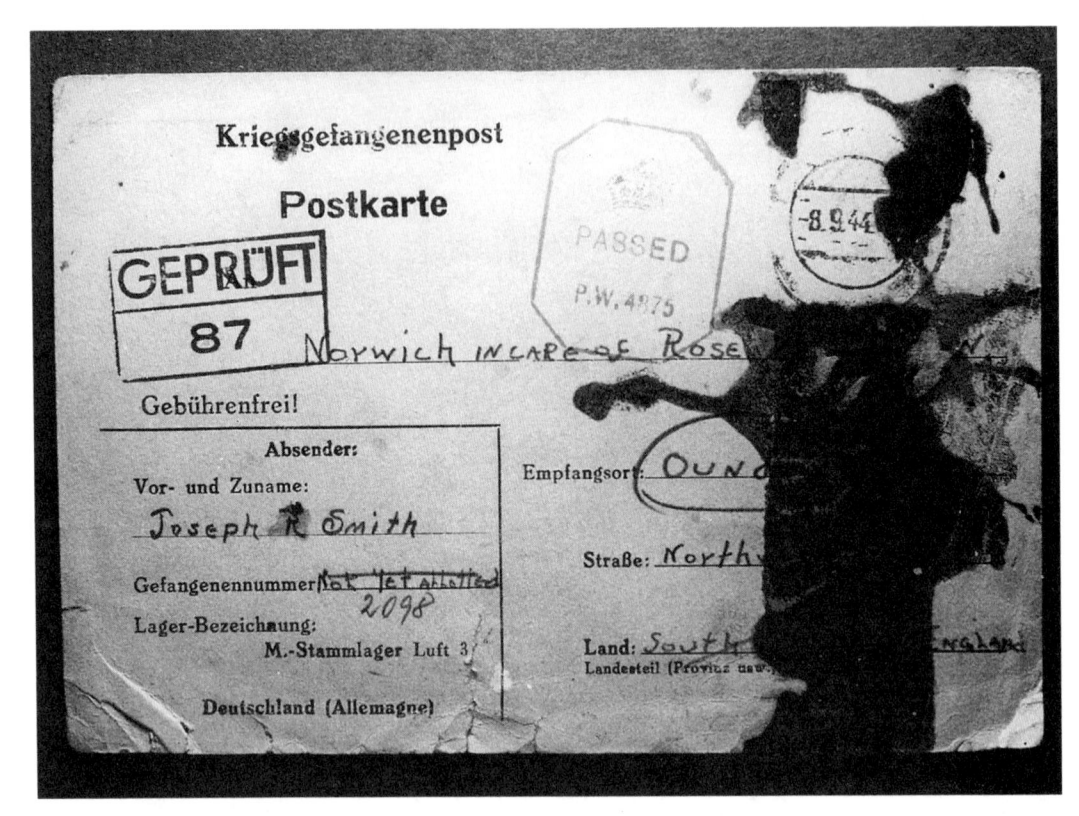

Postcard sent by 351st POWs to R. Norwood, licensee of the Rose and Crown pub in Oundle. (R. Norwood)

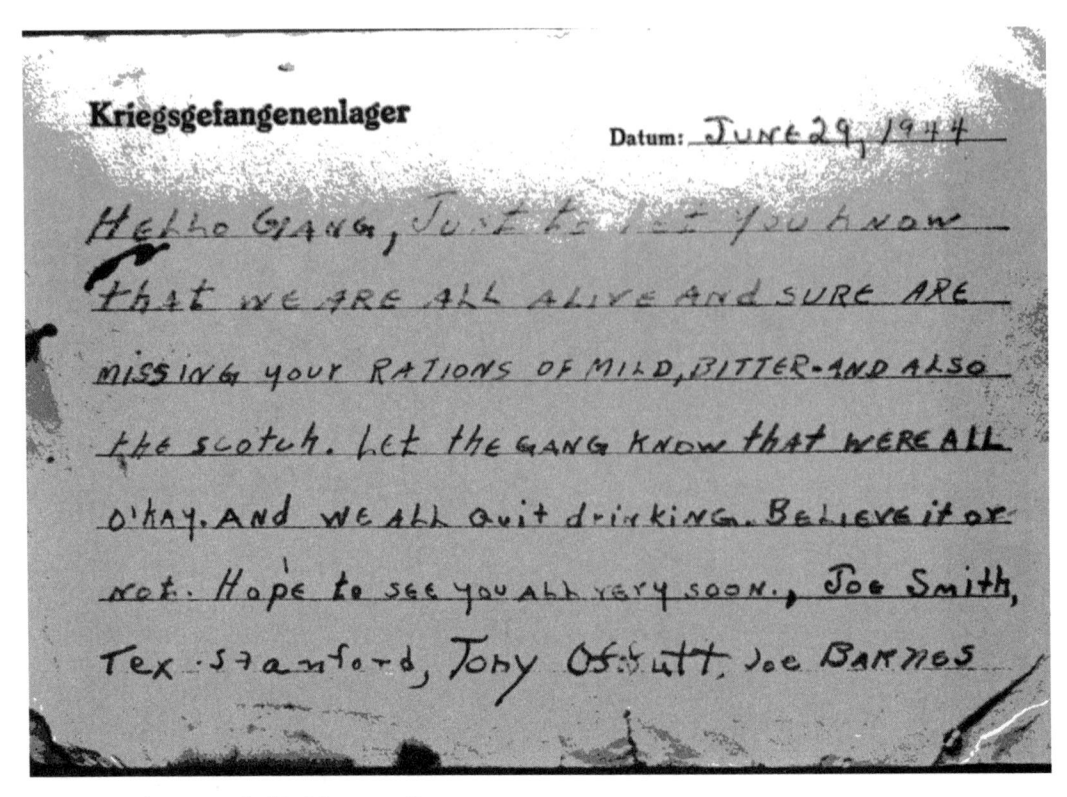

Reverse of postcard. (R. Norwood)

Red Cross Club, Polebrook. (C. Ball)

September 15, 1943: Officers bar. Lt. Joseph Turley serves Capt. Jerome Geiger, Lt. John Doyle and F.O. Borman. (F. Richardson)

L to R: Maj. Paul Fishburne, 509th Sqn. and brother, 1944. (F. Richardson)

Capt. William Baird, GP bombardier. (F. Richardson)

Capt. Donald Gaylord, 511th Sqn. (F. Richardson)

Capt. Marvin Brooksby, 509th Sqn. (F. Richardson)

Capt. Morris Harmon, 509th Sqn. (F. Richardson)

Capt. Jack Danby GP navigator 1943. (F. Richardson)

The base in the summer of 1944, taken from the south. (C. Ekblad)

Maj. John Carraway, 511th Sqn. (F. Richardson)

December 30, 1944: M/Sgt. Maynard V. Gibbs, 509th crew chief, after the presentation of the Bronze Star. (F. Richardson)

Maj. James Stewart 508th Sqn. (F. Richardson)

September 15, 1943: The *Major Ball*, the result of running out of fuel, Maj. James Stewart, pilot. (C. Ekblad)

511th crew. Rear: Duane Anderson P, Mark Rice CP, Milton Morisette N, Gerald Tracewitz B. Front: Raymond Mansell BT, Robert Jankowski RO, Stanley Klyve TG, John Lahr RW, Milton Griffin LW, Douglas Stewart TT. (C. Ball)

509th Lead crew. L to R: Lt. John Heck, Capt. Eli Fowler P, Lt. Seymour Levinson N, Lt. Arthur Bartzocas P. (F. Richardson)

509th Lead crew. L to R: Lt. Gerald Viste, Lt. George Decker, Lt. Thomas Gallagher. (F. Richardson)

Lead crew. Lt. Charles Henry, Lt. Charles Woodrum, Lt. James Lechner, Lt. William Custard. (F. Richardson)

Capt. Nick Lynch, 510th Sqn. (F. Richardson)

September 27, 1944: Result of a direct hit by flak over Cologne, pilot Capt. Jerome Geiger. (G. Geiger)

Brig. Gen. Lacey talking to Lt. Col. Robert Burns and Lt. Col. Clinton Ball. (F. Richardson)

Capt. Donald Floden, 508th Sqn. (F. Richardson)

Captain Lewis Maginn, 509th OPS. (F. Richardson)

Lt. Carl Engfer, 509th Sqn. (F. Richardson)

Maj. Ralph W. Menees GP Navigator. (F. Richardson)

Capt. Harry Holsapple, 510th OPS. (F. Richardson)

Lead crew. Capt. Eli Fowler, Lt. John Heck, Capt. William Logan, Lt. Seymour Levinson. (F. Richardson)

Capt. Wendell Secrest and his crew after his promotion. (F. Richardson)

Lead crew. Capt. James Lowery P, Lt. Rex Kinnucan, Lt. Alexander Kubetin, Capt. George Cobb P. (F. Richardson)

L to R: Lt. Carl Engfer, Lt William Balliot, Lt. John Roelhke, Lt. Charles Wolcott, 509th Sqn. (F. Richardson)

Capt. Wendell Secrest, 509th Sqn. (F. Richardson)

Capt. Lee Dennis, 510th Sqn. (F. Richardson)

509th party. L to R: unknown, Capt. Clement Hayes, Capt. William Nichols, Maj. Franklin Richardson, Maj. Leonard Roper, Maj. Robert Ramsey, Maj. Edward Smith. (F. Richardson)

Capt. William B. Lyttle, 509th Sqn. (F. Richardson)

Capt. Harold E. Kelley, 510th Sqn. (F. Richardson)

May 8, 1944: Lead crew. Capt. Allen Behrendt B, Capt. Nelson Matthews N, Lt. Col. Clinton Ball, Air Commander, Lt. James Wimmer P. (C. Ball)

Bigas Bird. Rear: Lt. Jerry Walters N, Lt. Harold Johnson P, Lt. George Brown CP, Lt. Elliott Reznik B. Front: Sgt. Adolph Smetana TG, Sgt. Leon Donnelly TT, M/Sgt. Thomas Hudson, Crew Chief, Sgt. Robert Flanagan WG, Sgt. George Flammer BT, Sgt. Gerald Pilcher RO. (Smetana)

September 3, 1943: Capt. Robert Rollman, 509th Engineering Officer. (F. Richardson)

Capt. William Winter, GP Bombardier. Killed on practice mission April 22, 1944. (F. Richardson)

Roman Catholic Chaplin Victor Kreutzer. (Langebahn)

509th Sqn. party. (F. Richardson)

Capt. Orville Oldham, 508th Sqn. After completing his tour he transferred to P-51s. He was later killed on a practice mission. (F. Richardson)

Maj. Leonard B. Roper, 510th Sqn. (F. Richardson)

509th crew. Rear: Lt. Herbert Banton, Lt. Jack Omohundro, Sgt. Orville Click, Sgt. P. O'Leary, Sgt. Harold Prezlomski, Lt. John Carson, Lt. Robert Matthews. Front: Sgt. John DeGraff, Sgt. Russell Nelson, Sgt. Gerald Brown, Sgt. Earl Smith. (J. Omohundro)

Capt. Leslie Cruthirds, 508th Sqn. (F. Richardson)

Chaplain "Honest Tom" Richards. (F. Richardson)

August 4, 1943: S/Sgt. Gorsuch being presented with the Silver Star.

Lt. Clark Gable and Maj. Keith Birlem, 508th Sqn. (C. Ball)

511th *The Battered Shack.* (E. Wiggs)

Polebrook main gate with Cpl. Oliver Clegg and Cpl. Charlie Langenbahn. (C. Langenbahn)

Capt. Harvey Wallace and Lt. Jack Doyle, 511th Sqn.
(F. Richardson)

Capt. John P. Carson, 509th Sqn. (F. Richardson)

Lt. George Reish and Lt. Robert Leimbeck, 509th Sqn.
(F. Richardson)

Brig. Gen. Lacey briefing lead crews. Capt. Ralph Menees on right. (F. Richardson)

Combat equipment locker room. (C. Stackhouse)

The bus to Peterborough outside the main gate. (C. Langenbahn)

Combat Officers Mess. (C. Stackhouse)

The marriage of Lt. Col. Robert Bowles. (F. Richardson)

Enlisted combat crews mess. The Polebrook caterers received citations for the best Air Corps Mess in the ETO, and for the best Mess of any American Unit in the ETO. (Seldon Fleming)

L to R: Lt. Col. Robert Burns, Capt. Harvey Wallace, Maj. Elzia Ledoux

Combat Equipment locker room. (C. Stackhouse)

Capt. Carl Ekblad, GP Engineering Officer. (C. Ekblad)

M/Sgt. Robert Bailey, 509th Sqn. Crew Chief. (R. Bailey)

Capt. George Sullivan N, Capt. Robert Lee B, 508th Sqn. (F. Richardson)

Officers Club. Carl B. Stackhouse second from the right, L.B. Roper fourth from the right. (C. Stackhouse)

351st Medical Detachment in Sgt. William Vorhies' office. (Nowack)

Officers Club. Front: Col. Robert Burns, Maj. Paul Fishburne, Lt. Col. Benoid Glawe, Maj. Carl Hinkle. Rear: Lt. Col. Clinton Ball, Maj. Franklin Richardson, Maj. John Carraway, Maj. James Stewart. (C. Ball)

Col. Merlin Carter, the Group's last C.O. (C. Ekblad)

Maj. Mortimore Korges, 509th Sqn. (C. Ekblad)

Capt. Charles Fuller and crew. (J. Tynan)

Robert L. Gelsleichter, Michael Kucsmas, Joseph L. Poltrone, Russell C. Patten, after 25th mission. (R. Hathaway)

Rear: Capt. Robert H. Johnson, T/Sgt. R. C. Stuart, T/Sgt. Millard Jantz, T/Sgt. George Gilliland, Lt. Robert Fontaine. Front: T/Sgt. Orrin Diltz, T/Sgt. William S. Heard, Lt. Stanley Taylor. (M. Jantz)

Rear: S/Sgt. Maurice Turner, Lt. Eugene Sylvester, Lt. Newton Wilbur, Lt. Gilbert Whitchurch, Lt. Richard Cox, S/Sgt. Frederick Vester. Front: S/Sgt. Frederick Gowen, S/Sgt. Robert Mondragon, S/Sgt. Donal Luse, S/Sgt. Andrew Boyarko. (F. Vester)

Rear: unknown, unknown, Seaborn Jones, James Dawsey. Front: Walter Karniewski, Ralph Montavon. (S. McClusky)

Rear: Charles Hull, Joseph Koffend, Frederick Nelson, Walter Johnson, John Swistak, Joseph "Zip" Turley, John Tynan. Front: Stanley Stanek, unknown, unknown. (J. Tynan)

Lt. Theodore Reed and crew. (J. Tynan)

511th crew. Rear: Sgt. Sebastian Nocera, Sgt. Harold Krause, Sgt. Mitchell Kirk, Sgt. Lester Adkins, Sgt. Myron Andersen, Sgt. Bob Casey. Front: Lt. Harlan Popp, Lt. Johnny Zimmerman, Lt. Orville Wolz, Lt. Robert Pacquer. (B. Nocera)

Lt. Robert Taylor and crew. (J. Tynan)

508th OPS. Rear: Capt. Earl Branaman, Capt. Lester Boardman, S/Sgt. Roland Holsen, Cpl. Brennen, Sgt. Carl Radcliff. Front: Sgt. Edmond Czarzasty, T/Sgt. Ralph Cowley, unknown, Cpl. Paul Piscotta. (J. Tynan)

508th Armorers. L to R: Cpl. James Cline, Cpl. Charles Harris, Cpl. Bryce Carswell, Cpl. Renato Bresson. (J. Tynan)

Unknown 508th crew. (J. Tynan)

Lt. Robert Lee, Lt. George Sullivan, Capt. Leslie Cruthirds, Capt. Daniel McCafferty, Lt. James Wimmer. (J. Tynan)

Lt. Donald "Pappy" Lord and crew. (J. Tynan)

Rear: William Mingos, James Thompson, John Keller, T. Warner, Mahlon Miller.
Front: W. Rolland, Kenneth Gable, Fred Wright, William Hepburn. (J. Kalita)

Rear: Honor Windes, George Kiely, John Duncan. Front: John Murzyn, G. C. Tilton, Daniel A. Johnson, Avery Stephens, Paul Reilly, Robert Jordan. (S. McClusky)

Lt. Robert Smith and crew, July 1943.

Rear: S/Sgt. Marvin Cameron, T/Sgt. William Elliot, S/Sgt. Harold Leyva, S/Sgt. D. McLain, S/Sgt. William Hazen, T/Sgt. George May. Front: Lt. Bernard Nelson, Lt. Samuel Consoli, Lt. Donald Rude, Lt. Donald Smith. (C. Ekblad)

Rear: Raeford Fulks, Bruce Penman, George Turley, William Laney, John Winton, Jose Jimenez.
Front: Wendell Olson, Zane Moore, Richard Hough, Robert Burleson. (B. Penman)

Lead crew. Anthony Zotollo, Robert Lawsen, Norman Gootee, John Dunnigan.
(J. Dunnigan)

Lead crew. Rear: Lee Dennis, Charlie Summers, Elmer Robinson, Clinton Ball. Front: unknown, Billy Gwyn, William Washburn. (E. Robinson)

511th Engineering. Rear: Bernard Duncan, George Stout, Robert Whitman, Oran Upton, Johnson, Howard Stickford. Front: Alberic Padula, William O'Connell, Elliot Atwood, William Riggs, Elias Vargas. (R. Chubb)

T. Mahoney, Lewis Darling, Clarence McCall, David Robinson, Homer Woods. (F. Arthur)

351st S-2 Officers. Rear: Capt. Smith, unknown, Lt. Rosenfeld, Lt. Harry Bleile, Capt. Harward Fisher, Capt. Michael Balkovich, Lt. Clay Snedeger, Lt. Higley. Front: Capt. Stephen Callahan, unknown, Capt. Erwin Cooper, Maj. Robert Ramsey, Capt. Charles Hillway, Capt. Blumfield, Capt. Leppert, unknown. (N. Morello)

Maj. Elzia Ledoux, 509th Sqn. (F. Richardson)

Rear: Robert McCann, Arthur Deimann, Willis Moore, James Douglas, M. Sturgel.
Front: Robert Burnett, Charles Tippel, Raymond Perry, John Primm, Robert Bell.
Seated: Raymond "Red" Pennell. (J. Primm)

Maj. John Gorham, 510th Sqn. (C. Ekbald)

Rear: Herbert Doty, Ralph Cator, Joseph Woolridge.
Front: J. P. Weston, Dale Worrell, Harold Christensen.
(J. Primm)

Col. William Hatcher at Polebrook on his return from POW camp.

Capt. Theodore Argiropulos and crew. (J. Tynan)

Roderick Roe, William Trask, Frank Mayarka, Abraham Silverman. (J. Tynan)

September 1944: crew of *Baby Butch*. Rear: Lt. E.C. Saur, Lt. Walter Culbert, Lt. Ed Hennegan, Lt. George Adams, S/Sgt. Charles Walters. Front: S/Sgt. Clair Carl, S/Sgt. Charles Johnson, S/Sgt. John Stick, S/Sgt. Karl Buschenfelt, S/Sgt. Emmett Bennett.

508th Engineering. Rear: James R. Curry, Louis Govreau, unknown, Karl Eaheart, R. Odgers, Charles Deutsch, John Dmichowski, unknown, Stanley Bodek, Harley Beck, R. Miele, unknown, Frank Cebrzynski, John McIntyre. Front: Fred Domine, unknown, Phillip Doucett, James Achilles, R. Penman, James J. Curry, Robert Dawson, E. Littler. (J. Billin)

Lt. Newman Van Tassel, 509th OPS, 1943. (F. Richardson)

Rear: J. Dmichowski, J. Curry, A. Bartholomew. Front: G. Beckstein, J. Bijak, W. Horan. (A. Bartholomew)

Rear: W. Scott, Gore Davis, Paul Fennell, F. Petrucci, Lawrence Jones, Samuel Silver. Front: Robert Gunster, William Whitten, Robert Condon, Joseph Isoardi. (R. Condon)

James D. Craven, Donald E. Floden, Ernest L. Watts, unknown. (G. Gross)

508th crew. Rear: Max Northern, Richard Cheswick, Gerald Kevorkian, Lloyd LeLand, Earl Maxwell. Front: John Hocevar, Henry Stine, William Nygren, Samuel Nocefara, John Williamson. (J. Tynan)

Rear: Sgt. Louis Walters, Lt. John Heck, Lt. Seymour Levinson, Capt. Eli Fowler, Lt. Grant Newby, Lt. James Lunan. Front: Sgt. Joseph Massara, Sgt. Arthur Disbrow, Sgt. Carl Borden, Sgt. Thomas Kolessar, Sgt. Frank Schmid. (J. Heck)

Rear: Harold Botkin, David Snyder, Leonard London, Joseph A. Berardi, B. Udell, G. T. Tiffin. Front: Jesse Nelson, Walther Wefel, John Greenwood. (J. Berardi)

509th Armament Section, Pueblo, Colorado. (E. Polgroszek)

Rear: Rubin Blanck, Harold Waite. Front: Edward Polgroszek, Herbert Schneider, unknown. (E. Polgroszek)

Rear: Harold Ruschmyer, Jackson Dubose, Cyril Shircel, Irving Geller, Andrew Graney, Kenneth Cox. Front: Charles Daugherty, Elmer Johnson, D. Stump, Elver Huntley. (C. Daugherty)

Crew of 42-31776 YB-H *Maggie's Drawers*. Rear: Tony Carbona N, Baltus Jancitus B, Jack Coyle CP, Robert Seaman P, Don Henderson. Front: unknown, unknown, Charles Fouzie, Henry Annucci. (R. Bromberg)

Rear: Kenneth Stephens, Thomas Miles, John Fortin, Richard Sutton, Roderick Roe.
Front: Wesley Clendenning, George Koudelka, Daniel Markiewicz, Donald Crandell, William Stormer. (W. Clendenning)

Capt. Richard Hathaway "B" Flight Commander 509th Sqn.
(F. Richardson)

Rear: S/Sgt. Peter Swangin, Lt. Clarence Horton, Lt. William Byers, Lt. Richard Moulton, Capt. Harold Edwards. Front: T/Sgt. John Floresta, S/Sgt. Raymond Schwabe, S/Sgt. B. Johnson, S/Sgt. Jack Wyatt. (J. Tynan)

Celestial Dixon, Daniel McCafferty, Leonard Roberts, James Wimmer, George Gross. (G. Gross)

Rear: unknown, Capt. Andrew Koszarek, T/Sgt. Albert Tokar, Lt. Walter McKinnon, S/Sgt. Edwin Lemley, T/Sgt. Torkief Knaphus, Lt. Nicholas Lynch. Front: unknown, S/Sgt. Everett Thomas, Lt. Eugene Meyer, T/Sgt. Reginald Nachriener. Seated: S/Sgt. William McMahon. (E. Meyer)

Rear: Lt. Robert E. Redman, Lt. Eldon Stear, Lt. John Bury, Lt. Richard Real, Lt. Thomas Miller. Front: T/Sgt. Kenneth Perry, T/Sgt. Edward Moreland, S/Sgt. Robert Lightner, T/Sgt. Francis Reed, S/Sgt. Robert Duvall. (E. Stear)

Rear: Lt. Leighton Zeiner, Lt. William Crockett, Lt. Joseph Adamiak, Lt. William Kelder. Front: Sgt. Grady Fuqua, Sgt. M. Asher, Sgt. Charles Ellman, Sgt. B. Almanzor, Sgt. Cleo Davis, Sgt. John Bone. (R. Wilcox)

Crew of *Ten Horsepower*. Rear: Sgt. Archie Mathies, Sgt. Joseph Rex, Sgt. Carl Moore, Sgt. Russell Robinson, Sgt. Thomas Sowell, Sgt. Magnus Hagbo. Front: Lt. Clarence Nelson, F.O. Ronald Bartley, Lt. Walter Truemper, Lt. Joseph R. Martin (H. Stickford)

Rear: Sgt. Jerry Engles, Sgt. Odie Sullivan, Sgt. Frank Marrek, Sgt. Walter Patterson, Sgt. Lester Barclay. Front: Lt. Samuel Ciraulo, Lt. Charles Best, Lt. Joseph Garner, Lt. Robert Brooks. (J. Brooks)

Rear: Robert G. Jones, E. Westrich, Ralph Geiselman, Edward Ohr, Samuel Davis, Kenneth Tate, Paul Salva, Henry Olson, William E. Davis, William Keith, Earl Peters. Front: Sylvester Brill, T. V. Meeres, G. Beigner, Hiram Marksberry, Allen Forrester, H. Miller, Walter Terry. (V. Neibuhr)

509th: Sgt. Clyde Coleman, unknown, Cpl. Joseph DeBruce. (J. DeBruce)

Lt. Joseph Sweeney, S/Sgt. R. Hutchinson, 1st Sgt. Robert Mills, Lt. Anthony Panehal. Kneeling: Cpl. John Kalita. (J. Kalita)

Rear: F.O. Richard Woodbury, Lt. John Bury, Lt. Eldon Stear, Capt. Donald Gaylord. Front: Capt. James Purcell, Lt. Benton Love, Lt. Richard Real. (E. Stear)

Rear: George Patterson, Harold Schulte, Leonard Lesch. Front: Thomas Kucskar, Leon Phelps. (G. Patterson)

Robert Whitman, Aubrey Delk, Walter Johnson, Heber Stamps. (F. Arthur)

Bernard Cole, William Halligan, Raymond Nagle,
Gerald Arens, Eugene Garske, George Burlow. (R. Nagle)

Edward Ohr, John Moen, Lebron Fox, Herber Yonker, Sylvester Brill, Francis Arthur, Warren Dorfler, Edward Westrich. (V. Neibuhr)

Rear: Lt. Robert Girardin, Lt. John Bury, Col. Merlin Carter, Capt. James Purcell.
Front: Lt. Richard Real, Lt. Joseph Galloway, Lt. Eldon Stear. (E. Stear)

Rear: Lt. Elmer Robinson, Lt. Charles Auten, Lt. James King. Front: Lt. Richard Hough, Capt. Harry Holsapple. (E. Robinson)

Rear: Maurice Marshall, Edward Falcey, John Carwile, Cleo Davis, Peter J. Schultz. Front: John Harper, Charles Harrison, Junior Edwards. (M. Marshall)

Lt. Vernon Evans and crew. (J. Kalita)

Rear: J. Winston, George Turley, Zane Moore, Wendell Olson. Front: Bruce Penman, Jose Jimenez, Raeford Fulks. (R. Fulks)

511th group includes: D. M. Morris, S. L. Wendt, Benjamin Fincher, Alejandro Chacon, Louis Boone, Ervin Schrock, P. Soderling, Louis Shadoan, Thomas Dye, Robert Marriott, Donald Briggs, Eugene Welch. (T. Dye)

Included in this 511th group: Brown, Eugene Garske, Gerald Arens, Bowman Bailey. (E. Garske)

Rear: Maj. John Gorham, Capt. James Purcell, Lt. Charles Hubbel, Lt. John Bury.
Front: Lt. Joseph Galloway, Lt. Richard Real, Lt. Eldon Stear, Lt. Joseph McGarity.
(E. Stear)

Rear: Martin, Jesse McGee, Alejandro Chacon, Hunter. Front: Thomas Dye, Joseph Shames, Elliot Atwood. (T. Dye)

Rear: William Marison, Walter Gorski, Ernest Marez, Wesley Kennard.
Front: Walter Shepherd, Paul Anderson, Wayne Livesay, Burton Davis. (B. K. Davis)

Rear: Thomas Kucskar, George Patterson, Leonard Lesch, D. Young, Leon R. Phelps.
Front: William Mawhorter, Aubrey Rhoden, Donald Appleford, Ralph Dickman, David Saltman. (G. Patterson)

511th Communications includes: Balgenorth, J. Crockett, Ross Viviano, Eugene Garske, Frederick Schick, Delford Grothe, Stanley Kazmierski, Gilbert Flaton, William Corcoran, George Schulman, James Lannon, Ronald Brown, Bernard Cole, Raymond Nagle, Howard McDonough. (R. Nagle)

Sharon Ann. L to R: George Feeney, Robert Condin, Harold Christensen, Calvin Adams. (J. Primm)

Lt. Col. Ledoux's farewell party. Rear: Lt. John Houck, Lt. Joseph Dickman, Capt. William Nicholls, Capt. Franklin Richardson, Col. Elzia Ledoux, Lt. Newman Van Tassel, Lt. George Decker. Front. Lt. Edwin Simon, Capt. Leinellen, Capt. Clement Hayes, Capt. William Smith, Lt. Herbert Schneider. (T. Cooper)

July 1944: crew of *Bedlam Ball* #2. Front: S/Sgt. Cecil Badgett, Lt. George Uttley, Lt. James Ralston, Lt. Milton Sheir, Lt. Charles Hayes, Sgt. Dick Carr. Front: Sgt. Marion Coverdale, Sgt. Joe Garza, Sgt. William Saunders, S/Sgt. Alvin Bernstein. (J. Freels)

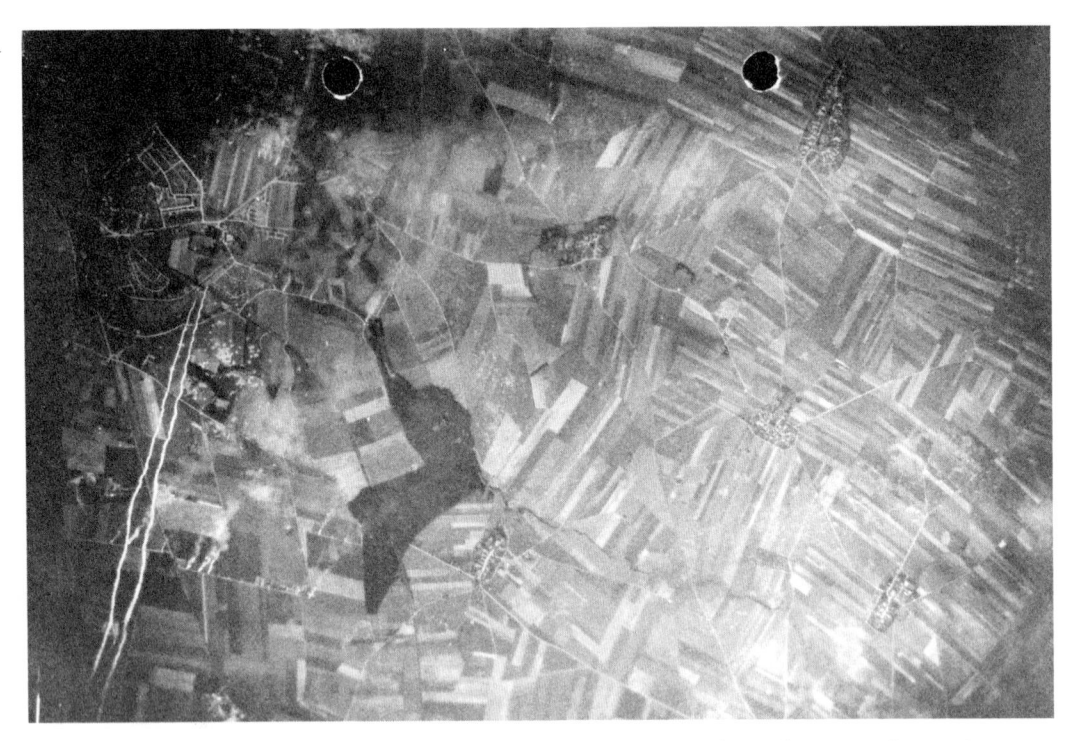

February 20, 1944: Leipzig, Germany. The white streaks at left are from smoke canisters dropped to mark the target.

1943: 510th crew members. S/Sgt. John Costello unknown, T/Sgt. Seymour Zeitler. (T. Costello)

Pvt. John Gantt. (R. Stamey)

Malcolm Higgins' crew.

Cpl. Calvert G. P'Pool, 509th. Killed on flight home June 8, 1945. (A. P'Pool)

Silver Ball. Rear: Sgt. James McCann, Lt. Owen Fitzgerald, Sgt. Frank Avry, Sgt. Isador Kaplowitz, Lt. Carl Miller. Front: Lt. Maurice Fikes, Sgt. Anthony Bushlow, Sgt. Albert Lien, Sgt. George Stafford. (F. Avry)

Silver Dollar. Rear: John Mack Jr., Clair Tracy, George Sullivan, Richard Gardner, Jack Fritzsinger, Joseph Heffner. Front: Dale Rodness, Herbert Sass, Raymond Hoydn. (C. Tracy)

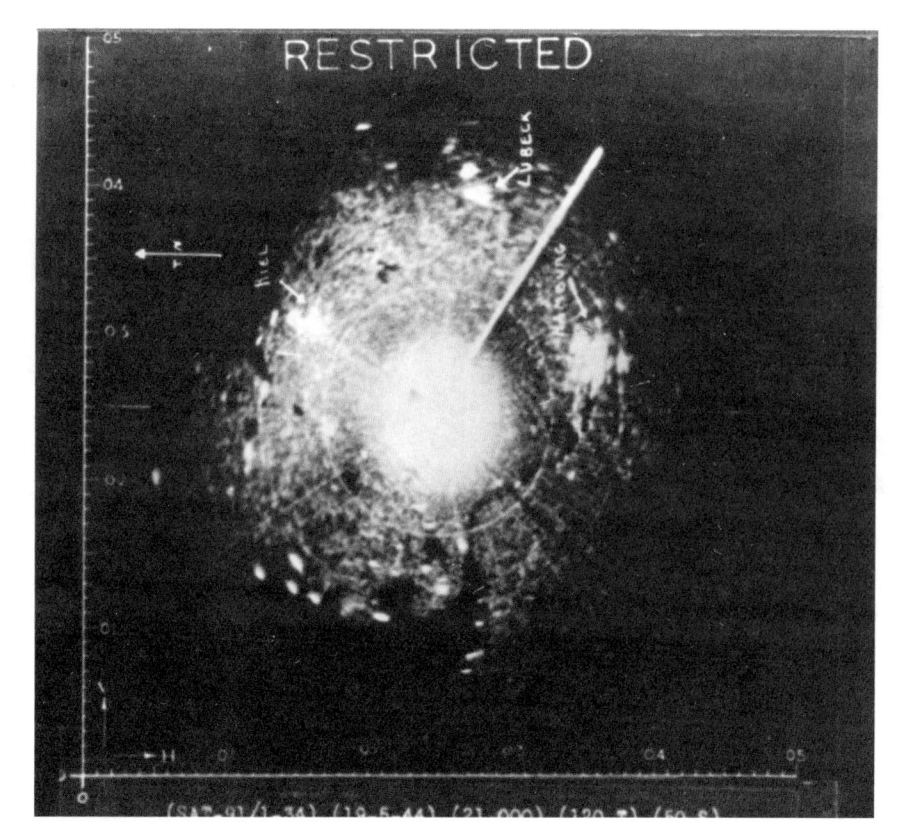

May 19, 1944: H2X radar of Keil.

L to R: Maj. Arren A. Akins, Capt. Otto R. Vasak, unknown.

Strike photo, location unknown.

October 28, 1943: 510th crew. Rear: Sgt. Thomas Sowell, Sgt. Russell Robinson, Sgt. Magnus Hagbo. Front: Sgt. Joseph Rex, Sgt. Archie Mathies, Sgt. Carl Moore.

September 12, 1944: Lt. Hadley's B-17, 44-6139 DS-K, after crash landing in Belgium. (T.Maki)

September 12, 1944: Lt. Hadley's B-17, two ladies from Belgium take this opportunity to look at a B-17 close up. (T. Maki)

Strike photo, Caen airfield.

511th ground crew. Rear: S/Sgt. William Davis, Cpl. Harold Hawkins, Sgt. Robinson. Front: M/Sgt. Samuel Davis, Sgt. Miller, Sgt. Ralph Geiselman. Note crew member painting group insignia in background.

The cathedral in Cologne, Germany after the war. (K. Menees)

September, 1943. Rear: Sgt. Angelocci, Lt. Carl Magness, Lt. Horace Hopkins, Lt. Everett Hale, Lt. Carl Habecker. Front: Sgt. Richard Atwood, Sgt. William Stroh, Sgt. Flanagan, Sgt. William Meighen, Sgt. Norman Bruning. (J. Heflin)

June 25, 1943: Lt. Boyd's crew.

Maj. Ralph Menees. (K. Menees)

Rear: Lt. Bill Bragg, Lt. Anthony Zotolla, Lt. Robert Lawsen, Sgt. Louis Cohen, Sgt. Edwin West, Sgt. Henry Fiengo. Front: Sgt. Leonard Barton, Lt. Joseph Loiacono, Sgt. Claudius Carter, Sgt. Bill Jordan. (E. West)

42-31776 YB-H *Maggie's Drawers*. Sgt. Lerseth, Sgt. Brotherton, Sgt. Jewel Hopper, Sgt. Lawrence Yanny.

Maj. General Eaker visits Polebrook.

Crew of *Prophet's Paradise*. Rear: Sgt. Junior Daniels, Lt. Clyde Armstrong, Lt. John McNamara, Lt. Richard Arceneaux, F.O. Herbert Mishkin, Sgt. Gene Baron. Back: Sgt. Alfred Jones, Sgt. Gregory Cluett, unknown, Sgt. Clive Barnes. (H. Mishkin)

December 31, 1944. Group includes: Lt. Clyde Armstrong, Lt. Howard Brown, Lt. Richard Arceneaux, Lt. Herbert Mishkin, Sgt. Carl Barnes, Sgt. Gene Baron, Sgt. Gregory Cluett, Sgt. Alfred Jones, Sgt. Stanley Klyve. (H. Mishkin)

February 28, 1945. Rear: Lt. Morris Turner, F.O. Paul Walker, Lt. Allen MacDonald. Front: Lt. O'Neal, Lt. Henry Rossen. (C. Walker)

1944: Forming up over England before heading to the target. (D. Marsey)

Rear: Sgt. William Moore, Sgt. George Tobolsky, Sgt. Robert Fry, Sgt. Daniel Coffey, Sgt. Dwain Little, Sgt. Charles Watkins. Front: Lt. Donald Marsey, Lt. Leo Cook, Lt. Frederick Kelley, Lt. Alan Reed. (D. Marsey)

May 25, 1944: 509th. Rear: Lt. Joseph Berardi, Lt. Arnold Goodman, Lt. Joseph Heard. Front: Lt. Marty Strom, S/Sgt. Clyde Risinger. (J. Berardi)

Rear: unknown, Capt. Julian Meadows, unknown. Front: Lt. Johnny Clark, Lt. Charles Sugg, Maj. William Bounds, Lt. Robert Schneider. (R. Schneider)

Rear: Sgt. Max Ross, Sgt. James Doyle, unknown, Sgt. Charles Pike, unknown, Sgt. Guy Lunsord. Front: Lt. John Crutcher, Lt. Paul Purvis, Lt. Roger Johnson, Lt. Lloyd Hunter. (R. Johnson)

December 31, 1943: 42-3093 TU-K *Nobody's Darling*. L to R: Sgt. Arthur Novaco, Sgt. Guy Merideth, Sgt. Winston Haggard, Sgt. Huber Butler, Lt. Francis Needham, Lt. Robert Chalmers, Sgt. Walter Skinner, Lt. Ferris Martin, Sgt. Charles Newberry. (W. Skinner)

511th crew. Rear: Sgt. Elmo Hancock, Sgt. Jack McGee, Lt. Raymond Butler, Sgt. Paul Malamed, Sgt. Walter Nolan. Front: Sgt. Theodore Mahas, Lt. George Dyer, Lt. Charles Kern, Sgt. Cecil Thrasher Jr. (R. Butler)

42-3152 TU-A *Sleepy Lagoon*. Standing: Cpl. George Berth, Sgt. Joseph Weber. Sitting: Sgt. Robert Braem, Cpl. Thaddeus Cieslak.

511th crew. Rear: Sgt. Herbert Goldstein, Lt. Anthony Nardone, Lt. George Holden, Lt. Claude Adams, Lt. Carl Kennedy, Sgt. Robert Hayes. Front: Sgt. Gus Siciliano Jr., Sgt. Charles Belmonte, Sgt. Anthony Salerno. (G. Siciliano)

508th ground crew. L to R: Sgt. William Bogue, Sgt. Paul Buntin, Sgt. Kent Burkett, Cpl. Rudolph Burrough, Sgt. Jack Billin, M/Sgt. Louis Frankart. (M. Gentry)

1943: 508th crew. Rear: Sgt. Victor Vlha, Lt. Howard Davis, Lt. Richard Perkins, Lt. Max Polin, F.O. William Warring. Front: Sgt. Ralph Haney, Sgt. Mearl Waswick, Sgt. Gordon Schmitt, Sgt. Carroll Bonnett, Sgt. James Quillin. (S. Schjodt)

Rear: Sgt. Wesley Creech, Sgt. Lloyd Bogle, Sgt. Gilbert Beyer, Sgt. Andredge Vinson, Sgt. Samuel Bell, Sgt. Vern Palmer. Front: Lt. Donald McLott, Lt. James Redmond, Lt. Martin Strom, Lt. Tony Wagner. (J. Redmond)

42-30499 RQ-Q *My Princess*. (J. Redmond)

November 1943. L to R: T/Sgt. Omer Theroux, T/Sgt. Elmer Ruschman, S/Sgt. Ivey Hullender. (E. Ruschman)

509th crew. Back: Sgt. Denvil Lykins, Sgt. James Williams, Sgt. Albert Omer, Sgt. Everett Sahlstrom, Sgt. Francis Reed, Sgt. James Young. Front: Lt. Gerald Viste, Lt. Daniel Mertzluft, Lt. Thomas Gallagher, Lt. Tomas Heck. (J. Young)

Lt. Frank Lubozynski, Lt. Dick Cramer, Lt. Orrin Goder. (F. Urbanek)

Rear: Sgt. Max Cole, Sgt. Archie Ward. Front: Sgt. Frank Urbanek, Sgt. Harry Kirker, Sgt. Calvin Heard. (F. Urbanek)

June 1943: Pyote, Texas. Rear: Sgt. Jerry Anderson, Sgt. W. Schmidt, Sgt. Walter Swarthout, Sgt. Joe Langstaff, Sgt. Norm Burke, Sgt. Dick Palmer. Front: Lt. George Arnold, Lt. David Mills, Lt. Jim O'Donoghue, Lt. Herman Jacoby. (N. Burke)

B-17 stuck in the mud. (W. Cosgrove)

Barracks and bikes in the winter. (W. Cosgrove)

Lt. Charles Henry, Lt. William Cosgrove. (W. Cosgrove)

Rear: Lt. Clifford Pryor, Lt. Charles Henry, Lt. William Cosgrove, Lt. Edwards, Lt. John Curley. Front: Sgt. Robert Rickenbacker, Sgt. Dewey Paxon, Sgt. Edward Poppe, Sgt. William Teel, Sgt. Earl McCracken. (W. Cosgrove)

Capt. Louis Maginn, 511th BS.

44-6082 TU-B *Wisconsin Beauty.* Rear: Sgt. Dwain Little, Sgt. Leo Cook, Sgt. Robert Fry. Front: Sgt. Charles Watkins, Lt. Donald Marsey, Sgt. Daniel Coffey. (D. Marsey)

July 1944: Hunter Field, Georgia. Rear row includes: Sgt. Kenneth Pfleging, Sgt. Johnnie Parsons, Sgt. Arnold Mitchell, Sgt. Edward Jull, Sgt. Lucien Benevich. Front: Lt. Harry Perry, Lt. Edward Anderson, Lt. William Ramsey, Lt. Harvey Powell. (P. Crawford)

508th crew. Rear: unknown, Lt. Robert Thoman, Lt. James Chapman, F.O. Raymond Latimer, Sgt. Harold Clapp. Front: Sgt. Eddie Herman, Sgt. Billie Abbogast, Sgt. Homer Mendez, Sgt. Henry Coile, Sgt. Salvatore Maggiore. (J. Chapman)

510th Sgt. Robert Braem attaching shackle to a bomb just before loading.

511th crew. Rear: Lt. Cliff Pryor, Lt. Bruce McKenzie, Sgt. Earl McCracken, Sgt. Walter Derrick, Lt. Jack Schadegg, Lt. Jack Stevens. Front: Sgt. Chester Galomski, Sgt. Jack Crumley, Sgt. William Covert, Sgt. Dewey Paxon. (S. Yopp)

September 23, 1943. Rear: Lt. John Duchesneau, Lt. Billy Gwyn, Lt. William Raser, Lt. Augustus Cesarini. Front: Sgt. William Lamb, Sgt. Omer Theroux, Sgt. Michael Bushco, Sgt. Ivey Hullender, Sgt. Elmer Ruschman. (E. Ruschman)

July 15, 1944: 511th BS, *Woodchoppers Ball*. Lt. Cosgrove and crew after completing first mission. (W. Cosgrove)

Cpl. Dominick Sarica, 508th. (D. Sarica)

Waiting for opening time "Rose and Crown in Oundle. (Reiss)

351st OPS. Pueblo, Colorado. Chesborough, Jackson, A. Geiss, Fred Sommer. (F. Sommer)

Buckshot. Rear: T/Sgt. James Ball, S/Sgt. Manuel Trujillo, S/Sgt. Fred Way, T/Sgt. Paul Kallas, S/Sgt. Wayne Kettleson. Front: Lt. George Farrell, Lt. John May, Lt. Harold Cannon, Lt. Norbert Wood. (M. Trujillo)

351st Photo Section: J. Marke, R. Hurst, G. Ahren, R. Rudy, J. Fawbush, E. Birtwell, H. Stewart, J. McDevitt, A. Solomon, D. Henderson. (R. Bromberg)

Lt. Keith Rhode and crew. (J. Tynan)

M/Sgt. Paul Muegge, S/Sgt. William M. Smith, Sgt. Beecher Weida, Cpl. William Parish. (R. Chubb)

511th group: William Davis, Ralph Geisleman, Kenneth Tait, Willard Teace, Edward Westrich, Edward Ohr, Paul Salva. (H. Stickford)

Lt. Walter Truemper, posthumous Medal of Honor recipient. Photo taken upon graduation from Navigator training in August of 1943.

Medal of Honor

July 4, 1944: Aurora, Illinois. Mrs. Friedericka Truemper, with Walter's Navigator's wings pinned on her blouse, accepts the Medal of Honor on behalf of her son, Walter. Walter's father Henry is at left, his sister Ann at right.

Sgt. Archibald Mathies, posthumous Medal of Honor recipient. Archie signed this photo "To the sweetest of all, My Mother." (D. Mathies)

Medal of Honor

July 23, 1944: First Presbyterian Church, Finleyville, Pennsylvania. Mrs. Mary Mathies accepts the Medal of Honor on behalf of her son, Archie. (D. Mathies)

February 20, 1944: 42-31763 TU-A *Ten Horsepower* after the attempted landing by Lt. Walter Truemper and Sgt. Archibald Mathies.

February 20, 1944: 42-31763 TU-A *Ten Horsepower* after crash on Denton Hill.

February 20, 1944: 42-31763 TU-A *Ten Horsepower* after crash on Denton Hill.

GLOSSARY

11th St. Comp.	11th Station Complement, responsible for airfield defense
1206th QM Co.	Quartermaster Company, responsible for supplying food and other requirements to maintain the airfield
150mm	150 millimeter anti-aircraft shells
20mm	20 millimeter cannon shells
500lb GP	General purpose bomb
8th AF	Eighth Air Force
94th C.B. Wing	Combat Bomb Wing, part of the First Division of the 8th Air Force
A/F	Airfield
A30	Twin-engine fighter/bomber
AFEC	Air Force European Command
ASR	Air Sea Rescue
ATC	Air Transport Command
Avn. F/F Pltn.	Aviation Fire Fighting Platoon
B	Bombardier
B.G.	Bomb Group
B.S.	Bomb Squadron
Bowser	Fuel truck
Brig. Gen.	Brigadier General
BT	Ball turret
Buncher	Transmitted signal to assist formation assembly
Buzz job	Low level flying
C.O.	Commanding Officer
Capt.	Captain

Catwalk	Walkway through the bomb bay
Chaff	Aluminum strips to confuse German RADAR
Chemical Co.	Chemical Company, responsible primarily for oxygen supplies
Chutes	Parachutes
Closed in	Low cloud and mist, making it difficult to land
Col.	Colonel
Combat Box	Self-protecting bomber formation
Comm.	Communication
CP	Copilot
Cpl.	Corporal
Crossbow	Code name for flying bomb sites in France
Darky	Manned radio station to be called in emergencies
Do 217	German twin-engine bomber
Ensign	Single-engine float plane
ETO	European Theater of Operations
F.O.	Flight Officer
Feather prop	Turn propeller to minimize wind resistance
Finance Sect.	Finance Section, responsible for payroll
Flak	Exploding shells from German anti-aircraft guns
FW 100	German single-engine fighter
FW 189	German single-engine fighter
FW 190	German single-engine fighter
GH	Navigation and bombing aid
GP	Group
H2X	Downward looking airborne RADAR
Hardstand	Dispersed concrete pads on which aircraft were parked
HE 111	German twin-engine bomber
HQ	Headquarters
I.P.	Initial point, start of bombing run
Int'd.	Aircrew interned in a neutral country such as Switzerland
Ju 88	German twin-engine fighter/bomber

KIA	Killed in action
L to R	Left to Right
Lead ship	First aircraft in formation
Lt.	Lieutenant
Lt. Col.	Lieutenant Colonel
LW	Left waist gunner
M.P.I.	Main Point of Impact (aiming point)
M/Sgt.	Master Sergeant
M17 incendiary	Bomb containing phosphorus and other combustible chemicals
Maj.	Major
Mayday	Emergency signal, similar to SOS
Me 109	German single-engine fighter
Me 163	German single-engine jet fighter
Me 210	German twin-engine fighter
Me 262	German twin-engine jet fighter
Me 410	German twin-engine fighter
Medical Disp.	Medical Dispensary i.e. sick quarters
MGM	Metro-Goldwyn-Meyer film company
MIA	Missing in action
Milk run	An unopposed mission
MO	Mickey operator (RADAR operator)
MOH	Medal of Honor
MP Company	Military Police
Mph	Miles per hour
N	Navigator
No-ball	Code name for V1 flying bomb sites in France
Non coms	Noncommissioned officers
OPS	Operations
Ord. S&M Co.	Ordnance Supply & Maintenance Company
P	Pilot
PCBW	Provisional Combat Bomb Wing

PFF ship	Pathfinder force aircraft carrying RADAR
POW	Prisoner of war
Prop wash	Turbulence caused by propellers
RAF	Royal Air Force
RO	Radio operator
RW	Right waist gunner
S/Sgt.	Staff Sergeant
Sgt.	Sergeant
Slipping an aircraft	Sliding the aircraft sideways to line up with the runway
Slow time	Flying to break in new engines
SOS	International code signal of extreme distress (Save our souls)
Split-S	A maneuver used by fighter pilots to turn inside the opposing fighter
Sqn.	Squadron
St. Comp.	Station Complement, responsible for airfield defense
Stand down	No flying activity
Sub-Depot	447th Sub-Depot, responsible for engine changes and other repairs to aircraft that could not be done out on the hardstands
T/Sgt.	Tech Sergeant
TG	Tail gunner
TT	Top turret
TWX machine	Teleprinter
U-boats	German submarines
UK	United Kingdom
VHF	Very High Frequency radio
WACS	Women's Army Corps
Wash	Area in England with bombing ranges
WAVES	Women Accepted for Volunteer Emergency Service
WG	Waist Gunner
WRENS	Women's Royal Naval Service
ZOI	Zone of the Interior (United States)

Quick Order Form

Fax orders: 920-730-8624.

Telephone orders: Call toll-free: 1-800-592-1243. Have your credit card ready.

E-mail orders: RSchool@Polebrook.com

Postal orders: Cross Roads, Rick School, PO Box 83, Kimberly, WI 54136-0083, USA. Telephone: 920-730-2715

Website: www.polebrook.com

Please send _____ (quantity) of *The 351st Bomb Group in WWII* hardcover book(s) @ $55.00 each $ _____

(WI residents add 5% sales tax ($2.75) for each) $ _____

Shipping $ _____
U.S.: $7 for the first book. Shipping is FREE when ordering 2 or more books delivered to the same address in the continental United States.

ORDER TOTAL $ _____

Payment: ☐ Check   ☐ Visa   ☐ MasterCard

Card Number: _____

Name on card: _____ Exp. Date: _____

~ COMPLETE SATISFACTION GUARANTEED ~

Ship to:

Name: _____ P.O. Box _____

Address: _____

City: _____ State: _____ Zip: _____

Telephone: _____ E-mail address: _____

Newcastle
Middlesbrough
York
Hull
Birmingham
351 B.G.
POLEBROOK
Cambridge
Ipswich
Oxford
London
Dover
Portsmouth
Calais
Boulogne
Ostende
Antwerp
Brussels
Amsterdam
Rotterdam
Duisburg
Dusseldorf
Cherbourg
Le Havre
Paris